ROGET'S

Pocket Thesaurus

BASED ON
*ROGET'S International Thesaurus
of English Words and Phrases*

Edited by
C. O. SYLVESTER MAWSON

Assisted by
KATHARINE ALDRICH WHITING

A POCKET CARDINAL EDITION
PUBLISHED BY POCKET BOOKS · NEW YORK

ROGET'S POCKET THESAURUS

Based on *Roget's International
Thesaurus of English Words and Phrases*

Crowell edition published December, 1923

A Pocket *Cardinal* edition

1st printing............July, 1946
92nd printing........August, 1969

This Pocket *Cardinal*® edition includes every word contained in the
original, higher-priced edition. It is printed from brand-new plates
made from completely reset, clear, easy-to-read type.
Pocket *Cardinal* editions are published by Pocket Books, a division of
Simon & Schuster, Inc., 630 Fifth Avenue, New York, N.Y. 10020.
Trademarks registered in the United States and other countries.

L

What Is a Thesaurus?

"A *Thesaurus* is the opposite of a dictionary. You turn to it when you have the meaning already but don't yet have the word. It may be on the tip of your tongue, but what it is you don't yet know. It is like the missing piece of a puzzle. You know well enough that the other words you try out won't do. They say too much or too little. They haven't the punch or have too much. They are too flat or too showy, too kind or too cruel. But the word which just fills the bill won't come, so you reach for the *Thesaurus*."

—*From the Introduction by* I. A. RICHARDS

INTRODUCTION

A *Thesaurus*, says the dictionary, is "a treasury or storehouse; hence a repository, especially of words, as a dictionary." But, in a sense, this book is the opposite of a dictionary. You turn to a dictionary when you have a word but are not sure enough what it means—how it has been used and what it may be expected to do. You turn to the *Thesaurus* when you have your meaning already but don't yet have the word. It may be on the tip of your tongue, or in the back of your mind or the hollow of your thought, but what it is you don't yet know. It is like the missing piece of a puzzle. You know well enough that the other words you try out won't do. They are not the right shape. They say too much or too little. They haven't the punch or have too much. They are too flat or too showy, too kind or too cruel. But the word which just fills the bill won't come, so you reach for the *Thesaurus*.

Like the dictionary, it is a dangerous book in all sorts of ways. Sometimes you wake up—after half an hour—and realize that the problem of the missing word is still where it was. You have just been wandering happily about in the treasure house looking its riches over, forgetting what you came in for. It has worse dangers. Sometimes the words you find start new streams of thought which wash everything out.

Then not the word only but the idea too will be missing. In this "Lost Chord" situation, the best thing to conclude is that so evanescent an idea was hardly worth keeping. Sometimes, worse still, Temptation assails you. Instead of the right word—the word your thought was yearning for as its mysterious predestined mate—some

v

brazen hussy or wastrel of a vocable, never met and
never thought of before, seizes your regard

> O these encounterers
> That give a coasting welcome ere it comes

Beware! As Confucius' pupil said, "For one word a man
is often deemed to be wise and for one word he is often
deemed to be foolish. We ought to be careful indeed
what we say."

A big vocabulary is a grand thing when well understood and resourcefully used. But all grandeurs have
their penalties. It is the business of a *Thesaurus* to take
us into all verbal company—to introduce us to every sort
and condition of word, with no guarantee, expressed or
implied, as to what they may not do to us if we trust
them without proper inquiry.

> Who hath given man speech
> Or who hath set therein
> A thorn for peril and a snare for sin

cries the Chorus in *Atalanta in Calydon*.

The great Railway strike in England turned upon the
phrase "definitive terms." One side took it to mean "unchangeable"; the other explained too late that they only
meant "full and detailed." Well does Peter Mark Roget
observe, "A misapplied or misapprehended term is sufficient to give rise to fierce and interminable disputes; a
misnomer has turned the tide of popular opinion; a verbal
sophism has decided a party question; an artful watchword, thrown among combustible materials has kindled
the flame of deadly warfare and changed the destiny of
an empire."

That is the tragic side. The comic possibilities more
concern us here. People who swagger about in borrowed
words may, like Porthos in *The Three Musketeers*, im-

press the inexperienced. They bring the wrong sorts of smiles to the lips of the discerning.

To know the words without the things is perilous indeed. "How often," said the lecturer, "have I dallied by the shores of Lac Leman or strolled on the delightful slopes overlooking Lake Geneva." "Pardon me," said a member of the audience, "but are they not synonymous?" "You may think so, Sir," replied the speaker, "but for my part I consider Lac Leman by far the more synonymous of the two." Awful warnings of this sort abound. "I always tell my children to look it up in the dictionary or the encyclopedia," said the Sea Captain. "That is what they are there for. Always be exact . . . No, I don't wear my ribbons in public places. Seems to me they are a bit promiscuous."

But when is a word our own? What is a mastery of language? How in fact do we acquire a vocabulary worthy of the name?

The answer of course is: By experience with words, by living with great books and good talkers, by watching their words at work and at play—in brief, by becoming *familiar* with words. Mere acquaintanceship with them is not profitable here. An acquaintance is one whose name and face you know, without more than a rough idea of his being and business. A familiar is one about whom you know as much as possible. Words are astonishingly like people. They have characters, they almost have personalities—are honest, useful, obliging . . . or treacherous, vain, stubborn . . . They shift, as people do, their conduct with their company. They are an endless study in which we are studying nature and ourselves at that meeting point where our minds are trying to give form to or take it from the world.

Peter Mark Roget a century ago had high hopes of the help his arrangement of words might be to thought and to the construction of a common second language such

as Basic English may become. There is nothing fantastic
about such hopes. In drawing up his scheme of divisions
his model was biological classification. He was a physician
and Secretary of the Royal Society. But we need not take
Roget's actual categories too seriously. To criticize them
would be to bring up all the hardest problems there are.
They serve their purpose—which is to remind us systematically of all that we know about words. "It is not suf-
ficiently considered," said Dr. Johnson, "that men require more often to be reminded than to be informed."
For information about words we go to the dictionary—
the bigger it is the better. We go to the *Thesaurus* in the
hope that something we really know already will come
back to us in our need. How vast is the realm of our current oblivion. "I know," said Benjamin Paul Blood, "as
having known, the secret of existence." Nothing will better make us realize how nearly true this is than an hour
spent in the treasury. How incredibly much we understand if only we can mobilize our understanding. Roget's
Thesaurus is one of the greatest of all *memoria technica*.
It is an astonishing thought that we can carry it in the
pocket.

I. A. RICHARDS

CONTENTS

POCKET THESAURUS AND WORD FINDER

CLASS I
WORDS EXPRESSING ABSTRACT RELATIONS

CLASS II
WORDS RELATING TO SPACE

CLASS III
WORDS RELATING TO MATTER

CLASS IV
WORDS RELATING TO THE INTELLECTUAL FACULTIES

CLASS V
WORDS RELATING TO THE VOLUNTARY POWERS

CLASS VI
WORDS RELATING TO THE SENTIENT & MORAL POWERS

ABBREVIATIONS USED IN THIS BOOK

abbr. abbreviated, abbreviation
adj. adjective, adjectival expression
adv. adverb, adverbial expression
Am. *or* Amer. America, American
Am. hist. American history
Am. Ind. American Indian
anat. anatomy
anon. anonymous
Ar. Arabic
arch. architecture
archæol. archæology
arith. arithmetic
astrol. astrology
astron. astronomy
Bib. Biblical
biol. biology
bot. botany
Brit. British
Can. Canada, Canadian
chem. chemistry
Chin. Chinese
class. classical
colloq. colloquial
com. commerce, commercial
conj. conjunction
Du. Dutch
Dan. Danish
dial. dialect, dialectal
dim. diminutive
E. East
eccl. ecclesiastical
Eng. English, England
erron. erroneous, -ly
esp. especially
exc. except
F. French
fem. feminine
fig. figurative, -ly
G. *or* Ger. German
Gr Greek
Gr Brit. Great Britain
her. heraldry
Hind. Hindustani
hist. history, historical
Icel. Icelandic
Ind. Indian
Ir. Irish, Ireland
int. interjection
It. Italian

Jap. Japanese
joc. jocular
L. Latin
l.c. lower case
masc. masculine
math. mathematics
mil. military
Moham. Mohammedan
myth. mythology
n. noun
naut. nautical
neut. neuter
Norw. Norwegian
obs. obsolete
opp. opposed
orig. original, -ly
parl. parliamentary
path. pathology
Pg. Portuguese
pharm. pharmacy
philos. philosophy
physiol. physiology
pl. plural
pol. *or* polit. political
pop. popular, -ly
prep. preposition
prov. proverb, provincial
psychol. psychology
R. C. Ch. Roman Catholic Church
relig. religion
rhet. rhetoric, rhetorical
Russ. Russian
S. Am. South American
Scand. Scandinavian
Scot. Scottish, Scotland
sing. singular
Skr. Sanskrit
Sp. Spanish
surg. surgery
Sw. Swedish
tech. technical
theat. theatrical
theol. theology
typog. typography
Univ. University
U. S. United States
v. verb
zool. zoology

HOW TO USE THE BOOK

I. To find a synonym or antonym for any given WORD:

Turn to the Index* and find the particular word or any term of kindred meaning; then refer to the category indicated (the numbers printed in bold face at the top outer corner of each page). There in its proper grouping, the indexed word will be found, together with a wide selection of related terms. Synonyms and antonyms are placed in adjoining positions. For example, suppose a synonym is wanted for the word "cold" in the sense of "indifferent." Turn to the Index, where the following references will be found:

> cold, *adj.*
> *frigid* 383
> *insensible* 823
> *indifferent* 866

The italicized words give the general sense of the synonyms in the respective categories. The bold-faced figures denote that the indexed word is itself the heading or keyword of a distinct group. Thus, in this example, under 383 we find a list of adjectives grouped under the word "cold" in the literal sense of the term.

Turning to No. 866 (the sense required), we read through the varied list of synonyms ("indifferent, frigid, lukewarm," etc.) and select the most appropriate expression. To widen the selection, suggested references are given to allied lists; while in the adjoining category (No. 865) are grouped the corresponding antonyms ("eager, keen, burning, ardent," etc.). The groups are arranged, not merely to supply synonyms for some special word, but also to suggest new lines of thought and to stimulate the imagination.

II. To find suitable words to express a given IDEA:

Find in the Index some word relating to the idea, and the categories referred to will supply the need.

For example, suppose a writer wishes to convey the idea of "rest." Turning to No. 265, he will find *nouns* giving such associated senses as "quiet," "pause," "resting place," or *verbs* with the sense of "be still," "remain," "quell," or *adjectives* such as "quiescent," "still," "silent," and the like. The mere reading of the entire list will help to crystallize the idea and give it utterance.

III. To find appropriate words or new ideas on any given SUBJECT:

Turn up the subject or any branch of it. The Index itself will frequently suggest various lines of thought, while reference to the indicated groups will provide many words and phrases that should prove helpful.

Thus, suppose "poetry" is the theme, No. 597 will be found most suggestive. Or again, the subject may be "the drama" (599), "music" (415), "the vegetable kingdom" (367), "national legislatures" (696), "psychical research" (992a), or

*(page 311)

"mythology" **(979)**. The writer may perhaps be hazy about the titles of the ruling chiefs of India. Reference to **875** will prevent his applying a Hindu title to a Mohammedan prince. He may wish to know the term for a "plain" in different parts of the world; No. **344** will tell him exactly. The subject may be such an everyday one as "food" **(298)**, "automobiles" **(272)**, "aviation" **(267 and 269a)**, or various kinds of "amusements" **(840)**; whatever it is, the search will not prove altogether unprofitable.

N.B.—To grasp the underlying principle of the classification, study the *Tabular Synopsis of Categories* (pp. xiv-xxviii).

The guide numbers always refer to the *section* numbers in the text, and *not* to pages.

PLAN OF CLASSIFICATION

xiii

TABULAR SYNOPSIS OF CATEGORIES

Class I. ABSTRACT RELATIONS

I. EXISTENCE

1. Existence	2. Nonexistence
3. Substantiality	4. Unsubstantiality
5. Subjectiveness	6. Objectiveness
7. State	8. Circumstance

II. RELATION

9. Relation	10. Irrelation
11. Consanguinity	
12. Correlation	
13. Identity	14. Contrariety
	15. Difference
16. Uniformity	16a. Want of Uniformity
17. Similarity	18. Dissimilarity
19. Imitation	20. Nonimitation
	20a. Variation
21. Copy	22. Prototype
23. Agreement	24. Disagreement

III. QUANTITY

25. Quantity	26. Degree
27. Equality	28. Inequality
	29. Mean
	30. Compensation
31. Greatness	32. Smallness
33. Superiority	34. Inferiority
35. Increase	36. Decrease
37. Addition	38. Deduction
39. Adjunct	40. Remainder
	40a. Decrement
41. Mixture	42. Simpleness
43. Junction	44. Disjunction
45. Vinculum	
46. Coherence	47. Incoherence
48. Combination	49. Decomposition
50. Whole	51. Part
52. Completeness	53. Incompleteness
54. Composition	55. Exclusion (from a compound)
56. Component	57. Extraneousness

IV. ORDER

58. Order	59. Disorder
60 Arrangement	61. Derangement
62. Precedence	63. Sequence
64. Precursor	65. Sequel

VII. CHANGE

140. Change
141. Permanence
142. Cessation
143. Continuance
144. Conversion

145. Reversion

146. Revolution
147. Substitution
148. Interchange
149. Changeableness
150. Stability
151. Present Events
152. Future Events

VIII. CAUSATION

153. Cause
154. Effect
155. Attribution
156. Chance
157. Power
158. Impotence
159. Strength
160. Weakness
161. Production
162. Destruction
163. Reproduction

164. Producer
165. Destroyer
166. Paternity
167. Posterity
168. Productiveness
169. Unproductiveness
170. Agency

171. Energy
172. Inertness
173. Violence
174. Moderation
175. Influence
176. Tendency
177. Liability
178. Concurrence
179. Counteraction

CLASS II.   SPACE

I. SPACE IN GENERAL

180. Space (indefinite)
181. Region (definite)
182. Place

183. Situation
184. Location
185. Displacement
186. Presence
187. Absence
188. Inhabitant
189. Habitation
190. Contents
191. Receptacle

II. DIMENSIONS

192. Size
193. Littleness
194. Expansion
195. Contraction
196. Distance
197. Nearness
198. Interval
199. Contact
200. Length
201. Shortness
202. Breadth. Thickness
203. Narrowness. Thinness
204. Layer
205. Filament
206. Height
207. Lowness

Class III. MATTER

I. MATTER IN GENERAL

II. INORGANIC MATTER

(1) Solids

(2) Fluids

CLASS IV. INTELLECT
I. FORMATION OF IDEAS

469. Qualification

470. Possibility
472. Probability
474. Certainty
476. Reasoning
478. Demonstration
480. Judgment
480a. Discovery
482. Overestimation
484. Belief
486. Credulity
488. Assent
490. Knowledge
492. Scholar
494. Truth
496. Maxim
498. Intelligence. Wisdom
500. Sage
502. Sanity

505. Memory
507. Expectation

471. Impossibility
473. Improbability
475. Uncertainty
477. Intuition. Sophistry
479. Confutation
481. Misjudgment

483. Underestimation
485. Unbelief. Doubt
487. Incredulity
489. Dissent
491. Ignorance
493. Ignoramus
495. Error
497. Absurdity
499. Imbecility. Folly
501. Fool
503. Insanity
504. Madman
506. Oblivion
508. Nonexpectation
509. Disappointment

510. Foresight
511. Prediction
512. Omen
513. Oracle
514. Supposition
515. Imagination

II. COMMUNICATION OF IDEAS

516. Meaning
518. Intelligibility

517. Unmeaningness
519. Unintelligibility

520. Equivocalness

521. Figure of Speech
522. Interpretation
524. Interpreter
525. Manifestation
527. Information
529. Disclosure
531. Publication
532. News
534. Messenger
535. Affirmation
537. Teaching

540. Teacher

543. Veracity

523. Misinterpretation

526. Latency
528. Concealment
530. Ambush

533. Secret

536. Negation
538. Misteaching
539. Learning
541. Learner

542. School

544. Falsehood

Class V. VOLITION

I. INDIVIDUAL VOLITION

600. Will
601. Necessity
602. Willingness
603. Unwillingness
604. Resolution
605. Irresolution
604a. Perseverance
606. Obstinacy

607. Apostasy
608. Caprice
609. Choice
609a. Absence of Choice
610. Rejection
611. Predetermination
612. Impulse
613. Habit
614. Desuetude
615. Motive
615a. Absence of Motive
617. Plea
616. Dissuasion
618. Good
619. Evil
620. Intention
621. Chance
622. Pursuit
623. Avoidance
624. Relinquishment

625. Business
626. Plan
627. Method
628. Mid-course
629. Circuit
630. Requirement
631. Instrumentality
632. Means
633. Instrument
634. Substitute
635. Materials
636. Store
637. Provision
638. Waste
639. Sufficiency
640. Insufficiency
641. Redundance
642. Importance
643. Unimportance
644. Utility
645. Inutility
646. Expedience
647. Inexpedience
648. Goodness
649. Badness
650. Perfection
651. Imperfection
652. Cleanness
653. Uncleanness
654. Health
655. Disease
656. Healthiness
657. Unhealthiness
658. Improvement
659. Deterioration
660. Restoration
661. Relapse
662. Remedy
663. Bane
664. Safety
665. Danger
666. Refuge
667. Pitfall
668. Warning
669. Alarm
670. Preservation

Class VI. AFFECTIONS

I. AFFECTIONS IN GENERAL

II. PERSONAL AFFECTIONS

V. RELIGIOUS AFFECTIONS

ROGET'S POCKET THESAURUS AND WORD FINDER

CLASS I

Words Expressing ABSTRACT RELATIONS

I. EXISTENCE

1. EXISTENCE. — *N.* existence, being, entity, subsistence, presence, omnipresence, ubiquity.

reality, actuality, fact, matter of fact, truth, verity.

essence, inner reality, vital principle.

Science of existence: ontology.

V. **exist,** be, subsist, live, breathe; vegetate; happen, take place; occur, prevail.

consist in, lie in; be comprised in.

abide, continue, endure, last, remain.

Adj. **existent,** subsistent, extant; afloat, on foot, current, prevalent.

real, actual, positive, absolute; veritable, true; substantial, essential.

well founded, well grounded, authentic.

Adv. **actually,** in fact, in reality; indeed.

2. NONEXISTENCE. — *N.* nonexistence, inexistence; nonentity; nullity; nihilism; blank; absence, emptiness, void, vacuum; nothingness.

annihilation, extinction, destruction, abolition, extirpation, nirvana, obliteration.

V. **not exist,** be null and void; cease to exist; pass away, perish, be *or* become extinct; die out; disappear, vanish, fade, melt away, dissolve, be no more; die, etc., 360.

annihilate, nullify; abrogate, etc., 756; destroy, etc., 162; remove, displace, vacate; obliterate, extirpate.

Adj. **inexistent,** nonexistent; negative, blank; null, missing, absent, etc., 187.

unreal, baseless, unsubstantial, shadowy, spectral, visionary.

unborn, uncreated, unbegotten.

1

extinct, gone, lost, departed; defunct, etc. (*dead*), 360.

fabulous, ideal, etc. (*imaginary*), 515.

3. SUBSTANTIALITY —*N* substantiality; person, thing, object, article; something, a being, creature, body, substance, matter, etc., 316; groundwork, materiality.

Adj. **substantial,** essential: personal. bodily, corporeal, tangible, etc. (*material*), 316.

4. UNSUBSTANTIALITY.—*N.* unsubstantiality, nothingness, nihility; bubble, etc., 353.

nothing, naught, *nil* [L.], nullity, zero, cipher; blank, void, hollowness.

thing of naught, man of straw, lay figure; nonentity.

phantom, apparition, specter, shadow, dream, vision, will-o'-the-wisp, *ignis fatuus* [L.].

V. **vanish,** evaporate, fade, sink, fly, dissolve, melt away; die away, die out; disappear, etc., 449.

Adj. **unsubstantial**; baseless, groundless; ungrounded; without foundation.

visionary, imaginary, immaterial, spectral, etc., 980*a*; dreamy; shadowy; ethereal, airy, gaseous, imponderable, tenuous, vague, vaporous, dreamlike, illusory, unreal.

vacant, vacuous; empty, void, blank, hollow.

5. SUBJECTIVENESS.—*N.* subjectiveness, intrinsicality, inherence, immanence, indwelling; ego; essence, quintessence, elixir; gist, pith, core, kernel, marrow, backbone, heart, soul, life, substance.

principle, nature, constitution.

temper, temperament; spirit, humor, quality, disposition.

aspect, mood, feature, peculiarity, idiosyncrasy.

Adj. **intrinsic,** subjective; fundamental, implanted, inherent, essential, natural; innate, inborn, inbred, ingrained, indwelling, immanent, inwrought; radical, incarnate, hereditary, inherited, congenital, indigenous, native; in the grain, bred in the bone, instinctive; characteristic, ineradicable, fixed.

Adv. **practically,** virtually, substantially, in effect.

6. OBJECTIVENESS.—*N.* objectiveness, extraneousness, extrinsicality.

Adj. **extrinsic,** objective; extraneous, external, incidental, accidental, nonessential. unessential, accessory; contingent, fortuitous, casual.

implanted, ingrafted; inculcated, infused.

7. STATE.—*N.* state, condition, category; estate, lot, mood, temper.

dilemma, pass, predicament, quandary, corner, fix [*colloq.*], plight.

frame, fabric, stamp, mold; constitution.

form, shape; tone, tenor, trim, guise, fashion, mode, style, character.

8. CIRCUMSTANCE.—*N.* circumstance, situation, phase, position; footing, standing, status.

occasion, juncture, contingency.

predicament, emergency; exigency, crisis, pinch, pass, plight.

Adj. circumstantial, conditional, provisional; contingent, incidental; adventitious.

Adv. thus, in such wise; in *or* under the circumstances (*or* conditions).

accordingly, that being the case; since, seeing that.

conditionally, provided, if, in case; if so, unless, in the event of; provisionally.

II. RELATION

9. RELATION.—*N.* relation, bearing, relativity, reference, connection, concern; analogy; similarity; homogeneity, affinity, alliance, nearness, association; consanguinity, etc., 11; relationship, relevancy.

ratio, proportion; comparison.

link, tie, bond.

V. relate to, refer to; bear upon, regard, concern, touch, affect, pertain to, belong to; correlate.

associate, connect; link, bind.

Adj. relative, relating to, referable to; belonging to.

related, connected, associated, affiliated; allied, collateral, cognate, affinitive.

relevant, applicable, in the same category.

Adv. as regards, concerning, with relation to, with regard to; by the way, in the matter of.

10. [Want or absence of relation] IRRELATION.—*N.* irrelation, dissociation; inapplicability; disconnection, disjunction; inconsequence, disagreement, heterogeneity; irrelevancy.

V. have no relation to, have no bearing upon, have nothing to do with.

Adj. unrelated, irrespective, unallied, disconnected, unconnected, heterogeneous; isolated.

extraneous, strange, alien, foreign, outlandish, exotic.

irrelevant, inapplicable, not pertinent, unessential, inapposite, beside the mark.

remote, farfetched, out-of-the-way, forced, detached, apart.
incidental, parenthetical, episodic.

Adv. **parenthetically,** by the way, by the by; incidentally, without regard to.

11. [Relations of kindred] CONSANGUINITY.—*N.* **consanguinity,** relationship, kindred, blood; parentage, paternity; lineage, connection, alliance; people [as, *my people*], family, ties of blood, blood relation.

kinsman, kinsfolk; kith and kin; relative, relation; connection; next of kin; near relation, distant relation.

family, fraternity; brotherhood, sisterhood.

race, stock, generation; clan, tribe; strain, breed.

V. **be related to,** claim kinship with.

Adj. **related,** akin, consanguineous, allied, affiliated; kindred.

12. [Double or reciprocal relation] CORRELATION.—*N.* **correlation,** interdependence, reciprocity, mutuality, correspondence, interchange, exchange, barter.

alternation, seesaw, to-and-fro.

V. **reciprocate,** alternate, interact; interchange, exchange; correlate.

Adj. **reciprocal,** mutual, correlative; correspondent, corresponding; alternate; interchangeable; equivalent, complementary.

13. IDENTITY.—*N.* **identity,** sameness, unity, convertibility; equality, etc., 27; homogeneity; self, oneself.

monotony, repetition, etc., 104.

facsimile, etc. *(copy),* 21; similarity, etc., 17; exactness, fidelity; same, selfsame, counterpart.

V. **coincide,** coalesce.

treat as identical *(or* the same), render identical; identify.

Adj. **identical,** self, selfsame, ditto.

coincident, coinciding, coalescent, indistinguishable; one; equivalent, convertible, equal.

14. CONTRARIETY.—*N.* **contrariety,** contrast, foil, antithesis, counterpart, complement; oppositeness; antagonism, opposition, clashing, repugnance, antipathy.

inversion, subversion, reversal, the opposite, the reverse, the inverse, the converse, antipodes.

V. **be contrary,** contrast with, oppose, differ from.

invert, reverse, turn topsy-turvy, turn upside down, transpose.

contradict, contravene; antagonize, etc., 708.

Adj. **contrary,** opposite, counter, adverse, averse, converse, reverse; opposed, antithetical, contrasted, antipodean, diametrically opposite; antagonistic, conflicting, inconsistent, contradictory; hostile, inimical.

15. DIFFERENCE.—*N.* difference, dissimilarity, variance, variation, variety; diversity, divergence, heterogeneity, contrast, antithesis; disagreement, disparity, inequality, distinction, contradiction, contrariety.

nice (*or* fine, subtle) distinction, discrimination; modification.

V. **differ,** vary; mismatch, contrast; diverge from, depart from, deviate from; modify, change, alter.

discriminate, distinguish, etc., 465.

Adj. **different,** diverse, heterogeneous; varied, variant, divergent, incongruous, modified; diversified, various.

other, another, not the same; unequal, etc., 28; unmatched, widely apart.

distinctive, characteristic, discriminative, distinguishing; diagnostic.

16. UNIFORMITY.—*N.* uniformity; homogeneity, stability, continuity, permanence, consistency, accordance, conformity; agreement, etc., 23; consonance.

regularity, constancy, evenness, sameness, unity, even tenor, routine.

V. accord with, etc., 23; conform to; assimilate; level, smooth.

Adj. **uniform,** homogeneous, of a piece, consistent; even, equable, constant, level; invariable, regular, unvaried, undiversified, unvarying, singsong, dreary, monotonous.

Adv. **always,** ever, evermore, perpetually, forever, everlastingly, invariably.

16a. WANT OF UNIFORMITY.—*N.* diversity, irregularity, unevenness; uncomformity, dissimilarity, dissimilitude, divergence, heterogeneity.

Adj. **diversified,** varied, irregular, checkered, uneven; multifarious, of various kinds.

17. SIMILARITY.—*N.* similarity, resemblance, likeness, semblance, affinity, approximation, parallelism; agreement, etc., 23; analogy, correspondence; brotherhood, family likeness.

repetition, etc., 104; sameness, etc. (*identity*), 13; uniformity, etc., 16.

the like; match, fellow, companion, pair, mate, twin, double, counterpart, brother, sister; one's second self, *alter ego* [L.]; chip of the old block, birds of a feather.

simile, parallel, type, image, etc. (*representation*), 554.

V. **resemble,** look like, favor [*colloq.*], follow, echo, reproduce, bear resemblance; savor of, smack of; approximate; parallel, match, rhyme with; take after; imitate, etc., 19.

Adj. **similar,** resembling, like, alike; twin.

analogous, parallel, of a piece; such as.

akin to, etc. (*consanguineous*), 11; correlative, corresponding, cognate, allied to.

approximate, near, close, something like, near [as, *near* silk, *colloq.*], mock, pseudo, simulating, representing.

exact, etc. (*true*), 494; lifelike, faithful, true to life; the very image of, cast in the same mold.

Adv. as if, so to speak; as it were, as if it were; *quasi* [L.], just as.

18. DISSIMILARITY.—*N.* **dissimilarity,** dissimilitude; unlikeness, diversity, disparity, divergence, variation; difference, etc., 15; no**velty,** originality.

V. **vary,** etc. (*differ*), 15; differ from; diversify.

Adj. **dissimilar,** unlike, disparate; divergent, nonidentical, unique, new, novel, unprecedented, original; diversified, etc., 16*a*.

Adv. **otherwise,** alias.

19. IMITATION.—*N.* **imitation,** copying; repetition, duplication; quotation; reproduction.

mockery, aping, mimicry.

simulation, impersonation; parrotism, parrotry; representation, etc., 554; semblance, pretense; copy, etc., 21.

paraphrase; parody, etc., 21.

plagiarism; forgery, etc., 544.

imitator, echo, cuckoo, parrot, ape, monkey, mimic; copyist.

V. **imitate,** copy, mirror, reflect, reproduce, repeat; do like, echo, re-echo, catch; match, parallel; forge, counterfeit.

mimic, ape, simulate, impersonate, act, etc. (*drama*), 599; represent, etc., 554; parody, travesty, caricature, burlesque, take off, mock; borrow.

follow in the steps (*or* wake) **of,** take pattern by, follow suit [*colloq.*], follow the example of, walk in the shoes of, take after, model after; emulate.

Adj. **imitative,** modeled after; molded on, borrowed, counterfeit, imitation, false, pseudo, near [as, *near* silk, *colloq.*]; mock, mimic.

Adv. **literally,** verbatim, word for word, exactly, precisely.

20. NONIMITATION.—*N.* **nonimitation,** originality, creativeness.

Adj. **unimitated,** uncopied; unmatched, unparalleled; inimitable, etc., 33; unique, original, primordial, creative; exceptional, rare, uncommon, unexampled, out-of-the-way, unwonted.

20a. VARIATION.—*N.* **variation,** alteration, change, imitation; modification; discrepancy.

divergency, deviation, deflection; aberration; innovation.

V. **vary,** etc. (*change*), 140; deviate, etc., 279; diverge; alternate.

Adj. **varied,** modified; diversified, etc., *16a;* dissimilar, etc., 18.

21. [Result of imitation] **COPY.**—*N.* **copy,** facsimile, counterpart, effigy, form, likeness, similitude, semblance, cast, tracing; imitation, etc., 19; model, representation, study; portrait, etc., 554; duplicate, transcript, transcription; reflection, shadow, echo; reprint, replica, transfer, reproduction, repetition.

servile copy, counterfeit, forgery.

parody, caricature, burlesque, travesty, paraphrase; cartoon.

Adj. **faithful,** lifelike, similar, close, exact.

22. [Thing copied] **PROTOTYPE.**—*N.* **prototype,** original, model, pattern, precedent, standard; type; archetype, exemplar, example.

copy, text, design; keynote.

die, mold; matrix, last, mint, seal, punch, stamp, intaglio, negative.

V. be an example, set an example.

23. AGREEMENT.—*N.* **agreement,** accord, accordance, unison, harmony, concord, union, unity, unanimity; understanding, *entente cordiale* [F.], concert [as, the *concert* of Europe].

conformity, uniformity, consistency; correspondence, parallelism, apposition.

fitness, aptness, relevancy; pertinence, aptitude, propriety, applicability, admissibility, compatibility.

adaptation, adjustment, accommodation; assimilation.

consent, etc. (*assent*), 488; concurrence, consensus; co-operation.

V. **agree,** accord, harmonize; correspond, tally, consent, etc. (*assent*), 488; suit, fit, befit; square with, dovetail, match, resemble, parallel.

adapt, accommodate, graduate; adjust, etc. (*render equal*), 27; regulate, reconcile.

Adj. **agreeing,** accordant, correspondent, congenial; coherent; harmonious, reconcilable, conformable; consistent, compatible; in accordance with, in harmony with, in keeping with.

apt, apposite, pertinent, pat; to the point; happy, felicitous, germane, applicable, relevant, admissible.

fit, adapted, appropriate, suitable; meet, etc. (*expedient*), 646.

24. DISAGREEMENT.—*N.* **disagreement,** discord, dissonance, disunion, discrepancy, unconformity, incongruity, dissension, conflict, opposition, antagonism, difference, misunderstanding.

disparity, disproportion; inequality, variance, divergence.

unfitness, inaptitude, impropriety, inapplicability, irrelevancy.

V. **disagree,** clash, conflict, dispute, quarrel, jar, interfere.

Adj. **disagreeing,** discordant, inharmonious; hostile, antagonistic, repugnant, clashing, jarring, factious, dissentient, incompatible, irreconcilable, inconsistent with; incongruous; repugnant to.

inapt, inept, inappropriate, improper, unsuited, unsuitable, inapplicable; unfit, unbefitting, unbecoming; ill-timed, unseasonable, ill-adapted, infelicitous, irrelevant.

uncongenial, unsympathetic, ill-assorted, mismatched.

Adv. in defiance of, in contempt of, in spite of.

III. QUANTITY

25. [Absolute quantity] QUANTITY.—*N.* quantity, magnitude; size, bulk, volume, mass, amount, measure, measurement, substance, strength.

[Science of quantity] mathematics.

[Definite quantity] armful, handful, mouthful, spoonful, stock, batch, lot, dose; quota, pittance, driblet.

Adj. quantitative, some, any, more or less.

26. [Relative quantity] DEGREE.—*N.* degree, grade, step, extent, measure, amount, ratio, standard, height, pitch; reach, mark, stage, rate, range, scope, caliber; gradation, shade; tenor, compass; sphere, station, rank, standing; interval, space [*music*]; intensity, strength.

V. graduate, calibrate, measure.

Adj. comparative, gradual, shading off.

Adv. by degrees, gradually, step by step, little by little, inch by inch, drop by drop; to some extent.

27. [Sameness of quantity or degree] EQUALITY.—*N.* equality, parity, symmetry, balance, poise; evenness, monotony, level; equivalence, equipoise, equilibrium; par, quits; distinction without a difference, identity, similarity.

tie, dead heat; drawn game, drawn battle; neck-and-neck race.

match, peer, compeer, equal, mate, fellow, brother; equivalent.

V. equal, match, keep pace with, run abreast; come up to; balance.

equalize, level, dress [*mil.*], balance, handicap, trim, adjust, poise; strike a balance; restore equilibrium.

Adj. equal, even, level, monotonous, symmetrical, co-ordinate; on a par with, on a level with, up to the mark.

equivalent, tantamount; quits; synonymous; convertible; all one, all the same; drawn [as, *a game*].

Adv. equally, to all intents and purposes.

28. [Difference of quantity or degree] INEQUALITY.—*N.* inequality, disparity, odds; difference, etc., 15; unevenness, shortcoming; superiority, etc., 33; inferiority, deficiency, inadequacy.

V. **be unequal,** have the advantage, turn the scale; overmatch, etc., 33; fall short of.

Adj. **unequal,** uneven, partial, inadequate, deficient; overbalanced, unbalanced, top-heavy, lopsided.

unequaled, unparalleled, unrivaled, unique, matchless, inimitable, peerless.

29. MEAN.—*N.* **mean,** medium, average, balance, rule, run, golden mean, middle; compromise, neutrality.

V. **average,** split the difference, strike a balance, pair off.

Adj. **mean,** intermediate; middle, etc., 68; average, normal, standard; neutral.

mediocre, middle class, bourgeois, commonplace.

Adv. **on an average,** in the long run; in round numbers.

30. COMPENSATION.—*N.* **compensation,** equation; indemnification; compromise, measure for measure, retaliation, equalization.

setoff, offset; makeweight, counterpoise, ballast; indemnity, equivalent, *quid pro quo* [L.]; amends, counterbalance, counterclaim.

pay, payment, reward, etc., 973.

V. **compensate,** indemnify; counterpoise, balance, counterbalance, offset, set off; square, make up for, equalize, etc., 27; recoup, redeem; pay, reward, etc., 973.

Adj. **compensating,** compensatory, equivalent, equal.

Adv. **notwithstanding,** but, however, yet, still, nevertheless, although, though; howbeit, albeit; at all events, in spite of, despite, on the other hand, at the same time.

31. GREATNESS.—*N.* **greatness,** vastness, magnitude; size, etc., 192; multitude; immensity, enormity, might, strength, intensity, fullness.

great quantity, quantity, deal [*colloq.*], volume, bulk, mass, heap; stock, store, load, shipload; abundance, sufficiency.

fame, distinction, grandeur, dignity; importance, etc., 642.

V. **be great,** soar, tower, loom, rise above, transcend; bulk, bulk large.

enlarge, etc. (*increase*), 35; wax, magnify, grow, expand, swell, dilate.

Adj. **great,** large, considerable, big, bulky, huge, etc., 192; titanic; voluminous, ample, abundant; many, etc., 102; full, intense; signal.

goodly, noble, precious, mighty; extraordinary; important, etc., 642; supreme, etc., 33; complete, etc., 52; arrant, downright; uttermost; profound, intense, consummate; rank, unmitigated, glaring, flagrant.

world-wide, widespread, far-famed, extensive.

august, grand, dignified, sublime, majestic.

vast, immense, enormous, extreme; inordinate, excessive, extravagant, monstrous, crass, gross; towering, stupendous, prodigious.

unlimited, etc. (*infinite*), 105; unutterable, indescribable, ineffable, unspeakable, inexpressible, fabulous.

absolute, positive, stark, decided, unequivocal, essential, perfect.

remarkable, notable, noticeable, noteworthy, renowned.

Adv. in a great or high degree: greatly, much, indeed, very, very much, most; pretty, enough, in a great measure, passing, richly; on a large scale; by wholesale; mightily, powerfully; extremely, exceedingly, intensely, indefinitely, immeasurably, incalculably, infinitely.

in a positive degree: truly, etc. (*truth*), 494; decidedly, unequivocally, absolutely, essentially, fundamentally, radically, downright, in all conscience.

in a complete degree: entirely, completely, wholly; abundantly, amply, fully, widely.

in a supreme degree: pre-eminently, superlatively, supremely, incomparably.

in a too great degree: immoderately, monstrously, preposterously, exorbitantly, excessively, enormously, out of all proportion.

in a marked degree: particularly, remarkably, singularly, curiously, uncommonly, unusually, peculiarly, notably, signally, strikingly, pointedly, chiefly; famously, egregiously, prominently, glaringly, emphatically, incredibly.

in a violent degree: furiously, violently, severely, desperately, tremendously, extravagantly.

in a painful degree: painfully, sadly, sorely, bitterly, piteously, grievously, miserably, cruelly, woefully, lamentably, shockingly, frightfully, dreadfully, fearfully, terribly, horribly, distressingly, balefully.

32. SMALLNESS.—*N.* smallness, littleness, paucity; fewness, sparseness, scarcity, insignificance, unimportance.

small quantity, modicum, minimum; atom, particle, trifle, electron, molecule, corpuscle, point, speck, dot, mote, jot, iota; minutiæ, details; tittle, spark; grain, scruple, minim; drop, sprinkling, dab, dash, tinge, dole, mite, bit, morsel, crumb, scrap, shred, tag, splinter, rag; snip, sliver, paring, shaving, hair; thimbleful, handful, capful, mouthful; fragment, fraction.

V. be small, lie in a nutshell.

diminish, etc. (*decrease*), 36; contract, shrink, dwindle, wane.

Adj. small, little, stunted; diminutive, etc. (*small in size*), 193; minute, miniature, inconsiderable, paltry, etc. (*unimportant*), 643; scanty, scant, limited, meager, sparing; few, etc., 103; moderate, modest.

inappreciable, infinitesimal, atomic, microscopic, molecular.

mere, simple, sheer, stark, bare.

Adv. **in a small degree:** to a small extent, on a small scale; a little, slightly, imperceptibly; miserably, wretchedly; insufficiently, imperfectly, faintly, feebly, passably.

in a certain or limited degree: partially, in part, in a certain degree, to a certain degree *or* extent; comparatively, rather, in some degree *or* measure; somewhat; simply, only, purely, merely; at least, at most, ever so little, thus far, after a fashion.

almost, nearly, well-nigh, not quite, all but, near upon, close upon, near the mark; within an ace (*or* inch) of, on the brink of; scarcely, hardly, barely, only just, no more than.

in an uncertain degree: about, thereabouts, somewhere about, nearly.

in no degree: noway, nowise, not at all, not in the least, not a bit, not a jot, in no wise, in no respect, by no means, on no account.

33. SUPERIORITY.—*N.* superiority, majority, plurality; advantage; preponderance, prevalence.

nobility, etc. (*rank*), 875; superman, overman.

supremacy, supremeness, primacy, pre-eminence, lead; maximum, record; crest, climax, culmination, summit, peak, transcendence; lion's share, excess, surplus, overweight, redundance.

V. **exceed,** excel, transcend, outdo, outbalance, overbalance, outweigh, outrank, outrival, out-Herod Herod; pass, surpass, overtop, overmatch; cap, culminate, beat, cut out [*colloq.*]; beat hollow [*colloq.*], outstrip, eclipse, throw into the shade; predominate, prevail; precede, take precedence, come first, bear the palm, break the record.

Adj. **superior,** greater, major, higher, exceeding; distinguished, ultra.

supreme, greatest, maximum, utmost, paramount, pre-eminent, foremost, crowning, excellent, peerless, matchless; unrivaled, unparalleled, unequaled, unapproached, unsurpassed; superlative, incomparable, transcendent.

Adv. **beyond,** more, over; over and above; at its height.

in a superior or supreme degree: eminently, pre-eminently, surpassing, superlatively, supremely, principally, especially, particularly, peculiarly.

34. INFERIORITY.—*N.* inferiority, shortcoming, deficiency; minimum; imperfection; meanness, poorness, baseness, shabbiness.

Personal inferiority: the people, etc., 876; subordination.

V. **be inferior,** fall short of, come short of, not come up to; become smaller, decrease, yield the palm, play second fiddle.

Adj. **inferior,** smaller; less, lesser, deficient, reduced, lower, subordinate, secondary, junior, minor, humble; second rate; unimportant, etc., 643.

Adv. less, short of, under.

35. INCREASE.—*N.* **increase,** augmentation, addition, enlargement, extension, expansion, growth, increment, accretion, development, accumulation, inflation, enhancement, aggravation, exaggeration.

gain, produce, product, profit, advantage, booty, plunder.

V. **increase,** augment, add to, enlarge, etc., 31; advance, rise, mount, ascend.

aggrandize, raise, exalt; deepen, heighten, lengthen, thicken; inflate, intensify, enhance, magnify, redouble, double; aggravate, exaggerate.

Adj. **increasing,** growing, crescent, multiplying, intensifying, intensive.

Adv. **crescendo,** increasingly.

36. DECREASE.—*N.* **decrease,** diminution, lessening, subtraction, reduction, abatement, declension; shrinkage, contraction, curtailment, abridgment.

subsidence, wane, ebb, decline; ebb tide, neap tide, ebbing.

V. **decrease,** diminish, lessen; abridge, shorten, shrink, contract; dwindle, fall away, waste, wear; wane, ebb, decline, subside, languish, decay, crumble.

discount, belittle, minimize, depreciate, extenuate, lower, weaken, attenuate; dwarf, reduce, shorten, subtract; mitigate, ease, moderate.

Adv. **decrescendo,** decreasingly.

37. ADDITION.—*N.* **addition,** annexation, accession, re-enforcement; increase, etc., 35; increment.

affix, codicil, tag, appendage, postscript, adjunct, supplement; accompaniment, insertion.

V. **add,** annex, affix, subjoin, tack to, append, tag, attach; interpose, introduce, insert.

compute, total, cast (*or* sum, count) up.

re-enforce, strengthen, augment.

Adj. **additional,** supplemental, supplementary; extra, spare, further, fresh, more, other, auxiliary, contributory, accessory.

Adv. **in addition,** more; and, also, likewise, too, furthermore, further; besides, to boot; over and above, moreover; as well as, together with, along with, in conjunction with.

38. DEDUCTION.—*N.* **deduction,** subtraction, retrenchment; abstraction, mutilation, amputation, curtailment, abbreviation.

rebate, etc. (*decrement*), 40*a*; minuend, subtrahend; decrease, etc., 36.

V. deduct, subtract, retrench; withdraw; take from, take away; detract, reduce, eliminate, diminish, curtail, shorten; deprive of, etc. (*take*), 789; weaken.

mutilate, amputate, cut off, cut away, excise.

pare, thin, prune, scrape, file.

Adv. less; short of; minus, without, except, excepting, with the exception of, save, exclusive of.

39. [Thing added] **ADJUNCT.**—*N.* adjunct, addition, affix, suffix, appendage, annex, augmentation, increment, re-enforcement, accessory, accompaniment, etc., 88; addendum (*pl.* addenda); complement, supplement, sequel.

rider, offshoot, episode, side issue, corollary, codicil, etc. (*addition*), 37.

V. add, annex, etc., 37.

Adj. additional, etc., 37.

40. [Thing remaining] **REMAINDER.**—*N.* remainder, residue, remains, remnant, rest, relic; leavings, odds and ends, residuum, dregs, refuse, stubble, ruins, wreck, skeleton, fossil, stump, rump.

surplus, excess; balance [*commercial slang*], result; superfluity, redundance; survival.

V. remain, survive, be left; exceed.

Adj. remaining, left, residual, residuary; over, odd; surviving; net; superfluous, etc. (*redundant*), 641.

40a. [Thing deducted] **DECREMENT.**—*N.* decrement, discount, rebate, defect, loss, deduction; waste.

41. MIXTURE.—*N.* mixture, admixture, junction, etc., 43; amalgamation, combination, etc., 48; infusion, transfusion; infiltration; interlarding, interpolation, etc., 228; adulteration.

Thing mixed: tinge, tincture, touch, dash, smack, spice, seasoning, infusion.

Compounds: alloy, amalgam; brass, pewter; miscellany, medley, mess, hash, hodgepodge, patchwork, jumble; potpourri, mosaic.

half-blood, half-breed, half-caste, crossbreed, mulatto, quadroon, octoroon, Eurasian; mule, cross, hybrid, mongrel.

V. mix, join, etc., 43; combine, etc., 48; mingle, commingle, intermingle, interlard, interpolate, intertwine, interweave; associate with.

imbue, infuse, diffuse, suffuse, transfuse, instill, infiltrate, dash, tinge, tincture, season, blend, cross; alloy, amalgamate, compound, adulterate.

Adj. mixed, composite, half-and-half, hybrid, mongrel, heterogeneous; motley, variegated, miscellaneous, promiscuous, indiscriminate.

Adv. among, amid, with; in the midst of.

42. [Freedom from mixture] **SIMPLENESS.**—*N.* simpleness, purity, homogeneity.

elimination, sifting, purification, etc. (*cleanness*), 652.

V. **render simple,** simplify.

sift, winnow, bolt, eliminate; exclude, get rid of; clear, purify, etc. (*clean*), 652.

Adj. **simple,** uniform, homogeneous, single, pure, clear; elemental, elementary.

43. JUNCTION.—*N.* junction, joining, union; connection, conjunction, annexation, attachment; marriage, wedlock; confluence, communication, meeting, reunion; assemblage, etc., 72; coherence, etc., 46; combination, etc., 48.

joint, joining, juncture, pivot, hinge, articulation; seam, gore, gusset, link, bond.

contingency, emergency, predicament, crisis, concurrence.

V. **join,** unite, connect; associate; put together, piece together, embody.

attach, fix, fasten, bind, secure, tighten, clinch, tie, strap, sew, lace, stitch, knit, button, buckle, hitch, lash, splice, gird, tether, moor, picket, chain; fetter, hook, link, yoke, bracket; marry; bridge over, span.

pin, nail, screw, bolt, hasp, clasp, clamp, rivet; solder, cement, etc., 46.

entwine, interlace, intertwine, interweave; entangle.

Adj. **joined,** joint; corporate, compact.

firm, fast, close, tight, taut, secure, inseparable, indissoluble.

Adv. **jointly,** in conjunction with, etc. (*in addition to*), 37; fast, firmly.

44. DISJUNCTION.—*N.* disjunction, disconnection, disunion, disengagement, dissociation, discontinuity, etc., 70; isolation, insularity, insulation, separateness; dispersion.

separation, parting; detachment, segregation; divorce; cæsura, division, subdivision, break, fracture, rupture; dismemberment, dissection, disintegration, severance, disruption, cleavage.

fissure, breach, rent, rift, crack, slit, cut, incision.

V. **disjoin,** disconnect, disengage, disunite, dissociate, divorce, part, detach, unfasten, separate, disentangle, cut off, segregate; set apart, keep apart; insulate, isolate; cut adrift, loose, set free. liberate.

divide, sunder, subdivide, sever, dissever, cut, chop, saw, snip, nip, cleave, rive, rend, slit, rip, split, splinter, chip, crack, snap, break, tear, burst; wrench, rupture, hack, hew, slash, slice, carve, quarter, dissect, anatomize; partition, parcel.

disintegrate, dismember, disband; disperse, etc., 73; dislocate, break up.

part, part company; separate, leave; alienate, estrange.

Adj. disjoined, discontinuous, disjunctive; isolated, insular; separate, apart, asunder, loose, free, adrift.

Adv. separately, one by one, severally, apart, asunder.

45. [Connecting medium] VINCULUM.—*N.* vinculum, link; connective, connection; junction, etc., 43; hyphen; bracket; bridge, steppingstone; bond, cord; rope, line, cable, hawser, painter; chain; string, etc. (*filament*), 205.

fastening, tie; ligament, ligature; strap; tackle, rigging; yoke, band, headband, fillet, snood, brace, thong, girdle, noose, lariat, lasso, knot, girth, cinch.

cement, glue, gum, paste, size, solder, mortar, plaster, putty.

shackle, rein, etc. (*means of restraint*), 752.

V. bridge over, span; connect, etc., 43.

46. COHERENCE.—*N.* coherence, cohesion, cohesiveness, adherence, adhesion, adhesiveness; conglomeration, aggregation, consolidation, soldering, connection; relativity.

tenacity, toughness; stickiness; inseparability.

conglomerate, concrete, etc., 321.

V. cohere, adhere, coagulate, stick, cling, cleave, hold, close with, clasp, hug.

glue, agglutinate, cement, paste, gum; solder, weld; cake, consolidate, solidify, agglomerate.

Adj. adhesive, cohesive, adhering, tenacious, tough; sticky, etc., 352.

47. INCOHERENCE.—*N.* incoherence, nonadhesion; looseness, laxity, relaxation; loosening, disjunction, etc., 44.

V. loosen, make loose, slacken, relax; unglue, etc., 46; detach, etc., 44.

Adj. nonadhesive, noncohesive, incoherent, detached, loose, baggy, slack, lax, relaxed, segregated, unconsolidated; uncombined, etc., 48.

48. COMBINATION.—*N.* combination, mixture, etc., 41; junction, etc., 43; union, unification, synthesis, incorporation, amalgamation, coalescence, fusion, brew, blend, blending; centralization.

alloy, compound, amalgam, composition, resultant.

V. **combine,** unite, incorporate, alloy, intermix, interfuse, interlard, amalgamate, embody, absorb, blend, merge, fuse, consolidate, coalesce, solidify, impregnate, centralize.

league, federate, confederate, fraternize, club, associate, amalgamate, couple, pair, ally.

Adj. **combined,** conjoint; ingrained, imbued.

allied, amalgamated, federate, confederate, corporate, leagued.

49. DECOMPOSITION.—*N.* **decomposition,** analysis, dissection, dissolution, breakup; disjunction, etc., 44; disintegration.

decay, rot, putrefaction, putrescence, putridity, caries, corruption.

V. **decompose,** analyze, dissolve; resolve into its elements, dissect, disintegrate, disperse; crumble into dust.

rot, decay, consume, putrefy.

50. [Principal part] WHOLE.—*N.* **whole,** totality, integrity, entirety, completeness; integer, integral.

all, the whole, total, aggregate, sum, sum total.

bulk, mass, lump, tissue, staple, body, greater part, main part; lion's share.

V. **form a whole,** embody, amass; aggregate, assemble; amount to.

Adj. **whole,** total, gross, entire; complete, etc., 52; wholesale, sweeping; comprehensive.

indivisible, indissoluble, indissolvable.

Adv. **wholly,** altogether; as a whole, totally, completely, entirely, all, all in all, wholesale, in a body, collectively, in the aggregate, in the main, on the whole, bodily, substantially.

51. PART.—*N.* **part,** portion; item, particular; aught, any; division; sector, segment; fraction, fragment; detachment, subdivision.

section, chapter, verse; article, clause.

piece, lump, bit, cut, cutting; chip, chunk, slice, scrap, crumb, morsel, moiety, particle; installment, dividend; share.

member, limb, arm, wing, scion, branch, bough, joint, link, offshoot, ramification, twig, spray, spring; runner, tendril; leaf, leaflet; stump.

V. **part,** divide, disjoin, etc., 44; partition, etc. (*apportion*), 786.

Adj. **fractional,** fragmentary, sectional; incomplete, partial.

divided, broken, cut, cropped, shorn.

divisible, dissoluble, dissolvable.

Adv. **partly,** in part, partially; piecemeal, by installments, in detail.

52. COMPLETENESS.—*N.* **completeness,** intactness, completion, etc., 729; fill, saturation, entirety; totality, integrity; perfection, etc., 650; solidarity, unity, all, high tide, flood tide, spring tide.

V. **complete,** etc. (*accomplish*), 729; fill, charge, load, replenish; make up, eke out, supply deficiencies; fill up, fill in, satiate; saturate.

Adj. **complete,** entire, whole, intact, perfect, full, absolute, thorough; solid, undivided.

brimful, brimming, chock-full; saturated, crammed; replete, etc. (*redundant*), 641; fraught, laden.

exhaustive, radical, sweeping, thoroughgoing.

regular, unmitigated, sheer, unqualified, unconditional, free, abundant, etc. (*sufficient*), 639.

completing, supplemental, supplementary.

Adv. **completely,** altogether, outright, wholly, totally, utterly, quite; effectually, fully, in all respects, in every respect; out and out; throughout, from first to last, from head to foot, from top to toe, every whit, every inch.

53. INCOMPLETENESS.—*N.* **incompleteness,** deficiency, shortcoming, want, lack, insufficiency, imperfection, etc., 651; immaturity.

Part wanting: defect, deficit, omission; shortage; break, etc. (*discontinuity*), 70; missing link.

V. **be incomplete,** fall short of, lack, etc. (*be insufficient*), 640.

Adj. **incomplete,** uncompleted, imperfect, unfinished; defective, deficient, wanting, failing, in arrear, short, short of; perfunctory, sketchy, crude, immature.

mutilated, garbled, hashed, mangled, butchered, docked, truncated.

in progress, in hand; going on, proceeding.

54. COMPOSITION.—*N.* **composition,** constitution; make-up; combination, etc., 48; embodiment; formation.

authorship, compilation, composition, production, invention; writing.

painting, etching, design, etc. (*painting*), 556; relief, etc. (*sculpture*), 557.

typesetting, typography, etc., 591.

V. **be composed of,** consist of.

include, etc., 76; contain, hold, comprehend, admit, embrace, embody.

compose, constitute, form, make; fabricate, weave, construct; compile, scribble, draw, write.

55. EXCLUSION.—*N.* **exclusion,** omission, exception, rejection, repudiation; exile, seclusion, lockout, ostracism, prohibition.

separation, segregation, elimination, expulsion.

V. **exclude,** bar; leave out, shut out; reject, repudiate, blackball, ostracize; lay aside, put aside, set apart; relegate, segregate; strike off, strike out; neglect, banish, etc. (*seclude*), 893; separate, etc. (*disjoin*), 44.

pass over, omit; eliminate, weed out.

Adj. **exclusive,** inadmissible, preclusive, preventive, prohibitive.

Adv. **except,** exclusive of, save.

56. COMPONENT.—*N.* **component,** integral part, element, constituent, ingredient, contents; feature; member, etc. (*part*), 51; personnel.

V. **enter into,** be *or* form part of, etc., 51; merge in, share in, participate; belong to, appertain to; combine, unite.

form, make, constitute, compose, fabricate, etc., 54.

Adj. **inherent,** intrinsic, essential.

inclusive, all-embracing, comprehensive.

57. EXTRANEOUSNESS.—*N.* **extraneousness,** extrinsicality; exclusion; alienism.

foreign body (substance *or* element).

alien, stranger, intruder, interloper, foreigner, newcomer; immigrant, emigrant; outsider, barbarian, tenderfoot [*slang*].

Adj. **extraneous,** foreign, alien, exterior, external; outlandish, barbaric, barbarian.

excluded, inadmissible; exceptional.

Adv. **abroad,** in foreign parts, in foreign lands; oversea, overseas.

IV. ORDER

58. ORDER.—*N.* **order,** regularity, uniformity, symmetry, harmony; course, routine; method, disposition, arrangement, array, system, economy, discipline, orderliness, subordination.

gradation, progression · series, etc. (*continuity*), 69.

rank, place, etc. (*term*), 71.

V. **adjust,** regulate, systematize, standardize; time.

Adj. **orderly,** regular; in order, in trim, neat, tidy, methodical, uniform, symmetrical, shipshape, businesslike, systematic, normal, habitual.

Adv. **in order,** methodically, in turn, in its turn; step by step; systematically, by clockwork.

59. DISORDER.—*N.* **disorder,** derangement; irregularity; untidiness; anomaly, etc. (*unconformity*), 83; anarchy, anarchism; disunion; discord.

confusion, disarray, jumble, botch, litter, farrago, mess, muddle, hodgepodge, imbroglio, chaos, clutter, medley.

complexity, complication, entanglement, intricacy; perplexity; network, maze, labyrinth; wilderness, jungle; tangled skein.

turmoil, ferment, etc. (*agitation*), 315; trouble, disturbance, convulsion, tumult, uproar, riot, rumpus [*colloq.*], fracas, pandemonium, Babel, saturnalia.

V. disorder, botch, disturb, derange, etc., 61; entangle, ravel, ruffle, rumple.

Adj. disorderly, out of order, out of place, irregular, desultory; anomalous, etc. (*unconformable*), 83; disorganized; straggling; unmethodical, unsystematic; untidy, slovenly, messy [*colloq.*], indiscriminate, chaotic, confused; deranged, etc., 61; topsy-turvy, disjointed, out of joint.

complex, intricate, complicated, perplexed, involved, entangled, knotted, tangled, inextricable.

troublous, tumultuous, turbulent; riotous, etc. (*violent*), 173.

60. [Reduction to Order] ARRANGEMENT.—*N.* arrangement, plan, etc., 626; preparation, provision; disposal, disposition; distribution, sorting, assortment, allotment, apportionment, graduation, organization, groupings; analysis, classification, division, systematization, codification.

Result of arrangement: orderliness, form, array, digest; synopsis, etc. (*compendium*), 596; table; register, etc. (*record*), 551; organism; stipulation, settlement.

V. arrange, dispose, fix, place; form; set in order, set out; compose, space, range, graduate, marshal, array, rank, group, parcel out, allot, apportion, distribute, assign the parts; dispose of, assort, sort; tidy [*colloq.*].

classify, class, file, list; register, etc. (*record*), 551; catalogue, tabulate, index, alphabetize, grade, codify.

methodize, regulate, systematize, co-ordinate, organize; unravel, disentangle.

Adj. arranged, embattled, in battle array; cut and dried; methodical, orderly, regular, systematic, on file; tabular.

61. [Bringing into disorder] DERANGEMENT.—*N.* derangement, muss [*colloq.* U. S.], mess; disorder, etc., 59; discomposure, disturbance; disorganization, dislocation; inversion, etc., 218; insanity, etc., 503.

V. derange, disarrange, discompose, displace, misplace; mislay, disorder; disorganize; embroil, convulse, unsettle, disturb, confuse, trouble, perturb, disconcert, jumble; muddle; unhinge, dislocate, put out of joint, throw out of gear.

turn topsy-turvy, etc. (*invert*), 218; bedevil; complicate, involve, perplex, confound; tangle, entangle; tousle [*colloq.*], dishevel, ruffle, rumple, etc. (*fold*), 258; become insane, etc., 503.

litter, scatter; mix, etc., 41.

62. [Consecutive Order] **PRECEDENCE.**—*N.* precedence, the lead, superiority, etc., 33; importance, consequence; premise; antecedence, precursor, etc., 64; priority, preference.

prefix, affix; preamble; prelude, overture, voluntary.

V. **precede,** forerun, come before, come first; head, lead, lead the way; introduce, usher in; rank, outrank; take precedence.

prefix; premise, prelude, preface; affix.

Adj. **preceding,** precedent, antecedent; anterior; prior, etc., 116; before; former, foregoing, aforesaid, said; introductory, etc., 64.

Adv. **before;** in advance, etc. (*precession*), 280.

63. **SEQUENCE.**—*N.* sequence, train; following, succession; afterclap, afterglow, aftermath, afterpiece, aftertaste.

continuation, prolongation; order of succession.

V. **succeed,** come after, ensue, come next.

follow, tag [*colloq.*], heel, dog, shadow, hound, hunt; trace, retrace.

append, place after, subjoin.

Adj. **succeeding,** sequent; subsequent; proximate, next; consecutive, etc. (*continuity*), 69.

latter, posterior, etc., 117.

Adv. **after,** subsequently; behind, etc. (*rear*), 235.

64. **PRECURSOR.**—*N.* precursor, antecedent, precedent, predecessor; forerunner, pioneer; outrider; leader, bellwether; herald, harbinger.

prelude, preamble, preface, prologue, foreword, proem, exordium, introduction; heading, frontispiece, groundwork; preparation, etc., 673; overture, voluntary; premises.

prefigurement, etc., 511; omen, etc., 512.

Adj. **introductory,** preludial, prefatory, precursory, inaugural, preliminary.

65. **SEQUEL.**—*N.* sequel, suffix, tail, queue, train, wake, trail, rear; retinue, suite; appendix, postscript, postlude, conclusion, epilogue; peroration; codicil; continuation; appendage, tag, aftergrowth, afterpiece, afterthought, second thoughts; outgrowth.

follower, successor, pursuer, adherent, partisan, disciple, client; sycophant, parasite.

66. **BEGINNING.**—*N.* beginning, commencement, opening, outset, incipience, inception; introduction, etc. (*prelude*), 64; initial; inauguration, embarkation, rising of the curtain; curtain raiser, maiden speech; exordium; outbreak, onset, brunt; initiative, first move; start, starting point; dawn, etc. (*morning*), 125.

origin, etc. (*cause*), 153; source, rise; bud, germ, egg, embryo, rudiment; genesis, birth, nativity, cradle, infancy.

head, heading; title page; van, etc. (*front*), 234.

entrance, entry; inlet, orifice, mouth, porch, portal, portico, door; gate, gateway; postern, wicket, threshold, vestibule; border, frontier.

rudiments, elements, outlines, grammar, alphabet, ABC.

V. **begin,** commence; rise, arise; originate, initiate, open, start; dawn, set in, take its rise, enter upon; set out, etc. (*depart*), 293; embark in; make one's debut; institute; set about, set to work; make a start; break ground, cross the Rubicon; undertake, etc., 676.

usher in, lead the way, take the lead *or* initiative; inaugurate, head; lay the foundations, etc. (*prepare*), 673; found, etc. (*cause*), 153; set up, set on foot, launch, broach; open up, open the door to.

come into existence, take birth; burst forth, break out; spring up, crop up.

recommence; begin at the beginning, begin again, start afresh.

Adj. **initial,** prime, introductory, incipient; inaugural; embryonic, rudimentary; primal, primary, primeval, etc. (*old*), 124; aboriginal; natal.

first, maiden, foremost, front, head, leading.

Adv. **first,** in the first place, in the bud, in embryo, from the beginning, formerly.

67. END.—*N.* **end,** close, termination, conclusion, finish, completion, finis, finale, period, term, terminus, last, extreme, extremity; fag end, tip, nib, point, tail, tag, peroration, appendix, epilogue; consummation, denouement, fall of the curtain; goal, destination, terminal, limit, stoppage; expiration; dissolution, death, etc., 360; doomsday.

last stage, evening (*of life*); *coup de grâce* [F.], deathblow; knockout.

V. **end,** close, finish, terminate, conclude; expire, die, etc., 360; come to a close, perorate; run out, pass away.

bring to an end, put an end to, make an end of; achieve, etc. (*complete*), 729; stop, etc., 142.

Adj. **final,** terminal; conclusive; crowning, etc. (*completing*), 729; last, ultimate; hindermost; rear, etc., 235.

ended, settled, decided, over.

Adv. **finally,** in fine; at the last; once for all.

68. MIDDLE.—*N.* **middle,** midst, thick, midmost; mean, etc., 29; medium, middle term; center, core, kernel, nucleus, hub, heart, bull's-eye; mid-course, neutrality, compromise.

equidistance, bisection; equator, diaphragm, midriff.

Adj. **middle,** medial, mid, midmost; intermediate, equidistant, central, pivotal, mediterranean, equatorial.

Adv. **midway,** halfway, in the middle; amidships.

69. [Uninterrupted sequence] CONTINUITY.—continuity, continuousness, succession, round, suite, progression, series, train, chain; scale; gradation, course; perpetuity.

procession, cavalcade, parade; column; retinue, cortege, funeral, ovation.

pedigree, genealogy, lineage, history, family tree, race; ancestry, descent, family, house; line, line of ancestors; strain.

rank, file, line, row, range, tier.

V. **arrange in a series,** string together, file, list, thread, tabulate.

Adj. **continuous,** continued; consecutive, progressive, gradual, serial, successive; uninterrupted, unbroken, entire; linear; perennial, constant.

Adv. **continuously,** in a line, in succession, in turn; running, gradually, in file, in single file, in Indian file.

70. [Interrupted sequence] DISCONTINUITY.—*N.* discontinuity, disconnectedness; disconnection, etc., 44; interruption, break, fracture, flaw, fault, crack, cut; gap, etc. (*interval*), 198; intermission, alternation.

V. **alternate,** interchange, intermit.

discontinue, pause, interrupt, intervene; break, break off; interpose, etc., 228; disconnect, etc. (*disjoin*), 44; dissever.

Adj. **discontinuous,** disconnected, broken, interrupted, fitful, irregular, spasmodic, desultory; intermittent, alternate, recurrent, periodic.

Adv. **at intervals,** by snatches, by jerks, by fits and starts.

71. TERM.—*N.* term, rank, station, stage, step; degree, etc., 26; scale, grade, status, state, position, standing, footing, place, mark, period, range.

72. [Collective Order] ASSEMBLAGE.—*N.* assemblage, collection, levy, gathering, ingathering, mobilization, meet, forgathering, muster, team; concourse, conflux, congregation.

meeting, levee, reunion, drawing room, at home; social gathering, 892; assembly, congress, house, senate, legislature, etc., 696; convocation, caucus, convention.

company, platoon, faction, caravan, posse, watch, squad, corps, troop, troupe; army, regiment.

miscellany, miscellanea, compilation; symposium; library, etc. (*store*), 636.

crowd, throng; flood, rush, deluge; rabble, mob, host, etc. (*multitude*), 102; rout, press, crush, horde, body, tribe; crew, gang, knot, squad, force, band, party; bunch, drive, roundup.

clan, brotherhood, association, etc. (*party*), 712.

group, cluster, clump, set, batch, lot, pack; budget, assortment, bunch; parcel, packet, bundle, package, bale, fagot, wisp, truss, tuft, shock, clump; grove, thicket; rick, stack, sheaf, swath; volley, shower, storm, cloud.

accumulation, etc. (*store*), 636; heap, lump, pile, mass, pyramid; drift, snowball, snowdrift; amassment; conglomeration, aggregation, concentration, convergence, congestion, quantity, etc. (*greatness*), 31.

V. **be** *or* **come together,** assemble, collect, muster; meet, unite, join, rejoin; cluster, flock, swarm, surge, stream, herd, crowd, huddle, throng, associate; congregate, concentrate, resort, forgather.

bring together, assemble, muster, collect, gather; hold a meeting, convene, convoke; rake up, dredge, heap, mass, pile; pack, cram, lump together; compile, group, concentrate, unite, amass, accumulate, hoard, store.

Adj. **dense,** serried, teeming, swarming, populous.

73. DISPERSION.—*N.* dispersion, disjunct on, etc., 44; divergence, radiation, broadcast, spread, dissemination, diffusion, dissipation, distribution; apportionment, allotment.

V. **disperse,** scatter, sow, disseminate, sow broadcast, diffuse, radiate, broadcast, shed, spread, bestrew, dispense, disband, dismember, distribute; apportion, etc., 786; dispel, cast forth, draft off; strew, cast, sprinkle; issue, deal out, retail, utter.

Adj. **scattered,** disseminated, strown, strewn, dispersed, diffuse, diffusive, sparse, broadcast, sporadic, widespread; epidemic, etc. (*general*), 78; adrift, stray; disheveled.

74. [Place of meeting] FOCUS.—*N.* focus, center, gathering place, rendezvous, rallying point, headquarters, resort, haunt, retreat, club; tryst, trysting place, place of meeting.

V. **focus,** bring to a point, bring to a focus; rally, meet.

75. [Distributive Order] CLASS.—*N.* class, division, subdivision, category, head, order, section; department, province, domain, sphere.

kind, sort, type, estate, genus, species, variety, family, race, tribe, caste, clan, breed, kin; clique, coterie, set; sect, gender, sex.

description, denomination, persuasion, connection, designation, character, stamp; selection, specification.

76. INCLUSION.—*N.* inclusion, admission, incorporation, comprisal, reception.

composition, embodiment, formation.

V. **include,** comprise, comprehend, contain, admit, embrace, receive, inclose, etc. (*circumscribe*), 229; incorporate, cover, embody, encircle; reckon among, number among; refer to; place under, arrange under, take into account.

Adj. **inclusive,** included, including; comprehensive, sweeping, all-embracing.

77. EXCLUSION [from a class].—*N.* **exclusion,** rejection, *see* exclusion (*from a compound*), 55.

78. GENERALITY.—*N.* **generality,** universality, catholicity, miscellany, miscellaneousness; common run, prevalence, rifeness.

everyone, everybody, all hands [*colloq.*], all the world and his wife [*humorous*], anybody.

V. **be general,** prevail.

render general, spread, broaden, universalize, generalize.

Adj. **general,** generic, collective; current, wide, broad, comprehensive, sweeping; encyclopedic, panoramic, widespread, etc. (*dispersed*), 73; common, prevalent, prevailing, rife, epidemic.

universal, catholic, world-wide.

every, all, unspecified, miscellaneous, indefinite.

Adv. **generally,** always, in general, generally speaking; for the most part.

79. SPECIALTY.—*N.* **specialty,** speciality, individuality, peculiarity; personality, characteristic, mannerism, idiosyncrasy, singularity, originality; trait, distinctive feature.

particulars, details, items, counts; minutiæ.

V. **specify,** particularize; individualize, specialize; designate, determine; denote, indicate, point out, select, differentiate; itemize, enter into detail.

Adj. **special,** especial, particular, individual, specific, proper, personal, original, private, respective, definite, minute, certain, peculiar, marked, appropriate, characteristic, exclusive, restricted; singular, exceptional; typical, representative.

Adv. **each,** apiece, one by one, severally, respectively, in detail. **namely,** that is to say, viz.; to wit.

80. RULE.—*N.* **regularity,** uniformity, constancy, clockwork precision, punctuality, etc. (*exactness*), 494; even tenor, rut; system, routine, custom; formula; canon, convention, maxim, rule, regulation; standard, model, precedent; conformity, etc., 82.

law, order of things; normality, normalcy, normal state, ordinary condition, standing order; hard and fast rule.

Adj. **regular,** uniform, symmetrical, constant, steady; according to rule, etc., 82; normal, habitual, customary, etc., 613; methodical, orderly, systematic.

81. MULTIFORMITY.—*N.* **multiformity,** variety, diversity

Adj. **multiform,** multifold, multifarious, multiplex; manifold, many-sided; protean, heterogeneous, motley, mosaic.

indiscriminate, irregular, diversified, diverse; of every description.

82. CONFORMITY.—*N.* **conformity,** observance; conventionality, etc. (*custom*), 613; agreement, accord.

example, instance, exemplification, illustration, specimen, sample.

conventionalist, formalist, bromide [*slang*], Philistine.

V. **conform to,** adapt oneself to.

be regular, travel in a rut; obey rules; agree with, comply with, fall in with; be guided by, harmonize, conventionalize, follow the fashion; do at Rome as the Romans do; swim with the stream.

exemplify, illustrate, cite, quote.

Adj. **conformable to rule,** adaptable, consistent, agreeable, compliant; regular, etc., 80; according to rule, well regulated, orderly, uniform, symmetric.

conventional, etc. (*customary*), 613; ordinary, common, habitual, usual; strict, rigid, uncompromising.

typical, normal, formal; canonical, orthodox, exemplary, illustrative, in point.

Adv. **conformably,** by rule; in accordance with, in keeping with; according to; as usual, as a matter of course.

invariably, etc. (*uniformly*), 16.

83. UNCONFORMITY.—*N.* **nonconformity,** unconformity, nonobservance, unconventionality, informality; anomaly, anomalousness, exception, peculiarity; breach *or* violation of custom; eccentricity, oddity, rarity.

individuality, singularity, originality, idiosyncrasy, mannerism.

aberration, irregularity; singularity; exemption; qualification, proviso.

nonconformist, Bohemian, nondescript character, original, freak, prodigy, wonder, miracle, curiosity.

mongrel, half-caste, etc., 41.

outcast, outlaw, Ishmael, pariah.

V. **be uncomformable,** leave the beaten path; break (*or* violate) a law *or* custom; stretch a point.

Adj. **uncomformable,** exceptional, eccentric; abnormal, unnatural, anomalous, misplaced, out of order, irregular, arbitrary, lawless; informal, stray, eccentric, peculiar, exclusive, egregious.

unusual, unaccustomed, unwonted, uncommon; rare, singular, unique, curious, odd, extraordinary, strange, monstrous; wonderful, etc., 870; remarkable, noteworthy, queer, quaint, nondescript, original, unorthodox, unconventional, Bohemian, unprecedented, unparalleled, unexampled, unheard of; fantastic, newfangled, eccentric, grotesque, bizarre; unfamiliar, outlandish.

heterogeneous, amorphous, mongrel, hybrid; unsymmetric, etc., 243.

Adv. unconformably; except, unless, save.

V. NUMBER

84. NUMBER.—*N.* number, symbol, numeral, figure, cipher, digit, integer, round number; series.

sum, product, total, aggregate, difference.

ratio, proportion, percentage; progression; arithmetical progression.

power, root, exponent, index, logarithm.

85. NUMERATION.—*N.* numeration, numbering; tale, tally, enumeration, reckoning, computation, calculation, calculus; measurement, etc., 466; statistics.

arithmetic, algebra, differential calculus, calculus of differences.

muster, poll, census, roll call; account, etc. (*list*), 86.

Instruments: abacus, calculating machine, adding machine, cash register.

arithmetician, calculator, algebraist, geometrician, trigonometrician, mathematician, actuary, statistician.

V. number, count, enumerate; call over, run over; take an account of, call the roll, muster, poll; sum up, cast up; tell off, cipher, reckon, reckon up, estimate, compute, calculate.

check, prove, demonstrate, balance, audit, overhaul, take stock.

total, amount to, come to.

Adj. numeral, numerical; arithmetical, analytic, algebraic, statistical, computable, calculable, commensurable, commensurate.

86. LIST.—*N.* list, catalogue, card index; inventory, schedule; register, etc. (*record*), 551; account; bill, bill of costs; tally, file, index, table, contents; book, ledger; synopsis, syllabus; scroll, screed, invoice, manifest, bill of lading; prospectus, program; bill of fare, menu; score, bulletin, census, statistics, returns; directory, atlas, gazetteer; calendar, almanac.

dictionary, lexicon, glossary, vocabulary, wordbook, thesaurus.

roll; muster roll; roll of honor; roster, slate, poll, panel.

V. list, enroll, schedule, inventory, register, catalogue, invoice, bill, book, slate, post, docket; empanel, tally, file, index, tabulate, enter, census.

87. UNITY.—*N.* unity, oneness; individuality; unification, etc., 48; completeness, completion.

one, unit; individual.

V. isolate, insulate.

render one; unite, etc. (*join*), 43, (*combine*), 48.

Adj. **one,** sole, lone, single, solitary; individual, apart, alone; unaccompanied, unattended, singlehanded; singular, odd, unique, isolated; insular.

88. ACCOMPANIMENT.—*N.* **accompaniment,** adjunct, accessory; context; appendage, appurtenance; attribute.

company, association, partnership; companionship.

attendant, companion, associate, colleague, partner; consort, spouse; satellite, hanger-on, shadow; escort, suite, train, retinue, convoy, follower, etc., 65.

V. **accompany,** attend, convoy, chaperon; associate with, couple with.

Adj. **accompanying,** fellow, twin, joint; associated with, coupled with; accessory, attendant.

Adv. **with,** withal; together with, along with, in company with; therewith, herewith; and, etc. (*addition*), 37.

together, in a body, collectively, in conjunction.

89. DUALITY.—*N.* **duality,** dualism; duplicity; polarity.

two, deuce, couple, couplet, both, twain, brace, pair, twins, Castor and Pollux, gemini, fellows; yoke, span; distich.

V. **pair,** mate, couple, bracket, yoke.

Adj. **two,** twain, both; dual, twin; duplex, etc., 90; tête-à-tête.

90. DUPLICATION.—*N.* **duplication,** doubling, reduplication; iteration, etc. (*repetition*), 104; renewal.

duplicate, facsimile, copy, replica, counterpart, etc. (*copy*), 21.

V. **double;** redouble, reduplicate; repeat, etc., 104; renew, renovate.

Adj. **double;** doubled; twofold, two-sided, duplex; double-faced, double-headed; twin, duplicate, second; dual.

Adv. **twice,** once more; over again, etc. (*repeatedly*), 104.

91. [Division into two parts] BISECTION.—*N.* **bisection,** halving, bifurcation, forking, branching, ramification, dichotomy.

half, moiety.

V. **bisect,** halve, divide, separate, split, cut in two, cleave.

fork, bifurcate, branch off *or* out, ramify.

Adj. **bisected,** cloven, cleft; bifurcated; semi-, demi-, hemi-.

92. TRIALITY.—*N.* **triality** [*rare*], trinity,[1] triunity.

three, triad, triplet, trio; triangle, trident, tripod, trireme, triumvirate.

third power, cube.

Adj. **three;** triform, tertiary.

93. TRIPLICATION.—*N.* **triplication,** triplicity; trilogy.

V. **treble,** triple; cube.

Adj. **treble,** triple; threefold, third.

[1] Trinity is hardly ever used except in a theological sense; *see* Deity, 976.

Adv. **three times,** thrice; in the third place, thirdly; threefold, triply, trebly.

94. [Division into three parts] **TRISECTION.**—*N.* trisection, tripartition, third, third part.

V. trisect, divide into three parts, third.

95. QUATERNITY.—*N.* quaternity [*rare*], four, quartet, quadruplet; square, quadrilateral; quadrangle.

V. square, biquadrate, reduce to a square.

Adj. **four;** quadratic; quadrangular, quadrilateral.

96. QUADRUPLICATION.—*N.* **quadruplication.**

V. **quadruplicate,** multiply by four.

Adj. **fourfold,** quadruple; fourth.

Adv. **four times,** in the fourth place, fourthly.

97. [Division into four parts] **QUADRISECTION.**—*N.* quadrisection, quadripartition; quartering; fourth; quart, quarter; farthing; quarto.

V. **quarter,** divide into four parts, quadrisect.

98. FIVE, ETC.—*N.* **five,** quintet, pentagon, pentameter.

six, half a dozen; hexagon, hexameter, sextet.

seven, heptagon, heptameter, heptarchy.

eight, octave, octagon, octameter, octavo, octet.

nine, nonagon.

ten, decade, decagon, decasyllable, decemvir, decemvirate, decennium.

twelve, dozen; **thirteen,** long dozen, baker's dozen; **twenty,** score; **fifty,** half a hundred; **sixty,** threescore; **seventy,** threescore and ten; **eighty,** fourscore; **ninety,** fourscore and ten.

hundred, centenary, century; bicentenary, tercentenary.

thousand, millennium; myriad.

V. quintuplicate, sextuple; centuplicate.

Adj. **five,** fifth, quintuple; pentangular, pentagonal. **sixth,** sextuple, hexagonal, hexangular. **seventh,** septuple, heptagonal, heptangular. **eight,** octuple, octagonal, octangular. **tenth,** tenfold, decimal, decagonal, decasyllabic. **eleventh,** undecennial, undecennary. **twelfth,** duodenary, duodenal. **sixtieth,** sexagesimal **seventieth,** septuagesimal.

centuple, centuplicate, centennial, centenary; hundredth, thousandth, millenary, millennial, etc.

99. QUINQUESECTION, ETC.—*N.* **quinquesection,** division by five, etc., 98; decimation; tithe; fifth, etc.

Adj. decimal, tenth; duodecimal, twelfth; sexagesimal, sexagenary; hundredth, centesimal; millesimal, etc.

100. [More than one] **PLURALITY.**—*N.* plurality, one or two, two or three, etc.; a few, several; multitude, etc., 102; majority.

Adj. **plural,** more than one, upwards of, some, certain.

100a. [Less than one] **FRACTION.**—*N.* fraction, fractional part; part, portion, fragment, etc., 51.

Adj. **fractional,** fragmentary, inconsiderable, partial.

101. ZERO.—*N.* **zero,** nothing; naught, nought; cipher; none, nobody.

102. MULTITUDE.—*N.* **multitude,** multitudinousness, multiplicity; profusion, etc. (*plenty*), 639; legion, host, array, army, galaxy; numbers, scores; heap, power, sight, lot, lots [*all five colloq.*], swarm, bevy, cloud, flock, herd, drove, shoal, school, flight, covey, hive, brood, litter, farrow, fry, nest; mob, crowd, etc. (*assemblage*), 72.

V. **be numerous,** swarm with, teem with, be alive with, crowd, swarm, outnumber, multiply; people.

Adj. **many,** several, sundry, various, alive with; numerous; profuse, manifold, multitudinous, teeming, populous, outnumbering, crowded, thick, galore [*colloq.*]; thick-coming, endless, etc. (*infinite*), 105.

103. FEWNESS.—*N.* **fewness,** paucity, scarcity, sparseness, sparsity; handful; small quantity, etc., 32; rarity, infrequency; minority.

Diminution of number: reduction, weeding, elimination; decimation; eradication.

V. **render few,** reduce, diminish, weed out, eliminate, thin, decimate.

Adj. **few,** scant, scanty; thin, rare, scarce, sparse, few and far between; exiguous; infrequent.

104. REPETITION.—*N.* **repetition,** iteration, recapitulation, reiteration; monotone; duplication, reduplication, monotony, harping, recurrence; reappearance, reproduction; periodicity, etc., 138; succession, run; alliteration; rhythm, tautology; diffuseness, redundancy.

echo, encore, burden of a song, refrain, undersong.

cuckoo, etc. (*imitation*), 19; reverberation, vibration, resonance; drumming, etc. (*roll*), 407; renewal, etc. (*restoration*), 660.

V. **repeat,** iterate, reiterate, redouble, reproduce, echo, re-echo, drum, harp upon, hammer; rehearse; resume, return to, recapitulate.

recur, revert, return, reappear; renew, etc. (*restore*), 660. duplicate, reduplicate.

Adj. **repeated,** repetitious, recurrent, recurring; frequent, incessant; redundant, tautological; another.

monotonous, harping, iterative, unvaried; habitual, etc., 613. **aforesaid,** aforenamed; said.

Adv. **repeatedly,** often, again, anew, afresh, once more; ditto, encore, again and again; over and over, frequently, etc., 136.

105. INFINITY.—*N.* infinity, infinitude, infiniteness; perpetuity, immortality; inexhaustibility, immensity, boundlessness.

V. **be infinite,** have no limits (*or* bounds), go on forever.

Adj. **infinite,** immense; numberless, countless, measureless, innumerable, immeasurable, incalculable, illimitable, interminable, unfathomable; without limit, without end, limitless, endless, boundless; untold, unnumbered, unmeasured, unbounded, unlimited; perpetual, etc., 112.

VI. TIME

106. TIME.—*N.* **time,** duration; period, term, stage, space, span, spell, snap, season; course.

intermediate time, while, interim, interval; intermission, interregnum, interlude; respite.

era, epoch, eon, cycle, age, reign, dynasty, administration.

V. **continue,** last, endure, stay, go on, remain, persist, abide, stand, stick [*colloq.*], hold out; intervene; elapse, etc., 109.

pass time, spend *or* while away time, tide over; employ time; seize an opportunity; linger on, drag on; tarry, etc., 110; waste time, etc. (*be inactive*), 683; procrastinate, etc., 133.

Adj. **permanent,** etc. (*durable*), 110; timely, opportune, seasonable.

Adv. **while,** whilst, during; in the course of; in the time of, when; meantime, meanwhile, in the meantime, in the interim; from day to day; for a time, for a season; till, until, up to, yet; the whole time, all the time; throughout; for good, permanently, always.

then, hereupon, thereupon, whereupon.

107. Absence of time.—*N.* no time.

Adv. **never,** ne'er; at no time, at no period; on no occasion, nevermore.

108. [Definite duration or portion of time] PERIOD.—*N.* **period;** octave, semester, quarter, moon, year, decennial, decennium; decade, lifetime, generation; epoch, era, century, age, millennium.

109. [Indefinite duration] COURSE.—*N.* **corridors** (*or* sweep, vista, halls, progress, process, lapse, flow, tide, march, flight) of time; duration, etc., 106.

Indefinite time: eon, age.

V. **elapse,** lapse, flow, run, proceed, advance, pass; fly, slip, slide, glide; crawl, drag; expire, go by, pass by, be past.

Adv. **in time,** in due time (*or* season, course); in course of time, in the fullness of time.

110. [Long duration] DURABILITY.—*N.* durability, durableness, permanence, continuance, persistence, lastingness, standing; immutability, stability; survival; longevity, etc. (*age*), 128; delay, etc. (*lateness*), 133; slowness.

an age, a long time, eon, century, an eternity; perpetuity, etc., 112.

V. **last,** endure, stand, remain, abide, continue, etc., 106.

tarry, etc., 133; drag on, protract, prolong; spin out, eke out, draw out; temporize, gain time.

outlast, outlive, survive.

Adj. **permanent,** durable, lasting; chronic, long-standing; persistent; lifelong, livelong; endless, fixed, long-lived, perennial; perpetual, etc., 112.

prolonged, protracted, spun out; lingering, long-winded; slow, etc., 275.

Adv. **long,** for a long time; long ago, etc. (*in a past time*), 122; all the day long, the livelong day; all the year round; permanently.

111. [Short duration] TRANSIENCE.—*N.* transience, transiency, evanescence, impermanence; changeableness, etc., 149; mortality; span; nine days' wonder, bubble; interregnum, interim.

velocity, etc., 274; suddenness, abruptness.

V. **be transient,** flit, pass away, fly, gallop, vanish, sink, melt, fade, evaporate.

Adj. **transient,** transitory, passing, evanescent, fleeting, fugitive; temporal, temporary, provisional, provisory; cursory; short-lived, ephemeral; deciduous; perishable, mortal; precarious; impermanent.

brief, quick, brisk, fleet; meteoric, volatile, summary; pressed for time, etc. (*haste*), 684; sudden, momentary, spasmodic, instantaneous.

Adv. **temporarily,** for the moment, for a time; awhile, soon, etc. (*early*), 132; briefly.

112. [Endless duration] PERPETUITY.—*N.* perpetuity, eternity, aye; immortality, perpetuation.

V. **eternalize,** immortalize, eternize, perpetuate.

Adj. **perpetual,** eternal, everlasting, continual, endless, unending; ceaseless, incessant, uninterrupted, unceasing; interminable; unfading, never-ending, deathless, immortal, undying, imperishable.

Adv. **perpetually,** always, ever, evermore, aye; forever, in all ages, without end, to the end of time; till doomsday; constantly, etc. (*very frequently*), 136.

113. [Point of time] INSTANTANEITY.—*N.* instantaneity, instantaneousness; suddenness, abruptness.

moment, instant, second, twinkling, flash, breath.

V. be instantaneous; flash.

Adj. instantaneous, momentary, extempore, sudden, abrupt.

Adv. instantaneously, in no time; presto, instanter, in a trice, in a jiffy [*colloq.*], suddenly, in the same breath; at once, plump; immediately, etc. (*early*), 132; extempore, on the spur of the moment; slapdash, etc. (*haste*), 684.

114. [Estimation, measurement, and record of time] CHRONOMETRY.—*N.* chronometry, chronology, horology.

almanac, calendar; register, registry; chronicle, annals, journal, diary.

timekeeper, clock, watch, repeater; chronometer, timepiece; dial, sundial, hourglass.

V. register, date, chronicle; measure time, beat time, mark time.

Adj. chronologic *or* chronological, temporal.

115. [False estimate of time] ANACHRONISM.—*N.* anachronism, error in time, error in chronology, misdate; anticipation; disregard (*or* neglect, oblivion) of time.

V. misdate; antedate, postdate, anticipate; take no note of time.

Adj. misdated; undated; overdue; out of date, anachronistic, behind time, ahead of time.

116. PRIORITY.—*N.* priority, predecessor, precedence, pre-existence; precursor, antecedent, forerunner; the past, etc., 122.

V. precede, come before; pre-exist, forerun; go before, lead, head; presage, herald, usher in, introduce, announce.

be beforehand, etc. (*be early*), 132; anticipate, forestall.

Adj. prior, previous, preceding, anterior, antecedent; pre-existent; former, aforementioned, foregoing, before-mentioned, aforesaid, said; introductory, etc. (*precursory*), 64.

Adv. before, prior to; earlier; previously, ere, already, yet, beforehand; on the eve of.

117. POSTERIORITY.—*N.* posteriority; succession, sequence; following, continuance, prolongation; futurity, future; successor; sequel, etc., 65; remainder.

V. follow after, pursue, come after, go after; succeed, supervene; ensue, result.

Adj. subsequent, posterior, following, after, later, succeeding, successive, ensuing, posthumous; future, etc., 121; after-dinner.

Adv. subsequently, after, afterward, since, later; next, close upon, thereafter, thereupon.

118. PRESENT TIME.—*N.* the present time, the present juncture *or* occasion; the times, time being; twentieth century.

Adj. present, actual, instant, current, latest, existing.

Adv. at this time, at this moment, etc., 113; now, at present; today, nowadays; already; even now, but now, just now; for the time being.

119. DIFFERENT TIME.—*N.* different time, other time.

Adv. then, at that time (*or* moment, instant); on that occasion. when; whenever, whensoever; whereupon, upon which; at various times.

once, formerly, once upon a time.

120. SIMULTANEOUSNESS.—*N.* simultaneousness, synchronism, coexistence, coincidence, concurrence.

contemporary, coeval.

V. coexist, concur, accompany, keep pace with; synchronize.

Adj. simultaneous, coexisting, coincident, synchronous, concomitant, concurrent; coeval; contemporary, contemporaneous.

Adv. simultaneously, together, in concert; in the same breath.

121. THE FUTURE.—*N.* future, futurity, hereafter, time to come; morrow, tomorrow, by and by, doomsday, day of judgment, crack of doom.

approach of time, advent; destiny, etc., 152.

heritage, heirs, posterity, descendants.

prospect, anticipation, expectation; foresight, etc., 510.

V. anticipate, expect, await, foresee; forestall, etc. (*be early*), 132.

approach, await, threaten; impend, etc. (*be destined*), 152; come on, draw near.

Adj. future, to come; coming, impending, overhanging, imminent; next, near, close at hand; eventual, ulterior; prospective, in prospect.

Adv. prospectively, hereafter, in future; in course of time, eventually, ultimately, sooner or later.

soon, early; on the eve of, on the point of, about to.

122. THE PAST.—*N.* the past, past time, days of yore, days of old, times past, former times, yesterday, the olden time; retrospection, memory, priority.

antiquity, antiqueness, time immemorial, history, remote time; remote past; paleontology, archeology, antiquarianism.

antiquary, antiquarian, archeologist.

ancestry, lineage, forefathers.

V. pass, lapse, blow over.

Adj. past, gone, gone by, over, passed away, bygone, elapsed,

lapsed, expired, extinct, exploded, forgotten, irrecoverable; obsolete, antiquated, outworn.

former, pristine, quondam, late; ancestral.

foregoing, last, latter; recent.

looking back, retrospective, retroactive; archeological.

Adv. **formerly,** of old, of yore, time was, ago; anciently, long ago; lately, latterly, of late; ere now, before now, hitherto, heretofore; already, yet, up to this time.

123. NEWNESS.—*N.* **newness,** novelty; youth, juvenility, immaturity.

innovation; renovation, restoration.

upstart, *nouveau riche* [F.], parvenu.

modernism, modernness, modernity; modernization; latest fashion.

V. **renew,** renovate; rejuvenate; modernize.

Adj. **new,** novel, recent, fresh, green; young, etc., 127; raw, immature; virgin, untried; **modern,** late; newborn, new-fashioned, newfangled, newfledged; just out [*colloq.*], unhandled; brand-new, up-to-date [*colloq.*], renovated, spick-and-span.

Adv. **newly,** afresh, anew, lately, just now, latterly, of late.

124. OLDNESS.—*N.* **oldness,** age, antiquity.

maturity, matureness, ripeness.

decline, decay; senility, superannuation, dotage.

archaism, antiquarianism; thing of the past, relic of the past.

tradition, custom, immemorial usage, common law; folklore.

V. **be old,** have had its day, have seen its day.

become old, age, fade.

Adj. **old,** ancient, antique; time-honored, venerable, hoary; elder, eldest; firstborn; senile, etc., 128.

primitive, prime, primeval, aboriginal; antediluvian, prehistoric, dateless, patriarchal, archaic, classic, medieval; ancestral.

immemorial, traditional, unwritten, inveterate, rooted.

antiquated, of other times, of the old school, old world; obsolete, out-of-date, out-of-fashion, gone by, stale, old-fashioned, exploded, extinct, timeworn, crumbling, secondhand.

125. MORNING. [Noon]—*N.* **morning,** morn, forenoon, antemeridian, A.M., prime, dawn, daybreak; dayspring, peep of day, break of day, aurora, sunrise, daylight, cockcrow.

noon, midday, noonday, noontide, meridian, prime; nooning, noontime.

spring, springtide, springtime, seedtime; vernal equinox.

summer, summertide, summertime, midsummer.

Adj. **matin,** matutinal.

noon, noonday, midday.

spring, vernal.
summer, estival.
126. EVENING. [Midnight]—*N.* evening, eve, decline of day,
close of day, eventide, vespers, nightfall, curfew, dusk, gloaming,
twilight, sunset, sundown, bedtime.
afternoon, post meridiem [L.], P.M.
midnight; dead of night, witching time.
autumn, fall; harvesttime; autumnal equinox; Indian summer.
winter.
Adj. vesper, nightly, nocturnal; autumnal.
wintry, winterly.
127. YOUTH.—*N.* youth; juvenility; infancy, babyhood; childhood; boyhood, girlhood; rising generation; minority, immaturity, teens, tender age, bloom.
cradle, nursery.
flower of life, springtide of life, seedtime of life, golden season of
life; heyday of youth, school days.
Adj. young, youthful, juvenile, green, callow, sappy, beardless,
underage, in one's teens; younger, junior; newfledged, unfledged,
unripe.
128. AGE.—*N.* age; oldness, old age, advanced age, senility,
years, gray hairs, declining years, decrepitude, superannuation,
second childhood, dotage; vale of years; decline of life; green old
age, ripe age; longevity.
seniority, eldership, primogeniture; elders, etc. (*veteran*), 130;
dean, father.
V. age, grow old, decline, wane.
Adj. aged; old, etc., 124; elderly, senile; ripe, mellow, declining,
waning, past one's prime; gray, gray-headed, hoar, hoary, venerable, patriarchal, timeworn, antiquated, effete, decrepit, superannuated; advanced in life (*or* years); stricken in years; doting,
etc. (*imbecile*), 499.
older, elder, oldest, eldest; senior; firstborn.
129. INFANT.—*N.* infant, babe, baby; nursling, suckling.
child, tot, mite, chick, kid [*slang*], little one, brat, pickaninny
[*colored child*], urchin, elf.
youth, boy, lad, laddie, slip, sprig, stripling, youngster, cub,
whippersnapper [*colloq.*], schoolboy, hobbledehoy, young hopeful,
cadet, minor.
girl, lass, lassie, wench, damsel; maid, maiden, virgin; nymph,
colleen, flapper, minx, schoolgirl; hoyden, tomboy, romp.
Adj. infantile, infantine, puerile, boyish, girlish, childish,
babyish, kittenish; boylike, girllike, newborn; young, etc., 127.
130. VETERAN.—*N.* veteran, old man, patriarch, graybeard;

grandfather, sexagenarian, octogenarian, nonagenarian, centenarian; Methuselah; elders, forefathers; dotard, etc., 501.

granny, crone, hag, beldam.

Adj. **veteran;** aged, etc., 128.

131. ADOLESCENCE.—*N.* **adolescence,** majority, adulthood, womanhood, manhood, virility; flower of age; full bloom; spring of life.

man, etc., 373; woman, etc., 374; adult.

middle age, maturity, full age, prime of life, meridian of life.

V. **come of age,** come to man's estate, come to years of discretion; attain majority; come out [*colloq.*].

Adj. **adolescent,** pubescent, of age, of full age, of ripe age; out of one's teens, grown up, full-grown, manly, manlike, virile, adult; womanly; marriageable.

middle-aged, mature, in one's prime; matronly.

132. EARLINESS.—*N.* **earliness,** punctuality, promptitude, readiness, expedition, quickness, haste, etc. (*velocity*), 274; suddenness.

prematurity, precocity, precipitation, anticipation.

V. **be early,** be beforehand.

anticipate, forestall, take time by the forelock, steal a march upon; bespeak, secure, engage, pre-engage.

accelerate, expedite, etc. (*quicken*), 274; make haste, etc. (*hurry*), 684.

Adj. **early,** timely, seasonable, punctual, forward; prompt, etc. (*active*), 682.

premature, precipitate, precocious, anticipatory.

sudden, instantaneous, immediate; unexpected, etc., 508.

imminent, impending, near.

Adv. **early,** soon, anon, betimes, ere long, before long; punctually, in time; on time, on the dot [*slang*].

beforehand; prematurely, too soon; precipitately, hastily; in anticipation; unexpectedly, unawares.

suddenly, etc. (*instantaneously*), 113; at short notice, extempore; on the spur of the moment, at once; on the spot, on the instant, at sight, offhand, straight, straightway; forthwith, immediately, quickly, speedily, apace; presently, by and by, directly.

133. LATENESS.—*N.* **lateness;** tardiness, etc. (*slowness*), 275.

delay, procrastination, postponement, adjournment, prorogation, retardation; protraction, prolongation; moratorium; aftertime; respite, truce, reprieve, stop, stay, suspension, remand.

V. **be late,** tarry, wait, stay, bide, take time; dawdle, etc. (*be inactive*), 683; linger, loiter, gain time; hang fire; stand over, lie over; hang.

put off, defer, delay, lay over, suspend; stave off; retard, postpone, adjourn, prorogue, procrastinate; dally, prolong, protract, spin out, draw out, table, lay on the table, shelve; reserve, temporize, filibuster, stall [*slang*].

be kept waiting, dance attendance; cool one's heels [*colloq.*]; await, expect, wait for.

Adj. late, tardy, dilatory; slow, leisurely, behindhand, backward, unpunctual; overdue, belated, delayed; posthumous.

Adv. late; backward, at the eleventh hour, at length, at last; ultimately; behind time; too late.

slowly, deliberately, at one's leisure.

134. TIMELINESS.—*N.* timeliness, opportunity, opening, occasion, show [*colloq.*]; suitable time *or* season, high time; nick of time; golden opportunity, clear stage, fair field; spare time, leisure.

crisis, turn, emergency, juncture, conjunction; turning point.

V. improve the occasion; seize an opportunity; use (*or* profit by) an opportunity; give (*or* grant) an opportunity; suit the occasion, etc. (*be expedient*), 646; strike the iron while it is hot, make hay while the sun shines.

Adj. timely, well timed, opportune, seasonable; appropriate, suitable.

lucky, providential, fortunate, happy, favorable, propitious, auspicious.

occasional, accidental, extemporaneous, extemporary; contingent, provisional.

Adv. opportunity, in due time; for the nonce; in the nick of time, just in time; at the eleventh hour, now or never.

by the way, by the by; while on this subject, speaking of; extempore; on the spur of the moment.

135. UNTIMELINESS.—*N.* untimeliness, unseasonableness, unsuitable time, improper time; evil hour; intrusion; anachronism.

V. be ill-timed, mistime, intrude, come amiss, break in upon; be busy, be occupied, be engaged.

lose an opportunity; neglect an opportunity; allow *or* suffer the opportunity to pass (*or* slip, go by, escape); waste time; let slip through the fingers.

Adj. ill-timed, mistimed, ill-fated, ill-omened, ill-starred; untimely, unseasonable, out of season; inopportune, inconvenient, untoward, unlucky, inauspicious, unpropitious, unfortunate, unfavorable, unsuited; inexpedient.

unpunctual, etc. (*late*), 133; premature, etc. (*early*), 132.

136. FREQUENCY.—*N.* frequency, repetition, iteration, reiteration.

V. **keep on;** reiterate, repeat, recur, etc., 104; do nothing but.

Adj. **frequent,** not rare, thick-coming, incessant, perpetual, continual, constant, habitual, etc., 613.

Adv. **often,** oft, ofttimes, frequently; repeatedly, in quick succession; daily, every day; habitually, commonly.

perpetually, continually, constantly, incessantly, at all times.

sometimes, occasionally, at times, now and then, again and again.

137. INFREQUENCY.—*N.* **infrequency,** infrequence, rarity; uncommonness.

Adj. **infrequent,** uncommon, sporadic; rare, few, scant, scarce; unprecedented.

Adv. **seldom,** rarely, scarcely, hardly; not often, infrequently, uncommonly, sparsely, scarcely ever, hardly ever.

138. REGULARITY [of recurrence].—*N.* **periodicity,** intermittence; oscillation, vibration; beat, pulse, pulsation; rhythm, alternation; round, revolution, rotation, regularity, bout, turn; routine; cycle.

anniversary, biennial, triennial, quadrennial, quinquennial, sextennial, septennial, octennial, decennial; tricennial; jubilee, centennial, centenary, bicentennial, bicentenary, tercentenary; birthday, natal day, fete day, saint's day, feast, festival, fast, holiday.

Christmas, Yuletide, New Year's Day, Ash Wednesday, Maundy Thursday, Good Friday, Easter; Halloween, All Saints' Day; All Souls' Day; Candlemas; Memorial *or* Decoration Day, Independence Day, Labor Day, Thanksgiving, ground-hog day, woodchuck day, leap year, St. Swithin's Day, Midsummer Day; May Day.

V. **return,** revolve, recur, come round again; beat, pulsate; alternate; intermit.

Adj. **periodic,** periodical; serial, recurrent, cyclic, cyclical, rhythmic, recurring, intermittent; alternate, every other; every.

regular, steady, constant, methodical, punctual.

Adv. **by turns,** in turn, in rotation, alternately, off and on, round and round.

139. IRREGULARITY [of recurrence].—*N.* **irregularity,** uncertainty, unpunctuality; fitfulness, capriciousness.

Adj. **irregular,** uncertain, unpunctual, capricious, erratic, desultory, fitful, flickering; rambling, spasmodic; unmethodical, unsystematic, unequal, uneven, variable.

Adv. **by fits and starts.**

VII. CHANGE

140. CHANGE.—*N.* **change,** alteration, mutation, permutation, variation, modification, modulation, inflection, mood, qualification, innovation, deviation, shift, turn; diversion, variety, break.

conversion, etc. (*gradual change*), 144; revolution, etc., 146; inversion, reversal; displacement, transposition, removal, transference.

transformation, metamorphosis, transfiguration, transmutation; transubstantiation; transmigration, metempsychosis; avatar.

changeableness, etc., 149.

V. **change,** alter, vary, modulate, diversify, qualify, tamper with; turn, shift, veer, jibe, jib, tack, chop, warp, swerve, deviate, dodge; turn aside; take a turn, turn the corner.

modify, work a change, patch, piece, transform, transfigure, transmute, convert, revolutionize; metamorphose, ring the changes; innovate, introduce new blood, shuffle the cards; shift the scene, turn over a new leaf.

recast, remodel; reverse, etc., 218; convert into, etc., 144.

Adj. **changed,** newfangled; changeable, changeful, variable, devious, transitional.

141. PERMANENCE.—*N.* **permanence,** fixity, persistence, endurance; durability; standing, *status quo* [L.]; maintenance, preservation, conservation; conservatism; stability, constancy; quiescence, etc., 265; obstinacy, inflexibility.

V. **endure,** persist, remain, stay, tarry, rest, hold, last, bide, abide, dwell, maintain, keep; stand fast, subsist, live, outlive, survive; hold one's ground (*or* footing).

Adj. **permanent,** stable, fixed, settled, established, irremovable, durable; unchanged, intact, inviolate; persistent; conservative; unfailing, unfading.

Adv. for good, at a stand, at a standstill, as you were!

142. CESSATION.—*N.* **cessation,** discontinuance; intermission, remission; suspense, suspension; interruption; stop; hitch [*colloq.*]; stoppage, halt.

pause, rest, lull, respite, truce, armistice, stay; interregnum. In debate: closure, cloture.

deadlock, checkmate, dead center, dead stand, dead stop; end.

punctuation: comma, semicolon, colon, period, full stop; cæsura.

V. **cease,** discontinue, desist, stay; break off, leave off; hold, stop, pull up, stop short; check, stick, hang fire; halt, pause, rest, come to a stand; arrive, etc., 292; go out, die away, wear away, pass away, lapse; be at an end.

have done with, give over; give up, etc. (*relinquish*), 624.

interrupt, suspend, intermit, remit; put an end to, bring to a stand (*or* standstill), stop, cut short, arrest.

143. CONTINUANCE [in action].—*N.* **continuance,** continuation; pursuance, maintenance, extension, perpetuation, prolongation; persistence, perseverance; repetition.

V. **continue,** persist, go on, keep on, hold on; abide, pursue; stick to; maintain its course; keep up, drag on, stick [*colloq.*], persevere, endure, carry on; keep the field, keep the ball rolling.

sustain, uphold, hold up, follow up, perpetuate, prolong, maintain; preserve.

Adj. **continuing,** uninterrupted, unvarying, persistent, unceasing, unvaried, sustained, chronic; undying, immortal, perpetual.

144. [Gradual change to something different] CONVERSION.
—*N.* **conversion,** reduction, transmutation, assimilation; chemistry, alchemy; growth, progress; naturalization; transportation.

passage, transit, transition, transmigration; shifting, flux; phase.

convert, neophyte, proselyte; pervert, renegade, apostate, turncoat.

V. **be converted into;** become, turn to *or* into; turn out, lapse, shift; pass into, grow into, merge into; melt, grow, wax, mature, mellow.

convert into, resolve into; make, render; mold, form, remodel, reform, reorganize; bring to, reduce to.

145. REVERSION.—*N.* **reversion,** return; revulsion; turning point, turn of the tide; alternation, rotation; inversion, etc., 218; recoil, reaction; retrospection, retrogression; restoration, relapse, atavism, throwback.

V. **revert,** reverse, return, turn back; relapse; invert; recoil; retreat; restore; undo, unmake; turn the scale.

146. [Sudden or violent change] REVOLUTION.—*N.* **revolution,** revolt; breakup; destruction, etc., 162; clean sweep, debacle, overturn, overthrow, rebellion, rising, uprising, mutiny, counterrevolution, bolshevism.

spasm, convulsion, throe, revulsion; earthquake, eruption, upheaval, cataclysm, explosion.

V. **revolutionize,** revolt, rebel, rise; remodel, recast.

Adj. **revolutionary,** catastrophic, cataclysmic, cataclysmal, insurgent, Red, insurrectionary, mutinous, rebellious; bolshevistic *or* bolshevik.

147. [Change of one thing for another] SUBSTITUTION.—*N.* **substitution,** commutation, supplanting.

substitute, scapegoat; alternative; makeshift, temporary expedient, shift, apology, stopgap; alternate; dummy, double; changeling; representative, deputy.

price, purchase money, consideration, equivalent.

V. **substitute,** put in the place of, change for, give place to; take the place of; supplant, supersede, replace, cut out [*colloq.*]; commute, redeem, compound for.

Adj. **substituted,** vicarious.

Adv. **instead;** by proxy; in place of, **in lieu of.**

148. [Double or mutual change] **INTERCHANGE.**—*N.* **interchange,** exchange; commutation, permutation; transposition, shuffle; alternation, reciprocity; swap [*colloq.*], barter, exchange; retaliation, reprisal; retort, requital, cross fire.

V. **interchange,** exchange, bandy, barter, transpose, swap [*colloq.*], reciprocate, commute; give and take, retaliate; retort; requite.

Adj. **reciprocal,** mutual; interchangeable.

international, interstate, interurban, interdenominational; interscholastic, intercollegiate.

Adv. in exchange, vice versa, conversely, by turns, turn about.

149. CHANGEABLENESS.—*N.* **changeableness,** mutability, inconstancy; versatility, mobility; instability, vacillation, irresolution, indecision; fluctuation, vicissitude; alternation, oscillation.

Comparisons: moon, kaleidoscope, chameleon, quicksilver, shifting sands, weathercock, vane, weathervane, harlequin, turncoat; wheel of fortune.

restlessness, fidgets, disquiet; disquietude, unrest; agitation, etc., 315.

V. **fluctuate,** vary, waver, flicker, flutter, shift, shuffle, shake, totter, tremble, vacillate, shift to and fro; oscillate, pulsate, vibrate; alternate.

Adj. **changeable,** changeful; changing, mutable, variable, kaleidoscopic; protean, versatile, mobile.

inconstant, unsteady, unstable, unfixed, unsettled; fluctuating, wavering, vibratory, restless, tremulous; erratic, fickle; mercurial, irresolute, indecisive; capricious, fitful, spasmodic; vagrant, wayward; desultory, transient, etc., 111.

150. STABILITY.—*N.* **stability,** immutability, unchangeableness, constancy; immobility; soundness, vitality, stabilization; stiffness, solidity; permanence, etc., 141; obstinacy, obduracy.

fixture, establishment; leopard's spots.

standpatter [*politics*].

V. **be firm,** stick fast; stand firm, remain firm; stand pat [*colloq.*].

establish, settle, fix, set, stabilize; retain, keep hold; make good, make sure; fasten, etc. (*join*), 43; perpetuate.

settle down; strike root, take root.

Adj. **unchangeable,** immutable; unaltered, unalterable, constant; permanent, persistent, invariable, undeviating; stable, durable, perennial; irretrievable, irrevocable, indissoluble, indestructible, imperishable, indelible.

fixed, steadfast, firm, solid; deep-rooted, ineradicable; fast, steady, confirmed, inveterate; immovable, rooted; settled, stereo-typed, established, vested; obstinate, etc., 606; incontrovertible, valid.

stuck fast, transfixed, aground, stranded.

151. PRESENT EVENTS.—N. eventuality, event, occurrence, incident, affair, transaction, proceeding, fact; phenomenon.

circumstance, particular; happening, adventure; crisis, pass, emergency, contingency; concern, business.

consequence, issue, result, termination, conclusion.

affairs, matters; the world, life, things, doings; the times.

V. happen, occur; take place, come to pass, take effect; present itself; fall out, turn out, befall, betide; turn up, crop up, arrive; ensue, result; arise, start; take its course, pass off.

experience; meet with; fall to the lot of; be one's lot; find, en-counter; undergo, pass through, go through, endure, bear, suffer, abide, stand, brook.

Adj. eventful, stirring, full of incident; memorable, momen-tous, signal; current, on foot, at issue, in question; incidental.

Adv. eventually, ultimately, finally; in the event of, in case.

152. FUTURE EVENTS.—N. destiny, fatality, fate, lot, doom, fortune; future, future state; future existence, hereafter· next world, world to come; life to come; prospect.

V. impend, hang over, threaten, loom, await, approach; fore-ordain, preordain; destine, predestine, doom.

Adj. impending, destined; coming, in store, to come, instant, at hand, near, imminent; in the wind, in prospect.

Adv. in time, in the long run; all in good time; eventually.

VIII. CAUSATION

153. CAUSE.—N. cause, origin, source, principle, element; prime mover, ultimate cause; author, producer, creator, determi-nant; mainspring, agent; leaven; groundwork, foundation, support.

causality, causation; origination; production, etc., 161.

spring, fountain, well; fountainhead, reservoir, wellspring; genesis; derivation; remote cause; influence.

pivot, hinge, turning point; heart, hub, focus.

reason, reason why; ground, occasion; final cause; under-currents.

rudiment, egg, germ, nucleus, seed.

nest, cradle, nursery, birthplace, hotbed.

V. cause, originate, give rise to, occasion, sow the seeds of; bring to pass, bring about; produce; create, develop; set on foot, entail; found, institute.

procure, induce, draw down, superinduce, evoke, elicit, provoke.
contribute, conduce to, have a hand in, influence; determine, decide, turn the scale.

Adj. **causal,** original; primary, originative, generative, productive, creative; formative; radical; in embryo, embryonic.

Adv. **from the beginning,** in the first place; because, etc., 155.

154. EFFECT.—*N.* effect, consequence; aftergrowth, afterclap, aftermath; derivative; derivation; result; resultant; upshot, issue, outcome, conclusion; catastrophe, end; development, outgrowth; fruit, crop, harvest, product.

production, work, handiwork, fabric, performance; creature, creation; offspring, offshoot; first fruits.

V. **be the effect of,** be due to, be owing to; originate in *or* from; rise from, spring from, emanate from, come from, issue from, flow from, result from; depend upon, hang upon, hinge upon, turn upon.

Adj. **owing to;** resulting from; due to; caused by; derived from, evolved from; derivative; hereditary.

Adv. **consequently,** it follows that, as a consequence, in consequence; necessarily, eventually.

155. [Assignment of cause] ATTRIBUTION —*N.* attribution, theory, assignment, reference to, accounting for; imputation; derivation.

explanation, interpretation, reason why.

V. **attribute to,** ascribe to, impute to, refer to, lay to, trace to; blame; saddle; account for, derive from; theorize.

Adj. **attributed;** attributable, referable; due to; owing to.

Adv. **hence,** thence, therefore, for, since, on account of, because, owing to; forasmuch as; whence.

why? wherefore? whence? how comes it? how is it? how so?

156. [Absence of assignable cause] CHANCE[1].—*N.* chance, accident, fortune, hazard, luck, fluke [*cant*], casualty, hit; fate, lottery, tossup [*colloq.*]; throw of the dice; heads or tails, wheel of fortune.

probability, possibility, contingency, odds, run of luck; main chance.

gamble, speculation, gaming, game of chance.

V. **chance,** turn up; fall to one's lot; be one's fate; stumble on, light upon; blunder upon, hit, hit upon.

Adj. **casual,** fortuitous, accidental, chance, haphazard, random, incidental, unintentional, unpremeditated.

---

[1]The word *chance* has two distinct meanings: the first, the absence of assignable *cause*, as above; and the second, the absence of *design*—for the latter see 621.

Adv. **by chance,** by accident; at random, casually; perchance, etc. (*possibly*), 470.

157. POWER.—*N.* **power;** potency, efficacy, puissance, might, energy, vigor, force; ascendancy, sway, almightiness, omnipotence; authority, weight, control; influence, predominance.

ability, competence, efficiency, efficacy; validity, cogency; vantage ground.

capability, capacity; faculty, quality, attribute, endowment, virtue, gift, property, qualification.

V. **empower;** give *or* confer power; invest, endue; endow, arm; strengthen, etc., 159.

electrify, magnetize, energize, galvanize.

Adj. **powerful,** puissant, potent, capable, able; cogent, valid, effective, effectual, efficient, efficacious, adequate, competent; predominant; mighty, omnipotent, almighty.

forcible, energetic; influential; productive.

electric, magnetic, galvanic, dynamic, potential.

Adv. by virtue of, by dint of.

158. IMPOTENCE.—*N.* **impotence;** inability, disability, incapacity, incapability; ineptitude; inefficiency, incompetence, disqualification; inefficacy, etc. (*inutility*), 645; failure, etc., 732.

helplessness, prostration, paralysis, collapse, exhaustion, senility, superannuation, decrepitude, imbecility, inanition.

mollycoddle, old woman, milksop, sissy [*colloq.*], mother's darling.

collapse, faint, swoon, drop; go by the board; end in smoke, etc. (*fail*), 732.

render powerless, disable, disarm, incapacitate, disqualify, unfit, invalidate, undermine, deaden, cramp, tie the hands; prostrate, paralyze, muzzle, cripple, maim, lame, throttle, strangle, silence, spike the guns; unhinge, unfit; put out of gear.

unman, unnerve, devitalize, attenuate, enervate.

shatter, exhaust; weaken, enfeeble.

Adj. **powerless,** impotent, helpless; incapable, incompetent, inefficient, ineffective, unfit, unfitted, unqualified, disqualified; crippled, disabled; senile, decrepit, superannuated; paralytic, paralyzed, nerveless, out of joint, out of gear; unnerved, unhinged; done up [*colloq.*], done for [*colloq.*], dead-beat [*colloq.*], exhausted, shattered, prostrate, demoralized, harmless; unarmed, weaponless, defenseless.

nugatory, null and void, inoperative, good for nothing, ineffectual, inadequate, inefficacious, etc. (*useless*), 645.

159. STRENGTH.—*N.* **strength;** power, etc., 157; energy, vigor, force; main (*or* physical, brute) force; spring, elasticity.

vitality, virility, lustihood, stamina, nerve, muscle, sinews, physique; grit.

athletics, athleticism; gymnastics, calisthenics.

athlete, gymnast, acrobat; Atlas, Hercules.

strengthening, invigoration, refreshment.

Science of forces: dynamics, statics.

V. strengthen, invigorate, brace, nerve, fortify, buttress, sustain, harden, steel; gird, set up, gird up one's loins; recruit, set on one's legs [*colloq.*]; vivify; refresh, reinforce, restore.

Adj. strong, mighty, vigorous, forcible; hard, stout, robust, sound, sturdy, husky [*colloq.*], hardy, powerful, potent, puissant.

resistless, irresistible, invincible, impregnable, unconquerable, indomitable, incontestable, valid; overpowering, overwhelming, all-powerful.

able-bodied; athletic, Herculean, muscular, brawny, wiry, well knit, sinewy, strapping, stalwart, lusty.

manly, manful; masculine, male, virile, in the prime of manhood.

Adv. strongly, by force, by main force.

160. WEAKNESS.—*N.* weakness, debility, relaxation, languor, enervation; impotence, etc., 158; infirmity, effeminacy; fragility; inactivity, etc., 683.

anemia, bloodlessness, deficiency of blood, poverty of blood.

loss of strength, delicacy; decrepitude; invalidism.

V. be weak; drop, crumble, give way; totter, dodder; tremble, shake; halt, limp; fade, languish, decline, flag, fail.

weaken, enfeeble, debilitate, shake, relax, sap, enervate, unnerve; cripple, unman; cramp, reduce, sprain, strain, dilute, impoverish.

Adj. weak, faint, feeble, infirm; impotent; relaxed, unnerved, unstrung, limp, strengthless, powerless; weakly, sickly, flaccid.

soft, effeminate, womanish.

frail, fragile; flimsy, sleazy, papery, unsubstantial, gimcrack, rickety, jerry-built; broken, decrepit, lame, shattered, shaken, crazy, shaky, tumbledown.

unsound, spent, effete; decayed, rotten, worn, seedy, languishing, wasted, laid low, the worse for wear; on its last legs.

161. [Power in operation] PRODUCTION.—*N.* production, creation, construction, formation, fabrication, manufacture; building, architecture, erection; organization; establishment; workmanship, performance; achievement; flowering, efflorescence, fruition; genesis, birth; evolution, development, growth; breeding; propagation.

publication; works, opus (*pl.* opera) [L.]; authorship.

structure, building, edifice, fabric, erection, pile.

V. **produce,** perform, operate, do, make, form, construct, fabricate, frame, contrive, manufacture; build, raise, rear, erect; establish, constitute, compose, evolve, coin, organize, institute; achieve, accomplish.

flower, blossom, bear fruit, bear, bring forth, give birth to, usher into the world; generate, propagate, engender, create; breed, develop, bring up.

induce, superinduce; cause, etc., 153.

Adj. **productive;** prolific, etc., 168; creative, formative, constructive; generative; teeming.

162. [Nonproduction] DESTRUCTION.—*N.* destruction; waste, dissolution, breaking up, disruption; disorganization; demolition, overthrow, subversion, suppression; abolition, etc., 756; sacrifice; ravage, devastation, incendiarism; revolution, etc., 146; road to ruin; sabotage.

fall, downfall, ruin, perdition; breakdown, breakup; cave-in [*colloq.*]; wreck, shipwreck, cataclysm.

extinction, extermination, annihilation; doom, crack of doom.

V. **perish,** fall, fall to the ground, tumble, topple; fall to pieces, break up, crumble, go to wrack and ruin; go by the board, be all over with, go to pieces, totter to its fall.

destroy, do (*or* make) away with, waste; nullify, annul, sacrifice, demolish, overturn, overthrow, overwhelm; upset, subvert, put an end to; do for [*colloq.*], undo, break down, cut down, pull down, dismantle, mow down, blow down; suppress, quash, put down, crush, blot out, efface, obliterate, cancel, erase, strike out, expunge, delete; dispel, dissipate, dissolve; consume.

smash, crash, quell, squash [*colloq.*], shatter, shiver, batter; tear (*or* pull, crush) to pieces; ruin, fell; sink, swamp, scuttle, wreck, shipwreck, engulf, submerged; lay in ruins, raze, level; deal destruction, lay waste, ravage, gut; devour, desolate, devastate, blast, exterminate, eradicate, annihilate.

Adj. **destructive,** subversive, cataclysmic, ruinous, incendiary, suicidal, deadly, all-destroying, all-devouring.

163. REPRODUCTION.—*N.* reproduction, renovation; restoration, etc., 660; renewal, revival, regeneration, revivification; apotheosis; resuscitation, reanimation, resurrection, reappearance.

V. **reproduce,** restore, etc., 660; revive, renovate, renew, repeat, regenerate, revivify, resuscitate, reanimate, refashion, multiply.

Adj. **reproductive,** resurgent, reappearing; renascent; Hydra-headed.

164. PRODUCER.—*N.* producer, originator, inventor, author, founder, generator, mover, architect, grower, raiser, introducer, creator; maker, etc. (*agent*), 690; prime mover.

165. DESTROYER.—*N.* destroyer, wrecker, annihilator; cankerworm, etc. (*bane*), 663; assassin, etc. (*killer*), 361; executioner, etc. (*punish*), 975; iconoclast, vandal, nihilist.

166. PATERNITY.—*N.* paternity, fathership, fatherhood; parentage.

parent, father, sire, dad [*colloq.*], papa, pater [*colloq.*], daddy [*colloq.*], paterfamilias; ancestor.

motherhood, maternity, mother, dam, mamma, mammy, mam [*colloq.*], matriarch, materfamilias.

stem, trunk, tree, stock, pedigree, house, lineage, line, family, race, tribe, clan; genealogy, family tree, descent, extraction, birth, ancestry; forefathers, forebears.

Adj. parental; paternal; maternal; ancestral, linear, patriarchal; racial.

167. POSTERITY.—*N.* posterity, progeny, breed, issue, offspring, brood, family, children, heirs; rising generation.

descendant, scion, offshoot, chip of the old block, heir, heiress, heir apparent, heir presumptive.

child, son, daughter, baby, kid [*colloq.*], imp, brat, cherub, tot, innocent, urchin, chit [*colloq.*]; infant, etc., 129.

lineage, line, straight descent, heredity, sonship, primogeniture.
Adj. hereditary, lineal.

filial, sonlike, daughterly, dutiful.

168. PRODUCTIVENESS.—*N.* productiveness, fecundity, fertility, luxuriance; multiplication, propagation, fructification.

V. fructify; generate, impregnate; teem, spawn, multiply; produce, etc., 161; conceive.

Adj. productive, prolific, copious; teeming, fertile, fruitful, plenteous, luxuriant; generative, life-giving; originative.

169. UNPRODUCTIVENESS.—*N.* unproductiveness, infertility, sterility, barrenness, unfruitfulness; unprofitableness, etc. (*inutility*), 645.

waste, desert, Sahara, wild, wilderness.

V. be unproductive; hang fire, flash in the pan, come to nothing.
Adj. unproductive, barren, unfertile, arid, sterile, unfruitful, fruitless, useless, fallow; unprofitable, etc. (*useless*), 645.

170. AGENCY.—*N.* agency, operation, force, function, office, maintenance, exercise, work, swing, play.

causation, impelling force; mediation, intervention, instrumentality; influence, etc., 175; action, etc. (*voluntary*), 680; method, procedure.

V. operate, work; act, perform, play, support, sustain, maintain, take effect, quicken, strike; have play, have free play; bring to bear upon.

Adj. operative, efficient, efficacious, practical, effectual; at work, on foot; acting, in operation, in force, in action.

171. ENERGY.—*N.* energy, force; intensity, vigor, strength, backbone [*colloq.*], vim [*colloq.*], mettle, pep [*slang*], fire, go [*colloq.*], high pressure; human dynamo.

activity, agitation, effervescence, ferment, fermentation, ebullition, stir, bustle; voluntary, energy, etc., 682; mental energy, etc., 604; resolution, stimulation; exertion, etc. (*effort*), 686.

V. give energy, energize, stimulate, strengthen, invigorate, kindle, excite, inflame, exert; sharpen, intensify.

Adj. energetic, strong, forcible, active, strenuous, brisk, forceful, mettlesome, enterprising, go-ahead [*colloq.*]; potent, etc. (*powerful*), 157; intense, keen, sharp, acute, incisive, trenchant.

poignant, virulent, caustic, corrosive, mordant; harsh, stringent, drastic.

172. INERTNESS.—*N.* inertness, inertia, inactivity, torpor, languor, quiescence, inaction, passivity, stagnation.

mental inertness; sloth; inexcitability, etc., 826; irresolution, indecision, vacillation; obstinacy, etc., 606.

V. be inert, hang fire, be inactive; smolder.

Adj. inert, inactive, passive; torpid, etc., 683; sluggish, logy, stagnant, dull, heavy, slack, tame, slow, lifeless, dead.

latent, dormant, smoldering, unexerted.

Adv. in suspense, in abeyance.

173. VIOLENCE.—*N.* violence, vehemence, might, impetuosity, boisterousness, disorder, effervescence, ebullition; turbulence, bluster; uproar, riot, row [*colloq.*], rumpus [*colloq.*].

ferocity, rage, fury, exasperation; malignity; severity, etc., 739; force, brute force; outrage.

fit, paroxysm, spasm, convulsion, throe; hysterics, passion, etc., 825.

outbreak, outburst, discharge, volley, explosion, blast, detonation, eruption, volcano, earthquake, thunderstorm.

fury, berserk, dragon, demon, tiger, wild beast; fire-eater [*colloq.*], etc. (*blusterer*), 887.

V. be violent; ferment, effervesce; rampage; run wild, run amuck, rage, roar, riot, storm; boil, boil over; fume, foam, ride roughshod, out-Herod Herod.

explode, go off, detonate, fulminate, let off, let fly, discharge, thunder, blow up, flash, flare, burst.

render violent; stir up, quicken, excite, incite, urge, lash, stimulate; irritate, inflame, kindle, foment, exasperate, convulse, infuriate, madden, lash into fury.

Adj. violent, vehement, acute, sharp; rough, tough [*colloq.*], rude, bluff, brusque, abrupt, boisterous, wild, impetuous, rampant; savage, fierce, ferocious.

turbulent, tumultuous; disorderly, raging, troublous, riotous, obstreperous, uproarious; frenzied, mad, insane; desperate, rash; infuriate, furious, frantic, outrageous; stormy, etc. (*wind*), 349.

fiery, flaming, scorching, hot, red-hot.

unbridled, unruly; headstrong, ungovernable, uncontrollable, irrepressible.

spasmodic, convulsive, explosive; detonating; volcanic, meteoric.

Adv. violently, amain; by storm, by force, by main force, with might and main, at one fell swoop; in desperation, with a vengeance.

174. MODERATION.—*N.* moderation; lenity, etc., 740; temperateness, temperance, gentleness, mildness, quiet, sobriety; mental calmness, composure, etc. (*inexcitability*), 826.

alleviation, assuagement, mitigation, relaxation, tranquilization, pacification.

moderator; sedative, lenitive, palliative; opiate, balm.

V. moderate, slacken, soften, mitigate, palliate, alleviate, allay, assuage, appease, temper, mollify, lull, soothe, compose, still, calm, cool, quiet, tranquilize, hush, quell, sober, pacify, smooth, deaden, smother; blunt, subdue, chasten; weaken, etc., 160; lessen, decrease; check, tame, curb, restrain.

Adj. moderate, gentle, mild; cool, sober, temperate, reasonable, lenient, measured; calm, unruffled, quiet, tranquil, still, halcyon; peaceful, peaceable, pacific.

Adv. in moderation, within bounds.

175. [Indirect Power] INFLUENCE.—*N.* influence; importance, etc., 642; weight, pressure, pull [*colloq. or slang*]; interest; preponderance, prevalence, sway; predominance, upper hand, ascendancy; dominance, reign; control, domination, hold; authority, power, potency, capability, spell, magic, magnetism.

footing; purchase, support; play, leverage, vantage ground, advantage.

patronage, protection, auspices; patron, etc. (*auxiliary*), 711; tower of strength.

V. be influential, carry weight, sway, bias, actuate, weight, tell; magnetize, work upon; take root, take hold; pervade, run through; be rife.

dominate, subject; predominate, outweigh; override, overbear; have *or* gain the upper hand, prevail.

lead, control, rule, manage, master, get control of, make one's influence felt; take the lead, pull the strings; turn the scale; set the fashion.

Adj. **influential,** effective, potent; important, etc., 642; weighty; prevalent, rife, rampant; dominant, predominant, authoritative, recognized.

Adv. with telling effect, with authority.

176. TENDENCY.—*N.* **tendency,** aptness, aptitude, proneness, proclivity, bent, turn, tone, bias, set, warp, leaning (*with* to *or* toward), predisposition, inclination, liability, propensity, susceptibility; quality, nature, temperament; idiosyncrasy; cast, vein, grain, humor, mood, trend, drift.

V. **tend,** contribute, conduce, lead, influence, dispose, incline, verge, bend to, warp, turn, work toward, gravitate toward, trend; affect; carry, redound to, bid fair to; promote, etc. (*aid*), 707.

Adj. **tending;** conducive, working toward, in a fair way to, likely to, calculated to; liable, etc., 177; subservient, instrumental, useful; subsidiary, accessory.

177. LIABILITY.—*N.* **liability,** susceptibility; possibility, contingency.

V. **be liable,** incur, lay oneself open to, be subjected to, run the chance, stand a chance; lie under, expose oneself to, open a door to.

Adj. **liable,** subject, in danger, open to, exposed to; answerable, responsible, accountable, amenable; apt to; dependent on.

contingent, incidental, possible, on the cards, within range of, at the mercy of.

178. CONCURRENCE.—*N.* **concurrence,** co-operation, collaboration; conformity, agreement, accord; alliance; complicity, collusion, partnership, union.

V. **concur,** conduce, conspire, contribute; agree, unite, harmonize, combine; hang *or* pull together, co-operate; keep pace with, run parallel.

Adj. **concurrent,** conformable, joint, co-operative, concordant, harmonious, in alliance with, of one mind, at one with.

179. COUNTERACTION.—*N.* **counteraction,** opposition; contrariety, contradiction; antagonism, polarity; clashing, collision, interference, resistance, friction; reaction, recoil; counterblast, neutralization, check, hindrance; repression, restraint.

V. **counteract,** clash, cross, interfere with, conflict with; contravene; jostle; militate against, stultify, antagonize, frustrate, oppose, overcome, overpower, withstand, resist, impede, hinder, repress, restrain; recoil, react.

neutralize, offset, undo, cancel; counterpoise, counterbalance.
Adj. **antagonistic,** conflicting, reactionary; contrary, etc., 14.
Adv. **although,** notwithstanding; in spite of; against.

CLASS II

Words Relating To SPACE

I. SPACE IN GENERAL

180. [Indefinite space] SPACE.—*N.* space, extension, extent, proportions, expanse, stretch; room, accommodation, capacity; scope, compass, range, latitude, field; sweep, play, swing; spread, expansion.

elbowroom, leeway, seaway, headway; margin; sphere, arena.

open space, free space, void, waste, desert, wild, wilderness; moor, down, downs, upland, moorland; prairie, steppe, llano, campagna.

unlimited space; heavens, ether, infinity; world, wide world.

Adj. **spacious,** roomy, extensive, extended, expansive, capacious, ample; widespread, vast, world-wide, wide, far-flung, boundless, limitless, endless, infinite; shoreless, trackless, pathless.

Adv. extensively; by and large; everywhere, far and near (*or* wide), here, there, and everywhere; from pole to pole, from the four corners of the earth, from all points of the compass; to the four winds, to the uttermost parts of the earth.

181. [Definite space] REGION.—*N.* region, sphere, ground, soil, area, realm, hemisphere, quarter, orb, circuit, circle; pale, etc. (*limit*), 233; tract, clearing; domain.

county, shire, canton, province, department, parish, diocese, township, commune, ward, bailiwick; principality, duchy, palatinate, archduchy, dukedom, dominion, colony, commonwealth, territory, country; fatherland, motherland; kingdom, empire.

precinct, arena, district, beat; patch, plot, inclosure, close, enclave, field, paddock, etc. (*inclosure*), 232; street.

clime, climate, zone, meridian, latitude.

Adj. **territorial,** provincial, regional, insular; local, parochial.

182. [Limited space] PLACE.—*N.* place, spot, whereabouts, point; niche, nook, corner, hole, pigeonhole, etc. (*receptacle*), 191; compartment; premises, courtyard, square, place, piazza, plaza, forum; hamlet, village, etc. (*abode*), 189; pen, etc. (*inclosure*), 232; location, site, locality, situation.

Adv. **somewhere,** in some place, here and there, in various places.

183. SITUATION.—*N.* situation, position, locality, latitude and longitude; footing, status, standing; standpoint; stage; aspect, attitude, posture, pose.

place, site; station, post, seat, whereabouts; environment, ground; bearings, direction, spot, etc. (*limited space*), 182.

topography, geography; map, plan, chart.

V. **be situated,** be situate, be located; lie; have its seat in.

Adj. **situate,** situated; local, topical, topographical.

Adv. hereabouts, thereabouts, whereabouts; in place, here, there.

184. LOCATION.—*N.* **location,** situation; lodgment; stowage; packing, lading; establishment, settlement, installation; insertion, etc., 300.

anchorage, roadstead, mooring.

settlement, plantation, colony; habitation, etc. (*abode*), 189.

domestication; colonization; naturalization.

V. **place,** situate, locate, localize, put, lay, set, seat; station, park (as, *an automobile*), lodge, quarter, post, install; house, stow, pack; load, lade; establish, fix, root; graft; plant, etc. (*insert*), 300; deposit, store, store away.

billet on, quarter upon, saddle with.

settle, domesticate, colonize, found, people; take root, strike root; anchor, cast anchor, moor, tether, picket; settle down; take up one's abode, establish *or* locate oneself; keep house; squat, burrow, get a footing; bivouac, encamp, pitch one's tent; inhabit, etc., 186.

Adj. **placed;** situate, ensconced, imbedded, rooted; moored, at anchor.

185. DISPLACEMENT.—*N.* **displacement,** misplacement, dislocation, derangement, transposition.

ejection, expulsion, eviction; exile, banishment, ostracism.

removal, etc. (*transference*), 270; transshipment, moving, shift.

V. **displace,** dislodge, disestablish; misplace, unseat, disturb; set aside, remove, take away, cart away, draft off; exile, etc. (*seclude*), 893.

unload, empty, etc. (*eject*), 297; transfer, etc., 270; dispel.

vacate, depart, evacuate.

Adj. **displaced;** unplaced, unhoused, unsettled; houseless, homeless, out of place; out of a situation.

186. PRESENCE.—*N.* **presence,** attendance; occupancy, occupation; ubiquity, omnipresence.

permeation, pervasion; diffusion.

bystander, etc. (*spectator*), 444.

V. **be present,** make one of; look on, attend, remain. find *or* present oneself; lie, stand.

inhabit, occupy, dwell, reside; stay, sojourn; live, abide; lodge, tenant; people.

frequent, resort to, haunt; revisit.

pervade, permeate; overspread; fill, run through.

Adj. **present;** situate; moored, at anchor; resident, domiciled; ubiquitous, omnipresent.

peopled, inhabited, populous.

Adv. here, there, everywhere; aboard, on board, at home, afield; on the spot; in presence of, before.

187. ABSENCE.—*N.* absence, nonresidence, absenteeism; nonattendance, cut [*colloq.*]; alibi.

emptiness; void, vacuum, vacancy.

interval, hiatus, interruption; interregnum.

truant, absentee.

V. **be absent;** keep away, play truant, absent oneself, stay away, hold aloof.

withdraw, retreat, retire; go away.

Adj. **absent,** not present, away, nonresident, gone, from home; missing; lost; wanting; omitted.

empty, void; vacant, vacuous, blank; untenanted, unoccupied, uninhabited, tenantless; desert, deserted, uninhabitable.

Adv. **without,** minus, nowhere; elsewhere; in default of; sans.

188. INHABITANT.—*N.* inhabitant; resident, dweller, indweller, addressee, occupier, occupant, householder; inmate; tenant, incumbent; settler, squatter, backwoodsman, planter, habitant, colonist; islander; denizen, citizen; burgher, townsman, burgess; villager; cottager, cotter; boarder, lodger.

native, aborigine, aboriginal.

people, etc. (*mankind*), 372; population; colony, settlement; household.

V. **inhabit,** dwell, etc., 186.

Adj. **indigenous,** native, domestic; domiciled; naturalized; vernacular.

189. HABITATION.—*N.* habitation, abode, dwelling, lodging, domicile, residence, address, berth, housing, quarters, headquarters.

home, fatherland, motherland, country; homestead, hearth, chimney corner; roof, household, housing, native soil, native land.

county, parish, etc. (*region*), 181.

retreat, haunt, habitat, resort; nest, arbor, bower, grotto; lair, den, cave, hole, hiding place, cell, sanctum sanctorum, eyrie, rookery, hive; covert, perch, roost.

anchorage, roadstead, roads; dock, basin, wharf, quay, port, harbor.

camp, bivouac, encampment, cantonment, barracks, quarters; tent, wigwam, tepee; igloo.

farm, farmhouse, grange.

cot, cabin, hut, hovel; shanty, dugout, chalet, log cabin, log house; shack![*colloq*], shed, booth, stall, pen, fold; stable, barn; kennel, sty, cote, dovecote, coop, hutch; cowhouse, cowshed.

house, mansion, place, villa, cottage, lodge, hermitage, rotunda, tower, château, castle, pavilion, hotel, court, manor house, hall, palace; kiosk, bungalow, country seat; apartment (*or* brownstone, duplex, frame, shingle, flat, tenement) house; three-decker; building, buildings.

hamlet, village, dorp [Dutch], rancho [Sp. Amer.].

town, borough, city, capital, metropolis; suburb; province, country; county town, county seat.

street, place, terrace, parade, esplanade, boardwalk, embankment, road, row, lane, alley, court, quadrangle, close, yard, passage.

square, polygon, circus, crescent, block, arcade, colonnade, cloister; market place.

assembly room, auditorium, concert hall, armory, gymnasium; cathedral, church, chapel, meetinghouse, etc. (*temple*), 1000; parliament, etc. (*council*), 696.

inn, hotel, tavern, caravansary, alehouse, saloon, club, clubhouse; grill room, chophouse, coffeehouse, eating house; canteen, restaurant, buffet, café, cabaret.

sanatorium, health resort, sanitarium; spa, watering place.

V. inhabit, etc., 186; take up one's abode, etc. (*locate oneself*), 184.

Adj. urban, metropolitan; cosmopolitan; suburban.

provincial, rural, rustic, country, countrified.

190. [Things contained] CONTENTS.—*N.* contents; cargo, lading, freight, shipment, load, bale, burden; cartload, shipload; stuffing.

V. load, lade, ship, pile, fill, stuff.

191. RECEPTACLE.—*N.* receptacle, container; inclosure, etc., 232; recipient, receiver; compartment, cell; hole, corner, niche, recess, nook; crypt; stall; pigeonhole; mouth.

stomach, paunch, belly, crop, craw, maw.

bag, sack, wallet, pocket, pouch; purse; knapsack, haversack, satchel, reticule; saddlebags; portfolio; valise, grip [*colloq.*], suitcase, handbag, schoolbag, brief case, traveling bag, Gladstone bag.

case, chest, box, coffer, caddy, casket; reliquary, shrine; caisson; desk, bureau; trunk, portmanteau, bandbox.

vessel, utensil; vase, canister, jar; basket, pannier, hamper; crate; creel; cradle, bassinet.

For liquids: cistern, reservoir; vat, caldron, barrel, cask, keg, tun, butt, firkin, tub; bottle, jar, decanter, ewer, carafe, canteen, flagon; demijohn; flask, vial, phial; cruet, caster; urn, percolator, coffeepot, teapot, samovar; bucket, pail; pot, tankard, jug, pitcher, mug, porringer; receiver, retort, alembic, crucible; can, kettle; bowl, basin; punch bowl, cup, goblet, beaker, chalice, tumbler, glass.

plate, platter, dish, tray, waiter, salver.

ladle, dipper; shovel, trowel, spatula.

cupboard, closet; locker, bin, buffet, sideboard; drawer, chest of drawers, chiffonier; till, safe; bookcase, cabinet.

chamber, apartment, room, cabin; office, court, hall, suite of rooms, apartment, flat, tenement; parlor, living (*or* sitting, drawing, reception) room; best room [*colloq*]; boudoir; sanctum; bedroom, dormitory; refectory, dining room; nursery, schoolroom; library, study; studio; smoking room, den.

attic, loft, garret; cellar, vault, hold, cockpit; cubbyhole; basement, kitchen, pantry, scullery; storeroom, lumber room; dairy, laundry; garage; hangar; outhouse, penthouse; lean-to, shed.

portico, porch, stoop, veranda, piazza.

bower, arbor, summerhouse; grotto; conservatory, greenhouse.

II. DIMENSIONS

192. SIZE.—*N.* size, dimensions, proportions; magnitude, bulk, volume; largeness, greatness; expanse, amplitude, mass; capacity; tonnage; cordage; caliber.

lump, block, mass; clod, mountain, mound; heap, etc. (*assemblage*), 72.

corpulence, obesity, plumpness.

immensity, hugeness, monstrosity, enormity.

giant, Titan, Hercules, Gargantua; monster, mammoth, whale, behemoth, leviathan, elephant, jumbo [*colloq.*]; colossus.

V. **be large,** become large, etc. (*expand*), 194.

Adj. **large,** big, great, considerable, bulky, voluminous, ample, massive; capacious, comprehensive, spacious; mighty, towering.

stout, corpulent, fat, plump, chubby; portly, burly, brawny, fleshy.

unwieldy, hulky, hulking, lumpish, overgrown; puffy, swollen, bloated.

huge, immense, enormous, titanic, mighty; vast; stupendous; monster, monstrous; gigantic; elephantine, mammoth; giant, colossal, cyclopean, Gargantuan.

193. LITTLENESS.—*N.* littleness, smallness; epitome; microcosm; vanishing point.

dwarf, pygmy, midget; Lilliputian, elf; doll, puppet, manikin; Tom Thumb.

mite, insect, arthropod, ephemerid, ephemera, bug [*pop.*], larva.
atom, monad, animalcule, animalculum (*pl.* animalcula), molecule, microbe, germ, micro-organism, bacterium (*pl.* bacteria), amoeba.

particle, speck, dot, mote; scrap; spark; scintilla; fragment, fraction; grain, powder, dust; minutiæ, etc. (*unimportance*), 643.

V. **belittle,** lie in a nutshell; become small, decrease; contract, etc., 195.

Adj. **little,** small, minute, diminutive, microscopic; inconsiderable, petty; limited, cramped; puny, runty, tiny, wee [*colloq.*], elfin, miniature, pocket; undersized, stunted, dwarf, dwarfed, dwarfish, pygmy; Lilliputian; invisible, infinitesimal, homeopathic.

Adv. in a small compass, in a nutshell; on a small scale.

194. EXPANSION.—*N.* expansion, dilation; growth, increase, enlargement, amplification; extension, augmentation, aggrandizement; spread, increment, development, swell, dilatation; obesity, corpulence; dropsy, swelling, distension, puffiness, inflation.

V. **enlarge,** expand, widen, extend, grow, increase, swell, fill out; dilate, stretch, spread; wax; bud, shoot, sprout, germinate, put forth, open, burst forth; outgrow; overrun.

spread, augment, aggrandize; distend, develop, amplify, spread out, widen, magnify; inflate, blow up; stuff, fatten, pad, cram, bloat; exaggerate.

Adj. **expanded,** larger; swollen, expansive, widespread, overgrown, exaggerated, bloated, fat, tumid, dropsical; corpulent, obese; puffy, distend, bulbous; full-blown, full-grown; big, etc., 192.

195. CONTRACTION.—*N.* **contraction,** reduction, diminution; decrease, etc., 36; lessening, shrinking; atrophy; emaciation, attenuation.

compression, condensation, constraint, compactness; compendium, abstract, epitome; strangulation; astringency.

V. **decrease,** lessen, grow less, dwindle, shrink, contract, narrow, shrivel, collapse, wither, fall away, waste, wane, ebb.

diminish, boil down; deflate, exhaust, empty; constrict, condense, compress, squeeze, crush; pinch, tighten, strangle; cramp; dwarf; shorten, etc., 201; circumscribe, limit, bound, confine.

pare, reduce; attenuate; rub down, scrape, file, grind, chip, shave, shear.

Adj. **contracting,** astringent; shrunk, shrunken, contracted; strangulated; wizened; stunted; waning; compact.

196. DISTANCE.—*N.* **distance,** remoteness; space, etc., 180; far cry to; elongation; drift, offing, background; remote region; reach, span.

outpost, outskirt; horizon, skyline; foreign parts, antipodes.

V. **be distant;** extend to, stretch to, reach to, spread to, stretch away to; range, outreach.

Adj. **distant,** far, far off, far away, remote; telescopic; yon, yonder; ulterior; transatlantic, transalpine; ultramundane, antipodean; inaccessible, out-of-the-way; unapproachable.

Adv. **far off,** far away, afar, afar off; away; beyond range, aloof; wide of, clear of; abroad, yonder, farther, further, beyond; far and wide, from pole to pole; out of range, out of hearing.

apart, asunder; at arm's length.

197. NEARNESS.—*N.* **nearness,** proximity, propinquity; vicinity, vicinage, neighborhood, contiguity, etc., 199.

short distance, short cut; earshot, close quarters, range, stone's throw; gunshot, hair's breadth, span.

purlieus, neighborhood, vicinage, environs, suburbs, confines.

bystander, spectator; neighbor.

approach, approximation, access; convergence, meeting.

V. **be near,** adjoin, abut, neighbor, trench on; border upon, verge upon; approximate; stand by, hang about; cling to, clasp, hug; huddle; hover over.

bring *or* draw near; converge, etc., 290; crowd, pack, huddle.

Adj. **near,** nigh, close (*or* near) at hand, close, neighboring, bordering upon, contiguous, adjacent, adjoining; proximate, approximate; at hand, handy; intimate.

Adv. **near,** nigh, hard by, close to, close upon; hard upon; at the point of; next door to; within reach (*or* call, hearing, earshot, range); on the verge of; in sight of; at close quarters; beside, alongside, side by side; in juxtaposition; at the heels of.

about; thereabouts; roughly, in round numbers; approximately, as good as, well-nigh.

198. INTERVAL.—*N.* **interval,** space; separation, division; hiatus, cæsura; interruption; interregnum; interstice.

parenthesis; void, vacuum; incompleteness, deficiency.

cleft, break, gap, opening; hole, puncture; chasm, mesh, crevice, chink, cranny, crack, slit, fissure, rift, fault, flaw, breach, fracture, rent, gash, cut.

gorge, defile, pass, ravine, canyon, crevasse; abyss, abysm; gulf; inlet, strait; furrow, etc., 259; gully, gulch, notch.

V. **gape,** yawn; separate, etc., 44.

199. CONTACT.—*N.* **contact,** contiguity, contiguousness, proximity, apposition, abuttal, abutment, juxtaposition, touching, meeting; conjunction, adhesion, etc., 46.

borderland; frontier, etc. (*limit*), 233.

V. **adjoin,** join, abut on, neighbor, border, march with; graze, touch, meet; coincide; coexist; adhere, etc., 46.

Adj. **contiguous,** touching, in contact, conterminous, end to end; close, etc. (*near*), 197.

200. [Linear Dimensions] LENGTH.—*N.* **length,** longitude, extent, span; mileage.

line, bar, rule, stripe, streak.

lengthening, prolongation, production, protraction; tension, extension.

Measures of length: line, nail, inch, hand, palm, foot, cubit, yard, ell, fathom, rood, pole, furlong, mile, knot, league; chain; meter, kilometer, centimeter, etc. pedometer, odometer, odograph, viameter, log [*naut.*], speedometer, telemeter, scale.

V. **be long,** stretch out, sprawl; extend to, reach to, stretch to.

lengthen, let out, extend, elongate; stretch; prolong, protract; draw out, spin out.

Adj. **long,** elongate, lengthy, outstretched, extended; lengthened, interminable.

linear, lineal; longitudinal.

lanky, lank, slab-sided [*slang*], rangy; tall; long-limbed.

Adv. **lengthwise,** at length, longitudinally, along; tandem; in a line; from end to end, from stem to stern, from head to foot, from top to toe; fore and aft; over all.

201. SHORTNESS.—*N.* **shortness,** brevity, littleness, etc., 193; a span.

abridgment, shortening, abbreviation, retrenchment, curtailment, epitomization, condensation; reduction, etc. (*contraction*), 195; epitome, etc. (*compendium*), 596.

elision, ellipsis; conciseness, brevity.

V. **shorten,** curtail, retrench, abridge, abbreviate; take in, reduce; compress, contract; epitomize, abstract, summarize, condense; cut, pare down, clip, dock, lop, prune, shear, shave, mow, crop, stunt; nip, check the growth of, foreshorten [*drawing*].

Adj. **short,** brief, curt; compendious, compact; stubby, pudgy, squatty; stumpy [*colloq.*], thickset, chunky, scrub, stocky, squat, dumpy; pug, turned up; little, etc., 193; concise, etc., 572; summary.

202. BREADTH, THICKNESS.—*N.* **breadth,** width, latitude, amplitude.

diameter, bore, caliber; radius.

thickness; corpulence, etc. (*size*), 192; expansion, dilatation.

V. **expand,** etc., 194; thicken, widen.

Adj. **broad,** wide, ample, extended, outspread, outstretched. thick, dumpy, squat, thickset, stubby, etc., 201.

203. NARROWNESS, THINNESS.—*N.* **narrowness,** slenderness; closeness.

line; hair's breadth.

thinness, tenuity; leanness, lankiness, emaciation.

shaving; strip, etc. (*filament*), 205; thread, skeleton, shadow, scrag, mere skin and bone.

narrowing, tapering; contraction, etc., 195.

V. **narrow,** taper; contract, etc., 195.

Adj. **narrow,** close; slender, thin, fine, delicate, threadlike, finespun, taper, slim; scant, scanty, spare; contracted.

lean, emaciated, skinny, scrawny, meager, gaunt, rawboned, lank, lanky, weedy [*colloq.*]; starved, starveling; attenuated, shriveled, pinched, spindle-legged, spindle-shanked, spindling; worn to a shadow; hatchet-faced; lantern-jawed.

204. LAYER.—*N.* **layer,** stratum, course, bed, coping, substratum, floor, stage, story, tier.

leaf, sheet, flake, scale, coat, peel, membrane, film, slice, shaving, wafer.

stratification, lamination, foliation; scaliness.

V. **slice,** shave, pare, peel.

plate, coat, veneer; cover, etc., 223.

Adj. scaly, filmy, membranous, flaky, foliated, stratified.

205. FILAMENT.—*N.* filament, line; fiber, vein, hair, cobweb, capillary, strand, tendril, gossamer.

thread, yarn, packthread, cotton.

string, twine, twist, cord, rope, tape, ribbon, wire.

strip, shred, slip, band, fillet, lath, splinter.

Adj. fibrous, threadlike, wiry, stringy, ropy; capillary, wire-drawn; hairy, etc. (*rough*), 256.

206. HEIGHT.—*N.* height, altitude, elevation, eminence, pitch; loftiness, sublimity.

tallness, stature; prominence, etc., 250; apex, zenith, culmination.

colossus, etc. (*size*), 192; giant.

height, mount, mountain, hill; headland, foreland, promontory; ridge, dune, rising ground, down, uplands, highlands; knoll, hummock, hillock, mound; bluff, cliff, peak.

tower, pillar, column, obelisk, monument, belfry, steeple, spire, minaret, campanile, turret, dome, cupola; pyramid, pagoda.

pole, pikestaff, Maypole, flagstaff; mast, mainmast, topmast.

high water; high (*or* flood, spring) tide.

V. tower, soar, hover; cap, culminate; overhang, surmount, rise above, command, overtop, rise, ascend.

heighten, uprear, uplift, upraise, elevate.

Adj. high, elevated, eminent, exalted, lofty, sublime; tall, gigantic, big, colossal; towering, beetling, soaring, elevated; higher, superior, upper, supernal; highest, etc. (*topmost*), 210. lanky, etc. (*thin*), 203.

upland, hilly, mountainous, alpine, heaven-kissing, cloud-capped.

overhanging, impending, incumbent, overlying; superimposed.

Adv. on high, high up, aloft, up, above, overhead; in the clouds.

207. LOWNESS.—*N.* lowness, levelness, flatness; debasement, prostration; depression, hollow; lowlands.

basement, cellar, vault, crypt, cavern; hold; base, etc., 211.

low water, low (*or* ebb, neap) tide.

V. be low, lie low, underlie; crouch, wallow, grovel; lower, etc. (*depress*), 308.

Adj. low, low-lying, level; flat; crouched, squat, prostrate, depressed, debased.

lower, inferior, under, nether.

lowest, nethermost, lowermost.

Adv. under, beneath, underneath, below, down, downward; underfoot, underground; downstairs, belowstairs; at a low ebb; below par.

208. DEPTH.—*N.* depth, profundity, depression, hollow.

pit, shaft, well, crater, chasm, crevasse, deep, abyss, bowels of the earth, bottomless pit.

soundings, draft, submersion, plunge, dive; plummet, lead.

V. **deepen**, sink, excavate, mine, sap, dig, burrow.

sound, heave the lead, take soundings.

Adj. **deep**, deep-seated, profound, buried; sunk, submerged, subaqueous, submarine, subterranean, underground.

bottomless, fathomless, unfathomed, unfathomable, abysmal, down-reaching, yawning.

Adv. **out of one's depth**, beyond one's depth; over head and ears.

209. SHALLOWNESS.—*N.* **shallowness**, superficiality; shoals.

Adj. **shallow**, slight, superficial; skin-deep, ankle-deep, knee-deep, shoal.

210. SUMMIT.—*N.* **summit**, top, vertex, apex, zenith, pinnacle, acme, crown; height, pitch, maximum; goal, consummation; climax, turning point; culmination; turn of the tide, fountainhead.

tip, tiptop; crest, crow's-nest, cap, peak; brow, head.

architrave, frieze, cornice, coping, coping stone, capital, headpiece, capstone, pediment, entablature; attic, loft, garret, housetop, upper story, roof (*covering*), 223.

V. **crown**, top, cap, crest, surmount, overtop; culminate.

Adj. **highest** (high, etc., 206), top, topmost, overmost, uppermost, tiptop; capital, head, polar; supreme, supernal.

211. Base.—*N.* **base**, basement; plinth, dado, wainscot; baseboard, mopboard; bedrock, hardpan; foundation, substructure, substratum, ground, earth, pavement, floor, paving; footing, groundwork, basis.

bottom, nadir, foot, sole, toe, hoof, root; keel.

Adj. **bottom**, undermost, nethermost; fundamental; founded on, based on.

212. VERTICALITY.—*N.* **verticality**, perpendicularity, erectness.

cliff, steep, crag, bluff, palisades; wall, precipice.

V. **be vertical**, stand erect *or* upright, stick up, cock up.

render vertical, set up, raise up, erect, rear, raise, pitch.

Adj. **vertical**; upright, erect, perpendicular, plumb, bolt upright.

Adv. on end; endwise; at right angles.

213. HORIZONTALITY.—*N.* **horizontality**; flatness; level, plane, stratum.

recumbency; lying down, reclination, proneness, supination, prostration.

V. **be horizontal**, lie, recline, lie flat; sprawl, loll.

render horizontal, lay, level, flatten, even, raze, smooth, align.

prostrate, knock down, floor, fell, ground, cut (*or* hew) down, mow down.

Adj. **horizontal,** level, even, plane, flush; flat, smooth.

recumbent, prone, supine, prostrate.

Adv. on one's back; on all fours; on its beam ends.

214. PENDENCY.—*N.* **pendency,** dependency; suspension, hanging.

pendant, drop, eardrop, tassel, lobe; tail, train, queue, pigtail; pendulum.

chandelier, gaselier.

V. **be pendent;** hang, depend, swing, dangle, lower, droop; flap, trail, beetle, jut, overhang.

suspend, hang, sling, hook up, hitch, fasten to, append.

Adj. **pendent,** pendulous, hanging; dependent; beetling, jutting over, overhanging; lowering; suspended.

215. SUPPORT.—*N.* **support,** ground, foundation, base, basis, fulcrum, purchase, footing, hold; stage, platform; rest, resting place; groundwork, substratum; floor.

supporter; aid, etc., 707; prop, truss, stand, stalk; bracket; ledge, shelf, table, trestle; rung, round; staff, stick, crook, crutch.

post, pillar, column, pediment, pedestal; caryatid; buttress, jamb, mullion, stile, abutment.

frame, framework; scaffold, skeleton, beam, rafter, girder, lintel, joist; keystone; arch; mainstay.

seat, throne, dais; divan, ottoman, sofa, davenport, couch, daybed; stall; chair, wing chair, armchair, easy chair, elbowchair, rocking chair, Morris chair; settee, form, bench; saddle, sidesaddle, pillion; packsaddle; pommel, horn.

stool, hassock, footstool.

bed, bedstead, four-poster; pallet; cot; hammock, shakedown; crib, trundle bed, cradle; litter, stretcher; bunk, berth; mat, rug, cushion; lap.

V. **support,** bear, carry, hold, sustain, shoulder; hold up, back up, bolster up, shore up, uphold, brace, truss, stay, prop; maintain; aid, etc., 707.

Adj. **supporting,** supported; fundamental.

216. PARALLELISM.—*N.* **parallelism,** equidistance, concentricity.

V. **be parallel,** parallel, equal.

Adj. **parallel,** coextensive, equidistant; collateral, concentric, concurrent; abreast, equal, even, alongside.

Adv. alongside, abreast, broadside on.

217. OBLIQUITY.—*N.* **obliquity,** inclination, incline, slope, slant; leaning, tilt; bias, diagonal, zigzag, list, twist, sag, cant, lurch; distortion, etc., 243; bend, curve.

acclivity, steepness; rise, ascent, pitch, grade, rising ground, hill, bank; cliff, precipice, etc. (*vertical*), 212; shelving beach; declivity, dip, fall.

V. **be oblique;** slope, slant, lean, cant, incline, shelve, decline, descend, bend; heel over, careen; sag, slouch, sidle, skid.

render oblique; sway, bias; slope, slant, tilt; incline, bend, crook; distort, etc., 243; zigzag, stagger [*mech.*].

Adj. **oblique,** inclined; sloping, tilted; askew, asquint, bias, aslant, diagonal, transverse, athwart; indirect, wry, awry, crooked; sinuous, zigzag; knock-kneed, etc. (*distorted*), 243.

uphill, rising, ascending; steep, abrupt, precipitous.

downhill, falling, descending; declining, shelving, declivitous.

Adv. **obliquely;** on one side, askew, askance, awry, edgewise, at an angle; sidelong, sidewise, slantwise.

218. INVERSION.—*N.* inversion, subversion, reversion; opposition, polarity; contrariety, contradiction, reversal, transposition, transposal; turn of the tide; overturn, revolution; somersault; revulsion.

V. **be inverted,** turn (*or* go, wheel) about, turn (*or* tilt, topple) over; capsize, turn turtle.

invert, subvert; reverse; upturn, overturn, upset, overset, turn topsy-turvy; transpose.

Adj. **inverted,** wrong side out (*or* up); inside out, upside down; on one's head, topsy-turvy.

inverse; reverse, etc. (*contrary*), 14; opposite.

Adv. **inversely,** conversely; heels over head, head over heels.

219. CROSSING.—*N.* crossing; intersection, grade crossing.

network, reticulation; net, web, mesh, netting, lace, plait; sieve, screen; wicker; mat, matting; trellis, lattice, grating, grille, gridiron, tracery, fretwork, filigree; entanglement.

crucifix, cross, rood, crisscross.

V. **cross,** intersect, interlace, intertwine, intertwist, interweave, interlink, crisscross; twine, entwine, weave, twist, wreathe; dovetail, mortise, splice, link.

plait, pleat, plat, braid; entangle, ravel; net, knot.

Adj. **crossed,** matted, transverse, intersected, cross; cross-shaped, cruciform; netlike, retiform, latticed, grated, barred, streaked.

Adv. **cross,** athwart, thwart, transversely; at grade; crosswise, across.

220. EXTERIORITY.—*N.* exteriority; outside, exterior; surface, superficies; skin, covering; face, facet.

V. **be exterior,** lie around, environ, encircle.

externalize, objectify, visualize, envisage, actualize.

Adj. **exterior,** external, extraneous; outer, outermost; outward, outlying, outside, outdoor.

outstanding; extrinsic, incidental; superficial, skin-deep.

Adv. **externally,** out, without, over, outwards, out of doors, in the open air.

221. INTERIORITY.—*N.* interiority; inside, interior; interspace, subsoil.

contents, etc., 190; substance, pith, marrow; heart, bosom, breast; recesses, innermost recesses; cave, etc. (*concavity*), 252.

inmate, intern, inhabitant, etc., 188.

V. inclose, etc. (*circumscribe*), 229; intern; embed, etc. (*insert*), 300; place within, keep within.

Adj. interior, internal; inner, intimate, inside, inward, inmost, innermost; deep-seated, inherent, ingrained, innate, inborn, inbred, intrinsic.

home, inland, domestic, family, indoor.

Adv. internally; inwards, within, indoors, withindoors; at home.

222. CENTRALITY.—*N.* centrality; centralization, concentration; center; middle, midst; focus; center of gravity.

core, kernel, nucleus; heart, pole, axis, bull's-eye, nave, hub; marrow, pith; metropolis.

V. centralize, concentrate; bring to a focus; converge, etc., 290.

Adj. central; middle, axial, pivotal, nuclear, focal, concentric; middlemost; metropolitan.

223. COVERING.—*N.* covering, cover; canopy, awning, tent, marquee, wigwam, tepee; umbrella, parasol, sunshade; veil; shield, etc. (*defense*), 717.

roof, ceiling, thatch, tiles, slates, leads, shingles; dome, cupola.

coverlet, counterpane, sheet, quilt, blanket, rug; eiderdown quilt, comforter; pillowcase, pillowslip; linoleum, oilcloth; tarpaulin.

integument: skin, pellicle, fleece, fur, leather, lambskin, sable, beaver, ermine, hide, coat, buff, pelt, peltry [*collective noun*]; cuticle, cutis, epidermis; clothing, etc., 225.

peel, rind, crust, bark, husk, shell.

sheath, sheathing, capsule, pod, casing, case, wrapping, wrapper; envelope; cornhusk, corn shuck.

veneer, facing; scale, layer; incrustation, coating, paint, stain, varnish, enamel, whitewash, plaster, stucco.

V. cover, superimpose, overlay, overspread; wrap, incase, face, case, veneer, paper; clapboard, shingle; conceal, etc., 528.

coat, paint, stain, varnish, incrust, crust, cement, stucco, plaster; smear, daub, besmear, bedaub; gild, plate, japan, lacquer, enamel, whitewash.

Adj. covered, hooded, cowled, armored, armor-plated; ironclad; scaly.

224. LINING.—*N.* lining, coating, inner coating; filling, stuffing, wadding, padding; facing, bushing; sheathing.

V. line, stuff, incrust, wad, pad, fill, face, ceil, bush, wainscot, sheathe.

225. CLOTHING.—*N.* clothing, dress; covering, etc., 223; raiment, costume, attire, toilet, habiliment; vesture, vestment;

garment, garb, wardrobe, apparel, wearing apparel, clothes, finery, etc. (*ornament*), 847.

outfit, equipment, trousseau; uniform, khaki; livery, gear, harness, turnout, accoutrement, caparison, suit, trappings.

dishabille, undress, tea gown, wrapper, negligee, dressing gown, kimono; rags, tatters, old clothes.

robe, habit, gown, dress, frock; blouse, middy blouse, waist, shirtwaist; suit; coat; toga, tunic, smock.

dress suit, dress clothes, evening dress, dinner coat, dinner jacket; Tuxedo [*colloq.*]; glad rags [*slang*].

cloak, mantle, shawl, veil; cape, plaid [Scot.], muffler, overcoat, greatcoat; oilskins, slicker, mackintosh, waterproof, ulster; poncho; pea-jacket; sweater, blazer, cardigan, jersey; Mackinaw coat.

jacket, vest, waistcoat; gaberdine.

skirt, petticoat, kilt; bloomers.

trousers, breeches, pants [*colloq.*]; overalls; shorts; tights; drawers; knickers [*colloq.*].

headdress, headgear, coiffure [F.], crush hat, opera hat; tam-o'-shanter, topee [India], sombrero; cap, hat, bonnet, panama, leghorn; derby; nightcap, skullcap; hood, coif; wimple; snood; crown, etc., 247; wig, front, peruke, periwig; turban, fez, tarboosh, shako, busby, bearskin; kepi, helmet; mask, domino.

body clothes, underclothing, linen; shirt, undervest, undershirt; smock, shift, chemise; nightgown, nightshirt, pajamas; bedgown.

tie, neckerchief, neckcloth; ruff, collar, cravat, stock, handkerchief, scarf; bib, tucker; boa; girdle, cummerbund [India].

shoe, Oxford shoe, Oxford tie, pump, sneakers, boot, slipper, moccasin, sandal, galosh, arctic, overshoe, rubber; patten, clog; snowshoes, ski.

stocking, hose, sock; hosiery.

glove, gauntlet; mitten, mitt.

V. **clothe,** array, dress, accouter, rig, fit out, deck, drape, robe, enrobe, gown, attire, apparel, equip; harness, caparison; cover, wrap, shroud, swathe, swaddle.

wear; don; put on, slip on; mantle.

Adj. **clothed,** clad, invested, habited.

226. DIVESTMENT.—*N.* divestment; nudity, bareness, nakedness; dishabille, etc., 225.

baldness, hairlessness.

V. **divest,** uncover, expose, lay open, lay bare, denude, bare, strip; undress, disrobe, dismantle; put off, take off, doff.

peel, bare, slough, excoriate, skin, scalp, flay, bark, husk.

Adj. **naked,** nude, bare, stark-naked, exposed; undressed, undraped, unclad, ungarmented, unclothed.

bald, hairless, beardless; shaven, clean-shaven.

227. ENVIRONMENT.—*N.* **environment,** encompassment; surroundings, outskirts, suburbs, purlieus, precincts, environs, entourage, neighborhood, vicinage, vicinity.

V. **environ,** surround, beset, compass, encompass, inclose, encircle, circle, girdle, hedge, embrace, gird, belt, engird; skirt, hem in; circumscribe, etc., 229; beleaguer, invest, besiege, beset, blockade.

Adj. **surrounding,** begirt; suburban.

Adv. **around,** about; without; on every side, on all sides.

228. INTERLOCATION.—*N.* interlocation, interjacence, interpenetration; interjection, interpolation, interlineation, interspersion, intercalation.

intervention, interference, interposition, intrusion; insinuation; insertion.

intermediary, go-between, interagent, middleman, medium.

partition, diaphragm, midriff; wall, party wall; panel, bulkhead.

V. **intervene,** come between, get between, interpenetrate.

introduce, import; throw in, edge in, run in, work in; interpose, insinuate, interject, interpolate, insert, intersperse, interlard, dovetail, splice, mortise.

interfere, intrude, obtrude; thrust in, etc. (*insert*), 300.

Adj. **intervening,** parenthetical, episodic; intrusive; embosomed.

Adv. **between,** among; amid, amidst; in the thick of; betwixt and between [*colloq.*]; parenthetically.

229. CIRCUMSCRIPTION.—*N.* circumscription, limitation, inclosure; confinement, etc. (*restraint*), 751; envelope, case.

V. **circumscribe,** limit, bound, confine, inclose; surround, etc., 227; hedge in, rail in, fence round, hedge round; picket; corral; imprison, restrain.

enfold, bury, incase, enshrine, enclasp; clothe, 225; embosom.

Adj. **circumscribed,** begirt, girt; lapped; buried in, immersed in; embosomed, imbedded, mewed up; imprisoned, etc., 751; landlocked.

230. OUTLINE.—*N.* outline, circumference; perimeter, periphery; circuit, lines, contour, profile, silhouette, lineaments, relief, bounds; coast line, horizon.

zone, belt, girdle; girth; band; baldric, zodiac; tire, pale, etc. (*inclosure*), 232; circlet, etc., 247.

V. **outline,** delineate, silhouette, block, sketch, circumscribe, etc., 229.

231. EDGE.—*N.* edge, verge, brink, brow, brim, margin, border, confine, skirt, rim, side; lip.

threshold, door, porch; portal, etc. (*opening*), 260.

shore, coast, strand, bank; quay, wharf, dock, mole, landing.

fringe, flounce, frill, furbelow; valance; trimming, edging, skirting, hem, selvage, welt; frame.

V. **edge,** coast, border, skirt; fringe, flounce, hem.

232. INCLOSURE.—*N.* inclosure, envelope; case, etc. (*receptacle*), 191; wrapper; girdle, etc., 230.

pen, fold; sty, paddock, pasture; pound; corral, yard; net, seine.

fence, pale, paling, balustrade, rail, railing, wall; hedge, hedgerow.

barrier, barricade, cordon, stockade; gate, gateway; weir; door, hatch, prison, etc., 752.

dike, ditch, trench, drain, moat.

V. **inclose,** circumscribe, etc., 229.

233. LIMIT.—*N.* **limit,** boundary, bounds, pale, confine, term, bourn, verge; termination, terminus, terminal; stint; frontier, border, marches.

boundary line, landmark; turning point.

V. **limit,** bound, compass, confine, define, circumscribe.

Adj. **definite;** terminal; frontier, bordering, border, boundary.

Adv. **thus far,** thus far and no further.

234. FRONT.—*N.* **front,** foreground, forefront; face, frontage, façade, proscenium, frontispiece; priority; obverse (*of a medal*).

van, vanguard, advanced guard; front rank; outpost; first line; scout.

brow, forehead; visage, physiognomy, features, countenance; bow, stem, prow; jib; bowsprit.

pioneer, etc. (*precursor*), 64.

V. **front,** face, confront, brave, dare, defy, oppose; breast; come to the front *or* fore.

Adj. **fore,** foremost, headmost; forward, anterior, front, frontal.

Adv. **before,** in front, in the van, in advance; ahead; in the foreground.

235. REAR.—*N.* **rear,** back; rear rank, rearguard; background, hinterland.

tail, scut (*as of a hare*), brush (*of a fox*).

afterpart; stern, poop; postern door; tailpiece, crupper.

wake; train, retinue, suite, cortege.

reverse; other side of the shield.

V. **be behind;** fall astern; bring up the rear; heel, tag, shadow, follow, pursue.

Adj. **back,** rear, hindmost; posterior; after.

Adv. **behind,** in the rear *or* background; at the heels of; after, aft, abaft, astern, rearward, backward.

236. SIDE.—*N.* **side,** flank, quarter, lee; wing; profile; gable, gable end; broadside.

points of the compass; East, sunrise, Orient, Levant; West, Occident, sunset.

V. **flank,** skirt, outflank; sidle; border; be on one side.

Adj. **lateral,** sidelong; collateral; flanking, skirting.

eastern, eastward, east, Orient, Oriental, auroral, Levantine.

western, west, westerly, westward, Occidental.

Adv. **sidewise,** sidelong, sideling, broadside on; abreast, alongside, beside; aside; by, by the side of; side by side; to windward, to leeward; laterally; right and left.

237. OPPOSITE.—*N.* **opposite,** opposite side, reverse, inverse; counterpart, antithesis; opposition, polarity; inversion, etc., 218.

antipodes, opposite poles; North and South.

Adj. **opposite,** reverse, converse; antipodal, diametrical, antithetic, counter; fronting, facing.

northern, north, northerly, northward, hyperborean, boreal, polar, arctic.

southern, south, southerly, southward, austral, antarctic.

Adv. **over,** over the way, over against; against; face to face, vis-à-vis [F.].

238. RIGHT.—*N.* **right,** right hand; offside, starboard.

Adj. **dextral,** dexterous, right-handed, dexter.

ambidexter, ambidextrous.

239. LEFT.—*N.* **left,** left hand, south paw [*slang*]; near side; larboard, port.

Adj. **left-handed,** sinistral.

III. FORM

240. FORM.—*N.* **form,** figure, shape, make, formation, frame, construction, cut, build, contour, outline, stamp, type, cast, mold, fashion; structure, etc., 329; sculpture, architecture.

feature, lineament, turn; phase, etc. (*aspect*), 448; posture, attitude, pose.

V. **form,** shape, figure, fashion, carve, cut, chisel, hew, cast; roughhew, sketch, block out; trim, model, knead, mold, sculpture; cast, stamp; build, etc. (*construct*), 161.

Adj. **structural;** plastic, formative, impressible; creative.

shapely, well proportioned, symmetrical, well made, well formed, trim, neat.

241. ABSENCE OF FORM.—*N.* **formlessness,** shapelessness, misproportion, uncouthness; rough diamond; disorder, etc., 59; deformity, etc., 243; disfigurement, defacement; mutilation.

V. **deface,** disfigure, deform, mutilate, derange, etc., 61; blemish, mar.

Adj. **formless,** shapeless, amorphous, unshapely, misshapen, unsymmetrical, malformed, unformed; anomalous.

rough, rude, barbarous, rugged, scraggy; in the rough.

242. [Regularity of form] SYMMETRY.—*N.* **symmetry,** shapeliness, finish; beauty, etc., 845; proportion, eurythmics, uniformity, parallelism; centrality; radiation, branching, ramification; regularity, evenness.

Adj. **symmetrical,** shapely, well set, finished; beautiful, etc., 845; classic, chaste, severe.

regular, uniform, balanced, equal, even, parallel.

243. [Irregularity of form] DISTORTION.—*N.* distortion, contortion; knot, warp, buckle, screw, twist; crookedness, obliquity; grimace, deformity, malformation; monstrosity, misproportion, ugliness, disfigurement.

V. **distort,** contort, twist, warp, buckle, screw, wrench, wrest, writhe, deform, misshape.

Adj. **distorted,** out of shape, irregular, unsymmetric, awry, wry, askew, crooked, gnarled; not true, not straight; deformed; misshapen, misproportioned, ill-proportioned; ill-made; humpbacked, hunchbacked; bandy-legged, bow-legged; knock-kneed.

244. ANGULARITY.—*N.* angularity, bifurcation; fold, etc., 258; notch, etc., 257; fork, crotch, angle, bend, elbow, knee, knuckle; zigzag; right angle, acute angle, obtuse angle; obliquity, etc., 217.

corner, nook, recess, niche.

triangle; rectangle, square; lozenge, diamond; rhomb, rhombus, rhomboid; quadrangle, quadrilateral; parallelogram; polygon, pentagon, hexagon, heptagon, octagon, oxygon, decagon; cube, prism, pyramid.

V. **fork,** branch, ramify, bifurcate, bend hook.

Adj. **angular,** bent, crooked, aquiline, jagged, serrated; forked, bifurcate, crotched, zigzag, hooked; akimbo; oblique, etc., 217.

245. CURVATURE.—*N.* curvature, curvedness, incurvature, bend; flexure, crook, hook, bending; deflection, turn; deviation, detour; sweep; curl; sinuosity, etc., 248.

curve, arc, arch, arcade, vault, bow, cresent, half-moon, horseshoe, loop, festoon; parabola, hyperbola; tracery.

V. **be curved,** sweep, sag; deviate, etc., 279; turn; re-enter.

render curved, bend, curve, deflect, inflect; crook; turn, round, arch, arch over, bow, coil, curl, recurve.

Adj. **curved,** curvate, devious; recurved, arched, vaulted; oblique, etc., 217; circular, etc., 247; bell-shaped; bow-shaped, embowed; crescent, crescent-shaped, horned; heart-shaped, cordate; hook-shaped, hooked, hooklike; moon-shaped, lunar, sickle-shaped.

246. STRAIGHTNESS.—*N.* straightness, directness; inflexibility; straight (*or* bee, right, direct) line; short cut.

V. **be straight,** have no turning, go straight, steer for.

render straight, straighten, rectify; set *or* put straight; unbend, unfold, uncurl, uncoil, unravel.

Adj. **straight,** rectilinear; direct, even, right, true, in a line; undeviating, unswerving, straight as an arrow; inflexible.

perpendicular, plumb, vertical, upright, erect.

247. [Simple circularity] **CIRCULARITY.**—*N.* circularity, roundness; rotundity, etc., 249.

circle, circlet, ring, hoop; bracelet, armlet; loop, wheel, cycle, orb, orbit, disk, circuit, zone, belt, cordon, band; hub, nave; sash, girdle, cestus, cincture, baldric, wreath, garland; crown, coronet, chaplet, snood, fillet; necklace, collar; noose, lasso.

ellipse, oval; ellipsoid, cycloid.

V. **round;** ring, encircle, etc., 227.

Adj. **round,** rounded, circular, oval, elliptic, elliptical, egg-shaped.

248. [Complex circularity] **CONVOLUTION.**—*N.* convolution, involution, winding, wave, undulation, sinuosity, sinuousness, meandering, twist, twirl; contortion.

coil, roll, curl, spiral, corkscrew, worm, tendril, scallop, kink; serpent, snake, eel; maze, labyrinth.

V. **wind,** twine, twirl, wreathe, entwine; wave, undulate, meander; twist, coil, roll; wrinkle; curl, friz, indent, scallop; wring, contort.

Adj. **winding,** twisted, convoluted; circling, snaky, serpentine, sinuous, undulating, undulated, wavy.

involved, intricate, mazy, tortuous, labyrinthine; circuitous, kinky, curly.

spiral, coiled, screw-shaped.

Adv. in and out, round and round.

249. ROTUNDITY.—*N.* rotundity, roundness, sphericity, globularity.

cylinder, barrel, drum; roll, roller, rolling pin, column.

sphere, globe, ball, spheroid, globule; bulb, bullet, pellet, pill, marble, pea, knob.

V. **sphere,** form into a sphere, roll into a ball, give rotundity, round.

Adj. **rotund;** round, etc. (*circular*), 247; cylindrical, conical, spherical, globular, bulbous; egg-shaped, ovoid, ovate; bell-shaped, etc., 245.

250. CONVEXITY.—*N.* convexity, prominence, projection, swelling, swell, bulge, protuberance, protrusion, excrescency.

excrescence, hump; bow; clump, bunch; bulb, bump, knob; knot; boss; tooth, peg; ridge, rib, snag; peak, etc. (*sharpness*), 253; growth, tumor; pimple, wart, wen; fungus, blister; nipple, teat, dug, breast.

proboscis, nose, beak, snout, nozzle.

belly, paunch; abdomen.

arch, cupola, dome, vault.

relief, cameo; low relief, bas-relief, high relief.

point of land, hill, mount, mountain; cape, promontory; fore-land, headland; hummock, ledge, spur.

V. project, bulge, protrude; bag, belly, pout, bunch; jut out, stand out, stick out, stick up; hang over, beetle.

raise, etc., 307; emboss.

Adj. prominent, protuberant, projecting; bossed, bossy, convex, bunchy, hummocky, bulbous; bloated, swollen, distended; bowed, arched; bold; bellied; gibbous; club-shaped, knobby, gnarled; salient, in relief, raised.

251. FLATNESS.—*N.* flatness; smoothness.

plane; level, plain, tableland, plateau; stratum; plate, table, tablet, slab.

V. flatten; level, etc., 213; fell.

Adj. flat, plane, even, smooth; flush; level, horizontal; recumbent, supine, prostrate.

Adv. flat, flatwise, lengthwise, horizontally.

252. CONCAVITY.—*N.* concavity, depression, dip; hollow, hollowness; indentation, intaglio, cavity, dent, dint, dimple; honeycomb.

excavation, pit, sap, mine, shaft; caisson; trough, etc. (*furrow*), 259; bay, etc. (*of the sea*), 343.

cup, basin, crater; punch bowl; cell, etc.(*receptacle*), 191; socket. valley, vale, dale, dell, dingle, glen.

cave, cavern, cove; grot, grotto; hole, burrow, kennel, tunnel; gully, etc., 198.

excavator, sapper, miner.

V. render concave; depress, hollow, gouge; stave in; scoop, scoop out; dig, delve, excavate, dent, dint, perforate; mine, sap, undermine, burrow, tunnel.

Adj. concave, hollow; funnel-shaped; retreating; cavernous; porous, perforated; honeycombed.

253. SHARPNESS.—*N.* sharpness, acuteness; saliency.

point, spike, spine, spit, needle, pin; prick, barb; spur; horn, antler; snag; tag; thorn, bristle; tooth, tusk; tine.

beard, porcupine, hedgehog, brier, bramble, thistle, bur; curry-comb, comb.

peak, crag, crest, cone, sugar loaf; spire, pyramid, steeple.

cutting edge, knife edge, blade, edge tool, cutlery, knife, pen-knife, razor; scalpel, lancet; plowshare, colter; hatchet, ax, pick, cleaver, scythe, sickle, scissors, shears; sword, etc. (*arms*), 727; bodkin, etc. (*perforator*), 262.

sharpener; hone, strop; grindstone, whetstone, steel, emery, carborundum.

V. be sharp; taper to a point; bristle with; cut, etc., 44.

sharpen, whet, point, barb, set, strop, grind.

Adj. **sharp,** keen; acute, pointed; tapering; spiked, spiky, studded, peaked, salient; prickly, spiny, thorny, bristling, barbed, spurred, bearded, thistly, briery; craggy, jagged, snaggy; cone-shaped, conical.

keen-edged, cutting; sharp-edged, knife-edged; sharpened.

254. BLUNTNESS.—*N.* **bluntness,** dullness.

V. **be** *or* **render blunt,** dull; take off the point *or* edge; blunt, turn.

Adj. **blunt,** dull, dullish, obtuse, pointless, unpointed; unsharpened.

255. SMOOTHNESS.—*N.* **smoothness;** polish, gloss; lubrication.

smoother; roller, steam roller; sandpaper, emery paper; flat-iron, sadiron; burnisher.

V. **smooth;** plane; file; mow, shave; level, roll; macadamize; polish, burnish, sleek, iron, press, mangle; lubricate, oil, grease, wax, anoint.

Adj. **smooth;** polished; even; sleek, glossy, silken, silky; velvety; slippery, glassy, oily.

256. ROUGHNESS.—*N.* **roughness,** asperity; corrugation.

hair, mat, thatch, mop; scalp lock; tress, lock, curl, ringlet; shag; mane; eyelashes, lashes; beard, whiskers; mustache; imperial, goatee; fringe; hair shirt.

plumage; plume, crest; feather, tuft.

nap, pile, grain, texture.

V. **roughen,** rough, rough up, crinkle, ruffle, crumple, rumple; corrugate; stroke the wrong way, rub the fur the wrong way.

Adj. **rough,** uneven; rugged, jagged; cross-grained, gnarled, gnarly, knotted, scraggly, scraggy; craggy, cragged; unkempt, unpolished, roughhewn; prickly, etc. (*sharp*), 253.

hairy, bristly, hirsute, tufted, bushy; nappy, bearded, shaggy.

Adv. **against the grain;** in the rough; on edge.

257. NOTCH.—*N.* **notch,** dent, nick, cut, indent, indentation; embrasure, battlement.

saw, tooth, scallop; jag.

V. **notch,** nick, mill, score, cut, dent, indent, jag, scarify, scallop.

Adj. **notched,** dentate, toothed, serrate *or* serrated.

258. FOLD.—*N.* **fold,** crease, flexure, pleat, plait, tuck, gather; joint, elbow, double; wrinkle, pucker, crow's-feet; crinkle, crumple; dog's-ear; ruffle, flounce; corrugation.

V. **fold,** double, pleat, plait, crease, wrinkle, cocker, crinkle, curl, shrivel, rumple, corrugate, ruffle, crumple, pucker; dog's-ear, tuck, ruck, hem, gather.

259. FURROW.—*N.* **furrow,** groove, rut, scratch, streak, crack, score, incision, slit.

trench, ditch, dike, moat, trough, channel, gutter, ravine, etc., 198; depression.

V. **furrow,** flute, groove, carve, corrugate, cut, chisel, plow; incise, engrave, etch, grave.

Adj. **furrowed,** ribbed, striated, fluted, corduroy.

260. OPENING.—*N.* **opening,** aperture, yawning; chasm, etc., 198.

outlet, inlet; pore; vent, venthole, blowhole, airhole; orifice, mouth, sucker, muzzle, throat, gullet, nozzle.

window, casement, lattice; embrasure; light; skylight, fanlight; bay window, bow window, oriel, dormer.

portal, porch, gate, postern, wicket, trapdoor, hatch, door; cellarway, driveway, gateway, doorway, hatchway, gangway.

way, path, etc., 627; thoroughfare; channel, gully; passage, passageway.

alley, lane, mall, aisle, glade, vista.

tube, pipe, main; water pipe, etc., 350; air pipe, etc., 351; vessel, canal, gut, fistula; smokestack, chimney, flue; bore, caliber.

tunnel, mine, pit, shaft; gallery.

hole, puncture, perforation; pinhole, loophole, peephole, eye, eyelet; slot.

sieve, strainer, colander, riddle, screen.

opener, key, master key; open-sesame.

V. **open,** gape, yawn, fly open.

perforate, pierce, tap, bore, drill; transpierce, transfix; enfilade, impale, spike, spear, gore, spit, stab, pink, puncture, lance; stick, prick, riddle.

uncover, unclose; punch, stave in; mine, etc. (*scoop out*), 252.

Adj. **open;** perforated, wide-open, agape, ajar, unclosed; gaping, yawning; patent.

tubular; pervious, permeable; porous, honeycombed.

261. CLOSURE.—*N.* **closure,** blockade, shutting up, sealing, obstruction; contraction, constipation; impermeability; blind alley; cul-de-sac [F.].

V. **close,** plug, block up, stop up, fill up, cork up, button up, stuff up, dam up; blockade; obstruct, bar, bolt, stop, seal; choke, throttle; ram down, dam, cram; clinch; shut, slam, snap.

Adj. **closed,** shut, unopened; unpierced, impervious, impermeable; impenetrable; impassable, pathless, wayless; untrodden.

tight, unventilated, airtight, watertight, hermetically sealed; snug.

262. PERFORATOR.—*N.* **perforator,** piercer, borer, auger, chisel, gimlet, drill, awl, scoop, corkscrew, dibble, trepan, lancet, probe, bodkin, needle, stiletto; punch, gouge; spear, etc. (*weapon*), 727; puncher; punching machine, punching press.

263. STOPPER.—*N.* stopper, stopple; plug, cork, bung, spike, spill, stopcock, tap, faucet; valve, spigot; rammer; ram, ramrod; piston; stopgap; wadding, stuffing, padding, sponge [*surg.*], tourniquet.

doorkeeper, gatekeeper, janitor, concierge [F.], porter, warder, beadle, usher, guard, sentinel; watchdog.

IV. MOTION

264. MOTION.—*N.* motion, movement; move; mobility, movableness, motive power; mobilization.

stream, flow, flux, run, course, stir.

rate, pace, tread, footfall, step, stride, gait; velocity, clip [*colloq.*]; progress, locomotion.

journey, etc., 266; voyage, sail, cruise, passage; transit, etc., 270. unrest, restlessness, etc., 149.

V. **move,** go, hie, budge, stir, pass, flit; hover around *or* about; shift, slide, glide, roll, flow, stream, run, drift, sweep along; wander, etc. (*deviate*), 279; walk, etc., 266.

put in motion, set in motion; impel, etc., 276; propel, etc., 284; mobilize.

Adj. **moving,** in motion, traveling; transitional, shifting, movable, mobile, motive, motor; mercurial; restless, etc. (*changeable*), 149; nomadic, etc., 266; erratic, etc., 279; evolutionary.

Adv. **under way;** on the move (*or* wing, fly, tramp, march).

265. REST.—*N.* rest; stillness, quiescence; stagnation, stagnancy, fixity, immobility, catalepsy; quietism.

quiet, tranquility, calm; repose, relaxation; dead calm; silence, peace, hush; sleep, etc. (*inactivity*), 683.

pause, lull, etc. (*cessation*), 142; stand, standstill; deadlock, dead stand; full stop; embargo.

resting place; bivouac; home, abode; bed, etc. (*support*), 215; haven, etc. (*refuge*), 666; goal, destination, bourn.

V. **be still,** stand still, stand fast, stand firm, lie still, keep quiet, repose, rest; vegetate, stagnate.

remain, stay; stand, tarry, mark time; pull up, draw up; hold, halt, stop, discontinue, stop short, pause; bring to, heave to, lay to; anchor, cast anchor, come to anchor, ride at anchor, lie to; rest on one's laurels, take breath.

dwell, etc., 186; settle, settle down; alight, dismount, arrive.

quell, becalm, hush, calm, still, tranquilize, stay, lull to sleep, lay an embargo on.

Adj. **quiescent,** still; silent, hushed, quiet; motionless, moveless; fixed; stationary; at rest, at a stand, at a standstill, at anchor; stock-still; sedentary, untraveled, stay-at-home; becalmed, stagnant, quiet; unmoved, calm, restful; immovable, stable; sleeping, etc. (*inactive*), 683.

266. [Locomotion by land] JOURNEY.—*N.* **travel,** traveling, wayfaring; campaigning.

excursion, journey, expedition, tour, trip, circuit, pilgrimage, march, walk, promenade, constitutional [*colloq.*], stroll, saunter, ramble, hike [*colloq.*], tramp, turn, stalk, perambulation; outing, ride, drive, airing, jaunt.

riding, equitation, horsemanship.

roving, vagrancy, nomadism; vagabondism, hoboism; migration; emigration, immigration. *Wanderlust*, [Ger.].

itinerary, route, guide; handbook; roadbook; Baedeker.

procession, parade, cavalcade, caravan, file, cortege, column.

vehicle, etc., 272.

traveler, etc., 268.

station, stop, stopping place, terminal, terminus, depot, railway station.

V. **travel,** journey, flit, take wing; migrate, emigrate, immigrate; trek; tour, peregrinate.

motor, bicycle, cycle [*colloq.*], spin, speed; trolley [*colloq.*].

motorize, electrify.

wander, roam, range, prowl, rove, jaunt, ramble, stroll, saunter, perambulate, meander, straggle; gad, gad about.

take horse, ride, drive, trot, amble, canter, gallop, prance, frisk, caracole.

walk, march, step, tread, pace; plod, trudge, wend; promenade; track; hike [*colloq.*], tramp; stalk, stride; strut, bowl along, toddle; paddle; peg on, jog on, shuffle on.

glide, slide, coast, skim, skate.

file off, march in procession, defile.

go to, repair to, resort to, hie to, betake oneself to.

Adj. **traveling,** journeying; itinerant, peripatetic, roving, rambling, vagrant, migratory, nomadic.

self-moving, automobile, automotive, locomotive.

wayfaring, wayworn; travel-stained.

267. [Locomotion by water or air] NAVIGATION.—*N.* **voyage,** cruise, sail, passage, aquatics; boating, yachting, cruising; ship, etc., 273.

headway, sternway, leeway; fairway.

oar, scull, sweep, pole; paddle, screw, propeller, turbine; sail, canvas.

aeronautics, aerial navigation, balloonery; balloon, etc., 273; ballooning; aviation, airmanship; flying, flight, volplaning, planing [*colloq.*], hydroplaning, volplane, glide, dive, nose-dive, spin, looping the loop; wing; pinion, aileron.

mariner, etc., 269; aviator, etc., 269a.

V. sail; embark, etc., 293; spread sail, gather way, make sail, carry sail; ride the waves, ride out the storm.

navigate, scud, boom, drift, course, cruise, steam; coast, hug the shore.

row, paddle, pull, scull, punt.

float, swim, skim, dive, wade.

Aeronautics: fly, soar, drift, hover, aviate; volplane, plane [*colloq.*], glide, dive, fly over, nose-dive, spin, loop the loop, land; take wing, take a flight.

Adj. nautical, maritime, naval; seafaring, seagoing; coasting; afloat; navigable.

aeronautic, aeronautical, aerial.

aquatic, natatory, natatorial.

Adv. under way (*or* sail, canvas, steam), in motion, in progress, on the wing; afloat.

268. TRAVELER.—*N.* traveler, wayfarer, voyager, passenger; commuter, straphanger [*colloq.*].

tourist, excursionist, globe-trotter [*colloq.*]; explorer, adventurer, mountaineer; wanderer, rover, straggler, rambler; landsman, landlubber, vagrant, loafer, tramp, hobo, vagabond, Bohemian, gypsy, nomad, Arab; pilgrim, palmer; immigrant; emigrant.

fugitive, refugee; runaway; renegade.

courier, messenger, runner; Mercury.

pedestrian, walker, foot passenger, hiker [*colloq.*], tramper.

rider, horseman, equestrian, cavalier; jockey, trainer, breaker, roughrider; huntsman, whip; postilion, postboy.

driver, coachman, charioteer, carter, wagoner, drayman, truckman; cabman, cab driver.

Railroad: engineer; fireman, stoker; conductor, motorman.

Automobile: driver, chauffeur, automobilist, motorist.

269. MARINER.—*N.* mariner, navigator; sailor, seaman, seafarer, seafaring man, sea dog [*colloq.*]; tar, bluejacket, gob [*slang*]; marine; midshipman, middy [*colloq.*]; able seaman, hand; crew; captain, commander, master mariner, skipper; mate, boatswain; boatman, ferryman, waterman, lighterman, longshoreman; gondolier; oar, oarsman, rower.

steersman, coxswain, cox [*colloq.*], helmsman, pilot.

269a. AERONAUT.—*N.* aeronaut, aviator, airman, flier, aviatress *or* aviatrix, pilot, observer, spotter [*mil. cant*], scout, bomber, ace; balloonist.

270. TRANSFERENCE.—*N.* transfer, transference; removal; deportation, extradition; conveyance, carriage; contagion, infection; transfusion; transfer, etc. (*of property*), 783.

transit, transition; passage, ferry; portage, carry; carting, cartage; shipment, freight; transmission, transport, transportation; translation; transposition, transposal.

deposit, moraine, drift, alluvium.

gift, bequest, legacy, deed, lease; quitclaim.

freight, cargo, mail, baggage, luggage, goods.

V. transfer, transmit, transport, transplant, transfuse; convey, carry, bear; hand, pass, forward; shift; bring, fetch, reach; conduct, convoy.

send, delegate, consign, relegate, deliver; ship, freight, embark; transpose; drag, etc., 285; mail, post.

Adj. transferable, assignable, negotiable, transmissible, movable, portable; contagious, infectious.

271. CARRIER.—*N.* carrier, porter, redcap, bearer, freighter, expressman; stevedore; coolie; conductor, chauffeur, truck driver; letter carrier, postman; pigeon post, carrier pigeon.

beast of burden, beast, cattle, horse, steed; charger, war horse; hunter; race horse, racer, courser, Arab, barb; blood horse, thoroughbred; palfrey, cob; nag, jade, hack; pack (*or* draft, cart, dray) horse; mare, filly, colt, foal.

pony, Shetland; broncho, cow pony, mustang.

ass, donkey, jackass, burro; mule.

reindeer; camel, dromedary, llama, elephant.

vehicle, etc., 272; ship, etc., 273.

Adj. equine, asinine; electric, motor, express.

272. VEHICLE.—*N.* vehicle, conveyance, carriage, caravan, car, van.

wagon, dray, cart, lorry, truck.

tumbrel, barrow, wheelbarrow, handbarrow; dump cart; baby carriage, gocart, perambulator; wheel chair; police van, patrol wagon, Black Maria [*colloq.*]; Conestoga wagon, prairie schooner; jinrikisha, ricksha [*colloq.*].

equipage, coach, chariot, phaeton, wagonette, break, drag, landau, barouche, victoria, brougham; sulky, runabout.

post chaise, mail stage, diligence, stage, stagecoach; horsecar, omnibus, bus [*colloq.*]; cab, hansom, four-wheeler, hack; dogcart, trap [*colloq.*], buggy, chaise.

team, pair, span, tandem, four-in-hand.

litter, palanquin, sedan; stretcher, hurdle; ambulance.

sled, bob, bobsled; toboggan; sledge, sleigh; ski, snowshoes, skates, roller skates.

cycle, bicycle, tricycle, tandem; machine [*colloq.*], wheel [*colloq.*], motorcycle; velocipede, hobbyhorse.

automobile, motorcar, limousine, sedan, touring car, roadster, coupé, motor [*colloq.*], machine [*colloq.*], car, auto [*colloq.*], autocar, runabout; truck, tractor; taxicab, taxi [*colloq.*], motorbus; flivver [*slang*], jitney [*colloq.*].

Allied automobile terms: tonneau, chassis, hood, top, ignition, spark plug, generator, distributor, magneto, self-starter, gear, gear box, differential, cylinder, manifold, intake, exhaust, carburetor, ammeter, speedometer, oil gauge, primer, clutch, universal joint, crank shaft, transmission, tire, rim; gasoline; trailer; garage; chauffeur, etc., 268.

train; express, mail; car, coach; baggage car; rolling stock; trolley, electric car, electric [*colloq.*].

Adj. vehicular; traveling, etc., 266.

273. SHIP.—*N.* ship, vessel, boat, sail; craft, bottom.

navy, marine, fleet, flotilla.

shipping, man-of-war, etc., 726; merchant ship, merchantman; packet, liner; whaler; slaver; collier; coaster, freight steamer, freighter, lighter; trawler, fishing boat; pilot boat; yacht.

ship, sailing vessel, clipper ship, windjammer [*colloq.*], bark; brig, brigantine, schooner; fore-and-after [*colloq.*]; sloop, cutter, revenue cutter, yawl, ketch, smack, lugger, barge, scow, cat, catboat.
steamer, steamboat, steamship; tug.
boat, rowboat; shallop, skiff, pinnace; launch; lifeboat, longboat, jolly boat, gig, cockboat, tender, cockleshell, dory, canoe, dugout, dinghy, punt, outrigger; float, raft, iceboat.
coracle, gondola, galley, argosy, galleon; junk, sampan [both Chinese]; dhow [Arab]; trireme; derelict.

Aeronautics: aircraft; balloon, airship, dirigible, zeppelin, airplane, monoplane, biplane, triplane; air cruiser, flying boat, hydroplane; kite, parachute.

Allied aeronautical terms: fuselage, gondola, wings, controls, aileron, lifting power, rudder; tail, hangar.

Adj. marine, maritime, naval, nautical, seafaring, ocean-going; seaworthy.

aeronautic, aerial; airworthy.

Adv. afloat, aboard; on board, on shipboard.

274. VELOCITY.—*N.* velocity, speed, celerity, swiftness, rapidity; expedition, etc. (*activity*), 682; acceleration; haste, etc., 684.

spurt, sprint, rush, dash, race, steeplechase; round pace; flight.

pace, gallop, canter, trot, round trot, run, hand gallop.

V. speed, hie, hasten, spurt, sprint, scamper, scuttle, trip, post; scud, scurry, whiz; run, dart, swoop, fly, race, shoot, tear, whisk, sweep, skim, scorch [*colloq.*], rush, dash; bolt, run away; ride hard; hurry, hasten, haste; accelerate, quicken; carry sail, crowd sail.

Adj. fast, speedy, swift, rapid, quick, fleet; nimble, agile, expeditious; express; active, brisk, light-footed, nimble-footed; winged.

Adv. apace; at full speed, full gallop; posthaste; in double-quick time; whip and spur; by leaps and bounds; in high (gear *or* speed) [*automobiling*].

275. SLOWNESS.—*N.* **slowness,** tardiness; languor, etc. (*inactivity*), 683; drawl.

jog trot, dogtrot; amble, rack, pace, single-foot, walk; mincing steps; dead march, slow march.

retardation; slackening; delay, etc. (*lateness*), 133.

slow goer, slowpoke [*colloq.*]; loiterer, sluggard, dawdler; tortoise, snail.

V. **move slowly;** creep, crawl, lag, walk, linger, loiter, saunter; plod, trudge, lumber; trail, drag; dawdle, etc., 683; worm one's way, inch, inch along, jog on, toddle, waddle, slouch, shuffle, halt, hobble, limp, shamble; flag, falter, totter, stagger; mince, take one's time.

retard, relax, slacken, check, moderate, rein in, curb; reef, shorten *or* take in sail; brake, slacken speed, backwater, back pedal.

Adj. **slow,** slack; tardy; dilatory, etc. (*inactive*), 683; leisurely; deliberate, gradual; languid, sluggish, apathetic, phlegmatic, lymphatic; moderate.

dull, slow [*colloq.*], prosaic, boring, wearisome, uninteresting, humdrum.

Adv. at half speed, in slow time; with clipped wings; in low (gear *or* speed) [*automobiling*].

gradually, by degrees, step by step, bit by bit.

276. [Motion conjoined with force] IMPULSE.—*N.* **impulse,** impetus; momentum; push, thrust, shove, boom, boost, explosion, etc. (*violence*), 173; propulsion, etc., 284.

clash, collision, encounter, shock, brunt, crash, bump; impact; charge, onset; percussion, concussion.

blow, stroke, knock, tap, rap, slap, smack, pat, dab; fillip; bang; hit, whack, thwack, cuff, buffet, punch, thump, kick, cut, thrust, lunge; carom, cannon; jab.

Science of mechanical forces: mechanics, dynamics.

V. **impel,** push; start, set going; drive, urge; boom, boost; thrust, prod; elbow, shoulder, jostle, hurtle, shove, butt, jog, jolt; throw, etc. (*propel*), 284.

strike, knock, thump, beat, bang, slam, dash, punch, thwack, whack; batter, tamp, buffet, cudgel, belabor; lunge, jab, kick; hit, tap, rap, slap, pat.

collide, foul; telescope; bump, butt.

Adj. **impulsive,** propulsive, dynamic.

277. RECOIL.—*N.* **recoil,** rebound, ricochet, backlash, boomerang: kick; elasticity, etc., 325; reflex, reflux; reverberation, resonance, repulse; reaction, revulsion.

reactionary, recalcitrant.

V. recoil, react; balk, jib; rebound, reverberate, echo; ricochet.

Adj. refluent, recalcitrant, reactionary.

278. DIRECTION.—*N.* direction, bearing, course, set, trend, run, drift, tenor; tendency, etc., 176; dip, tack, aim.

points of the compass, cardinal points.

line, path, road, range, line of march, alignment; airline, beeline.

V. tend toward, conduct to, go to; point to, bend, verge, incline, dip; steer for, make for, aim at, level at; take aim; hold a course; be bound for; make a beeline for.

Adj. bound for; direct, straight; undeviating, unswerving.

directable, steerable, dirigible, guidable.

Adv. toward, on the road to; hither, thither, whither; **directly;** straight, point-blank; in a bee (*or* direct, straight) line to, as the crow flies; windward, in the wind's eye.

through, via, by way of.

279. DEVIATION.—*N.* deviation; warp, refraction; sweep; deflection, zigzag.

diversion, digression, aberration, drift, sheer, divergence, ramification, forking; detour.

Oblique motion: tack, yaw [*both naut.*]; echelon [*mil.*]; knight's move [*chess*].

V. deviate, alter one's course, turn, bend, curve, swerve, heel, bear off; jibe, yaw, wear, sheer, tack [*all naut.*]; sidle, edge, veer, diverge; wind, twist; turn aside, wheel, steer clear of; dodge, step aside, shy, jib; glance off.

deflect; divert, shift, switch, shunt; sidetrack.

stray, straggle; digress, wander, meander; go astray, ramble, rove, drift.

Adj. deviating, errant; excursive, discursive; devious, desultory, rambling; stray, vagrant, circuitous, roundabout, sidelong, indirect, crooked, zigzag; oblique.

280. PRECEDING.—*N.* preceding, leading, heading, precedence, priority, the lead, van, front; precursor, etc., 64.

V. precede, go before, forerun; introduce, herald; head, take the lead; lead, steal a march, get ahead, outstrip; take precedence.

Adv. in advance, before, ahead, in the van, in front.

281. FOLLOWING.—*N.* following, attendance; pursuant; sequence, sequel.

follower, attendant, satellite, pursuer, shadow, dangler, train.

V follow; pursue, etc., 622; go after; attend, dance attendance on, dog, shadow; hang on the skirts of; camp on the trail.

lag, loiter, linger, fall behind.

Adv. behind; in the rear; after, etc. (*order*), 63 (*time*), 117.

282. [Motion forward] PROGRESSION.—*N.* progression, progress, progressiveness; advance, advancement, headway; march, etc., 266; rise, improvement, etc., 658.

V. advance; proceed, go, go on, progress, get on, gain ground, forge ahead, press onward, step forward, make progress (*or* head, headway); go ahead, shoot ahead; distance.

Adj. progressive, advanced, up-to-date; enterprising, go-ahead [*colloq.*].

Adv. forward, onward; forth, on, ahead, under way.

283. [Motion backward] REGRESSION.—*N.* regression, retrogression, retreat, retirement, recession, withdrawal.

reflux, refluence, backwater, ebb, return; reflexion, recoil.

countermotion, countermovement, countermarch; tergiversation, backsliding, fall; deterioration, relapse, reversion.

V. recede, return, revert, retreat, retire; retrograde, back, back out [*colloq.*], back down [*colloq.*], balk; withdraw; recoil, rebound; turn back, fall back, put back; lose ground; drop astern; backwater, put about [*naut.*], veer, shy, double, wheel, countermarch; ebb, regurgitate.

Adj. retrograde, retrogressive; regressive, refluent, reflex, contraclockwise, counterclockwise; balky, perverse, reactionary.

284. PROPULSION.—*N.* propulsion, projection; push, etc. (*impulse*), 276; ejection; throw, fling, toss, shot, discharge, shy.

Science of propulsion: gunnery, ballistics.

missile, projectile; gun, etc. (*arms*), 727.

marksman, rifleman, good shot, dead shot, crack shot; sharpshooter, etc. (*combatant*), 726; gunner; archer, bowman.

V. propel, project, throw, fling, cast, pitch, toss, jerk, heave, shy, hurl.

dart, lance, tilt; drive, sling, pelt, pitchfork.

send; let off, fire off, discharge, shoot; launch, send forth, let fly; dash.

start, put *or* set in motion, set going, trundle, bundle off; impel, etc., 276; expel, eject.

Adj. propulsive, projectile, ballistic.

285. TRACTION.—*N.* traction, draft, pull, haul.

V. draw, pull, haul, lug, rake, trawl, draggle, drag, tug, tow, trail, train; take in tow.

Adj. tractile, tractional, ductile.

286. [Motion toward] APPROACH.—*N.* approach, approximation; access; advent.

pursuit, chase, hunt.

V. **approach,** converge, near, get (*or* draw) near; move toward, drift; gain upon; pursue, etc., 622; make land.

Adj. approximate, convergent; impending, imminent.

287. [Motion from] RECESSION.—*N.* **recession,** retirement, withdrawal; retreat; regression, etc., 283; departure, etc., 293; flight.

V. **recede,** go, go back, move back, retire, withdraw, ebb; shrink; drift away; depart, etc., 293; retreat, retire, fall back; run away, fly, flee.

288. ATTRACTION.—*N.* **attraction,** attractiveness; pull, magnetism, gravity.

loadstone, lodestar, polestar, magnet.

lure, bait, charm, decoy.

V. **attract,** pull, drag, draw, magnetize, bait, trap, decoy, charm, lure, allure.

Adj. **attractive,** attracting, seductive.

289. REPULSION.—*N.* **repulsion;** antipathy; repulse, abduction.

V. **repel,** push *or* drive from, etc., 276; chase, dispel; abduct; send away; repulse; keep at arm's length, turn one's back upon.

Adj. **repellent,** repulsive.

290. [Motion nearer to] CONVERGENCE.—*N.* **convergence,** confluence, concourse, concurrence, concentration; meeting.

assemblage, etc., 72; resort, etc., 74.

V. **converge,** concur; come together, unite, meet, close in upon; center, concentrate.

Adj. **convergent,** confluent, concurrent; centripetal.

291. [Motion farther off] DIVERGENCE.—*N.* **divergence,** ramification, forking; separation, detachment, dispersion, deviation, etc., 279.

V. **diverge,** ramify, branch off, fly off; spread, scatter, disperse, etc., 73; part, sever, separate, sunder.

Adj. **divergent,** radial, centrifugal.

Adv. broadcast.

292. ARRIVAL.—*N.* **arrival,** advent; landing; debarkation, disembarkation.

destination, bourn, goal; harbor, haven, port; terminus, terminal; home, journey's end; anchorage, refuge.

meeting, joining, encounter, rejoining; return, re-entry.

V. **arrive,** get to, come to; come; reach, attain; overtake; make, fetch; join, rejoin; return; enter, appear, drop in, visit.

alight, light, dismount, detrain.

land, cast anchor, put in, debark, disembark.

meet, encounter, come across; come (*or* light) upon.

Adv. **here,** hither.

293. DEPARTURE.—*N.* **departure,** embarkation; outset, start; removal; exit, etc. (*egress*), 295; exodus, hegira, flight.

leave-taking, adieu, farewell, good-by, Godspeed; valediction, valedictory, valedictorian.

V. **depart;** go, go away, go off, set out, start, issue, march out, debouch, sally forth; sally, go forth; retire, withdraw, remove; cut [*colloq. or slang*], take flight, take wing; fly, flit; strike tents, decamp, break camp, take leave; disappear, etc., 449; entrain; saddle, bridle, harness up, hitch up [*colloq.*].

quit, vacate, evacuate, abandon.

embark, go abroad; set sail, put to sea, sail, take ship; get under way, weigh anchor.

Adv. **hence,** whence, thence.

294. [Motion into] INGRESS.—*N.* **ingress;** entrance, entry; influx, inroad, incursion, invasion, irruption; penetration, infiltration; insinuation, insertion, etc., 300.

immigration, incoming, foreign influx.

import [*used esp. in pl.*], importation.

immigrant, incomer, newcomer, colonist.

inlet; mouth, door, etc. (*opening*), 260; path, etc., 627; conduit, etc., 350.

V. **enter;** come in, pour in, flow in; set foot on; burst *or* break in upon, invade; penetrate, infiltrate.

Adj. **incoming,** inbound, inward.

295. [Motion out of] EGRESS.—*N.* **egress,** exit, issue; emergence; outbreak; outburst, eruption; emanation; evacuation; leakage, percolation, oozing, drain, drainage; gush, outpour, effluence, outflow, discharge.

export [*used esp. in pl.*], exportation; shipment.

emigration, exodus, departure.

emigrant, migrant, colonist.

outlet, vent, spout, faucet, tap, sluice, floodgate; mouth, opening, door; pathway; conduit.

V. **emerge,** emanate, issue; go (*or* come, pass, pour, flow) out of.

exude, discharge, leak; run through, percolate; strain, distill; perspire, sweat; drain, seep, ooze, filter, infiltrate, gush, spout, flow out; pour, trickle; find vent; escape, etc., 671.

Adj. **eruptive,** porous, pervious, leaky; outgoing, outbound, outward bound.

296. [Motion into, actively] RECEPTION.—*N.* **reception;** admission, admittance, entree; importation; initiation, introduction, absorption; suction, sucking; eating, drinking, etc. (*food*), 298; insertion, etc., 300.

V. **give entrance to,** introduce, usher, admit, initiate; receive, import, bring in; absorb, imbibe, instill, implant, induct, inhale; let in, take in.

swallow, gulp; eat, drink, etc., 298.

Adj. **introductory,** initiatory, preliminary.

297. [Motion out of, actively] **EJECTION.**—*N.* **ejection,** rejection, expulsion, eviction, dislodgment, banishment, exile, deportation, expedition; discharge, evacuation, eruption, eruptiveness; tapping, drainage; emetic; vomiting.

V. **eject,** reject; expel, discard; ostracize, boycott; banish, exile, fire [*slang*], throw away *or* aside, push out *or* off, send off *or* away; discharge, dismiss, turn *or* cast adrift; turn out, throw overboard.

evict, oust, dislodge; turn out of doors, deport, expatriate.

emit, send out, pour out, dispatch, shed, void, evacuate; give vent to; tap, draw off; pour forth; squirt, spurt, spill; breathe, blow, exhale.

empty; drain, sweep off; clear off, draw off; clean out, purge; tap, broach.

root out, root up, unearth, eradicate; weed out, get out; eliminate, get rid of, do away with, shake off.

vomit, spew; cast up, bring up; disgorge.

unpack, unlade, unload, unship; dump.

298. [Eating] **FOOD.**—*N.* **eating,** mastication, rumination; gastronomy, carnivorousness, vegetarianism, gluttony, etc., 957.

mouth, jaws, mandible [*esp. of birds*], chops.

drinking, potation, draft, libation; carousal, etc. (*amusement*), 840; drunkenness, etc., 959.

food, meat, nourishment, nutriment, sustenance, nurture, subsistence, provender, corn, feed, fodder, provision, ration, board; commissariat, etc. (*provisions*), 637; prey, forage, pasture, pasturage; fare, cheer; diet, dietary; regimen; staff of life, bread.

eatables, victuals, edibles, grub [*slang*], meat; bread, viands, delicacy, dainty, creature comforts, ambrosia; good cheer, good living.

table, cuisine [F.], bill of fare, menu, table d'hôte [F.], à la carte [F.].

meal, repast, feed [*colloq.*], spread [*colloq.*]; mess; refreshment, entertainment; refection, collation, picnic, feast, banquet, potluck.

mouthful, tidbit, morsel.

drink, beverage, liquor, potion, dram, draft.

restaurant, café, eating house.

V. **eat,** fare, feed, fare, devour, swallow, take; gulp, bolt; fall to; dispatch; tuck in [*slang*], dine, banquet, gormandize, etc., 957; crunch, chew, masticate, nibble, gnaw, mumble.

live on; feed upon; browse, graze, crop; bite, champ, munch, ruminate.

drink, quaff, sip, sup; lap; tipple, guzzle, carouse.

cater, purvey, etc., 637.

Adj. eatable, edible, esculent; dietetic; culinary; nutritive, nutritious; succulent.

underdone, rare; well done; overdone; high [*of game*]; ripe [*of cheese*].

drinkable, potable; bibulous.

omnivorous, carnivorous, flesh-eating, herbivorous, graminivorous, piscivorous.

299. EXCRETION.—*N.* excretion, discharge, emanation, exhalation, secretion, effusion, perspiration, sweat.

hemorrhage, bleeding; outpouring, etc. (*egress*), 295; diarrhea.

saliva, spittle, sputum (*pl.* sputa), spit; catarrh; lava.

V. excrete, etc. (*eject*), 297; secrete; exhale, emanate, etc. (*come out*), 295.

300. [Forcible ingress] INSERTION.—*N.* insertion, implantation, introduction; interpolation, interlineation, insinuation, etc. (*intervention*), 228; injection, inoculation, infusion; ingress, etc., 294; immersion; submersion, dip, plunge.

V. insert, introduce, put in (*or* into), run into; inject; imbed, inlay, inweave; interject, etc., 228; infuse, instill, inoculate, impregnate, imbue.

graft, ingraft, bud, plant, implant.

obtrude; thrust in, stick in, ram in, stuff in, tuck in, press in, drive in; pierce, etc. (*make a hole*), 260.

immerse, merge; bathe, soak, etc. (*water*), 337; dip, plunge, etc., 310.

301. [Forcible egress] EXTRACTION.—*N.* extraction; removal, elimination, extrication, eradication, extirpation, extermination; ejection, etc., 297; export, etc. (*egress*), 295; wrench.

V. extract, draw; take out, draw out, pull out, tear out, pluck out, pick out, get out; wring from, wrench; extort; root up, weed out; eradicate, uproot, pull up, extirpate.

elicit, evolve, bring forth, draw forth; extricate.

eliminate, etc. (*eject*), 297; remove.

express, squeeze out, press out, distill.

302. [Motion through] PASSAGE.—*N.* passage, transmission; permeation, penetration; infiltration; ingress; egress, exit, issue; path, road, way; conduit, opening; journey, voyage, sail, cruise.

V. pass, pass through; perforate, penetrate, permeate, thread, cut across; ford, cross; make (*or* work, thread, worm, force) one's way; find a way (*or* vent); transmit, make way, traverse.

303. [Motion beyond] OVERRUNNING.—*N.* overrunning, overrun, inroad, advance, infraction, transgression, encroachment, infringement; transcendence; redundance, etc., 641.

V. **overrun,** pass, go beyond, go by, shoot ahead of; steal a march upon, gain upon.

outstrip, override, overshoot the mark; outrun, outride, outrival, outdo; beat; distance; throw into the shade; exceed, transcend, surmount; tower above, surpass.

encroach, overstep, transgress, trespass, infringe, intrude, invade.

Adv. **ahead,** beyond the mark.

304. [Motion short of] SHORTCOMING.—*N.* shortcoming, failure, falling short; default, defalcation; delinquency; fizzle [*colloq.*], slump [*colloq.*]; flash in the pan.

incompleteness, deficiency; defect, imperfection, fault; insufficiency, etc., 640; noncompletion, nonfulfillment; failure, etc., 732.

V. **fall short,** come short of, not reach; want; keep within bounds (*or* the mark, compass).

collapse, fail, break down, flat out [*colloq.*], come to nothing; fall down, slump, fizzle out [*all colloq.*]; fall through, fall to the ground; cave in [*colloq.*], end in smoke, miss the mark.

Adj. **deficient;** at fault; short, short of; out of depth; perfunctory, remiss.

305. [Motion upward] ASCENT.—*N.* ascent, ascension; rising, rise, upgrowth, upward flight; upgrade; leap, etc., 309; grade, ramp, acclivity, hill, etc., 217.

stairway, staircase, stairs; flight of steps *or* stairs; ladder, scaling ladder; companionway [*naut.*]; escalator, elevator.

V. **ascend,** rise, mount, arise, uprise; go up, get up, work one's way up, start up, spring up, shoot up; aspire, aim high.

climb, shin [*colloq.*], swarm [*colloq.*], clamber, scramble, escalade, surmount, wind upward, scale.

tower, soar, spire, go aloft, fly aloft; surge; leap, etc., 309.

Adj. **rising;** ascendant; upcast; buoyant.

Adv. **up,** upward, skyward, heavenward; upturned; uphill.

306. [Motion downward] DESCENT.—*N.* descent, inclination, declension, declination; drop; cadence; subsidence, lapse; downcome, comedown, setback, fall; slump [*colloq.*], downfall, tumble, stumble, slip, tilt, trip, lurch.

avalanche, landslide, slide, snowslide, glissade.

declivity, dip, decline, pitch, drop, downgrade.

V. **descend,** go (*or* drop, come) down, fall, gravitate, drop, slip, skid, slide, settle; decline, sink, subside, droop, slump [*colloq.*].

get down, dismount, alight, light; swoop; stoop, etc., 308; fall prostrate, precipitate oneself; let fall.

tumble, trip, stumble, lurch, pitch, topple; tilt, sprawl.

Adj. **steep**, sloping, declivitous; beetling, overhanging; bottomless, fathomless, abysmal.

descending; down, downcast, descendent; deciduous.

Adv. downward, downhill.

307. ELEVATION.—*N.* **elevation**; raising; erection, lift; upheaval; sublimation, exaltation; prominence, relief.

lever, crowbar, crane, derrick, windlass, capstan, winch; dredge, dredger.

elevator, dumbwaiter; escalator.

V. **elevate**, raise, heighten, lift, erect; set up, tilt up; rear, hoist, heave; uplift, upraise, uprear; buoy, mount, exalt; sublimate.

take up, drag up, fish up; dredge.

Adj. **elevated**, upturned, stilted, rampant.

308. DEPRESSION.—*N.* **depression**, lowering; dip, etc. (*concavity*), 252.

overthrow, overturn; upset; prostration, reduction, abasement, subversion.

bow, curtsy, dip [*colloq.*], bob, duck, genuflexion, kowtow, obeisance, salaam.

V. **depress**, lower, cast down, let drop, let fall; sink, debase, bring low, abase, reduce, precipitate.

overthrow, overturn, overset, upset, prostrate, level, fell; down [*colloq.*], cast (*or* throw, fling, dash, pull, knock, hew) down, raze.

sit, sit down, squat; recline, sprawl.

crouch, stoop, bend, cower.

bow, curtsy, genuflect, kowtow, duck, bob, dip, kneel; incline, make obeisance, salaam, prostrate oneself, bow down.

Adj. **depressed**; at a low ebb; prostrate, horizontal.

309. LEAP.—*N.* **leap**, jump, hop, spring, bound, vault.

caper, dance, gambol, frisk, prance, curvet, caracole, buck; hop, skip, and jump.

V. **leap**, jump, hop, spring, bound, vault, clear, ramp, skip.

prance, dance, caper; buck; curvet, caracole, bob, bounce, flounce; frisk, jump about, romp, frolic, gambol; cavort, cut capers [*colloq.*].

Adj. **leaping**, saltatorial; frisky, lively, frolicsome.

Adv. on the light fantastic toe.

310. PLUNGE.—*N.* **plunge**, dip, dive, nose-dive [*aviation*], header [*colloq.*]; submergence, submersion, immersion.

diver; diving bird.

V. **plunge**, dip, souse, duck; dive, plump; take a header [*colloq.*]; make a plunge; bathe; pitch.

submerge, submerse; immerse; douse, sink, engulf, send to the bottom.

founder,welter,wallow; get out of one's depth; go to the bottom.

Adj. submergible, submersible.

311. CIRCULAR MOTION.—*N.* circulation, turn, excursion, circumnavigation, circumflexion; wheel, compass, lap, circuit; turning, evolution; coil, spiral.

V. **turn,** bend, wheel; go about, put about [*both naut.*]; go (*or* turn) round, round, turn a corner; double a point [*naut.*]; make a detour.

circle, encircle, circumscribe, circuit, describe a circle, circumnavigate; go the round.

wind, circulate, meander; whisk, twirl, twist, coil.

wallow, welter, roll.

Adj. circuitous, roundabout, devious.

312. ROTATION—*N.* rotation, revolution, gyration, circulation, roll; pirouette, convolution.

eddy, vortex, whirlpool, maelstrom; swirl, surge; whir, whirl; cyclone, tornado; vertiginousness, vertigo.

V. **rotate,** roll, revolve, spin, turn, turn round, encircle, circulate, swirl, gyrate,wheel,whirl, twirl, roll up, furl; box the compass.

Adj. rotating, rotary; vertiginous.

313. UNFOLDMENT.—*N.* **unfoldment,** unfolding, development; evolvement, evolution; inversion.

V. **evolve;** unfold, unroll, unwind, uncoil, untwist, unfurl, untwine, unravel; disentangle; develop.

Adj. evolutional, evolutionary.

314. [Motion to and fro] OSCILLATION.—*N.* oscillation, vibration, undulation, pulsation; pulse, beat, throb.

alternation; coming and going; ebb and flow, flux and reflux, systole and diastole; ups and downs.

fluctuation; vacillation, irresolution, indecision.

swing, wave, beat, shake, wag, seesaw, teeter.

V. **oscillate,** vibrate, undulate, wave; rock, teeter, sway, swing, dangle; pulsate, beat; wag, waggle; nod, bob, curtsy; wobble.

fluctuate, reel, quake; quiver, quaver, shake, flicker; wriggle; roll, toss, pitch; flounder, stagger, totter.

alternate, pass and repass, shuttle, ebb and flow, come and go; vacillate.

Adj. **oscillating;** undulatory, vibratory; pendulous.

Adv. **to and fro,** up and down, back and forth, in and out, seesaw, zigzag, from side to side, shuttlewise.

315. [Irregular motion] AGITATION.—*N.* agitation, stir, tremor, shuffling, shake, ripple, jog, jolt, jar, jerk, shock, trepidation, quiver, quaver, dance; tarantella; twitter, flicker, flutter.

disquiet, perturbation, commotion, turmoil, turbulence; tumult, hubbub, rout, bustle, fuss, racket.

twitching, chorea, St. Vitus' dance; staggers, blind staggers; epilepsy, fits.

spasm, throe, throb, palpitation, convulsion, paroxysm, seizure, grip, cramp.

disturbance, disorder; restlessness, changeableness, instability.

ferment, fermentation, ebullition, effervescence, hurly-burly; tempest, storm, whirlpool, vortex, etc., 312; whirlwind, tornado, cyclone, typhoon.

V. be agitated; shake, tremble, flutter, flicker; quiver, quaver, quake; shiver, writhe, toss; shuffle, tumble, stagger, bob, reel, sway; wag, waggle, wriggle; stumble, shamble, flounder, totter, flounce, flop, dance, curvet, prance, cavort; squirm; twitch; bustle.

throb, pulsate, beat, palpitate, go pitapat.

ferment, effervesce, foam, boil, boil over, bubble, bubble up; simmer.

agitate, shake, convulse, toss, tumble, wield, brandish, flap, flourish, whisk, jerk, jolt, jog, joggle, disturb, stir, shake up, churn.

Adj. agitated, shaking, tremulous; convulsive, jerky; effervescent, unquiet, restless.

Adv. by fits and starts; in convulsions, in fits, in a flutter.

CLASS III

Words Relating to MATTER

I. MATTER IN GENERAL

316. MATERIALITY.—*N.* materiality, corporality; substantiality, material existence; incarnation, flesh and blood.

matter, body, substance, protoplasm, stuff, element, principle, material, substratum.

object, article, thing, something; still life; materials, etc., 635.
Science of matter: physics; natural philosophy; physical science.
materialist, physicist.

V. materialize, substantiate, incorporate, embody, incarnate.

Adj. material, bodily, corporeal, corporal, physical, incarnate, materialized, embodied; sensible, tangible, ponderable, palpable, substantial; unspiritual, materialistic.

objective, impersonal, nonsubjective.

317. IMMATERIALITY.—*N.* immateriality, insubstantiality, incorporality, unsubstantiality, spirituality; astral plane.

personality; I, myself, me.

ego, spirit, etc. (*soul*), 450; astral body, etheric double, subliminal self, subconscious self, higher self.

spiritualism, spiritism; animism.

spiritualist, spiritist; animist.

V. **dematerialize,** disembody, spiritualize.

Adj. **immaterial,** incorporeal, incorporate, unsubstantial; spiritistic, animistic; discarnate, bodiless, disembodied; extramundane, unearthly; spiritual, etc. (*psychical*), 450.

subjective, personal, nonobjective.

318. WORLD.—*N.* world, creation, nature, universe; earth, globe, sphere, wide world; cosmos, macrocosm.

heavens, sky, empyrean, starry cope (*or* host); firmament.

heavenly bodies, luminaries, stars, asteroids; galaxy, Milky Way; constellations, planets, satellites; comet, meteor, falling (*or* shooting) star; solar system.

sun, orb of day, daystar [*poetic*], Helios, Apollo, Phoebus, etc. (*sun god*), 423.

moon, Diana, Luna, Phoebe, Cynthia, Selene, silver-footed queen.

Adj. **cosmic,** mundane, terrestrial, earthly, sublunary.

celestial, empyreal, heavenly, solar; lunar; starry, stellar, sidereal, astral; nebular.

Adv. in all creation, on the face of the globe, here below, under the sun.

319. GRAVITY.—*N.* gravity, gravitation; weight, heft, heaviness, ponderousness, specific gravity, pressure, load, burden, ballast, counterpoise; mass.

Weighing instrument: balance, scales, steelyard, beam, weighbridge.

Science of gravity: statics.

V. **weigh,** load, press; counterweigh, poise; gravitate.

Adj. **weighty,** heavy, ponderous, ponderable; cumbersome, burdensome, cumbrous, unwieldy, massive; static.

320. LEVITY.—*N.* levity, lightness, imponderability, buoyancy, volatility.

ferment, leaven, yeast, pepsin.

V. **be light,** float, swim.

render light, lighten.

ferment, work, raise, leaven.

Adj. **light,** subtle, imponderous, imponderable, ethereal, airy, feathery, gossamery; volatile, vaporous, buoyant, floating, foamy, frothy; portable.

fermenting, fermentative, yeasty.

II. INORGANIC MATTER

(1) Solids

321. DENSITY.—*N.* **density**, solidity, solidness; impenetrability, impermeability; costiveness, constipation.

condensation; solidification, consolidation, concretion, coagulation; cohesion, etc., 46; petrifaction, etc. (*hardening*), 323; thickening, crystallization, precipitation.

solid body, mass, block, lump; concretion, concrete, conglomerate; stone, rock, cake; card.

sediment, lees, dregs, settlings.

V. **be dense**, compress, squeeze, ram down; solidify; cement, set, consolidate, condense, congeal, coagulate, curd, curdle; fix, clot, thicken, cake, candy, precipitate, deposit, cohere, crystallize; petrify, harden, stiffen.

compress, squeeze, ram down.

Adj. **dense**, solid, solidified; coherent, cohesive, compact; close, serried, thickset; substantial, massive, impenetrable, concrete, hard; crystalline, thick, stodgy.

undissolved, unmelted, unliquefied, unthawed.

indivisible; indissoluble, insoluble.

322. RARITY.—*N.* **rarity**, tenuity; subtlety.

rarefaction, attenuation, expansion, inflation; ether, etc. (*gas*), 334.

V. **rarefy**, expand, dilate, attenuate, thin.

Adj. **rare**, subtle, thin, fine, tenuous, compressible, flimsy, slight, light, porous; rarefied, unsubstantial.

323. HARDNESS.—*N.* **hardness**, firmness, rigidity, inflexibility, temper, callosity; induration, petrifaction, ossification; crystallization.

V. **harden**, render hard, temper, stiffen, cement, indurate, petrify, ossify.

Adj. **hard**, rigid, stubborn, stiff, firm; stark, unbending, unyielding, inflexible, tense.

adamantine, stony, granitic, rocky, horny, callous, bony, cartilaginous.

324. SOFTNESS.—*N.* **softness**, pliableness, flexibility, pliancy, pliability, malleability, ductility, tractility, plasticity, flaccidity, laxity, flabbiness, mollification, softening.

V. **soften,** render soft, mollify, mellow; mash; knead, massage. bend, give, yield, relent, relax.

Adj. **soft,** tender; mollified; supple, pliant, pliable, flexible, lithe, lithesome, limber; plastic; ductile, malleable, tractable; yielding; flabby, flaccid, lax, limp, flimsy; mellow; spongy.

downy, woolly, fluffy, feathery.

325. ELASTICITY.—*N.* **elasticity,** springiness, spring, resilience *or* resiliency, buoyancy; recoil, rebound, reflex.

V. **be elastic;** spring back, recoil.

Adj. **elastic,** springy, resilient, buoyant.

326. INELASTICITY.—*N.* **inelasticity,** flaccidity, laxity; want of elasticity, etc., 325.

Adj. **inelastic,** flaccid, yielding; not elastic.

327. TENACITY.—*N.* **tenacity,** toughness, strength; cohesiveness, cohesion, adhesion; stubbornness, etc. (*obstinacy*), 606; gumminess, glutinousness, viscidity.

Adj. **tenacious,** cohesive, tough, strong, resisting; adhesive, stringy, viscid, gummy, glutinous, gristly, cartilaginous; stubborn, etc. (*obstinate*), 606.

328. BRITTLENESS.—*N.* **brittleness,** fragility; frailty; shortness.

V. **break,** crack, snap, split, shiver, splinter, crumble, crash, crush, burst, give way; fall to pieces; crumble to dust.

Adj. **brittle,** breakable, delicate, fragile, frail; splintery; crisp, short [*as of pastry*].

329. STRUCTURE.—*N.* **structure,** organization, constitution, organism, anatomy, frame, mold, fabric, construction; framework, architecture; stratification.

texture, contexture; tissue, grain, web, surface, nap; roughness; warp and woof (*or* weft); fineness (*or* coarseness) of grain.

Adj. **structural,** organic; anatomic *or* anatomical.

textile; fine-grained, coarse-grained, ingrained; ingrain; fine, delicate, subtile, subtle, gossamer, gossamery, filmy; coarse; homespun, linsey-woolsey.

330. POWDERINESS.—*N.* **powderiness,** grittiness, sandiness, friability.

powder, dust, sand, shingle; sawdust; grit; meal, bran, flour, rice, spore; crumb, seed, grain; particle.

Reduction to powder: pulverization, comminution, granulation, disintegration, abrasion, detrition; mill, grater, rasp, file, pestle and mortar, grindstone, quern, millstone.

V. **pulverize,** powder, comminute, granulate, reduce to powder; scrape, file, abrade, grind, grate, rasp, pound, bruise, beat, crush, craunch, crunch, crumble, disintegrate.

Adj. **powdery,** granular, mealy, floury, farinaceous, branny, dusty, sandy, gritty.

pulverable *or* pulverizable, friable, crumbly, shivery.

331. FRICTION.—*N.* friction, rubbing, abrasion, rub; massage; erasure; elbow grease [*colloq.*].

eraser, rubber, India rubber.

V. **rub,** abrade, scratch, scrape, scrub, fray, rasp, graze, curry, scour, polish, rub out, erase, file, grind, etc. (*pulverize*), 330; massage.

332. [Absence or prevention of friction] LUBRICATION.—*N.* **lubrication,** anointment, oiling.

smoothness, polish, gloss; unctuousness.

lubricant, lubricator; ointment, salve, balm, unguent.

V. **lubricate,** oil, grease; lather, soap; wax; anoint.

(2) Fluids

333. FLUIDITY.—*N.* **fluidity,** liquidity, liquidness; liquefaction; solubility; gaseity, etc., 334.

solution; fluid; liquid; juice, sap, lymph, serum.

Science of liquids at rest: hydrostatics, hydrodynamics, hydrokinetics.

V. **be fluid;** run; flow, etc. (*water in motion*), 348; liquefy, etc., 335.

Adj. **liquid,** fluid; juicy, succulent, sappy; rheumy; fluent, flowing; liquefied, uncongealed; soluble.

334. GASEITY.—*N.* **gaseity,** gaseousness, vaporousness; volatility; aeration; gasification; flatulence.

elastic fluid, gas, air, vapor, ether, steam, fume, effluvium; cloud, etc., 353.

Science of elastic fluids: pneumatics, aerostatics, aerodynamics, aerography, aeromechanics.

V. **gasify,** render gaseous; aerate; vaporize, etc., 336.

Adj. **gaseous,** ethereal, aery, aerial, airy, vaporous, volatile, flatulent.

335. LIQUEFACTION.—*N.* **liquefaction,** liquescence; deliquescence; melting, fusion; thaw; solubleness; solution.

mixture, decoction, infusion, solution.

V. **dissolve,** liquefy; run; melt, thaw, fuse; hold in solution; percolate

Adj. **liquefied;** soluble, dissolvable; solvent, dissolvent.

336. VAPORIZATION.—*N.* **vaporization,** atomization; fumigation, steaming; distillation; gasification; evaporation.

vaporizer, atomizer, spray, evaporator, still, retort.

V. **vaporize,** gasify, atomize; spray; distill, sublimate, evaporate; exhale, emit vapor; fumigate; fume, smoke, reek, steam.

Adj. **volatile,** vapory, vaporous, gaseous; volatilized.

337. WATER.—*N.* **water,** lymph; aqua [L.], *eau* [F.]; fluid, etc., 333.

washing, bathing, bath, immersion; dilution; infiltration, irrigation, seepage.

deluge, etc. (*water in motion*), 348; high water, flood tide, spring-tide.

sprinkler, shower *or* shower bath; nozzle; atomizer, etc., 336.

water, dilute, add water; moisten, etc., 339; steep, soak, drench, wet, dip, immerse, submerge; duck; drown; wash, lave, bathe, sprinkle, dabble; inundate, deluge; irrigate; infiltrate, percolate, seep.

inject; gargle, syringe.

Adj. **watery,** aquatic, lymphatic; infiltrative, seepy; drenching; diluted, weak; wet, etc. (*moist*), 339.

338. AIR.—*N.* **air,** etc. (*gas*), 334; atmosphere; ventilation.
the open, open air; sky, blue sky.

weather, climate; rise and fall of the barometer (*or* mercury).

Science of air: aerology, aerometry, aerography; meteorology, climatology; pneumatics; aeronautics, etc., 267.

aeronaut, etc., 269*a*.

barometer, aneroid, weatherglass, weather gauge.

weather vane, weathercock, vane.

V. **air,** ventilate, fan, etc. (*wind*), 349.

fly, soar, drift, hover; aviate, etc. (*aeronautics*), 267.

Adj. **containing air,** flatulent, effervescent; windy, etc., 349.
atmospheric, airy; aerial, aeriform; aery, pneumatic.

meteorological, barometric, aerographic, weatherwise.

Adv. **in the open air,** in the open, under the stars, out of doors, outdoors; alfresco [It.].

339. MOISTURE.—*N.* **moisture;** moistness, humidity; dew; marsh, etc., 345.

V. **moisten,** wet, sponge, damp, bedew; infiltrate, saturate; soak, sodden, seethe, sop; drench, etc. (*water*), 337.

perspire, etc. (*exude*), 295.

Adj. **moist,** damp; watery, etc., 337; undried, humid, wet, dank, muggy; dewy; juicy.

sodden, soppy, soggy, dabbled; reeking, dripping, soaking, saturated, soft, sloppy, muddy: swampy, etc. (*marshy*), 345; irriguous.

340. DRYNESS.—*N.* **dryness,** aridness, aridity, drought.
desiccation, evaporation; drainage.

V. **dry**, dry up, soak up; sponge, swab, wipe, drain, parch, sear; desiccate, evaporate.

Adj. **dry**, rainless, fair, pleasant, fine; arid, sear, droughty, waterless, dried, desiccated; juiceless, sapless; corky; husky, parched; waterproof, watertight.

341. OCEAN—*N.* **ocean**, sea, main, high seas, deep, salt water; waters, waves, billows; tide, etc. (*water in motion*), 348; offing, watery waste, pond [*humorous for Atlantic*], the seven seas; ocean lane, steamer track.

Neptune, Poseidon, Oceanus, Thetis, Triton, naiad, Nereid; sea nymph, siren, mermaid, merman; trident, dolphin.

oceanography; oceanographer.

Adj. **oceanic**, marine, maritime; seaworthy, seagoing.

342. LAND.—*N.* **land**, earth, ground, soil, dry land, terra firma [L.].

continent; mainland, main; peninsula, chersonese; delta; neck of land, isthmus; oasis; promontory, etc. (*projection*), 250; highland, etc. (*height*), 206; plain, etc., 344.

realty, real estate, property, acres.

coast, shore, strand, beach; bank; seaboard, seaside, seacoast, seashore; reclamation, made land.

fatherland, home, country, native land; region, etc., 181.

soil, glebe, clay, loam, marl, gravel, mold, subsoil, clod.

rock, crag, cliff, boulder.

landsman, landlubber, tiller of the soil; agriculturist, etc., 371.

V. **land**, disembark, debark, come to land, come (*or* go) ashore.

Adj. **earthy**; continental, midland; earthly, terrestrial; littoral, alluvial; landed, territorial; geographic *or* geographical.

Adv. **ashore**, on shore, on land, on dry land, on terra firma.

343. GULF, LAKE.—*N.* **gulf**, bay, inlet, bight, estuary, bayou, fiord, frith *or* firth; mouth; lagoon, cove, creek; natural harbor; roads; sound, strait, narrows.

lake, loch [Scot.], mere, tarn, pond, pool; well, artesian well; ditch, dike, dam, race, millrace; tank, reservoir.

344. PLAIN.—*N.* **plain**, open country; basin, downs, waste, desert, wild, steppe [*Russia*], grassland; tundra [*Arctic*], pampas [*esp. in Argentina*], savanna [*as in Brazil; also, a treeless plain, as in Florida*], campo [*S. Amer.*], llano [*S. Amer.*], prairie, heath, common, moor, moorland; bush; plateau, tableland, mesa; uplands; reach, stretch, expanse; alkali flat.

meadow, mead, pasture, lea, pasturage, field.

lawn, green, plot, grassplot.

greensward, sward, turf, sod, grass; heather.

grounds; estate, park, common, campus.

345. MARSH.—*N.* **marsh,** swamp, morass, peat bog, fen, bog, quagmire, slough; mud, slush.

Adj. **marsh,** marshy, fenny, swampy, boggy, soft; muddy, squashy, spongy.

346. ISLAND.—*N.* **island,** isle, islet; reef, atoll; archipelago; islander.

V. **insulate,** island.

Adj. **insular,** seagirt; archipelagic.

347. [Fluid in motion] STREAM.—*N.* **stream,** etc. (*of water*), 348 (*of air*), 349.

V. **flow,** etc., 348; blow, etc., 349.

348. [Water in motion] RIVER.—*N.* **running water,** jet, squirt, spout, splash, rush, gush, sluice.

waterspout, waterfall; fall, cascade, Niagara; cataract, inundation, deluge; chute, washout.

rain, rainfall; drizzle, shower; downpour, cloudburst; rains, rainy season, monsoon.

stream, course, flux, flow, current, tide, race, millrace, tiderace.

spring; fount, fountain; rill, rivulet, streamlet, brooklet; branch; brook, river; reach; tributary.

body of water, torrent, rapids, flood; spring (*or* high, flood, full) tide; bore, eagre; ebb, reflux; undercurrent, undertow; eddy, vortex, whirlpool, maelstrom.

wave, billow, surge, swell, ripple; tidal wave; comber, rollers, ground swell, surf, breakers, white horses.

Science of fluids in motion: hydrodynamics; hydraulics, hydrostatics, hydrokinetics, hydromechanics.

V. **flow,** run; meander; gush, pour, spout, roll, jet, well, issue; drop, drip, dribble, plash, trickle, distill, percolate; stream, surge, swirl, overflow, inundate, deluge, flow over, splash, swash; murmur, babble, purl, gurgle, spurt, ooze, flow out, etc. (*egress*), 295.

flow into, fall into, open into, drain into; discharge itself, disembogue.

Cause a flow: pour; pour out, etc. (*emit*), 297; shower down; irrigate, drench, etc. (*wet*), 337; spill, splash.

Stop a flow: stanch; dam, plug, stop up, cork, dam up, obstruct, choke, cut off.

rain; pour; shower, sprinkle, drizzle; set in.

Adj. **flowing,** fluent, meandering, flexuous; choppy, rolling; tidal.

rainy, showery, drizzly, drizzling, wet.

349. [Air in motion] WIND.—*N.* **wind,** draft, air; breath, puff, whiff, zephyr, blow, stream, current.

gust, blast, breeze, squall, half a gale, gale.

trade wind, trades, monsoon.

storm, tempest, hurricane, whirlwind, tornado, cyclone, typhoon, simoom [*as in Asia Minor*], harmattan [*W. coast of Africa*], sirocco [*as in W. Africa, Texas, and Kansas*], khamsin [*Egypt*], mistral [*Mediterranean*]; blizzard, norther, northeaster, northeast gale.

wind gauge, anemometer, anemograph; weathercock, weather vane, vane.

breathing, respiration, inspiration, inhalation, expiration, exhalation; blowing, fanning, inflation; ventilation.

V. blow, waft; storm.

respire, breathe, inhale, exhale; inspire, expire; puff, gasp, wheeze; snuff, snuffle; sniff, sniffle; sneeze, cough, hiccup.

inflate, pump, blow up.

whistle, scream, roar, howl, sing, sing in the shrouds, growl.

Adj. windy, breezy, gusty, squally.

stormy, tempestuous, blustering, cyclonic, typhonic; boisterous, violent.

350. [Channel for the passage of water] CONDUIT.—*N.* conduit, channel, duct, watercourse, canyon, coulee, water gap, gorge, ravine, chasm; race; aqueduct, canal; flume, dike, main; arroyo, gully, gulch; moat, ditch; gutter, drain, sewer, culvert; scupper; funnel, trough, siphon, pump, hose; pipe, tube; artery; spout, gargoyle; weir, floodgate, water gate, sluice, lock, valve.

Anatomy: artery, vein, blood vessel, pore; aorta; intestines, bowels; esophagus, gullet; throat.

351. [Channel for the passage of air] AIR PIPE—*N.* air pipe, airhole, blowhole, breathing hole, touchhole, venthole, spilehole, bung, bunghole; shaft, air shaft, smoke shaft, flue, chimney, funnel, vent, ventilator.

nostril, nozzle, throat; windpipe, trachea.

352. SEMILIQUIDITY.—*N.* semiliquidity; stickiness, pastiness, adhesiveness; thickening, jellification.

mud, slush, slime, ooze; moisture, humidity; marsh, etc., 345.

V. thicken, coagulate, gelatinize; jellify, jelly, jell [*colloq.*]; emulsify; mash, squash [*colloq.*], churn, beat up.

Adj. semifluid, semiliquid; half-melted, half-frozen; milky, muddy, curdled; thick, gelatinous, mucilaginous, glutinous, sticky; ropy; clotted.

353. [Mixture of air and water] BUBBLE, CLOUD.—*N.* bubble; foam, froth, spray, surf; spume, scum; lather, suds, yeast.

effervescence, babbling, fermentation; evaporation.

cloud, vapor, fog, mist, haze, steam; scud, rack, cumulus; nebula, cirrus, curl cloud; thunderhead; stratus.

V. **bubble,** boil, foam, spume, froth; effervesce, ferment, fizz; aerate.

cloud, overcast, overcloud, befog, becloud, mist, fog, overshadow, shadow.

Adj. **bubbling,** frothy, effervescent, sparkling, fizzy, heady. **cloudy,** nebulous; vaporous; overcast.

354. PULPINESS.—*N.* **pulpiness;** fleshiness; pulp, paste, dough, sponge, batter, curd, pap, jam, poultice.

V. **pulp,** mash, squash [*colloq.*], macerate; coagulate, etc., 352.

Adj. **pulpy;** [*of fruit*] fleshy, succulent.

355. UNCTUOUSNESS.—*N.* **unctuousness,** oiliness; lubrication; unguent, salve, cerate; ointment, etc. (*oil*), 356; anointment; lubricant.

V. **oil,** anoint, lubricate, etc., 332; smear, salve, grease, lard.

Adj. **unctuous,** oily, oleaginous, fat, fatty, greasy; waxy, soapy, slippery.

356. OIL.—*N.* **oil,** fat, butter, cream, grease, tallow, suet, lard, dripping, blubber; glycerin; coconut butter; soap, soft soap; wax; paraffin, benzine, kerosene, naphtha, gasoline, petroleum; ointment, pomade, unguent, liniment.

356a. RESIN.—*N.* **resin,** rosin, gum; shellac, varnish, mastic, lacquer, sealing wax; amber, ambergris; bitumen, pitch, tar, asphalt.

V. **varnish,** etc. (*overlay*), 223; rosin, resin.

Adj. **resinous,** lacquered, tarred, tarry, pitched, pitchy, gummed, gummy, waxed; bituminous, asphaltic.

III. ORGANIC MATTER

(1) Vitality

357. ORGANIZATION.—*N.* **organization,** structure, organized nature, animated nature; living beings; organic remains; organism; animal and plant life, fauna and flora.

fossils; fossilization, petrifaction; paleontology; paleontologist.

Science of living beings: biology, natural history;[1] zoology, etc., 368, botany; physiology, anatomy, organic chemistry; evolution, Darwinism.

protoplasm, bioplasm; cell, proteid, protein, albumen, germinal matter, germ plasm, germ cell; amoeba, protozoan.

naturalist, biologist, zoologist, botanist, bacteriologist, embryologist.

---

[1]The term *natural history* is also used as relating to all the objects in nature whether organic or inorganic, and including, therefore, *mineralogy, geology, meteorology,* etc.

V. **organize,** systematize, form, arrange, construct.

fossilize, petrify, mummify.

Adj. **organic,** organized, structural; cellular, protoplasmic.

fossilized, petrified.

358. INORGANIZATION.—*N.* **mineral kingdom,** mineral world; unorganized (*or* inorganic) matter.

Science of the mineral kingdom: mineralogy, geology, metallurgy.

V. **mineralize;** pulverize, turn to dust.

Adj. **inorganic,** inanimate, unorganized, mineral.

359. LIFE.—*N.* **life;** vitality; existence, etc.; animation.

vital spark, vital flame, lifeblood; respiration, breath, breath of life.

vivification; oxygen; life force; vitalization; revival; revivification, etc., 163; life to come, etc. (*destiny*), 152.

Science of life: physiology, biology, embryology.

nourishment, nutriment, etc. (*food*), 298.

V. **live,** be alive, breathe, subsist, exist, walk the earth.

be born, see the light, come into the world; quicken; revive; come to life.

give birth to, etc. (*produce*), 161; bring to life, put life into, vitalize; vivify, reanimate, restore, resuscitate.

Adj. **living,** alive; in life, in the flesh, breathing, quick, animated; lively, etc. (*active*), 682; vital, vivifying.

360. DEATH.—*N.* **death,** decease, demise; mortality; dying, dissolution, departure, release, rest, eternal rest; loss, bereavement.

cessation (*or* loss, extinction) **of life.**

river of death; Jordan, Stygian shore; the great adventure.

angel of death, death's bright angel; death, doom, fate, destiny.

death song, dirge, requiem, elegy, threnody.

V. **die,** expire, perish; breathe one's last; lose *or* lay down one's life; die a violent death; give (*or* yield) up the ghost.

die for one's country, make the supreme sacrifice, go West [*First World War euphemism*].

Adj. **dead,** lifeless, inanimate; deceased, late; departed, defunct; gone, no more; bereft of life.

deadly, mortal, fatal.

dying, moribund, at the point of death, at death's door, at the last gasp.

361. [Destruction of life; violent death] KILLING.—*N.* **killing;** homicide, manslaughter; murder, assassination; effusion of blood; bloodshed, slaughter, carnage, butchery, massacre.

war, warfare, organized murder; battle; war to the death, etc. (*warfare*), 722; Armageddon; deadly weapon, etc. (*arms*), 727.

deathblow, finishing stroke, *coup de grace* [F.], quietus; execution, etc. (*capital punishment*), 972; martyrdom.

suffocation, strangulation, garrote; hanging, etc., *v.*

slayer, butcher, murderer, Cain, assassin, cutthroat, garroter, thug, gallows, executioner, etc. (*punishment*), 975; apache, gunman [*colloq.*], bandit.

regicide, parricide, fratricide [*these words refer to both doer and deed*].

suicide, self-murder, self-destruction, hara-kiri [Jap.], suttee; immolation, holocaust.

fatal accident, violent death, casualty, disaster, calamity.

Destruction of animals: slaughtering, sport; the chase, venery; hunting, coursing, shooting, fishing; pigsticking.

sportsman, huntsman, hunter, Nimrod; fisherman, angler.

shambles, slaughterhouse.

V. kill, put to death, slay, shed blood; murder, assassinate, butcher, slaughter, immolate; massacre, decimate; put an end to; dispatch, do to death, do for [*colloq.*]; hunt, shoot, saber, stab, bayonet, put to the sword.

strangle, garrote, hang, throttle, choke, stifle, suffocate; smother, asphyxiate, drown.

execute; behead, guillotine; hang; electrocute.

die a violent death; commit suicide; kill (*or* make away with, put an end to) oneself.

Adj. murderous, slaughterous, sanguinary, bloody-minded, bloodthirsty; homicidal; red-handed, bloody, bloodstained, gory.

mortal, fatal, deadly, lethal; mutually destructive, internecine; suicidal.

362. CORPSE.—*N.* corpse, carcass, skeleton, relics, remains, dust, ashes, earth, clay; mummy; carrion.

ghost, shade, phantom, specter, apparition, spirit, revenant, spook [*colloq.*].

363. INTERMENT.—*N.* interment, burial, sepulture, entombment; obsequies, funeral, funeral rite, wake; knell, passing bell, death bell, tolling; dirge, etc. (*lamentation*), 839; dead march, muffled drum; pall, bier, litter, hearse, catafalque.

cremation, burning; pyre, funeral pile.

undertaker, funeral director.

mourner, mute; pallbearer, bearer.

graveclothes, shroud, winding sheet; cerecloth, cerements.

coffin, casket; urn; sarcophagus.

burial place, grave, pit, sepulcher, tomb, vault, crypt, catacomb, mausoleum; cemetery, burial ground, graveyard, churchyard; God's acre; potter's field; barrow, tumulus; charnel house, dead-house; morgue, mortuary; burning ghat [India]; crematorium, crematory.

gravedigger, sexton.

monument; gravestone, headstone, tombstone; hatchment, stone, marker, cross; epitaph, inscription.

autopsy, post-mortem examination *or* post mortem [L.].

disinterment, exhumation.

V. inter, bury, entomb; inurn; cremate.

disinter, exhume, unearth.

Adj. funereal, funeral, mortuary, sepulchral, cinerary; burial; elegiac.

364. ANIMAL LIFE.—*N.* animal life, animalism.

human system; breath; flesh, flesh and blood; physique, strength, power, vigor, force; spring, elasticity, tone.

V. incarnate, incorporate.

Adj. fleshly, carnal, human, corporeal.

365. VEGETATION.—*N.* vegetation, vegetable life, growth, herbage, flowerage.

V. vegetate, germinate, sprout, grow, shoot up, luxuriate, grow rank, flourish, flower, blossom; cultivate.

Adj. vegetative, vegetal, vegetable; leguminous, etc., 367.

luxuriant, rank, dense, lush, wild.

366. ANIMAL.—*N.* animal kingdom, fauna, brute creation.

animal, creature, created being, living thing; dumb animal, dumb friend, dumb creature; brute, beast.

mammal, quadruped, bird, reptile, fish, crustacean, shellfish, mollusk, worm, insect, zoophyte; animalcule, etc., 193.

beasts of the field, fowls of the air; flocks and herds, livestock, domestic animals, wild animals, game.

Domestic animals: horse, etc. (*beast of burden*), 271; cattle, ox; bull, bullock; cow, milch cow, Jersey, calf, heifer, shorthorn, yearling, steer; sheep; lamb, ewe, ram; pig, swine, boar, hog, sow; yak, zebu, buffalo.

dog, hound, canine; pup, puppy; whelp, cur [*contemptuous*], mongrel.

cat, feline, puss, pussy, tabby; tomcat *or* tom; mouser; Angora, Persian, Maltese, tortoise-shell; kitten, kitty.

Wild animals: deer, buck, doe, fawn, stag, hart, hind, roe, roebuck, caribou, elk, moose, reindeer, wapiti *or* American elk, fallow deer, red deer.

antelope, gazelle, American antelope *or* pronghorn, chamois.

ape, monkey, gorilla, marmoset, chimpanzee, lemur, baboon, orangutan.

fox, reynard, vixen [*fem.*]; dingo, coyote; wildcat, lynx, bobcat; skunk.

lion, tiger, etc. (*wild beast*), 913.

rat, mouse.

lizard, saurian, iguana, newt, chameleon, Gila monster, dragon; crocodile, alligator.

whale, shark, porpoise, walrus, seal, octopus, devilfish; swordfish; pike; salmon, trout, etc.

Birds: feathered tribes, singing bird, warbler, dickybird [*colloq.*].

canary, vireo, linnet, finch, goldfinch, siskin, crossbill, chewink, peewee, titmouse *or* chickadee, nightingale, lark; magpie, cuckoo, mocking bird, catbird, starling; robin, sparrow, swallow, etc.

swan, cygnet, goose, gander, duck, drake, wild duck, mallard.

gull, sea gull, albatross, petrel, stormy petrel *or* Mother Carey's chicken; owl, bird of night; hawk, vulture, buzzard; eagle, bird of freedom.

game, ruffed grouse, grouse, blackcock, duck, plover, rail, snipe, pheasant.

poultry, fowl, cock, rooster, chanticleer, barndoor fowl, barnyard fowl, hen, chicken, chick; guinea fowl, guinea hen; peafowl, peacock, peahen.

Insects: bee, honeybee, queen bee, drone; ant, white ant, termite; wasp, locust, grasshopper, cicada, cicala, cricket; dragonfly; beetle; butterfly, moth; fly, mosquito; earwig; bug, buffalo bug, gypsy moth, weevil.

vermin, lice, cooties [*slang*], flies, fleas, cockroaches *or* roaches, water bugs, bugs, bedbugs, mosquitoes; rats, mice, weasels.

snake, serpent, viper; asp, adder, coral snake *or* harlequin snake, krait [India], cobra, cobra de capello, king cobra, rattlesnake *or* rattler, copperhead, constrictor, boa constrictor, boa, python.

Mythological: basilisk, cockatrice, salamander; griffin; chimera; Python, Hydra, Cerberus.

Adj. **animal;** zoological; equine; bovine; canine; feline; fishy, piscatorial; ophidian, reptilian, snakelike.

367. VEGETABLE.—*N.* **vegetable,** vegetable kingdom; flora.

organism, plant, tree, shrub, bush, creeper, vine; herb, seedling; exotic; annual, perennial; pulse, greens.

foliage, leafage, verdure; branch, bough, stem, trunk; leaf, spray, leaflet, frond, pad, flag, petal, needle, sepal; spray, runner, shoot, tendril.

flower, blossom, bud, floweret, flowering plant.

tree, sapling, seedling; oak, elm, beech, birch, timber tree, pine, palm, spruce, fir, hemlock, yew, larch, cedar, juniper, chestnut, maple, alder, ash, myrtle, magnolia, walnut, olive, poplar, willow, linden, lime; fruit tree; arboretum, etc., 371.

banyan, teak, acacia, deodar, fig tree, eucalyptus, gum tree.

woodlands, virgin forest, forest primeval, forest, wood, timberland, timber, wood lot; weald, park, greenwood, grove, copse, coppice, thicket, chaparral, jungle, bush.

undergrowth,'underwood, brushwood, brake, scrub, heath, heather, fern, bracken, furze, gorse, broom, sedge, rush, bulrush, bamboo; weed, moss, lichen, turf, grass, herbage.

grassland, plain, etc., 344.

seaweed, alga (*pl.* algae), dulse, kelp, rockweed, sea lettuce, gulfweed, sargasso, sargassum; Sargasso Sea.

V. **vegetate,** grow, flourish, bloom, flower, blossom; bud, etc. (*expand*), 194; timber, retimber, plant, trim, graft, prune, cut.

Adj. **vegetable,** vegetative, vegetarian; leguminous, herbaceous, herbal, botanic *or* botanical; arboreous, arboreal, sylvan; grassy, verdant, verdurous; floral; ligneous, wooden, woody; bosky, copsy; mossy, turfy, deciduous, evergreen.

native, domestic, indigenous, native-grown, home-grown.

368. [Science of animals] ZOOLOGY.—*N.* **zoology,** zoography, morphology, anatomy, histology, embryology; comparative anatomy, animal physiology, comparative physiology, anthropology, ornithology, ichthyology, entomology, paleontology.

zoologist, zoographer, zoographist, anatomist, anthropologist, ornithologist, ichthyologist, entomologist, paleontologist.

Adj. zoological, zoologic; zoographical.

369. [Science of plants] BOTANY.—*N.* botany, phytology, phytobiology, vegetable chemistry; vegetable physiology, dendrology; flora; botanic garden, etc. (*garden*), 371.

botanist, phytologist, phytobiologist, dendrologist; horticulturist, etc., 371; herbalist, herbist, herbarian.

V. botanize, herborize.

Adj. botanic *or* botanical, dendroid, dendriform, herby, herbal; horticultural.

370. MANAGEMENT OF ANIMALS.—*N.* domestication, domesticity, manège, veterinary art; breeding, taming.

menagerie, zoological garden, zoo [*colloq.*]; bear pit; aviary; apiary, beehive, hive; aquarium, fishery, fish hatchery, fish pond; hennery, incubator.

Keeper: herder, cowherd, grazier, drover, cowkeeper; shepherd, shepherdess; gamekeeper; trainer, breeder; cowboy, cowpuncher; horse trainer, bronchobuster [*slang*]; beekeeper, apiarist, apiculturist.

veterinarian, veterinary surgeon, vet [*colloq.*], horse doctor, horseshoer.

inclosure, stable, barn; sheepfold, sty; cage, hencoop.

V. tame, domesticate; corral, round up; break in, gentle, break, bust [*slang*], break to harness, train; ride, drive; spur, prick, lash, goad, whip; yoke, harness, harness up [*colloq.*], hitch, hitch up [*colloq.*], cinch.

groom, tend, rub down, brush, currycomb; water, feed, fodder; bed down, litter.

tend stock, milk, shear; water, etc. (*groom*), *v.*; herd; raise, bring up.

hatch, incubate, sit, brood, cover.

Adj. tame, domestic, domesticated, housebroken, broken, gentle, docile.

371. MANAGEMENT OF PLANTS.—*N.* agriculture, cultivation, husbandry, farming; tillage, gardening, vintage; horticulture, arboriculture, forestry; floriculture; landscape gardening.

husbandman, horticulturist, gardener, florist; agriculturist, yeoman, farmer, granger, cultivator, tiller of the soil, plowman; logger, lumberman, lumberjack, forester, woodcutter, pioneer, backwoodsman.

garden: botanic (*or* flower, kitchen, market, truck) garden; nursery; greenhouse, hothouse, conservatory; grassplot, lawn; shrubbery, arboretum, orchard; vineyard, orangery.

field, meadow, mead, green, common.

V. cultivate, till, till the soil, farm, garden, sow, plant; reap, mow, cut; manure, dress the ground; dig, spade, delve, hoe, plow, harrow, rake, weed; force, seed, turf; transplant, thin out, bed, prune, graft.

Adj. **arable,** plowable, tillable.

rural, rustic, country, agrarian, pastoral, bucolic, Arcadian.

372. MANKIND.—*N.* mankind, man; human race (*or* species, kind, nature); humanity, mortality, generation.

Science of man: anthropology, ethnology, ethnography.

human being; person, personage; individual, creature, fellow creature, mortal, body, somebody, one, someone; soul, living soul; party [*slang or vulgar*].

people, persons, folk, public, society, world; community, general public; nation, state, realm, republic; commonweal, commonwealth; body politic; the masses, etc. (*commonalty*), 876; population; lords of creation; ourselves.

Adj. **human,** mortal, personal, individual; national, civic, public social.

373. MAN.—*N.* man, male; gentleman, sir, master; yeoman, chap [*colloq.*], swain, fellow, blade, beau; husband, etc. (*youth*), 129.

mister, Mr., *monsieur* (*abbr.* M., *pl.* Messrs.) [F.], *Herr* [Ger.], *signor* [It., *used before name*], *signore* [It.], *signorino* [It., *dim. of signore*], *señor* [Sp.], *senhor* [Pg.].

Male animal: cock, drake, gander, dog, boar, stag, hart, buck, horse, stallion, gelding; tom, tomcat; he-goat, billy goat [*colloq.*]; ram; bull, bullock; capon; ox, steer.

Adj. **male,** masculine, manly, virile; unwomanly, unfeminine.

374. WOMAN.—*N.* woman, female, petticoat.

womankind, womanhood; the sex, fair sex, softer sex.

dame [*archaic except as an elderly woman or as slang*], madam, lady, donna, belle, matron, dowager, good woman, squaw; wife.

spinster, old maid, bachelor girl, new woman, girl, etc. (*youth*), 129.

mistress, Mrs., *madame* (*pl.* mesdames) [F.], *Frau* [Ger.], *signora* [It.], *señora* [Sp.], *senhora* [Pg.]; miss, *mademoiselle* (*pl.* mesdemoiselles) [F.], *Fräulein* [Ger.], *signorina* [It.], *señorita* [Sp.], *senhorita* [Pg.].

Effeminacy: betty, molly, mollycoddle, old woman, tame cat [*all contemptuous*].

Female animal: hen; bitch, slut; sow, doe, roe, mare; she-goat, nanny goat [*colloq.*], nanny [*colloq.*]; ewe, cow; lioness, tigress; vixen.

harem, seraglio, purdah [India].

Adj. **female,** feminine, womanly, ladylike, matronly, girlish, maidenly; womanish, effeminate, unmanly.

(2) Sensation

375. PHYSICAL SENSIBILITY.—*N.* sensibility, sensitiveness, feeling, impressibility, susceptibility.

sensation, impression; consciousness.

V. feel, perceive, be sensitive to.

render sensitive, sharpen, refine, excite, stir, cultivate, tutor.

cause sensation, impress, excite (*or* produce) an impression.

Adj. sensitive, sensuous; perceptive, sentient, sensible; conscious, alive, alive to impressions, impressionable, responsive.

acute, sharp, keen, vivid, lively.

Adv. to the quick; on the raw [*slang*].

376. PHYSICAL INSENSIBILITY.—*N.* insensibility, obtuseness, paralysis, anesthesia, hypnosis, stupor, coma, sleep.

anesthetic; opium, ether, chloroform, chloral; nitrous oxide, laughing gas; cocaine, novocain; refrigeration.

V. render insensible, blunt, cloy, satiate; benumb, numb, deaden, freeze, paralyze; anesthetize; put to sleep, hypnotize, stupefy, stun.

Adj. insensible, unfeeling, senseless, callous, hard, hardened, casehardened, proof, obtuse, dull; paralytic, palsied, numb, dead.

377. PHYSICAL PLEASURE.—*N.* pleasure, bodily enjoyment, animal gratification, gusto, relish, delight, sensual delight, sensuality; luxuriousness, dissipation, round of pleasure; comfort, ease, luxury, lap of luxury; creature comforts; purple and fine linen; bed of roses.

treat; diversion, entertainment, banquet, refreshment, feast.

happiness, felicity, bliss, beatitude, etc. (*mental enjoyment*), 827.

V. enjoy, relish; luxuriate in, revel in, bask in, wallow in; feast on, gloat over, smack the lips.

please, charm, delight, enchant, etc., 829.

Adj. comfortable, cosy, snug, luxurious, in comfort, at ease, in clover [*colloq.*].

agreeable, etc., 829; grateful, refreshing, comforting, cordial, genial; gratifying, sensuous; palatable, delicious, sweet; fragrant; melodious, harmonious; lovely, etc. (*beautiful*), 845.

Adv. in comfort, on a bed of roses, on flowery beds of ease.

378. PHYSICAL PAIN.—*N.* pain, suffering, dolor, ache, smart; shoot, shooting, twinge, pang, gripe, hurt, cut; sore, soreness; discomfort.

spasm, cramp; crick, stitch; convulsion, throe; throb, colic, gripes.

torment, torture, agony, anguish, rack, crucifixion, martyrdom.

V. **suffer,** feel (*or* suffer, undergo) pain; ache, smart, bleed, tingle, shoot, twinge; writhe, wince.

pain, give pain, inflict pain; lacerate; hurt, chafe, sting, bite, gnaw, stab, grate, gall, fret, prick, pierce, wring, convulse; torment, torture; rack, agonize; crucify; flog, etc. (*punish*), 972.

Adj. **painful,** aching, poignant, excruciating, biting; on the rack; sore, raw.

(1) *Touch*

379. [Sensation of pressure] **TOUCH.**—*N.* **touch,** contact, tangency, impact, feeling; graze, glance, brush, lick; manipulation, rubbing, kneading, massage.

V. **touch,** feel, handle, finger, thumb, paw, fumble, grope; stroke, massage, rub, knead, manipulate, wield; throw out a feeler.

Adj. **tactual,** tangible, palpable, tangent, lambent.

380. SENSATIONS OF TOUCH.—*N.* **itching,** tickling, titillation.

itch, scabies; mange.

V. **itch,** tingle, creep, thrill, sting; prick, prickle.

tickle, titillate.

Adj. **ticklish,** titillative.

itchy, mangy; creepy, crawly.

381. [Insensibility to touch] **NUMBNESS.**—*N.* **numbness;** physical insensibility, etc., 376; anesthesia.

V. **benumb,** etc., 376; stupefy, drug, deaden, paralyze.

Adj. **numb,** benumbed, insensible, unfeeling, deadened; intangible, impalpable; dazed, comatose, narcotic.

(2) *Heat*

382. HEAT.—*N.* **heat,** caloric; temperature, warmth, incandescence.

summer, dog days, heat wave, broiling sun; sun, etc. (*luminary*), 423.

flush, glow, blush, redness; fever.

fire, spark, scintillation, flash, flame, blaze; bonfire; wildfire; sheet of fire, lambent flame.

hot springs, geysers; thermae, hot baths, Turkish bath; steam.

V. **be hot,** glow, flush, sweat, swelter, bask, smoke, reek, stew, simmer, seethe, boil, burn, singe, scorch, scald, broil, blaze, flame; smolder, parch, pant.

heat, etc. (*make hot*), 384; incandesce.

thaw, fuse, melt, liquefy.

Adj. **warm,** mild, genial; tepid, lukewarm.

hot, heated, fervid, fervent, baking, ardent, sunny, sunshiny, torrid, tropical, thermal.

close, sultry, stifling, stuffy, suffocating, oppressive, sweltering.

fiery; incandescent, ebullient, glowing, aglow, reeking, smoking; live; on fire, blazing, in flames, in a blaze; alight, afire, ablaze, smoldering.

feverish, febrile, inflamed, burning; in a fever.

383. COLD.—*N.* **cold,** coldness, frigidity, inclemency.

winter; depth of winter; hard winter; arctic, antarctic.

ice; sleet; hail, hailstone; frost, rime, hoarfrost; icicle, thick-ribbed ice; iceberg, floe, berg, ice field, ice pack, glacier.

snow, snowflake, snowball, snowdrift, snowstorm, snowslip, snow avalanche.

chill, chilliness, shivering, goose flesh, chilblains, frostbite, chattering of teeth.

V. **be cold,** shiver, quake, shake, tremble, shudder, chill, freeze.

Adj. **cold,** cool, chill, chilly, frigid; fresh, keen, bleak, raw, inclement, bitter, biting, cutting, nipping, piercing, pinching; shivering, anguish; frostbitten.

icy, glacial, frosty, freezing, wintry, boreal, arctic, snowbound, icebound, frost-bound, frozen.

Adv. with chattering teeth.

384. CALEFACTION.—*N.* **calefaction,** tepefaction, heating, melting, fusion, liquefaction, combustion; cremation; calcination; incineration; carbonization; cauterization.

ignition, kindling, inflammation, conflagration; incendiarism, arson; auto-da-fé [Pg.], the stake, burning at the stake; suttee.

incendiary, arsonist, pyromaniac, fire bug.

boiling, ebullition, ebullience, decoction; hot spring, geyser.

crematory, crematorium, incinerator; furnace, etc., 386.

wrap, blanket, flannel, wool, fur; wadding, lining, interlining; clothing, etc., 225.

Products of combustion: cinder, ash, embers, slag, clinker; coke, carbon, charcoal.

V. **heat,** warm, chafe, foment; make hot; sun oneself, bask in the sun.

fire, set fire to, set on fire; kindle, enkindle, light, ignite; rekindle.

melt, thaw, fuse; liquefy, dissolve.

burn, scorch; inflame; roast, toast, fry, grill, singe, parch, bake; brand, cauterize, sear, burn in; corrode, char, carbonize, calcine, incinerate, smelt; reduce to ashes.

take *or* catch fire; blaze, etc. (*flame*), 382.

boil, stew, cook, seethe, scald, parboil, simmer.

Adj. heated, warmed; burnt, scorched; molten; volcanic.

inflammable, inflammatory, combustible.

385. REFRIGERATION.—*N.* refrigeration, cooling, congelation, glaciation; solidification; ice; icebox, ice chest; refrigerator.

fire extinguisher, asbestos; fireman, fire brigade, fire department, fire engine.

V. cool, fan, refresh; ice, refrigerate, congeal, freeze, benumb, chill, petrify, pinch, nip, cut, pierce, bite.

extinguish, put out, stamp out; damp, slack, quench.

Adj. incombustible, asbestic, unflammable, uninflammable; fireproof.

386. FURNACE.—*N.* furnace, stove; cookstove, cooker, oven, brick oven, tin oven, Dutch oven, range, fireless cooker; forge, fiery furnace; volcano; kiln, brickkiln, limekiln.

brasier, tripod, salamander, heater, warming pan, footstove, foot warmer; radiator, register, coil; boiler, caldron, pot; urn, kettle; chafing dish; retort, crucible, alembic, still; flatiron, sadiron; toasting fork, toaster.

galley, caboose; hothouse, conservatory; bakehouse; washhouse, laundry.

fireplace, hearth, grate, firebox; andiron, firedog, fire irons; poker, tongs, shovel, hob, trivet; damper, crane, pothooks, chains, turnspit, spit, gridiron.

hot bath; thermae; Turkish (*or* Russian, vapor, electric, sitz, hip, shower) bath; bathroom, lavatory.

387. REFRIGERATOR.—*N.* refrigerator, icebox, ice chest; cold storage; refrigerating plant; icehouse; ice-cream freezer, freezer; ice bag, ice pack, cold pack; ice pail, cooler, wine cooler.

refrigerant, freezing, mixture, ice, ammonia.

388. FUEL.—*N.* fuel, firing, combustible, coal, anthracite, bituminous coal; carbon, slack, cannel coal *or* cannel, lignite, coke, charcoal; turf, peat; oil, gas, natural gas, electricity; ember, cinder, ash, slag, clinker; tinder, touchwood; punk.

log, backlog, yule log, firewood, fagot, kindling wood, kindlings, brushwood.

fumigator, incense, joss stick; smudge; disinfectant.

brand, firebrand, torch; fuse, wick; spill, match, light.

V. coal, stoke; feed, fire, etc., 384.

Adj. carbonaceous; combustible, inflammable; slow-burning, free-burning.

389. THERMOMETER.—*N.* thermometer, thermometrograph, thermostat, thermoscope; differential thermometer, telethermometer, pyrometer.

(3) *Taste*

390. TASTE.—*N.* taste, flavor, gusto, savor, relish; smack, tang; aftertaste.

palate; tongue; tooth; stomach.

V. taste, flavor, savor, smack; tickle the palate, etc. (*savory*), 394.

Adj. tasty, savory, flavored, spiced; palatable, etc., 394.

391. INSIPIDITY.—*N.* insipidity; tastelessness, unsavoriness.

Adj. insipid; tasteless, unsavory, unflavored, jejune, savorless; weak, stale, flat, vapid, wishy-washy [*colloq.*].

392. PUNGENCY.—*N.* **pungency,** piquancy, poignancy, tang, nip.

sharpness, acridity; sourness, unsavoriness.

dram, cordial, nip, bracer [*colloq.*], pick-me-up [*colloq.*], potion, liqueur.

tobacco, nicotine; smoke, cigar, cheroot, stogy; cigarette, fag [*slang*], Havana, Cuban tobacco; weed [*colloq.*]; snuff.

V. **season,** spice, bespice, salt, pepper, pickle, brine, devil, curry.

Adj. **pungent,** strong, high-flavored, full-flavored, high-seasoned; gamy, high; sharp, piquant, racy; biting, mordant; spicy; seasoned, spiced; hot, peppery; acrid, bitter; sour, acid, etc., 397; unsavory, etc., 395.

salt, saline, brackish, briny.

393. CONDIMENT.—*N.* **condiment,** flavoring, seasoning, sauce, spice, relish; pickle; chutney; appetizer.

V. season, etc. (*render pungent*), 392.

394. SAVORINESS.—*N.* **savoriness,** tastiness, palatability; delectability; relish, zest.

appetizer, hors d'oeuvre [F.].

delicacy, titbit, dainty, ambrosia, nectar.

V. **be savory;** tickle the palate (*or* appetite); tempt the appetite, taste good.

relish, like, smack the lips.

Adj. **savory,** tasty; good, palatable; pleasing, nice, dainty, exquisite, delicate; delectable, toothsome, appetizing, delicious; rich, luscious, ambrosial, nectareous; distinctive.

395 UNSAVORINESS.—*N.* unsavoriness; acridness, sourness, etc., 397; acerbity; gall and wormwood.

V. **be unpalatable,** sicken, disgust, nauseate, pall, turn the stomach.

Adj. **unsavory,** unpalatable, ill-flavored; bitter, acrid, acrimonious.

offensive, repulsive, nasty, sickening, nauseous; loathsome; unpleasant, etc., 830.

396. SWEETNESS.—*N.* **sweetness,** saccharinity.

sugar, saccharin; preserve, jam, sugar candy, sugarplum.

sweets, confectionery, caramel, lollipop, bonbon, jujube, comfit, sweetmeat, confection; honey, manna; glucose, sirup, treacle, molasses, maple sirup, maple sugar; taffy, butterscotch.

Sweet beverages: nectar; mead, liqueur, sweet wine.

pastry, cake, pie, tart, puff, pudding.

V. sweeten, sugar, sugar off [*local*]; candy.

Adj. sweet, sugary, saccharine, candied, honied, luscious, cloying, honey-sweet, nectareous; dulcet, mellifluous.

397. SOURNESS.—*N.* sourness, acerbity, acidity; acid.

V. render sour, acidify, acidulate, acetify; ferment.

Adj. sour; acid, acidulated; subacid; tart, crabbed; hard, unripe, green; astringent, styptic.

(4) *Odor*

398. ODOR.—*N.* odor, smell, scent; effluvium; emanation, exhalation; fume, trail, redolence.

V. have an odor (*or* scent); smell, exhale; give out a smell (*or* odor); scent.

smell, scent, snuff, sniff, inhale.

Adj. odorous, odoriferous; strong-scented, redolent, pungent.

Relating to the sense of smell: olfactory; quick-scented, keen-scented.

399. INODOROUSNESS.—*N.* inodorousness, absence (*or* want) of smell.

deodorization; deodorizer, deodorant.

V. be inodorous (*or* scentless); not smell.

Adj. inodorous, scentless; without smell (*or* odor).

400. FRAGRANCE.—*N.* fragrance, aroma, redolence, perfume, bouquet; sweet smell (*or* odor), scent.

perfumery; incense, frankincense; musk, myrrh, attar, bergamot, balm, civet, potpourri, tuberose, hyacinth, heliotrope, rose, jasmine, lily, lily of the valley, violet, pomander; toilet water; eau de cologne [F.], cologne, cologne water.

bouquet, nosegay, posy [*colloq.*], boutonniere [F.], buttonhole [*colloq.*].

spray; wreath, garland, chaplet.

Scent containers: smelling bottle, scent bottle, vinaigrette; scent bag, sachet; thurible, censer, incense burner, atomizer, spray.

V. be fragrant (*or* scented); have a perfume (*or* aroma); smell sweet, scent, perfume; embalm.

Adj. fragrant, aromatic, redolent, spicy, balmy, scented; sweet-smelling, sweet-scented; perfumed; incense-breathing, ambrosial.

401. FETOR—*N.* fetor, bad smell (*or* odor), stench, stink, fetidness, fustiness, mustiness; rancidity; foulness.

V. have a bad smell, smell, stink, smell strong, smell offensively.

Adj. fetid; strong-smelling; high, bad, strong, offensive, noisome, rank, rancid, moldy, tainted, musty; smelling, stinking; putrid, rotten, foul; suffocating.

(5) *Sound*

402. SOUND.—*N.* sound, noise; sonority, sonorousness; strain; accent, twang, intonation; tune, cadence; audibility; resonance, vibration; voice, etc., 580.

Science of sound: acoustics, phonetics, phonology, phonography; telephony, radiophony.

V. **sound,** make a noise; give out sound, emit sound; resound.

Adj. **sounding,** sonorous, resonant, audible, distinct; auditory, acoustic.

phonetic, phonic, sonant.

403. SILENCE.—*N.* silence, stillness, quiet, peace, hush, lull; rest [*music*]; muteness; silence of the tomb (*or* grave).

V. **silence,** still, hush, stifle, muffle, gag, stop; muzzle, put to silence.

Adj. **silent;** still, stilly; noiseless, quiet, calm, soundless, hushed; speechless; aphonic, surd, mute.

solemn, soft, awful, deathlike.

Adv. in dead silence.

404. LOUDNESS.—*N.* loudness, power, vociferation, uproariousness.

din, loud noise, clang, clangor, clatter, noise, roar, uproar, hubbub, racket, hullabaloo, pandemonium; fracas; outcry, etc., 411; explosion, detonation.

blare, trumpet blast, flourish of trumpets, fanfare, blast; peal, swell, alarum, boom; resonance, etc., 408.

V. **be loud** (*or* deafening); peal, swell, clang, boom, thunder, roar; deafen, stun, rend the air, awake the echoes; resound, etc., 408; speak up, shout, etc. (*vociferate*), 411; bellow, etc. (*cry as an animal*), 412.

Adj. **loud,** sonorous, deep, full, powerful; noisy, blatant; clangorous, thundering, deafening, earsplitting, piercing; shrill, etc., 410; obstreperous, uproarious; clamorous, vociferous, fullmouthed, stentorian.

Adv. **loudly,** noisily; aloud; at the top of one's lungs, lustily, in full cry.

405. FAINTNESS.—*N.* faintness, inaudibility; faint sound, whisper, breath; undertone; murmur, hum, buzz, purr, lap [*of waves*], plash; sough, moan, rustle; tinkle.

hoarseness, huskiness.

silencer, muffler; soft pedal, damper, mute, sordine [*all music*].

V. **whisper,** breathe; mutter, etc. (*speak imperfectly*), 583.

murmur, purl, hum, gurgle, ripple, babble, flow; rustle; tinkle.

muffle, deaden, mute, subdue.

Adj. faint, low, dull; stifled, muffled; inaudible; hoarse, husky; gentle, soft; floating; purling, flowing; muttered; whispered; liquid; soothing; dulcet, etc. (*melodious*), 413.

Adv. in a whisper, with bated breath, *sotto voce* [It.]; between the teeth; aside; piano, pianissimo [*both music*]; out of earshot; inaudibly, faintly.

406. [Sudden and violent sounds] **SNAP.**—*N.* snap, etc., *v.*; toot, shout, yell, yap [*dial.*], yelp, bark.

report, thump, knock, clap, thud; burst, thunderclap, thunderburst, eruption, blowout [*tire*], explosion, discharge, detonation, firing, salvo, volley.

V. snap, rap, tap, knock; click; clash; crack, crackle; crash; pop; slam, bang, clap; thump, toot, yelp, bark, fire, explode, rattle, burst on the ear.

407. [Repeated and protracted sounds] **ROLL.**—*N.* roll, etc., *v.*; drumming, rumbling, howl, dingdong; ratatat, rubadub, tattoo; pitapat; quaver, clutter, charivari, racket; peal of bells, devil's tattoo; drumfire, barrage; whir, rattle, drone; reverberation.

V. roll, drum, boom; whir, rustle, tootle, roar, drone, rumble, rattle, clatter, patter, clack.

hum, trill, shake; chime, peal, toll; tick, beat.

408. RESONANCE.—*N.* resonance; ring, chime, ringing, clangor, bell note, tintinnabulation, vibration, reverberation.

bass; basso [It.], basso profundo [It.]; baritone, contralto; pedal point, organ point; snoring, snore.

V. resound, reverberate, re-echo; ring, sound; chink, clink; jingle, tinkle; chime; gurgle, mutter, murmur; plash, echo, ring in the ear.

Adj. resonant, reverberant, resounding, reverberating; deep-toned, deep-mouthed; hollow, sepulchral; gruff, etc. (*harsh*), 410.

408a. NONRESONANCE.—*N.* nonresonance, dead sound; thud, thump, muffled drums, cracked bell; damper, sordine, mute; muffler, silencer.

V. muffle, deaden, mute; sound dead; stop (*or* deaden) the sound.

Adj. nonresonant, dead, mute; muffled, deadened.

409. [Hissing sounds] **SIBILATION.**—*N.* sibilation, hissing; zip; hiss, buzz; sneezing, sternutation.

V. hiss, buzz, whiz; rustle; fizz, fizzle; wheeze, whistle, sizzle, swish.

Adj. sibilant; hissing; rustling; wheezy.

410. [Harsh or high sounds] **STRIDENCY.**—*N.* stridency; stridor, harshness, raucousness; sharpness; creak, jar; creaking, grating; discord, dissonance.

high note, shrill note; soprano, treble, tenor, alto, falsetto; head voice, head tone; shriek, yell, cry, wail, pipe.

V. **grate,** creak, saw, snore, jar, burr, pipe, twang, jangle, clank; scream, etc. (*cry*), 411; set the teeth on edge, pierce (*or* split) the ears; yelp, etc. (*animal sound*), 412; buzz, etc. (*hiss*), 409.

Adj. **grating,** creaking, jangling, jarring, strident, harsh, coarse, hoarse, raucous; metallic; rough, rude; gruff, grum, sepulchral, hollow.

high, sharp, acute, shrill; piercing, high-pitched; cracked; discordant.

411. CRY.—*N.* **cry,** shout; shriek; hubbub; bark, etc. (*animal*), 412.

outcry, vociferation, ejaculation, hullabaloo, chorus, clamor, hue and cry, plaint; lungs; stentor.

V. **cry,** roar, shout, bawl; halloo, halloa, yo-ho, whoop; yell, bellow, hoot, boo; howl, scream, screech, shriek; shrill, squeak, squeal, squall; whine, pipe.

cheer, huzza, hurrah, yell.

moan, grumble, groan.

snort, snore; grunt, etc., 412.

vociferate, raise (*or* lift) the voice; yell out, call out, sing out, cry out; exclaim, give cry, clamor; rend the air; make the welkin ring; shout at the top of one's voice.

Adj. **clamorous,** clamant, vociferous; stentorian, etc. (*loud*), 404; open-mouthed; full-mouthed.

412. [Animal sounds] ULULATION.—*N.* **ululation,** howling, cry, roar; call, note, howl, bark, yelp, bowwow, belling; woodnote; insect cry; twittering, drone.

V. **ululate,** howl; cry, roar, bellow; bark, yelp; bay, bay the moon; yap, growl, snarl, howl; grunt, snort, squeak; neigh, bray; mew, purr, caterwaul; bleat, low, moo; crow, screech, croak, caw, coo, gobble, quack, cackle, cluck; chirp, cheep, chirrup, peep, sing, twitter; chatter, hoot, wail; hum, buzz; hiss; blat [*colloq.*].

413. MELODY. CONCORD.—*N.* **melody,** rhythm, measure; rhyme, etc. (*poetry*), 597; euphony.

Musical terms: pitch, timbre, intonation, tone, overtone.
orchestration, harmonization, modulation, phrasing.
staff *or* stave, line, space, brace; bar, rest; passage, phrase; trill *or* shake, turn, arpeggio [It.].
note, musical note, notes of a scale; sharp, flat, natural; high note, etc., 410; low note, etc., 408; interval; semitone.
breve, semibreve *or* whole note, minim *or* half note, crotchet *or* quarter note, quaver *or* eighth note, semiquaver *or* sixteenth note, demisemiquaver *or* thirty-second note; sustained note, drone.
scale, gamut; diapason; key, clef, chord.
harmony, concord; tonality; consonance; part; unison; chime.
Science of harmony: harmony, harmonics; thorough bass, counterpoint; composer.

opus (*pl. opera*) [L.], piece of music, etc., 415.

V. **harmonize,** chime, symphonize, transpose, orchestrate; blend, put in tune, tune, accord, string.

Adj. **harmonious,** harmonic, in concord, in tune, in concert, in unison.

melodious, musical, tuneful, tunable; sweet, dulcet, mellow, mellifluous; soft; clear, silvery; euphonious; enchanting, etc. (*pleasure-giving*), 829; fine-toned, silver-toned, full-toned, deep-toned.

414. DISCORD.—*N.* **discord,** dissonance, want of harmony; harshness, etc., 410; charivari, racket; Babel, pandemonium.

V. **be discordant** (*or* harsh); jar, etc. (*sound harshly*), 410.

Adj. **discordant,** dissonant, out of tune, tuneless; unmusical, untunable; unmelodious, inharmonious; singsong; harsh, etc., 410; jarring.

415. MUSIC.—*N.* **music;** minstrelsy; strain, tune, air, melody; piece of music; rondo, rondeau, pastoral; cavatina, fantasia, toccata [It.]; fugue, canon; potpourri, medley; incidental music; variations, roulade, cadenza, cadence, trill; serenade, nocturne.

instrumental music; orchestral score, full score; composition, opus (*pl. opera*) [L.]; concert piece; concerto [It.]; symphony, sonata, symphonic poem, tone poem; chamber music; movement; overture, prelude, voluntary; string quartet (*or* quintet).

lively music, polka, reel, etc. (*dance*), 848; ragtime, jazz; syncopation, martial music, march; allegro, presto.

slow music, Lydian measures; adagio, largo, andante; lullaby, cradle song, berceuse [F.]; dirge, etc. (*lament*), 839; dead march; minuet.

vocal music, vocalism; chant; psalm, psalmody, hymnology; hymn; canticle; oratorio; opera, operetta; cantata; song, lay, ballad, ditty, carol; recitative, aria.

solo, duet, trio, quartet, quintet, sestet, septet, double quartet, chorus; part song, descant, glee, madrigal, catch, round, chorale; antiphon; accompaniment; inside part, second, alto, tenor, bass; score, piano score, vocal score.

concert, musicale, recital, chamber concert, popular concert *or* pop [*colloq.*], open-air concert; serenade; community singing, singsong [*colloq.*].

method, solfeggio [It.], tonic sol-fa, sight singing, sight reading.

V. **compose,** write, etc., 416; attune, tune.

perform, execute, play, etc., 416.

Adj. **musical;** instrumental, vocal, choral, lyric, melodic; operatic; classic, modern, orchestral, symphonic, contrapuntal; program, imitative; harmonious, etc., 413.

416. MUSICIAN. [Performance of music]—*N.* **musician,** virtuoso, performer, player, minstrel; bard, etc. (*poet*), 597; accompanist, instrumentalist, organist, pianist, violinist, fiddler; flutist, harpist, fifer, trumpeter, cornetist, piper, drummer.

orchestra; strings, woodwind, brass; band, brass band, military band, German band, jazz band; street musicians.

vocalist, singer, warbler; songbird; songster, songstress; chorister; chorus singer; choir, chorus.

Orpheus, Apollo, the Muses, Polyhymnia, Erato, Euterpe, Terpsichore.

conductor, choirmaster, bandmaster, concertmaster, drum major, song leader, precentor.

performance, execution, touch, expression.

V. play, tune, tune up, pipe, pipe up, strike up, sweep the chords, fiddle, strike the lyre, beat the drum; blow (*or* wind) the horn; twang, pluck, pick; pound, thump; drum, thrum, strum, beat time; execute, perform; accompany.

compose, set to music, arrange, harmonize, orchestrate.

sing, troll, chant, intone, hum, warble, twitter, carol, chirp, chirrup, lilt, quaver, trill, shake.

Adj. musical; lyric, dramatic; bravura, florid, brilliant.

417. MUSICAL INSTRUMENTS.—*N.* musical instruments; orchestra (*including* strings, woodwind, brass, and percussive instruments); band; string band, military band, brass band.

418. [Sense of sound] HEARING.—*N.* hearing, audition; audibility; acoustics; ear for music.

ear; eardrum, tympanum.

Instruments: ear trumpet, audiphone, dentiphone, speaking trumpet; phonograph, gramophone, graphophone, microphone, victrola; stethoscope; telephone, radiophone, wireless telephone, radio.

hearer, auditor, audience, listener; eavesdropper.

V. hear, overhear; hark, hearken; list, listen; strain one's ears, attend to, give attention, prick up one's ears; give ear, give a hearing to.

Adj. hearing, auditory, acoustic, phonic; auricular; auditive.

419. DEAFNESS—*N.* deafness, hardness of hearing, inaudibility; deaf-mute; deaf-and-dumb alphabet.

V. deafen, render deaf, stun, split the ears (*or* eardrum).

Adj. deaf, hard (*or* dull) of hearing; stunned, deafened; stone-deaf; inattentive.

inaudible, out of earshot (*or* hearing).

(6) *Light*

420. LIGHT.—*N.* light, ray, beam, stream (*of light*), gleam, streak; sunbeam, moonbeam; aurora, dawn, daylight, day, sunshine; glint, glare, glow, afterglow; sun, etc., 423.

reflection, refraction, dispersion.

halo, glory, nimbus, aureole, aura.

spark, scintilla, scintillation, flash, blaze, coruscation; flame, glare, blaze; lightning; phosphorescence.

luster, sheen, shimmer, gloss, brightness, brilliancy, splendor, effulgence; illumination, radiance, radiation.

Science of light: optics, radiometry; photography; phototelegraphy, radiotelegraphy; actinic rays, radioactivity; Röntgen rays, X rays, ultraviolet rays.

illuminant, gas, etc., 423.

V. **shine,** glow, beam, glitter, glisten, gleam; flare, blaze, glare, shimmer, glimmer, flicker, sparkle, scintillate, coruscate, flash.

daze, dazzle, bedazzle.

lighten, enlighten, light, irradiate, illume, illumine, illuminate; kindle, etc., 384.

Adj. **luminous,** lucent; light, sunny, bright, vivid, splendid, resplendent, refulgent, lustrous, brilliant, radiant, lambent; aglow.

shiny, glossy, burnished, glassy.

clear, cloudless, unclouded.

421. DARKNESS.—*N.* **darkness,** duskiness; blackness, swarthiness; obscurity, gloom, murk, murkiness; dusk; dimness, etc., 422.

night; midnight; dead of night.

shadow, shade; obscuration, adumbration; eclipse; radiograph.

V. **darken,** obscure, shade, dim; lower, overcast, overshadow, cloud, becloud, bedim.

extinguish, put out, blow out, snuff out.

Adj. **dark,** darkling, obscure; black, etc. (*color*), 431; nocturnal.

somber, dusky; dingy, lurid, gloomy, murky; shady, umbrageous; overcast, etc. (*dim*), 422; cloudy, etc., 426.

422. DIMNESS.—*N.* **dimness,** paleness, dullness, duskiness, mistiness.

twilight, dusk, nightfall, gloaming; dawn, daybreak, break of day, Aurora; moonlight, moonshine [*poetic*], starlight.

V. **cloud over,** gloom, lower.

twinkle, glimmer, flicker.

pale, fade, grow dim.

dim, bedim, obscure, shade, shadow, darken, cloud, becloud.

Adj. **dim,** dull, dingy, dusky, lackluster; cloudy, misty, hazy.

leaden, lurid, dun; overcast, dirty.

423. [Source of light] LUMINARY.—*N.* **luminary;** light, ray, beam; flame, etc. (*fire*), 382; spark, scintilla; phosphorescence.

Heavenly bodies: sun, orb of day, daystar [*poetic*]; star; constellation; galaxy, Milky Way; polestar, Polaris; morning star, Lucifer; evening star, Venus; moon, etc., 318.

sun god, Helios, Phoebus, Apollo, Hyperion, Ra [*Egypt*].

phosphorus; *ignis fatuus* [L.]; jack-o'-lantern, will-o'-the-wisp.

polar lights, northern lights, aurora borealis [L.], aurora australis [L.]; aurora.

Artificial light: gas, gaslight, electric light, electric torch; headlight, searchlight; spotlight, flashlight, limelight, calcium light; lamplight, lamp, lantern, dark lantern, bull's-eye; candle, taper, rushlight; torch, flambeau, brand; gaselier, chandelier; candelabrum, sconce, luster, candlestick; fireworks, pyrotechnics.

signal light, rocket, balefire, beacon fire; lighthouse.

V. illuminate, etc. (*light*), 420.

Adj. self luminous; phosphorescent; radiant, etc. (*light*), 420.

424. SHADE.—*N.* shade; awning, etc. (*cover*), 223.

screen, curtain, portiere [F.]; shutter, blind.

veil, mantle, mask.

cloud, mist, shadow; smoke screen [*mil.*].

blinkers, blinders; smoked glasses, colored spectacles.

V. veil, draw a curtain; cast a shadow, etc. (*darken*), 421.

Adj. shady, umbrageous, shadowy.

425. TRANSPARENCY.—*N.* transparency, transparence, translucence, diaphanousness; lucidity, limpidity; fluorescence; translumination.

V. be transparent (*or* pellucid); transmit light.

Adj. transparent, pellucid, lucid, diaphanous; translucent, limpid, clear, serene, crystalline.

426. OPACITY.—*N.* opacity, opaqueness; cloudiness; film; cloud, etc., 353.

V. be opaque; obstruct the passage of light.

Adj. opaque, impervious to light; dim, etc., 422; turbid, thick, muddy, cloudy, foggy, vaporous; smoky, murky, smeared, dirty.

427. SEMITRANSPARENCY.—*N.* semitransparency, opalescence, milkiness, pearliness; mist, haze, steam.

V. cloud, frost, cloud over, frost over.

Adj. semitransparent, semidiaphanous, semiopaque; opalescent, opaline; pearly, milky; frosted, hazy, misty.

428. [Specific Light] COLOR.—*N.* color, hue, tint, tinge, dye, complexion, shade, tincture; coloration; glow, flush; tone, key.

primary color, complementary color; coloring, keeping, tone, value.

spectrum, spectrum analysis; prism, spectroscope, kaleidoscope.

pigment, coloring matter, paint, dye, wash, distemper, stain; medium.

V. color, dye, tinge, stain, tint, tone; paint, wash, distemper, ingrain, grain, illuminate, emblazon.

Adj. colored, dyed; chromatic; prismatic; double-dyed.

bright, vivid, intense, deep; fresh, rich, gorgeous; bright-colored, gay.

gaudy, florid; garish; showy, flaunting; flashy; many-colored, parti-colored, variegated; raw, crude; glaring, flaring.

mellow, harmonious, pearly, sweet, delicate, subtle, tender.

dull, sad, somber, sad-colored, grave, gray, dark.

429. ABSENCE OF COLOR.—*N.* decoloration, discoloration; pallor, paleness, sallowness.

neutral tint, monochrome, black and white.

V. **lose color,** fade, become colorless, turn pale; pale, fade out.

deprive of color, decolor, wash out, tone down; whiten, bleach, blanch.

Adj. **colorless,** uncolored, hueless, pale, pallid; pale-faced, anemic; faint, dull, cold, muddy, leaden, dun, wan, sallow, dingy, ashy, ashen, ghastly, cadaverous, glassy, lackluster; discolored.

light-colored, fair, blond, ash-blond; white, etc., 430; towheaded.

430. WHITENESS.—*N.* whiteness, showiness, hoariness.

whitewash, whiting, whitening, calcimine.

V. **whiten,** bleach, blanch, silver, frost.

whitewash, calcimine, white.

Adj. **white,** snow-white, snowy, frosted, hoar, hoary; silvery, silver, milk-white, milky.

whitish, creamy, pearly, ivory, fair, blond, ash-blond; blanched; light.

431. BLACKNESS.—*N.* **blackness,** darkness, obscurity; swarthiness, swartness; lividness.

Negro, Negress, blackamoor, man of color, colored man, colored woman, nigger [*colloq., usually contemptuous*], darky [*colloq.*], black, Ethiop, Ethiopian, Hottentot, Pygmy, Bushman, African.

V. **black,** blacken, blot, blotch, smut, smudge, smirch; darken, etc., 421.

Adj. **black,** sable, somber, livid, dark, inky, ebon, pitchy, sooty; swart, swarthy, dusky, dingy, murky; blotchy, smudgy; low-toned.

432. GRAY.—*N.* gray, etc., *adj.*; grayness; neutral tint, silver, dove color, pepper and salt, chiaroscuro [It.].

V. **render gray,** gray.

Adj. **gray;** iron-gray, dun, drab, dingy, leaden, pearly, dove-colored, silver, silvery, silvered; dapple-gray; ashen, ashy; grizzly, grizzled.

433. BROWN.—*N.* brown, etc., *adj.*; brownness.

V. **render brown,** brown, tan, embrown, bronze.

Adj. **brown,** nut-brown, seal-brown, mahogany, chocolate; fawn, ecru, tawny; tan, fawn-colored, snuff-colored, liver-colored.

reddish-brown, terra cotta, russet, foxy, bronze, coppery, copper-colored, maroon; bay, roan, sorrel; chestnut, henna, auburn, hazel.

sunburned; tanned, etc., *v.*

434. RED.—*N.* red, etc., *adj.*; flesh color, flesh tint, color, warmth; redness, ruddiness, blush.

V. redden, rouge, crimson, incarnadine; ruddle, rust.

blush, flush, color, color up, mantle, redden.

Adj. red, scarlet, cardinal, vermilion, carmine, crimson, pink, rose, cerise, cherry, salmon, maroon, carnation, magenta, solferino, damask.

reddish; sanguine, bloody, gory; coral, coralline, rosy, roseate; blood-red, wine-red, wine-colored, ruby, rufous, bricky, reddish-brown, etc., 433; rose (*or* ruby, cherry, claret, flame, flesh, peach, salmon, brick, rust) -colored.

red-complexioned, red-faced, florid, burned, rubicund, ruddy, red, high-colored, glowing, sanguine, blooming, rosy, hectic, flushed, inflamed.

Of hair: sandy, carroty, brick-red, Titian, auburn, chestnut.

435. GREEN.—*N.* green, etc., *adj.*; greenness, verdancy, verdure.

Adj. green, verdant, olive; verdurous; emerald (*or* pea, grass, apple, sea, leaf, bottle, Irish, Kelly) green; greenish, aquamarine, blue-green.

436. YELLOW.—*N.* yellow, etc., *adj.*; yellowness; jaundice.

V. render yellow, yellow, gild.

Adj. yellow, aureate, golden, gold, gilt, gilded, lemon, fallow; sallow, jaundiced; tawny, cream, creamy; flaxen, yellowish, buff; gold (*or* saffron, citron, lemon, amber, straw, primrose, cream) -colored.

437. PURPLE.—*N.* purple, etc., *adj.*; royal purple; gridelin, amethyst; damson, heliotrope.

V. render purple, purple, empurple.

Adj. purple, violet, plum-colored, lavender, lilac, puce, mauve, purplish, amethystine, magenta, solferino, heliotrope; livid; purplish.

438. BLUE.—*N.* blue, etc., *adj.*; azure [*her.*]; indigo; sapphire, blueness, bluishness; bloom.

Adj. blue, azure, cerulean, sky-blue, navy-blue, midnight-blue, cadet-blue, robin's-egg-blue, baby-blue, ultramarine, aquamarine, electric-blue, steel-blue; bluish; cold.

439. ORANGE.—*N.* orange, old gold; gold color, etc., *adj.*

Adj. orange, orange (*or* gold, brass, apricot) -colored; warm, hot, glowing, flame-colored.

440. VARIEGATION.—*N.* variegation; iridescence, play of colors, spottiness; tricolor.

check, plaid, tartan, patchwork; marquetry, parquet, parquetry, mosaic, checkerwork; chessboard, checkers; harlequin.

V. variegate, stripe, streak, checker, fleck, speckle, besprinkle,

sprinkle; stipple, dot, tattoo, inlay, tessellate; damascene; embroider, quilt.

Adj. **variegated,** many-colored, many-hued, divers-colored, parti-colored, polychromatic; kaleidoscopic.

iridescent, opaline, opalescent, prismatic, pearly, shot, tortoise-shell.

mottled, pied, piebald, skewbald; motley, marbled, pepper-and-salt, dappled.

checkered, checked, plaid, mosaic, tessellated.

spotted, spotty; powdered; speckled, freckled, flea-bitten, studded; flecked.

barred, veined, brindled, tabby, watered.

441. [Perception of light] VISION.—*N.* **vision,** sight, optics, eyesight.

view, look, glance, ken, glimpse, glint, peep, peek; gaze, stare, leer; contemplation, regard, survey; inspection, reconnaissance, watch, espionage, autopsy; sight-seeing, globe-trotting [*colloq.*].

viewpoint, standpoint, point of view; loophole, watchtower.

field of view; theater, amphitheater, arena, vista, horizon; bird's-eye view, panoramic view.

eye, visual organ, organ of vision, naked eye; clear (*or* sharp, quick, eagle) sight.

V. **see,** behold, discern, perceive, descry, sight, make out; discover, distinguish, recognize, spy, espy, command a view of; witness, contemplate, look on, see at a glance.

look, view, eye, survey, scan, inspect; reconnoiter, glance, cast a glance; observe, etc. (*attend to*), 457; watch, keep watch; watch for, etc. (*expect*), 507; peep, peek, peer, pry, take a peep.

look intently; strain one's eyes; rivet the eyes upon; stare, gaze; pore over, gloat on, gloat over; leer, ogle, glare; goggle; squint, gloat, look askance.

Adj. **ocular,** visual, optic *or* optical; ophthalmic; visible, etc., 446.

clear-sighted, clear-eyed, farsighted; eagle-eyed, hawk-eyed, lynx-eyed, keen-eyed, Argus-eyed.

Adv. **at sight,** at first sight, at a glance, at the first blush.

442. BLINDNESS.—*N.* **blindness,** sightlessness, benightedness, cataract; dim-sightedness, etc., 443; Braille.

V. **be blind,** not see; lose one's sight; grope in the dark.

blind, blindfold, hoodwink, dazzle; put one's eyes out; throw dust into one's eyes; screen, hide.

Adj. **blind,** eyeless, sightless, visionless; dark; stone-blind, stark-blind, undiscerning; dim-sighted, etc., 443.

Adv. **blindly,** blindfold; darkly.

443. DIM-SIGHTEDNESS.—*N.* **Imperfect vision:** dim (*or* short, near, long) -sightedness; purblindness, bleardness, myopia, astigmatism; color blindness, snow blindness; ophthalmia; cataract.

squint, cross-eye, cast in the eye, swivel eye, cockeye, goggle-eyes.

Limitation of vision: blinker, blinder; screen, curtain, veil.

Fallacies of vision: refraction, distortion, illusion, mirage, phantasm, phantom; vision; specter, apparition, ghost; will-o'-the-wisp, etc., 423.

V. **be dim-sighted,** see double; see through a glass darkly; wink, blink, squint, look askance, screw up the eyes, glare, glower.

dazzle, glare, swim, blur.

Adj. **dim-sighted,** myopic, nearsighted, shortsighted, astigmatic; blear-eyed, goggle-eyed, one-eyed; half-blind, purblind; cockeyed [*colloq.*], dim-eyed, mole-eyed.

444. SPECTATOR.—*N.* **spectator,** beholder, observer, looker-on, onlooker, witness, eyewitness, bystander, passer-by; sight-seer; rubberneck [*slang*].

spy, scout; sentinel, etc. (*warning*), 668.

grandstand [*fig.*], bleachers [*fig.*], gallery.

V. **witness,** behold, etc. (*see*), 441; look on, etc. (*be present*), 186.

445. OPTICAL INSTRUMENTS.—*N.* **optical instruments;** lens, magnifier, microscope; spectacles, glasses, goggles, eyeglass, pince-nez; periscope; telescope, glass, lorgnette, binocular; spyglass, opera glass, field glass; burning glass, convex lens; prism.

camera, hand camera, kodak [*trade name*]; moving-picture machine, magic lantern, stereopticon; stereoscope, kaleidoscope.

mirror, reflector, speculum; looking glass, pier glass, cheval glass.

optics, optician; photography, photographer; optometry, optometrist; microscopy, microscopist.

446. VISIBILITY.—*N.* **visibility,** perceptibility, conspicuousness, distinctness, appearance, etc., 448; exposure; manifestation, etc., 525; ocular demonstration; field of view, vista, horizon.

V. **appear,** open to the view; catch the eye; present (*or* show, manifest, reveal, expose, betray) itself; stand forth, stand out; materialize; show; arise; peep out, peer out; start up, spring up; gleam, glimmer; glitter, glow, loom; glare; burst forth; burst upon the view; heave in sight [*naut. or colloq.*]; come into view, come out, come forth, come forward; attract the attention, etc., 457.

expose to view, show, display.

Adj. **visible,** perceptible, discernible, apparent; in view, in full view, in sight; exposed to view.

distinct, plain, clear, definite; obvious, etc. (*manifest*), 525; recognizable; glaring, palpable, staring, conspicuous.

Adv. before one, under one's very eyes, in sight of.

447. INVISIBILITY.—*N.* invisibility, imperceptibility; indistinctness; mystery; latency, obscurity; concealment, mystification.

V. **be invisible** (*or* imperceptible); be hidden, etc. (*hide*), 528; escape notice.

render invisible; conceal, etc., 528; put out of sight.

Adj. **invisible,** imperceptible; out of sight, not in sight, unseen; viewless; inconspicuous; covert, latent.

indistinct; dim; mysterious, dark, obscure; confused, indistinguishable, shadowy, indefinite, undefined, ill-defined, blurred, out of focus; misty, veiled, concealed.

448. APPEARANCE.—*N.* **appearance,** phenomenon, sight, show, scene, view; lookout, outlook, prospect, vista, perspective, bird's-eye view, scenery, landscape, seascape, picture, tableau; display, exposure, rising of the curtain.

spectacle, pageant; peep show, magic lantern, biograph, cinematograph, cinema [*colloq.*], moving pictures, movies [*colloq.*], photoplay, photodrama; panorama.

aspect, angle, phase, shape, form, guise, look, complexion, color, image, mien, air, cast, carriage, port, demeanor; presence, expression, point of view, light.

lineament, feature, trait, lines; outline, outside; contour, silhouette, face, countenance, visage, profile; physiognomy.

V. **appear,** be visible, seem, look, show; cut a figure, figure; present to the view; show, etc. (*make manifest*), 525; look like, resemble.

Adj. **apparent,** seeming, ostensible; on view.

Adv. **to all appearance,** ostensibly, seemingly, on the face of it, at the first blush, at first sight, to the eye.

449. DISAPPEARANCE.—*N.* **disappearance,** evanescence, eclipse; departure, exit; vanishing point.

V. **disappear,** vanish, dissolve, fade, melt away, pass, go, depart, be gone, leave no trace; be lost to view (*or* sight), pass out of sight.

efface, etc., 552.

Adj. **disappearing,** evanescent; missing, lost; lost to sight.

CLASS IV

WORDS RELATING TO THE INTELLECTUAL FACULTIES

I. FORMATION OF IDEAS

450. INTELLECT.—*N.* **intellect**, mind, understanding, reason; rationality; intellectual faculties (*or* powers); senses, consciousness, observation, intellectuality, mentality, intelligence; conception, judgment, wits, brains, parts, capacity, genius; wit; ability; wisdom; ideality, idealism.

ego, soul, spirit; heart, breast, bosom; subconscious self, subliminal consciousness.

seat of thought, brain; head, headpiece; skull, cranium.

Science of mind: psychology, psychoanalysis; psychophysics; metaphysics; philosophy.

psychical research; telepathy, thought transference, thought reading; clairaudience; clairvoyance, mediumship; spiritualism, etc., 992*a*.

V. **reason**, understand, think, reflect, cogitate, conceive, judge, contemplate, meditate; ruminate, etc. (*think*), 451.

note, notice, mark; take notice of; be aware of, realize; appreciate.

Adj. **intellectual**, mental, rational; psychological; conscious, percipient, brainy [*colloq.*].

hyperphysical, subconscious, subliminal; telepathic, clairvoyant; psychic *or* psychical, spiritual, metaphysical, transcendental.

450a. ABSENCE OF INTELLECT.—*N.* **want of intellect** (*or* mind, understanding); unintellectuality; imbecility, etc., 490.

Adj. **unendowed with** (*or* void of) reason; unintelligent, etc. (*imbecile*), 499.

451. THOUGHT.—*N.* **thought**; reflection, cogitation, consideration, meditation, study, speculation, deliberation, brainwork, cerebration; close study, application.

mature thought; afterthought, reconsideration, second thoughts; retrospection, examination.

abstraction, abstract thought, contemplation, musing; reverie, etc , 458; depth of thought.

V. **think**, reflect, cogitate, consider, reason, deliberate; contemplate, meditate, ponder, muse, dream, ruminate, speculate; brood over, con over, study; bend (*or* apply) the mind; digest, discuss, hammer at, hammer out; weigh, realize, appreciate; fancy.

harbor, cherish, entertain, nurture (*as an idea*), imagine; bear in mind; reconsider.

suggest itself, present itself, occur to; come into one's head; strike one, come uppermost; enter (*or* cross, flash across, occupy) the mind.

Adj. **thoughtful,** pensive, meditative, reflective, cogitative, contemplative, speculative, deliberative, studious, introspective, philosophical.

absorbed, rapt; lost in thought; engrossed in, intent.

Adv. all things considered, taking everything into consideration (*or* account).

452. ABSENCE OF THOUGHT.—*N.* **vacancy of mind,** poverty of intellect; thoughtlessness, etc. (*inattention*), 458; inanity, fatuity, vacuity.

V. **put away thought;** relax (*or* divert) the mind; make the mind a blank, let the mind lie fallow; indulge in reverie, etc. (*be inattentive*), 458.

Adj. **vacant,** inane, unintellectual, unoccupied, unthinking, irrational, unreasoning, thoughtless, inattentive; diverted; bigoted, narrow-minded.

453. [Object of thought] IDEA.—*N.* **idea,** notion, conception, thought; apprehension, impression, perception; sentiment, reflection, observation, consideration; abstract idea.

view, opinion, theory; conceit, fancy; fantasy, etc., 515.

viewpoint, point of view; aspect, angle; field of view.

454. [Subject of thought] TOPIC.—*N.* **subject,** subject matter; matter, motif, theme, topic, thesis, text, business, affair, matter in hand, argument; motion, resolution, case, point; proposition, theorem; field of inquiry; moot point, point at issue; problem, etc. (*question*), 461.

V. enter the mind, etc., 451.

Adv. **under consideration,** under advisement; in question, in the mind; at issue, before the house, on foot, on the carpet.

455. [Desire of knowledge] CURIOSITY.—*N.* **curiosity;** inquisitiveness; interest, thirst for knowledge, mental acquisitiveness; inquiring mind.

investigator, inquirer, etc., 461.

busybody, newsmonger; Peeping Tom, Paul Pry, eavesdropper; gossip.

V. **be curious;** take an interest in, investigate; stare, gape; see the sights.

pry, nose, search, ferret out.

Adj. **curious,** inquiring, etc., 461; inquisitive, burning with curiosity, overcurious, prying; inquisitorial; agape, expectant.

456. [Absence of curiosity] INCURIOSITY.—*N.* **incuriosity;** incuriousness; apathy, unconcern, indifference.

V. **be incurious** (*or* indifferent); have no curiosity, etc., 455; be bored by, take no interest in.

Adj. **incurious,** uninquisitive, indifferent; impassive, etc., 823; uninterested, bored.

457. ATTENTION.—*N.* **attention;** intentness, alertness; thought, etc., 451; observance, observation; consideration, reflection; heed; heedfulness; notice, regard; circumspection, etc. (*care*), 459; study, scrutiny; inspection, revision, revisal.

minuteness, circumstantiality, attention to detail.

V. **attend,** watch, observe, look, see, view, notice, regard, take notice, mark; pay attention to, give heed to; occupy oneself with; contemplate, etc. (*think of*), 451; look to, see to; heed, mind, take cognizance of, entertain, recognize; make (*or* take) note of; note.

examine, scan, scrutinize, consider; overhaul, revise, pore over; inspect, review.

revert to, hark back to; come to the point.

meet with attention; attract notice, fall under one's notice; be under consideration.

call attention to, bring under one's notice; point out (*or* to, at), indicate; direct attention to; show; bring forward.

Adj. **attentive,** mindful, heedful, observant, regardful; alive to, awake to, on the job [*colloq.*], alert; taken up with, occupied with; engrossed in, wrapped in, absorbed, rapt; watchful; intent on, open-eyed; on the watch.

458. INATTENTION.—*N.* **inattention,** inconsideration, want of consideration, inconsiderateness; oversight; inadvertence, disregard; want of thought; heedlessness, etc. (*neglect*), 460; unconcern.

abstraction; absence of mind, absorption, preoccupation, distraction, reverie, brown study [*colloq.*], woolgathering.

V. **be inattentive** (*or* unobservant); overlook, disregard; pass by, neglect; think little of; pay no attention to; dismiss from one's mind; drop the subject, think no more of; turn a deaf ear to.

confuse, disconcert, discompose, perplex, bewilder, fluster, flurry; call off *or* distract the attention (thoughts, mind); put out of one's head.

Adj. **inattentive,** unobservant, undiscerning, unmindful, unheeding, regardless; listless, apathetic; blind, deaf; volatile, scatter-brained, flighty, giddy; unreflecting; inconsiderate, thoughtless; wild, harum-scarum [*colloq.*], heedless, careless, neglectful.

abstracted, absent, distrait [F.], woolgathering, dreamy; dazed, absent-minded; lost in thought; rapt, in the clouds, daydreaming; preoccupied, engrossed; in a reverie; off one's guard; caught napping.

459. CARE. [Vigilance]—*N.* care, solicitude, anxiety; heed, concern, heedfulness; scruple.

vigilance; watchfulness, surveillance, watch, vigil, lookout, watch and ward; espionage, reconnoitering; watching.

alertness, attention, prudence, forethought, circumspection, precaution, caution; accuracy, exactness; minuteness, attention to detail.

watcher, watchman, watchdog.

V. be careful, take care, be cautious; take precautions; pay attention to, etc., 457; take care of; look *or* see to, look after, keep an eye upon; chaperon, matronize, keep watch, mount guard, watch.

Adj. careful, regardful, heedful; prudent, discreet, cautious; considerate, thoughtful; provident; alert; sure-footed.

guarded, on one's guard; on the alert (*or* watch, lookout); awake, vigilant; watchful, wakeful, Argus-eyed, lynx-eyed.

scrupulous, punctilious, conscientious; tidy, orderly; clean; accurate, exact.

Adv. carefully, with care, gingerly.

460. NEGLECT.—*N.* neglect; carelessness; negligence; omission, procrastination; supineness, apathy; inattention, etc., 458; imprudence, improvidence, recklessness; slovenliness, untidiness; dirt; inexactness, inaccuracy.

trifler, waiter on providence; Micawber; slacker.

V. neglect, take no care of, let slip, let go; lose sight of.

delay, defer, procrastinate, postpone, adjourn, pigeonhole, shelve, table, lay on the table.

overlook, disregard; pass over, pass by; let pass; wink at, connive at.

scamp; trifle, slight, slur; skim, skip, take a cursory view of, run over, dip into; slur *or* slip over; push aside, throw into the background, sink; ignore; forget.

Adj. neglectful, negligent, remiss; heedless, careless; thoughtless, inconsiderate; perfunctory, offhand.

unwary, unwatchful, unguarded, off one's guard.

supine, apathetic; inattentive, etc., 458; nonchalant, indifferent; imprudent, reckless; slovenly, disorderly; dirty; inexact, inaccurate; improvident, unthrifty.

neglected, unheeded, uncared for, unattended to; abandoned, shunted, shelved.

461. INQUIRY. [Subject of inquiry. QUESTION.]—*N.* inquiry; request, etc., 765; search, research, quest; pursuit, prosecution.

examination, review, scrutiny, investigation; inquest, inquisition; trial; exploration; exploitation, ventilation; sifting; calculation, analysis, dissection; study, consideration.

reconnoitering, reconnaissance, espionage.

questioning, interrogation, interrogatory; challenge, examination, third degree [*colloq.*], cross-examination; discussion; catechism.

question, query, problem, poser, desideratum, point (*or* matter) in dispute; moot point; issue, question at issue; bone of contention, enigma, etc. (*secret*), 533; knotty point.

inquirer, investigator, inquisitor, inspector, querist, examiner, catechist; scrutator, scrutinizer; analyst.

V. inquire, seek, search, make inquiry, look for, scan, reconnoiter, explore, sound, rummage, ransack, pry, peer, look round; overhaul; look behind the scenes; nose, nose out, trace up; hunt out, fish out, ferret out; unearth.

track, seek a clue; hunt, trail, shadow, mouse, dodge, trace, pursue, experiment, etc., 463.

examine, study, consider, calculate; dip *or* dive into, probe, sound, fathom, scrutinize, analyze, anatomize, dissect, parse, resolve, sift, winnow, thresh out; investigate, look into, discuss, canvass, subject to examination, quiz, pose; audit, tax, pass in review.

question, ask, demand; interrogate, catechize, pump; cross-question, cross-examine; grill [*colloq.*], put through the third degree [*colloq.*].

Adj. inquiring, inquisitive, catechetical, inquisitorial, analytic; interrogative.

undetermined, undecided, tentative; in question, in dispute, in issue, under consideration; moot, proposed; doubtful, etc. (*uncertain*), 475.

462. ANSWER.—*N.* answer, response, reply, rejoinder; retort, repartee; antiphon, acknowledgment; password; echo; counterstatement, countercharge, contradiction.

[Law] defense, plea, reply, rejoinder, rebutter, surrebutter, surrejoinder.

solution, explanation; discovery, disclosure; cause; clue.

oracle, etc., 513.

V. answer, respond, reply, rebut, retort, rejoin; give answer; acknowledge, echo.

[Law] defend, reply, surrejoin, surrebut, plead, rebut.

explain, interpret; solve, etc. (*unriddle*), 522; discover, fathom, hunt out, inquire; satisfy, set at rest, determine.

Adj. responsive, respondent, antiphonal; oracular; conclusive.

463. EXPERIMENT.—*N.* experiment, essay, trial, attempt;

analysis, investigation; verification, probation, proof, criterion, diagnosis, test, crucial test; assay, ordeal.

speculation, random shot, leap in the dark; feeler, pilot balloon.

experimenter, experimentalist, assayer, analyst; prospector, adventurer; speculator, gambler, stock gambler, plunger [*slang*].

V. experiment, essay, try, venture, make an experiment, make trial of; rehearse; put to the test, prove, verify, test.

grope, grope for, feel one's way, fumble, throw out a feeler; send up a pilot balloon; see how the land lies (*or* wind blows); feel the pulse; fish for, angle, trawl, cast one's net.

Adj. experimental, probationary; analytic, speculative, tentative, empirical.

on trial, on examination, on *or* under probation, under suspicion; on one's trial.

464. COMPARISON.—*N.* comparison, contrast, parallelism, balance; identification; simile, similitude, allegory, etc. (*metaphor*), 521.

V. compare, collate, confront, contrast, balance; parallel.

Adj. comparative, relative, contrastive; metaphorical, etc., 521.

Adv. relatively; as compared with.

465. DISCRIMINATION.—*N.* discrimination, distinction, differentiation, diagnosis, nice perception; estimation; nicety, refinement, taste, judgment; tact, discernment, acuteness, penetration.

V. discriminate, distinguish, separate; draw the line, sift; estimate, etc. (*measure*), 466; sum up, criticize; take into account, weigh carefully.

Adj. discriminating, critical, diagnostic, perceptive, discriminative, distinctive; nice, acute.

465a. INDISCRIMINATION.—*N.* indiscrimination, indistinction; want of discernment; uncertainty, etc. (*doubt*), 475.

V. confound, confuse, jumble, heap indiscriminately; swallow whole.

Adj. indiscriminate, indistinguishable, lacking distinction, undistinguished, undistinguishable; promiscuous, undiscriminating.

466. MEASUREMENT.—*N.* measurement, mensuration, survey, valuation, appraisement, assessment, estimate, estimation; dead reckoning [*naut.*]; reckoning, gauging; horsepower, candle power.

measure, gauge; yard measure, standard, rule, foot rule, spirit level, plumb line; square, T-square, steel square, compass, dividers, calipers; log, log line, patent log [*naut.*]; meter, line, rod, check.

flood mark, high-water mark, load-line mark.

scale; graduation, graduated scale; vernier, quadrant, theodolite; beam, steelyard, weighing machine, balance.

latitude and longitude, altitude and azimuth.

geometry; topography, cartography; surveying, land surveying.

surveyor, land surveyor, topographer, cartographer.

V. **measure,** meter; value, assess, rate, appraise, estimate, form an estimate; standardize; span, pace, step, inch, divide, gauge, balance, poise, weigh; plumb, probe, sound, fathom; survey, plot, block in, block out, rule, draw to scale.

Adj. **metrical,** metric; measurable; topographic *or* topographical, cartographic *or* cartographical.

467. [Materials for reasoning] EVIDENCE.—*N.* **evidence;** facts, premises, data, grounds, proof; confirmation, corroboration, ratification, authentication.

testimony, attestation; affirmation, declaration; deposition.

authority, warrant, credential, diploma, voucher, certificate, document, deed, warranty; autograph, handwriting, signature, seal, countersign; exhibit; citation, reference, quotation; admission, etc. (*assent*), 488.

witness, eyewitness, deponent [*law*]; sponsor.

writ, summons, etc. (*lawsuit*), 696.

V. **evince,** show, betoken, indicate, denote, imply, involve, argue, bespeak.

have weight, carry weight; tell, speak volumes, speak for itself.

testify, bear witness, give evidence, depose, witness, vouch for; certify, attest, acknowledge.

confirm, ratify, corroborate, indorse, support, bear out, vindicate, uphold, warrant.

adduce, evidence, cite, quote; refer to, call, call to witness; bring forward, bring into court; allege, plead.

establish, make out a case; authenticate, substantiate, verify, make good.

Adj. **evidential,** indicative, deducible, inferential, firsthand, authentic, documentary; cumulative, corroborative, confirmatory; significant, weighty, overwhelming, conclusive.

oral, hearsay, circumstantial, presumptive.

Adv. **by inference;** according to, in corroboration of.

468. COUNTEREVIDENCE.—*N.* **counterevidence,** rejoinder, disproof, refutation, negation, denial; plea, etc., 617; vindication.

V. **refute,** rebut, oppose; confute, etc. (*refute*), 479; subvert; destroy, check, weaken; contravene; contradict, deny, alter the case; turn the tables; prove a negative.

Adj. **contradictory,** conflicting; unattested, unauthenticated, unsupported, supposititious, trumped up.

Adv. **on the other hand** (*or* side), in opposition; in rebuttal.

469. QUALIFICATION.—*N.* **qualification,** limitation, modification, coloring; allowance, consideration, extenuating circumstances; mitigation.

condition, proviso, exception; exemption; saving clause.

V. **qualify,** limit, modify, affect, give a color to, narrow, temper; allow for, take into account.

Adj. **qualifying,** extenuating, palliative; conditional; exceptional; hypothetical, contingent.

Adv. **provided,** if, unless, but, yet; according as; conditionally, admitting, supposing; even, although, though.

470. POSSIBILITY.—*N.* **possibility,** potentiality, practicability, feasibility, workableness; potency; compatibility, etc. (*agreement*), 23.

contingency, chance, etc., 156.

V. **be possible,** stand a chance; admit of, bear.

render possible, put in the way of, bring to bear, bring together.

Adj. **possible,** conceivable, imaginable, credible; compatible, etc., 23; likely.

practicable, feasible, workable, achievable; within reach, accessible, surmountable; attainable, obtainable.

Adv. **possibly,** perhaps, perchance, peradventure, haply.

471. IMPOSSIBILITY.—*N.* **impossibility,** impracticability, incredibility, hopelessness, infeasibility; discrepancy.

V. **attempt impossibilities;** square the circle, find the elixir of life, discover the philosopher's stone, discover the grand panacea, find the fountain of youth, discover the secret of perpetual motion; make bricks without straw; weave a rope of sand; be in two places at once; gather grapes from thorns.

Adj. **impossible,** not possible, absurd, contrary to reason, unlikely, unreasonable, incredible, visionary, impractical, inconceivable, improbable, unimaginable, unthinkable.

impracticable, unachievable, infeasible; insuperable, insurmountable, inaccessible, unattainable, unobtainable; out of the question; incompatible, etc., 24; impassable, impervious, self-contradictory.

472. PROBABILITY.—*N.* **probability,** likelihood, likeness, verisimilitude, plausibility; color, semblance, show of; presumption; credibility; prospect; chance, etc., 156.

V. **be probable,** lend color to; point to; imply, bid fair, promise, stand (*or* run) a good chance.

presume, infer, venture, suppose, take for granted, flatter oneself; expect, etc., 507; count upon, etc. (*believe*), 484.

Adj. **probable,** likely, hopeful, presumable, presumptive, apparent.

plausible, specious, ostensible, colorable, reasonable, credible.

Adv. **in all probability,** most likely, apparently, seemingly, to all appearance.

473. IMPROBABILITY.—*N.* **improbability,** unlikelihood; bare possibility; long odds; incredibility.

V. **be improbable,** go beyond reason, strain one's credulity; have a small chance.

Adj. **improbable,** unlikely, rare, unheard of, inconceivable; unimaginable, incredible.

474. CERTAINTY.—*N.* **certainty;** necessity, etc., 601; certitude, sureness, surety, assurance; infallibility, reliability, inevitableness; fact; positive fact, matter of fact.

bigotry, positiveness, dogmatism, dogmatization; fanaticism.

dogmatist, doctrinaire, bigot; zealot, fanatic.

V. **render certain,** insure, assure; clinch, make sure; determine, decide; know, etc. (*believe*), 484.

Adj. **certain,** sure, inevitable, assured, solid, well founded.

unqualified, absolute, positive, definite, clear, unequivocal, categorical, unmistakable, decisive.

conclusive, undeniable, unquestionable; indisputable, incontestable, indubitable; irrefutable; final; undoubted, unquestioned, undisputed; questionless.

authoritative, authentic, official.

evident, manifest; self-evident, axiomatic.

infallible, unerring; unchangeable, etc., 150; trustworthy, reliable.

dogmatic, opinionated, dictatorial, doctrinaire; fanatical, bigoted.

Adv. **certainly,** undoubtedly, indubitably; for certain, surely, no doubt, doubtless, to be sure, of course, as a matter of course, in truth, truly, without fail.

475. UNCERTAINTY.—*N.* **uncertainty,** incertitude, doubt, doubtfulness, dubiousness.

hesitation, suspense, perplexity, embarrassment, dilemma, bewilderment; puzzle, quandary; timidity, etc. (*fear*), 860; vacillation, wavering, indetermination.

vagueness, haze, fog, obscurity, ambiguity, open question, blind bargain, pig in a poke, leap in the dark.

fallibility, unreliability, untrustworthiness; precariousness.

V. **hesitate,** flounder, miss one's way, wander aimlessly, beat about; lose oneself, lose one's head.

perplex, pose, puzzle, confuse, confound, bewilder, nonplus.

doubt, etc. (*disbelieve*), 485.

Adj. **uncertain,** unsure; casual, random, aimless, doubtful, dubious; insecure, unstable, indecisive, irresolute; unsettled, undecided, undetermined, in question; experimental, tentative.

vague, indefinite, ambiguous, equivocal, undefined, confused; mysterious, cryptic, veiled, obscure, undefinable; oracular.

perplexing, enigmatic, paradoxical, apocryphal, problematical.

fallible, questionable, debatable, untrustworthy, unreliable.

puzzled, perplexed; lost, astray, adrift, at sea, at fault, at a loss, at one's wit's end, distracted, distraught.

476. REASONING.—*N.* **reasoning,** ratiocination; inference, induction, generalization.

logic, art of reasoning, dialectics; deduction, induction; **syn**thesis, analysis; syllogism.

discussion, comment; ventilation; inquiry, etc., 461.

argumentation, controversy, debate; polemics, wrangling, **con**tention.

argument, case, plea, proposition, terms, premises, data, **prin**ciple.

arguments, reasons, pros and cons.

reasoner, logician, dialectician, casuist; disputant, **contro**versialist; wrangler, arguer, debater.

V. **reason,** argue, discuss, debate, dispute, contend, wrangle, chop logic; controvert, deny; canvass; consider, examine.

Adj. **reasoning,** rational; argumentative, controversial, dialectic, polemical; disputatious.

logical, syllogistic, inductive, deductive, synthetic *or* synthetical, analytic *or* analytical; relevant, germane.

Adv. **for,** because, hence, whence, seeing that, since, then, thence, so; whereas, considering, therefore, wherefore; **conse**quently, *ergo* [L.], thus, accordingly.

finally, in conclusion, in fine, after all, on the whole.

477. [Absence of reasoning] INTUITION. [Specious reasoning] **SOPHISTRY.—***N.* **intuition;** instinct, association of ideas; rule of thumb; presentiment.

sophistry, casuistry, equivocation, evasion, mental reservation, chicanery; perversion, mystification; speciousness; nonsense, etc., 497; hairsplitting, quibbling; begging of the question.

sophism, quibble, quirk, fallacy, subterfuge, shift, subtlety; inconsistency; claptrap.

V. **pervert,** quibble, equivocate, mystify, evade, elude; gloss over, varnish; misteach, etc., 538; mislead, etc. (*error*), 495; misrepresent, etc. (*lie*), 544; cavil, refine, split hairs; misjudge, etc., 481; beg the question, reason in a circle.

Adj. **intuitive,** instinctive, impulsive.

illogical, unreasonable, false, unsound, invalid; unwarranted, gratuitous; incongruous, inconsequent, inconsequential; unconnected; inconsistent; unscientific; untenable, inconclusive, incorrect, fallacious, groundless, unproved.

specious, sophistic *or* sophistical, casuistic; deceptive, illusive, illusory, hollow, plausible; evasive; irrelevant, inapplicable.

weak, feeble, poor, flimsy, loose, vague, irrational; nonsensical, absurd, foolish, etc. (*imbecile*), 499; frivolous; pettifogging, quibbling.

478. DEMONSTRATION.—*N.* demonstration, proof; conclusiveness; evidence, etc., 467; verification, etc., 462.

V. **demonstrate,** prove, establish, make good; show, evince, verify, etc., 467; settle the question.

follow; stand to reason; hold good, hold water [*colloq.*].

Adj. **demonstrative;** demonstrable; unanswerable, conclusive, decisive, convincing; irresistible, irrefutable, undeniable.

demonstrated, proved; unconfuted, unanswered, unrefuted; evident, self-evident, axiomatic.

deducible, inferential, following.

Adv. **of course,** in consequence, consequently, as a matter of course.

479. CONFUTATION.—*N.* confutation, refutation; answer, disproof, conviction, invalidation; exposure, exposé [F.], retort.

V. **confute,** refute, parry, negative, disprove, expose, show up; rebut, defeat, demolish, upset, subvert, overthrow, overturn, confound; invalidate; convince, silence; clinch an argument.

Adj. **confutable,** refutable; capable of refutation.

480. [Results of reasoning] JUDGMENT.—*N.* **judgment,** decision, determination, finding, verdict, sentence, decree; opinion, etc. (*belief*), 484; good judgment.

result, conclusion, upshot; deduction, inference, corollary.

estimation, valuation, appreciation; arbitrament, arbitration; assessment.

estimate, award; review, criticism, critique, notice, report.

plebiscite, voice, casting vote; vote, suffrage, election.

arbiter, arbitrator; judge, umpire; assessor, referee; inspector; censor.

reviewer, critic; connoisseur; commentator, annotator.

V. **judge,** conclude, opine; come to (*or* arrive at) a conclusion; ascertain, determine.

deduce, derive, gather, collect, infer.

estimate, form an estimate, appreciate, value, count, assess, rate, rank, account; regard, consider, think of; size up [*colloq.*].

decide, settle; try, pronounce, rule; find, pass judgment, sentence, doom, decree; give (*or* deliver) judgment; adjudge, adjudicate; arbitrate, award; confirm.

review, comment, criticize; examine, etc., 457; investigate, etc., 461.

Adj. **judicious,** judicial; determinate, conclusive, confirmatory.

critical, hypercritical, hairsplitting, censorious.

Adv. on the whole, all things considered, therefore, wherefore.

480a. [Result of search or inquiry] **DISCOVERY.**—*N.* discovery, detection, disclosure, find, revelation.

V. **discover,** find, determine, evolve; fix upon; find (*or* trace, make, root) out; spot [*colloq.*], fathom, bring out, draw out, educe, elicit, bring to light, dig up, unearth, disinter.

solve, resolve; unriddle, unravel, find a clue to; interpret; disclose; see through, detect; catch; scent, smell out.

recognize, realize, verify, make certain of, identify.

481. MISJUDGMENT.—*N.* **misjudgment,** obliquity of judgment, warped judgment; miscalculation, misconception, misinterpretation, etc., 523; hasty conclusion.

preconception, prejudgment, foregone conclusion; presumption, preconceived idea; prejudice, predilection, prepossession; presentiment, foreboding; fixed idea, obsession.

partisanship, clannishness; *esprit de corps* [F.], prestige, party spirit, class prejudice, class consciousness, race prejudice, provincialism.

quirk, shift, quibble, equivocation, evasion, subterfuge.

bias, warp, twist; hobby, whim, craze, cult, fad, crotchet, partiality.

V. **misjudge,** misconjecture, misconceive, misunderstand; miscalculate, misreckon; overestimate, etc., 482; underestimate, etc., 483.

prejudge, dogmatize; have a bias, run away with the notion; jump to a conclusion; blunder, etc., 699.

bias, warp, twist; prejudice, prepossess.

Adj. **misjudging,** ill-judging, wrong-headed; superficial; prejudiced, prepossessed; shortsighted, purblind; partial, one-sided; warped.

narrow, narrow-minded, provincial, parochial, insular; mean-spirited, confined, illiberal, intolerant, infatuated, fanatical, positive, dogmatic, dictatorial, pragmatic; egotistical, conceited, opinionated; bigoted, etc. (*obstinate*), 606; unreasonable, stupid, etc., 499; credulous, gullible.

482. OVERESTIMATION.—*N.* **overestimation,** exaggeration, hyperbole; optimism, much ado about nothing; tempest in a teacup; fine writing, rodomontade, gush [*colloq.*], hot air [*slang*].

egoism, egotism, bombast, conceit; vanity; megalomania.

egoist, egoist, megalomaniac; optimist; braggart, boaster, braggadocio, swaggerer.

V. **overestimate,** overrate, overpraise; strain, magnify; exaggerate, etc., 549.

eulogize, gush over [*colloq.*], boost; puff [*colloq.*]; extol.

Adj. inflated, puffed up; grandiose, stilted, pompous, pretentious, bombastic.

483. UNDERESTIMATION.—*N.* underestimation, underval-
uation; depreciation, etc. (*detraction*), 934; pessimism, self-de-
traction, self-depreciation; modesty, etc., 881

pessimist, depreciator, knocker [*slang*], crapehanger [*slang*]

V. underrate, underestimate, undervalue. depreciate, disparage, detract, decry, ridicule, deride; slight, etc. (*despise*), 930,
neglect; slur over.

make light (*or* little) of, belittle, run down [*colloq.*], minimize,
set no store by, set at naught, disregard.

Adj. depreciating, depreciative, depreciatory; pessimistic.

depreciated, unappreciated, unvalued, unprized.

484. BELIEF.—*N.* belief, credence; credit; assurance; faith,
trust, confidence, presumption; hope.

conviction, principle; persuasion, certainty, opinion, view, conception, impression, surmise; conclusion.

doctrine, tenet, dogma, articles, canons: view. gospel article
(*or* declaration, profession) of faith, creed; assent, avowal. confession; propaganda.

credibility, probability; plausibility.

V. believe, credit, give faith (*or* credit, credence) to, realize;
assume, take it; consider, presume; count (*or* depend, rely. build)
upon; take for granted.

confide in, believe in, put one's trust in, place reliance on, trust.

think, hold, opine, conceive; have (*or* hold, entertain, adopt,
embrace, foster, cherish) a belief *or* an opinion.

persuade, assure, convince, satisfy, bring to reason, convert,
indoctrinate; wean, bring round, bring (*or* win) over; carry conviction.

Adj. certain, sure, assured, positive, cocksure [*colloq.*], satisfied,
confident, unhesitating, convinced, secure.

confiding, trustful, unsuspecting, unsuspicious; credulous,
gullible.

believed, trusted, unsuspected, undoubted.

credible, reliable, trustworthy, accredited, satisfactory; probable.

485. UNBELIEF. DOUBT.—*N.* unbelief, disbelief, incredulity; infidelity, etc. (*irreligion*), 989; wrangling, nonconformity;
dissent, change of opinion; retractation, etc., 607.

doubt, uncertainty, skepticism, misgiving, demur discredit;
distrust, mistrust; misdoubt, suspicion, jealousy, scruple, qualm.

incredibility, incredibleness, unbelievability.

agnostic, skeptic; unbeliever, etc., 487.

V. **disbelieve,** discredit, misbelieve, dissent; refuse to believe.

doubt, distrust, mistrust; question, challenge, dispute; deny, etc., 536; cavil, wrangle; suspect, scent, smell, smell a rat [*colloq.*], harbor suspicions; have one's doubts.

demur, stick at, pause, hesitate, shy at, scruple; waver.

stagger, startle; shake one's faith, stagger one's belief.

Adj. **unbelieving,** skeptical, incredulous; distrustful of, suspicious of.

doubtful, etc. (*uncertain*), 475; disputable, questionable, suspicious; incredible, unbelievable, inconceivable.

Adv. with caution, with grains of allowance.

486. CREDULITY.—*N.* credulity, credulousness, gullibility; infatuation; self-delusion, self-deception; superstition; bigotry.

credulous person, dupe, gull.

V. **be credulous;** follow implicitly; swallow, swallow whole, gulp down; take on faith.

impose upon, etc. (*deceive*), 545.

Adj. **credulous,** gullible, easily deceived *or* convinced; simple, silly, childish; infatuated, superstitious; confiding, trustful, unsuspicious.

487. INCREDULITY.—*N.* **incredulity,** incredulousness; skepticism, doubt, disbelief, etc., 989; unbelief, etc., 485.

unbeliever, skeptic, doubting Thomas, disbeliever, agnostic, infidel, misbeliever; heretic, etc. (*heterodox*), 984.

V. **be incredulous,** distrust, doubt, suspect, refuse to believe; turn a deaf ear to.

Adj. **incredulous,** skeptical, suspicious; dissenting, unbelieving; heterodox.

488. ASSENT.—*N.* **assent,** acquiescence, admission; nod; consent, compliance; agreement, understanding; affirmation; recognition, acknowledgment, avowal, confession.

unanimity, common consent, consensus, acclamation, chorus; public opinion; concurrence, accord.

ratification, confirmation, corroboration, approval, acceptance; indorsement.

consenter, indorser, subscriber; upholder, etc. (*auxiliary*), 711.

V. **assent,** give assent, acquiesce, agree, accept, accede, accord, concur, consent, coincide, echo, reciprocate, go with; recognize; subscribe to, conform to, defer to; go with the stream; be in the fashion, join in the chorus.

acknowledge, own, admit, confess; concede, yield; abide by; permit, etc., 760.

confirm, ratify, approve, indorse, countersign; corroborate, etc., 467.

Adj. **assenting,** of one accord (*or* mind); of the same mind, at one with, agreed, acquiescent.

uncontradicted, unchallenged, unquestioned, unanimous.

Adv. **yes,** yea, aye, true; granted; even so, just so; to be sure, as you say; surely, assuredly; exactly, precisely, certainly, of course, unquestionably, no doubt, doubtless.

unanimously, by common consent, to a man, as one man; with one consent (*or* voice, accord).

489. DISSENT.—*N.* **dissent,** nonconsent, discordance, disagreement.

nonconformity, heterodoxy, protestantism, schism; disaffection, secession, recantation.

dissension, discord, caviling, wrangling; discontent, etc., 832.

protest, contradiction, denial; noncompliance, rejection.

dissentient, dissenter, nonconformist; sectary; separatist, protestant; heretic, etc., 984.

V. **dissent,** demur, call in question, disagree, refuse to admit; cavil, wrangle, protest, repudiate; contradict, deny.

secede; recant, etc., 607.

Adj. **dissenting,** negative; contradictory; dissentient; unconvinced, unconverted.

sectarian, denominational, schismatic; heterodox; intolerant.

Adv. at variance with, at issue with; under protest.

490. KNOWLEDGE.—*N.* **knowledge;** cognizance; cognition, acquaintance, experience, ken, insight, familiarity; comprehension, apprehension; recognition; appreciation, judgment, etc., 480; intuition, consciousness, perception.

enlightenment, light; impression, perception, discovery, revelation.

learning, erudition, lore, scholarship; letters, literature; book learning, bookishness, general information; education, culture, cultivation, attainments, acquirements, accomplishments, proficiency.

V. **know,** be aware of; conceive, apprehend, comprehend; realize, understand, appreciate; fathom, make out, recognize, discern, perceive, see, experience.

learn, imbibe knowledge; discover, evolve

Adj. **aware of,** cognizant of, conscious of, acquainted with, privy to, in the secret; alive to; apprized of, informed of; undeceived.

educated, erudite, instructed, learned, lettered, well informed, well versed, well read, well grounded, well educated; high-brow [*slang*], bookish, scholastic, profound, deep-read, book-learned, accomplished; self-taught, self-educated, knowing, shrewd.

known, ascertained, well known, recognized, noted, received, notorious, proverbial; familiar, hackneyed, trite, commonplace.

Adv. to the best of one's knowledge; as every schoolboy knows.

491. IGNORANCE.—*N.* ignorance, illiteracy, unlearnedness, unacquaintance, unconsciousness, darkness, blindness; incomprehension, simplicity.

sealed book; virgin soil, unexplored ground; dark ages.

Imperfect knowledge: smattering, superficiality, half learning, shallowness, glimmering; incapacity.

Affectation of knowledge: pedantry, charlatanry, charlatanism.

V. **be ignorant** (*or* uninformed); be uneducated; know nothing of; ignore, be blind to.

Adj. **ignorant;** unknowing, unaware, unacquainted, uninformed, uninitiated, unwitting, unconscious; witless, unconversant.

illiterate, unread, low [*slang*], uncultivated, uninstructed, untaught, untutored, unschooled, uneducated, unlearned, unlettered, empty-headed.

shallow, superficial, green, rude, empty, half-learned, half-baked [*colloq.*], unscholarly.

in the dark; benighted, blinded, blindfold, hoodwinked; misinformed.

unknown, unapprehended, unexplained, uninvestigated, unexplored, unheard of; concealed, etc., 528.

Adv. unawares; for aught one knows; not that one knows.

492. SCHOLAR.—*N.* scholar, savant [F.], pundit [India], schoolman, professor, academician, doctor, fellow, don [Eng.], graduate, postgraduate, classicist, philosopher, scientist, linguist, etymologist, philologist, lexicographer; man of learning.

bookworm, bibliophile, bibliomaniac, bluestocking [*colloq.*], high-brow [*slang*].

pedant, doctrinaire; pedagogue, **Dr. Pangloss;** instructor, etc., 540.

student, learner, pupil, schoolboy, etc. (*learner*), 541.

Adj. **learned,** etc., 490.

493. IGNORAMUS.—*N.* ignoramus, illiterate, dunce, duffer, numskull [*colloq.*]; no scholar.

smatterer, dabbler, half scholar; charlatan; wiseacre.

novice, greenhorn, plebe [*West Point cant*]; tyro, etc. (*learner*), 541.

Adj. **bookless,** shallow, simple, dull, dumb [*colloq.*], dense, crass; illiterate, etc., 491.

494. [Object of knowledge] TRUTH.—*N.* **truth,** verity; fact, reality, authenticity, gospel; veracity, etc., 543.

accuracy, exactitude, exactness, preciseness, precision, regularity, fidelity, nicety.

V. hold true, stand the test, have the true ring, hold good.

trace, solve, etc. (*discover*), 480a.

Adj. true, real, actual, veritable; certain, etc., 474; unimpeachable; veracious, etc., 543.

pure, sound, sterling, true-blue; natural, unsophisticated, unadulterated, simon-pure [*colloq.*], unvarnished, undisguised.

exact, accurate, definite, concrete, precise, well defined, just, right, correct, strict, severe, rigid, rigorous, scrupulous, literal, punctilious, mathematical, scientific, unromantic; faithful, constant, unerring; particular, nice, meticulous, delicate, fine; clean-cut, clear-cut.

authentic, genuine, legitimate; orthodox, etc., 983a; official.

valid, well grounded, well founded, solid, substantial, tangible.

Adv. truly, verily, indeed, in reality; in very truth, in fact, as a matter of fact, beyond doubt.

495. ERROR.—*N.* error, fallacy, misconception, misapprehension, misunderstanding; aberration, inexactness, laxity; misconstruction, misinterpretation; misjudgment, heresy, misstatement, anachronism; fable, etc. (*untruth*), 546.

mistake, fault, blunder, oversight, misprint, erratum (*pl.* errata), slip, blot, flaw, trip, stumble, bungle; slip of the tongue, slip of the pen, clerical error; bull, etc. (*absurdity*), 497; spoonerism, malapropism.

delusion, illusion, false impression; bubble; self-deceit, self-deception; hallucination, mirage, etc., 443; dream, etc. (*fancy*), 515.

V. mislead, misguide, lead astray, beguile, misinform, delude; falsify, misstate; deceive, etc., 545; lie, etc., 544.

err, be in error, be mistaken, be deceived; mistake, deceive oneself, blunder, misapprehend, misconceive, misunderstand, miscalculate, misjudge.

trip, stumble, lose oneself, go astray; fail, etc., 732; take the shadow for the substance.

Adj. erroneous, untrue, false, faulty, erring, fallacious, unreal, ungrounded, groundless, unsubstantial, unsound, inexact, inaccurate, incorrect.

illusive, illusory, delusive; mock, imaginary, spurious, etc., 545; deceitful, etc., 544; untrustworthy.

exploded, refuted, discarded.

mistaken, in error, deceived, out in one's reckoning; wide of the mark, at fault, at cross-purposes, at sea, bewildered.

496. MAXIM.—*N.* maxim, aphorism, dictum, saying, adage, saw, proverb, motto, epigram, sentence, mot [*Gallicism*], commonplace, moral.

axiom, theorem, formula, truism.

principle, profession of faith, conclusion, etc. (*judgment*), 480.

Adj. aphoristic, proverbial, axiomatic; hackneyed, trite.

Adv. as the saying is, as they say.

497. ABSURDITY.—*N.* absurdity, absurdness, imbecility, etc., 499; nonsense, paradox, inconsistency.

blunder, muddle, Irish bull; anticlimax, bathos.

farce, burlesque, parody, limerick; farrago, extravagance.

pun, sell [*colloq.*], catch [*colloq.*], verbal quibble, joke.

jargon, gibberish, balderdash, bombast, claptrap, twaddle, moonshine, stuff.

tomfoolery, mummery, monkeyshine [*slang*], monkey trick, frisk, practical joke, escapade.

V. play the fool, blunder, muddle; be guilty of absurdity; romance, talk nonsense, exaggerate; be absurd, frisk, caper, joke, play practical jokes.

Adj. absurd, nonsensical, farcical, burlesque, preposterous, egregious, senseless, inconsistent, ridiculous, extravagant, self-contradictory, paradoxical; foolish, etc., 499; meaningless, fantastic, bombastic, high-flown.

498. [Faculties] INTELLIGENCE. WISDOM.—*N.* intelligence, capacity, comprehension, understanding; intellect, etc., 450; brains, parts, sagacity, mother wit, wit, gumption [*colloq.*], acuteness, acumen, longheadedness, subtlety, penetration, perspicacity, discernment, good judgment; discrimination, cunning, refinement.

wisdom, sapience, sense, common sense, clear thinking, rationality, reason; reasonableness, judgment, solidity, depth, profundity, caliber.

genius, inspiration, talent, etc., 698.

Wisdom in action: prudence, etc., 864; vigilance, etc., 459; tact, etc., 698; foresight, etc., 510; sobriety, self-possession, ballast, mental poise, balance.

V. have all one's wits about one; be brilliant, scintillate, coruscate; understand, etc. (*intelligible*), 518.

penetrate, see through, see at a glance, discern; foresee, etc., 510; discriminate.

Adj. Applied to persons: intelligent, quick of apprehension, keen, acute, alive, awake, bright, quick, sharp, quick-witted, wide-awake; shrewd, astute; clearheaded, long-sighted, calculating, thoughtful, farsighted, discerning, perspicacious, penetrating, piercing; sharp as a needle; alive to, etc. (*cognizant*), 490; clever, etc. (*apt*), 698.

wise, sage, sapient [*often in irony*], sagacious, rational, sensible, judicious, strong-minded; worldly-wise, sophisticated.

impartial, unprejudiced, unbiased, unbigoted, equitable, fair.

prudent, etc. (*cautious*), 864; sober, staid, solid; watchful; provident, prepared, etc., 673.

Applied to actions: wise, sensible, judicious, well judged, well advised; prudent, politic; expedient, etc., 646.

499. IMBECILITY, FOLLY.—*N.* imbecility, want of intelligence (*or* intellect), shallowness, silliness, foolishness, stupidity, stolidity; incompetence.

simplicity, puerility; senility, dotage, second childhood; fatuity; idiocy.

folly, frivolity, irrationality, trifling, ineptitude, inconsistency, giddiness; eccentricity, etc., 503; extravagance, etc. (*absurdity*), 497; rashness, etc., 863.

V. trifle, drivel, dote; ramble, play the fool, fool, stultify oneself, talk nonsense.

Adj. Applied to persons: unintelligent, unintellectual, unreasoning; mindless, brainless; half-baked [*colloq.*], bovine, thick [*colloq.*], blockish, unteachable; ungifted, unenlightened, unwise; thickskulled, muddleheaded, addleheaded, weak-minded, feebleminded.

stupid, dull, heavy, obtuse, blunt, stolid, asinine, inapt.

childish, childlike; infantine, infantile, babyish, puerile, senile, anile; simple, credulous.

imbecile, fatuous, idiotic, driveling; vacant, bewildered.

foolish, silly, senseless, irrational, insensate, nonsensical, maudlin.

narrow-minded, bigoted, etc., 606; rash, etc., 863; eccentric, odd.

Applied to actions: foolish, unwise, injudicious, improper, unreasonable, ill-advised, ridiculous, silly, stupid, asinine; inconsistent, irrational; extravagant, nonsensical, frivolous, trivial; useless, etc., 645; inexpedient, etc., 647.

500. SAGE.—*N.* sage, wise man; master mind, thinker, philosopher, savant [F.]; pundit, etc. (*scholar*), 492; wiseacre [*ironical*]; expert, etc., 700.

authority, oracle, mentor, Solon, Solomon, Buddha, Confucius.

Adj. venerable, venerated, reverenced, revered, honored; authoritative, oracular; wise, erudite, etc., 490.

501. FOOL.—*N.* fool, idiot, tomfool, wiseacre, simpleton,

Simple Simon; donkey, ass, owl, goose, dolt, booby, noodle, imbecile, nincompoop [*colloq.*], oaf, lout, blockhead, bonehead [*slang*], calf [*colloq.*], colt, numskull [*colloq.*], clod, clodhopper; soft *or* softy [*colloq. or slang*], mooncalf, saphead [*slang*], gawk, rube [*slang*].

greenhorn, etc. (*dupe*), 547; dunce, etc. (*ignoramus*), 493; lubber, etc. (*bungler*), 701; madman, etc., 504; dotard, driveler, old fogy [*colloq.*].

502. SANITY.—*N.* **sanity**, soundness, rationality, sobriety, lucidity, senses, common sense, horse sense [*colloq.*], sound mind.

V. **become sane**, come to one's senses, sober down, cool down, see things in proper perspective.

render sane, bring to one's senses, sober, bring to reason.

Adj. **sane**, rational, normal, wholesome, right-minded, reasonable, sound, sound-minded, in possession of one's faculties.

Adv. **sanely**, in reason, within reason, within bounds.

503. INSANITY.—*N.* **insanity**, lunacy; madness, mania, dementia, idiocy; delirium tremens, d.t.'s, the horrors [*colloq.*]; frenzy, raving, wandering, delirium, delusion, obsession, hallucination, derangement, unsoundness of mind.

vertigo, dizziness, swimming, sunstroke.

oddity, eccentricity, twist, monomania; fanaticism, infatuation, craze.

V. **be *or* become insane**, lose one's senses (*or* reason), go mad, rave, dote, ramble, wander; lose one's head, drivel.

derange, render *or* drive mad, madden, infatuate, obsess, befool; turn the brain, turn one's head.

Adj. **insane**, mad, lunatic; crazy, crazed, crackbrained, cracked [*colloq.*], touched; bereft of reason; unhinged, insensate, beside oneself, demented, maniacal, daft, frenzied, deranged, maddened, moonstruck, off one's head.

giddy, vertiginous, wild, flighty, distracted, distraught, bewildered.

odd, fanatical, infatuated, eccentric.

delirious, lightheaded, rambling, wandering, frantic, raving, stark mad.

504. MADMAN.—*N.* **madman**, lunatic, maniac; crank [*colloq.*], nut [*slang*].

dreamer, visionary, rhapsodist, seer, enthusiast, fanatic; Don Quixote, Ophelia.

idiot, etc., 501.

505. [The Past] MEMORY.—*N.* **memory**, remembrance; retention, retentiveness; retentive (*or* tenacious, trustworthy, ready) memory.

recollection, retrospect, reminiscence; recognition; afterthought.

reminder, hint, suggestion, memorandum (*pl.* memoranda), token, memento, souvenir, keepsake, relic; memorial, monument; commemoration, jubilee.

mnemonics; art of memory, artificial memory; Mnemosyne.

fame, celebrity, renown, reputation; repute, notoriety.

V. **remember,** retain the memory of, keep in mind; bear in mind, haunt one's mind (*or* thoughts); rankle; keep the wound open, brood over.

recollect, recall, call up, conjure up, retrace; look back upon, review; call (*or* bring) to mind.

remind, suggest, hint, prompt; put (*or* keep) in mind; bring to mind, call up, summon up, renew; redeem from oblivion; commemorate.

memorize, commit to memory; con, con over; fix in the mind, engrave upon the memory; learn by heart, know by rote, have at one's fingers' ends.

make a note of, put down, record.

Adj. **remembering,** mindful, reminiscent; fresh, still vivid; enduring, unforgotten; never to be forgotten, indelible; within one's memory; memorable, suggestive.

Adv. **by heart,** by rote, without book, word for word.

506. OBLIVION.—*N.* **oblivion;** forgetfulness; Lethe; obliteration of the past; short (*or* treacherous, untrustworthy, slippery, failing) memory; decay (*or* failure, lapse) of memory; amnesia.

amnesty, general pardon.

V. **forget,** be forgetful; fall (*or* sink) into oblivion; have a short memory; lose, lose the memory of, lose sight of.

efface, from the memory; unlearn; consign to oblivion, think no more of; let bygones be bygones.

Adj. **forgotten,** unremembered, out of mind; buried (*or* sunk) in oblivion.

forgetful, oblivious; heedless, deaf to the past; Lethean.

507. [The Future] EXPECTATION.—*N.* **expectation,** expectancy, anticipation, prospect, contingency, reckoning, calculation; foresight; suspense; abeyance.

assurance, confidence, reliance, hope, trust, presumption; prognostication; prediction, etc., 511.

V. **expect;** look for, look out for, look forward to; hope for, anticipate; have in prospect, keep in view; contemplate; wait for, watch for, await; foresee, prepare for, forestall.

predict, prognosticate, forecast.

Adj. **expectant;** expecting, in expectation, vigilant; open-eyed, open-mouthed; agape, gaping, on tenterhooks, on tiptoe; ready, prepared, provided for, provident.

expected, foreseen; in prospect, prospective, provisional; future, coming; in view, on the horizon; impending.

Adv. **expectantly,** on the watch, with muscles tense, on edge [*colloq.*], with eyes (*or* ears) strained, with bated breath.

soon, shortly, forthwith, presently.

508. NONEXPECTATION.—*N.* **nonexpectation,** unforeseen contingency, the unforeseen; miscalculation, false expectation; disappointment; disillusion.

surprise, blow, shock; bolt out of the blue; astonishment, amazement; wonder, bewilderment.

V. **be unexpected,** come unawares, turn up, burst *or* flash upon one; take by surprise, catch unawares.

surprise, startle, stun, stagger, astound; throw off one's guard; spring upon, astonish, etc. (*strike with wonder*), 870.

Adj. **nonexpectant,** surprised; unwarned, unaware; off one's guard.

unexpected, unanticipated, unlooked for, unforeseen; unheard of; startling; sudden.

Adv. **unexpectedly,** abruptly, suddenly, unawares; without notice *or* warning.

509. DISAPPOINTMENT.—*N.* **disappointment,** blighted hope, disillusion, balk; blow, false (*or* vain) expectation; miscalculation; fool's paradise.

V. **be disappointed;** look blank, look *or* stand aghast; find to one's cost.

disappoint, crush (*or* dash, blight) one's hope, balk *or* disappoint one's expectation, balk, tantalize; dumfounder, dumfound, disconcert, disillusionize; dissatisfy; disgruntle.

Adj. **aghast;** disgruntled; out of one's reckoning.

510. FORESIGHT.—*N.* **foresight,** prevision, long-sightedness, farsightedness; anticipation; prudence; forethought.

foreknowledge, prescience; presentiment, foreboding; second sight.

prospect; foregone conclusion; forecast.

V. **foresee;** look forward to, look ahead *or* beyond; look into the future; see one's way; see how the land lies.

anticipate, expect, surmise, contemplate; predict; forewarn.

Adj. **foreseeing,** prescient, anticipatory; farseeing, farsighted, long-sighted; provident; weatherwise; prospective; expectant.

Adv. against the time when; for a rainy day.

511. PREDICTION.—*N.* **prediction,** announcement; program;

platform; premonition, presage, foreboding; phophecy, prognostication, augury, forecast; omen, etc., 512; horoscope; soothsaying,
fortunetelling, divination; oracle, etc., 513.

astrology; spell, charm, etc., 993; sorcery, magic, etc., 992.

V. predict, forecast, prognosticate, prophesy, divine, foretell;
tell fortunes, cast a horoscope (*or* nativity); forewarn.

presage, augur, bode, forebode; foretoken, betoken; portend,
signify, point to.

herald, usher in, announce; lower; threaten.

Adj. prophetic, oracular, sibylline; weatherwise.

ominous, portentous; auspicious; premonitory, significant of.

512. OMEN.—*N.* omen, portent, presage, augury; sign, token;
harbinger; bird of ill omen; halcyon birds; signs of the times;
warning, etc., 668.

Adj. auspicious, favorable, halcyon, of good omen.

inauspicious, ill-boding, ill-omened, ill-starred.

513. ORACLE.—*N.* oracle; prophet, seer, soothsayer, proph-
etess, witch, sibyl; augur, haruspex; medium, clairvoyant, palm-
ist; fortuneteller; sorcerer, etc., 994; interpreter, etc., 524.

Delphic oracle; Cumaean Sibyl, Sibyl, Cassandra, Witch of
Endor, Sphinx.

weather prophet, weather bureau.

514. [Creative Thought] SUPPOSITION.—*N.* supposition,
assumption, presumption, condition, hypothesis, postulate,
theory, data; thesis, theorem; conjecture, guess, guesswork, speculation; surmise, suspicion, inkling, suggestion, hint.

theorist, theorizer, doctrinaire, doctrinarian.

V. suppose, conjecture; surmise, suspect, guess, divine; theorize, speculate; presume, presuppose, assume, predicate; believe,
take for granted.

propound, propose, put forth; put a case, submit; move, make a
motion; hazard *or* put forward a suggestion (*or* supposition); suggest, allude to, hint.

Adj. assumed, given; conjectural, presumptive, hypothetical;
theoretical, academic.

suggestive, allusive, stimulating.

Adv. if, if so be; on the supposition, in case, in the event of; as
if, provided; perhaps, for aught one knows.

515. IMAGINATION.—*N.* imagination, originality, invention;
fancy; inspiration.

ideality, idealism; romanticism, utopianism, castle-building,
dreaming; frenzy, rhapsody, ecstasy, reverie, daydream.

conception; flight of fancy; creation of the brain; imagery;
word painting.

fantasy, conceit; figment, myth; romance, extravaganza; dream, vision; shadow, chimera, phantasm, illusion, phantom, fancy, whim, vagary; bugbear, nightmare; flying Dutchman, great sea serpent, man in the moon, castle in the air, castle in Spain, Utopia, fairyland; land of Prester John.

Creative works: work of fiction, etc. (*novel*), 594; poetry, etc., 597; drama, etc., 599; music, etc., 415; painting, sculpture, architecture; art.

idealist, romanticist, visionary, romancer, daydreamer, dreamer, castle-builder; creative artist.

V. imagine, fancy, conceive; idealize, realize; dream, dream of; indulge in reverie; fancy (*or* represent, picture, figure) to oneself.

create, originate, devise, invent, make up, coin, fabricate; improvise.

Adj. imaginative, original, inventive, creative, productive.

extravagant, romantic, high-flown, flighty, preposterous; unreal; unsubstantial.

ideal; intellectual, impracticable, imaginary, visionary, utopian, quixotic.

fanciful; fantastical; fictitious; fabulous, legendary, mythic *or* mythical, mythological, chimerical; whimsical; fairy, fairylike.

II. COMMUNICATION OF IDEAS

516. MEANING.—*N.* meaning [*idea to be conveyed*], signification, significance; sense, import, purport; pith, essence; force; drift, bearing, tenor, spirit; allusion; suggestion, interpretation; acceptation.

Thing signified: matter, subject, subject matter, substance, gist, argument.

V. mean, signify, denote, express; import, purport; convey, imply, indicate; tell of, speak of; touch on; point to, allude to; drive at; involve; declare; affirm, state.

paraphrase, state differently; express by a synonym.

Adj. meaning, expressive, significant, pithy; intelligible, explicit, clear; suggestive; allusive.

literal, word-for-word, verbatim; exact, real.

synonymous; tantamount, equivalent.

implied; understood, tacit.

Adv. to that effect; that is to say.

517. UNMEANINGNESS.—*N.* unmeaningness, absence of meaning, drivel, senselessness; empty sound.

nonsense, jargon, gibberish, mere words, rant, bombast, balderdash, babble, inanity, twaddle, trash, rubbish; absurdity; imbecility, folly; ambiguity, vagueness, etc., 519.

V. mean nothing; be unmeaning; gibber; jabber, twaddle, rant, babble.

scribble, scrawl, scratch.

Adj. unmeaning, meaningless, senseless; nonsensical; inexpressive; vague; not significant.

trashy, inane, trumpery, trivial, insignificant.

518. INTELLIGIBILITY.—*N.* intelligibility; comprehensibility; clearness, clarity, explicitness, lucidity, perspicuity; precision; plain speaking.

V. render intelligible, popularize, simplify, elucidate, explain, interpret.

understand, comprehend; take in, catch, grasp, follow; master.

Adj. intelligible; clear, lucid; perspicuous, transparent.

plain, distinct, clear-cut, hard-hitting, to the point, explicit; positive; definite, precise; unequivocal, legible, obvious, etc., 525.

graphic, telling, vivid; expressive.

519. UNINTELLIGIBILITY.—*N.* unintelligibility, incomprehensibility, vagueness, obscurity, ambiguity, confusion; mystification; jargon.

enigma, riddle; sealed book.

V. render unintelligible, conceal, darken, confuse, mystify, perplex.

Adj. unintelligible, incomprehensible, unaccountable, undecipherable, unfathomable, inexplicable, inscrutable, insoluble, impenetrable; puzzling, enigmatic; indecipherable, illegible.

obscure, crabbed, dark, muddy, dim, nebulous, mysterious, hidden, latent, occult; abstruse; indefinite, vague, loose, ambiguous.

inexpressible, unutterable, ineffable.

520. [Having a double sense] **EQUIVOCALNESS.**—*N.* equivocalness, equivocation, double meaning; ambiguity; quibble; conundrum, riddle; pun, word play; sphinx, Delphic oracle.

equivocation, etc. (*duplicity*), 544; white lie, mental reservation, etc., 528.

V. equivocate, etc. (*palter*), 544; prevaricate; have a double meaning.

Adj. equivocal, ambiguous; double-tongued; enigmatical; indeterminate, doubtful.

521. FIGURE OF SPEECH.—*N.* figure, trope, phrase, expression; euphemism; image, imagery; personification, metaphor; simile, satire, irony.

allegory, apologue, parable, fable.

V. employ figures of speech; personify, allegorize, fable, shadow forth, allude to.

Adj. figurative, metaphorical, euphuistic, allusive; allegoric *or* allegorical, ironic, ironical, satiric *or* satirical; euphemistic.

522. INTERPRETATION.—*N.* interpretation, definition, explanation; elucidation, diagnosis; solution, answer; meaning, etc., 516; clue.

translation; rendering, rendition; metaphrase, literal (*or* word-for-word) translation; free translation; key; crib, horse, pony, trot [*school cant*].

comment, commentary; exegesis, exposition; inference, deduction; illustration, exemplification; gloss, annotation, note, construction, version, reading.

equivalent, equivalent meaning, synonym; paraphrase, convertible terms.

dictionary, etc., 562.

prediction, etc., 511; chiromancy, palmistry; astrology.

V. **interpret**, explain, define, construe, translate, render; decipher, make out, unravel, disentangle, solve; read between the lines.

elucidate, account for, throw *or* shed light upon; clear up, popularize, simplify; illustrate, exemplify; unfold, expound, comment upon, annotate.

Adj. **explanatory**, expository; interpretative, elucidative, inferential, illustrative.

equivalent, convertible, synonymous.

metaphrastic, literal, word-for-word.

Adv. **in explanation;** that is to say, to wit, namely.

literally, strictly speaking; in plain terms (*or* words).

523. MISINTERPRETATION.—*N.* misinterpretation, misapprehension, misconception, misunderstanding, misconstruction; misapplication; cross-purposes; mistake, etc., 495.

misrepresentation, perversion, misstatement, exaggeration; abuse of terms; play upon words, pun, parody, travesty; falsification, etc. (*lying*), 544.

V. **misinterpret**, misapprehend, misunderstand, misconceive; misjudge, misspell; mistranslate, misconstrue, misapply; mistake, etc., 495.

misrepresent, pervert, misstate, garble, falsify, distort; travesty, play upon words; stretch (*or* strain, twist, wrest) the sense *or* meaning.

Adj. **misinterpreted,** mistranslated; confused, tangled, snarled, mixed.

dazed, perplexed, bewildered, rattled [*slang*], benighted.

Adv. **at cross-purposes,** at sixes and sevens [*colloq.*]; in a maze.

524. INTERPRETER.—*N.* **interpreter,** translator, expositor, expounder, exponent; demonstrator; commentator, annotator; oracle, etc., 513.

spokesman, speaker, mouthpiece, foreman of the jury, mediator, advocate, delegate, representative, diplomatic agent, ambassador, plenipotentiary.

guide, courier, cicerone, showman, barker [*colloq.*].

525. MANIFESTATION.—*N.* **manifestation,** indication, expression; plain speaking, candor, openness; showing, exposition, demonstration; séance, materialization; exhibition, production, display, show.

Thing shown: exhibit, exhibition, exposition, show [*colloq.*], performance.

publicity, etc., 531; disclosure, etc., 529; openness, candor; saliency, prominence.

V. **make manifest,** materialize, express, represent, set forth, evidence, exhibit, produce, show, show up, expose; hold up, show forth, unveil, display, demonstrate, lay open; draw out, bring out; manifest oneself; speak out, proclaim, publish.

indicate, point out; disclose, discover; translate, transcribe, decipher, decode; elicit, bring to light, disinter.

be manifest *or* plain, appear, etc., 446; transpire, come to light, be disclosed; go without saying, be self-evident.

Adj. **manifest,** apparent; salient, striking, prominent, in the foreground, ostensible, notable, pronounced.

plain, intelligible, clear, defined, definite, distinct, conspicuous, obvious, evident, unmistakable; conclusive, indubitable, palpable, self-evident; open, patent, express, explicit; naked, bare, literal, downright, unreserved, frank, plain-spoken.

barefaced, brazen, bold, shameless, daring, flaunting, loud [*colloq.*]; flagrant, arrant, notorious; glaring.

Adv. **manifestly,** openly, plainly, above board, in plain sight, in the open, in broad daylight; without reserve.

526. LATENCY.—*N.* **latency,** hidden meaning; obscurity, ambiguity; secret, mystery, occultism, mysticism, symbolism; reserve, reticence; concealment, mystification, suppression, evasion; Delphic oracle; undercurrent; snake in the grass.

allusion, insinuation, implication; innuendo.

latent influence, power behind the throne, friend at court, wire-puller [*colloq.*], kingmaker.

V. **lurk,** smolder, underlie, make no sign; escape observation (*or* detection, recognition); lie hid, lie in ambush.

keep back, etc. (*conceal*), 528.

involve, imply, connote, import, allude to, leave an inference; symbolize.

Adj. **latent,** lurking; dormant, secret, occult; esoteric, recondite, veiled, symbolic, cryptic, mystic, mystical.

unapparent, unknown, unseen, unsuspected; invisible; unexpressed, undisclosed, tacit.

indirect, crooked, underhand, underground; by inference, by implication; implied, implicit, understood, tacit; allusive, covert, undercover, concealed.

Adv. secretly, stealthily, incognito; in the background; behind the scenes, between the lines; below the surface.

527. INFORMATION.—*N.* information, enlightenment, acquaintance, knowledge; publicity, notoriety.

mention; instruction, communicativeness, intercommunication.

notification, intimation, communication, notice, annunciation, announcement, communiqué; representation; message, etc., 532.

report, advice, monition; news, tidings, return, record, account, description; statement, estimate, specification.

informant, authority, teller, harbinger, herald, reporter, exponent, mouthpiece; spokesman, etc. (*interpreter*), 524; spy, informer, eavesdropper, detective, sleuth [*colloq.*]; newsmonger; messenger, etc., 534.

guide, cicerone; pilot; guidebook, handbook; map, plan, chart, gazetteer; itinerary.

hint, suggestion, insinuation, innuendo, inkling, whisper, cue, byplay; gesture; word to the wise.

V. tell, inform, acquaint, impart, apprise, advise, instruct, enlighten.

mention, express, intimate, represent, communicate, make known; publish, disseminate; notify, signify, specify; retail, describe; state, declare, assert, affirm.

announce, report, bring (*or* send, leave) word; telegraph, wire [*colloq.*], telephone, phone [*colloq.*].

disclose, etc., 529; explain.

hint, insinuate, allude to, glance at, let fall, indicate; suggest, prompt, give the cue.

undeceive, set right, correct, disabuse.

Adj. informational, advisory.

expressive, explicit, plain-spoken; declaratory; expository; communicative.

528. CONCEALMENT.—*N.* concealment, mystification; reticence, reserve, reservation; mental reservation, aside; suppression, evasion, white lie; silence, closeness, secretiveness, mystery.

screen, cloak; ambush, ambuscade; stowaway; blind baggage [*slang*].

cipher, code, sympathetic ink.

stealth, stealthiness, slyness, caution, cunning.

secrecy, privacy, secretness; disguise, mask, masquerade; incognito (*fem.* incognita).

masquerader, masker, mask, domino.

V. conceal, hide, secrete; lock up; cover, screen, cloak, veil, shroud; curtain, muffle; mask, camouflage, disguise; ensconce.

keep from, keep to oneself, keep secret; bury; sink, suppress; keep in the background; stifle, hush up; withhold, reserve.

code, use a code *or* cipher, reduce to a code.

hoodwink, blind, blindfold; mystify, puzzle, deceive, lead astray.

be concealed, hide oneself, couch; lie in ambush, lurk, sneak, skulk, slink, prowl, gumshoe [*slang*].

Adj. concealed, hidden, secret, private, privy; recondite, mystic, mystical, occult, dark, cryptic; in secret, tortuous; close, inviolate, confidential, behind a screen, undercover, in ambush, in hiding, in disguise; undisclosed, untold, covert, mysterious.

furtive, stealthy, skulking, surreptitious, underhand, sly, cunning, evasive; secretive, clandestine; reserved, reticent, uncommunicative, close, taciturn.

Adv. secretly, in secret, in private, incognito.

behind closed doors, under the rose, *sub rosa* [L.]; on the sly [*colloq.*]; in a whisper.

confidentially, in strict confidence, between ourselves, between you and me.

underhand, by stealth, like a thief in the night; stealthily.

529. DISCLOSURE.—*N.* disclosure, revelation, divulgence, exposition, exposure, publication, exposé.

acknowledgment, avowal, confession, confessional.

narrator, etc., 594; talebearer, etc., 532; informant, etc., 527.

V. disclose, discover, unmask, unveil, unfold, uncover, unseal, lay bare, expose, bare, bring to light, disabuse, open the eyes of, turn informer.

divulge, reveal, let into the secret, tell, etc. (*inform*), 527; breathe, utter, peach [*slang*]; let slip *or* drop, betray; blurt out, vent, whisper about, speak out, break the news, publish, etc., 531.

acknowledge, allow, concede, grant, admit, own, confess, avow, make a clean breast, unbosom oneself; turn informer.

be disclosed, transpire, come to light, become known, escape the lips; ooze out, leak out, come to one's ears.

530. AMBUSH. [Means of concealment]—*N.* ambush, ambuscade, lurking place, trap, snare, pitfall, etc., 667.

hiding place, secret place, recess, hole, cubbyhole, crypt; safe, safe-deposit box, safety-deposit box.

screen, cover, shade, blinker; veil, curtain, blind, cloak, cloud.

mask, visor, disguise, masquerade, domino.

V. **ambush,** ambuscade, lie in ambush, lie in wait for; set a trap for, ensnare.

531. PUBLICATION.—*N.* **publication,** public announcement, promulgation, propagation, proclamation, pronouncement, edict.

publicity, notoriety, currency, flagrancy, cry, hue and cry, bruit; report, etc. (*news*), 532; telegram, etc., 532.

the press, the fourth estate, public press; newspaper, journal, gazette.

advertisement, placard, bill, flier [*cant*], leaflet, handbill, poster; circular, notice, program, manifesto.

V. **publish,** make public, broach, utter, circulate, propagate, promulgate, spread, spread abroad, rumor, diffuse, disseminate; issue; bring before the public; give to the world; report, voice, bruit; proclaim, herald, blazon, noise abroad, advertise.

telegraph, cable, wireless [*colloq.*], broadcast, wire [*colloq.*].

Adj. **published,** current; public, notorious, flagrant.

Adv. **publicly,** in public, in open court, with open doors.

532. NEWS—*N.* **news,** information, etc., 527; intelligence, tidings; beat *or* scoop [*newspaper cant*], story, copy [*cant*].

message, word, advice, communication, bulletin, broadcast, dispatch; telegram, cable [*colloq.*], wire [*colloq.*], radio, radiogram, wireless telegram, wireless [*colloq.*]; telephone, radiophone, wireless telephone.

report, rumor, hearsay, cry, bruit, fame; talk, scandal, gossip; tittle-tattle.

narrator, historian; newsmonger, scandalmonger; talebearer, telltale, gossip, tattler, tattletale; chatterer, busybody; informer.

V. **transpire,** etc. (*be disclosed*), 529; rumor, etc. (*publish*), 531.

Adj. **rumored,** rife, current, in circulation.

533. SECRET.—*N.* **secret,** mystery; problem, etc. (*question*), 461; unintelligibility, etc., 519.

enigma, riddle, puzzle, conundrum, charade, rebus.

maze, labyrinth, intricacy.

Adj. **secret,** concealed, etc., 528; involved, tortuous, circuitous, labyrinthine; enigmatic *or* enigmatical.

534. MESSENGER.—*N.* **messenger,** intermediary, go-between; envoy, emissary, legate, nuncio, delegate; angel; Gabriel, Hermes, Mercury.

courier, runner; commissionaire, errand boy; herald, crier, trumpeter, bellman.

mail, post, post office; air mail; postman, mailman, letter carrier; carrier pigeon.

telegraph, cable, wire [*colloq.*], radiotelegraph, wireless telegraph, wireless [*colloq.*], radio.

telephone, phone [*colloq.*], radiotelephone, radiophone, wireless telephone.

reporter, newspaperman, journalist; gentleman (*or* representative) of the press; special correspondent; scout, spy, informer.

535. AFFIRMATION.—*N.* **affirmation,** statement, allegation, profession, assertion, declaration; confirmation; asseveration, swearing, oath, affidavit, deposition; assurance, protest, protestation.

positiveness, emphasis, peremptoriness, dogmatism, weight.
vote, voice; ballot, suffrage.
remark, observation, saying, dictum, sentence.

V. assert, say, affirm, declare, state; protest, profess; acknowledge; put forward; advance, allege, propose, propound; announce, enunciate, broach, set forth, maintain, contend, pronounce.

depose, aver, avow, avouch, asseverate, swear, affirm; take one's oath; make an affidavit; vow, vouch, warrant, certify, assure; attest, adjure.

emphasize, insist upon, lay stress on; lay down the law; dogmatize, repeat, reassert, reaffirm.

Adj. affirmative, declaratory, positive; unmistakable, clear; certain, etc., 474; express, explicit, absolute, emphatic, decided, insistent, dogmatic, formal, solemn, categorical, peremptory.

Adv. with emphasis, ex cathedra, without fear of contradiction.

536. NEGATION.—*N.* **negation,** denial; disavowal, disclaimer; contradiction, protest; dissent, etc., 489.

qualification, etc., 469; repudiation, rejection, recantation, revocation; retractation, rebuttal, confutation; refusal, etc., 764.

V. deny; contradict, contravene; controvert, gainsay, negative, give the lie to, belie.

disclaim, disown, repudiate, disaffirm, disavow, abjure, forswear, renounce; recant, revoke.

dispute, impugn, confute, rebut, join issue upon; bring (*or* call) in question, set aside, ignore; refuse, etc., 764.

Adj. contradictory; negative; recusant, dissentient, at issue upon.

Adv. no, nay, not, nowise, not at all, not in the least, quite the contrary, by no means.

537. TEACHING.—*N.* **teaching,** pedagogics, pedagogy, instruction, edification, education, tuition, tutorship, tutelage; direction, guidance.

preparation, qualification, training, schooling, discipline; drill, practice.

lesson, lecture, recitation, sermon, homily, harangue, disquisition; apologue, parable; discourse; explanation; exercise, task; curriculum; course.

V. **teach,** instruct, educate, edify, school, tutor, cram [*colloq.*], grind [*colloq.*], prime, coach; enlighten, inform, etc., 527; direct, guide.

inculcate, infuse, instill, imbue, impregnate, implant; disseminate, propagate.

expound, etc. (*interpret*), 522; lecture; hold forth, preach; sermonize, moralize.

train, discipline, form, ground, prepare, qualify, drill, exercise, practice, familiarize with, inure, initiate, graduate.

Adj. **educational,** scholastic, academic, disciplinary, instructive, pedagogic, didactic; cultural, humanistic, humane; pragmatic, practical, utilitarian.

538. MISTEACHING.—*N.* misteaching, misinformation, misguidance, misdirection, perversion, sophistry; the blind leading the blind.

V. **misinform,** misteach, misinstruct, misdirect, misguide, pervert; deceive, mislead, misrepresent, lie.

render unintelligible, bewilder, mystify, conceal.

539. LEARNING.—*N.* learning, acquisition of knowledge, acquirement, attainment; mental cultivation, scholarship, erudition; lore; wide reading; study, grind [*colloq.*]; inquiry, etc., 461. **apprenticeship,** tutelage, novitiate.

V. **learn,** acquire (*or* gain, imbibe, pick up, obtain) knowledge *or* learning; master, grind [*college slang*], cram [*colloq.*], get up, learn by heart.

study, read, peruse; con, pore over, wade through, plunge into. burn the midnight oil; be taught.

Adj. **studious;** industrious, etc., 682; scholastic, scholarly, well read, widely read, erudite, learned.

540. TEACHER.—*N.* teacher, preceptor, instructor, master, tutor, schoolmaster, dominie, pedagogue; kindergartner, governess, mistress; coach [*colloq.*], crammer [*colloq.*]; professor, don [*Univ. cant*], lecturer, reader, preacher; pastor, etc. (*clergy*), 996; schoolmistress.

guide, counselor, adviser, mentor, pioneer, apostle, missionary, propagandist; example.

professorship, chair, fellowship, tutorship, mastership, instructorship.

Adj. **pedagogic,** tutorial, professorial; scholastic, etc., 537.

541. LEARNER.—*N.* learner, scholar, student, alumnus (*pl.* alumni; *fem.* alumna, *pl.* alumnae), pupil, schoolboy, schoolgirl;

monitor, prefect; undergraduate, freshman; graduate student, postgraduate student.

class, form, grade, room; promotion, graduation.

disciple, follower, apostle, proselyte.

classmate, fellow student, schoolmate, schoolfellow, fellow pupil.

novice, beginner, tyro, recruit, tenderfoot [*slang or colloq.*], neophyte, probationer; apprentice.

Adj. in leading strings, pupillary, probationary.

542. SCHOOL.—*N.* school, academy, lyceum, seminary, college, educational institution, institute; university, varsity [*colloq.*], alma mater [L.].

General: day (*or* boarding, preparatory, elementary, denominational, secondary, military, naval, technical, library, secretarial, business, correspondence) school; kindergarten, nursery school; Sunday (*or* Sabbath, Bible) school.

United States: district (*or* grade, parochial, public, primary, grammar, junior high, high, Latin) school; private school, normal school, kindergarten training school; summer school; military academy (West Point); naval academy (Annapolis); college, fresh-water college [*colloq.* or *slang*], state university; graduate school, postgraduate school.

class, division, form, etc., 541; seminar.

classroom, room, schoolroom, recitation room; lecture room, lecture hall, theater, amphitheater.

desk, reading desk, pulpit, forum, stage, rostrum, platform.

schoolbook, textbook; grammar, primer, reader.

Adj. scholastic, academic, collegiate; educational, cultural; gymnastic, athletic, physical, eurythmic.

543. VERACITY.—*N.* veracity, truthfulness, frankness, truth, sincerity, candor, honesty, fidelity, love of truth; probity, etc., 939.

V. speak the truth, tell the truth; speak on oath; speak without equivocation (*or* mental reservation), make a clean breast, disclose, etc., 529; speak one's mind.

Adj. truthful, true; veracious, scrupulous, punctilious; sincere, candid, frank, open, outspoken, straightforward, unreserved, truth-telling, honest, trustworthy; guileless, pure, truth-loving; true-blue, as good as one's word; unfeigned, ingenuous.

544. FALSEHOOD.—*N.* falsehood, falseness, falsity, falsification, misrepresentation, deception, etc., 545; untruthfulness, lying; untruth, etc., 546; mendacity, guile, perjury, false swearing; forgery, invention, fabrication; perversion, distortion, exaggeration, prevarication, equivocation, evasion, fraud; simulation, dissimulation, dissembling; deceit; sham, pretense; malingering.

duplicity, double dealing, insincerity, hypocrisy, cant, pharisaism; casuistry, Machiavellism; lip service, hollowness, mere show; quackery, charlatanism, charlatanry; humbug; cajolery, flattery; Judas kiss; perfidy, etc., 940; cunning, etc., 702; misstatement, false report.

V. **lie,** tell a lie (*or* an untruth), fib, swear falsely, forswear, perjure oneself, bear false witness.

falsify, misstate, misquote; misrepresent, etc., 523; belie; garble, gloss over, disguise, color, varnish, doctor [*colloq.*], dress up, embroider; exaggerate, etc., 549.

prevaricate, equivocate, quibble; trim, shuffle, fence, beat about the bush.

fabricate, invent; trump up; forge; coin; hatch, concoct; romance.

dissemble, dissimulate; feign, assume; pretend, make believe; play false, play a double game; coquet; act *or* play a part; affect, pose; simulate, pass off for; counterfeit, sham; malinger; deceive, etc., 545.

Adj. **false,** untrue, deceitful, mendacious, lying, untruthful, fraudulent, dishonest; faithless, forsworn; evasive, disingenuous, hollow, insincere; artful, cunning, tricky, wily, sly; perfidious, treacherous, perjured; spurious, etc., 545; falsified.

hypocritical, canting, pharisaical; Machiavellian, double-tongued, double-dealing; two-faced, double-faced; smooth-spoken, smooth-tongued; plausible, mealy-mouthed; affected, canting, insincere.

545. DECEPTION.—*N.* **deception;** falseness, etc., 544; untruth, etc., 546; imposition, imposture; fraud, deceit, guile, fraudulence, misrepresentation, bluff; trickery, knavery, sharp practice, collusion, chicanery; treachery, double-dealing.

delusion, jugglery, sleight of hand, legerdemain, conjuring.

trick, cheat, wile, blind, feint, chicane, juggle, swindle; stratagem, artifice; hoax; bunk [*slang*], gold brick [*colloq.*].

snare, trap, pitfall, gin; bait, decoy duck, stool pigeon; cobweb, net, meshes, toils; ambush, ambuscade.

disguise, false colors, camouflage, masquerade, mask, mummery, borrowed plumes; dissembler, hypocrite, etc., 548.

sham, mockery, copy, counterfeit, make-believe, forgery, fraud, untruth, etc., 546; hollow mockery; whited sepulcher, tinsel, paste.

illusion, delusion, self-deception, *ignis fatuus* [L.], mirage, etc., 443.

V. **deceive,** mislead, lead astray, take in, defraud, cheat, cozen, swindle, victimize; betray, play false; lie, etc., 544; mystify; blind, hoodwink; throw dust into the eyes; impose upon, practice upon, palm off on; bluff.

outwit, circumvent, overreach, steal a march on.

insnare, ensnare, entrap, decoy, waylay, lure, beguile, delude, inveigle, trick.

fool, befool, dupe, gull, hoax, humbug, stuff [*slang*], sell [*slang*]; trifle with, cajole, flatter; dissemble, dissimulate, sham, counterfeit.

practice chicanery, live by one's wits, juggle, conjure, play off, palm off, foist off.

Adj. deceptive, deceitful, tricky, cunning, etc., 702; elusive, insidious; delusive, illusory.

make-believe; untrue, etc., 546; mock, sham, counterfeit, pseudo, spurious, so-called, pretended, feigned, bogus [*colloq.*], fraudulent, surreptitious, illegitimate, contraband; adulterated, disguised; unsound, meretricious, jerry-built; tinsel.

Adv. under false colors, under cover of.

546. UNTRUTH.—*N.* untruth, falsehood, lie, story, fib, whopper [*colloq.*].

fabrication, forgery, invention; misstatement, misrepresentation, perversion, falsification, false coloring, exaggeration.

fiction; fable, nursery tale, fairy tale, romance, extravaganza; canard; yarn [*colloq.*], fish story [*colloq.*], traveler's tale, cock-and-bull story, myth, moonshine, bosh [*colloq.*].

half truth, white lie, pious fraud; suppression; irony.

pretense, pretext, subterfuge, evasion, shift, shuffle, make-believe, sham, etc., 545; profession, Judas kiss, cajolery, flattery; disguise, etc., 530.

V. feign, make-believe, pretend, sham, counterfeit; lie, etc., 544.

Adj. untrue, false, trumped up; unfounded, invented, fictitious, fabulous, fabricated, fraudulent, forged; evasive.

547. DUPE.—*N.* dupe, gull, victim, April fool; sucker [*slang*]; laughingstock, etc., 857; greenhorn; fool, etc., 501; puppet, cat's-paw.

V. be deceived, be the dupe of; fall into a trap; swallow *or* nibble at the bait; swallow whole; bite.

Adj. credulous, gullible, etc., 486.

mistaken, etc. (*error*), 495.

548. DECEIVER.—*N.* deceiver, dissembler, hypocrite, Pharisee; sophist; serpent, snake in the grass, Judas, wolf in sheep's clothing.

liar, storyteller, perjurer, false witness, faker [*slang*], fraud, four-flusher [*slang*], confidence man, decoy, stool pigeon; rogue, knave, cheat, swindler.

impostor, pretender, malingerer, humbug; adventurer, adventuress.

trickster, conjurer, juggler, necromancer, sorcerer, magician, wizard, medicine man, witch doctor; quack, charlatan, mountebank.

549. EXAGGERATION.—*N.* **exaggeration,** expansion, amplification; fringe, embroidery; extravagance, hyperbole, stretch, high coloring, caricature; yarn [*colloq.*], traveler's tale, fish story [*colloq.*]; tempest in a teacup; much ado about nothing; puffery, etc. (*boasting*), 884; rant, etc., 577.

V. **exaggerate,** magnify, pile up, aggravate; amplify, expand, overestimate, overstate, overdraw, overshoot the mark, overpraise; stretch a point; draw a long bow [*colloq.*], out-Herod Herod; overcolor, heighten; embroider, color; puff, etc. (*boast*), 884.

Adj. **exaggerated,** overwrought; bombastic, etc. (*magniloquent*), 577; hyperbolical, extravagant; preposterous, egregious.

550. [Means of communication] INDICATION.—*N.* **indication,** sign, symbol; index, indicator, pointer, cue, note, token, symptom; type, figure, emblem, cipher, device; motto, epitaph.

means of recognition; lineament, feature, trait, trick, earmark, characteristic.

gesture, gesticulation; pantomime; wink, glance, leer; nod, shrug, beck; touch, nudge; byplay, dumb show; deaf-and-dumb alphabet, dactylology.

track, spoor, trail, footprint, scent; clue, key.

signal, rocket, watch fire, beacon fire, watchtower; telegraph, semaphore; fiery cross; calumet, peace pipe; heliograph; searchlight, flashlight.

mark, line, stroke, score, streak, scratch, tick, dot, notch, nick, blaze; red letter, underlining, impression.

Map drawing: hachure, contour line; isobar, isopiestic line, isobaric line; isotherm, isothermal line; latitude, longitude, meridian, equator.

For identification: badge, countercheck, countersign, counterfoil, stub, duplicate, tally; label, ticket, counter, check, chip, voucher, stamp; trade-mark, hallmark; card, visiting card; credentials; handwriting, sign manual, autograph, signature; monogram, seal, signet; fingerprint; brand; caste mark; mortarboard [*colloq.*], cap and gown, hood; shibboleth; watchword, catchword, password, cue; sign, countersign, pass, grip; open-sesame.

Insignia: banner, flag, colors, streamer, pennant, pennon, ensign, standard; eagle, oriflamme, blue peter, jack, Union Jack; Old Glory [*colloq.*], Stars and Stripes.

Heraldry: crest, arms, coat of arms, armorial bearings; hatchment, escutcheon *or* scutcheon; shield, supporters; livery, uniform; cockade, brassard, epaulet, chevron; garland, chaplet, love knot, favor.

Of locality: beacon, flagstaff, hand, pointer, vane, cock, weathercock, weather vane; guidepost, signpost; sign, signboard; North Star, polestar; landmark, seamark; lighthouse; address, direction, name.

Of the future: warning, premonition; omen, portent, sign.

Of the past: trace, record.

Of danger: warning, alarm, fire alarm, burglar alarm.

Of authority: scepter, etc., 747.

Of triumph: trophy, etc., 733.

Of mourning: mourning, etc., 839.

Of quantity: gauge, etc., 466.

Of distance: milestone, milepost.
Of disgrace: brand, foolscap, mark of Cain, stigma, stripes, broad arrow.
   call, word of command; bugle call, trumpet call; bell, alarum, battle cry, reveille, taps, last post; sacring bell, Sanctus bell, angelus; dirge.

V. **indicate,** denote, betoken, connote, signify; represent, stand for; typify, symbolize; mark, note, stamp, nick, blaze; label, ticket.

   make a sign, signalize; beckon, nod, wink, glance, leer, nudge, shrug, gesticulate.

   sign, seal, attest, underscore, underline; call attention to.

Adj. **indicative,** indicatory; connotative, denotative, representative, typical, individual, symbolic *or* symbolical, symptomatic, characteristic, significant, diagnostic, emblematic, armorial.

551. RECORD.—*N.* trace, vestige, relic, remains; scar, cicatrix; footstep, footmark, footprint; track, mark, wake, trail, scent, spoor.

   monument, hatchment; escutcheon *or* scutcheon; slab, tablet, trophy, obelisk, pillar, column, monolith; memorial; memento; testimonial, medal, Congressional medal; cross, Victoria cross [Eng.], iron cross [Ger.]; ribbon, garter; commemoration, etc. (*celebration*), 883.

   record, note, minute; register, registry; roll; list; entry, memorandum, endorsement, inscription, copy, duplicate, docket; mark, etc., 550; deed; document; deposition, affidavit; certificate.
   notebook, memorandum book; bulletin, bulletin board, scoreboard, score sheet; card index, file, letter file, pigeonholes.
   newspaper, daily, gazette, magazine, paper [*colloq.*].
   calendar, diary, log, journal, daybook, ledger, cashbook.
   archive, scroll, state paper, return, bluebook; almanac, gazetteer, census report; statistics; Congressional Records; minutes, chronicle, annals; legend; history, biography, etc., 594.
   registration; registry, enrollment, tabulation; entry, booking; signature, sign manual; recorder, etc., 553; journalism.
   mechanical record, recording instrument; phonograph, etc., 418; speedometer, pedometer, patent log [*naut.*]; ticker, tape; time clock; turnstile; cash register.

V. **record,** put *or* place upon record, chronicle, calendar, hand down to posterity; commemorate, etc. (*celebrate*), 883; report, commit to writing, note, put *or* set down; mark, etc. (*indicate*), 550; sign, etc. (*attest*), 467; enter, book, post, insert; mark off, tick off; register, list, enroll, inscroll; file.

552. [Suppression of sign] OBLITERATION.—*N.* obliteration, erasure, cancellation, deletion; blot; effacement, extinction.

V. **efface,** obliterate, erase, expunge, cancel; blot (*or* rub, scratch, strike, wash, wipe) out; deface, render illegible; rule out.
   be effaced, leave no trace.

Adj. **obliterated,** erased; unrecorded, unregistered.

553. RECORDER.—*N.* recorder, notary, clerk; registrar, register; amanuensis, secretary, recording secretary, stenographer, bookkeeper, scribe.

   annalist, historian, historiographer, chronicler; biographer, etc.

(*narrator*), 594; antiquary, antiquarian, archeologist; memorialist.

journalist, newspaperman, reporter, interviewer; publicist, author, editor.

554. REPRESENTATION.—*N.* representation, depiction, imitation, illustration, delineation, imagery, portraiture; design, designing; art, fine arts; painting, etc., 556; sculpture, etc., 557; engraving, etc., 558.

photography; radiography, X-ray photography, skiagraphy.
personation, impersonation; personification; drama, etc., 599.

drawing, picture, sketch, draft; tracing; copy, etc., 21.
photograph, photo [*colloq.*], daguerreotype, print, cabinet, snapshot.
image, effigy, icon, portrait, likeness, facsimile.
figure, figurehead, puppet, doll, manikin, lay figure, model, marionette, statue, statuette, bust.
map, plan, chart; diagram; ground plan, projection, elevation; atlas; outline, view.
radiograph, radiogram, skiagraph, skiagram, X-ray photograph, Xray [*colloq.*].
delineator, draftsman; artist, etc., 559; photographer, radiographer, X-ray photographer, skiagrapher, daguerreotypist.

V. represent, delineate, depict, portray, picture, limn, photograph, snapshot; figure, shadow forth, adumbrate; describe, etc., 594; trace, copy; mold; illustrate, symbolize; paint, etc., 556; sculpture, etc., 557; engrave, etc., 558.

personate, impersonate, dress up [*colloq.*], pose as, act; personify; play, etc. (*drama*), 559; mimic, etc. (*imitate*),19.

Adj. representative; illustrative; imitative, figurative; similar, like, etc., 17; descriptive, etc., 594.

555. MISREPRESENTATION.—*N.* misrepresentation, misstatement, falsification, exaggeration, distortion; bad likeness, daub, scratch.

burlesque, travesty, parody, take-off, caricature, extravaganza.

V. misrepresent, distort, overdraw, exaggerate, daub; falsify, understate, overstate, stretch.

burlesque, travesty, parody, caricature.

556. PAINTING. BLACK AND WHITE.—*N.* painting, depicting, drawing; design; perspective; composition; treatment; arrangement, values, atmosphere, tone, technique.

palette; easel; brush, pencil, stump, black lead, charcoal, crayons, chalk, pastel; paint, etc. (*coloring matter*), 428; water (*or* oil) colors; oils, oil paint; varnish; distemper, fresco, enamel, mosaic, encaustic painting; batik.
style, school; the grand style, high art; futurist, cubist, vorticist.
picture, painting, piece, tableau, canvas; fresco, cartoon; drawing, draft; still life, genre (*or* landscape) painting; sketch, outline, study.
portrait; head; miniature; silhouette; profile.

view, landscape, seascape, sea view, seapiece; scene, prospect; interior; panorama, bird's-eye view.

picture gallery, art gallery, art museum; studio, atelier [F.].

photograph, radiography, etc., 554; photograph, radiograph, etc., 554.

V. **paint,** design, limn, draw, sketch, pencil, color; stencil; depict, etc. (*represent*), 554.

Adj. **pictorial,** graphic; picturesque, historical; futurist, cubist, vorticist; in the grand style.

557. SCULPTURE.—*N.* **sculpture,** carving, modeling, statuary; ceramics.

marble, bronze, terra cotta; ceramic ware, pottery, porcelain, china, earthenware; cloisonné, enamel, faïence.

relief, low relief, bas-relief, high relief; intaglio; cameo; medal, medallion.

statue, statuette, bust; cast.

V. **sculpture,** carve, cut, chisel, model, mold; cast.

558. ENGRAVING.—*N.* **engraving,** etching, chiseling; plate (*or* copperplate, steel, half-tone, wood) engraving; lithography, chromolithography, photolithography.

printing; color printing, lithographic printing; type printing; three-color process.
impression, print, engraving, plate; steel-plate, copperplate; etching; aquatint, mezzotint; cut, woodcut; lithograph, chromolithograph, photolithograph.
illustration, illumination; half-tone; photogravure; rotogravure; vignette, initial letter, tailpiece.

V. **engrave,** grave, etch; bite; bite in; lithograph; print.

559. ARTIST.—*N.* **artist;** painter, drawer, sketcher, designer, engraver, graver, line engraver, draftsman; chaser; copyist; enameler, enamelist; cartoonist, caricaturist.

historical (*or* landscape, marine, flower, portrait, genre, miniature, scene) painter; carver, modeler, statuary, sculptor.

(1) Language generally

560. LANGUAGE.—*N.* **language;** phraseology, etc., 569; speech, etc., 582; tongue, lingo [*chiefly humorous or contemptuous*], vernacular, mother (*or* vulgar, native) tongue; king's English; dialect, brogue, patois, idiom.

confusion of tongues, Babel; universal language, Esperanto, Ido; pantomime, dumb show.

literature, letters, polite literature, belles-lettres [F.], muses, humanities, republic of letters, dead languages, classics.

linguist, etc. (*scholar*), 492.

V. **express,** say, express by words.

Adj. **lingual,** linguistic; dialectal, dialectic; vernacular, current; bilingual; polyglot; literary; colloquial, slangy.

561. LETTER.—*N.* **letter;** character; hieroglyphic; alphabet,

ABC; consonant, vowel, diphthong, mute, surd, sonant, liquid, labial, palatal, cerebral, dental, guttural.

syllable; monosyllable, dissyllable, polysyllable; prefix, suffix.

spelling, orthography; phonetic spelling, phonetics.

cipher, code; monogram, anagram; acrostic, double acrostic.

V. spell; transliterate.

cipher, decipher; code, decode.

Adj. literal; alphabetical, syllabic.

phonetic, voiced, tonic, sonant; voiceless, surd; mute, labial, palatal, cerebral, dental, guttural, liquid.

562. WORD.—N. word, term, vocable; name, etc., 564; phrase, etc., 566; root, derivative; part of speech.

dictionary, lexicon, vocabulary, wordbook, index, glossary, thesaurus.

Science of language: etymology, philology; terminology; pronunciation, orthoëpy; lexicography.

verbosity, verbiage, wordiness; loquacity, etc., 584.

V. vocalize; etymologize, derive; index; translate.

Adj. verbal, literal; derivative.

verbose, wordy, etc., 573; loquacious, etc., 584.

563. NEOLOGY.—N. neology, neologism; barbarism; corruption.

dialect, brogue, patois, provincialism, broken English, Anglicism, Briticism, Gallicism, Americanism; gypsy lingo, Romany.

lingua franca, pidgin English, Hindustani; Esperanto, Ido.

jargon, dog Latin, gibberish; confusion of tongues, Babel; lingo, slang, cant, argot, billingsgate.

pseudonym, pen name; nickname; alias.

neologist, word coiner, coiner of words.

V. coin words; Americanize, Anglicize, Gallicize.

Adj. neologic, neological; slang, cant, barbarous.

564. NOMENCLATURE.—N. nomenclature; naming, nicknaming; baptism.

name, appellation, appellative, designation, denomination; nickname, etc., 565; epithet; title, head, heading; style, proper name, cognomen, patronymic, surname; title, handle to one's name; namesake.

term, expression, noun; technical term; cant.

V. name, call, term, denominate, designate, style, entitle, dub [colloq. or humorous], christen, baptize, nickname, characterize, specify, label.

Adj. named, yclept [humorous]; known as; titular, nominal.

565. MISNOMER.—N. misnomer; malapropism, Mrs. Malaprop.

nickname, sobriquet, pet name, assumed name, alias; stage name; *nom de guerre* [F.], nom de plume [English formation], pen name, pseudonym.

V. **misname,** miscall, nickname; take an assumed name.

Adj. **misnamed;** self-styled; so-called, quasi.

nameless, anonymous; unacknowledged; pseudo.

566. PHRASE.—*N.* phrase, expression, locution; sentence, paragraph; paraphrase, metaphor, euphemism, euphuism; motto, proverb; figure of speech; idiom, turn of expression; phraseology, etc., 569.

V. **express,** phrase; word, voice; put into (*or* express by) words; call, denominate, designate, dub.

Adv. in round (*or* set) terms; in set phrases; by the card.

567. GRAMMAR.—*N.* grammar, accidence, syntax, analysis, parts of speech; inflection, case, declension, conjugation; philology.

V. parse, analyze, conjugate, decline.

Adj. grammatical, syntactic *or* syntactical, inflectional, declensional, synthetic *or* synthetical.

568. SOLECISM.—*N.* solecism; grammatical blunder; error, slip; slip of the pen, slip of the tongue, bull; barbarism, impropriety.

V. **solecize,** commit a solecism; murder the king's English.

Adj. **ungrammatical,** incorrect, inaccurate, faulty; improper.

569. STYLE.—*N.* style, diction, phraseology, wording; manner, strain; composition; mode of expression, idiom, choice of words; mode of speech, literary power, command of language; authorship, artistry.

V. **word,** phrase, express by words, write; apply the file.

Various Qualities of Style

570. PERSPICUITY.—*N.* perspicuity, perspicacity, explicitness, lucidness, lucidity, limpidity, clearness; plain speaking, expression, definiteness, definition; exactness, etc., 494.

Adj. **lucid,** intelligible, etc., 518; limpid, pellucid, clear, explicit; exact, etc., 494.

571. OBSCURITY.—*N.* obscurity, unintelligibility, involution, confusion; hard words; ambiguity, indefiniteness, vagueness, inexactness, inaccuracy; darkness of meaning.

Adj. **obscure,** involved, confused.

572. CONCISENESS.—*N.* conciseness, terseness, brevity, laconicism, abridgment, compression, condensation, epitome, etc., 596.

Portmanteau word [Lewis Carroll]; brunch [breakfast + lunch], slithy, *adj.* [slimy + lithe], torrible, *adj.* [torrid + horrible].

V. **be concise,** telescope, compress, condense, abridge, abbreviate, abstract, etc., 596; come to the point.

Adj. **concise,** brief, short, laconic, succinct, curt, compact, summary, compendious, etc., 596; terse, to the point; compressed, condensed, pointed; pithy, crisp, trenchant, epigrammatic, sententious.

Adv. **briefly,** summarily; in brief, in short, in a word.

573. DIFFUSENESS.—*N.* **diffuseness,** profuseness, amplification, verbosity, wordiness; verbiage, flow of words, etc. (*loquacity*), 584; looseness; tautology, exuberance, redundance, prolixity, periphrase, expletive; padding [*editors' cant*]; drivel, twaddle.

V. **expand,** expatiate, enlarge, dilate, amplify, inflate, pad [*editors' cant*], rant; maunder, prose; harp upon, dwell on.

digress, ramble, beat about the bush, protract.

Adj. **diffuse,** profuse, wordy, verbose, copious, exuberant; lengthy, long, long-winded, protracted, prolix, diffusive, roundabout, digressive, discursive, loose; rambling, frothy.

574. VIGOR.—*N.* **vigor,** power, force; boldness, intellectual force; spirit, punch [*slang*], point, piquancy, raciness; verve, ardor, enthusiasm, glow, fire, warmth; gravity, weight.

loftiness, elevation, sublimity, grandeur.

eloquence; command of words, command of language.

Adj. **vigorous,** nervous, powerful, forcible, forceful; mordant, biting, trenchant, incisive; graphic, impressive.

spirited, lively, glowing, sparkling; racy, bold, pungent, piquant, pithy.

lofty, elevated, sublime, poetic, grand, weighty, ponderous; eloquent.

vehement, passionate, burning, impassioned, petulant.

575. FEEBLENESS.—*N.* **feebleness,** baldness, enervation, flaccidity, vapidity, poverty.

Adj. **feeble,** tame, meager, insipid, watery, nerveless, vapid, trashy, poor, dull, dry, languid; bald, colorless, enervated; prosy, prosaic, weak, slight; careless, slovenly, loose, lax; slipshod, inexact; puerile, childish; rambling, etc. (*diffuse*), 573.

576. PLAINNESS.—*N.* **plainness,** homeliness, simplicity, severity; household words.

V. **speak plainly,** waste no words, come to the point.

Adj. **plain,** simple, unornamented, unadorned, unvarnished; homely, homespun; neat; severe, chaste, pure, Saxon; commonplace, matter-of-fact, natural, prosaic, sober.

Adv. point-blank; in plain English; in common parlance.

577. ORNAMENT.—*N.* ornament, floridness, grandiloquence, magniloquence, declamation, well-rounded periods; elegance, etc., 578; flourish, trope; euphuism, euphemism.

bombast, inflation, pretension; rant, fustian, highfalutin [*slang*], buncombe, balderdash; fine writing; purple patches.

V. ornament, overcharge, overload; euphuize, euphemize.

Adj. ornate; ornamented, beautified, florid, rich, flowery; euphuistic, euphemistic; sonorous, inflated, swelling, tumid; turgid, pedantic, pompous, stilted, high-flown, sententious, rhetorical, declamatory; grandiose; grandiloquent, magniloquent, bombastic; frothy, flashy, flamboyant.

578. ELEGANCE.—*N.* elegance, distinction, clarity, purity, grace, felicity, ease; gracefulness, euphony; taste, good taste, restraint, propriety, correctness.

purist, classicist, stylist.

Adj. elegant, polished, classic *or* classical, correct, artistic; chaste, pure; graceful, easy, fluent, unaffected, natural, mellifluous, euphonious; restrained.

felicitous, happy, neat; well expressed.

579. INELEGANCE.—*N.* inelegance, impurity, vulgarity; poor diction, poor choice of words; loose construction; ill-balanced sentences; barbarism, slang; solecism, mannerism, affectation.

Adj. inelegant, graceless, ungraceful; harsh, abrupt; dry, stiff, cramped, formal, forced, labored; artificial, mannered, affected, ponderous, awkward; unpolished; turgid, barbarous, uncouth, rude, crude, halting, vulgar.

(2) Spoken Language

580. VOICE.—*N.* voice; intonation; utterance; vocalization; cry, exclamation, expletive, ejaculation; vociferation, enunciation, articulation; distinctness; clearness; delivery, attack.

accent, accentuation; emphasis, stress; pronunciation; euphony, etc. (*melody*), 413.

V. speak, utter, breathe; cry, etc. (*shout*), 411; ejaculate, rap out; articulate, enunciate, vocalize, pronounce, accentuate, deliver, emit; whisper, murmur.

Adj. vocal, phonetic, oral; ejaculatory, articulate, distinct, euphonious, melodious.

581. DUMBNESS.—*N.* dumbness; silence, etc. (*taciturnity*), 585; deaf-mutism, deaf-muteness, deaf-dumbness, mute, dummy, deaf-mute.

V. **silence,** muzzle, muffle, suppress, smother, gag, strike dumb, dumfound.

Adj. **dumb,** mute, mum; tongue-tied; voiceless, speechless, wordless; silent, etc. (*taciturn*), 585; inarticulate.

582. SPEECH.—*N*. **speech,** locution, talk, parlance, word of mouth, prattle.

oration, recitation, delivery, speech, address, discourse, lecture, harangue, sermon, tirade, soliloquy, etc., 589; conversation, etc., 588; salutatory; valedictory.

oratory, elocution, eloquence, rhetoric, declamation; grandiloquence.

speaker, spokesman, mouthpiece, orator, rhetorician, lecturer, preacher, elocutionist, reciter, reader; spellbinder.

V. **speak,** talk, say, utter, pronounce, deliver, breathe, let fall, rap out, blurt out.

soliloquize, etc., 589; tell, etc. (*inform*), 527; address, etc., 586; converse, etc., 588.

declaim, hold forth, harangue, stump [*colloq*.], spout, rant; recite, lecture, sermonize, discourse, expatiate.

Adj. **oral,** lingual, phonetic, unwritten, spoken.

eloquent, oratorical, rhetorical, elocutionary, declamatory, grandiloquent.

583. [Imperfect Speech] STAMMERING.—*N*. **inarticulateness;** stammering, hesitation, impediment in one's speech; lisp, drawl, nasal accent; twang; falsetto, brogue.

V. **stammer,** stutter, hesitate, falter.

mumble, mutter, maunder; mince, lisp; jabber, gabble, gibber; splutter, sputter; drawl, mouth; croak.

murder the language, murder the king's English; mispronounce.

Adj. **inarticulate;** stammering, guttural, throaty, nasal; tremulous.

584. LOQUACITY.—*N*. **loquacity,** loquaciousness, effusion; talkativeness, garrulity.

gabble, gab [*colloq*.], jaw [*low*], hot air [*slang*]; jabber, chatter; prate, prattle, twaddle, small talk.

fluency, volubility, flow of words; verbosity, etc. (*diffuseness*), 573; eloquence.

talker; chatterer, chatterbox; babbler, ranter, proser, driveler, gossip, magpie.

V. **be loquacious,** talk glibly, pour forth, prate, palaver, prose, maunder, chatter, blab, gush, prattle, jabber, jaw [*low*], babble, gabble; expatiate, gossip, talk at random, talk nonsense.

Adj. **loquacious,** talkative, garrulous, chattering, chatty, declamatory, fluent, voluble, effusive, glib, flippant.

585. TACITURNITY.—*N.* taciturnity, silence, muteness, curtness; reserve, reticence.

man of few words; Spartan.

V. be silent, keep silence; hold one's tongue, say nothing; render mute.

Adj. silent, mute, mum, still, dumb.

taciturn, laconic, concise, sententious, close, close-mouthed, curt; reserved; reticent.

586. ADDRESS.—*N.* address, allocution; speech, etc., 582; appeal, invocation, salutation, salutatory.

V. address, speak to, accost, apostrophize, appeal to, invoke; hail, salute; call to, halloo.

lecture, preach, harangue, spellbind.

587. RESPONSE, etc., *see* Answer 462.

588. CONVERSATION.—*N.* conversation, colloquy, converse, interlocution, talk, discourse, dialogue, duologue.

chat, tattle, gossip, tittle-tattle; babble.

conference, parley, interview, audience, reception; congress, etc. (*council*), 696; powwow.

debate, palaver, war of words, controversy.

talker, gossip, tattler; chatterer, etc. (*loquacity*), 584; speaker, etc., 582; conversationalist.

V. converse, talk together, hold (*or* carry on, join in, engage in) a conversation; parley; palaver; chat, gossip, tattle; prate, etc., 584.

confer with, discourse with, commune with, talk it over.

Adj. conversational, conversable; chatty, colloquial.

589. SOLILOQUY.—*N.* soliloquy, monologue, apostrophe.

V. soliloquize, monologize, talk to oneself; think aloud, apostrophize.

Written Language

590. WRITING.—*N.* writing, chirography, penmanship; typewriting; manuscript; script; character, letter, etc., 561.

shorthand, stenography, phonography; secret writing, cipher, cryptography.

handwriting; signature, mark, autograph, hand, fist [*colloq.*]; calligraphy.

composition, authorship; lucubration, production, work, screed, article, paper; book, etc., 593; essay, theme, thesis; novel, textbook; poem, book of poems (*or* verse), anthology.

writer, scribe; author, etc., 593; amanuensis, secretary, clerk, penman, copyist; stenographer, typewriter, typist.

V. **write,** pen, typewrite, type [*colloq.*]; copy, engross; transcribe; scribble, scrawl, scratch; note down, write down, record.

compose, indite, draw up, draft, formulate; dictate; inscribe.

Adj. **written,** in writing, in black and white; stenographic.

591. PRINTING.—*N.* printing, typography; type, linotype, monotype; composition, print, letterpress, text, context, matter; copy, impression, proof, galley, galley proof, page proof.

printer, compositor; reader, proofreader, corrector of the press; printer's devil; copyholder, copyeditor.

V. **print;** compose; go to press; publish, issue, bring out.

Adj. **typographical,** printed, in type.

592. CORRESPONDENCE.—*N.* correspondence, letter, epistle, missive, note, post card, postal card; dispatch; bulletin, circular.

correspondent, writer, letter writer.

V. **correspond,** write to, send a letter to; communicate, communicate by writing (*or* letter); circularize, follow up, bombard; reply.

593. BOOK.—*N.* book, booklet; writing, work, volume, tome, tract, treatise, brochure, monograph, pamphlet, libretto; handbook, manual, novel, etc. (*composition*), 590; publication; magazine, periodical.

work of reference, encyclopedia, cyclopedia, dictionary, thesaurus, concordance, anthology, compilation.

writer, author, essayist, contributor; hack writer, hack; journalist, publicist, reporter, correspondent; editor, scribe, etc., 590; playwright, etc., 599; poet, etc., 597.

publisher, bookseller; librarian; bookworm.

bookstore, bookshop, bookseller's shop, publishing house.

library, public library, lending library.

594. DESCRIPTION.—*N.* description, account, statement, report, record; brief, etc. (*abstract*), 596; delineation, sketch, pastel, vignette; monograph; narration, recital, rehearsal, relation.

narrative, history, memoir; annals, etc., (*chronicle*), 551; journal, letters, biography, autobiography, life, adventures.

Fiction: novel, romance, story, tale, short story, anecdote; detective story, fairy tale, fable, parable, allegory.

narrator, historian, biographer, novelist, storyteller, romancer, anecdotist, word painter; writer, etc., 593.

V. **describe,** set forth, picture, portray, characterize, delineate, narrate, relate, recite, recount, romance, tell, report; detail, particularize.

Adj. **descriptive,** graphic, narrative, epic, romantic, historic *or* historical, biographical, autobiographical; traditional, legendary, mythical, fabulous; anecdotic, idealistic; realistic, true to life –

595. DISSERTATION.—*N.* dissertation, treatise, essay, thesis, theme; tract, discourse, memoir, disquisition, lecture, sermon, homily, investigation, study, discussion, exposition.

commentary, review, critique, criticism, article, leader, editorial.

commentator, critic, essayist, publicist, reviewer, leader writer, editor.

V. comment, explain, interpret, criticize, illuminate; treat of (*or* ventilate, discuss, deal with, go into) a subject.

596. COMPENDIUM.—*N.* compendium, abstract, précis, epitome, analysis, digest, brief, condensation, abridgment, abbreviation, etc., 201; summary, draft, minute, note; excerpt, extract; synopsis, textbook, outlines, syllabus, contents, heads, prospectus.

fragments, extracts, cuttings; fugitive pieces, anthology, miscellany, compilation.

recapitulation, résumé, review; symposium.

V. abridge, abstract, epitomize, summarize; abbreviate, etc. (*shorten*), 201; condense, etc. (*compress*), 195.

compile, etc. (*collect*), 72; note down, collect, edit.

recapitulate, review, skim, run over, sum up.

Adj. compendious, synoptic, abridged, analytic *or* analytical.

Adv. in short, in substance, in few words, in a nutshell.

597. POETRY.—*N.* poetry, poetics, poesy. muse, Apollo, Parnassus, inspiration, fire of genius.

poem; epic, ballad, lyric, ode, idyl, eclogue, pastoral, sonnet, elegy; dramatic (*or* didactic, satirical, narrative, lyric) poetry; satire; anthology.

versification, rhyming, prosody; scansion, scanning.
canto, stanza, verse, line, couplet, triplet, quatrain; refrain, chorus, burden; octave, sextet.
verse, rhyme, assonance, alliteration, meter, measure; foot, numbers, rhythm; ictus, beat, accent, accentuation, iambus, iambic, dactyl, spondee, trochee, anapest, etc.; hexameter, pentameter; Alexandrine; blank verse, heroic verse; doggerel.

poet, genius, creator; poet laureate; laureate; bard, lyrist, sonneteer, rhapsodist, satirist, troubadour; minstrel; minnesinger, Meistersinger; jongleur, versifier, rhymer, rhymester, minor poet, poetaster.

V. poetize, sing, write poetry; string verses together, versify, make verses, rhyme.

Adj. poetic *or* poetical; lyric *or* lyrical; tuneful; metrical; elegiac, iambic, dactylic, spondaic, trochaic, anapestic.

598. PROSE.—*N.* prose, prosaicness; poetic prose; narrative, etc., 594.

prose writer, essayist, novelist, etc., 594.

V. prose; write prose (*or* in prose).

Adj. prosaic, prosy, unpoetical, unrhymed, in prose.

599. THE DRAMA.—*N.* the drama, the stage, the theater, the play; theatricals, histrionic art.

play, drama, piece, tragedy, comedy, opera, vaudeville, curtain raiser, interlude, afterpiece, farce, extravaganza, harlequinade, pantomime, burlesque, ballet, spectacle, masque, melodrama; comedy of manners; charade, mystery, miracle play, morality play.

act, scene, tableau, curtain; introduction, prologue, exposition, epilogue; libretto, book, text, prompter's copy.

performance, representation, show [*colloq.*], stage setting, stagecraft; acting; impersonation, stage business; slapstick [*slang*], buffoonery.

theater, playhouse, amphitheater, moving-picture theater, moving pictures, movies [*colloq.*]; puppet show, marionettes, Punch and Judy.

cast, dramatis personae [L.], role, part, character; repertoire, repertory.

actor, player, performer; masker, mime, mimic; star, headliner; comedian, tragedian.

buffoon, mummer, pantomimist, clown; pantaloon, harlequin, columbine; punch.

company, first tragedian, prima donna, leading lady; lead; leading man; comedian, comedienne; juvenile lead, juvenile; villain, heavy lead, heavy, heavy father; ingenue, soubrette; character man, character woman, extra, mute, supernumerary, super [*theat. cant*].

dramatist, playwright, playwriter; dramatic author (*or* writer).
audience, house; orchestra, gallery.

V. act, play, perform; put on the stage, dramatize, stage, produce, set; personate, mimic, enact; rehearse, spout, rant; tread the stage (*or* boards); make one's debut, take a part, star.

Adj. dramatic; theatrical; scenic, histrionic, comic, tragic, farcical, tragicomic, melodramatic, operatic; stagy, spectacular.

Adv. on the stage, on the boards; in the limelight, in the spotlight; before the footlights, before an audience; behind the scenes.

CLASS V

Words Relating to the VOLUNTARY POWERS

I. Individual Volition

600. WILL.—*N.* will, volition, free will; freedom, etc., 748; discretion; choice, inclination, intent, purpose, option, etc. (*choice*), 609; spontaneity, spontaneousness; originality.

determination, etc. (*resolution*), 604; force of will, will power, autocracy, bossiness [*colloq.*].

wish, desire, pleasure, mind, disposition, etc., 602; intention, etc., 620.

V. will, see fit, think fit; determine, etc. (*resolve*), 604; enjoin; settle, etc. (*choose*), 609; volunteer; do what one chooses, etc. (*freedom*), 748; have one's own way; use one's discretion; boss, [*colloq.*]; originate.

Adj. **voluntary,** volitional, willful; free, etc., 748; optional, discretionary; autocratic, dictatorial, bossy [*colloq.*].

willing, etc., 602; unbidden, spontaneous; original.

Adv. **voluntarily,** at will, at pleasure.

of one's own accord, on one's own responsibility; by choice, purposely, intentionally.

601. NECESSITY.—*N.* **necessity,** obligation; compulsion, etc., 744; subjection, etc., 749; stern (*or* dire) necessity, last resort.

instinct, blind impulse, natural tendency (*or* impulse), predetermination.

destiny, fatality, fate, kismet, doom, election, predestination; lot, fortune; fatalism.

Fates, God's will, heaven, will of heaven; stars; planets; wheel of fortune.

V. **be obliged,** be forced, be driven; be fated, be doomed, be destined, have no alternative.

destine, doom, foredoom, devote; predestine, preordain; necessitate; compel, etc., 744.

Adj. **necessary,** needful, etc. (*requisite*), 630; compulsory, etc. (*compel*), 744; inevitable, unavoidable, irresistible, irrevocable, inexorable, binding.

fated; destined, fateful, set apart, devoted, elect.

involuntary, instinctive, automatic, blind, mechanical; unconscious, unwitting, unthinking; unintentional.

Adv. **necessarily,** of necessity, of course; willy-nilly.

602. WILLINGNESS.—*N.* **willingness,** disposition, inclination, liking, turn, propensity, leaning, frame of mind, humor, mood, vein, bent, aptitude.

geniality, cordiality, good will; alacrity, readiness, zeal, enthusiasm, earnestness, eagerness.

assent, etc., 488; compliance, etc., 762.

volunteer, unpaid worker, amateur, nonprofessional.

V. **be willing,** incline, lean to, mind, hold to, cling to; desire, etc., 865; acquiesce, assent, comply with; jump at, catch at; take up, plunge into, have a go at [*colloq.*].

volunteer, offer, proffer.

Adj. **willing,** fain, disposed, inclined, favorable, content, well disposed; ready, forward, earnest, eager, zealous, enthusiastic; bent upon, desirous.

docile, amenable, easily persuaded, facile, easygoing, tractable, genial, gracious, cordial.

voluntary, gratuitous, free, unconstrained, spontaneous, unasked, unforced.

Adv. **willingly,** fain, freely, with pleasure, of one's own accord; graciously, with a good grace, without demur.

603. UNWILLINGNESS.—*N.* unwillingness, indisposition, disinclination, aversion, averseness, reluctance; indifference, etc., 866; backwardness, slowness; obstinacy, etc., 606.

scruple, scrupulousness, delicacy, qualm, shrinking, recoil; hesitation, fastidiousness.

dissent, etc., 489; refusal, etc., 764.

V. **be unwilling,** dislike, etc., 867; demur, stick at, scruple, stickle; hang fire, shirk, slack, recoil, shrink, hesitate; avoid, etc., 623; oppose, etc., 708; dissent, etc., 489; refuse, etc., 764.

Adj. **unwilling,** loath, disinclined, indisposed, averse, reluctant, opposed, adverse, laggard, backward, remiss, slack, indifferent, scrupulous; repugnant, restive; grudging, forced, under compulsion, irreconcilable.

Adv. **unwillingly,** grudgingly, with an ill grace; against one's will, against the grain; under protest.

604. RESOLUTION.—*N.* determination, will, decision, resolution; backbone; clear grit, grit; sand [*slang*]; strength of mind, resolve, firmness, energy, manliness, vigor, resoluteness; zeal, devotion.

self-control, self-mastery, self-command, self-reliance, self-restraint, self-denial.

tenacity, perseverance, etc., 604a; obstinacy, etc., 606; pluck.

V. **resolve,** will, determine, decide, form a resolution, conclude, fix, bring to a crisis, take a decisive step, take upon oneself.

take one's stand, stand firm, insist upon, make a point of, set one's heart upon; stick at nothing, make short work of, not stick at trifles; persevere, etc., 604a.

Adj. **resolved,** determined; strong-willed, strong-minded; resolute, self-possessed, earnest, serious; decided, peremptory, unflinching, firm, iron, game, plucky, tenacious, gritty, indomitable, inexorable, relentless; obstinate, etc., 606; unyielding; grim, stern, inflexible, irrevocable.

Adv. **resolutely,** in earnest, earnestly; on one's mettle, manfully, like a man.

604a. PERSEVERANCE.—*N.* perseverance, continuance, constancy, steadiness, persistence, patience; pertinacity, industry.

grit, bottom, pluck, stamina, backbone, sand [*slang*]; tenacity, staying power, endurance; bulldog courage.

V. **persevere,** persist, hold on, hold out; stick to, cling to, adhere to; keep on, carry on, hold on; bear up, keep up, hold up; plod; continue, die in harness, die at one's post.

Adj. **persevering,** constant; steady, steadfast, unwavering, unfaltering, unflinching, unflagging, plodding; industrious, etc., 682; strenuous, pertinacious, persistent; indomitable, indefatigable.

Adv. **without fail,** through thick and thin, through fire and water; sink or swim, rain or shine, fair or foul.

605. IRRESOLUTION.—*N.* **irresolution,** indecision, indetermination, instability, uncertainty; demur, suspense, hesitation, hesitancy, vacillation, changeableness, fluctuation; caprice, etc., 608; lukewarmness.

fickleness, levity, pliancy, weakness, timidity; cowardice, etc., 862.

waverer, shilly-shally, turncoat, opportunist, timeserver.

V. **be irresolute,** remain neuter; dilly-dally, hesitate, hover, shilly-shally, hem and haw, demur, debate, balance; dally with, coquet with; go halfway, compromise, be afraid.

vacillate, falter, waver, fluctuate, change, alternate, shuffle, palter, shirk, trim.

Adj. **irresolute,** drifting, halfhearted; undecided, undetermined, uncertain, at a loss; fickle, unreliable, irresponsible, unstable; capricious, etc., 608.

weak, feeble-minded, frail, timid, cowardly, pliant.

Adv. **irresolutely,** in faltering accents; off and on.

606. OBSTINACY.—*N.* **obstinacy,** tenacity, cussedness; perseverance, etc., 604*a*; immovability, inflexibility, obduracy, doggedness, stubbornness, self-will, contumacy, perversity; resolution, etc., 604.

bigotry, intolerance, dogmatism; fixed idea, fanaticism, zealotry, infatuation, monomania.

bigot, dogmatist, zealot, fanatic, bitter-ender [*colloq.*]; mule.

V. **be obstinate,** stickle, take no denial, be wedded to an opinion, persist, die hard, not yield an inch, stand out.

Adj. **obstinate,** tenacious, stubborn, obdurate, inflexible, balky; immovable, unchangeable, inexorable, determined, mulish, dogged; sullen, sulky; unmoved.

arbitrary, dogmatic, positive, bigoted, opinionated, stiff-necked, hidebound, unyielding; incorrigible.

willful, self-willed, perverse; ungovernable, wayward, refractory, unruly, headstrong; contumacious; cross-grained.

Adv. **with set jaw;** no surrender.

607. APOSTASY.—*N.* **apostasy,** recantation; renunciation; abjuration, defection, retraction, withdrawal, disavowal, revocation, tergiversation, reversal; backsliding.

turncoat, apostate, renegade, pervert, deserter, backslider, crawfish [*slang*].

timeserver, trimmer, double-dealer; weathercock.

V. **apostatize,** veer round, turn round; change one's mind, abjure, renounce, relinquish, back down, shift one's ground, change sides, go over, recant, retract, revoke, rescind, forswear.

trim, shuffle, blow hot and cold, be on the fence, straddle.

Adj. **changeful,** irresolute, ductile, slippery, trimming, timeserving.

608. CAPRICE.—*N.* **caprice,** fancy, humor, whim, fit, crotchet, quirk, freak, fad, vagary, prank, escapade.

V. **be capricious,** take it into one's head, blow hot and cold, play fast and loose.

Adj. **capricious,** erratic, eccentric, fitful, inconsistent, fanciful, whimsical, crotchety, freakish, wayward, wanton; contrary, captious, unreasonable, arbitrary; fickle, etc. (*irresolute*), 605.

Adv. **by fits,** by fits and starts, without rhyme or reason.

609. CHOICE.—*N.* **choice,** option, selection, pick; discretion, alternative, preference, adoption, decision.

Scylla and Charybdis.

election, poll, ballot, vote, voice, suffrage, plebiscite, referendum; electioneering; voting, elective franchise; ticket; ballot box.

voter, elector, constituent, electorate, constituency.

V. **choose;** elect, make one's choice; make choice of, fix upon, settle, decide, make up one's mind; adopt, take up, embrace, espouse.

vote, poll, hold up one's hand, give a (*or* the) voting sign; divide.

select, pick, cull, glean, winnow; pitch upon, indulge one's fancy; set apart, mark out for.

prefer, fancy, have rather, had (*or* would) as lief; reserve.

Adj. **optional,** discretional, at choice, on approval.

chosen, choice, elect, select, popular; preferential.

Adv. **optionally,** at pleasure, at the option of.

by choice, by preference; in preference; rather, before.

609a. ABSENCE OF CHOICE.—*N.* **no choice;** Hobson's choice; first come first served; necessity, etc., 601.

neutrality, indifference; indecision, etc. (*irresolution*), 605.

V. **be neutral,** have no preference, waive, not vote.

Adj. **neutral,** neuter; indifferent; undecided, etc. (*irresolute*), 605.

610. REJECTION.—*N.* **rejection,** repudiation, exclusion; refusal, etc., 764.

V. **reject,** set (*or* lay) aside, give up; decline, etc. (*refuse*), 764; exclude, except; pluck up, spurn, cast out; repudiate, scout, disclaim, discard.

Adv. **neither,** neither the one nor the other.

611. PREDETERMINATION.—*N.* **predetermination,** predestination, premeditation, foregone conclusion; resolve, project; intention, etc., 620; fate, necessity.

list, schedule, calendar, docket, slate [*pol. cant*], register, roster, poll, muster, draft.

V. **predetermine,** predestine, premeditate, resolve beforehand.

list, schedule, docket, slate, register, poll, empanel, draft.

Adj. **premeditated,** predesigned, prepense [*as,* malice *prepense*], studied, designed, calculated, aforethought; foregone.

well laid, well devised, well weighed; maturely considered; cut-and-dried.

Adv. **deliberately,** with eyes open, in cold blood; intentionally.

612. IMPULSE.—*N.* **impulse,** sudden thought; impromptu, improvisation; inspiration, flash, spurt.

V. **improvise,** extemporize; say what comes uppermost, act on the spur of the moment, rise to the occasion; spurt.

Adj. **extemporaneous,** impulsive, snap, improvised, unpremeditated, unprompted, natural, unguarded; spontaneous.

Adv. **extempore,** extemporaneously; offhand, impromptu.

613. HABIT.—*N.* **habit,** addiction, wont, run, way, matter of course, beaten path, second nature; trick, knack, skill.

custom, use, usage, prescription, practice; prevalence, observance; conventionalism, conventionality, mode, fashion, vogue, etiquette.

rule, standing order, precedent, routine, red tape, rut, groove.

V. **habituate,** inure, harden, season, caseharden; accustom, familiarize; acclimatize.

cling to, adhere to; acquire a habit; follow the beaten track (*or* path), move in a rut.

prevail; come into use, become a habit, take root; grow upon one.

Adj. **habitual,** customary, accustomed, wonted, usual, general, ordinary, common, frequent, everyday, household, familiar, trite, hackneyed, commonplace, conventional, regular, set, stock, established, stereotyped; fixed, rooted, permanent, inveterate, besetting, ingrained, current.

wont; used to, given to, addicted to, in the habit of; seasoned, imbued with, devoted to, wedded to.

Adv. **as usual,** as things go, as the world goes; as you were [*mil.*].

as a rule, for the most part, generally, most frequently.

614. DESUETUDE.—*N.* **desuetude,** disusage; disuse, etc., 678; want of practice.

V. **be unaccustomed,** leave off (*or* break off, shake off, violate) a habit *or* custom; be weaned from; disuse, etc., 678; wear off.

Adj. **unaccustomed,** unused, unwonted, unseasoned, untrained; new, fresh, original; unskilled.

unconventional, unfashionable, unusual; disused, etc., 678.

615. MOTIVE.—*N.* **motive,** reason, ground, call, principle, mainspring, pro and con, reason why; ulterior motive; intention, etc., 620.

inducement, consideration; attraction, loadstone, magnet, magnetism, temptation, enticement, allurement, glamour, witchery; charm, spell; fascination, blandishment, cajolery; seduction.

influence, prompting, dictate, instance; impulse, incitement, press, insistence, instigation; inspiration, persuasion, encouragement, exhortation, advice, solicitation, pull [*slang*].

incentive, stimulus, spur, fillip, whip, goad, provocative, whet.

bribe, lure, sop, decoy, bait, bribery and corruption.

tempter, prompter, instigator, coaxer, wheedler, siren; firebrand.

V. **induce,** move, draw, inspire; put up to [*slang*], prompt; stimulate, rouse, arouse, animate, whet, incite, provoke, instigate, actuate, encourage, advocate.

influence, bias, sway, incline, dispose, predispose; lead, lobby.

persuade, prevail upon, overcome, carry, bring round, conciliate, win (*or* talk) over; enlist; engage; invite, court.

tempt, overpersuade, entice, allure, captivate, fascinate, bewitch, hypnotize, charm, magnetize, wheedle, coax, lure, inveigle.

bribe, tamper with, suborn, grease the palm, corrupt.

enforce, force, impel, propel, whip, lash, goad, spur, prick, urge, egg on, hound on, hurry on.

Adj. **persuasive,** inviting, tempting, suasive, seductive, attractive, fascinating; provocative.

Adv. **because,** therefore, for, by reason of, for the sake of, on account of; out of, from, as, forasmuch as.

615a. ABSENCE OF MOTIVE.—*N.* **absence of motive;** caprice, etc., 608; chance, etc. (*absence of design*), 621.

V. **scruple,** etc. (*be unwilling*), 603; have no motive.

Adj. **aimless,** capricious, without rhyme or reason.

Adv. **capriciously,** out of mere caprice.

616. DISSUASION.—*N.* **dissuasion,** expostulation, remonstrance; deprecation, etc., 766; discouragement, damper, wet blanket.

curb, restraint, constraint, check.

V. **dissuade,** cry out against, remonstrate, expostulate, warn.

disincline, indispose, shake, stagger; discourage, dishearten, disenchant; deter, hold back, restrain, repel, turn aside, damp, cool, chill, blunt, calm, quiet, quench.

Adj. averse, etc. (*unwilling*), 603; repugnant, etc. (*dislike*), 867.

617. [Ostensible motive, ground, or reason] **PLEA.**—*N.* plea, pretext; allegation, excuse, vindication, justification; color; gloss, guise.

pretense, subterfuge, dust thrown in the eye; blind, lame excuse, makeshift, shift.

V. **plead,** allege, excuse, vindicate; color, gloss over, make a pretext of, use as a plea, take one's stand upon; pretend.

Adj. ostensible, alleged, pretended.

Adv. ostensibly; under the plea of, under the pretense of.

618. GOOD.—*N.* good, benefit, advantage; improvement, etc., 658; interest, service, behoof, behalf; commonweal; gain, profit, harvest; boon, etc. (*gift*), 784; good turn, blessing, prize, windfall, godsend, good fortune; happiness, etc., 827; goodness, etc., 648.

V. **benefit,** profit, advantage, serve, help, avail, do good to.

gain, prosper, flourish, thrive.

Adj. commendable, etc., 931; useful, etc., 644; good, beneficial, etc., 648.

Adv. **well,** aright, satisfactorily, favorably, in one's interest.

619. EVIL.—*N.* evil, ill, harm, hurt, mischief, nuisance, drawback, disadvantage; ills that flesh is heir to, mental suffering, pain; bane, etc., 663.

badness, etc., 649; painfulness, etc., 830; evildoer, etc., 913.

blow, buffet, stroke, scratch, bruise, wound, gash, mutilation; mortal blow (*or* wound); damage, loss.

disaster, accident, casualty, mishap, misfortune, calamity, woe, fatal mischief, catastrophe, tragedy, ruin; adversity, etc., 735.

outrage, wrong, injury, foul play; bad turn, disservice, grievance.

V. **harm,** injure, hurt, do disservice to.

Adj. **disastrous;** hurtful, etc., 649; disadvantageous, injurious, harmful.

Adv. **amiss,** wrong, ill; to one's cost.

620. INTENTION.—*N.* intention, intent, purpose; project, etc., 626; undertaking, design, ambition; view, proposal; contemplation.

object, aim, end; drift, tendency; destination, mark, point, goal, target, prey, quarry, game.

decision, determination, resolve; fixed purpose, resolution; ultimatum.

V. **intend,** purpose, design, mean, have in view, bid for, labor for, aspire to, aim at; contemplate, meditate, think of, dream of, talk of; premeditate, destine, propose; project, etc. (*plan*), 626; desire, etc., 865; pursue, etc., 622.

Adj. **intentional,** advised, express, determinate; bound for; disposed, inclined, bent upon, at stake; in prospect.

Adv. **intentionally,** advisedly, wittingly, knowingly, designedly, purposely, on purpose, by design, studiously, pointedly; deliberately.

621. [Absence of purpose] CHANCE.[1]—*N.* chance, etc., 156; lot, destiny, etc., 601; luck; hoodoo [*colloq.*], jinx [*slang*], Jonah, voodoo; wheel of chance, fortune's wheel; mascot.

speculation, venture, random shot, blind bargain, leap in the dark; fluke [*sporting cant*], flier [*slang*]; flutter [*slang*]; futures.

gambling, betting, drawing lots; wager; gamble, risk, stake, bet.

gambler, gamester, speculator; bookmaker, man of the turf.

V. **chance,** etc., 156; toss up, cast (*or* draw) lots; tempt fortune; speculate.

risk, venture, hazard, stake; wager, bet, gamble, game, play for.

Adj. **chance;** fortuitous, etc., 156; unintentional, unintended, accidental; random, undesigned, purposeless.

Adv. **at random,** at a venture, by chance, as it may happen.

622. [Purpose in action] PURSUIT.—*N.* pursuit, prosecution; pursuance, enterprise, undertaking, business, etc., 625; adventure, quest, hobby.

chase, hunt, race, steeplechase; hunting, coursing, sport, shooting, angling, fishing.

pursuer; hunter, huntsman, the field; sportsman, Nimrod; hound.

V. **pursue,** prosecute, follow, shadow; carry on, undertake, engage in, set about, endeavor, seek, trace, aim at, fish, fish for; press on, follow up, take up; go in for.

chase, give chase, stalk, course, hunt, hound.

Adj. **in quest of,** in pursuit, in full cry, on the scent.

623. [Absence of pursuit] AVOIDANCE.—*N.* avoidance, evasion, flight; escape, retreat, recoil, departure.

abstention, abstinence; forbearance; inaction, etc., 681; neutrality.

shirker, slacker [*colloq.*], shirk, quitter, truant; fugitive, refugee, runaway, deserter, renegade; backslider.

V **abstain,** refrain, spare; eschew, keep from, let alone.

avoid, shun, steer (*or* keep) clear of; fight shy of, evade, elude, shirk.

shrink, hang (*or* hold, draw) back; recoil, retire, flinch, shy, dodge, parry.

[1] See note on 156.

beat a retreat; turn tail, take to one's heels; run, run away, cut and run [*colloq.*]; fly, flee, take flight; desert, make off, sneak off, sheer off; slip, play truant, decamp, flit, bolt, abscond; escape, etc., 671; abandon, etc., 624.

Adj. **elusive,** evasive; fugitive, runaway; shy, wild.

624. RELINQUISHMENT.—*N.* **relinquishment,** abandonment; desertion, defection, secession, withdrawal; discontinuance, renunciation, abrogation, resignation, retirement; cession, etc. (*of property*), 782.

V. **relinquish,** give up, abandon, desert, forsake, leave in the lurch; go back on [*colloq.*]; leave, quit, vacate, resign.

renounce, forego, have done with, drop, discard, give up the point (*or* argument), table, table the motion.

625. BUSINESS.—*N.* business, occupation, employment, undertaking, pursuit; affair, concern, matter, case.

task, work, job, chore, errand, commission, mission, charge, duty; avocation, hobby.

function, part, role, capacity, province, department, sphere, field, line; walk, round, routine; race, career.

office, place, position, post, incumbency, living; situation, berth, billet, appointment, engagement; undertaking, etc., 676.

vocation, calling, profession; cloth, faculty; craft, handicraft; trade.

V. **occupy oneself with;** employ oneself in *or* upon; undertake, etc., 676; turn one's hand to; be engaged in, be occupied with, be at work on; have in hand; ply one's trade.

officiate, serve, act, do duty; discharge (*or* perform) the duties of; hold (*or* fill) an office; hold a portfolio.

Adj. **businesslike;** workaday; professional, official, functional; busy.

in hand, on hand, afoot, on foot, going on; acting.

626. PLAN.—*N.* plan, scheme, design, project, proposal, proposition, suggestion; resolution, motion; organization, arrangement, system.

outline, sketch, skeleton, draft, rough draft, copy; forecast, program, prospectus; order of the day, memoranda, platform, plank, slate, ticket; role; policy.

contrivance, invention, expedient, receipt, nostrum, artifice, device; stratagem, trick; shift.

measure, step; stroke, master stroke; trump, trump card.

intrigue, cabal, plot, conspiracy, machination; mine.

promoter, designer, organizer, founder, projector; author, artist.

V. **plan,** scheme, design, frame, contrive, project, forecast, sketch, devise, invent, hatch, concoct; hit upon; map out, shape out a course; prepare, etc., 673.

systematize, organize; cast, recast, arrange; digest, mature.

plot, intrigue; counterplot, mine, countermine, lay a train.

Adj. under consideration, on the carpet, on the table.

627. METHOD. [Path]—*N.* method, way, manner, form, mode, fashion, guise; procedure.

path, road, route, course, tack; trajectory, orbit, track, beat.

means of access, entrance, approach, passage, cloister, covered way, lobby, corridor, aisle; alley, lane, avenue, artery, channel; gateway, door; secret passage; covert way.

roadway, thoroughfare; highway, turnpike, state road, causeway, king's highway; parkway, boulevard, speedway; walk, footpath, pathway, pavement, sidewalk, byroad, crossroad; railroad, railway, trolley track, tramway; towpath; street, etc. (*abode*), 189; bridge, viaduct.

Adv. how; in what way, in what manner; by what mode; so, thus; anyhow.

628. MID-COURSE.—*N.* mid-course, middle way, middle course; moderation; mean, etc., 29; golden mean.

compromise, half measures, neutrality.

V. keep the golden mean, steer a middle course; go straight. compromise, make a compromise, concede half, go halfway.

Adj. neutral, average, even; impartial, moderate; straight.

Adv. in the mean; in moderation.

629. CIRCUIT.—*N.* circuit, roundabout way, digression, detour, loop, winding.

V. go round about, make a circuit, make a detour; meander, deviate.

Adj. circuitous, indirect, roundabout; zigzag.

Adv. in a roundabout way; by an indirect course.

630. REQUIREMENT.—*N.* requirement, need, wants, necessities; stress, exigency, pinch, case of need; desideratum; necessity, indispensability, urgency.

requisition, demand, request, claim; run, call for.

charge, command, injunction, precept, mandate, order, ultimatum.

V. require, need, want, stand in need of, lack; desire, etc., 865.

Adj. necessary, requisite, needful, imperative, essential, indispensable, called for; in demand, in request.

urgent, exigent, pressing, instant, crying.

Adv. of necessity; at a pinch.

631. INSTRUMENTALITY.—*N.* instrumentality; aid, etc., 707; subservience, mediation, intervention; pull [*slang*], influence; medium, intermediary, vehicle, tool, agency; instrument, expedient; means, etc., 632.

minister, handmaid, servant; friend at court, go-between.

V. **mediate,** minister, intervene, come (*or* go) between; interpose; use one's influence, be instrumental; subserve.

Adj. **instrumental;** useful, etc., 644; subservient, serviceable; intermediary, intermediate, intervening; conducive.

Adv. **through,** by, whereby, thereby, hereby; by the agency of, by dint of; by (*or* in) virtue of; by means of.

somehow, by fair means or foul; somehow or other; by hook or by crook.

632. MEANS.—*N.* means, resources, wherewithal, ways and means; capital, etc. (*money*), 800; revenue, income; stock in trade, provision, reserve, remnant, last resource, appliances, conveniences; expedients, wheels within wheels; sheet anchor; aid, etc., 707; medium, etc., 631.

V. **provide the wherewithal,** find (*or* possess) means, have powerful friends, have friends at court; have something to draw on.

Adj. **instrumental,** etc., 631; **mechanical,** etc., 633.

trustworthy, reliable, efficient; honorable, etc. (*upright*), 939.

Adv. **by means of,** with; wherewith, herewith, therewith; wherewithal.

633. INSTRUMENT.—*N.* **instrument,** organ, tool, implement, utensil, machine, engine, lathe, gin, mill; motor; machinery, mechanism.

equipment, gear, tackle, tackling; rigging, apparatus, appliances; plant, harness, trappings, fittings, accouterments, appointments, furniture, upholstery; chattels; paraphernalia.

mechanical powers; leverage; fulcrum, lever, crow, crowbar, jimmy, marline spike, handspike; arm, limb, wing; wheel and axle; wheelwork, clockwork; wheels within wheels; pinion, crank, winch, capstan, wheel, flywheel, turbine, water wheel, pump; pulley, crane, derrick; inclined plane; wedge; screw; jack; spring, mainspring; loom, shuttle, jenny.

handle, hilt, haft, shaft, shank; tiller, rudder, helm; treadle, pedal.

Adj. **mechanical;** propulsive, driving, hoisting, elevating, lifting.

useful, labor-saving, ingenious; well made, well fitted, well equipped.

634. SUBSTITUTE.—*N.* **substitute,** etc., 147; proxy, alternate, understudy; deputy, etc., 759.

635. MATERIALS.—*N.* **material,** raw material, stuff, stock, staple; ore.

636. STORE.—*N.* **store,** accumulation, hoard; stock, fund, mine, vein, lode, quarry; spring, fount, fountain; well; orchard, garden, farm; stock in trade, supply; treasure; reserve, reserve fund, savings.

crop, harvest, vintage, yield, product, gleaning.

storehouse, storeroom, store closet; depository, depot, cache, warehouse, magazine; garner, granary, grain elevator, silo; safe-deposit vault; armory; arsenal; stable, barn.

reservoir, cistern, tank, pond, millpond; gasometer.

V. store, put by, lay by, set by, stow away, store up, hoard up, treasure up, lay up, save, preserve, save up, bank; cache, deposit; stow, stack, load; harvest; accumulate, amass, hoard.

reserve; keep back, hold back; husband, husband one's resources.

Adj. in store, in reserve, spare, supernumerary.

Adv. for a rainy day, for a nest egg, to fall back upon; on deposit.

637. PROVISION.—*N.* provision, supply; grist, resources, etc. (*means*), 632; groceries, purveyance, commissariat.

caterer, purveyor, commissary, quartermaster, steward, purser, housekeeper; innkeeper, landlord, mine host; grocer, fishmonger, provision merchant.

V. provide, make provision, lay in, lay in a stock (*or* store).

supply, furnish; cater, victual, provision, purvey, forage; stock, make good, replenish, fill; recruit, feed.

store, etc., 636; conserve, keep, preserve, lay by, gather into barns.

638. WASTE.—*N.* consumption, expenditure, exhaustion; dispersion, leakage, loss, wear and tear, waste; prodigality.

V. consume, spend, expend, use, swallow up; exhaust, spill, drain, empty, deplete; disperse, etc., 73; waste; squander.

labor in vain, etc. (*useless*), 645; cast pearls before swine; waste powder and shot.

run to waste; ebb, leak, melt away, run dry, dry up.

Adj. wasted, gone to waste, useless, run to seed; dried up.

wasteful, etc. (*prodigal*), 818; penny wise and pound foolish.

639. SUFFICIENCY.—*N.* sufficiency, adequacy, enough, wherewithal, competence.

abundance, plenitude, plenty, copiousness, amplitude, profusion, full measure; fill; luxuriance, affluence, fat of the land.

rich man, etc. (*wealth*), 803; financier, banker, plutocrat.

V. suffice, do, just do [*both colloq.*], satisfy, pass muster; have enough, have one's fill.

abound, teem, flow, stream, rain, shower down; pour, pour in; swarm; bristle with.

Adj. sufficient, enough, adequate, up to the mark, commensurate, competent, satisfactory; ample, plenty, plentiful, plenteous; copious, abundant; replete, unstinted, inexhaustible.

rich, affluent, etc. (*wealthy*), 803; luxuriant, etc. (*fertile*), 168.

Adv. without stint; to the good.

640. INSUFFICIENCY.—*N.* **insufficiency,** inadequacy, incompetence, deficiency, imperfection, shortcoming; paucity, stint, bare subsistence; poverty, etc., 804.

scarcity, dearth; want, need, lack, poverty, starvation, famine, drought.

dole, mite, pittance; short allowance; half rations.

depletion, emptiness, vacancy; ebb tide; low water; insolvency, etc. (*nonpayment*), 808.

poor man, pauper, etc., 804; bankrupt.

V. **want,** lack, need, require; be in want, etc. (*poor*), 804; live from hand to mouth.

impoverish, drain, drain of resources; stint, etc., 819.

Adj. **insufficient,** inadequate, too little, not enough; incompetent, perfunctory, deficient, wanting; imperfect; ill-furnished, ill-provided, ill-stored.

short of, out of, destitute of, devoid of, bereft of, slack, at a low ebb; empty, vacant, bare; dry, drained.

unprovided, unsupplied, unfurnished; unfed; empty-handed.

meager, poor, thin, spare, stinted, starved, emaciated, undernourished, underfed, half-starved, famine-stricken, famished.

scarce, scant, not to be had, scurvy, stingy, etc., 819; at the end of one's tether; without resources, in want.

Adv. in default of, for want of; failing.

641. REDUNDANCE.—*N.* **redundance,** too much, too many, superabundance, superfluity, exuberance, profuseness; profusion, plenty, repletion, plethora, glut, congestion, surfeit, overdose, oversupply, overflow; excess, surplus, remainder.

V. **superabound,** overabound, swarm; bristle with, overflow, run over; run riot; overrun, overstock, overdose, overfeed, overload, overburden, overwhelm, overshoot the mark; gorge, glut, load, drench, inundate, deluge, flood; send (*or* carry) coals to Newcastle.

cloy, choke, suffocate; pile up, lay on thick, lavish.

Adj. **redundant,** turgid; exuberant, inordinate, superabundant, excess, overmuch, replete, profuse, lavish, prodigal; exorbitant, extravagant, overflowing; gorged, stuffed.

superfluous, unnecessary, needless, over and above, supernumerary, spare, duplicate, supererogatory.

Adv. **over and above;** over much, too much; too far; over, too; over head and ears, over one's head; up to one's eyes; extra.

642. IMPORTANCE.—*N.* **importance,** consequence, moment, prominence, consideration, mark; weight, influence; value, usefulness; greatness, etc., 31; superiority, etc., 33; notability.

salient point, outstanding feature; cardinal point: substance, gist, sum and substance, cream, salt, core, kernel, heart, nucleus; key, keynote; keystone.

import, significance, concern; emphasis, interest.

gravity, seriousness, solemnity; pressure, urgency, stress.

V. **be important,** be somebody, be something; import, signify, matter, carry weight; come to the front, lead the way, take the lead.

value, care for, set store upon *or* by.

accentuate, emphasize, lay stress on; mark, underline, underscore.

Adj. **important,** of importance, momentous, material, considerable, weighty, influential, notable, prominent, salient, signal; memorable, remarkable; stirring, eventful.

grave, serious, earnest, grand, solemn, impressive, commanding, imposing.

urgent, pressing, critical, crucial, instant.

foremost, principal, leading, chief, main, prime, primary; capital; superior, etc., 33; marked, rare; paramount, essential, vital, radical, cardinal.

significant, telling, trenchant, emphatic, pregnant.

Adv. **in the main;** above all, in the first place, before everything else.

643. UNIMPORTANCE.—*N.* **unimportance,** insignificance, nothingness, immateriality.

triviality, levity, frivolity, paltriness, smallness, matter of indifference; no object.

nothing, small (*or* trifling) matter; joke, jest, snap of the fingers, fudge, fiddlestick, incident, mere nothing, nonentity.

toy, plaything, gewgaw, bauble, trinket, bagatelle, kickshaw, knickknack.

trumpery, trash, rubbish, stuff, frippery; chaff, dross, froth, scum, bubble, smoke; weed; refuse.

trifle, straw, pin, fig, button, feather, continental, jot, mote, rap, old song; cent, red cent; picayune [*colloq.*].

nine days' wonder, flash in the pan, much ado about nothing, tempest in a teapot.

minutiae, details, minor details.

V. **be unimportant,** not matter, matter (*or* signify) little, not matter a straw.

make light of, catch at straws, make mountains out of molehills.

Adj. **unimportant,** immaterial; nonessential, unessential, irrelevant; indifferent, mediocre, passable, fair, tolerable, commonplace; mere, common, ordinary, insignificant.

trifling, trivial; slight, slender, light, airy, flimsy, idle, shallow, weak, powerless, frivolous, petty, finical.

paltry, poor, pitiful, contemptible, puerile; sorry, mean, meager, shabby, miserable, wretched, vile, niggardly, scurvy, beggarly, worthless, two-by-four [*colloq.*], cheap, trashy, catchpenny, gimcrack, trumpery; one-horse [*colloq.*]

Adv. rather, somewhat, fairly, fairly well, tolerably.

644. UTILITY.—*N.* utility, usefulness, efficacy, efficiency, adequacy; helpfulness, service, use, help, aid, applicability, subservience; value, worth, productiveness, utilization.

commonweal, public good; utilitarianism.

V. avail, serve, conduce, tend, answer (*or* serve) one's turn; benefit, bear fruit, profit, remunerate.

act a part, etc. (*action*), 680; discharge a function, render a service; bestead, stand one in good stead; help, etc., 707.

Adj. useful, of use, serviceable, subservient, conducive, helpful.

advantageous, beneficial, profitable, gainful, remunerative, valuable; invaluable, beyond price; prolific.

adequate; efficient, efficacious; effective, effectual.

applicable, available, ready, handy, at hand, commodious, adaptable.

645. INUTILITY.—*N.* inutility, uselessness, inefficacy, futility; ineptitude, inadequacy, unfitness; inefficiency, incompetence, unskillfulness, labor in vain; worthlessness; triviality, etc., 643.

rubbish, junk, lumber, litter, odds and ends, shoddy; rags, leavings, dross, trash, refuse, sweepings, offscourings, waste, rubble, debris; chaff, stubble, dregs, weeds, tares.

V. labor in vain; seek (*or* strive) after impossibilities; use vain efforts, beat the air, pour water into a sieve, bay at the moon; cast pearls before swine, carry coals to Newcastle.

render useless, dismantle, dismast, disqualify; disable, hamstring, cripple, lame; spike guns, clip the wings; put out of gear.

Adj. useless, inutile, futile, unavailing, bootless; inoperative, inadequate, inept, inefficient, ineffectual, incompetent.

worthless, valueless, unsalable; not worth a straw, good for nothing, dear at any price; vain, empty, inane; gainless, profitless, fruitless; unserviceable, unprofitable; ill-spent; effete, barren, sterile, impotent, worn out, unproductive; uncalled for; unnecessary, unneeded, superfluous.

646. EXPEDIENCE.—*N.* expedience, desirability, fitness, propriety, utility, advantage, opportunity; opportunism; pragmatism.

V. be expedient, suit, befit; suit (*or* befit) the occasion.

Adj. expedient, desirable, advisable, acceptable; convenient; worth while, meet; fit, fitting, due, proper, eligible, seemly, becoming, befitting; opportune, advantageous, etc., 644; suitable.

practical, practicable, effective, pragmatic, pragmatical.

Adv. in the nick of time; in the right place.

647. INEXPEDIENCE.—*N.* inexpedience, undesirability, impropriety, unfitness, inutility, disadvantage, inconvenience, inadvisability.

V. be inexpedient, come amiss, embarrass, put to inconvenience.

Adj. inexpedient, undesirable; inadvisable, ill-advised, unsuitable, troublesome, objectionable, ineligible, inadmissible, inconvenient, discommodious, disadvantageous; inappropriate, unfit; unsatisfactory, unprofitable, inept, inopportune, improper, unseemly.

clumsy, awkward; cumbrous, cumbersome, lumbering, unwieldy, hulky.

648. [Good qualities] GOODNESS.—*N.* goodness, excellence, merit; beneficence, benevolence, etc., 906; virtue, etc., 944; value, worth, price.

perfection, quintessence; superiority, etc., 33; prime, flower, cream, elite, pick, A 1 *or* A number 1 [*colloq.*], pick of the crop, salt of the earth; prodigy, wonder; gem of the first water, treasure, one in a thousand.

good man, etc., 948.

V. be beneficial, produce (*or* do) good, profit, benefit, improve, be the making of, make a man of; do a good turn, confer an obligation.

be good, be pure gold, look good to [*colloq.*]; excel, transcend, stand the test; pass muster, pass an examination.

vie, challenge, comparison, emulate, rival.

Adj. beneficial, valuable, of value; useful, etc., 644; advantageous, profitable; edifying, salutary.

harmless, innocuous, innocent, inoffensive.

favorable; propitious, etc. (*hope-giving*), 858; fair.

good, excellent; better; superior, etc., 33; above par; nice, fine; genuine, etc. (*true*), 494.

choice, best, select, picked, elect, rare, priceless, matchless, peerless, unequaled, unparalleled, inimitable, crack [*colloq.*], crackajack [*slang*], gilt-edge [*colloq.*]; superfine, of the first water; first-rate, first-class; high-wrought, exquisite, admirable, capital, estimable, precious, priceless, invaluable, inestimable.

satisfactory, up to the mark, unexceptionable, unobjectionable.

Adv. for one's benefit.

649. [Bad qualities] BADNESS.—*N.* badness, hurtfulness, virulence; abomination, pestilence, guilt, depravity, vice, etc., 945; malignity, malevolence.

bane, etc., 663; plague spot, evil star, ill-wind; hoodoo [*colloq.*], jinx [*slang*], Jonah; snake in the grass, skeleton in the closet; thorn in the flesh.

ill-treatment, annoyance, molestation, abuse, oppression, persecution, outrage, misusage, scathe, injury.

bad man, etc., 949; evildoer, etc., 913.

V. hurt, harm, scathe, injure; pain, etc., 830.

wrong, aggrieve, oppress, persecute, trample upon; overburden, weigh down; victimize.

maltreat, abuse; ill-use, ill-treat; buffet, bruise, scratch, maul; smite, molest, do violence; stab, pierce.

Adj. hurtful, harmful, baneful, baleful, injurious, deleterious, detrimental, noxious, pernicious, mischievous, mischief-making, malignant, prejudicial; oppressive, burdensome, onerous; malign.

corrupting, virulent, venomous, corrosive; poisonous, deadly, destructive.

bad, ill, arrant, dreadful; horrid, horrible; dire; rank, foul, rotten.

unsatisfactory, indifferent, deteriorated, below par, imperfect, ill-conditioned.

deplorable, wretched, sad, grievous, lamentable, pitiful, pitiable, woeful.

evil, wrong; depraved, wicked, etc., 945; shocking; reprehensible.

hateful, abominable, vile, base, villainous, detestable, execrable, cursed, accursed, damnable, diabolic.

Adv. to one's cost; where the shoe pinches.

650. PERFECTION.—*N.* perfection; paragon, pink, pink (*or* acme) of perfection.

model, standard, pattern, mirror.

masterpiece, master stroke, prize winner, prize; superexcellence.

V. perfect, bring to perfection, ripen, mature; consummate, crown, put the finishing touch to (*or* upon); complete.

Adj. perfect, faultless, immaculate, spotless, impeccable, unblemished, sound, scathless, intact; consummate, finished.

best, model, standard; inimitable, unparalleled, beyond all praise.

Adv. clean as a whistle; with a finish; to the limit.

651. IMPERFECTION.—*N.* imperfection; deficiency, inadequacy, defection, badness, immaturity.

fault, defect, weak point; screw loose; flaw, taint, blemish, weakness, shortcoming, drawback.

V. be imperfect, have a defect, lie under a disadvantage; not pass muster, fall short.

Adj. imperfect, deficient, defective, faulty, unsound, tainted, out of order; warped, injured; inadequate, crude, incomplete, below par.

indifferent, middling, ordinary, mediocre, average, tolerable, fair, passable; decent; not bad, not amiss; admissible, bearable.

inferior, secondary, second-rate, one-horse [*colloq.*]; two-by-four [*colloq.*].

Adv. to a limited extent, pretty, moderately, considering.

652. CLEANNESS.—*N.* cleanness, purity, purification, purgation; ablution, lavation; disinfection, drainage, sewerage.

bath, bathroom, swimming pool, swimming bath, public bath, baths, bathhouse, lavatory; laundry, washhouse.

cleaner, washerwoman, laundress, laundryman, washerman; scavenger, sweeper; street sweeper, white wing [*local*]; dustman.

brush; broom, vacuum cleaner, carpet sweeper; mop, swab, hose.

cathartic, purgative, aperient, laxative.

V. **clean,** cleanse; rinse, flush, mop, sponge, scour, swab, scrub; wash, lave, launder; purify; purge, expurgate, clarify, refine.

strain, separate, filter, filtrate, drain; percolate.

sift, winnow, sieve, bolt, screen, riddle; pick, weed.

comb, rake, scrape, rasp; card.

sweep, brush, brush up, rout out; clean house, spruce up [*colloq.*].

disinfect, fumigate, ventilate, deodorize; whitewash.

Adj. **clean,** cleanly, pure, immaculate, spotless, stainless, unspotted, unsoiled, unsullied, untainted, sweet.

neat, spruce, tidy, trim, cleaned.

653. UNCLEANNESS.—*N.* uncleanness, impurity; defilement, contamination, abomination; taint.

decay, putrefaction; corruption; mold, mildew, dry rot, caries [*med.*].

squalor, squalidness, slovenliness.

dirt, filth, soil, slop; dust, smoke, soot, smudge, smut, grime.

dregs, grounds, lees, sediment, heeltap; dross, ashes, cinders; scum, froth.

sty, pigsty, lair, den, Augean stable, sink of corruption; slum, rookery.

mud, mire, quagmire, silt, slime, slush.

V. **rot,** putrefy, fester, rankle, reek; mold, molder, go bad.

soil, smoke, tarnish, spot, smear; daub, blot, blur, smudge, smutch, smirch; drabble, besmear, befoul, splash, stain, sully.

pollute, defile, debase, contaminate, taint, corrupt.

Adj. **unclean,** dirty, filthy, grimy, soiled, dusty, smutty, sooty; mussy [*colloq.*].

uncleanly, slovenly, slatternly, untidy, frowzy, sluttish, unkempt, unwashed, squalid.

offensive, nasty, coarse, foul, impure, abominable, beastly, reeky, fetid; moldy, musty, rancid, bad, touched, rotten, corrupt, tainted, putrid; gory, bloody.

654. HEALTH.—*N.* **health,** sanity; soundness, vigor; good (*or* perfect, excellent, robust) health; bloom, convalescence, strength, poise.

V. **be in health,** bloom, flourish, enjoy good health.

return to health; recover, etc., 660; get better, convalesce, be convalescent, recruit; restore to health, cure.

Adj. **healthy,** healthful, in health, well, sound, whole, strong, blooming, hearty, hale, fresh, green, florid, hardy, robust, vigorous, in fine fettle; chipper [*colloq.*].

uninjured, unscathed, unmarred, without a scratch, safe and sound.

655. DISEASE.—*N.* **disease;** illness, sickness; infirmity, ailment, indisposition; complaint, disorder, malady, loss of health, delicacy, delicate health, invalidism, malnutrition, want of nourishment; prostration, decline, collapse, decay.

visitation, attack, seizure, stroke, fit, epilepsy, apoplexy, palsy, paralysis; shock; shell shock.

taint, virus, pollution, infection, contagion; epidemic, plague, pestilence.

Science of disease: pathology, therapeutics; diagnostics, diagnosis.

V. **ail,** suffer, be affected with, droop, flag, languish, sicken, pine, dwindle; waste away, fail, lose strength, be laid by the heels; lie helpless.

Adj. **sick,** ill, not well, indisposed, ailing, squeamish, poorly, seedy [*colloq.*], laid up, confined, bedridden, in hospital, on the sick list; out of health, out of sorts [*colloq.*], under the weather [*colloq.*]; valetudinary.

sickly, infirm, unsound, unhealthy, weakly, drooping, flagging, lame, halt, crippled, halting.

diseased, morbid, tainted, poisoned, septic; mangy, leprous, cankered; rotten, withered; palsied, paralytic; consumptive, tubercular, tuberculous.

656. HEALTHINESS.—*N.* **healthiness,** wholesomeness; healthfulness, salubrity.

Preservation of health: hygiene, pure air, exercise, nourishment, tonic; immunity; sanitarium, sanatorium.

V. **be salubrious,** make for health, conduce to health; be good for, agree with.

Adj. **healthy,** healthful; salubrious, salutary, wholesome, sanitary, prophylactic; benign, bracing, tonic, invigorating, nutritious; hygienic.

innocuous, innocent; harmless, uninjurious, immune.

657. UNHEALTHINESS.—*N.* **unhealthiness,** plague spot; malaria, insalubrity; contagion; poisonousness.

V. **be unhealthy,** disagree with; shorten one's days.

Adj. **unhealthy,** insalubrious, unwholesome, noxious, noisome; pestiferous, pestilential; virulent, venomous, poisonous, septic, toxic, deadly.

infectious, contagious, catching, communicable, epidemic, sporadic, endemic; epizootic [*of animals*].

658. IMPROVEMENT.—*N.* **improvement,** amelioration, betterment; recovery, mend, amendment, emendation; advancement, advance, promotion, preferment, elevation, increase.

cultivation, culture, march of intellect, civilization.

reform, reformation; revision, radical reform; correction, refinement, elaboration; purification, repair.

reformer, progressive, radical.

V. **improve,** mend, amend, better, ameliorate, relieve; correct, repair, restore.

improve upon; rectify; enrich, mellow, elaborate, fatten.

refresh, revive; invigorate, strengthen, recruit, renew, revivify, freshen.

promote, cultivate, advance, forward, enhance, bring forward, foster.

revise, edit, review, make corrections, make improvements.

reform, remodel, reorganize, reclaim, civilize, lift, uplift, inspire.

Adj. **better,** better off, all the better for; improving, progressive, improved.

corrigible, improvable, curable.

Adv. **on consideration,** on reconsideration, on second thought.

659. DETERIORATION.—*N.* **deterioration,** debasement; wane, ebb, recession, retrogradation, decrease.

degeneracy, degeneration, degradation, depravation, depravity, demoralization.

injury, damage, loss, detriment, harm, impairment, outrage, havoc, inroad, ravage, vitiation, discoloration, pollution, poisoning, contamination, canker, corruption, adulteration, alloy.

decline, declension, declination; decadence, falling off; senility, decrepitude.

decay, dilapidation, wear and tear, erosion, corrosion, rottenness; moth and rust, dry rot, blight, atrophy.

V. **deteriorate,** degenerate, fall off, wane, ebb; retrograde, decline, droop, run to seed *or* waste, lapse, break down, crack, shrivel, fade, wither, molder, rot, rankle, decay, go bad; rust, crumble, shake, totter, perish.

corrupt, taint, infect, contaminate, poison, envenom, canker, blight, rot, pollute, defile, vitiate, debase, deprave, degrade; alloy, adulterate, tamper with, prejudice; pervert, demoralize, brutalize.

embitter, exasperate, irritate.

injure, impair, damage, harm, hurt, spoil, mar, despoil, waste; overrun, ravage, pillage.

wound, stab, pierce, maim, lame, cripple, hamstring, mangle, mutilate, disfigure, blemish, deface, warp.

Adj. deteriorated, unimproved, injured, degenerate, imperfect; battered, weathered, weather-beaten, stale, dilapidated, faded, worn, wasted, wilted, shabby, threadbare, frayed.

decayed, moth-eaten, worm-eaten, mildewed, rusty, moldy, seedy [*colloq.*], timeworn, effete, crumbling, moldering, rotten, cankered, blighted, tainted; decrepit, broken-down, worn-out, used up [*colloq.*].

stagnant, backward, unprogressive.

Adv. on the downgrade, on the downward track; beyond hope.

660. RESTORATION.—*N.* restoration, replacement, rehabilitation, reconstruction, reproduction, renovation, renewal, revival, resuscitation, reanimation, reorganization; redemption, restitution, relief, redress, retrieval, reclamation, recovery, convalescence, resumption.

renaissance, renascence, rebirth, new birth, regeneration, regeneracy, resurrection.

repair, repairing, reparation, mending; recruiting.

mender, repairer, tinker, cobbler.

V. recover, rally, revive; come to, come round, come to oneself; pull through, weather the storm, be oneself again; get well, survive, reappear.

restore, put back, reinstate, replace, rehabilitate, re-establish, reconstruct, rebuild, reorganize, convert, recondition, renew, renovate; regenerate; rejuvenate.

redeem, reclaim, recover, retrieve; rescue, etc. (*deliver*), 672.

cure, heal, remedy, doctor, bring round, set on one's legs.

resuscitate, revive, reanimate, revivify, reinvigorate, refresh.

repair, mend, put in repair, retouch, tinker, cobble, patch up, darn; stanch, calk, splice.

Adj. restored, convalescent, rejuvenated, renascent.

restorative, recuperative, curative, remedial.

restorable, remediable, retrievable, curable.

661. RELAPSE.—*N.* relapse, lapse; falling back, retrogradation; deterioration, etc., 659; backsliding.

V. relapse, lapse, fall (*or* slip) back, have a relapse, be overcome, be overtaken, yield again to, fall again into, return, retrograde.

Adj. backsliding, retrograde.

662. REMEDY.—*N.* remedy, help, redress, febrifuge; antipoison, antidote, emetic; stimulant, tonic; prophylactic, antiseptic, germicide, disinfectant; restorative; specific; cure, sovereign remedy, panacea.

materia medica, pharmacy, pharmaceutics; pharmacopoeia.

narcotic, opium, morphine, cocaine, hashish, dope [*slang*]; sedative.

physic, medicine, simples, drug, potion, draft, dose, pill, medicament; recipe, receipt, prescription; patent medicine, nostrum; elixir, balm, balsam, cordial.

salve, ointment, oil, lenitive, lotion, embrocation, liniment.

treatment, regimen, diet; dietary, dietetics; operation, the knife [*colloq.*], surgical operation; major operation.

healing art, practice of medicine, therapeutics; allopathy, homeopathy, osteopathy, eclecticism, surgery; faith cure, faith healing, mind cure, psychotherapy, psychotherapeutics; vocational therapy; dentistry.

hospital, surgery, infirmary, clinic, sanitarium, sanatorium; springs, baths, spa; asylum, home; Red Cross; ambulance.

dispensary, drugstore.

doctor, physician, medical man, general practitioner; specialist, consultant; surgeon.

intern, anesthetist, aurist, oculist, dentist, dental surgeon; osteopath, osteopathist; nurse, sister, nursing sister; apothecary, druggist, pharmacist, pharmaceutical chemist, Hippocrates, Galen; masseur (*fem.* masseuse), rubber.

V. **apply a remedy,** doctor [*colloq.*], dose, physic, nurse, minister to, attend, dress the wounds; relieve, palliate, heal, cure, remedy, restore.

Adj. **remedial,** restorative, corrective, palliative, healing; sanatory, sanative; prophylactic; medical, medicinal; therapeutic, surgical; tonic, sedative, lenitive; allopathic, homeopathic, eclectic; aperient, laxative, cathartic, purgative; septic; aseptic, antiseptic.

dietetic, dietary, alimentary; nutritious, nutritive; digestive, digestible.

663. BANE.—*N.* **bane,** curse, thorn in the flesh; bête noir [F.], bugbear; evil, scourge; fungus, mildew; dry rot; canker, cancer; poison, virus, venom; stench, fetor, poison gas.

sting, fang, thorn, bramble, brier, nettle.

Science of poisons: toxicology.

Adj. baneful, poisonous, etc. (*unwholesome*), 657.

664. SAFETY.—*N.* **safety,** security, surety, impregnability, invulnerability, escape, means of escape; safeguard, palladium; sheet anchor; rock, tower.

guardianship, wardship, wardenship; tutelage, custody, safekeeping, protection; auspices.

protector, guardian; warden, warder: preserver, lifesaver, custodian, duenna, chaperon.

safe-conduct, escort, convoy; guard, shield, guardian angel; tutelary deity (*or* saint).

watchman, patrolman, policeman, police officer, officer [*collog.*]; cop, copper [*both slang*], bluecoat [*collog.*], constable; detective, spotter [*slang*]; sheriff, deputy; sentinel, sentry, scout.

armed force, garrison, lifeguard, state guard, militia, regular army, navy; volunteer; marine, etc., 726; battleship, man-of-war, etc., 726.

judge, justice, judiciary, magistrate, justice of the peace.

V. protect, watch over, take care of, preserve, cover, screen, shelter, shroud, flank, ward, guard; defend, take precautions.

escort, support, accompany, convoy.

watch, mount guard, patrol, scout, spy.

Adj. safe, secure, sure, on terra firma [L.]; on the safe side; undercover, under lock and key; out of danger, protected; at anchor, high and dry, above-water; safe and sound.

snug, seaworthy, watertight, weatherproof, waterproof, fireproof; bombproof, shellproof.

defensible, tenable, proof against, invulnerable, unassailable, impregnable.

guardian, tutelary, protective.

Adv. with impunity.

665. DANGER.—*N.* danger, peril, insecurity, jeopardy, risk, hazard, venture, precariousness, instability; exposure, vulnerability, vulnerable point, heel of Achilles; forlorn hope.

Sense of danger: apprehension, etc., 860.

V. endanger, expose to danger, imperil, jeopardize, beard the lion in his den; sail too near the wind.

risk, hazard, venture, adventure, stake, set at hazard; run the gantlet.

Adj. dangerous, hazardous, perilous, unsafe, unprotected, insecure.

defenseless, guardless, unsheltered, unshielded; vulnerable, exposed; at bay.

precarious, critical, ticklish; slippery, between Scylla and Charybdis, between two fires; under fire; at stake, in question.

unsteady, unstable, shaky, tottering, top-heavy, tumble-down, ramshackle, crumbling, helpless, trembling in the balance; nodding to its fall.

threatening, ominous, ill-omened, alarming.

666. [Means of safety] REFUGE.—*N.* refuge, sanctuary, retreat, fastness, stronghold, fortress, castle, keep; asylum, shelter, covert, ark, home, hiding place.

anchorage, roadstead; breakwater, port, haven, harbor, pier, jetty, embankment, quay, wharf.

anchor, sheet anchor, grapnel, grappling iron, mainstay, support, safeguard.

667. [Source of danger] PITFALL.—*N.* pitfall, ambush, trap, snare, mine, spring gun.

rocks, reefs, sunken rocks, snags; sands, quicksands; breakers, shoals, shallows, lee shore, rockbound coast.

abyss, abysm, pit, void, chasm.

whirlpool, eddy, vortex, rapids, undertow; current, tiderace, maelstrom; eagre, bore, tidal wave.

pest, ugly customer, incendiary, firebug [*slang*]; firebrand; hornet's nest.

sword of Damocles; wolf at the door, snake in the grass, snake in one's bosom.

668. WARNING.—*N.* warning, caution, notice, premonition, prediction; symptom; lesson, admonition; handwriting on the wall, monitor, warning voice; stormy petrel, bird of ill omen, gathering clouds.

watchtower, beacon, signal post; lighthouse, etc., 550.

sentinel, sentry; watch, watchman; watch and ward; watchdog; patrol, picket, scout, spy, lookout, flagman.

V. warn, caution; forewarn, admonish, forbode, give warning; put on one's guard; sound the alarm.

beware, take warning, look out, keep watch and ward.

Adj. premonitory, cautionary; ominous, threatening, lowering, minatory; symptomatic.

Adv. with alarm, on guard, after due warning, with one's eyes open.

669. [Indication of danger] ALARM.—*N.* alarm; alarum, alarm bell, tocsin, beat of drum, sound of trumpet, hue and cry; signal of distress, SOS; fog signal, siren; yellow flag; danger signal; red light, red flag; fire alarm, still alarm; burglar alarm; police whistle.

V. alarm, give (*or* raise, sound) an alarm, warn, ring the tocsin.

670. PRESERVATION.—*N.* preservation, safekeeping, conservation, economy, maintenance, support, salvation, deliverance, etc., 672.

Means of preservation: prophylaxis; preserver, preservative; hygiene, hygienics; ensilage; dehydration, evaporation, drying, canning, pickling.

V. preserve, maintain, keep, sustain, support; save, rescue, make safe, take care of, guard; husband, economize.

embalm, dry, cure, salt, pickle, season, bottle, pot, tin, can; dehydrate, evaporate.

Adj. preserved, unimpaired, unbroken, uninjured, unhurt, unmarred; safe, safe and sound, intact, with a whole skin.

671. ESCAPE.—*N.* **escape**, flight, evasion, loophole, retreat; narrow (*or* hairbreadth) escape; close call [*colloq.*]; impunity.

refugee, etc. (*fugitive*), 623.

V. **escape**, make one's escape; break jail; get off, get clear off, elude, make off, give one the slip; wriggle out of; break loose, break away.

Adj. stolen away; fled; scot-free.

672. DELIVERANCE.—*N.* **deliverance**, extrication, rescue, ransom, reprieve, respite; armistice, truce; liberation, emancipation; redemption, salvation.

V. **deliver**, extricate, rescue, save, free, liberate, set free, release, emancipate, redeem, ransom; come to the rescue.

673. PREPARATION.—*N.* **preparation**, provision, arrangement, anticipation, precaution, forecast, rehearsal; dissemination, propaganda.

groundwork, steppingstone; foundation; scaffold, scaffolding.

elaboration, ripening, evolution; concoction, digestion; hatching, incubation.

Preparation of men: training, education, equipment, inurement; novitiate.

Preparation of food: cooking, cookery, culinary art; brewing.

Preparation of the soil: tilling, plowing, sowing, cultivation.

preparedness, readiness, ripeness, mellowness; maturity.

preparer, trainer, coach, teacher, pioneer; prophet; forerunner, etc. (*precursor*), 64; sappers and miners.

V. **prepare**, prime, get (*or* make) ready, arrange, make preparations, settle preliminaries, get up; prepare the ground, lay the foundations, erect the scaffolding.

elaborate, mature, ripen, mellow, season, bring to maturity; nurture; cook, brew.

equip, arm, man; fit out, fit up; furnish, rig, dress, accouter, array.

prepare for, guard against, forearm; make provision for; provide, provide against; set one's house in order, make all snug; clear decks, clear for action.

be prepared, be ready, watch and pray, keep one's powder dry, lie in wait for, anticipate, foresee.

Adj. **preparatory**, precautionary, provident; provisional, preliminary; in embryo, in hand, in train; afoot, afloat; on foot, brewing, hatching, forthcoming.

prepared, ready, cut and dried; available, at one's elbow, ready for use, all ready; handy.

ripe, mature, mellow; seasoned, practiced, experienced.

elaborate, labored, high-wrought, worked up.

Adv. **in preparation,** in anticipation of; afoot, astir, abroad.

674. NONPREPARATION.—*N.* **nonpreparation,** unpreparedness; improvidence.

immaturity, crudity, rawness; disqualification.

Absence of art: nature, state of nature; virgin soil, unweeded garden; rough diamond; raw material.

improvisation, etc. (*impulse*), 612.

V. **be unprepared;** lie fallow; live from hand to mouth.

extemporize, improvise; cook up, fix up.

surprise, drop in [*colloq.*], take (*or* catch) unawares; take by surprise.

Adj. **unprepared,** incomplete, premature, rudimental, embryonic, immature, unripe, callow, unfledged, unhatched; uncooked, raw, green, crude; coarse; rough, roughhewn; in the rough.

untaught, uneducated, untrained, untutored, unlicked.

fallow, unsown, untilled, uncultivated.

unfitted, disqualified, unqualified, ill-digested; unready, unorganized, unfurnished, unprovided, unequipped.

shiftless, improvident, unthrifty, thriftless, happy-go-lucky; slack, remiss.

Adv. **inadvertently,** by surprise, without premeditation; extempore.

675. ESSAY—*N.* **essay,** trial, endeavor, attempt; aim, struggle, venture, adventure, speculation, probation, experiment.

V. **try,** essay; experiment, etc., 463; endeavor, strive; tempt, attempt, venture, adventure, speculate, tempt fortune.

Adj. **tentative,** experimental, empirical, problematic, probationary.

Adv. **on examination,** on trial, at a venture; by rule of thumb.

676. UNDERTAKING.—*N.* **undertaking,** adventure, venture, engagement, compact, enterprise; pilgrimage.

V. **undertake,** engage in, embark in, launch (*or* plunge) into, volunteer; apprentice oneself to; engage, contract, devote oneself to, take up, take on, take in hand; tackle [*colloq.*]; set about; launch forth; betake oneself to, turn one's hand to, have in hand, begin, broach, institute.

Adj. **energetic;** full of pep [*slang*]; enterprising, adventurous, venturesome.

677. USE.—*N.* **use,** employ, exercise, application, appliance; disposal; consumption; agency, usefulness, etc., 644; benefit, recourse, resort, avail.

Conversion to use: utilization, utility, service, wear.

Way of using: usage, employment, *modus operandi* [L.].

user, consumer, market, demand.

V. **use,** make use of, employ, put to use, apply, put in action, set in motion, set to work; ply, work, wield, handle, manipulate; exert, exercise, practice, avail oneself of, profit by; resort to, have recourse to, recur to, take up, try.

utilize, turn to account (*or* use); exploit; administer, apply, bring into play; task, tax, put to task; devote, dedicate, consecrate.

consume, use up, devour, swallow up; absorb, expend; wear.

Adj. **useful,** etc., 644; instrumental, subservient, utilitarian, pragmatic.

678. DISUSE.—*N.* disuse; forbearance, abstinence; relinquishment, abandonment; desuetude, disusage.

V. **not use;** do without, dispense with, let alone, forbear, abstain, spare, waive, neglect; keep back, reserve.

disuse; lay up, lay by, shelve; set aside, lay aside, leave off, have done with; supersede, discard, throw aside, relinquish; destroy, make away with, cast (*or* throw) overboard; dismantle.

Adj. **disused,** done with, run down, worn out; unemployed, unapplied, unexercised, uncalled for, not required.

679. MISUSE.—*N.* misuse, misusage, misapplication, misappropriation; abuse, profanation, desecration; waste.

V. **misuse,** misemploy, misapply; exploit; misappropriate; desecrate, abuse, profane.

overtask, overtax, overwork; squander, waste.

680. ACTION.—*N.* action, performance, perpetration, exercise, movement, operation, evolution, work, employment; labor, exertion, execution; procedure, conduct; handicraft; business, agency.

deed, act, stitch, touch, transaction, job, doings, dealings, proceeding, measure, step, maneuver, bout, passage, move, stroke, blow; feat, exploit, achievement; handiwork, craftsmanship, workmanship; manufacture; stroke of policy.

doer, worker, agent, etc., 690.

V. **do,** perform, execute, achieve, transact, enact; commit, perpetrate, inflict; exercise, prosecute, carry on, work, labor, practice, play; employ oneself, ply one's task; officiate, have in hand; shape one's course.

act, operate, take action, take steps, take in hand, put in practice, carry into execution, act upon.

Adj. **in action,** acting, in harness, on duty; at work; operative.

Adv. in the act, in the midst of; red-handed.

681. INACTION.—*N.* inaction, passiveness, watchful waiting; noninterference; neglect, etc., 460; inactivity, etc., 683; stagnation, vegetation, rest, loafing, want of occupation, unemployment; sinecure; soft snap, cinch [*both slang*].

V. **not do,** not act, not attempt; be inactive, abstain from doing, do nothing, hold, spare; leave (or let) alone; let be, let pass, let things take their course, live and let live; rest upon one's oars; stand aloof; refrain, relax one's efforts; desist, stop, pause, wait; waste time.

undo, do away with; take down, take to pieces; destroy, etc., 162.

Adj. **passive;** unoccupied, unemployed, out of employ (or work, a job); uncultivated, fallow.

Adv. at a stand.

682. ACTIVITY.—*N.* **activity,** animation, life, vivacity, spirit, verve, pep [*slang*], dash, go [*colloq.*], energy, snap, vim.

smartness, nimbleness, agility; quickness, velocity, alacrity; promptitude; dispatch, expedition, haste, etc., 684; punctuality.

eagerness, zeal, ardor, enthusiasm, earnestness, intentness, vigor, devotion, exertion.

industry, assiduity, assiduousness, sedulousness, laboriousness, drudgery, diligence, perseverance, etc., 604*a*.

vigilance, etc., 459; wakefulness; sleeplessness, restlessness; insomnia.

bustle, hustle [*colloq.*], movement, stir, fuss, ado, bother, fidget, flurry.

officiousness, dabbling, meddling; interference, intermeddling; butting in [*slang*], intrusiveness, intrigue.

man of action, busy bee; new broom; devotee, enthusiast, fanatic, zealot, hustler [*colloq.*], live wire, human dynamo [*both colloq.*].

meddler, intriguer, busybody.

V. **be active,** busy oneself in; stir, stir about, bestir oneself; speed, hasten, bustle, fuss; push, go ahead, push forward; make progress; toil, moil, drudge, plod, persist, persevere, hustle [*colloq.*], push [*colloq.*], keep moving, seize the opportunity, lose no time, dash off, make haste.

have a hand in, take an active part, put in one's oar, have a finger in the pie, dabble, intrigue; agitate.

meddle, tamper with, interfere, interpose; obtrude; butt in, horn in [*both slang*].

Adj. **active,** brisk, lively, animated, vivacious, alive, frisky, spirited; nimble, agile, light-footed, nimble-footed.

quick, prompt, instant, ready, alert, spry [*colloq. and dial.*], sharp, smart; fast, etc. (*swift*), 274; capable, expeditious, awake, go-ahead [*colloq.*], live [*colloq.*], hustling [*colloq.*], wide-awake.

enterprising, eager, ardent, strenuous, zealous, resolute.

industrious, assiduous, diligent, sedulous, painstaking, intent, indefatigable, persevering, unwearied, sleepless; busy, occupied; hard at work, hard at it; plodding, hard-working, businesslike.

bustling, restless, fussy, fidgety, pottering.

meddlesome, pushing, officious.

astir, stirring, afoot, on foot, in full swing; on the alert.

Adv. with life and spirit, with might and main, full tilt.

683. INACTIVITY.—*N.* **inactivity;** inaction, etc., 681; inertness, lull, quiescence; rust.

idleness, remissness, sloth, indolence, dawdling, puttering, relaxation.

languor, dullness, sluggishness, procrastination, torpor, stupor, somnolence, drowsiness, heaviness, hypnotism, lethargy.

sleep, **slumber;** Morpheus; coma, trance, catalepsy, hypnosis, dream; **nap,** doze, siesta; hibernation.

idler, drone, dawdler, truant; dead one [*slang*], dummy, bum [*slang*], tramp, hobo, beggar, lounge lizard [*slang*], lounger, loafer, slow-poke, laggard, sluggard.

V. **be inactive,** do nothing; dawdle, drawl, lag, hang back, slouch, loll, lounge, loaf, loiter; sleep at one's post; take it easy.

dally, dilly-dally, idle (*or* fritter, fool) away time; putter, dabble.

sleep, slumber, be asleep, oversleep, hibernate; doze, drowse, nap, take a nap; fall asleep, drop asleep; get sleepy, nod, go to bed, turn in.

languish, expend itself, flag, hang fire; relax.

Adj. **inactive,** motionless; unoccupied, unemployed.

indolent, lazy, slothful, idle, remiss, slack, inert, torpid, sluggish, logy, languid, listless; lackadaisical, maudlin; heavy, dull, leaden; dilatory, laggard, slow, flagging; puttering.

sleeping, asleep, comatose; in the arms (*or* lap) of Morpheus.

sleepy, dozy, drowsy, somnolent, lethargic, heavy, heavy with sleep; soporific, hypnotic; dreamy.

Adv. with half-shut eyes, half asleep; in dreams, in dreamland.

684. HASTE.—*N.* **haste,** urgency, dispatch, acceleration, spurt, forced march, rush, scurry, scuttle, dash; velocity, etc., 274; precipitancy, precipitation, impetuosity; hurry, drive, scramble, bustle, fidget, flurry.

V. **haste,** hasten, make haste, dash on, push on, press on *or* forward, hurry, scurry, bustle, flutter, scramble, plunge, dash off, rush, express; bestir oneself, etc. (*be active*), 682; lose no time, make short work of; work against time, work under pressure.

quicken, accelerate, expedite, precipitate, urge, whip, spur, flog, goad.

Adj. **hasty,** hurried, cursory, precipitate, headlong, furious, boisterous, impetuous, hotheaded; feverish, pushing.

in haste, in a hurry, in hot haste, breathless, hard-pressed, urgent.

Adv. **with haste,** with speed, in haste, apace, amain; at short notice, immediately, posthaste; by cable, by telegraph, by wire-less [*colloq.*], by airplane, by return mail, by forced marches.

hastily, precipitately, helter-skelter, hurry-scurry, slapdash, slap-bang; full-tilt, full-drive; heels over head, headlong.

685. LEISURE.—*N.* leisure, convenience; spare time, vacant hour; time, time to spare; holiday, ease.

V. **have leisure,** take one's time (*or* leisure, ease); repose, etc., 687; move slowly, while away the time, be master of one's time, be an idle man.

686. EXERTION.—*N.* exertion, effort, strain, stress, tug, pull, throw, stretch, struggle, spell, spurt; dead lift, heft [*dial.*]; trouble, pains, duty; energy, etc. [*physical*], 171.

exercise, practice, play, gymnastics, field sports; breather [*colloq.*].

labor, work, toil, manual labor, sweat of one's brow, drudgery, slavery.

worker, plodder, laborer, drudge, slave; man of action; Hercules.

V. **labor,** work, toil, sweat, fag, drudge, slave, strive, strain; pull, tug, ply; ply the oar; exert oneself, bestir oneself (*be active*), 682.

work hard; rough it; put forth one's strength, buckle to, set one's shoulder to the wheel, do double duty; burn the candle at both ends, work (*or* fight) one's way; do one's best, do one's ut-most; take pains; strain every nerve; spare no efforts *or* pains.

Adj. **laborious,** elaborate; strained; toilsome, wearisome, bur-densome; uphill; herculean.

hard-working, painstaking, strenuous, energetic, never idle.

Adv. with might and main, with all one's might, to the best of one's abilities, tooth and nail, hammer and tongs, heart and soul.

687. REPOSE.—*N.* repose, rest, sleep, etc., 683; relaxation, breathing time; halt, stay, pause, respite.

day of rest, Sabbath, Lord's day, Sunday; holiday, red-letter day, gala day; vacation, recess.

V. **repose,** rest, take rest, take one's ease; lie down, recline, go to rest (*or* bed, sleep).

relax, unbend, slacken, take breath, rest upon one's oars; pause, etc. (*cease*), 142; stay one's hand.

take a holiday, shut up shop; lie fallow.

Adj. **holiday,** festal; sabbatic *or* sabbatical.

688. FATIGUE.—*N.* fatigue; weariness, etc., 841; yawning, drowsiness, lassitude, tiredness, sweat.

faintness, fainting, swoon, exhaustion, collapse, prostration.

V. **be fatigued,** yawn, droop, sink; flag; gasp, pant, puff, blow, drop, swoon, faint, succumb.

fatigue, tire, bore, weary, flag, jade, harass, exhaust, wear out, prostrate.

tax, task, strain; overtask, overwork, overburden, overtax, overstrain, fag, fag out.

Adj. fatigued; weary, etc., 841; drowsy, haggard, toilworn, way-worn, footsore, faint; done up [*colloq.*], exhausted, prostrate, spent, ready to drop, all in [*slang*], dog-tired, tired to death, played out.

worn, worn out; battered, shattered, seedy [*colloq.*], enfeebled.

breathless, short of (*or* out of)breath, blown, puffing and blowing, short-breathed, broken-winded.

689. REFRESHMENT.—*N.* recuperation; recovery of strength, restoration, revival, etc., 660; repair, refreshment; relief, etc., 834.

V. refresh, brace, strengthen, reinvigorate; air, freshen up, recruit, regale, repair, restore, revive; get better, recover (*or* regain) one's strength, recuperate.

Adj. refreshing, recuperative.

690. AGENT.—*N.* agent, doer, actor, performer, perpetrator, operator; executor, executrix; practitioner, worker; minister, etc. (*instrument*), 631; representative, etc. (*commissioner*), 758, (*deputy*), 759; factor, steward; servant, etc., 746; factotum.

workman, artisan, craftsman, handicraftsman, mechanic, operative; working-man, laboring man; hewers of wood and drawers of water; laborer; hand, man, day laborer, journeyman, hack, drudge, roustabout.

maker, artificer, artist, wright, manufacturer, architect, contractor, builder, smith.

machinist, engineer, electrician.

workwoman, charwoman, dressmaker, modiste, seamstress, needlewoman, milliner, laundress, washerwoman.

coworker, associate, fellow worker, co-operator, colleague, confrere; force, staff, personnel.

691. WORKSHOP.—*N.* workshop, laboratory, manufactory, armory, arsenal, mill, factory, studio, atelier; hive, hive of industry, beehive; bindery; dock, dockyard, slip, yard, wharf; foundry, forge, furnace.

melting pot, crucible, caldron, mortar, alembic; matrix.

692. CONDUCT.—*N.* conduct, behavior; deportment, carriage, demeanor, guise, bearing, manner; course of conduct, line of action; role; process, ways, practice, procedure, method; dealing, transaction, business.

policy, tactics, game, generalship, statesmanship, strategy, plan.

management; government, etc., 693; stewardship, husbandry; housekeeping, ménage, regime, regimen, economy; economics, political economy.

career, life, course, walk, province, race, record; execution, treatment; campaign.

V. **transact,** execute; dispatch, proceed with, discharge; carry on (*or* through, out, into effect); work out; go through, get through; enact.

adopt a course, shape one's course, play one's part; shift for oneself, paddle one's own canoe; conduct; manage, etc. (*direct*), 693.

behave, conduct (*or* acquit, carry, comport, bear, demean) oneself.

Adj. **directive,** methodical, businesslike, practical, executive, strategic, economic.

693. DIRECTION.—*N.* **direction;** management, government, conduct, legislation, regulation, guidance, reins; steerage, pilotage, helm, rudder, needle, compass; guiding star, lodestar, polestar, cynosure.

ministry, administration; stewardship, proctorship; chair; agency.

supervision, superintendence; surveillance, oversight; eye of the master; control, charge; auspices; command, etc. (*authority*), 737.

statesmanship, statecraft, kingcraft, reins of government; director, etc., 694; seat, portfolio.

V. **direct,** manage, govern, conduct; order, prescribe, head, lead, regulate, guide, steer, pilot, take the helm, be at the helm; hold the reins, drive.

superintend, supervise; overlook, oversee, control, handle, look after, see to, administer, patronize; rule, etc. (*command*), 737; hold office.

Adj. **directing,** executive, gubernatorial, supervisory; statesmanlike.

Adv. **in charge of,** under the guidance of, under the auspices of; in control of, at the helm, at the head of.

694. DIRECTOR.—*N.* **director,** manager, governor, controller, superintendent, supervisor, overseer, supercargo, inspector, foreman, surveyor, taskmaster; master, etc., 745; leader, ringleader, agitator, demagogue, conductor, precentor, bellwether, file leader.

guide, pilot; helmsman, steersman; adviser, etc., 695.

driver, whip, charioteer; coachman, carman, cabman; postilion, muleteer, teamster; chauffeur, motorman, engine driver.

head, headman, chief, principal, president, speaker; chair, chairman; captain, etc. (*master*), 745; superior; prime minister, premier.

officer, functionary, minister, official, bureaucrat, officeholder.

statesman, strategist, legislator, lawgiver, politician, boss [*slang*], political dictator, wirepuller [*colloq.*], power behind the throne, kingmaker.

steward, factor, agent, bailiff, factotum, major-domo, seneschal, housekeeper, shepherd; proctor, curator, librarian.

695. ADVICE.—*N.* **advice,** counsel, word to the wise, suggestion, recommendation, advocacy; consultation; exhortation, expostulation, dissuasion, admonition; guidance.

instruction, charge, injunction, message, speech from the throne.

adviser, prompter; counsel, counselor; monitor, mentor, sage, wise man; teacher, etc., 540; physician; arbiter, referee, judge.

consultation, conference, parley, powwow; reference.

V. **advise,** counsel, suggest, prompt, recommend, prescribe, advocate, exhort, persuade.

enjoin, enforce, charge, instruct, call, call upon, request, dictate.

expostulate, dissuade, admonish, warn.

confer, consult, refer to, call in; follow, take (*or* follow) advice.

696. COUNCIL.—*N.* **council,** committee, privy council, court, chamber, cabinet, board, directorate, syndicate, bench, staff.

Ecclesiastical: convocation, synod, congregation, church, chapter, vestry, consistory, conventicle, conclave, convention.

legislature, parliament, congress, national council, states-general, diet.

Duma [Russia], Storthing *or* Storting [Norway], Rigsdag [Denmark], Riksdag [Sweden], Cortes [Spain], Reichsrath *or* Reichsrat [Austria], Volksraad [Dutch], Dail Eireann [Sinn Fein].

upper house, upper chamber, first chamber, senate, legislative council, House of Lords, House of Peers; Bundesrath *or* Bundesrat [Ger.], federal council, Lagting [Nor.], Landsthing [Den.].

lower house, lower chamber, second chamber, house of representatives, House of Commons, the house, legislative assembly, chamber of deputies; Odelsting [Nor.], Folkething [Den.], Reichstag [Ger.].

assembly, caucus, clique; meeting, sitting, séance, conference, hearing, session, palaver; council fire, powwow.

Representatives: congressman, M.C., senator, representative; member, member of parliament, M.P., assemblyman, councilor.

Adj. **curule,** congressional, senatorial, parliamentary; synodic *or* synodical.

697. PRECEPT.—*N.* **precept,** direction, instruction, charge; prescript, prescription; recipe, receipt; golden rule; maxim, etc., 496.

rule, canon, law, code, convention; unwritten law; canon law; act, statute, rubric, stage direction, regulation; model, form, formula, technicality.

order, etc. (*command*), 741.

698. SKILL.—*N.* **skill,** skillfulness, address, dexterity, adroitness, expertness, proficiency, competence, craft; facility, knack, trick, sleight; mastery, excellence, sleight of hand, etc. (*deception*), 545.

accomplishment, acquirement, attainment; art, science; finish, technique.

worldly wisdom, knowledge of the world, *savoir-faire* [F.]; tact; mother wit, discretion, finesse; management.

cleverness, talent, ability, ingenuity, capacity, talents, faculty, endowment, forte, turn, gift, genius, intelligence, sharpness, readiness, aptness, aptitude, resourcefulness; felicity, capability, qualification.

expert, adept, etc., 700.

masterpiece, masterwork, chef-d'oeuvre [F.].

V. **be skillful,** excel in, be master of; have a turn for.

take advantage of, make the most of, profit by, make a hit, make a virtue of necessity, make hay while the sun shines.

Adj. **skillful,** dexterous, adroit, expert, apt, handy, quick, deft, ready, smart, proficient, good at, at home in, master of, conversant with; masterly, crack [*colloq.*], crackajack [*slang*], accomplished.

experienced, practiced, skilled, up in, in practice, competent, efficient, qualified, capable, fitted, fit for, trained, initiated, sophisticated, prepared, primed, finished.

clever, able, ingenious, felicitous, gifted, talented, resourceful, inventive; shrewd, sharp, cunning; neat-handed, fine-fingered; nimble-fingered, ambidextrous, sure-footed.

technical, artistic, scientific, workmanlike, businesslike, statesmanlike.

Adv. **skillfully,** artistically, with skill, with fine technique, with consummate skill; like a machine.

699. UNSKILLFULNESS.—*N.* unskillfulness, want of skill, incompetence, inability, infelicity, clumsiness, inaptitude, inexperience; disqualification.

mismanagement, misconduct, bad policy, impolicy; maladministration; misrule, misgovernment.

blunder, act of folly, bungle, botch, bad job, sad work.

bungler, etc., 701; fool, etc., 501.

V. **bungle,** blunder, muff [*esp. baseball*], boggle, fumble, botch, mar, spoil, flounder, stumble, trip; mismanage, misdirect, misapply.

mistake, take the shadow for the substance, bark up the wrong tree; be in the wrong box [*colloq.*]; lose one's way, miss one's way; fall into a trap.

Adj. **unskillful,** unskilled, inexpert, incompetent, bungling, awkward, clumsy, gawky, unhandy, maladroit; stupid, ill-qualified, unfit; raw, green, inexperienced; rusty, out of practice.

unaccustomed, unused, untrained, uninitiated; unbusinesslike, unpractical, shiftless; unstatesmanlike.

ill-advised, misadvised; ill-devised, ill-judged, ill-contrived, ill-conducted; misguided, foolish, wild; infelicitous.

700. EXPERT.—*N.* **expert,** adept, proficient, connoisseur, master, master hand; top sawyer; prima donna, first fiddle; past master.

picked man; medalist, prizeman.

veteran, old stager, old campaigner, man of business, man of the world.

genius; mastermind, master spirit; prodigy of learning, walking encyclopedia, mine of information.

man of cunning, diplomatist, diplomat, Machiavellian; politician, tactician strategist.

701. BUNGLER.—*N.* **bungler,** blunderer, blunderhead; fumbler, lubber, clown, lout, duffer [*colloq.*]; butter-fingers, muff, muffer [*all colloq.*]; awkward squad; novice, greenhorn.

landlubber, fresh-water sailor, fair-weather sailor, horse marine.

sloven, slattern, slut.

702. CUNNING.—*N.* **cunning,** craft, subtlety, maneuvering, temporization; circumvention; chicane, chicanery; sharp practice, knavery, jugglery, concealment, a nigger in the woodpile [*colloq.*], guile, duplicity, foul play.

diplomacy, politics, Machiavellianism; gerrymander, jobbery, back-stairs influence.

artifice, art, device, machination; plot, maneuver, stratagem, dodge, wile, trick, trickery, ruse, finesse, subterfuge, evasion, white lie, gold brick [*colloq.*], imposture, deception, net, trap.

schemer, trickster, sly boots [*humorous*], fox, reynard; intriguer, man of cunning.

V. **intrigue,** live by one's wits; maneuver, gerrymander, finesse, double, temporize, circumvent, outdo, get the better of, throw off one's guard; surprise, waylay, undermine, flatter; have an ax to grind.

Adj. **cunning,** crafty, artful, skillful; subtle, feline, deep, profound, designing, timeserving, tricky, wily, sly, insidious, stealthy, underhand, double-faced, shifty, deceptive; deceitful, crooked; shrewd, acute; sharp, canny, astute, knowing.

703. ARTLESSNESS.—*N.* **artlessness,** unsophistication, simplicity, innocence, candor, sincerity, singleness of purpose, honesty.

rough diamond, matter-of-fact man; *enfant terrible* [F.].

V. **be artless,** think aloud; speak one's mind; be free with one, call a spade a spade; tell the truth, the whole truth, and nothing but the truth.

Adj. **artless,** natural, pure, confiding, simple, plain, unsophisticated, unaffected, naïve; sincere, frank, open, candid, ingenuous, guileless; unsuspicious, honest, childlike; innocent. straightforward, aboveboard; single-minded.

matter-of-fact, plain-spoken, outspoken; blunt, downright, direct, unflattering, unvarnished.

Adv. in plain words (*or* English); without mincing the matter.

704. DIFFICULTY.—*N.* difficulty, hardness, impracticability, uphill work, herculean task; dead weight, dead lift.

dilemma, predicament, fix [*colloq.*], quandary, embarrassment, deadlock, perplexity, intricacy, entanglement, knot, Gordian knot, maze, coil, strait, pass, pinch, rub, critical situation, exigency, crisis, trial, emergency, scrape, slough, quagmire, hot water [*colloq.*], pickle, stew, imbroglio, mess, muddle, botch, hitch, stumbling block.

vexed question, poser, puzzle, knotty point, paradox; hard nut to crack, crux.

V. be difficult, go against the grain, try one's patience, go hard with one, pose, perplex, bother, nonplus.

flounder, boggle [*local*], struggle, stick fast; come to a deadlock.

render difficult, enmesh, encumber, embarrass, entangle; spike one's guns.

Adj. difficult, hard, tough [*colloq.*]; troublesome, toilsome, irksome; laborious, onerous, arduous, herculean, formidable.

awkward, unwieldy, unmanageable, intractable, stubborn, perverse, refractory, knotted, knotty, thorny; pathless, trackless, intricate.

embarrassing, perplexing, delicate, ticklish, critical, thorny.

in difficulty, in hot water [*colloq.*], in a fix [*colloq.*], in a scrape, between Scylla and Charybdis; on the horns of a dilemma; on the rocks; reduced to straits; hard-pressed; run hard; pinched; straitened; hard up [*slang*]; puzzled, at a loss, at one's wits' end, at a standstill; nonplused, stranded, aground.

Adv. with much ado; uphill, upstream; in the teeth of; against the grain.

705. FACILITY.—*N.* facility, ease, easiness, capability, feasibility, practicability; flexibility, pliancy, smoothness, plain sailing; mere child's play; cinch, snap [*both slang*].

V. be easy, run smoothly; have full play, obey the helm, work well, work smoothly.

facilitate, smooth, ease, lighten, free, clear, disencumber, disembarrass, disentangle, extricate, unravel, unknot; humor, leave a loophole, leave the matter open; give full play, make way for, pave the way, bridge over.

Adj. easy, facile; feasible, practicable, within reach, gettable, accessible.

manageable, tractable; submissive; yielding, ductile, tractable, pliant.

unburdened, unencumbered, unloaded, unobstructed, untrammeled; unrestrained, free, at ease, light.

Adv. **easily,** readily, expertly, adroitly, smoothly, swimmingly, with no effort.

706. HINDRANCE.—*N.* **prevention,** obstruction, stoppage, interruption, interception, hindrance, embarrassment, constriction, restriction, restraint, etc., 751.

interference, interposition, obtrusion; discouragement, disapproval, disapprobation, opposition.

impediment, obstacle, obstruction, knot, snag, hitch, contretemps, stumbling block, lion in the path.

check; encumbrance; clog, brake, anchor; bit, snaffle, curb; drag, load, burden, onus, impedimenta; dead weight; lumber, pack; nightmare, incubus; stay, stop; preventive, prophylactic.

drawback, objection; difficulty, etc., 704; obstacle; ill-wind, head wind; trammel, tether.

damper, wet blanket, kill-joy, dog in the manger, usurper, interloper, opponent; filibusterer.

V. **hinder,** impede, filibuster, embarrass.

avert, keep off, stave off, ward off; obviate; turn aside, draw off, prevent, nip in the bud; retard, slacken, check, counteract, countercheck, preclude, debar, inhibit, restrict.

obstruct, stop, stay, bar, bolt, lock; block, barricade; dam up, put on the brake, put a stop to, interrupt, intercept, oppose, interfere, interpose.

encumber, cramp, hamper; clog, cumber, handicap; choke, saddle with, load with, overload, overwhelm, lumber, entrammel, trammel, incommode, discommode, discompose, corner.

thwart, frustrate, disconcert, balk, foil; circumvent, baffle, override, defeat, spoil, mar, clip the wings of, cripple, damp, dishearten, discountenance, undermine.

Adj. **obstructive,** intrusive, meddlesome; onerous, burdensome; cumbrous, cumbersome.

Adv. **in the way,** with everything against one, through all obstacles, under many difficulties.

707. AID.—*N.* **aid,** assistance, help, succor; support, lift, advance, furtherance, promotion.

patronage, auspices, countenance, favor, interest, advocacy.

sustenance, maintenance, nutrition, nourishment; manna in the wilderness, food, means, subsidy, bounty.

relief, rescue; ministry, ministration; supernatural aid; *deus ex machina* [L.].

supplies, re-enforcements, contingents, recruits, support, ally.

V. **aid,** assist, help, succor, lend a hand; contribute, subscribe to;

take by the hand, take in tow; relieve, rescue; set on one's legs, give new life to, be the making of; re-enforce, recruit; promote, further, forward, advance; speed, expedite, quicken, hasten.

support, sustain, uphold, prop, hold up, bolster.

nourish, nurture, nurse, cradle, dry-nurse, suckle, foster, cherish, cultivate.

serve; do service to, tender to, pander to, minister to; tend, attend, wait on; take care of; entertain, regale.

oblige, accommodate, consult the wishes of; humor, cheer, encourage.

second, stand by, back, back up; abet, work for, stick up for [*colloq.*], stick by, take up (*or* espouse) the cause of; advocate, countenance, patronize, smile upon, favor, befriend, side with.

Adj. aiding, auxiliary, adjuvant, helpful, subservient, accessary, accessory, subsidiary.

friendly, amicable, favorable, propitious, well disposed, neighborly, obliging, at one's beck.

Adv. in aid of, on (*or* in) behalf of, in favor of, in the name of, in furtherance of, on account of, for the sake of.

708. OPPOSITION.—*N.* opposition, antagonism, contrariness, contrariety; contravention, counteraction; resistance, etc., 719; hindrance, restraint, etc., 751.

collision, conflict, discord, want of harmony; filibuster, clashing.

competition, rivalry, emulation, race, contest; tug of war.

V. oppose, counteract, withstand, etc. (*resist*), 719; hinder, restrain; obstruct, etc., 706; antagonize, cross, thwart, pit against, face, confront, cope with; protest (*or* vote) against; disfavor; contradict, contravene, belie.

encounter, meet, stem, breast, resist, grapple with, kick against the pricks; contend with (*or* against), do battle with (*or* against).

compete, emulate, rival; force out, drive one out of business.

Adj. adverse, antagonistic, oppugnant, contrary, at variance, at issue, at war with, in opposition, at daggers drawn.

unfavorable, unpropitious, unfriendly, hostile, inimical, cross.

competitive, emulous, cutthroat; in rivalry with, in friendly rivalry.

Adv. against, counter to, in conflict with, at cross-purposes.

in spite, in despite, in defiance; in the teeth (*or* face) of; across; athwart.

709. CO-OPERATION.—*N.* co-operation, concert, concurrence, complicity, collusion; participation; union, combination.

association, alliance, joint stock, partnership, pool, gentleman's agreement; confederation, coalition, federation, fusion; logrolling; freemasonry.

unanimity, *esprit de corps* [F.], party spirit, school spirit; clanship, partisanship; concord.

V. co-operate, concur; conduce, combine, pool, unite one's efforts, pull together, stand shoulder to shoulder; act in concert, join forces, fraternize; conspire, concert.

side with, take sides with, go along with, join hands with, make common cause with, unite with, join with, take part with, cast in one's lot with; rally round.

participate, be a party to, lend oneself to; chip in [*colloq.*], bear part in, second, espouse a cause.

Adj. co-operating, in league, hand in glove with; favorable to, unopposed.

Adv. unanimously, as one man, shoulder to shoulder.

710. OPPONENT.—*N.* opponent, antagonist, adversary; opposition; assailant, enemy, etc., 891.

oppositionist, wrangler, disputant; filibuster, filibusterer, extremist, bitter-ender, irreconcilable, obstructionist.

malcontent; demagogue, reactionist; anarchist, Red.

rival, competitor, contestant: the field.

711. AUXILIARY.—*N.* auxiliary, recruit, assistant, help, helper, helpmate, helping hand; colleague, partner, confrere, co-operator, coadjutor, collaborator, associate, right hand, right-hand man.

ally; friend, etc., 890; confidant (*fem.* confidante), alter ego [L.], pal [*slang*], chum [*colloq.*], mate.

puppet, cat's-paw, creature, tool; satellite, adherent, parasite, dependent.

confederate; accomplice; accessory.

upholder, seconder, backer, supporter, abettor, advocate, partisan, champion, patron, friend at court, mediator.

friend in need, special providence, guardian angel, fairy godmother, tutelary genius.

712. PARTY.—*N.* party, faction, denomination, class, communion, side, crew, team; band, horde, posse, phalanx; caste, family, clan.

community, body, fellowship, party spirit, solidarity, freemasonry; fraternity, sodality, brotherhood, sisterhood, sorority; fraternal order.

gang, tong [Chin.], bolsheviki, bolshevists, ring, machine, junto, cabal.

clique, knot, circle, set, coterie; club, casino.

corporation, corporate body, guild, company, partnership, firm, house; combine [*colloq.*], trust; holding company, merger.

society, association; institute, institution; union; trade-union;

league, syndicate, alliance, combination, coalition, federation, confederation, confederacy.

staff; cast, dramatis personae [L.].

V. unite, join, band together, club together, co-operate, etc., 709; associate, federate, federalize.

Adj. joint, federal, corporate, confederated, organized, leagued, syndicated; fraternal, Masonic, institutional, denominational; cliquish, cliquy.

Adv. side by side, hand in hand, shoulder to shoulder, in the same boat.

713. DISCORD.—*N.* discord, dissidence, dissonance, disagreement, jar, clash, break, shock.

variance, difference, dissension, misunderstanding, cross-purposes, odds, division, split, rupture, disruption, disunion, breach, schism, feud, faction.

polemics; litigation, strife, warfare, outbreak, open rupture, declaration of war.

quarrel, dispute, tiff, bicker, squabble, altercation, words, high words, family jars.

broil, brawl, row [*colloq.*], racket, hubbub, imbroglio, fracas, scrimmage, rumpus [*colloq.*], squall, riot, disturbance, commotion.

subject of dispute, ground of quarrel, battleground, disputed point, bone of contention, apple of discord, question at issue.

V. disagree, clash, jar, conflict, misunderstand, live like cat and dog; differ; dissent, etc., 489.

quarrel, fall out, dispute, litigate; controvert, squabble, altercate, row [*colloq.*], wrangle, bicker, nag, spar, brawl.

split, break with; declare war, try conclusions, join issue, pick a quarrel; sow dissension, embroil, entangle, disunite, widen the breach; set (*or* pit) against.

Adj. discordant, dissident, out of tune, dissonant, harsh, grating, jangling, unmelodious; on bad terms, dissentient, unreconciled, unpacified; inconsistent, contradictory, incongruous.

quarrelsome, heated, unpacific, controversial, polemic, disputatious, factious.

at strife, at odds, at loggerheads, at daggers drawn, at variance, at issue, at cross-purposes, at sixes and sevens, embroiled, torn, disunited.

714. CONCORD.—*N.* concord, accord, harmony, homologue, correspondence, agreement, sympathy, response; union, unison, unity, peace, unanimity; happy family.

amity, etc. (*friendship*), 888; alliance, *entente cordiale* [F.], good understanding, conciliation, arbitration, reunion.

peacemaker, intercessor, interceder, mediator.

V. agree, accord, harmonize with, fraternize, go hand in hand, run parallel, concur, co-operate, pull together, sing in chorus.

side with, sympathize with; go with, chime in with, fall in with; assent, etc., 488; reciprocate.

smooth, pour oil on the troubled waters, keep in good humor, meet halfway; mediate, intercede.

Adj. concordant, congenial; in accord, harmonious, united, cemented, allied, friendly, fraternal, conciliatory, of one mind.

Adv. unanimously, with one voice, in concert with, hand in hand.

715. DEFIANCE.—*N.* defiance, dare, defial; challenge; threat, etc., 909; war cry, war whoop.

V. defy, dare, beard, brave, set at defiance, set at naught, hurl defiance at; laugh to scorn; disobey, etc., 742; threaten; challenge.

Adj. defiant; rebellious, bold, insolent, reckless, contemptuous, greatly daring, regardless of consequences.

Adv. in the teeth of; under one's very nose; in open rebellion.

716. ATTACK.—*N.* attack, assault, onset, onslaught, charge.

aggression, offense; incursion, inroad, invasion; irruption, outbreak; sally, sortie, raid, foray.

storm, storming, boarding, escalade; siege, investment, bombardment, cannonade, barrage; zero hour.

fire, volley, fusilade; sharpshooting, broadside, cross-fire.

thrust, lunge, pass, home thrust; cut.

assailant, aggressor, invader; sharpshooter, dead shot.

V. attack, assault, assail; set upon, pounce upon, fall upon, charge; enter the lists.

show fight, take the offensive; strike at, thrust at; aim (*or* deal) a blow at; be the aggressor, strike the first blow, fire the first shot; advance (*or* march) against, march upon, invade, harry.

close with, come to close quarters, bring to bay, come to blows.

fire upon, fire at, draw a bead on, shoot at, pop at, level at, open fire, pepper, bombard, shell, fire a volley.

besiege, beset, beleaguer, invest; sap, mine; storm, board, scale the walls, go over the top.

cut and thrust, bayonet, butt; kick, strike, etc., 276; horsewhip, whip.

Adj. aggressive, offensive; up in arms; amuck.

Adv. on the warpath; over the top; at bay.

717. DEFENSE.—*N.* defense, protection, guard, ward; guardianship.

self-defense, self-preservation; resistance, etc., 719.

safeguard, screen, fortification, bulwark, trench, mine, dugout;

moat, ditch, intrenchment; rampart, dike; parapet, battlement, bastion, redoubt, embankment, mound, bank, breastwork, earthwork, fieldwork; buttress, abutment, fence, wall, paling, palisade, stockade; barrier, barricade, boom; portcullis, barbed-wire entanglements.

stronghold, hold, fastness, asylum, keep, donjon, citadel, capitol, castle; tower, fortress, fort, barrack; blockhouse.

[protective devices] buffer, fender, cowcatcher, armor; mail, shield, buckler.

defender, protector, guardian, bodyguard, champion; knight-errant, paladin; garrison.

V. defend, guard, ward (or beat) off, shield, screen, shroud; garrison, man; fence, intrench, arm, accouter.

repel, parry, put to flight; hold (or keep) at bay; resist invasion, stand siege, stand (or act) on the defensive, show fight; stand one's ground, hold, stand in the gap.

Adj. defensive; armed, armed at all points (or to the teeth); panoplied, accoutered; iron-plated, ironclad; bulletproof, bombproof; protective.

Adv. on the defensive, in defense, in self-defense; at bay.

718. RETALIATION.—N. retaliation, reprisal, retort; counter-stroke, counterblast; retribution.

requital, desert; tit for tat, give-and-take, blow for blow, an eye for an eye; boomerang.

recrimination, accusation; revenge, etc., 919; compensation.

V. retaliate, retort, turn upon; pay, pay off, pay back; cap, match; reciprocate, turn the tables upon, return the compliment; exchange blows; give and take, be quits, be even with; pay off old scores.

Adj. retaliatory, retaliative, retributive, recriminatory, reciprocal.

719. RESISTANCE.—N. resistance, stand, front, opposition, recalcitrance, repugnance, repulsion.

repulse, rebuff, snub.

insurrection, revolt, etc., 742; strike, lockout; boycott; riot.

V. resist; withstand; stand, stand firm (or fast, one's ground), stick it out [colloq.].

face, confront, breast the wave, stem the tide; grapple with; show a bold front, make a stand.

oppose, etc., 708; fly in the face of; withstand an attack, rise up in arms, strike, turn out, boycott; revolt, rebel; repel, repulse.

Adj. resistant, resistive, refractory, repugnant, recalcitrant, repulsive, repellent; up in arms.

unconquerable, stubborn, unconquered; indomitable, unyielding.

720. CONTENTION.—*N.* **contention,** strife, contest, struggle; belligerency, pugnacity, opposition.

controversy, polemics; debate, war of words, paper war, high words, quarrel, litigation.

competition, rivalry, match, race; athletics, athletic sports; games of skill.

conflict, skirmish; encounter, rencounter, rencontre, collision, affair, brush, fracas, etc. (*discord*), 713; clash of arms; tussle, scuffle, bout, broil, fray, affray, fight, battle, combat, action, engagement, joust, tournament, tourney; pitched battle; guerrilla (*or* irregular) warfare; death struggle, Armageddon.

duel, single combat, satisfaction, passage of arms, affair of honor; hostile meeting, appeal to arms.

V. **contend,** contest, strive, struggle, scramble, wrestle; spar, exchange blows, tussle, tilt, box, fence; skirmish, fight; wrangle; oppose, etc., 708; join issue.

compete (*or* cope, vie, race) with, emulate, rival; run a race.

Adj. **contentious,** combative, bellicose, belligerent, warlike, quarrelsome, pugnacious, pugilistic.

athletic, gymnastic, competitive, rival.

721. PEACE.—*N.* **peace,** amity, etc. (*friendship*), 888; harmony, concord, tranquillity, truce, pipe of peace, calumet.

piping time of peace, quiet life; neutrality; pacifism.

V. **be at peace,** keep the peace, make peace, pacify; be a pacifist.

Adj. **pacific;** peaceable, peaceful; calm, tranquil, untroubled, halcyon; bloodless; neutral, pacifistic.

722. WARFARE.—*N.* **warfare,** fighting, hostilities; war, arms, the sword, bloodshed; Mars.

appeal to arms (*or* the sword); ordeal (*or* wager) of battle; declaration of war.

battle array, campaign, crusade, expedition; warpath.

art of war, rules of war, the war game, tactics, strategy, generalship.

battle, conflict, etc. (*contention*), 720; service, campaigning, active service, tented field; war to the death (*or* knife).

war medal, military medal, Congressional Medal, Victoria Cross, V. C. [Eng.], *Croix de guerre* [F.], *Médaille militaire* [F.], Iron Cross [Ger.].

V. **war,** make war, go to war, declare war, wage war, arm, take up (*or* appeal to) arms; take the field, give battle, engage, fight, combat, contend, battle with.

serve; enroll, enlist; be on service (*or* active service), campaign;

smell powder, be under fire; be on the warpath, keep the field; take by storm; go over the top [*colloq.*]; sell one's life dearly.

Adj. **armed,** in (*or* under) arms, in battle array, in the field; embattled; battled.

warlike, belligerent, combative, bellicose, martial, military, militant; soldierly, chivalrous; civil, internecine; irregular, guerrilla.

Adv. in the thick of the fray, in the cannon's mouth; at the sword's point, at the point of the bayonet.

723. PACIFICATION.—*N.* **pacification,** conciliation, reconciliation, reconcilement; accommodation, arrangement, adjustment; terms, compromise; amnesty.

peace offering; olive branch; calumet, peace pipe.

truce, armistice; suspension of arms (*or* hostilities); truce of God; flag of truce, white flag.

V. **pacify,** tranquillize, compose, allay, reconcile, propitiate, placate, conciliate, meet halfway, hold out the olive branch, heal the breach, make peace, restore harmony, bring to terms.

raise a siege, sheathe the sword, bury the hatchet, lay down one's arms, turn swords into plowshares.

Adj. **conciliatory,** pacificatory.

724. MEDIATION.—*N.* **mediation,** mediatorship, intervention, interposition, interference, intercession; parley, negotiation, arbitration, good offices.

mediator, intercessor, peacemaker, negotiator, go-between, diplomatist, propitiator; umpire, arbitrator.

V. **mediate,** intercede, interpose, interfere, intervene; step in, negotiate; meet halfway; arbitrate, propitiate.

Adj. **mediatory,** propitiatory, diplomatic.

725. SUBMISSION.—*N.* **submission,** yielding, acquiescence, compliance, submissiveness, deference, nonresistance, obedience.

surrender, cession, capitulation, resignation, backdown [*colloq.*].

obeisance, homage, kneeling, genuflection, curtsy, kowtow [Chinese], salaam [Oriental], prostration.

V. **submit,** succumb, yield, defer to; bend, stoop; accede, resign oneself.

surrender, cede, capitulate, come to terms, lay down one's arms, strike one's flag, give way (*or* ground, in, up); obey.

yield obeisance, kneel to, bow to, pay homage to, cringe to, truckle to; kneel, bow submission, curtsy, kowtow [Chinese].

Adj. **submissive,** resigned, crouching, prostrate; unresisting, humble.

untenable, indefensible, insupportable, unsupportable.

726. COMBATANT.—*N.* **combatant;** belligerent, assailant, swashbuckler, duelist, swordsman; competitor, rival.

fighter, fighting man, prize fighter, pugilist, bruiser; gladiator.

soldier, warrior, brave, man at arms, guardsman, gendarme [F.]; campaigner, veteran; military man; knight; myrmidon, mercenary, irregular, free lance, franctireur; private, Tommy Atkins [Brit.], doughboy [*slang*], rank and file; sepoy [India], spearman, pikeman; archer, bowman; musketeer, rifleman, sharpshooter, skirmisher; grenadier, fusileer, infantryman, foot soldier, chasseur, zouave, artilleryman, gunner, cannoneer, engineer; cavalryman, trooper, dragoon; cuirassier, hussar, lancer; recruit, rookie [*slang*], conscript, drafted man, enlisted man.

officer, etc. (*commander*), 745; subaltern, ensign, standard-bearer.

horse and foot; cavalry, horse, light horse; infantry, foot, rifles; artillery, horse artillery, field artillery, gunners; military train.

armed force, troops, soldiery, military, forces, the army, standing army, regulars, the line; militia, national guard, state guard, yeomanry, volunteers, minutemen [*Am. hist.*]; posse; guards, yeomen of the guard, beefeaters [Eng.], lifeguards, household troops, bodyguard.

levy, draft; raw levies, awkward squad.

army, army corps; division, column, wing, detachment, garrison, flying column, brigade, regiment, battalion, squadron, company, battery, section, platoon, squad; picket, guard, legion, phalanx, cohort.

navy, first line of defense, wooden walls, naval forces, fleet, flotilla, armada, squadron; man-of-war's man, etc. (*sailor*), 269; marines.

man-of-war, line-of-battle ship, ship of the line, battleship, warship, ironclad, war vessel, superdreadnought, dreadnought, cruiser; torpedo boat, destroyer, gunboat, submarine, submersible, U-boat [Ger.]; submarine chaser, monitor; frigate, sloop of war, corvet, flagship; privateer; troopship, transport, tender.

airplane, hydroplane, seaplane, flying boat; glider; divebomber, bomber, Flying Fortress; dirigible, blimp [*cant*]; zeppelin, etc. (*aeronautics*), 273.

727. ARMS.—*N.* arms; arm, weapon, deadly weapon; armament; armor.

side arms, sword, cold steel, naked steel, steel, blade; broadsword, saber, cutlass, scimitar, rapier, foil, dagger, poniard, dirk, stiletto, bowie knife, bayonet.

ax, battle-ax, poleax, halberd, tomahawk, bill, partisan.

spear, lance, pike, assagai, javelin, dart, arrow; harpoon, boomerang; oxgoad, ankus.

club, war club, mace, truncheon, staff, bludgeon, cudgel, shillelagh, quarterstaff; billy, life preserver, blackjack.

bow, crossbow, long bow; catapult, sling.

firearms; gun, piece; artillery, ordnance; park, battery; cannon, fieldpiece, field gun, siege gun, mortar, howitzer, pompom, seventy-five [*French rapid-fire 75-mm. field gun*]; Lewis gun.

small arms; musketry; musket, firelock, fowling piece, rifle, carbine, blunderbuss, matchlock, harquebus, shotgun, breechloader, muzzle-loader, magazine rifle, automatic pistol, automatic, revolver, repeater; shooting iron [*slang*], six-shooter [*colloq.*], gun [*colloq. for revolver or pistol*], pistol.

missile, bolt, projectile, shot, ball, slug; grape, shrapnel, grenade, shell, bomb, depth bomb, smoke bomb, gas bomb; bullet; dumdum (*or* explosive, expanding) bullet; torpedo.

ammunition; powder, powder and shot; explosive; gunpowder; dynamite, cordite; cartridge; poison gas, mustard gas, chlorine gas, tear gas, etc.

728. ARENA.—*N.* arena, field, platform; scene of action, theater, walk, course; hustings; stage, boards, amphitheater, coliseum, colosseum; hippodrome, circus, race course, turf, cock-pit, bear garden, gymnasium, ring, lists; campus, playing field, playground.

battlefield, battleground, field of battle; no man's land [*First World War*]; theater (*or* seat) of war.

729. COMPLETION.—*N.* **completion;** accomplishment, achievement, fulfillment, performance, execution; dispatch, consummation, culmination; finish, conclusion; limit, close, finale, denouement, issue, upshot, result.

V. **complete,** perfect, effect, accomplish, achieve, compass, consummate, bring to maturity (*or* perfection); elaborate.

do, execute, make, work out, enact, dispatch, knock off [*colloq.*], finish off, dispose of, perform, discharge, fulfill, realize; carry out (*or* into effect).

do thoroughly, not do by halves, drive home; carry through, deliver the goods [*colloq.*].

finish, bring to a close, wind up, clinch, seal, put the last (*or* finishing) touch to; crown, crown all; cap.

Adj. **conclusive,** final, crowning, exhausting, complete, mature, perfect, consummate, thorough.

Adv. to crown all, as a last stroke, as a fitting climax.

730. NONCOMPLETION.—*N.* **noncompletion,** nonfulfill-ment, nonperformance, neglect, etc., 460; shortcoming, incom-pleteness; drawn battle, drawn game.

V. **leave unfinished,** leave undone, neglect, etc., 460; let alone, let slip; lose sight of.

fall short of, do things by halves, hang fire; collapse.

Adj. **incomplete,** uncompleted, unfinished, unaccomplished, unperformed, unexecuted; sketchy; sterile.

Adv. without (*or* lacking) the final touches.

731. SUCCESS—*N.* **success,** successfulness; progress; ad-vance; good fortune, prosperity, etc., 734; profit.

trump card; hit, stroke, master stroke; ten-strike [*colloq.*]; checkmate; prize.

mastery, advantage over; upper hand, whip hand; ascendancy, conquest, victory, walkover [*colloq.*], triumph.

victor, conqueror, master, champion, winner; master of the situation (*or* position).

V. **succeed,** be successful, gain one's end (*or* ends); crown with success; gain (*or* attain, carry, secure) a point *or* an object; get there [*slang*]; manage to, contrive to; accomplish, effect; come off successfully, take (*or* carry) by storm; gain the day (*or* prize, palm); carry all before one, score a success.

make progress, etc. (*advance*), 282; win (*or* make, work) one's way; speed; turn to account, prosper, etc., 734; strike oil [*slang*], make one's fortune.

triumph, be triumphant, gain a victory (*or* an advantage); surmount (*or* overcome) a difficulty, stem the torrent, weather the storm, master; distance, surpass, win.

defeat, conquer, discomfit, vanquish, overcome, overthrow, overpower, overmaster, outwit, outdo, outmaneuver, outgeneral, checkmate, beat, rout, floor, worst, lick to a frazzle [*colloq.*]; settle [*colloq.*], do for [*colloq.*], subdue, subjugate, reduce.

quell, silence, put down, confound, nonplus, baffle, circumvent, elude; drive to the wall.

avail, answer, answer the purpose; prevail, take effect, do, turn out well, take [*colloq.*], tell, bear fruit.

Adj. **successful;** prosperous, etc., 734; triumphant, crowned with success, victorious; unbeaten.

Adv. **successfully,** with flying colors, in triumph, swimmingly.

732. FAILURE.—*N.* **failure,** unsuccess, nonsuccess, nonfulfillment; labor in vain, no go [*colloq.*], inefficacy; vain attempt; frustration, disappointment.

blunder, error, etc., 495; fault, omission, miss, oversight, slip, trip, stumble; step, *faux pas* [F.]; scrape, mess, muddle, botch, fiasco.

mishap, etc. (*misfortune*), 735; split, collapse, smash, blow, explosion.

repulse, rebuff, defeat, rout, overthrow, discomfiture; beating, drubbing; subjugation, checkmate.

fall, downfall, ruin, perdition, wreck; deathblow; bankruptcy.

V. **fail,** be unsuccessful, make vain efforts, labor in vain; flunk [*colloq.*]; bring to naught, make nothing of, fall short of, go to the wall [*colloq.*], lick the dust; be defeated, have the worst of it, lose the day, lose; succumb.

miss, miss one's aim (*or* the mark), slip, trip, stumble, blunder, miscarry.

flounder, falter, limp, halt, hobble, fall, tumble, run aground, split upon a rock, break down, sink, drown, founder, come to grief.

come to nothing, end in smoke; flat out [*colloq.*]; fall through, hang fire, flash in the pan, collapse, go to wrack and ruin.

Adj. **unsuccessful,** successless, at fault; unfortunate, etc., 735; abortive, sterile, fruitless, bootless; ineffectual, ineffective, inefficient, lame, insufficient, unavailing.

stranded, aground, grounded, swamped, wrecked, shipwrecked, foundered, capsized.

undone, lost, ruined, broken, bankrupt, played out; done up, done for [*colloq.*]; broken down, overborne, overwhelmed; all up with [*colloq.*].

frustrated, thwarted, crossed, disconcerted; unhorsed, hard hit, stultified, befooled, dished [*colloq.*], foiled, defeated, victimized, sacrificed.

Adv. to little or no purpose, in vain.

733. TROPHY.—*N.* trophy; medal, prize, palm, laurel, laurels, bays, crown, chaplet, wreath; eulogy, citation; scholarship; garland; triumphal arch; war medal, etc., 722; Carnegie medal, Nobel prize; blue ribbon; decoration, etc., 877.

734. PROSPERITY.—*N.* prosperity, welfare, well-being; affluence, etc. (*wealth*), 803; success, etc., 731; luck, good fortune, good luck, blessings, godsend; bed of roses; fat of the land.

upstart, parvenu, *nouveau riche* [F.], mushroom.

V. prosper, thrive, flourish, swim with the tide; rise (*or* get on) in the world; light on one's feet; bask in the sunshine; have a run of luck; make one's fortune, feather one's nest, make one's pile [*slang*].

flower, blossom, bloom, fructify, bear fruit; fatten, batten.

Adj. prosperous, thriving, well off, well to do, at one's ease; rich, etc., 803; fortunate, lucky; palmy, halcyon.

auspicious, propitious, providential.

Adv. prosperously, swimmingly; as good luck would have it.

735. ADVERSITY.—*N.* adversity, evil, etc., 619; failure, etc., 732; bad (*or* ill, evil, adverse, hard) fortune *or* luck, frowns of fortune; broken fortunes; slough of despond; evil day, hard times, rainy day, cloud, gathering clouds, ill-wind; affliction, trouble, hardship, curse, blight, load, pressure, humiliation.

misfortune, mishap, mischance, misadventure, disaster, calamity, catastrophe; accident, casualty, blow, trial, sorrow, visitation, infliction, reverse, check, setback, contretemps [F.].

downfall, fall; losing game; ruin, undoing, extremity.

V. come to grief, go downhill, go to wrack and ruin, go to the dogs [*colloq.*]; fall, decay, sink, decline, go down in the world; have seen better days; be all up with [*colloq.*].

Adj. unfortunate, unblest, unhappy, unlucky, unprosperous, hoodooed [*colloq.*], luckless, hapless, out of luck; under a cloud; badly off; in adverse circumstances; poor, etc., 804; decayed, undone, on the road to ruin.

ill-fated, ill-starred, ill-omened; devoted, doomed; inauspicious, ominous, sinister, unpropitious, unfavorable.

adverse, untoward; disastrous, calamitous, ruinous, dire, deplorable.

Adv. from bad to worse, out of the frying pan into the fire.

736. MEDIOCRITY.—*N.* mediocrity, golden mean, moderation; moderate (*or* average) circumstances; respectability.

middle classes, *bourgeoisie* [F.].

V. strike the golden mean; preserve a middle course.

jog on, get along [*colloq.*], get on tolerably (*or* respectably).

Adj. middling, so-so, fair, medium, moderate, mediocre, ordinary.

Adv. with nothing to brag about.

II. INTERSOCIAL VOLITION[1]

737. AUTHORITY.—*N.* authority; influence, patronage, power, prestige, prerogative, jurisdiction.

right, divine right, authoritativeness, royalty, absolutism, despotism, tyranny.

command, empire, sway, rule; dominion, domination; sovereignty, supremacy, suzerainty, kingship; lordship, headship, leadership, mastership, government, dictation, control, hold, grasp; grip, iron sway, rod of empire.

reign, dynasty, administration; dictatorship, protectorate, presidency, presidentship, consulship, magistracy.

Governments: empire; monarchy; limited (*or* constitutional) monarchy; aristocracy; oligarchy, democracy, republic; triumvirate; autocracy; dictatorship, totalitarian state.

representative government, constitutional government, home rule, dominion rule [Brit.], colonial government; self-government, autonomy, self-determination; republicanism, federalism; socialism; communism; authoritarianism; totalitarianism; bureaucracy; martial law; feudal system, feudalism.

state, realm, commonwealth, country, power, body politic.

ruler, person in authority, lord, etc., 745; judicature, etc., 965; cabinet, etc. (*council*), 696; seat of government, headquarters.

V. authorize, empower, etc., 760; warrant, dictate.

rule, sway, command, control, administer, govern, direct, lead, preside over, be at the head of, reign.

dominate, have the upper (*or* whip) hand; preponderate, boss [*colloq.*]; override, overrule, overawe; lord it over, keep under, bend to one's will, have it all one's own way, be master of the situation, take the lead, lay down the law.

Adj. ruling, regnant, dominant, paramount, supreme, predominant, preponderant, in the ascendant, influential; imperious, dictatorial, peremptory; authoritative, executive, administrative, official, gubernatorial, bureaucratic, departmental.

sovereign; regal, royal, royalist, monarchical, kingly; dynastic, imperial, autocratic; oligarchic, democratic, republican.

[1]Implying the action of the will of one mind over the will of another.

Adv. in the name of, by the authority of, at one's command, in virtue of, under the auspices of.

738. [Absence of authority] LAXITY.—*N.* **laxity;** laxness, looseness, slackness; toleration, lenity, etc., 740; relaxation; freedom, etc., 748.

anarchy, interregnum; misrule, license, insubordination, mob rule, mob law, lynch law, nihilism, reign of violence.

Deprivation of power: dethronement, impeachment, deposition, abdication; usurpation.

V. **be lax,** hold a loose rein; give the reins to, give rope enough, give free rein to; tolerate; relax; misrule.

have one's fling, act without authority, act on one's own responsibility, usurp authority.

dethrone, depose; abdicate.

Adj. **lax,** loose; slack, remiss, negligent, etc., 460; weak.

relaxed, licensed, unbridled; anarchic *or* anarchical, nihilistic; unauthorized.

739. SEVERITY.—*N.* **severity;** strictness, harshness, rigor, stringency, austerity, inclemency; arrogance, etc., 885.

arbitrary power; absolutism, despotism; dictatorship, autocracy, tyranny, domination, oppression, assumption, usurpation; inquisition, reign of terror, iron rule, coercion, etc., 744; martial law.

bureaucracy, red-tapism, officialism.

tyrant, disciplinarian, martinet, stickler, despot, autocrat, oppressor, inquisitor, extortioner.

V. **arrogate,** assume, usurp, take liberties; domineer, bully, tyrannize, put on the screw, be hard upon, ill-treat, rule with a rod of iron, oppress, override, trample under foot, ride roughshod over; coerce, etc., 744.

Adj. **severe,** strict, hard, harsh, dour [Scot.], rigid, stern, rigorous, uncompromising, exacting, searching, inexorable, inflexible, obdurate, austere, relentless, stringent, strict, strait-laced, peremptory, absolute, arbitrary, imperative, coercive, tyrannical, extortionate, oppressive, cruel, arrogant; formal, punctilious.

Adv. with a high (*or* strong, tight, heavy) hand.

740. MILDNESS.—*N.* **mildness,** lenity, moderation, temperateness; tolerance, toleration, mildness, gentleness; favor; indulgence, clemency, mercy, forbearance, quarter, compassion, etc., 914.

V. **be lenient,** tolerate, bear with; spare the vanquished, give quarter; indulge, spoil.

Adj. **lenient,** mild, gentle, tolerant, indulgent, easy, moderate, complaisant, easygoing; clement, compassionate, forbearing; long-suffering.

741. COMMAND.—*N.* command, order, ordinance, act, fiat, bidding, word, call, beck, nod; direction, injunction, charge, instructions; dispatch, message.

demand, exaction, imposition, requisition, claim, requirement, ultimatum; request, etc., 765.

decree, dictate, dictation, mandate, precept; prescript, writ, ordination, bull, edict, dispensation, prescription, enactment, law, act; warrant, passport, summons, subpoena, citation; word of command, order of the day.

V. command, order, decree, enact, ordain, dictate, direct, give orders, issue a command; call to order; assume the command.

prescribe, set, appoint, mark out; set (*or* prescribe, impose) a task; set to work.

bid, enjoin, charge, instruct; require, demand, exact, impose, tax.

claim, lay claim to, reclaim.

cite, summon, call for, send for; subpoena; beckon.

Adj. commanding, authoritative, imperative, decisive, final.

Adv. in a commanding tone; by a stroke (*or* dash) of the pen; by order.

742. DISOBEDIENCE.—*N.* disobedience, insubordination, contumacy; infraction, infringement, violation.

revolt, rebellion, mutiny, outbreak, rising, uprising, insurrection, riot, tumult, strike.

sedition, treason; lese majesty; defection, secession, revolution; bolshevism.

insurgent, mutineer, rebel, traitor, communist, Fenian, Sinn Feiner, Red, Bolshevist, seceder, Secessionist [esp., U. S. hist.] *or* Secesh [*colloq. or slang*, U. S.]; apostate, renegade, anarchist.

V. disobey, violate, infringe; shirk, slack; defy, set at defiance, run riot, take the law into one's own hands; kick over the traces; refuse to support, bolt [*politics*].

resist, strike, rise, rise in arms; secede, mutiny, rebel.

Adj. disobedient, unruly, ungovernable; insubordinate, restive, refractory, defiant, contumacious; recusant, recalcitrant.

lawless, riotous, mutinous, seditious, insurgent, revolutionary.

743. OBEDIENCE.—*N.* obedience, observance, compliance; submission, subjection; nonresistance, passivity, resignation, submissiveness, ductility, obsequiousness, servility.

allegiance, loyalty, fealty, homage, deference, devotion; constancy, fidelity.

V. obey, submit, etc., 725; comply, do one's bidding, attend to orders, serve faithfully (*or* loyally, devotedly, without question); be resigned to, be submissive to; serve, etc., 746; play second fiddle.

Adj. **obedient,** law-abiding, complying, compliant; loyal, faithful, devoted; under beck and call, under control.

resigned, passive; submissive, etc., 725; unresisting, pliant.

Adv. as you please, if you please; in compliance with, in obedience to.

744. COMPULSION.—*N.* **compulsion,** coercion, constraint; restraint, etc., 751; enforcement, draft, conscription; eminent domain.

force; brute (*or* main, physical) force; the sword; mob law, martial law.

necessity, etc., 601; spur of necessity, Hobson's choice.

V. **compel,** force, make, drive, dragoon, coerce, constrain, enforce, necessitate, oblige.

extort, wring from, force upon, drag into; bind, pin down; require; tax, put in force; commandeer; restrain, etc., 751.

Adj. **compelling,** coercive, inexorable, compulsory, obligatory, stringent, peremptory, binding.

Adv. **forcibly,** by force, by force of arms; on compulsion, perforce, under protest, in spite of, in one's teeth; against one's will.

745. MASTER.—*N.* **master,** lord, commander, commandant, captain, chief, chieftain; paterfamilias [*Rom. law*], patriarch; sahib [India], head, senior, governor, ruler, dictator, leader, director, boss; sachem, sagamore.

potentate; liege, liege lord, suzerain, overlord, sovereign, monarch, crowned head, emperor, king, majesty, protector, president; autocrat, despot, tyrant, oligarch, dictator.

caesar, kaiser, czar, sultan, caliph, mogul, great mogul, mikado, inca; prince, duke, etc. (*nobility*), 875; archduke, doge; maharaja, raja, emir, nizam, nawab [*Indian ruling chiefs*].

empress, queen, sultana, czarina, princess, infanta, duchess, maharani, rani [both Hindu], begum [Moham.].

regent, viceroy, khedive, pasha, bey, mandarin.

the authorities, the powers that be, the government; staff, official, man in office, person in authority.

Military authorities: marshal, field marshal, generalissimo; commander in chief, general, brigadier general, brigadier, lieutenant general, major general, colonel, lieutenant colonel, major, captain, lieutenant, sublieutenant; officer, staff officer, aide-de-camp, adjutant, ensign, cornet, cadet, subaltern; noncommissioned officer; sergeant, top sergeant, corporal.

Civil authorities: mayor, prefect, chancellor, magistrate, syndic; burgomaster, seneschal, alderman, warden, constable.

Naval authorities: admiral, admiralty; commodore, captain, commander, lieutenant; skipper, master, mate.

746. SERVANT.—*N.* **servant,** retainer, follower, henchman, servitor, domestic, menial, help [*local*], employee; attaché [F.], official.

subject, liege, liegeman.

retinue, suite, cortege, staff, court; office force, clerical staff, clerical force, workers, associate workers, employees, the help.

attendant, squire, usher, apprentice; page, buttons [*colloq.*]; trainbearer, cup-bearer; waiter, butler, lackey, footman, flunky [*colloq.*]; boy [*any colored male servant, as in the Orient, South Africa, etc.*]; valet, equerry, groom, jockey, hostler or ostler, orderly, messenger, caddie; secretary, stenographer, clerk, agent, under-ling, understrapper; man.

maid, maidservant; girl, help [*local*], handmaid, lady's maid, nurse, ayah [India], nursemaid; cook, scullion, Cinderella; general servant [Brit.], general-housework maid [U. S.], general [*colloq.*]; washerwoman, laundress, charwoman.

dependent, hanger-on, satellite, parasite, protégé [F.], ward, hireling, mercenary, puppet, creature; serf, vassal, thrall, slave, Negro, helot; bondsman, bondswoman; bondslave; villein [*hist.*], churl [*hist.*].

V. **serve,** minister to, help, co-operate; wait (or attend, dance attendance) upon; squire, valet, tend, do for [*colloq.*].

Adj. **serviceable,** useful, helpful, co-operative; at one's call.

servile, slavish, subject, thrall, bond; subservient, obsequious, base, fawning, truckling, sycophantic, parasitic, cringing.

747. [Insignia of authority] SCEPTER.—*N.* Regal: scepter, orb; pall; robes of state, ermine, purple; crown, coronet, diadem; triple plume; flail [Egyptian]; signet seal.

Ecclesiastical: tiara, triple crown; ring, keys; miter, crozier, crook, staff; cardi-nal's hat; bishop's apron (or sleeves, lawn, gaiters), fillet.

Military: epaulet, star, bar, eagle, crown [Brit.], oak leaf, Sam Browne belt; chevron, stripe.

caduceus; Mercury's staff (or rod, wand); mace, fasces, ax, truncheon, staff, baton, wand, rod; flag, etc. (*insignia*), 550; regalia; toga, mantle; decoration, title, etc., 877; portfolio.

throne, divan; woolsack [*seat of English Lord Chancellor in the House of Lords*], chair, seat, dais.

talisman, amulet, charm, sign.

748. FREEDOM.—*N.* freedom, liberty, independence; license, indulgence.

scope, range, latitude, play, free play (or scope), swing, full swing, elbowroom, margin, rope, wide berth.

franchise; prerogative, etc., 924.

freeman, freedman, citizen, denizen.

immunity, exemption; emancipation, etc., 750; right, privilege.

autonomy, self-government; free trade; self-determination, non-interference; Monroe Doctrine [U. S.].

independent, free lance, freethinker, free trader.

V. **be free,** have scope (or one's own way), do what one likes, go at large, feel at home, stand on one's rights.

free, liberate, set free, etc., 750; give the reins to; make free of, enfranchise.

Adj. **free,** independent, at large, loose, scot-free; unconstrained, unconfined, unchecked, unhindered, unobstructed, uncontrolled, ungoverned, unchained, unshackled, unfettered, unbridled, uncurbed, unmuzzled, unvanquished.

unrestricted, unlimited, unconditional; absolute; with unlimited power (*or* opportunity); discretionary.

unbiased, unprejudiced, uninfluenced; spontaneous.

free and easy, at ease, at one's ease; quite at home.

exempt, immune, freed, freeborn; autonomous, freehold.

gratuitous, gratis, etc., 815; for nothing, for love.

Adv. **freely,** at will, with no restraint.

749. SUBJECTION.—*N.* **subjection;** dependence, subordination; thrall, thralldom, subjugation, bondage, serfdom; feudalism, vassalage, slavery, enslavement; conquest.

service; servitude, employ, tutelage, constraint, yoke, submission, obedience.

V. **be subject,** be at the mercy of, depend upon; fall a prey to, fall under, play second fiddle; serve, etc., 746; obey, etc., 743; submit, etc., 725.

subjugate, subject, tame, break in; master, tread down, weigh down, keep under, enthrall, enslave, lead captive, rule, etc., 737; hold in bondage (*or* leading strings).

Adj. **subject,** dependent, subordinate; feudal, feudatory; under control; in leading strings, in harness; servile, slavish, enslaved, downtrodden; henpecked; under one's thumb, tied to one's apron strings, at one's beck and call; liable.

Adv. **under;** under orders (*or* command), at one's orders.

750. LIBERATION.—*N.* **liberation,** disengagement, release, emancipation, Emancipation Proclamation; enfranchisement, manumission; discharge, dismissal.

deliverance, etc., 672; redemption, extrication, acquittance, absolution, acquittal, escape.

V. **liberate,** free, set free, emancipate, release; enfranchise, manumit; demobilize, disband, discharge, dismiss; let go, let loose, let out, deliver, etc., 672; absolve, acquit.

unfetter, untie, loose, loosen, relax; unbolt, unbar, unhand, unbind, unchain, disengage, disentangle; clear, extricate; reprieve.

Adj. **liberated,** freed; foot-loose, one's own master.

Adv. **at large,** at liberty; adrift.

751. RESTRAINT.—*N.* **restraint;** hindrance, etc., 706; coercion, compulsion, constraint, repression; discipline, control; limitation, restriction, protection, monopoly; prohibition, economic pressure.

confinement, durance, duress; imprisonment, incarceration, thrall, thralldom, limbo, captivity; blockade.

keep, care, charge, custody, ward.

repressionist, monopolist, protectionist.

V. **restrain**, check, restrict, debar, hinder, constrain, coerce, compel, curb, harness, control; hold in leash, withhold, repress, suppress, keep under; smother, pull in, rein in, hold, prohibit.

fasten, enchain, fetter, shackle, trammel; bridle, muzzle, gag, pinion, manacle, handcuff, hobble, bind, swathe, swaddle; tether, picket, tie, secure.

confine, shut up (*or* in), lock up, box up, bottle up, cork up, seal up, blockade, hem in, bolt in, wall in, rail in; impound, pen, coop; inclose, cage, imprison, immure, incarcerate, entomb; put in irons, cast into prison.

arrest, take into custody; take (*or* make) prisoner, lead captive, send to prison, commit; give in charge (*or* custody).

Adj. **restrained**, constrained, repressive, suppressive; imprisoned, pent up, wedged in; on parole; doing time [*colloq. or slang*], in custody.

stiff, narrow, prudish, strait-laced, hidebound.

Adv. **under restraint** (*or* lock and key, hatches), under discipline; in prison, in jail, in durance vile, in confinement; behind bars, in captivity, under arrest.

752. [Means of restraint] **PRISON.**—*N.* **prison**, prisonhouse; jail, cage, coop, den, cell; stronghold, fortress, keep, donjon, dungeon, Bastille, penitentiary, state prison, lockup, station house, station [*colloq.*], pen [*also slang for penitentiary*], pound; penal settlement; workhouse [U. S.; *in England, a workhouse is a poorhouse*], reformatory, reform school.

Restraining devices: shackle, bond, gyve, fetter, irons, pinion, manacle, handcuff, straight jacket, stocks, pillory; vise, bandage, splint, strap; yoke, collar, halter, harness; muzzle, gag, bit, curb, snaffle, bridle; rein, reins, lines [U. S. and dial. Eng.], ribbons [*colloq.*]; tether, picket, band, chain, cord.

bar, bolt, lock, padlock; rail, paling, palisade; wall, fence, barrier, barricade.

drag, brake, check, etc. (*hindrance*), 706.

753. KEEPER.—*N.* **keeper**, custodian, ranger, gamekeeper, warder, jailer, turnkey, castellan, guard; watch, watchdog, watchman, concierge [F.], sentry, sentinel; coastguard.

escort, bodyguard; convoy.

guardian, protector, governor; duenna, governess, nurse.

754. PRISONER.—*N.* **prisoner**, convict, captive, close prisoner.

V. stand committed; be imprisoned.

Adj. **imprisoned**, in prison, in custody, in charge, behind bars, under lock and key, under hatches.

755. [Vicarious authority] **COMMISSION.**—*N.* **commission**, delegation; consignment, assignment; proxy, power of attorney, deputation, legation, mission, embassy; agency.

errand, charge, brevet, diploma, permit.

appointment, nomination, charter; ordination; installation, inauguration, investiture; accession, coronation, enthronement.

V. **commission**, delegate, depute; consign, assign, commit, charge, intrust, authorize.

accredit, engage, hire, bespeak, appoint, name, nominate, return; ordain, install, induct, inaugurate, invest, crown; enroll, enlist; employ, empower.

Adv. **instead of**, in one's stead, in one's place; as proxy for.

756. ANNULMENT.—*N.* **annulment**, nullification, cancellation, abrogation, revocation, repeal.

dismissal, *congé* [F.], sack [*slang*], deposition, dethronement; disestablishment, disendowment.

countermand, repudiation, retractation, recantation; abolition, abolishment; dissolution.

V. **annul**, cancel, destroy, abolish, abrogate, revoke, repeal, rescind, reverse, retract, recall; overrule, override; set aside; disannul, dissolve, quash, nullify, nol-pros [*law, short for nolle prosequi*], disestablish; countermand, counterorder, throw overboard.

disclaim, deny, ignore, repudiate; recant, break off.

dismiss, discard; turn out, cast off (*or* adrift, aside, away); send off, send away, discharge, get rid of, bounce [*slang*]; fire, sack [*both slang*].

cashier, oust, unseat, dethrone, depose, unfrock, strike off the roll, disbar.

757. RESIGNATION.—*N.* **resignation**, retirement, abdication; renunciation, retractation, retraction, disclaimer, abandonment, relinquishment.

V. **resign**, give up, throw up, lay down, abjure, renounce, forego, disclaim, retract, deny, desert.

vacate, abdicate, retire; tender (*or* hand in) one's resignation.

758. CONSIGNEE.—*N.* **consignee**, trustee, nominee; committee.

functionary, curator; treasurer, etc., 801; agent, factor, steward, bailiff, clerk, secretary, attorney, solicitor, proctor, broker, underwriter, commission agent, factotum, caretaker, employee; servant, etc., 746.

negotiator, go-between; middleman.

delegate, commissioner; emissary, envoy, messenger.

diplomatist, diplomat, ambassador, plenipotentiary, diplomatic agent, representative, resident, consul, legate, etc., 534; attaché [F.].

salesman, traveler, traveling salesman, commercial traveler, drummer, traveling man.

759. DEPUTY.—*N.* deputy, substitute, proxy, delegate, representative, alternate; vice-president.

regent, vicegerent, viceroy, minister, premier, chancellor, provost, warden, lieutenant, consul, ambassador; delegate, etc., 758.

team, eight, nine, eleven; captain, champion.

V. **represent,** stand for, appear for, hold a brief for, answer for; stand in the shoes of; stand in the stead of.

delegate, depute, empower, commission, substitute, accredit.

Adj. **acting,** vice, viceregal; accredited to; delegated, representative.

Adv. **in behalf of,** in the place of, as representing, by proxy.

760. PERMISSION.—*N.* permission, leave, allowance, sufferance, tolerance, toleration, connivance; liberty, law, license, concession, grace; indulgence, favor, dispensation, exemption, release; authorization, accordance, admission.

permit, warrant, sanction, authority, pass, passport; license, carte blanche [F.], grant, charter, patent.

V. **permit,** let, allow, admit; suffer, tolerate, recognize; concede, etc., 762; accord, vouchsafe, favor, humor, gratify, indulge, wink at, connive at.

grant, empower, charter, enfranchise, privilege, license, authorize, warrant, sanction; intrust, commission.

absolve, release, exonerate, dispense with.

Adj. **permitted,** permissible, allowable, lawful, legitimate, legal, legalized, chartered, unforbidden.

Adv. by (*or* with) leave, under favor of, by all means.

761. PROHIBITION.—*N.* prohibition, inhibition; veto, interdict, interdiction, injunction, embargo, ban, taboo, proscription, restriction; contraband; forbidden fruit; Volstead Act, 18th amendment [all U. S.].

V. **prohibit,** inhibit, forbid, disallow; bar, debar, hinder, restrain, etc., 751; withhold, limit, circumscribe, clip the wings of, restrict; interdict, taboo, proscribe; exclude, shut out.

Adj. **prohibitive,** prohibitory; proscriptive; restrictive, exclusive.

prohibited, unlicensed, contraband, taboo, illegal, unauthorized.

762. CONSENT.—*N.* consent; assent, etc., 488; acquiescence, approval, compliance, agreement, concession, accession, acknowledgment, acceptance; permit, etc. (*permission*), 760; promise, etc., 768.

settlement, adjustment, ratification, confirmation.

V. **consent;** assent, etc., 488; yield assent, admit, allow, concede, grant, yield; acknowledge, give consent, comply with, acquiesce, agree to, accede, accept, close with, satisfy, settle, come to terms; deign, vouchsafe, promise.

Adj. willing, compliant, agreeable [*colloq.*], eager.

763. OFFER.—*N.* **offer,** proffer, tender, bid, overture, proposal, proposition; motion, invitation, offering.

V. **offer,** proffer, present, tender; bid; propose, move, make a motion, start, invite, place at one's disposal; make possible, put forward, press, urge upon, hold out.

volunteer, come forward, be a candidate, offer (*or* present) oneself, stand for, bid for; seek; be at one's service.

Adj. in the market, for sale, to let, disengaged, on hire; at one's disposal.

764. REFUSAL.—*N.* **refusal,** rejection, denial, declension, flat (*or* point-blank) refusal; repulse, rebuff; discountenance, disapprobation.

negation, abnegation, protest, renunciation, disclaimer; dissent, etc., 489; revocation, annulment.

V. **refuse,** reject, deny, decline, turn down [*slang*], dissent, etc., 489; negative, withhold one's assent, grudge, begrudge; stand aloof, be deaf to, turn one's back upon, discountenance, forswear, set aside.

resist, repel, repulse, rebuff, deny oneself, discard, repudiate, rescind, disclaim, protest.

Adj. **uncomplying,** deaf to, noncompliant, unconsenting; recusant, dissentient.

Adv. on no account, not for the world, not on your life! [*colloq.*].

765. REQUEST.—*N.* **request,** requisition; claim, demand, etc., 741; petition, suit, prayer, solicitation, invitation, entreaty, importunity, supplication, invocation.

motion, overture, application, canvass, address, appeal, imprecation; proposal, proposition.

V. **request,** ask, beg, crave, sue, pray, petition, solicit, canvass, invite, beg leave, beg a boon, apply to, call to, call for; make a request, make application, claim, demand; offer up prayers.

entreat, beseech, plead, supplicate, implore; conjure, adjure; apostrophize, cry to, kneel to, appeal to; invoke, evoke; press, urge, importune, dun, clamor for, cry aloud, cry for help.

Adj. **importunate,** clamorous, urgent, solicitous; cap in hand.

Adv. **please,** prithee, do, pray; be so good as, be good enough; have the goodness, vouchsafe, will you, I pray thee, if you please.

766. [Negative request] DEPRECATION.—*N.* **deprecation,** expostulation; intercession, mediation, protest, remonstrance.

V. **deprecate,** protest, expostulate, enter a protest, remonstrate.

Adj. **deprecatory,** expostulatory, intercessory.

unsought, unbesought; unasked.

767. PETITIONER.—*N.* **petitioner,** solicitor, applicant, suppliant, supplicant, suitor, candidate, claimant, aspirant, competitor, bidder; place hunter.

salesman, drummer, etc., 758; canvasser.

beggar, mendicant, panhandler [*slang*], cadger.

hotel runner, runner [*both cant*], steerer [*colloq.*], barker [*colloq.*].

sycophant, parasite, etc. (*servility*), 886.

768. PROMISE.—*N.* **promise,** undertaking, word, troth, plight, pledge, parole, word of honor, vow, oath, profession, assurance, warranty, guarantee, insurance, obligation, contract, stipulation.

engagement, affiance, betrothal, marriage contract (*or* vow); plighted faith.

V. **promise,** undertake, engage; make (*or* form, enter into) an engagement; bind (*or* pledge) oneself; vow, swear, give (*or* pledge) one's word; betroth, plight faith.

assure, warrant, guarantee, covenant, agree, vouch for, attest; answer for, be answerable for; secure, give security, underwrite.

Adj. **promissory,** votive, under hand and seal, upon oath, upon affirmation.

promised, affianced, pledged, bound, committed, compromised.

Adv. as true as I live; in all soberness; upon my honor; my word for it.

769. COMPACT.—*N.* **compact,** contract, specialty, deal [*colloq.*], agreement, bargain; pact, bond, covenant, indenture [*law*]; stipulation, settlement, convention; compromise, negotiation.

treaty, protocol, concordat, charter, Magna Charta, pragmatic sanction.

ratification, completion, signature, seal, bond.

V. **contract,** covenant, agree for; engage, etc. (*promise*), 768.

negotiate, treat, stipulate, make terms; bargain.

conclude, close, close with, complete, strike a bargain; come to terms (*or* an understanding); compromise, settle; confirm, ratify, clinch, subscribe, underwrite; indorse, sign, seal.

Adj. **contractual,** complete, agreed; signed, sealed, and delivered.

Adv. **as agreed upon,** as promised, according to the contract.

770. CONDITIONS.—*N.* **conditions,** terms, articles, articles of agreement; memorandum, clauses, provisions, proviso, covenant, stipulation, obligation, ultimatum.

V. **condition,** stipulate, insist upon, make a point of; bind, tie up; fence in, hedge in, make (*or* come to) terms.

Adj. **conditional,** provisional, guarded, fenced, hedged in.

Adv. **conditionally,** provisionally, on condition; with a string to it [*colloq.*], with a reservation.

771. SECURITY.—*N.* **security,** guaranty, guarantee; gage, bond, tie, pledge, mortgage, debenture; bill of sale, lien, collateral, bail, stake, deposit, earnest.

promissory note; bill, bill of exchange; I O U; personal security, covenant.

acceptance, indorsement, signature, execution, stamp, seal.

sponsor, surety, bail, hostage; godchild, godfather, godmother.

authentication, verification, warrant, certificate, voucher, receipt.

deed, instrument, title deed, indenture; charter, paper, parchment, settlement, will, testament, codicil.

V. **give security,** give bail, go bail; pawn, put in pawn, pledge, mortgage.

guarantee, warrant, assure; accept, indorse, underwrite, insure.

execute, stamp; sign, seal.

Adj. **pledged,** pawned, in pawn, at stake, on deposit, as earnest.

772. OBSERVANCE.—*N.* **observance,** performance, compliance, acquiescence, concurrence; obedience, etc., 743; fulfillment, satisfaction, discharge; acquittance, acquittal; adhesion, ackowledgment; fidelity.

V. **observe,** comply with, respect, acknowledge, abide by; cling to, adhere to, be faithful to, act up to; meet, fulfill, carry out, execute, perform, discharge, keep one's word (*or* pledge).

Adj. **observant,** faithful, true, loyal, honorable, etc., 939; punctual, punctilious, scrupulous, as good as one's word.

Adv. to the letter.

773. NONOBSERVANCE.—*N.* **nonobservance,** noncompliance, evasion, failure, omission, neglect, slackness, laxness, laxity, informality; lawlessness, disobedience, etc., 742; bad faith, etc., 940.

infringement, infraction; violation, transgression; piracy, literary theft.

V. **evade,** fail, neglect, omit, elude, cut [*colloq.*], set aside, ignore; shut (*or* close) one's eyes to.

infringe, transgress, violate, steal, pirate [*a book, etc.*].

discard, repudiate, protest, nullify, declare null and void, cancel, forfeit.

Adj. **elusive,** evasive, slack, lax, casual, slippery; nonobservant.

774. COMPROMISE.—*N.* **compromise,** composition, middle term, compensation, adjustment, mutual concession.

V. **compromise,** commute, compound, split the difference, meet one halfway, give and take, come to terms, submit to arbitration, patch up, arrange, straighten out, adjust, agree, make the best of, make a virtue of necessity.

POSSESSIVE RELATIONS[1]

(1) Property

775. ACQUISITION.—*N.* **acquisition,** procurement; purchase, inheritance; gift, etc., 784.

recovery, redemption, salvage, find.

gain, thrift, money-making, pelf, lucre, filthy lucre, the main chance.

profit, earnings, wages, salary, emolument, income, remuneration; winnings, pickings, perquisite; proceeds, produce, product; outcome, output; return, fruit, crop, harvest; benefit; prize; wealth, etc., 803.

V. **acquire,** get, gain, win, earn, obtain, procure, gather; collect, pick, pick up, glean, find, light upon, come across, come at; scrape up (*or* together); get in, net, bag, secure; derive, draw, get in the harvest.

profit, turn to profit (*or* account), make capital out of, make money by, obtain a return, reap the fruits of; gain an advantage; make (*or* coin, raise) money, raise funds; realize, clear, produce, take, receive, come by, inherit.

recover, get back, regain, retrieve, redeem.

Adj. **profitable,** productive, advantageous, gainful, remunerative, paying, lucrative.

Adv. in the way of gain; for money; at interest.

776. LOSS.—*N.* **loss,** forfeiture, lapse; privation, bereavement, deprivation, riddance; damage, squandering, waste.

V. **lose,** incur a loss, miss, mislay, let slip, be deprived of, be without, forfeit.

squander, lavish, get rid of, waste.

Adj. **bereft,** bereaved, deprived of, shorn of, denuded, minus [*colloq., exc. in math.*], cut off; rid of, quit of, out of pocket, lost.

777. POSSESSION.—*N.* **possession,** ownership, proprietorship, occupancy, hold, holding, tenure, tenancy, dependency.

exclusive possession, monopoly, retention, corner.

future possession, heritage, inheritance, heirship, reversion; primogeniture.

V. **possess,** have, hold, occupy, enjoy, be possessed of, own, command, inherit.

[1]That is, relations which concern property.

monopolize, corner, engross, forestall, appropriate.

belong to, appertain to, pertain to; be in one's possession, vest in.

Adj. possessing, worth, possessed of, master of, in possession of; endowed (*or* blest, fraught, laden, charged) with.

possessed, on hand, in hand, in store, in stock; at one's command, at one's disposal.

777a. EXEMPTION.—*N.* exemption, exception, immunity, privilege, release.

V. not have, not possess, not own, be without.

Adj. devoid of, exempt from, without, unpossessed of, unblest with; immune from.

unpossessed; untenanted, vacant, without an owner.

778. [Joint possession] PARTICIPATION.—*N.* participation, joint tenancy; joint (*or* common) stock; partnership; communion; community of possessions, communism, collectivism, socialism; co-operation.

participator, sharer, partner; shareholder; joint tenant; tenants in common; coheir.

communist, communalist, collectivist, socialist.

V. participate, partake, share, share in, join in, go shares, go cahoots [*slang*], go halves; share and share alike.

communize, communalize; have (*or* possess) in common.

Adj. communistic, socialistic; co-operative, profit-sharing.

Adv. in common, share and share alike; on shares.

779. POSSESSOR.—*N.* possessor, holder, occupant, occupier, tenant, tenant at will, lessee, lodger.

owner; proprietor, proprietress, master, mistress, lord.

landholder, landowner, landlord, landlady; lord of the manor, laird [*Scot.*], landed gentry.

Future possessor: heir, heir apparent, heir presumptive; inheritor, heiress, inheritrix.

780. PROPERTY.—*N.* property, possession, tenure; ownership, etc., 777.

estate, interest, right, title, claim, demand, holding, vested interest; use, trust, benefit; term, lease, settlement; remainder, reversion.

dower, dowry, jointure, inheritance, heritage, patrimony, legacy.

assets, belongings, means, resources, circumstances; wealth, etc., 803; money, etc., 800; estate and effects.

realty, real estate, land, lands, landed (*or* real) property; tenements; plant, fixtures; ground; freehold, copyhold, leasehold.

manor, domain, demesne; farm, plantation, ranch.

territory, state, kingdom, principality, realm, empire, protectorate, dependency, sphere of influence, mandate.

personalty, personal property (*or* estate, effects), chattels, goods, effects, movables; stock, stock in trade, things, paraphernalia, equipage, appurtenances; income, etc., 810.

baggage, luggage [esp. in Eng.], impedimenta, bag and baggage; cargo.

V. possess, etc., 777; be the possessor, own; inherit.

Adj. landed, hereditary, entailed, real, personal.

Adv. to one's credit, to one's account; to the good.

781. RETENTION.—*N.* **retention,** detention, custody; tenacity, firm hold, grasp, gripe, grip, clutches, talon, claw, fang, tentacle.

captive, prisoner, bird in hand.

V. **retain,** keep, hold, hold fast, clinch, clench, clutch, grasp, gripe, hug; secure, withhold, detain; hold (*or* keep) back; husband, reserve; have (*or* keep) in stock; entail, tie up, settle.

Adj. **retentive,** tenacious.

782. RIDDANCE.—*N.* **riddance,** relinquishment, abandonment, renunciation, dereliction; cession, surrender, dispensation; resignation.

derelict, jetsam; abandoned farm [U. S.]; waif, foundling.

V. **relinquish,** give up, surrender, yield, cede; let go, let slip; spare, drop, resign, forego, renounce, abandon, give away, dispose of, part with; lay aside, set aside, discard, cast off, dismiss; maroon.

cast (*or* throw, fling) away, jettison.

supersede, give notice to quit, give warning; be (*or* get) rid of; eject.

divorce, cut off, desert, disinherit; separate.

Adj. **relinquished,** cast off, derelict; disowned, disinherited, divorced.

783. TRANSFER [of property].—*N.* **transfer,** conveyance, assignment, alienation, conveyancing, transmission, sale, lease, release, exchange, barter; succession, reversion.

V. **transfer,** convey, alienate, assign, grant, consign; make over, hand over, transmit, negotiate; hand down; exchange.

change hands, devolve, succeed; require, come into possession.

disinherit; dispossess, etc., 789; substitute.

Adj. **transferable,** alienable, negotiable, reversional, transmissive; inherited.

784. GIVING.—*N.* **giving,** bestowal, presentation, concession, cession; delivery, consignment, dispensation, endowment; investment, investiture; award, recompense, etc., 973.

charity, almsgiving, liberality, generosity.

gift, donation, present, boon, favor, benefaction, grant, offering, bonus, oblation, sacrifice.

allowance, contribution, subscription, subsidy, tribute.

bequest, legacy, devise, will, dot, dowry, dower.

gratuity, alms, largess, bounty, dole, help, offertory, honorarium, Christmas box, tip, baksheesh, consideration.

bribe, bait, peace offering; graft [colloq.].

giver, grantor, donor, testator; investor, subscriber, contributor; fairy godmother.

V. deliver, hand, pass, assign, hand (*or* make, deliver, turn) over.

pay, etc., 807; render, impart, communicate.

concede, cede, yield, part with, shed; spend, sacrifice.

give, bestow, donate, confer, grant; accord, award, assign, offer; present, give away, dispense, dispose of; give (*or* deal) out, fork out [*slang*]; allow, contribute, subscribe.

invest, endow, settle upon; bequeath, leave, devise.

furnish, supply, help, administer to, afford, spare, accommodate with, indulge with, favor with; lavish, pour on, thrust upon.

bribe, tip; grease the palm [*slang*].

Adj. charitable, eleemosynary, tributary; gratis, etc., 815; donative.

785. RECEIVING.—*N.* receiving, acquisition, etc., 775; reception, acceptance, admission.

recipient, receiver; assignee, legatee, grantee, lessee; beneficiary, pensioner.

income, etc. (*receipt*), 810.

V. receive; take, etc., 789; pocket; acquire, etc., 775; admit, take in, catch, accept.

be received; come in, come to hand, go into one's pocket; fall to one's lot (*or* share), accrue.

Adj. receiving, recipient; stipendiary, pensionary.

received, given, allowed; secondhand.

786. APPORTIONMENT.—*N.* apportionment, allotment, consignment, assignment, allocation, appropriation; distribution, division, deal; partition, administration.

portion, dividend, share, allotment, lot, measure, dose; dole, meed, pittance; ration; ratio, proportion, quota, modicum, allowance.

V. apportion, divide; distribute, administer, dispense; allot, allocate, detail, cast, share, mete; portion (*or* parcel, dole) out; deal, carve.

partition, assign, appropriate, appoint.

Adv. respectively, each to each; by lot; in equal shares.

787. LENDING.—*N.* lending, loan, advance, accommodation, mortgage, etc., 771; investment.

lender, pawnbroker, my uncle [*slang*], moneylender, usurer, Shylock.

V. lend, advance, accommodate with; lend on security; loan; pawn.

invest, intrust, place (*or* put) out to interest; place, put; embark, risk, venture, sink.

let, lease, sublet, sublease.

Adv. in advance; on loan, on security.

788. BORROWING.—*N.* borrowing, pledging, pawning.

V. borrow, pledge, pawn, put up the spout [*slang*], raise money, raise the wind [*slang*]; run into debt.

hire, rent, farm; take a lease.

appropriate, adopt, apply, imitate, make use of, take; plagiarize, pirate.

789. TAKING.—*N.* taking, reception, appropriation, capture, apprehension, seizure; abduction, abstraction.

dispossession; deprivation, bereavement, disinheritance; attachment, execution, sequestration, confiscation, eviction.

rapacity, rapaciousness, extortion, bloodsucking; theft, etc.,791.

taker, captor, capturer; extortioner *or* extortionist; vampire.

V. take, catch, hook, bag, sack, pocket, receive, accept.

reap, crop, cull, pluck, gather, draw.

appropriate, assume, possess oneself of; commandeer [*colloq.*]; help oneself to, make free with, lay under contribution; intercept; scramble for; deprive of.

seize, snatch, abstract, take away (*or* off), run away with; abduct, kidnap, capture, steal, pounce (*or* spring) upon; swoop down upon; take by storm; take prisoner; grapple, embrace, grip, gripe, clasp, grab [*colloq.*], clutch, collar, throttle, claw.

dispossess, take from, take away from; tear from, tear away from, wrench (*or* wrest, wring) from, extort; deprive of, bereave; disinherit, oust, evict, eject, divest; levy, distrain [*law*], confiscate; sequester, sequestrate, usurp; despoil, strip, fleece, bleed [*colloq.*].

Adj. predatory, wolfish, rapacious, ravening, ravenous; parasitic; all-devouring, all-engulfing.

790. RESTITUTION.—*N.* restitution, return, restoration, reinstatement, reinvestment, rehabilitation, reparation, atonement; compensation, indemnification; recovery.

V. restore, return, give back, render, give up, let go, release, remit; disgorge, recoup, reimburse, compensate, indemnify, reinvest, reinstate, rehabilitate, repair, make good.

recover, get back, retrieve, redeem; take back again.

Adj. compensatory, indemnificatory; reversionary, redemptive.

Adv. in full restitution; as partial compensation; to atone for.

791. STEALING.—*N.* stealing, theft, thievery, robbery, rapacity, thievishness, abstraction, appropriation, plagiarism, depredation; kidnaping.

pillage, spoliation, plunder, sack, rapine, brigandage, highway robbery, holdup [*slang*]; raid, foray, piracy, privateering, buccaneering, filibustering; burglary, housebreaking; shoplifting, blackmail.

peculation, embezzlement, fraud, forgery, larceny, pilfering; kleptomania.

V. steal, thieve, rob, purloin, pilfer, filch, bag, crib [*colloq.*], palm; abstract; appropriate, plagiarize.

abduct, convey away, carry off, kidnap, impress, make (*or* run) off with, run away with, spirit away, seize.

plunder, pillage, filibuster, rifle, sack, loot, ransack, spoil, despoil, strip, sweep, gut, forage, levy blackmail, maraud, poach, smuggle, bunko; hold up.

swindle, peculate, embezzle; sponge, pluck, fleece, defraud, obtain under false pretenses.

counterfeit, forge, coin, circulate bad money.

Adj. thievish, light-fingered, piratical; predatory, raptorial.

792. THIEF.—*N.* thief, robber, spoiler, depredator, pillager, marauder; pilferer, plagiarist; harpy, shark [*slang*], smuggler, poacher, kidnaper; crook [*slang*], shoplifter.

pirate, corsair, viking, buccaneer, privateer.

brigand, bandit, filibuster, freebooter, thug, cattle thief, bushranger, mosstrooper [*hist.*], highwayman, footpad, strong-arm man.

pickpocket, cutpurse, light-fingered gentry; sharper; cardsharper, trickster.

swindler, peculator, forger, coiner, counterfeiter; fence, receiver of stolen goods.

burglar, housebreaker, yegg [*slang*], cracksman [*slang*], sneak thief; second-story thief (*or* man).

793. BOOTY.—*N.* booty, spoil, plunder, prize, prey, loot, swag [*cant*]; perquisite, boodle [*polit. cant*], graft [*colloq.*], pork barrel [*polit. cant*], pickings; blackmail; stolen goods.

Adj. looting, plundering, spoliative.

794. BARTER.—*N.* barter, exchange, interchange, Indian gift [*colloq.*].

trade, commerce, buying and selling, traffic, business, custom, transaction, negotiation, bargain; speculation, jobbing, stockjobbing.

free trade [*opp. to* protection].

V. barter, exchange, truck, swap *or* swop [*colloq. and dial.*]; interchange.

trade, traffic, buy and sell, give and take, carry on (*or* ply) a trade; deal in, speculate.

bargain; drive (*or* make, strike) a bargain; negotiate, bid for; haggle, stickle, dicker, cheapen, beat down, underbid; outbid.

Adj. commercial, mercantile, trading; marketable, staple, in the market, for sale; at a bargain, marked down; retail; wholesale.

Adv. across the counter; in the marts of trade.

795. PURCHASE.—*N.* purchase, buying, purchasing, shopping.

buyer, purchaser, client, customer, patron, clientele.

V. buy, purchase, invest in, procure; shop, market, go a-shopping; rent, hire, repurchase, buy in.

796. SALE.—*N.* sale, disposal; auction, custom.

salableness, salability, marketability, vendibility.

seller, vender, vendor [*law*]; merchant, auctioneer.

salesmanship, selling ability.

V. sell, vend, dispose of, make a sale, effect a sale; auction, sell at auction, put up to (*or* at) auction; hawk, dump, unload, place, undersell; dispense, offer, retail; deal in, sell off (*or* out), turn into money, realize.

Adj. salable, marketable, staple, in demand, popular.

unsalable, unpurchased, unbought, on the shelves, on one's hands.

797. MERCHANT.—*N.* merchant, trader, dealer, salesman; money-changer, shopkeeper, shopman; tradesman, tradespeople, tradesfolk.

peddler, hawker, huckster, sutler, vivandière; costermonger; canvasser, solicitor; faker [*slang*].

moneylender, usurer, banker; money-changer, money broker.

jobber, broker; buyer, seller; bear, bull [*Stock Exchange*].

firm, company, house, corporation, concern, trust.

798. MERCHANDISE.—*N.* merchandise, ware, commodity, effects, goods, article, stock, produce, staple commodity; stock in trade, cargo.

799. MART.—*N.* mart, market, market place; fair, bazaar, exchange, stock exchange, Wheat Pit [*Chicago*]; bourse, curb.

shop, store, department store, chain store, warehouse, depot, emporium, establishment; stall, booth; office, chambers, counting-house, bureau; counter.

(2) Monetary Relations

800. MONEY.—*N.* money, finance, funds, treasure, capital, stock; assets, wealth, etc., 803; supplies, ways and means, wherewithal *or* wherewith, sinews of war, almighty dollar, cash.

solvency, responsibility, reliability, solidity, soundness.

sum, amount; balance, balance sheet; sum total; proceeds, receipts.

currency, circulating medium, specie, coin, piece, hard cash; dollar, sterling; pounds, shillings, and pence, £ s. d.; guinea; wallet, roll, wad [*slang*]. purse, ready money.

precious metals, gold, silver, copper, bullion, ingot, bar, nugget.

petty cash, pocket money, pin money, spending money, change, small coin. wampum.

great wealth, money to burn [*colloq.*]; power *or* mint of money [*colloq.*], good sum, millions, thousands.

Science of coins: numismatics.

paper money; bill, money order; note, note of hand; bank note, promissory note; I O U, bond; bill of exchange; draft, check, order, warrant, coupon, debenture, greenback.

V. **total,** amount to, come to, mount up to.

issue, utter, circulate; fiscalize, monetize.

demonetize, deprive of standard value; cease to issue.

Adj. **monetary,** pecuniary, fiscal, financial; sterling.

solvent, sound, substantial, good, reliable, responsible, solid, having a good rating; able to pay 100 cents to the dollar.

801. TREASURER.—*N.* **treasurer,** bursar, purser, banker, financier; receiver, liquidator, steward, trustee, accountant, expert accountant, almoner, paymaster, cashier, teller; money-changer.

802. TREASURY.—*N.* **treasury,** bank, exchequer, bursary; strongbox, stronghold, strong room; coffer, chest, safe, depository, cash register, cashbox, money box, till.

purse, moneybag, pocketbook, wallet; pocket.

securities, stocks; public stocks (*or* funds, securities); bonds, government bonds, Liberty bonds [U. S.], gilt-edged securities.

803. WEALTH.—*N.* **wealth,** riches, fortune, opulence, affluence; easy circumstances; independence, competence.

capital, money; great wealth, bonanza, El Dorado; philosopher's stone; the golden touch.

pelf, mammon, lucre, filthy lucre.

means, resources, substance, command of money; property, income, livelihood.

rich man, moneyed man, man of substance; capitalist, millionaire, multimillionaire, plutocrat; nabob, Croesus, Midas.

V. **be rich,** roll (*or* wallow) in wealth, have money to burn [*colloq.*]; afford, well afford, command money.

become rich, fill one's pocket, feather one's nest, make a fortune; make money; worship mammon, worship the golden calf.

Adj. **wealthy,** rich, affluent, opulent, moneyed, well-to-do, well off, rolling in riches.

804. POVERTY.—*N.* **poverty,** indigence, penury, pauperism, destitution, want; need, neediness; lack, necessity, privation, distress, difficulties, wolf at the door, straits; low water [*slang*], impecuniosity.

mendicancy, beggary, mendicity; broken (*or* loss of) fortune; insolvency.

poor man, pauper, mendicant, beggar.

V. be poor, want, lack, starve, live from hand to mouth, have seen better days, go to rack and ruin; beg one's bread, run into debt.

impoverish, reduce, reduce to poverty, pauperize, fleece, ruin.

Adj. poor, indigent; poverty-stricken, badly off, moneyless, penniless; impecunious, short of money, hard up, seedy [*colloq.*]; barefooted, beggarly, beggared, destitute, reduced, needy, necessitous, distressed, pinched, straitened, embarrassed, involved, insolvent.

805. CREDIT.—*N.* credit, trust, score, tally, account.

paper credit, letter of credit, circular note; duplicate; mortgage, lien, draft, securities.

creditor, lender, lessor [*law*], mortgagee; dun, usurer.

V. credit, accredit, intrust, keep (*or* run up) an account with; place to one's credit (*or* account); give (*or* take) credit.

Adj. accredited; of good credit, of unlimited credit; well rated; credited.

Adv. on credit, to the account of, to the credit of.

806. DEBT.—*N.* debt, obligation, liability, debit, score.

arrears, deferred payment, deficit, default, insolvency; bad debt.

interest; premium, usury.

debtor; mortgagor, defaulter, borrower.

V. be in debt, owe; incur (*or* contract) a debt, run up a bill, (*or* an account); borrow, run into debt, be in difficulties.

answer for, go bail for; back one's note.

Adj. liable, chargeable, answerable for.

indebted, in debt, in embarrassed circumstances, in difficulties; encumbered, involved; insolvent.

unpaid; unrequited, unrewarded; owing, due, in arrear, outstanding.

807. PAYMENT.—*N.* payment, discharge, settlement, clearance, liquidation, satisfaction, reckoning, arrangement.

acknowledgment, release; receipt, voucher.

repayment, reimbursement, retribution; pay, money paid.

V. pay, defray, make payment; pay one's way, expend, put down, lay down; discharge, settle, foot the bill [*colloq.*]; settle with, satisfy, pay in full, clear, liquidate, pay up; cash, honor a bill, acknowledge; redeem.

repay, refund, reimburse, disgorge, make repayment.

Adj. out of debt, owing nothing, all clear, clear of debt, above-water; solvent.

Adv. money down, cash down, cash on delivery, C.O.D.

808. NONPAYMENT.—*N.* **nonpayment;** default, defalcation; protest, repudiation.

insolvency, bankruptcy, failure; run upon a bank; overdrawn account.

defaulter, bankrupt, insolvent, insolvent debtor; absconder, welsher [*slang*].

V. **not pay,** fail, break, stop payment; become insolvent (*or* bankrupt), swindle, run up bills.

protest, dishonor, repudiate, nullify.

Adj. **in debt,** behindhand, in arrear; beggared, insolvent, bankrupt, ruined.

809. EXPENDITURE.—*N.* **expenditure,** outgoings, outlay, expenses, disbursement; circulation.

Money paid: payment, etc., 807; pay, etc. (*remuneration*), 973; fee, footing, subsidy, tribute, ransom, bribe, donation, gift; investment; purchase.

deposit, earnest, installment.

V. **expend,** spend; run (*or* get) through, pay, disburse; lay out, fork out [*slang*]; invest, sink money.

reward, fee, remunerate; give, subscribe, subsidize; bribe.

Adj. **lavish,** free, liberal; beyond one's income.

expensive, costly, dear, high-priced, precious, high.

810. RECEIPT.—*N.* **receipt,** value received, income, revenue, return, proceeds; earnings.

rent, rent roll; rental.

premium, bonus, prize, drawings, handout [*slang*].

pension, annuity, pittance, jointure, alimony.

V. **receive,** get, be in receipt of, have coming in; take money; draw from, derive from; acquire, take.

yield, bring in, afford, pay, return; accrue.

Adj. **remunerative,** profitable, gainful, well paying, interest-bearing, well invested.

Adv. within one's income.

811. ACCOUNTS.—*N.* **accounts,** money matters, finance, budget, bill, score, reckoning, account.

bookkeeping, audit, single entry, double entry; ledger, cash-book, journal; balance sheet; receipts, assets; expenditure, liabilities; profit and loss account (*or* statement).

accountant, auditor, actuary, bookkeeper; expert accountant, certified accountant; bank examiner.

V. **keep accounts,** enter, post, post up, book, credit, debit, balance.

812. PRICE.—*N.* **price,** amount, cost, expense, charge, figure, demand, fare, hire; wages.

dues, duty, toll, tax, impost, tariff, levy; capitation, poll tax; custom, excise, assessment, taxation, tithe, ransom, salvage, towage; brokerage, wharfage, freightage.

worth, rate, value, par value, valuation, appraisement, money's worth; price current, market price, quotation.

V. **price,** set (*or* fix) a price, appraise, assess, charge, demand, ask, require, exact.

fetch, sell for, cost, bring in, yield, afford.

Adj. **taxable,** dutiable, assessable.

813. DISCOUNT.—*N.* **discount,** abatement, concession, reduction, depreciation, allowance, qualification, setoff, drawback, percentage, rebate.

V. **discount,** bate, rebate, abate, deduct, strike off, mark down, reduce, take off, allow, give, make allowance; depreciate.

Adv. **at a discount,** at a bargain, below par.

814. DEARNESS.—*N.* **dearness,** expensiveness, costliness, high price; overcharge, extravagance, exorbitance, extortion.

V. **overcharge,** bleed [*colloq.*], skin [*slang*], fleece, extort, profiteer.

pay too much, pay dearly, pay through the nose [*colloq.*].

Adj. **dear,** high, high-priced, expensive, costly, precious; extravagant, exorbitant, extortionate.

at a premium, beyond price, above price; priceless, of priceless value.

Adv. **dear,** dearly; at great cost, at heavy cost, at a high price.

815. CHEAPNESS.—*N.* **cheapness,** low price, depreciation, bargain, drug in the market.

V. **be cheap,** cost little; come down (*or* fall) in price, be marked down.

buy at a bargain, buy dirt-cheap, have one's money's worth; beat down, cheapen.

Adj. **cheap,** low-priced, low, moderate, reasonable, inexpensive, cheap at the price; dirt-cheap, catchpenny.

reduced, half-price, depreciated, shopworn, marked down, unsalable.

gratuitous, gratis, free, for nothing; costless, without charge, scot-free, complimentary, honorary.

Adv. **at a bargain,** for a mere song; at cost price, at prime cost.

816. LIBERALITY.—*N.* **liberality,** generosity, munificence;

bounty, bounteousness, hospitality, charity, open (*or* free) hand, open (*or* large) heart.

cheerful giver, free giver, patron; benefactor.

V. **be liberal,** spend freely; shower down upon, spare no expense, give with both hands; keep open house.

Adj. **liberal,** free, generous, charitable, hospitable; bountiful, bounteous, ample, handsome; unsparing, ungrudging; unselfish; open-handed, large-hearted; munificent, princely.

Adv. ungrudgingly; with open hands, with both hands.

817. ECONOMY.—*N.* **economy,** frugality; thrift, thriftiness; care, husbandry, retrenchment.

savings; prevention of waste, save-all; parsimony, etc., 819.

V. **economize,** save; retrench, cut down expenses; make both ends meet, meet one's expenses, pay one's way; husband, save (*or* invest) money; provide against a rainy day.

Adj. **economical,** frugal, careful, thrifty, saving, chary, spare, sparing; parsimonious, etc., 819; sufficient; plain.

818. PRODIGALITY.—*N.* **prodigality,** wastefulness, unthriftiness, waste; profusion, profuseness; extravagance, lavishness.

prodigal, spendthrift, waster, high roller [*slang*], squanderer, spender, prodigal son.

V. **squander,** lavish, sow broadcast, pay through the nose, spill, waste, dissipate, exhaust, drain, overdraw, spend money like water.

Adj. **prodigal,** profuse, thriftless, unthrifty, improvident, wasteful, extravagant, lavish, dissipated; penny-wise and pound-foolish.

Adv. with an unsparing hand.

819. PARSIMONY.—*N.* **parsimony,** parsimoniousness, stinginess, stint, illiberality; avarice, avidity, rapacity, extortion, venality, cupidity, selfishness.

miser, niggard, churl, screw, skinflint, curmudgeon, harpy, extortioner, extortionist, usurer.

V. **grudge,** begrudge, stint, pinch, gripe, screw, dole out, hold back, withhold, starve, famish.

drive a bargain, cheapen, beat down; have an itching palm, grasp, grab.

Adj. **parsimonious,** penurious, stingy, miserly, mean, shabby, near, niggardly, close, sparing, grudging, illiberal, ungenerous, churlish, sordid, mercenary, venal, covetous, avaricious; greedy, grasping, extortionate, rapacious.

Adv. with a sparing hand.

CLASS VI

WORDS RELATING TO THE SENTIENT AND MORAL POWERS

I. AFFECTIONS IN GENERAL

820. AFFECTIONS.—*N.* character, qualities, disposition, affections, nature, spirit, temper, temperament, idiosyncrasy, predilection, turn of mind, bent, bias, predisposition, proneness, proclivity, propensity, vein, humor, mood, sympathy.

soul, heart, bosom, inner man; inmost recesses of the heart.

passion, pervading spirit; ruling passion, fullness of the heart.

energy, fervor, fire, verve, force.

Adj. characterized, affected, formed, molded, cast, tempered; framed.

prone, predisposed, disposed, inclined; having a bias.

inborn, inbred, ingrained; deep-rooted, congenital, inherent.

Adv. at heart; in the vein, in the mood.

821. FEELING.—*N.* feeling, suffering, endurance, sufferance, response; sympathy, impression, inspiration, affection, sensation, emotion, pathos.

fervor, unction, gusto, vehemence, heartiness, cordiality, earnestness, eagerness, gush [*colloq.*], ardor, warmth, zeal, passion, enthusiasm, ecstasy.

excitement; thrill, shock, agitation, quiver, flutter, flurry, fluster, twitter, tremor, throb, throbbing, pulsation, palpitation, panting; blush, flush.

V. feel, receive an impression, be impressed with, respond, enter into the spirit of.

bear, suffer, support, sustain, endure, brook, brave, stand, abide, experience, taste, prove.

be agitated, be excited, glow, flush, blush, crimson, change color, mantle; darken, whiten, pale, tingle, thrill, heave, pant, throb, palpitate, tremble, quiver, flutter, shake, stagger, reel; wince.

Adj. sentient, sensuous, emotional; of (*or* with) feeling.

keen, sharp, lively, quick, acute, cutting, piercing, incisive, trenchant, pungent, racy, piquant, poignant, caustic.

impressive, deep, profound, indelible, deep-felt, heartfelt, soul-stirring, electric, thrilling, rapturous, ecstatic, rapt; pervading, penetrating, absorbing.

earnest, wistful, eager, fervent, fervid, gushing [*colloq.*], warm, passionate, hearty, cordial, sincere, zealous, enthusiastic, glowing, ardent.

rabid, raving, feverish, fanatical, hysterical, impetuous.

Adv. **heartily,** heart and soul, from the bottom of one's heart, devoutly.

822. SENSITIVENESS.—*N.* **sensitiveness,** sensibleness, sensibility, impressibility, susceptibility, vivacity, tenderness, sentimentality, sentimentalism.

excitability, etc., 825; physical sensibility, etc., 375.

V. **be sensitive,** have a tender heart; take to heart, shrink, wince, blench, quiver.

Adj. **sensitive,** sensible, impressible, impressionable; susceptive, susceptible; warmhearted, tenderhearted, softhearted, tender; sentimental, romantic; enthusiastic, impassioned, spirited, mettlesome, vivacious, lively, expressive, mobile, excitable, oversensitive, thin-skinned, fastidious.

Adv. to the quick, on the raw.

823. INSENSITIVENESS.—*N.* **insensitiveness,** insensibility, insensibleness, inertness, inertia, impassibility, impassivity, apathy, dullness, insusceptibility, lukewarmness.

coldness, coolness, frigidity, stoicism, nonchalance, unconcern, indifference, callousness, heart of stone.

torpor, torpidity, lethargy, coma, trance; sleep, stupor, stupefaction; paralysis, numbness.

stoic, Indian, man of iron.

V. **be insensitive,** not mind, not care, not be affected by; take no interest in; disregard.

blunt, numb, benumb, paralyze, deaden, stun, stupefy; brutalize.

inure; harden, steel, caseharden, sear.

Adj. **insensitive,** insensible, unconscious, impassive, insusceptible, unimpressible; passionless, spiritless, heartless, soulless, unfeeling.

apathetic, unemotional, phlegmatic; dull, frigid; cold, cold-blooded, coldhearted; inert, supine, sluggish, torpid, sleepy, languid, halfhearted; numb, numbed; comatose.

indifferent, lukewarm, careless, mindless, inattentive, unconcerned, nonchalant.

unaffected, unruffled, unimpressed, unexcited, **unmoved,** unstirred, untouched, unshocked, unblushing.

callous, thick-skinned, impervious, hard, hardened, inured, casehardened; imperturbable, unfelt.

Adv. in cold blood; with dry eyes.

824. EXCITEMENT.—*N.* **excitement,** excitation, stimulation, piquancy, provocation, inspiration, animation, agitation, perturbation; fascination, intoxication, impressiveness; irritation, passion, thrill.

emotional appeal, melodrama, sensationalism, yellow journalism.

V. **excite,** affect, touch, move, impress, strike, interest, animate, inspire, smite, infect, awake, wake; awaken, waken; call forth; evoke, provoke; raise up, summon up, call up, wake up, raise; rouse, arouse, stir, fire, kindle, enkindle, illumine, illuminate, inflame.

stimulate, inspirit; stir up, infuse life into, give new life to; introduce new blood, quicken; sharpen, whet, fillip; fan, foster, heat, warm, foment, revive, rekindle.

penetrate, pierce; go to one's heart, touch to the quick, possess the soul, rivet the attention; prey on the mind.

agitate, perturb, ruffle, fluster, flutter, flurry, shake, disturb, startle, shock, stagger, strike dumb, stun, astound, electrify, galvanize, petrify.

irritate, sting, cut, pique, infuriate, madden, lash into fury.

flare up, flash up, seethe, boil, simmer, foam, fume, flame, rage, rave.

Adj. **excited,** wrought up, overwrought, hot, red-hot, flushed, feverish; raging, flaming, ebullient, seething, foaming, fuming, stung to the quick; wild, raving, frantic, mad, distracted, beside oneself.

exciting, impressive, telling, warm, glowing, fervid, spirit-stirring, thrilling; soul-stirring, heart-stirring, agonizing, sensational, yellow [*colloq.*], melodramatic, hysterical; overpowering, overwhelming.

piquant, spicy, appetizing, stinging, provocative, tantalizing.

Adv. at a critical moment, under a sudden strain.

825. [Excess of sensitiveness] EXCITABILITY.—*N.* **excitability,** impetuosity, vehemence, boisterousness, turbulence; impatience, intolerance, irritability; disquiet, disquietude, restlessness, fidgets, agitation.

trepidation, perturbation, ruffle, hurry, fuss, flurry, fluster, flutter; ferment; whirl; stage fright, thrill.

passion, excitement, flush, heat, fever, fire, flame, fume, tumult, effervescence, ebullition; gust, storm, tempest; burst, fit, paroxysm, explosion, outbreak, scene, outburst; agony.

fury; violence, fierceness, rage, furor, desperation, madness, distraction, raving, delirium; frenzy, hysterics; intoxication; towering rage, anger, etc., 900.

fixed idea, monomania; fascination, infatuation; fanaticism; quixotism, quixotry.

V. fidget, fuss.

fume, rage, foam; bear ill, wince, chafe, champ the bit, lose one's temper, break out, burst out, fly out, explode, flare up, flame up, fire up, boil, rave, rant, tear, go into hysterics; run riot, run amuck; raise Cain [*slang*].

Adj. **excitable,** easily excited, mettlesome, high-mettled, skittish, high-strung, nervous, irritable, hasty, impatient, intolerant, moody; feverish, hysterical, delirious, mad.

restless, unquiet, mercurial, galvanic, fidgety, fussy.

vehement, demonstrative, violent, wild, furious, fierce, fiery, hotheaded; overzealous, enthusiastic, impassioned, fanatical; rabid, rampant, clamorous, uproarious, turbulent, tempestuous, boisterous.

impulsive, impetuous, passionate, uncontrolled, uncontrollable, ungovernable, irrepressible, volcanic.

Adv. in confusion, pellmell.

826. INEXCITABILITY.—*N.* inexcitability, imperturbability, even temper, tranquil mind, dispassion; toleration, tolerance, patience; passiveness, inertia, etc., 172; impassibility, etc. (*insensibility*), 823; stupefaction.

calmness, composure, placidity, *sang-froid* [F.], coolness, tranquillity, serenity, content; quiet, quietude; peace of mind.

equanimity, poise, staidness, gravity, sobriety, philosophy, stoicism, self-possession, self-control, self-command, self-restraint; presence of mind.

resignation, submission, sufferance, endurance, long-sufferance, forbearance, longanimity, fortitude, patience of Job, moderation, restraint.

V. **endure,** bear, go through, support, brave, disregard; tolerate, suffer, stand, bide; abide, bear with, put up with, acquiesce, submit, resign oneself to, brook, digest, eat, swallow, pocket, stomach; carry on, carry through; make light of, make the best of, put a good face on.

compose, appease, assuage, propitiate, repress, restrain, master one's feelings, set one's mind at ease (*or* rest), calm down, cool down.

Adj. **inexcitable,** imperturbable; unsusceptible, dispassionate, cold-blooded, enduring, stoical, philosophical, staid, sober, grave; sedate, demure, coolheaded, levelheaded.

easygoing, peaceful, placid, calm; quiet, tranquil, serene, cool, undemonstrative.

composed, collected, temperate, unstirred, unruffled, unperturbed.

meek, mild, tame, subdued, unoffended, unresisting, submissive, gentle, patient, tolerant, clement, long-suffering.

Adv. in cold blood; more in sorrow than in anger.

II. PERSONAL AFFECTIONS[1]

827. PLEASURE.—*N.* **pleasure,** gratification, enjoyment, delectation, relish, zest, gusto, satisfaction, complacency; well-being; good, etc., 618; comfort, ease, luxury; physical pleasure, etc., 377.

joy, gladness, delight, glee, cheer, sunshine; cheerfulness, etc., 836; treat, luxury; amusement, etc., 840.

happiness, felicity, bliss, beatitude, enchantment, transport, rapture, ecstasy; paradise, heaven.

V. **enjoy oneself,** joy, be in clover [*colloq.*], tread on enchanted ground; go into raptures; feel at home, breathe freely, bask in the sunshine.

enjoy, like, relish, be pleased with, derive pleasure from, take pleasure in, delight in, rejoice in, indulge in, gloat over, love; take to, take a fancy to [*both colloq.*].

Adj. **pleased,** gratified, glad, gladsome; comfortable, etc. (*physical pleasure*), 377; at ease; content, etc., 831.

happy, blessed, blissful, beatified, joyful, in raptures, in ecstasies.

overjoyed, entranced, enchanted; raptured, enraptured, ravished, transported; fascinated, captivated.

pleasing, delightful, ecstatic, beatific, painless, unalloyed, cloudless.

828. PAIN.—*N.* **pain,** mental suffering, dolor, suffering, ache; physical pain, etc., 378.

displeasure, dissatisfaction, discomfort, discomposure, disquiet; inquietude, uneasiness, discontent.

annoyance, irritation, worry; infliction, visitation; plague, bore; bother, vexation, mortification, chagrin.

care, anxiety, solicitude, concern, trouble, trial, ordeal, shock, blow, fret, burden, load.

grief, sorrow, distress, affliction, woe, bitterness, heartache, heavy (*or* aching, bleeding, broken) heart.

misery, unhappiness, infelicity, tribulation, wretchedness, desolation; despair, etc., 859; extremity, prostration, depth of misery, slough of despond; nightmare, incubus.

anguish, pang, agony, torture, torment; crucifixion, martyrdom, rack, hell upon earth; reign of terror.

sufferer, victim, prey, martyr, wretch, shorn lamb.

V. **suffer,** ail, feel (*or* suffer, undergo, bear, endure) pain, smart, ache, bleed, bear the cross; fall on evil days, come to grief.

fret, chafe, sit on thorns, wince, worry oneself, fret and fume; take to heart.

[1] Or those which concern one's own state of feeling.

grieve, mourn, lament, etc., 839; yearn, repine, pine, droop, languish, sink, despair, break one's heart.

Adj. **pained,** afflicted, suffering, worried, displeased, aching, griped, sore, raw, on the rack.

uneasy, uncomfortable, ill at ease; disturbed; discontented; weary, etc., 841.

unfortunate, etc., 735; doomed, devoted, accursed, undone, crushed, lost, stranded; victimized, ill-used.

unhappy, infelicitous, poor, wretched, miserable, woebegone, comfortless, cheerless, etc. (*dejected*), 837; careworn; heavy-laden, stricken.

sorry, concerned, sorrowful, cut up [*colloq.*], chagrined, horrified, horror-stricken; heartbroken, brokenhearted.

829. [Capability of giving pleasure] PLEASURABLENESS.— *N.* **pleasurableness,** pleasantness, agreeableness, pleasure giving, amusement, etc., 840; treat, etc. (*physical pleasure*), 377; dainty titbit, sweets, sweetmeats, nuts, salt, savor.

attraction, attractiveness, charm, fascination, captivation, enchantment, witchery, seduction, winning ways, winsomeness; loveliness, beauty, etc., 845.

V. **delight,** charm, gladden, bless, captivate, fascinate; enchant, entrance, enrapture, transport, bewitch, ravish.

please, satisfy, gratify, satiate, quench, indulge, humor, flatter, tickle; tickle the palate, refresh, enliven, treat, amuse, take one's fancy; attract, allure; stimulate, excite, interest.

Adj. **pleasurable,** pleasure-giving, pleasing, pleasant, amiable, agreeable, grateful, gratifying; acceptable; dear, beloved, welcome, favorite.

refreshing, comfortable, cordial, genial, glad, gladsome; sweet, delectable, nice, dainty, delicate, delicious.

attractive, inviting, prepossessing, engaging; winning, winsome, magnetic, fascinating, seductive; alluring, enticing, appetizing, cheering, bewitching, enchanting, entrancing.

delightful, charming, felicitous, exquisite, lovely, ravishing, rapturous; heartfelt, thrilling, ecstatic, heavenly.

Adv. to one's delight, in utter satisfaction; at one's ease; in clover [*colloq.*].

830. [Capability of giving pain] PAINFULNESS.— *N.* **painfulness,** trouble, care, trial, affliction, infliction, misfortune, mishap; cross, blow, stroke, burden, load, curse.

annoyance, pique, grievance, nuisance, vexation, mortification, worry, bore, bother, hornet's nest, plague, pest, wound; sore subject, skeleton in the closet, thorn in the flesh.

V. **pain,** hurt, wound, cause (*or* occasion, give, inflict) pain;

pierce, prick, cut, etc. (*physical pain*), 378; pierce (*or* break, rend) the heart; make the heart bleed.

sadden, make unhappy, grieve, afflict, distress; cut up [*colloq.*], cut to the heart.

annoy, incommode, displease, discompose, trouble, disturb, cross, thwart, perplex, molest; tease, tire, irk, fret, vex, mortify, worry, plague, bother, pester, bore, harass, harry, badger, heckle [*Brit.*], bait, beset, infest, persecute.

torment,wring, harrow, torture, rack, crucify, convulse, agonize.

irritate, provoke, sting, nettle, pique, fret, roil, rile [*colloq.* & *dial.*], chafe, gall; aggrieve, affront, enrage, ruffle, give offense.

maltreat, bite, snap at, assail, smite, etc., 972.

repel, revolt, sicken, disgust, nauseate, disenchant, offend, shock, rankle, gnaw, corrode, horrify, appall.

Adj. **painful,** hurtful, dolorous; distressing, cheerless, dismal, disheartening, depressing, dreary, melancholy, grievous, piteous, woeful, mournful, deplorable, pitiable, lamentable, sad; affecting, touching, pathetic.

unpleasant, unpleasing, displeasing, disagreeable, unpalatable, bitter, distasteful, uninviting, unwelcome, undesirable, obnoxious; unacceptable.

inauspicious, unlucky, ill-starred, unsatisfactory; untoward.

irritating, provoking, annoying, aggravating [*colloq.*], exasperating, galling, vexatious; troublesome, tiresome, irksome, wearisome.

importunate, pestering, bothering, harassing, worrying, tormenting.

insufferable, intolerable, insupportable, unbearable, unendurable.

shocking, terrific, grim, appalling, crushing; dreadful, fearful, frightful, tremendous, dire, heartbreaking, heart-rending, harrowing, rending.

odious, hateful, execrable, repulsive, repellent, horrid, horrible; offensive; nauseous, disgusting, revolting, nasty, loathsome, vile, hideous.

acute, sharp, sore, severe, grave, hard, harsh, cruel, biting, caustic; cutting, corroding, consuming, excruciating, agonizing.

cumbrous, cumbersome, burdensome, onerous, oppressive.

desolating, withering, tragical, disastrous, calamitous, ruinous.

Adv. in agony, out of the depths.

831. CONTENT.—*N.* **content,** contentment, contentedness; complacency, satisfaction, ease, peace of mind, serenity, cheerfulness; comfort.

patience, moderation, endurance; conciliation, reconciliation; resignation.

V. **be content,** rest satisfied, let well enough alone; take in good part; be reconciled to, take heart, take comfort.

content, set at ease, comfort; conciliate, reconcile, win over, propitiate, disarm, beguile; content, satisfy; gratify, etc., 836.

Adj. **content,** contented, satisfied, at ease, at one's ease, easy-going, not particular; conciliatory, unrepining, resigned, cheerful, serene, at rest; snug, comfortable.

satisfactory, adequate, sufficient, ample, equal to; satisfying.

Adv. to one's heart's content.

832. DISCONTENT.—*N.* **discontent,** dissatisfaction; disappointment, mortification; cold comfort; regret, repining, inquietude, vexation of spirit, soreness; heartburning.

malcontent, grumbler, growler, grouch [*slang*], croaker, faultfinder.

the opposition; bitter-enders [*politics,* U. S.], die-hards.

V. **be discontented,** repine, regret, take to heart, make a wry face, look blue, look black, look glum.

grumble, take ill, take in bad part; fret, chafe, croak; lament.

dissatisfy, disappoint, mortify, put out [*colloq.*], disconcert, dishearten.

Adj. **discontented,** dissatisfied, unsatisfied, regretful, dejected, etc., 837; dissentient, malcontent, exacting.

glum, sulky, in high dudgeon, in a fume, in the sulks (*or* dumps), in bad humor; sour, soured, sore; out of humor, out of temper.

833. REGRET.—*N.* **regret,** repining; homesickness, nostalgia; bitterness, heartburning; lamentation, penitence, etc., 950.

V. **regret,** deplore, bewail, lament, etc., 839; repine, rue, rue the day; repent, etc., 950; leave an aching void.

Adj. regretful, rueful; homesick.

834. RELIEF.—*N.* **relief,** deliverance, alleviation, mitigation, palliation, solace, consolation, comfort, unction; encouragement.

V. **relieve,** ease, alleviate, mitigate, palliate, soothe; salve; soften, assuage, allay; remedy, cure, restore, refresh.

cheer, comfort, console; enliven; encourage, give comfort, inspirit, invigorate.

Adj. **soothing,** assuaging, balmy, lenitive, palliative, curative.

835. AGGRAVATION.—*N.* **aggravation,** heightening, intensification, overestimation, exaggeration.

V. **aggravate,** render worse, heighten, embitter, sour, intensify, enhance [*Note:* aggravate *in the sense of* provoke *is colloquial*].

Adj. aggravated, worse, unrelieved, aggravative.

Adv. from bad to worse, worse and worse.

836. CHEERFULNESS.—*N.* **cheerfulness,** geniality, gayety, cheer, good humor, spirits; high spirits, animal spirits, glee, high glee, light heart.

liveliness, life, alacrity, vivacity, animation, joviality, jollity, levity, jocularity.

mirth, merriment, hilarity, exhilaration, laughter, merrymaking, rejoicing, etc., 838.

optimism, hopefulness, etc., 858.

V. **be cheerful,** have the mind at ease, smile, keep up one's spirits, cheer up, take heart, cast away care, perk up; rejoice, etc., 838; carol, chirp, chirrup, lilt.

cheer, enliven, elate, exhilarate, gladden, delight, inspirit, animate, inspire.

Adj. **cheerful;** happy, etc., 827; cheery, sunny, smiling; blithe, in good spirits, chipper [*colloq.*], gay, debonair, light, lightsome, lighthearted; buoyant, bright, airy, jaunty, sprightly, spirited, lively, animated, vivacious, sparkling, sportive.

merry, joyful, joyous, jocund, jovial; jolly, blithesome, gleeful, hilarious.

winsome, bonny, hearty, buxom.

playful, tricksy, frisky, frolicsome, jocose, jocular, waggish, mirthful, rollicking.

elate, elated; exulting, jubilant, flushed, rejoicing.

cheering, inspiriting, exhilarating, pleasing, palmy, flourishing.

Adv. **cheerfully,** cheerily, with relish, with zest.

837. DEJECTION.—*N.* **dejection,** depression, mopishness, low (*or* depressed) spirits; heaviness, gloom; weariness, disgust of life; prostration, broken heart; despair, hopelessness.

melancholy, sadness, melancholia, blue devils [*colloq.*], blues [*colloq.*], dumps [*chiefly humorous*], doldrums, horrors, hypochondria, pessimism; despondency, slough of despond; disconsolateness, hope deferred.

gravity; demureness, solemnity; long face, grave face.

hypochondriac, self-tormentor, croaker, pessimist, damper, wet blanket.

V. **be dejected,** grieve, mourn, lament, give way, lose heart, despond, droop, sink, despair.

lower, frown, pout; look blue, lay to heart, take to heart.

mope, brood over, fret, sulk, pine, pine away; yearn, repine.

depress, discourage, dishearten, dispirit, damp, dull, deject, sink, dash, unman, prostrate, break one's heart; sadden, dash one's hopes, prey on the mind, damp the spirits.

Adj. **cheerless,** joyless, spiritless; unhappy, etc., 828; melancholy, dismal, dreary, depressing, somber, dark, gloomy, lowering, frowning, funereal, mournful, lamentable, dreadful.

downcast, downhearted, down in the mouth [*colloq.*], down on one's luck [*colloq.*], heavyhearted; sullen, mopish, moody, glum; sulky, etc. (*discontented*), 832; out of heart (*or* spirits); lowspirited; weary, etc., 841; discouraged, disheartened, despondent, crestfallen.

sad, pensive, doleful, woebegone, melancholic, bilious, jaundiced, saturnine, lackadaisical.

serious, sedate, staid, earnest, grave, sober, solemn, demure, grim, grim-faced, rueful, wan, long-faced.

disconsolate, forlorn, comfortless, desolate, sick at heart, heartsick.

overcome, broken-down, prostrate, cut up [*colloq.*], unnerved, unmanned; downfallen, downtrodden; brokenhearted; careworn.

Adv. with a long face, with tears in one's eyes.

838. [Expression of pleasure] REJOICING.—*N.* rejoicing, exultation, triumph, jubilation, heyday, flush, reveling, merrymaking, pæan, *Te Deum* [L.]; congratulation.

smile, simper, smirk, grin; broad grin, sardonic grin.

laughter, giggle, titter, snicker, snigger, crow, cheer, chuckle, shout; guffaw, burst (*or* fit, shout, roar, peal) of laughter.

cheer, huzza, hurrah, cheering; shout, yell [U. S. and Can.], college yell; tiger [*colloq.*].

V. rejoice, congratulate oneself, hug oneself, clap one's hands; skip; sing, carol, chirrup, chirp, hurrah, cry for joy, leap with joy; exult, triumph; make merry.

smile, simper, smirk, grin, laugh in one's sleeve.

laugh, giggle, titter, snigger, snicker, chuckle, cackle; burst out, shout, roar, shake (*or* split) one's sides.

Adj. rejoicing, jubilant, exultant, triumphant, flushed, elated; laughing, convulsed with laughter.

laughable, ludicrous, etc. 853.

Adv. in fits of laughter; in triumph.

839. [Expression of pain] LAMENTATION.—*N.* lamentation, lament, wail, complaint, plaint, murmur, mutter, grumble, groan, moan, whine, whimper, sob, sigh; frown, scowl.

cry, scream, howl; outcry, wail of woe.

weeping, flood of tears, fit of crying, crying; melting mood. plaintiveness; languishment; condclence, etc., 915.

mourning, weeds [*colloq.*], widow's weeds, crape, deep mourning; sackcloth and ashes; death song, dirge, requiem, elegy, threnody, jeremiad, keen [Ir.].

mourner, keener [Ir.]; Niobe.

V. **lament,** mourn, deplore, grieve, keen [Ir.], weep over; bewail, bemoan, condole with, etc., 915; fret.

sigh, give (*or* heave) a sigh; wail.

cry, weep, sob, blubber, snivel, whimper, shed tears, burst into tears.

scream, groan, moan, whine, yelp, howl, yell, roar; rend the air.

complain, murmur, mutter, grumble, growl, clamor, croak, grunt.

Adj. **lamenting,** in mourning, in sackcloth and ashes, clamorous, sorrowing, sorrowful, mournful, lamentable, tearful, lachrymose, plaintive, querulous; in tears.

840. AMUSEMENT.—*N.* **amusement,** entertainment, diversion, reaction, relaxation, solace; pastime, sport; labor of love; pleasure, etc., 827.

fun, frolic, merriment, jollity, joviality, laughter, etc., 838; pleasantry, quip, jocoseness; drollery, buffoonery, tomfoolery; mummery, pageant.

play, game, gambol, romp, prank, antic, lark [*colloq.*], spree, skylarking, vagary, monkey trick, escapade, practical joke.

dance, hop [*colloq.*], ball, masquerade, ballet; step dance, skirt dance, folk dance, morris dance; gavot, minuet, Highland fling, reel, jig, hornpipe, sword dance, cakewalk; country dance, Scotch reel, Virginia reel, quadrille, lancers, cotillion; waltz, polka, mazurka, schottische, one-step, two-step, fox-trot.

festivity, fete, festival, merrymaking; party, etc. (*social gathering*), 892; revels, revelry, reveling, carnival, saturnalia, jollification [*colloq.*], junket, picnic.

holiday, red-letter day, play day; high days and holidays; high holiday.

place of amusement, theater; concert hall, ballroom, dance hall, assembly room; moving-picture theater; movies [*colloq.*]; music hall; vaudeville theater; circus, hippodrome.

Sports and games: athletic sports, track events, gymnastics; tournament.
skating, tobogganing; cricket, tennis, lawn tennis, rackets, squash, fives; croquet, golf, curling, hockey, polo, football, Rugby, rugger [*colloq.*]; association, soccer [*colloq.*]; quoits, discus, putting the weight (*or* shot), tug of war; baseball, basketball, pushball, lacrosse.
billiards, pool, pyramids, bagatelle; bowls, skittles, ninepins, tenpins; chess, draughts, checkers, dominoes, dice; card games, etc.

toy, plaything, doll, bauble.

sportsman (*fem.* sportswoman), hunter, Nimrod.

gamester, sport, gambler; dicer, punter, plunger.

devotee, enthusiast, follower, fan [*slang*], rooter [*slang or cant*].

V. **amuse,** entertain, divert, enliven, raise a smile, excite (*or* convulse with) laughter; cheer, rejoice, solace, please, interest.

amuse oneself, sport, disport, revel, junket, feast, carouse.

banquet, make merry; frolic, gambol, frisk, romp, caper, dance.

Adj. amusing, entertaining, diverting, recreative, pleasant, laughable, etc. (*ludicrous*), 853; witty, etc., 842; festive, festal, jovial, jolly, roguish, arch, playful, sportive.

Adv. at play, in sport.

841. WEARINESS.—*N.* **weariness**, ennui, boredom, lassitude, fatigue, etc., 688; drowsiness, languor.

disgust, nausea, loathing, sickness; satiety, repletion.

tedium, wearisomeness, tediousness, monotony.

bore, buttonholer, proser, dry-as-dust, fossil [*colloq.*], wet blanket.

V. **weary**, tire, fatigue, bore, send to sleep; buttonhole.

pall, sicken, nauseate, disgust; harp on the same string.

Adj. **wearying**, wearing, wearisome, tiresome, irksome, uninteresting, stupid, monotonous, dull, dry, arid, tedious, humdrum, flat; prosy, prosing; slow, soporific, somniferous.

weary, tired, drowsy, sleepy, etc., 683; uninterested, flagging, used up, worn out, blasé [F.].

842. WIT.—*N.* **wit**, wittiness, Attic salt, Atticism; point, fancy, whim, humor, drollery, pleasantry.

buffoonery, fooling, farce, tomfoolery, broad farce, fun.

jocularity, jocoseness, facetiousness, waggishness, comicality.

smartness, ready wit, banter, persiflage, retort, repartee.

witticism, smart saying, sally, flash, scintillation, flash of wit; jest, joke, epigram, conceit.

wordplay, play upon words, pun, riddle, conundrum, quibble.

V. **joke**, jest, cut jokes; crack a joke, pun; make merry with.

retort, flash back, flash, scintillate; banter, etc. (*ridicule*), 856.

Adj. **witty**, clever, keen, keen-witted, brilliant, pungent, quick-witted, smart, jocular, jocose, funny, waggish, facetious, comic, whimsical, humorous, sprightly, sparkling, epigrammatic.

843. DULLNESS.—*N.* **dullness**, heaviness, flatness, stupidity, want of originality, dearth of ideas; matter of fact, commonplace, platitude.

V. **be dull**, hang fire, fall flat, platitudinize, prose.

depress, damp, throw cold water on, lay a wet blanket on.

Adj. **dull**, jejune, dry, uninteresting, heavy-footed, elephantine; insipid, tasteless, unimaginative; prosy, prosaic, matter-of-fact, commonplace, platitudinous, pointless.

stupid, slow, flat, humdrum, monotonous, stolid.

844. HUMORIST.—*N.* **humorist**, wag, wit, epigrammatist, punster; life of the party; joker, jester, buffoon, comedian, merry-andrew, mime, tumbler, acrobat, mountebank, harlequin, pantaloon, punch, punchinello, clown; motley fool; caricaturist.

845. BEAUTY.—*N.* beauty, form, elegance, grace, symmetry, bloom, delicacy, refinement, charm, style; comeliness, fairness, polish, gloss; good effect, good looks.

brilliancy, radiance, splendor, gorgeousness, magnificence; sublimity.

beau ideal, Venus, Aphrodite, Hebe, the Graces, peri, houri, Cupid, Apollo, Hyperion, Adonis; Helen of Troy, Cleopatra; Venus de Milo, Apollo Belvedere.

loveliness, pleasurableness, etc., 829.

beautifying, decoration, ornamentation, etc., 847.

V. beautify, set off, grace; decorate, etc., 847.

Adj. beautiful, beauteous, handsome; pretty; lovely, graceful, elegant, exquisite, delicate, dainty.

comely, fair, goodly, bonny, good-looking, well favored, well formed, well proportioned, shapely, symmetrical, harmonious.

bright, bright-eyed; rosy-cheeked, rosy, ruddy, blooming, in full bloom.

trim, trig, tidy, neat, spruce, smart, jaunty, dapper.

brilliant, shining, sparkling, radiant, splendid, resplendent, dazzling, glowing, glossy, sleek; rich, gorgeous, superb, magnificent, grand, fine.

artistic, aesthetic, picturesque, pictorial, enchanting, attractive, becoming, ornamental.

perfect, unspotted, spotless, immaculate; undeformed, undefaced.

passable, presentable, tolerable, not amiss.

846. UGLINESS.—*N.* ugliness, deformity, inelegance, disfigurement, blemish, want of symmetry, distortion; squalor.

eyesore, object, figure, sight [*colloq.*], fright, scarecrow, hag, harridan, satyr, witch, monster.

V. deface, disfigure, deform, distort, blemish, injure, spoil; soil.

Adj. ugly, inartistic, unsightly, unseemly, uncomely, unshapely, unlovely; unbeautiful; coarse, plain, homely.

misshapen, misproportioned, shapeless, monstrous, gross; ill-made, ill-shaped, ill-proportioned, crooked, distorted.

unprepossessing, hard-featured, ill-favored, ill-looking; squalid, haggard; grim, grisly, ghastly, cadaverous, gruesome.

uncouth, ungainly, graceless, inelegant, ungraceful, stiff, rough, gross, rude, awkward, clumsy, gawky, lumbering, unwieldy.

repellent, forbidding, frightful, hideous, odious, repulsive; horrid, horrible, shocking.

disfigured, tarnished, smeared, besmeared, discolored, spotted, spotty.

showy, specious, pretentious, garish.

847. ORNAMENT.—*N.* **ornament,** ornamentation, ornateness, adornment, decoration, embellishment.

embroidery, needlework; lace, trimming, drapery; tapestry, arras; millinery.
wreath, festoon, garland, chaplet, flower, nosegay, bouquet, posy [*colloq.*].
tassel, knot; shoulder knot, epaulet, star, rosette, bow; feather, plume, fillet, snood.
jewelry: tiara, crown, coronet, diadem; jewel, gem, precious stone, trinket.

finery, frippery, tinsel, spangle, excess of ornament; pride, show, ostentation.

illustration, illumination; purple patches.

virtu, article of virtu, work of art, bric-a-brac, curio; rarity, a find.

V. **ornament,** embellish, enrich, decorate, adorn, beautify; garnish, furbish, polish, gild, varnish, enamel, paint.

spangle, bespangle, bead, embroider, chase, tool; emblazon, blazon, illuminate.

smarten, trim, bedizen, prink, trick up, trick out, deck, bedeck, array; spruce up [*colloq.*]; smarten up, dress, dress up.

Adj. **ornamental,** ornate, ornamented, rich, gilt, begilt, festooned.

smart, gay, flowery, glittering, new-spangled, fine, well groomed.
showy, gorgeous, flashy, gaudy, garish, tawdry, etc., 851.

848. BLEMISH.—*N.* **blemish,** disfigurement, deformity, defect, flaw, injury, eyesore.

stain, blot, spot, speck, speckle, blur, freckle, patch, blotch, smudge, birthmark, scar, mole, pimple, blister.

V. **disfigure,** etc. (*injure*), 659.

Adj. **disfigured,** imperfect, injured; discolored, specked, speckled, freckled, pitted, bruised.

849. SIMPLICITY.—*N.* **simplicity,** plainness, homeliness; chasteness, chastity, restraint, severity, naturalness, unaffectedness.

V. **simplify,** reduce to simplicity, strip of ornament, chasten, restrain.

Adj. **simple,** plain, homelike, homely, homespun [*fig.*], ordinary.

unaffected, natural, native; inartificial, free from affectation; chaste, severe; unadorned, unornamented.

simple-minded, childish, credulous, etc., 486.

850. [Good taste] TASTE.—*N.* **taste,** good (*or* refined, cultivated) taste; delicacy, refinement, fine feeling, discrimination, tact, polish, elegance, grace, culture, cultivation.

Science of taste: aesthetics.

man of taste, connoisseur, judge, critic, virtuoso, amateur, dilettante; purist, precisian.

V. display taste, appreciate, judge, criticize, discriminate.

Adj. in good taste, tasteful, unaffected, pure, chaste, classical, cultivated; graceful, attractive, charming, aesthetic, artistic.

refined, elegant, prim, precise, formal.

Adv. with quiet elegance; with elegant simplicity; without ostentation.

851. [Bad taste] VULGARITY.—*N.* vulgarity, vulgarism, barbarism, vandalism, bad taste; want of tact; ill-breeding, coarseness, indecorum, misbehavior, boorishness.

lowness, low life, brutality, blackguardism, rowdyism, ruffianism; ribaldry.

Excess of ornament: gaudiness, tawdriness, cheap jewelry; flashy clothes (*or* dress), finery, frippery, trickery, tinsel.

vulgarian, rough diamond, clown, Goth, vandal; snob, cad [*colloq.*], cub; parvenu, upstart; frump [*colloq.*], dowdy, slattern.

V. be vulgar, misbehave; show a want of tact (*or* consideration); be a vulgarian.

Adj. in bad taste, vulgar, unrefined, coarse, indecorous, ribald, gross; unseemly, unpresentable, ungraceful; dowdy, slovenly; low, extravagant, monstrous, horrid, shocking.

ill-mannered, ill-bred, underbred, snobbish, uncourtly, uncivil, discourteous, ungentlemanly, unladylike.

uncouth, unkempt, unpolished, plebeian; rude, awkward; homely, homespun, provincial, countrified, rustic; boorish, clownish; savage, brutish, blackguardly, rowdy, wild; barbarous, barbaric, outlandish; uncultivated.

antiquated, obsolete, out of fashion, old-fashioned, out of date, unfashionable.

newfangled, fantastic, fantastical, odd, affected.

tawdry, gaudy, meretricious, obtrusive, flaunting, loud, crass, showy, flashy, garish.

852. FASHION.—*N.* fashion, style, society, good (*or* polite) society, civilized life, civilization; court, high life, world, fashionable world; upper ten [*colloq.*], elite, smart set [*colloq.*], the four hundred; Vanity Fair; Mayfair.

manners, breeding, politeness; air, demeanor, *savoir-faire* [F.], gentility, decorum, propriety, Mrs. Grundy; convention, conventionality, the proprieties, punctiliousness, form, formality, etiquette.

mode, vogue, style, the latest thing, the rage, prevailing taste; custom.

V. be fashionable, be the rage, have a run, pass current, follow the fashion, go with the stream

Adj. fashionable, in fashion, *à la mode* [F.], presentable; punctilious, genteel, decorous, conventional; well bred, gentlemanly, ladylike.

polished, refined, thoroughbred, gently bred, courtly, distinguished, aristocratic, self-possessed, poised, easy, frank, unconstrained.

modish, stylish, swell [*slang*], all the rage, all the go [*colloq.*].
Adv. for fashion's sake; in the latest style (*or* mode).

853. RIDICULOUSNESS.—*N.* ridiculousness, comicality, oddity, drollery; farce, comedy, burlesque, buffoonery, bull, Irish bull, spoonerism; bombast, anticlimax, bathos; absurdity, laughingstock.

V. **be ridiculous,** play the fool, make a fool of oneself, commit an absurdity.

Adj. **ridiculous,** ludicrous, comic *or* comical, waggish, quizzical, droll, funny, laughable, farcical, seriocomic, tragicomic.

odd, grotesque, whimsical, fanciful, fantastic, queer, quaint, bizarre, eccentric, strange, outlandish, out-of-the-way.

extravagant, monstrous, preposterous, absurd, bombastic, inflated, stilted, burlesque, mock heroic.

854. FOP.—*N.* fine gentleman, fop, swell [*colloq.*], dandy, exquisite, coxcomb, beau, man about town, spark, popinjay, puppy [*contemptuous*], prig, jackanapes, carpet knight; dude [*colloq.*].
fine lady, belle, flirt, coquette, toast.

855. AFFECTATION.—*N.* affectation, affectedness, pretense, pretension, airs, pedantry, stiffness, formality, mannerism, euphuism; boasting, charlatanism, quackery.

prudery, demureness, mock modesty, false shame; sentimentalism.

foppery, dandyism, coxcombry, puppyism, conceit; coquetry.

poser, actor; pedant, pedagogue, doctrinaire, purist, euphuist, mannerist; bluestocking, prig, charlatan; prude, puritan, precisian, formalist.

V. **affect,** act a part, give oneself airs, boast, simper, mince, attitudinize, pose, languish; overact, overdo.

Adj. **affected,** pretentious, pedantic, stilted, stagy, theatrical, canting, insincere, unnatural; self-conscious, artificial; overdone, overacted.

stiff, formal, prim, smug, complacent; demure, puritanical, prudish.

priggish, conceited, foppish, finical, finicking, mincing, simpering, namby-pamby, sentimental, languishing.

856. RIDICULE.—*N.* ridicule, derision, snicker *or* snigger, grin, scoffing, mockery, banter, irony, persiflage, raillery, chaff.
squib, satire, skit, quip.

burlesque, parody, travesty, farce, caricature.

buffoonery, practical joke, horseplay, roughhouse [*slang*].

V. ridicule, deride; laugh at, grin at, smile at; snicker *or* snigger; banter, chaff, joke, guy [*colloq.*], rag [*slang*], haze [*colloq.*].

burlesque, satirize, parody, caricature, travesty.

Adj. derisive, sarcastic, ironical, satirical, quizzical, burlesque, mock.

Adv. as a joke, to raise a laugh.

857. [Object and cause of ridicule] LAUGHINGSTOCK.—*N.* laughingstock, butt, game, fair game, April fool, original, oddity; queer fish [*colloq.*], figure of fun [*colloq.*]; monkey; buffoon.

858. HOPE.—*N.* hope; desire, etc., 865; trust, confidence, reliance, faith, assurance, security; reassurance.

hopefulness, buoyancy, optimism, enthusiasm, aspiration; assumption, presumption; anticipation.

optimist, utopian.

daydream, castles in the air, utopia, millennium; golden dream, airy hopes, fool's paradise, fond hope.

mainstay, anchor, sheet anchor; staff.

V. hope, trust, confide, rely, lean upon; live in hope, rest assured.

hope for, etc. (*desire*), 865; anticipate; presume, aspire; promise oneself; expect.

be hopeful, look on the bright side of, make the best of it, hope for the best; hope against hope, take heart, flatter oneself.

encourage, hearten, inspirit, hold out hope, cheer, assure, reassure, buoy up, embolden; promise, bid fair, augur well.

Adj. hopeful, confident, in hopes, secure, sanguine, buoyant, elated, flushed, exultant, enthusiastic.

fearless, unsuspecting, unsuspicious, undespairing, self-reliant; dauntless, etc. (*courageous*), 861.

propitious, promising; probable, auspicious, reassuring; encouraging, cheering, inspiriting, bright, roseate.

859. HOPELESSNESS.—*N.* hopelessness, despair, desperation; despondency, dejection, etc., 837; pessimism, hope deferred, dashed hopes.

pessimist, hypochondriac; bird of ill omen.

V. despair; lose (*or* give up, abandon) all hope, give up, give over, yield to despair; falter; despond.

Adj. hopeless, desperate, despairing, gone, in despair, forlorn, inconsolable, brokenhearted.

undone, ruined; incurable, cureless, incorrigible; irreparable, irrecoverable, irretrievable, irreclaimable, irredeemable, irrevocable.

unpropitious, unpromising, inauspicious, ill-omened, threatening, lowering, ominous.

860. FEAR.—*N.* **fear,** timidity, diffidence, apprehensiveness, fearfulness, solicitude, anxiety, care, apprehension, misgiving, mistrust, suspicion, qualm; hesitation.

trepidation, flutter, fear and trembling, perturbation, tremor, quivering, shaking, trembling, palpitation, nervousness, restlessness, disquietude, funk [*colloq.*].

fright, alarm, dread, awe, terror, horror, dismay, consternation, panic, scare; stampede [*of horses*].

intimidation, bullying; terrorism, reign of terror; terrorist, bully.

V. **fear,** be afraid, apprehend, dread, distrust; hesitate, falter, funk [*colloq.*], cower, crouch, skulk, take fright, take alarm; start, wince, flinch, shy, shrink, fly.

tremble, shake, shiver, shudder, flutter, quake, quaver, quiver, quail.

frighten, fright, terrify, inspire (*or* excite) fear, bulldoze [*colloq.*], alarm, startle, scare, dismay, astound; awe, strike terror, appall, unman, petrify, horrify.

daunt, intimidate, cow, overawe, abash, deter, discourage; browbeat, bully, threaten, terrorize.

haunt, obsess, beset, besiege; prey (*or* weigh) on the mind.

Adj. **afraid,** frightened, alarmed, fearful, timid, timorous, nervous, diffident, fainthearted, tremulous, shaky, afraid of one's shadow, apprehensive; aghast, awe-struck, awe-stricken, horror-stricken, panic-stricken.

dreadful, alarming, redoubtable, perilous, dread, fell, dire, direful, shocking, frightful, terrible, terrific, tremendous; horrid, horrible, ghastly, awful, awe-inspiring, revolting.

861. [Absence of fear] COURAGE.—*N.* **courage,** bravery, valor, resoluteness, boldness, spirit, daring, gallantry, intrepidity, prowess, heroism, chivalry, audacity, rashness, dash, defiance, confidence, self-reliance; manhood, manliness, nerve, pluck, mettle, grit, virtue, hardihood, fortitude, firmness, backbone, resolution, tenacity.

exploit, feat, deed, act, achievement.

brave man, man of courage, a man, hero, demigod; Hercules, Achilles, Sir Galahad.

brave woman, heroine; Amazon, Joan of Arc.

V. **dare,** venture, make bold; face (*or* front, confront, brave, defy, despise) danger; face; meet, brave, beard, defy.

nerve oneself, summon up (*or* pluck up) courage, take heart, stand to one's guns, bear up, hold out; present a bold front, show fight, face the music.

hearten, inspire courage, reassure, encourage, embolden, inspirit, cheer, nerve, rally.

Adj. **courageous,** brave, valiant, valorous, gallant, intrepid, spirited, high-spirited, mettlesome, plucky; manly, manful, stout-hearted, lionhearted, bold, daring, audacious, fearless, dauntless, undaunted, undismayed, unflinching, unshrinking, confident, self-reliant.

enterprising, adventurous, venturous, venturesome; dashing, chivalrous, warlike, soldierly, heroic.

fierce, savage, pugnacious, bellicose.

strong-minded, strong-willed, hardy, doughty [*archaic or humorous*]; firm, resolute, determined, dogged, indomitable.

862. [Excess of fear] COWARDICE.—*N.* cowardice, pusillanimity, cowardliness, timidity, effeminacy; baseness, abject fear, funk [*colloq.*]; fear, etc., 860; white feather, cold feet [*slang*], yellow streak [*slang*].

coward, poltroon, dastard, sneak, recreant, cur [*contemptuous*], craven.

alarmist, terrorist, pessimist.

shirker, slacker; fugitive, etc., 623.

V. **quail,** funk [*colloq.*], cower, skulk, sneak; flinch, shy, fight shy, slink, run away; show the white feather.

Adj. **cowardly,** coward, fearful, shy, timid, timorous, spiritless, soft, effeminate, fainthearted; white-livered; dastard, dastardly, base, craven, sneaking, recreant; unwarlike.

Adv. with fear and trembling, in fear of one's life, in a blue funk [*colloq.*].

863. RASHNESS.—*N.* rashness, temerity, imprudence, indiscretion; overconfidence, presumption, audacity, precipitancy, impetuosity, foolhardiness, heedlessness, thoughtlessness, carelessness, desperation.

gaming, gambling; blind bargain, leap in the dark.

desperado, madcap, daredevil; scapegrace, Don Quixote, knight-errant, adventurer; fire-eater, bully, bravo.

gambler, gamester, etc. (*chance*), 621.

V. **be rash,** stick at nothing, play a desperate game, run into danger, play with fire (*or* edged tools); rush on destruction, tempt providence, go on a forlorn hope.

Adj. **rash,** incautious, indiscreet, injudicious, imprudent, improvident, uncalculating, impulsive, heedless, careless, without ballast.

reckless, wild, madcap, desperate, devil-may-care, death-defying, hotheaded, headlong, headstrong; breakneck, foolhardy, harebrained, precipitate.

overconfident, overweening; venturesome, venturous, adventurous, quixotic.

Adv. posthaste, headforemost.

864. CAUTION.—*N.* caution, cautiousness, discretion, prudence, heed, circumspection, calculation, deliberation, foresight, etc., 510; vigilance, etc., 459; warning, etc., 668.

worldly wisdom; safety first, Fabian policy, watchful waiting.

coolness, self-possession, self-command; presence of mind, *sangfroid* [F.].

V. be cautious, take care, take heed, mind, be on one's guard; think twice, look before one leaps, count the cost, feel one's way, see how the land lies; pussyfoot [*colloq.*], keep out of harm's way, stand aloof; keep (*or* be) on the safe side.

warn, caution, etc., 668.

Adj. cautious, wary, guarded, on one's guard, suspicious, vigilant, careful, heedful, chary, sure-footed, circumspect, prudent, noncommittal, canny [Scot.], discreet, politic, strategic.

unenterprising, unadventurous, cool, steady, self-possessed; overcautious.

865. DESIRE.—*N.* desire, wish, fancy, inclination, leaning, bent, mind, whim, partiality, predilection, propensity, liking, love, fondness, relish.

longing, hankering, yearning, aspiration, ambition, eagerness, zeal, ardor, solicitude, anxiety.

need, want, exigency, urgency, necessity.

appetite, keenness, hunger, stomach, thirst, drought.

avidity, greed, greediness, covetousness, ravenousness, grasping, craving, rapacity, voracity.

mania, passion, rage, furor, frenzy, itching palm, cupidity, kleptomania, dipsomania; monomania.

Person desiring: lover, votary, devotee, aspirant; parasite, sycophant.

attraction, magnet, loadstone, lure, allurement, fancy, temptation, fascination; hobby.

V. desire, wish, wish for, care for, affect, like, take to, cling to, fancy; prefer, have an eye to, have a mind to; have a fancy for, have at heart, be bent upon; set one's heart (*or* mind) upon, covet, crave, hanker after, pine for, long for; hope, etc., 858.

woo, court, ogle, solicit; fish for.

want, miss, need, lack, feel the want of.

attract, allure, whet the appetite; appetize, take one's fancy, tempt, tantalize, make one's mouth water.

Adj. desirous, desiring, appetitive, inclined, fain, wishful, longing, wistful; anxious, solicitous, sedulous.

eager, keen, burning, fervent, ardent; agog; breathless; impatient.

ambitious, aspiring, vaulting.

craving, hungry, sharp-set, peckish [*colloq.*], ravening, famished; thirsty, athirst, dry [*colloq. when meaning thirsty*], droughty.

greedy, voracious, ravenous, omnivorous, covetous, rapacious, grasping, extortionate, exacting, sordid, insatiable, insatiate.

desirable, desired, in demand, popular, pleasing, appetizing.

Adv. fain; with eager appetite.

866. INDIFFERENCE.—*N.* **indifference,** neutrality; unconcern, nonchalance, apathy, supineness, disdain, inattention, coldness.

V. **be indifferent,** stand neuter, take no interest in, have no desire for, have no taste for, not care for, care nothing for (*or* about); not mind; spurn, disdain.

Adj. **indifferent,** cold, frigid, lukewarm; cool, neutral, unconcerned, phlegmatic, easygoing, careless, listless, halfhearted, unambitious, undesirous, unsolicitous.

unattractive, unalluring, undesired, undesirable, unwished.

867. DISLIKE.—*N.* **dislike,** distaste, disrelish, disinclination, unwillingness, reluctance, backwardness.

repugnance, disgust, nausea, loathing, aversion, abomination, antipathy, abhorrence, horror, hatred, detestation; hate, etc., 898.

V. **dislike,** disrelish; mind, object to, have no taste for, shudder at, turn up the nose at, look askance at; shun, avoid, eschew, shrink from.

loathe, abominate, detest, abhor; hate, etc., 898.

repel, disincline, sicken, pall, nauseate, disgust, shock, make one's blood run cold.

Adj. **loath,** averse; shy of, sick of, disinclined, heartsick.

repugnant, repulsive, repellent, abhorrent, insufferable, fulsome, nauseous, loathsome, offensive, disgusting.

unpopular, undesirable, uncared for, disliked, out of favor.

uneatable, inedible, unappetizing, unsavory.

Adv. to satiety, to one's disgust.

868. FASTIDIOUSNESS.—*N.* **fastidiousness,** nicety, hypercriticism, epicurism.

discrimination, discernment, perspicacity, keenness, sharpness, insight.

epicure, gourmet.

Excess of delicacy: prudery, prudishness, primness.

V. **be fastidious,** split hairs; mince the matter; turn up one's nose at, disdain.

discriminate, have nice discrimination; have exquisite taste; be discriminative.

Adj. fastidious, nice, delicate, meticulous, finicking *or* finicky, exacting, hard to please, difficult, dainty, squeamish, thin-skinned; querulous; particular, scrupulous; critical, hypercritical, overcritical.

prudish, strait-laced, prim.

discriminative, discriminating, discerning, judicious, keen, sharp, perspicacious.

869. SATIETY.—*N.* satiety, satisfaction, saturation, repletion, glut, surfeit, satiation.

V. sate, satiate, satisfy, saturate, cloy, quench, slake, pall, glut, gorge, surfeit; bore, tire, spoil.

Adj. satiated, overgorged, overfed, blasé [F.], sick of.

870. WONDER.—*N.* wonder, astonishment, amazement, wonderment, bewilderment, admiration, awe; stupor, stupefaction, fascination, surprise.

V. wonder, marvel, admire, be surprised, start, stare; gape, hold one's breath, stand aghast.

astonish, surprise, amaze, astound; dumfound, dumfounder, startle, dazzle, daze, strike, electrify, stun, stupefy, petrify, confound, bewilder, stagger, fascinate, take away one's breath, strike dumb.

Adj. astonished, surprised, aghast, breathless, agape, open-mouthed, thunderstruck, spellbound; lost in amazement (*or* wonder, astonishment).

wonderful, wondrous, surprising, striking, marvelous, miraculous; unexpected, mysterious, monstrous, prodigious, stupendous, inconceivable, incredible, strange.

indescribable, inexpressible, ineffable; unutterable, unspeakable.

Adv. for a wonder, strange to say, to one's great surprise.

871. [Absence of wonder] EXPECTANCE.—*N.* expectance, expectancy, expectation, etc., 507.

calmness, imperturbability, *sang-froid* [F.], coolness, steadiness, lack of nerves, want of imagination.

V. expect, etc., 507; not wonder, make nothing of, take it coolly.

Adj. expecting, unamazed, astonished at nothing, blasé [F.], expected, foreseen.

calm, imperturbable, nerveless, cool, coolheaded, unruffled, steady, unimaginative.

common, ordinary, etc. (*habitual*), 613.

872. PRODIGY.—*N.* prodigy, phenomenon, wonder, wonderment, marvel, miracle; freak, freak of nature, monstrosity, monster; curiosity, infant prodigy, lion, sight, spectacle; sign, portent.

873. REPUTE.—*N.* **repute,** reputation, distinction, mark, name, figure, note, notability, éclat, vogue, celebrity, fame, renown, popularity; credit, prestige, account, regard, respect, fair name.

dignity, stateliness, solemnity, grandeur, luster, splendor, nobility, majesty, sublimity, glory, honor.

rank, standing, precedence, station, place, status, position, order, degree, caste, condition.

eminence, greatness, height, importance, pre-eminence, supereminence, elevation, exaltation.

celebrity, worthy, hero, man of mark (*or* rank), lion, notability, somebody.

scholar, savant; paragon, star; elite.

ornament, honor, feather in one's cap, halo, aureole, nimbus; laurels.

posthumous fame, memory, celebration, canonization, enshrinement, glorification, immortality, immortal name.

V. **be distinguished,** shine, etc. (*light*), 420; shine forth, figure, cut a figure, flourish, flaunt, play first fiddle, bear the palm, take precedence; win laurels (*or* golden opinions).

surpass, outshine, outrival, outvie, eclipse; throw into the shade, overshadow.

rival, emulate, vie with.

honor, give (*or* do, pay) honor to, accredit, dignify, glorify, pledge, toast, look up to, exalt, aggrandize, elevate, enthrone, signalize, immortalize, deify.

consecrate; dedicate to, devote to; enshrine, inscribe, blazon, lionize.

Adj. **distinguished,** noted, of note, honored, popular, remarkable, notable, celebrated, renowned, famous, famed, far-famed, conspicuous, foremost.

reputable, in good odor, in favor, in high favor, respectable, creditable, worthy.

imperishable, deathless, immortal, never fading, fadeless.

illustrious, glorious, splendid, brilliant, radiant; bright, etc.,420.

eminent, prominent, high, etc., 206; peerless, pre-eminent, great, dignified, proud, noble, honorable, lordly, grand, stately, august, princely, imposing, solemn, transcendent, majestic, sacred, sublime.

874. DISREPUTE.—*N.* **disrepute,** discredit, ill-repute, ill-favor, ingloriousness, derogation, abasement, debasement, degradation; odium, obloquy, opprobrium, ignominy, dishonor, disgrace, shame, humiliation, scandal, infamy.

stigma, brand, reproach, imputation, slur, stain, blot, spot, blur, tarnish, taint, badge of infamy.

V. be inglorious, have a bad name; disgrace oneself, lose caste; fall from one's high estate, cut a sorry figure.

shame, disgrace, put to shame, dishonor; tarnish, stain, blot, sully, taint; discredit, degrade, debase, expel.

stigmatize, vilify, defame, slur, brand, post, send to Coventry, snub, show up [*colloq.*], reprehend.

disconcert, put out [*colloq.*], upset, discompose; put to the blush.

Adj. disgraced, overcome, downtrodden, in bad repute, under a cloud, in the shade (*or* background); down in the world, down and out [*colloq.*].

inglorious, nameless, obscure, unknown to fame, unnoticed, unnoted, unhonored, unglorified.

discreditable, questionable, shameful, disgraceful, disreputable, despicable; unbecoming, unworthy, derogatory, degrading, humiliating, scandalous, infamous, opprobrious, arrant, shocking, outrageous, notorious, ignominious, base, abject, vile.

beggarly, pitiful, mean, petty, shabby.

875. NOBILITY.—*N.* nobility, rank, condition, distinction, blood, birth, high descent, order, quality.

high life, upper classes, upper ten [*colloq.*], the four hundred; elite, aristocracy, fashionable world.

celebrity, bigwig [*humorous*], magnate, great man, star, great gun [*colloq.*].

The nobility: peerage, baronage; House of Lords (*or* peers); lords, noblesse.
peer, noble, nobleman; lord, grandee, don, hidalgo; aristocrat, swell [*colloq.*], gentleman, squire, patrician.
gentry, gentlefolk, magnates.
king, etc., 745; prince, duke, marquis, earl, viscount, baron, baronet, knight, chevalier, count, esquire, laird [Scot.]; signior, seignior; *signor* [It.], *señor* [Sp.], *senhor* [Pg.]; sheik, pasha, sahib.
empress, queen, princess, duchess, marchioness, viscountess, countess; lady, *doña* [Sp.], *dona* [Pg.]; *signora* [It.], *señora* [Sp.], *senhora* [Pg.].
Hindu titles: raja, rana (*fem.* rani), maharaja, maharana (*fem.* maharani), Gaekwar [*lit.* cowherd; *Baroda*].
Mohammedan titles: nawab, sultan (*fem.* sultana), amir.
Rank or office: kingship, dukedom, marquisate, earldom; viscountship, county, lordship, baronetcy, knighthood.

Adj. noble, exalted, princely, titled, patrician, aristocratic; highborn, well born, courtly.

Adv. in high quarters.

876. THE PEOPLE.—*N.* the people, commonalty, democracy; obscurity; *bourgeoisie* [F.], the four million; lower classes (*or* orders), common herd, rank and file, the many, the general, the crowd, the ruck, the populace, the multitude, the million, the masses, the mobility [*humorous*], the peasantry, proletariat; *hoi polloi* [Gr.].

rabble, horde, canaille, dregs of society, mob, trash, riffraff, ragtag and bobtail.

commoner, one of the people, democrat, plebeian, republican, bourgeois [F.].

peasant, countryman, boor, churl, serf; swain, clown, clodhopper, yokel, lout, bumpkin; plowman, hayseed [*slang*], rustic, lunkhead [*colloq.*], rube [*slang*]; tiller of the soil; hewers of wood and drawers of water; gamin, street Arab.

rough, rowdy, roughneck [*slang*], ruffian, tough [*colloq.*], scullion, low fellow, cad.

upstart, parvenu, nobody, snob, mushroom, adventurer, *nouveau riche* (*pl. nouveaux riches*) [F.].

vagabond, beggar, caitiff, ragamuffin, pariah, outcast, tramp, panhandler [*slang*], bum [*slang*], hobo.

Adj. ignoble, common, mean, low, base, vile, sorry, scrubby, beggarly; vulgar, low-minded; snobbish, parvenu, low-bred; menial, servile.

plebeian, proletarian, lowborn, baseborn, risen from the ranks, obscure, untitled.

rustic, country, uncivilized; loutish, boorish, clownish, churlish, rude.

barbarous, barbarian, barbaric.

Adv. below the salt.

877. TITLE.—*N.* title, honor; earldom, etc. (*nobility*), 875.

highness, excellency, grace, lordship, reverence; reverend; esquire, sir, master, Mr., *signor* [It.], *señor* [Sp.], etc., 373; your (*or* his) honor.

madam, etc. (*mistress*), 374; empress, queen, etc., 875.

decoration, laurel, palm, wreath, garland, bays; medal, ribbon, cordon, cross, crown, coronet, star, garter; epaulet, chevron, colors, cockade; livery; order, arms, coat of arms, shield, escutcheon *or* scutcheon, crest; handle to one's name.

878. PRIDE.—*N.* pride, haughtiness, high notions, hauteur, vainglory, arrogance, self-importance, pomposity, side [*slang*], swagger, toploftiness [*colloq.*].

dignity, self-respect, self-esteem, decorum, stateliness, seemliness.

V. be proud, presume, swagger, strut, hold one's head high, look big, carry with a high hand; ride the high horse, give oneself airs.

Adj. dignified, stately, lordly, lofty-minded, high-souled, high-minded, high-mettled, high-flown.

proud, haughty, lofty, high, mighty, swollen, puffed up, flushed, vainglorious; purse-proud, fine.

supercilious, disdainful, bumptious, magisterial, imperious, high and mighty, overweening, consequential; pompous, toplofty [*colloq.*]; arrogant.

stiff, stiff-necked; starched, stuck up [*colloq.*]; strait-laced, prim, affected, etc., 855.

Adv. with head erect, with nose in air, with nose turned up; with a sneer, with curling lip.

879. HUMILITY.—*N.* humility, humbleness, meekness, lowliness, abasement, self-abasement, submission, resignation.

modesty, timidity; confusion, humiliation, mortification.

V. be humble, deign, vouchsafe, condescend, humble oneself, stoop, submit, yield the palm, sing small [*colloq.*], hide one's face.

be humiliated, be put out of countenance, be shamed, be put to the blush, receive a snub, eat humble pie.

humble, humiliate, snub, abash, abase, strike dumb, lower, cast into the shade, put to the blush, confuse, shame, mortify, disgrace, crush.

Adj. humble, lowly, meek, modest, etc., 881; humble-minded, sober-minded; submissive, servile.

humbled, bowed down, abashed, ashamed, dashed, crestfallen, shorn of one's glory.

Adv. with downcast eyes, with bated breath, on bended knee.

880. VANITY.—*N.* vanity, conceit, conceitedness, self-conceit, self-sufficiency, self-praise, self-glorification, self-applause, self-admiration; selfishness, etc., 943.

pretension, airs, affected manner, mannerism; egoism, egotism, priggishness; vainglory, arrogance, pride, ostentation.

egoist, egotist; peacock; coxcomb.

V. be vain, pique oneself, have too high opinion of oneself, strut, put oneself forward; give oneself airs, boast, etc., 884.

render vain, inflate, puff up, turn one's head.

Adj. vain, conceited, overweening, forward, vainglorious, high-flown, ostentatious, etc., 882; puffed up, inflated, flushed, elate.

self-satisfied, complacent, self-confident, self-sufficient, self-admiring, pretentious, priggish, egotistic *or* egotistical, arrogant, assured.

881. MODESTY.—*N.* modesty; humility, etc., 879; diffidence, demureness, timidity, bashfulness, retiring disposition, unobtrusiveness; blush, blushing; reserve, constraint.

V. be modest, retire, give way to, hide one's face; keep in the background; hide one's light under a bushel.

Adj. modest, diffident, retiring, humble, etc., 879; timid, timorous, bashful, shy, coy, demure, sheepish, shamefaced, blushing.

unpretending, unpretentious, unobtrusive, unassuming, unostentatious; reserved, constrained.

Adv. modestly, quietly, privately; without ceremony.

882. OSTENTATION.—*N.* ostentation, display, show, flourish, parade, pomp, magnificence, splendor, pageantry, array, state, solemnity; dash [*colloq.*], splash [*colloq.*], glitter, pomposity, pretense, pretensions.

demonstration, pageant, spectacle, exhibition, exposition, procession, turnout [*colloq.*]; fete, field day, review, march past, promenade.

ceremony, ceremonial, ritual, form, formality, etiquette, punctilio.

V. **flaunt,** show off, parade, display, exhibit, brandish, blazon forth; dangle, emblazon.

Adj. **ostentatious,** showy, dashing, pretentious, grand, pompous; garish, gaudy, flaunting, glittering, gay.

splendid, magnificent, sumptuous, palatial.

theatrical, theatric, dramatic, spectacular, scenic.

ceremonial, ceremonious, ritualistic; solemn, stately, majestic, formal, punctilious.

Adv. with flourish of trumpet, with beat of drum, with flying colors.

883. CELEBRATION.—*N.* **celebration,** solemnization, commemoration; jubilation, ovation, triumph; inauguration, installation, presentation; coronation; debut, coming out [*colloq.*].

birthday, anniversary, biennial, triennial, etc.; centenary, centennial; bicentenary, bicentennial; tercentenary, tercentennial, etc.; festivity, festival, fete, holiday.

triumphal arch; salute, salvo, salvo of artillery; flourish of trumpets, fanfare; colors flying; illuminations.

jubilee, 50th anniversary; diamond jubilee.

V. **celebrate,** keep, signalize, do honor to, commemorate, solemnize; rejoice, etc., 838; paint the town red [*colloq.*].

inaugurate, install, instate, induct, chair.

Adj. **commemorative,** celebrated, kept in remembrance; immortal.

Adv. in honor of, in commemoration of, in celebration of, in memory of, in memoriam [L.].

884. BOASTING.—*N.* **boasting,** boast, vaunt, pretensions, braggadocio, puff [*colloq.*], flourish, bluff, highfalutin, swagger, jingoism, chauvinism, brag, bounce, bluster, bravado, buncombe [*cant or slang*]; rodomontade, bombast, hot air [*slang*], tall talk [*colloq.*], exaggeration, magniloquence, heroics.

boaster, braggart, pretender, bluffer, hot-air artist [*slang*]; chauvinist, jingo, jingoist; blusterer, swaggerer.

V. **boast,** brag, vaunt, puff, show off, flourish, strut, swagger, bluff; talk big, draw the long bow, blow one's own trumpet.

exult, crow [*colloq.*], triumph, glory, rejoice, cheer; gloat, gloat over, chuckle.

Adj. **boastful,** braggart, pretentious, vainglorious, highfalutin.

elate, elated, jubilant, triumphant, exultant; in high feather.

885. [Undue assumption of superiority] INSOLENCE.—*N.* insolence, brazenness, haughtiness, arrogance, airs; bumptiousness, assumption, presumption; disdain, insult, bluster, swagger.

impertinence, cheek [*colloq. or, slang*], nerve [*slang*], sauce [*colloq.*], abuse; flippancy.

impudence, self-assertion, assurance, audacity, hardihood, gall [*slang*], shamelessness, effrontery.

V. **be insolent,** bluster, swagger, give oneself airs, arrogate, assume, presume; make bold, make free, take a liberty.

outface, outlook, outstare, outbrazen, brazen out; look big.

domineer, bully, dictate, hector; lord it over; snub, browbeat, intimidate; dragoon, bulldoze [*colloq.*], terrorize.

Adj. **insolent,** haughty, arrogant, imperious, dictatorial, arbitrary, highhanded, supercilious, overbearing, toplofty [*colloq.*], intolerant, domineering, overweening, bumptious.

pert, flippant, fresh [*slang*], saucy, forward, impertinent, assuming, impudent, audacious, presumptuous.

brazen, shameless, unblushing, unabashed; barefaced, brazen-faced; lost to shame.

blustering, swaggering, hectoring, rollicking, roistering, devil-may-care.

jingo, jingoistic, chauvinistic.

Adv. with nose in air; with arms akimbo; with a high hand.

886. SERVILITY.—*N.* **servility,** slavery, obsequiousness, toadying, subserviency; abasement, prostration, toadeating, fawning, flunkyism, sycophancy; humility, etc., 879.

sycophant, parasite, toady, toadeater, flunky, hanger-on, timeserver, flatterer, tool; beat [*slang*], dead beat [*slang*]; heeler, ward heeler [*both polit. cant*]; sponge, sponger, truckler.

V. **cringe,** bow, stoop, kneel; fawn, crouch, cower, sneak, crawl, sponge, toady, grovel; be servile.

go with the stream, follow the crowd, worship the rising sun; be a timeserver.

Adj. **servile,** obsequious, oily, pliant, cringing, fawning, slavish, groveling, sniveling, mealy-mouthed; sycophantic, parasitical; abject, prostrate, base, mean, sneaking, timeserving.

887. BLUSTERER.—*N.* **blusterer,** swaggerer, braggart; roisterer, brawler, bully, terrorist, rough, ruffian, roughneck [*slang*], tough [*colloq.*], rowdy, hoodlum [*colloq.*], hooligan [*slang*], swashbuckler; desperado, daredevil, fire-eater [*colloq.*], jingo.

dogmatist, doctrinaire, stump orator.

III. SYMPATHETIC AFFECTIONS

888. FRIENDSHIP.—*N.* **friendship,** amity, friendliness; harmony, concord, peace, etc., 721; cordiality, *entente cordiale* [F.], good understanding, sympathy, fellow feeling, response; affection, etc. (*love*), 897; benevolence, good will; partiality, favoritism.

brotherhood, fraternization, association; acquaintance, familiarity, intimacy, intercourse, fellowship.

fraternity, sodality; sisterhood, sorority, sorosis.

V. be friendly, be friends, be acquainted with, know; have dealings with, sympathize with, have a leaning to, bear good will, love, befriend.

become friendly, make friends with, break the ice, be introduced to, make (*or* scrape) acquaintance with, get into favor, gain the friendship of; shake hands with, fraternize.

Adj. friendly, amicable, neighborly; brotherly, fraternal, sisterly; ardent, devoted, sympathetic, harmonious, hearty, cordial, warmhearted.

friends with, at home with, on good (*or* friendly, amicable, cordial, familiar, intimate) terms, on speaking terms, on visiting terms.

acquainted, familiar, intimate, hail fellow well met, free and easy; welcome.

Adv. with open arms; arm in arm.

888. ENMITY.—*N.* enmity, hostility, antagonism, unfriendliness; discord, etc., 713; bitterness, rancor; heartburning, animosity; malevolence, etc., 907.

alienation, estrangement; dislike, aversion, hate, etc., 898.

V. be unfriendly, keep (*or* hold) at arm's length; be at loggerheads, bear malice, fall out; take umbrage; alienate, estrange.

Adj. unfriendly, inimical, hostile; at enmity, at variance, at daggers drawn, up in arms against.

on bad terms, not on speaking terms; cool, cold, estranged, alienated, disaffected, irreconcilable.

890. FRIEND.—*N.* friend, alter ego [L.], other self; intimate, confidant (*masc.*), confidante (*fem.*); best (*or* bosom, fast) friend, well-wisher; neighbor, acquaintance.

patron, backer, tutelary saint, good genius, advocate, partisan, sympathizer; ally, friend in need.

associate, comrade, mate, companion, confrere, colleague, partner, consort, chum [*colloq.*], pal [*slang*], buddy [*slang, First World War*]; playfellow, playmate, schoolmate, schoolfellow, classmate; bedfellow, bunkie [*colloq.*], roommate, shopmate, shipmate, messmate; fellow (*or* boon) companion.

Famous friendships: Pylades and Orestes, Castor and Pollux, Achilles and Patroclus, Damon and Pythias, David and Jonathan; Soldiers Three, the Three Musketeers.

host, hostess (*fem.*).

guest, visitor, frequenter, habitué, protégé.

compatriot, countryman, fellow countryman; fellow townsman.

891. ENEMY.—*N.* **enemy,** antagonist, foe, foeman, open (*or* bitter) enemy, opponent; mortal aversion (*or* antipathy); snake in the grass.

public enemy, enemy to society; anarchist, seditionist, traitor, traitress (*fem.*).

892. SOCIALITY.—*N.* **sociality,** sociability, social intercourse, intercourse, companionship, comradeship, fellowship; urbanity, intimacy, familiarity, condescension, *esprit de corps* [F.]; morale.

conviviality, good fellowship, joviality, jollity, festivity, merry-making; hospitality, heartiness; cheer.

welcome, greeting; hearty (*or* warm) reception; hearty welcome (*or* greeting), the glad hand [*slang*].

social gathering, social reunion, assembly, barbecue; bee; cornhusking, corn shucking [U. S.]; husking, husking-bee [U. S.]; hen party [*colloq.*]; house raising, housewarming, hanging of the crane, smoker [*colloq.*]; Dutch treat [*colloq.*]; stag, stag party [*both colloq.*]; sociable [U. S.], party, entertainment, reception, levee, at home, soiree, matinee; garden party, coming-out party [*colloq.*], surprise party; ball, hunt ball, dance festival.

Social meals: breakfast, wedding breakfast, hunt breakfast; luncheon, lunch; picnic lunch, basket lunch, picnic; tea, afternoon tea, five-o'clock tea, cup of tea, dish of tea [esp. Brit.], coming-out tea [*colloq.*]; tea party, tea fight [*slang*]; dinner, potluck, bachelor dinner, stag dinner [*colloq.*], hunt dinner; church supper, high tea, banquet.

visit, visiting; round of visits; call, morning call, interview; tryst, appointment.

V. **be sociable,** know, be acquainted, associate with, consort with, club together, join; make advances, fraternize.

visit, pay a visit, call at, call upon, leave a card, drop in, look in.

entertain, give a party; see one's friends, keep open house, do the honors, receive, welcome; kill the fatted calf.

Adj. **sociable,** companionable, clubbable [*colloq.*], cozy, chatty, conversational; convivial, festive, festal, jovial, jolly, hospitable.

free and easy, hail fellow well met, familiar, intimate, social, neighborly.

Adv. **en famille** [F.], in the family circle; on terms of intimacy; in the social whirl.

893. SECLUSION. EXCLUSION.—*N.* **seclusion,** privacy, retirement, concealment, rustication, solitude, isolation, loneliness, voluntary exile, aloofness.

retreat, cell, hermitage, cloister, convent; sanctum sanctorum [L.], study, library, den [*colloq.*].

exclusion, excommunication, banishment, exile, ostracism, cut.

unsociability, unsociableness, inhospitality, domesticity, self-sufficiency.

recluse, hermit; caveman, cave dweller, troglodyte, cynic, Diogenes.

outcast, pariah, leper; outsider, rank outsider; castaway, foundling.

V. seclude oneself, keep aloof, shut oneself up; deny oneself, rusticate, retire, retire from the world; take the veil.

exclude, repel, cut; send to Coventry, turn one's back upon, shut the door upon; blackball, excommunicate, exile, expatriate; banish, outlaw, maroon, ostracize, keep at arm's length; boycott, embargo, blockade, isolate.

Adj. secluded, sequestered, retired, private, out of the world.

unsociable, unsocial, inhospitable; domestic, stay-at-home.

excluded, unfrequented, unvisited, uninvited, unwelcome, under a cloud.

friendless, homeless, desolate, lorn, forlorn; solitary, lonely, lonesome, isolated, single, estranged; derelict, outcast, deserted, banished.

uninhabited, unoccupied, untenanted, tenantless, abandoned.

894. COURTESY.—*N.* courtesy; respect, etc., 928; good manners (*or* behavior, breeding); manners, politeness, urbanity, gentility, breeding, gentle breeding, cultivation, culture, polish, civility, amenity, suavity; good temper, good humor, amiability, complacency, affability, complaisance, compliance, gallantry, chivalry.

pink of courtesy, pink of politeness; flower of knighthood; Chesterfield; Lancelot.

ceremonial; salutation, reception, presentation, introduction, welcome, greeting; respects, regards, remembrances; deference, love.

Forms of greeting: bow, curtsy, salaam, kowtow [China], obeisance, bowing and scraping; kneeling, genuflection; capping, pulling the forelock, nod, shaking hands; embrace, hug, squeeze, kiss; salute, accolade.

V. be courteous, show courtesy; behave oneself, conciliate, speak one fair, take in good part.

do the honors, usher, usher in, receive, greet, hail, bid welcome, welcome; bid Godspeed; speed the parting guest.

salute; nod to; smile upon; uncover, touch (*or* raise) the hat, doff the cap, bow, make one's bow, curtsy, bob a curtsy, kneel; bow (*or* bend) the knee; salaam, kowtow [China], prostrate oneself.

Adj. courteous, polite, civil, mannerly, urbane; well behaved, well mannered, well bred, gently bred, of gentle breeding; polished, cultivated, refined; gallant, chivalrous, chivalric, knightly.

tactful, ingratiating, winning; gentle, mild; good-humored,

cordial, gracious, amiable, familiar; neighborly; obliging, complacent, conciliatory.

bland, suave, affable, honey-tongued; oily, unctuous, obsequious.

Adv. with a good grace; with open arms, with outstretched arms, with perfect courtesy, in good humor.

895. DISCOURTESY.—*N.* **discourtesy,** ill-breeding, bad manners; tactlessness; discourteousness, rusticity, incivility, lack (*or* want) of courtesy, disrespect, impudence, misbehavior, barbarism, barbarity; vulgarity, brutality, blackguardism, conduct unbecoming a gentleman.

bad temper, ill-temper, peevishness, surliness, churlishness, perversity; moroseness, etc., 901*a*; sternness, austerity; moodishness, captiousness, tartness, acrimony, asperity.

scowl, black looks, frown; sulks, short answer, rebuff; hard words, unparliamentary language, personality.

bear, brute, blackguard, beast; unlicked cub; crosspatch [*colloq.*], grouch [*slang*].

V. **be rude,** insult, treat with discourtesy, make bold with, make free with; take a liberty; stare out of countenance, ogle, point at.

sulk, frown, scowl, glower, pout; snap, snarl, growl.

cut; turn one's back upon, turn on one's heel; give the cold shoulder, keep at a distance.

Adj. **discourteous,** uncourteous, uncourtly, ill-bred, ill-mannered, ill-behaved, unmannerly, uncivil, impolite, unaccommodating, unneighborly, ungallant, ungracious, unpolished; ungentlemanly; unladylike; vulgar.

pert, forward, obtrusive, impudent, rude, saucy, flippant.

rough, rugged, bluff, blunt, short, gruff; churlish, boorish, bearish; brutal, brusque, stern, harsh, austere; cavalier.

bad-tempered, ill-tempered, ill-humored, crusty, tart, sour, crabbed, sharp, trenchant, sarcastic, caustic, virulent, bitter, acrimonious, venomous, contumelious, snarling, surly, perverse, grim, sullen, peevish, bristling, thorny.

Adv. with a bad grace.

896. CONGRATULATION.—*N.* **congratulation,** felicitation, compliment; compliments of the season; good wishes, best wishes.

V. **congratulate,** felicitate, wish one joy, compliment, tender (*or* offer) one's congratulations; wish many happy returns of the day.

897. LOVE.—*N.* **love,** affection, sympathy, fellow feeling; tenderness, heart, brotherly love; charity, good will, benevolence; attachment, fondness, liking, inclination; regard, admiration, fancy.

yearning, tender passion, gallantry, passion, flame, devotion, fervor, enthusiasm, rapture, enchantment, infatuation, adoration, idolatry.

mother love, maternal love, natural affection.

attractiveness, charm; popularity; idol, favorite, etc., 899.

god of love, Cupid, Eros, Venus; myrtle.

lover, suitor, fiancé [F.], follower [colloq.], admirer, adorer, wooer, beau, sweetheart, swain, young man [colloq.], flame [colloq.], love, truelove.

ladylove, sweetheart, mistress, inamorata, darling, idol, angel, goddess; betrothed, fiancée [F.].

flirt, coquette.

V. love, like, fancy, care for, take an interest in, sympathize with; be in love with, regard, revere, take to, set one's affections on, adore, idolize, dote on (or upon), make much of, hold dear, prize; hug, cling to, cherish, caress, fondle, pet.

charm, attract, attach, fascinate, captivate, bewitch, enrapture, turn the head.

Adj. loving, affectionate, tender, sympathetic, amorous, love-sick, fond, ardent, passionate, rapturous, devoted, motherly.

loved, beloved, well beloved, dearly beloved; dear, precious, darling, pet; favorite, popular.

lovable, adorable, lovely, sweet, attractive, winning, winsome, charming, enchanting, captivating, fascinating, bewitching, amiable.

898. HATE.—N. hate, hatred, vials of hate; hymn of hate; disaffection, disfavor; alienation, estrangement, coolness; enmity, etc., 889; animosity, malice, implacability.

umbrage, pique, grudge, spleen, bitterness, bitterness of feeling; ill-blood, bad blood; acrimony.

repugnance, etc. (dislike), 867; odium, unpopularity; detestation, abhorrence, loathing, execration, abomination, aversion, antipathy.

object of hatred, an abomination, an aversion, bête noire [F.]; enemy, etc., 891; bitter pill.

V. hate, detest, abominate, abhor, loathe; recoil at, shudder at; shrink from, revolt against, execrate; dislike, etc., 867.

alienate, estrange, repel, horrify, set against, sow dissension, set by the ears, envenom, incense, irritate, ruffle, vex.

Adj. abhorrent, averse from, set against; bitter, etc. (acri-monious), 895; implacable.

unloved, unbeloved, unlamented, undeplored, unmourned, un-cared for, unvalued; disliked.

lovelorn, jilted, crossed in love, forsaken, rejected.

hateful, obnoxious, odious, abominable, repulsive, offensive, shocking; disgusting, reprehensible.

invidious, spiteful; malicious, etc., 907.

899. FAVORITE.—*N.* **favorite,** pet, idol, jewel, spoiled child, apple of one's eye, man after one's own heart.

love, dear, darling, duck, honey, sweetheart, etc. (*ladylove*), 897.

general (*or* universal) favorite; idol of the people; matinee idol.

900. RESENTMENT.—*N.* **resentment,** displeasure, animosity, anger, wrath, ire, indignation; exasperation, vexation, wrathful, indignation.

pique, umbrage, huff, soreness, acerbity, virulence, bitterness, acrimony, asperity; irascibility, etc., 901; sulks, etc., 901*a*; hate, etc., 898; revenge.

irritation; warmth, ferment, excitement, ebullition; angry mood, pet, tiff, passion, fit, tantrum [*colloq.*].

rage, fury, towering rage, passion; outburst, explosion, paroxysm, storm, violence, vials of wrath; hot blood, high words.

Furies, Erinyes (*sing.* Erinys), Eumenides.

provocation, affront, offense, indignity, insult, grudge; last straw, sore subject; ill-turn, outrage; buffet, blow, box on the ear, rap on the knuckles.

V. **resent,** take amiss, take offense (*or* umbrage, exception); pout, frown, scowl, lower, snarl, growl, gnash, snap; redden, color; look black, look daggers.

be angry, fly into a rage, bridle up, fire up, flare up; chafe, mantle, fume, kindle, fly out, boil, boil with indignation (*or* rage), rage, storm, foam; hector, bully, bluster; lose one's temper; raise Cain [*slang*]; breathe revenge.

anger, affront, offend, give offense (*or* umbrage); hurt the feelings; insult, ruffle, heckle [Brit.], nettle, huff, pique; excite, irritate, fret, sting, provoke, chafe, wound, incense, inflame, enrage, envenom, embitter, exasperate, infuriate, madden; rankle.

Adj. **angry,** wroth, irate, ireful, wrathful; irascible, etc., 901; bitter, virulent, acrimonious, offended, indignant, hurt, sore.

fuming, raging, hot under the collar [*slang*]; convulsed with rage; fierce, wild, furious, fiery, rabid, savage, violent.

Adv. in the height (*or* heat) of passion; in an ecstasy of rage.

901. IRASCIBILITY.—*N.* **irascibility,** temper; crossness, petulance, irritability, tartness, acerbity, acrimony, asperity, pugnacity, excitability.

shrew, vixen, virago, dragon, scold, spitfire, fury.

V. **be irascible,** have a temper, be possessed of the devil, have the temper of a fiend; fire up, flare up.

Adj. **irascible,** bad-tempered, irritable, excitable; thin-skinned, sensitive; hasty, quick, warm, hot, testy, touchy, huffy, pettish, petulant, fretful, querulous, captious, moody, cross, fractious, peevish.

quarrelsome, contentious, disputatious, pugnacious, cantankerous [*colloq.*], cross-grained; waspish, peppery, fiery, passionate, choleric, shrewish.

901a. SULLENNESS.—*N.* sullenness, moroseness, spleen; churlishness, irascibility, moodiness, perversity, obstinacy, crabbedness.

sulks, dudgeon, dumps [*humorous*], doldrums; black looks, scowl; grouch [*slang*], huff.

V. **sulk**, frown, scowl, lower, glower, pout, grouch [*slang*].

Adj. **sullen**, sulky, ill-tempered, ill-humored, ill-disposed; crusty, crabbed, sour, sore, surly, moody, cross, cross-grained; perverse, wayward, refractory, restive, ungovernable, cussed [*vulgar or euphemistic*]; grumpy, glum, grum, grim, morose, grouchy [*slang*].

902. [Expression of affection] ENDEARMENT.—*N.* endearment, caress, blandishment, fondling, billing and cooing, dalliance, caressing, embrace, salute, kiss, smack, osculation.

courtship, wooing, suit, addresses, love-making; calf love [*colloq.*]; amorous glances, ogle, side glance, sheep's eyes, goo-goo eyes [*slang*].

flirting, flirtation, gallantry; coquetry, spooning [*slang*].

engagement, betrothal; marriage, etc., 903; honeymoon; love letter, billet-doux; valentine.

flirt, coquette; male flirt, philanderer; spoon [*slang*].

V. **caress**, fondle, pet; smile upon, coax, wheedle, coddle, make much of, cherish, foster.

clasp, hug, cuddle; fold to the heart, press to the bosom, fold in one's arms; snuggle, nestle, nuzzle; embrace, kiss, salute.

court, make love, bill and coo, spoon [*slang*], toy, dally, flirt, coquet, philander, pay court to; serenade; woo.

propose, make (*or* have) an offer, pop the question [*colloq.*]; become engaged, become betrothed; plight one's troth.

Adj. **lovesick**, spoony [*slang*].

903. MARRIAGE.—*N.* **marriage**, matrimony, wedlock, union, intermarriage; nuptial tie, nuptial knot; match; betrothment.

wedding, nuptials, Hymen, bridal, espousals; leading to the altar; honeymoon.

bridesmaid, maid of honor, matron of honor; attendant, usher, best man, bridesman, groomsman; bride, bridegroom.

married man, partner, spouse, mate, husband, man [*dial.*], consort.

married woman, wife, wedded wife, spouse, helpmeet, helpmate, better half, lady [*obs. or uncultivated*]; squaw; matron.

married couple, man and wife, wedded pair, wedded couple, Darby and Joan.

Kinds of marriage: monogamy, bigamy, polygamy, polyandry; Mormonism; morganatic (*or* left-handed) marriage, *mésalliance* [F.].

matchmaker, matrimonial agency (*or* agent, bureau).

V. **marry,** wive, take to oneself a wife; be married, be spliced [*colloq.*]; wed, espouse, lead to the altar, join, couple, be made one.

Adj. **engaged,** betrothed, plighted, affianced.

Matrimonial, marital, conjugal, connubial, wedded; nuptial, hymeneal, spousal, bridal.

904. CELIBACY.—*N.* celibacy, singleness, single blessedness; bachelorhood, bachelorship; misogyny.

virginity, maidenhood, maidenhead.

unmarried man, bachelor, old bachelor; misogamist, misogynist; monk, priest, celibate, religious.

unmarried woman, maid, maiden, virgin, spinster, old maid; nun, sister, vestal, vestal virgin; Diana.

Adj. **unmarried,** unwedded; wifeless, spouseless; single, celibate, virgin.

905. DIVORCE. WIDOWHOOD.—*N.* divorce, divorcement; separation, judicial separation, separate maintenance.

widowhood, weeds.

widow, relict, dowager; divorcée; grass widow.

widower; grass widower.

V. live separate; separate, divorce, put away.

906. BENEVOLENCE.—*N.* benevolence, Christian charity; God's grace; good will, philanthropy, unselfishness, kindness, kindliness, good nature, loving-kindness, benignity, brotherly love, charity, humanity, kindly feelings, fellow feeling, sympathy, goodness of heart, warmheartedness, kindheartedness, amiability, tenderness, love, friendship; tolerance, consideration; mercy.

charitableness, bounty, almsgiving; good works, beneficence, generosity, a good turn.

philanthropist, salt of the earth; good Samaritan, sympathizer, well-wisher, altruist.

V. **bear good will,** wish well, take (*or* feel) an interest in; be interested in, sympathize with, feel for; treat well, give comfort, do good, do a good turn, benefit, assist, render a service, render assistance, aid.

enter into the feelings of others, practice the golden rule, do as you would be done by.

Adj. **benevolent,** kind, kindly, well meaning, amiable, cordial, obliging, accommodating, indulgent, gracious, tender, considerate, warmhearted, kindhearted, tenderhearted, largehearted, softhearted, merciful; sympathizing, sympathetic.

full of natural affection, fatherly, motherly, brotherly, sisterly; paternal, maternal, fraternal; friendly.

charitable, beneficent, philanthropical, generous, humane, benignant, unselfish, altruistic, bountiful.

Adv. with the best intentions; out of deepest sympathy.

907. MALEVOLENCE.—*N.* **malevolence,** bad intent, bad intention, unkindness, uncharitableness, ill-nature, ill-will, enmity, hate, malice, malignance, malignity, maliciousness; spite, resentment; gall, venom, rancor, virulence, hardness of heart, heart of stone, obduracy; evil eye, cloven foot (*or* hoof).

ill-turn, bad turn; affront, indignity; tender mercies (*ironical*).

cruelty, brutality, savagery, ferocity; outrage, atrocity, illusage, persecution; barbarity, inhumanity, truculence, ruffianism; inquisition, torture.

V. **bear malice,** harbor a grudge; hurt, annoy, injure, harm, wrong, outrage, malign; molest, worry, harass, harry, bait, hound, persecute, oppress, grind, maltreat, ill-treat; give no quarter, have no mercy.

Adj. **malevolent,** ill-disposed, ill-intentioned, ill-natured, ill-conditioned, evil-minded, evil-disposed, venomous, malicious, malign, malignant, maleficent; rancorous, spiteful, treacherous, caustic, bitter, envenomed, acrimonious, virulent; grinding, galling, harsh; disobliging, unkind, unfriendly; ungracious, churlish, surly, sullen.

cold-blooded, coldhearted, hardhearted, stonyhearted, cold, unnatural; ruthless, pitiless, relentless.

cruel, brutal, brutish, savage, ferocious, inhuman; barbarous, fell, truculent, bloodthirsty, atrocious, fiendish, diabolic *or* diabolical, devilish, infernal, hellish.

Adv. with bad intent; with the ferocity of a tiger.

908. MALEDICTION.—*N.* **malediction,** malison, curse, imprecation, denunciation, execration; anathema, ban, proscription, excommunication, commination, fulmination; disparagement, vilification, vituperation.

abuse, evil speaking, foul (*or* bad, strong, unparliamentary) language, billingsgate, blackguardism, cursing, profane, swearing, expletive, oath, foul invective, ribaldry, scurrility, invective.

V. **curse,** imprecate, damn, swear at; execrate, vituperate, scold; anathematize, denounce, proscribe, excommunicate, fulminate, thunder against.

909. THREAT.—*N.* **threat,** menace, defiance, abuse, intimidation, denunciation, fulmination, etc., 908; gathering clouds.

V. **threaten,** threat, menace; snarl, growl, mutter, bully; defy, intimidate, shake the fist at; thunder, fulminate, bluster.

Adj. **threatening,** menacing, minatory, abusive; ominous, defiant.

910. PHILANTHROPY.—*N.* **philanthropy,** altruism, humanity, humanitarianism, benevolence; public welfare.

public spirit, patriotism, nationality, love of country.

philanthropist, altruist, etc., 906; humanitarian, patriot.

Adj. **philanthropic,** altruistic, humanitarian, public-spirited; patriotic; humane, largehearted, benevolent, etc., 906; generous, liberal, etc., 942.

911. MISANTHROPY.—*N.* **misanthropy,** hatred of mankind; selfishness, egoism, egotism; sullenness, moroseness, cynicism; want of patriotism.

misanthrope, misanthropist, egoist, egotist, cynic, man hater. woman hater, misogynist.

Adj. **misanthropic,** antisocial, unpatriotic; egoistical, egotistical, selfish; morose, sullen, cynical, etc., 901*a*.

912. BENEFACTOR.—*N.* **benefactor,** savior, protector, good genius, tutelary saint, guardian angel, good Samaritan; friend in need; salt of the earth; philanthropist, etc., 910; fairy godmother.

913. [Maleficent being] EVILDOER.—*N.* **evildoer,** evil worker, wrongdoer, etc., 949; mischiefmaker, marplot; oppressor, tyrant; incendiary, etc., 384; anarchist, nihilist, destroyer, vandal, iconoclast, terrorist.

savage, brute, ruffian, barbarian, desperado; apache, gunman, hoodlum [*colloq.*], redskin, tough [*colloq.*], bully, rough, hooligan [*slang*], dangerous classes; thief, etc., 792; cutthroat.

wild beast, tiger, leopard, panther, hyena, catamount [U. S.], catamountain, lynx, cougar, jaguar, puma; bloodhound, hellhound, sleuthhound; gorilla; vulture.

cockatrice, adder; snake, serpent, cobra, asp, viper, rattlesnake, boa; alligator, crocodile, octopus.

hag, hellhag, beldam, Jezebel.

monster, fiend, demon, etc , 980; devil incarnate, Frankenstein's monster; cannibal; bloodsucker, vampire, ogre, ghoul.

914. PITY.—*N.* **pity,** compassion, commiseration, sympathy, fellow feeling, tenderness, softheartedness, yearning, forbearance, humanity, mercy, clemency; leniency, lenity, charity, ruth, longsuffering; quarter, grace.

sympathizer; advocate, friend, partisan, patron, well-wisher, defender, champion.

V. **pity,** have (*or* take) pity, commiserate, condole, sympathize, feel for, be sorry for.

forbear, relent, relax, give quarter.

excite pity, touch, soften, melt, melt the heart; propitiate.

Adj. **pitying,** pitiful, compassionate, sympathetic, touched. merciful, clement, humane, humanitarian; tender, tender-hearted, softhearted, lenient, forbearing.

914a. PITILESSNESS.—*N.* **pitilessness,** inclemency, inexorability, inflexibility, hardness of heart; want of pity, severity, malevolence, etc., 907.

V. **be pitiless,** turn a deaf ear to; claim one's pound of flesh; have no mercy, give no quarter.

Adj. **pitiless,** merciless, ruthless, unpitying, unmerciful, inclement, grim-faced, grim-visaged; inflexible, relentless, inexorable, harsh, cruel, etc., 907.

915. CONDOLENCE.—*N.* **condolence,** sympathy, consolation; lamentation, etc., 839.

V. **condole with,** console, sympathize, express pity; afford consolation; lament with, express sympathy for, feel for, send one's condolences; share one's sorrow.

916. GRATITUDE.—*N.* **gratitude,** gratefulness, thankfulness; sense of obligation; acknowledgment, recognition, thanksgiving, giving thanks.

thanks, praise, benediction; paean; *Te Deum* [L.], grace, requital, thank offering.

V. **be grateful,** thank; give (*or* render, return, offer, tender) thanks, acknowledge, requite; lie under an obligation; never forget, overflow with gratitude.

Adj. **grateful,** thankful, obliged, beholden, indebted to, under obligation.

917. INGRATITUDE.—*N.* **ingratitude,** thanklessness, unthankfulness; thankless task, thankless office.

V. **be ungrateful,** feel no obligation, owe one no thanks, forget benefits, have a short memory for.

Adj. **ungrateful,** unmindful, unthankful; thankless, ingrate. forgotten; unacknowledged, unthanked, unrequited, unrewarded, ill-requited; ill-rewarded.

918. FORGIVENESS.—*N.* **forgiveness,** pardon, grace, remission, absolution, amnesty, oblivion; reprieve.

conciliation; reconciliation, forbearance, propitiation.

exoneration, excuse, quittance, release, indemnity; acquittal, exculpation.

V. **forgive,** pardon, think no more of, let bygones by bygones, bury the hatchet. start afresh.

remit, exculpate, exonerate, absolve, give absolution; blot out one's sins (*or* offenses, transgressions), wipe the slate clean; reprieve, acquit.

excuse, pass over, overlook; condone, wink at; bear with, allow for, make allowances for; pocket the affront.

conciliate, propitiate, placate; beg (*or* ask) pardon, make up a quarrel.

Adj. **forgiving**, placable, conciliatory.

919. REVENGE.—*N.* **revenge,** vengeance; vendetta, death feud, eye for an eye, tooth for a tooth, retaliation; day of reckoning.

rancor, vindictiveness, implacability, ruthlessness; malevolence, etc., 907.

avenger, nemesis, Eumenides.

V. **revenge,** avenge, take revenge, have one's revenge; breathe vengeance; give no quarter, take no prisoners.

keep the wound open, harbor revenge, bear malice; rankle, rankle in the breast.

Adj. **revengeful,** vengeful, vindictive, rancorous; pitiless, ruthless, rigorous, avenging, retaliative; unforgiving, unrelenting, inexorable, implacable, relentless, remorseless.

920. JEALOUSY.—*N.* **jealousy,** distrust, mistrust, heartburn; envy, etc., 921; doubt, suspicion; green-eyed monster.

V. **be jealous,** view with jealousy, grudge, begrudge.

doubt, distrust, mistrust, suspect, misdoubt.

Adj. **jealous,** jaundice, yellow-eyed, envious.

921. ENVY.—*N.* **envy,** enviousness; rivalry; ill-will, spite; jealousy, etc., 920.

V. **envy,** covet, grudge, begrudge, break the tenth commandment.

Adj. **envious,** invidious, covetous, grudging, begrudged; belittling.

IV. MORAL AFFECTIONS

922. RIGHT.—*N.* **right;** what ought to be, what should be; fitness.

justice, equity, equitableness, propriety, fairness, fair play, square deal [*colloq.*], impartiality; lawfulness, legality.

morals, etc. (*duty*), 926; law, etc., 963; honor, etc., 939; virtue, etc., 944.

V. **be right,** stand to reason.

do right, see justice done, see fair play; do justice to, recompense, hold the scales even, give everyone his due.

Adj. **right,** good; just, reasonable; fit, etc., 924; equal, equable, equitable; even-handed, fair, square.

legitimate, justifiable, rightful, as it ought to be; lawful, legal.

Adv. in justice, in equity, in reason; upon even terms.

923. WRONG.—*N.* **wrong,** iniquity; what ought not to be, what should not be; unreasonableness, grievance; shame.

injustice, unfairness, foul play, partiality, leaning, favor, favoritism, partisanship; undueness, unlawfulness, illegality.

dishonor, etc., 939; vice, etc., 945.

V. **do wrong,** be inequitable, show partiality, favor, lean toward; encroach; impose upon; reap where one has not sown.

Adj. **wrong,** wrongful, iniquitous, bad, unjust, unfair, inequitable, unequal, partial, one-sided; injurious.

unjustifiable, unreasonable, unwarrantable, objectionable, improper, unfit, unjustified; unlawful; illegal, immoral.

924. AUTHORIZATION.—*N.* **authorization,** sanction, authority, charter, warrant; constitution; bond.

right, dueness, due, privilege, prerogative, prescription, title, claim, pretension, legality, demand, birthright.

immunity, license, liberty, franchise; vested interest (*or* right).

deserts, merits, dues.

claimant, appellant; plaintiff, etc., 938.

V. **deserve,** merit, be worthy of, make good.

demand, claim, lay claim to, reclaim, exact; insist on (*or* upon), make a point of, require, assert, assume, arrogate.

entitle, give (*or* confer) a right, authorize, sanction, legalize, ordain, prescribe, allot.

Adj. **privileged,** allowed, sanctioned, warranted, authorized; ordained, prescribed, constitutional, chartered, enfranchised.

prescriptive, presumptive, absolute, inalienable, inviolable, sacrosanct.

merited, due to, deserved, condign [*archaic, except of punishment*].

right, creditable, fit, fitting, correct, square, due, proper, meet, befitting, becoming, seemly; decorous.

lawful, legitimate, legal, legalized, allowable.

Adv. by right, by divine right; on the square [*colloq.*].

925. [Want of authorization] IMPROPRIETY.—*N.* **impropriety,** undueness, unrightfulness, illegality, unlawfulness; falseness, invalidity of title; illegitimacy.

loss of right, disfranchisement, forfeiture.

assumption, usurpation, tort [*law*], violation, breach, encroachment, seizure, exaction, imposition.

usurper, pretender, impostor.

V. infringe, encroach, trench on, exact, arrogate, usurp, violate; get under false pretenses, sail under false colors.

disentitle, disfranchise, disqualify; invalidate.

Adj. undue, unlawful, illegal, illicit, unconstitutional, unauthorized, unwarranted, unsanctioned, unjustified; disqualified, unqualified; unprivileged, unchartered.

undeserved, unmerited, unearned.

illegitimate, bastard, spurious, false; usurped.

improper, unfit, unbefitting, unseemly, unbecoming, misbecoming; preposterous, pretentious, would-be.

926. DUTY.—*N.* duty, moral obligation, accountability, liability, onus, responsibility.

allegiance, fealty, tie; engagement; function, part, calling.

observance, fulfillment, discharge, performance, acquittal, satisfaction, redemption; good behavior.

morality, morals, decalogue; conscientiousness, conscience, inward monitor, still small voice within, sense of duty.

propriety, fitness, seemliness, decorum, the thing, the proper thing.

Science of morals: ethics, moral (*or* ethical) philosophy, casuistry, polity.

V. behoove, become, befit, beseem; belong to, pertain to; rest with, fall to one's lot, devolve on.

take upon oneself, be (*or* become) sponsor for, incur a responsibility; perform (*or* discharge) a duty *or* an obligation; act one's part, redeem one's pledge, be at one's post, do one's duty.

impose a duty, enjoin, require, exact; bind, bind over; saddle with, prescribe, assign, call upon, look to, oblige.

Adj. obligatory, binding, imperative, peremptory, stringent, incumbent on.

amenable, liable, accountable, responsible, answerable.

right, meet, etc. (*due*), 924; moral, ethical, conscientious.

Adv. with a safe conscience, as in duty bound, on one's own responsibility, at one's own risk.

927. DERELICTION OF DUTY.—*N.* dereliction, nonobservance, nonperformance, nonco-operation; indolence, neglect, infraction, violation, transgression, failure, evasion; fault, etc. (*guilt*), 947.

slacker, loafer, time killer; eyeserver, eyeservant; striker; nonco-operator.

V. violate, break, break through; infringe, set aside, set at naught; encroach upon, trench upon, trample on; slight, get by [*slang*], neglect, evade, escape, transgress, fail.

927a. EXEMPTION.—*N.* exemption, freedom, irresponsibility, immunity, liberty, license, release, discharge, excuse, dispensation, absolution, exculpation, exoneration.

V. **exempt,** release, acquit, discharge, remit; free, set at liberty, let off [*colloq.*], pass over, spare, excuse, dispense with, license; absolve, exonerate.

Adj. **exempt,** free, immune, at liberty, scot-free, released, unbound; irresponsible, not accountable, excusable.

928. RESPECT.—*N.* **respect,** regard, consideration, courtesy, attention, deference, reverence, honor, esteem, estimation, veneration, admiration; approbation, etc., 931.

homage, fealty, obeisance, genuflection, kneeling, prostration; salaam, etc., 894.

V. **respect,** regard; revere, reverence, honor, venerate, hallow; esteem, think much of, entertain respect for, look up to, defer to, pay attention to, pay respect to, do honor to; do the honors, hail, show courtesy, pay homage to.

command respect, inspire respect; awe, impose, overawe, dazzle.

Adj. **respectful,** deferential, decorous, reverential, ceremonious, bareheaded, cap in hand; prostrate.

respected, estimable; time-honored, venerable.

Adv. **in deference to;** with all respect, with due respect, with the highest respect; with submission.

929. DISRESPECT.—*N.* **disrespect,** disfavor, disrepute, want of esteem, low estimation, disparagement, detraction; irreverence, slight, indignity, contumely, affront, dishonor, insult, outrage, discourtesy, scoffing; hiss, hissing, hoot, derision; mockery.

gibe, flout, jeer, scoff, taunt, sneer, fling.

V. **slight,** disregard, undervalue, humiliate, depreciate, trifle with, pass by, push aside, overlook, be discourteous.

disparage, call names; throw mud at; point at, indulge in personalities.

dishonor, desecrate; insult, affront, browbeat, outrage.

deride, scoff, sneer, laugh at, ridicule, gibe, mock, jeer, taunt, twit, flout, roast [*colloq.*], guy [*colloq.*], rag [*dial. Eng.* and *college slang*], burlesque, scout, hiss, hoot.

Adj. **disrespectful,** disparaging, etc., 934; insulting, supercilious, rude, derisive, sarcastic, scurrilous, contemptuous, insolent, disdainful; irreverent.

unrespected, unregarded, disregarded, unenvied, unsaluted.

930. CONTEMPT.—*N.* **contempt,** disdain, scorn, contemptuousness, derision, etc. (*disrespect*), 929; contumely; slight, sneer, spurn, byword.

V. **despise,** contemn, scorn, disdain, disregard, scout, slight, pass by, look down upon, sneer at, laugh at, curl up one's lip, think nothing of, make light of, underestimate, esteem slightly, care nothing for, set no store by; pooh-pooh, damn with faint praise.

spurn, turn one's back upon, trample underfoot; kick; fling to the winds, repudiate.

Adj. **contemptuous**, disdainful, scornful, withering, supercilious, cynical, haughty, cavalier; derisive; with the nose in air.

contemptible, despicable, despised, pitiable, pitiful, downtrodden.

931. APPROBATION.—*N.* **approbation**, approval, sanction, advocacy; esteem, estimation, good opinion, admiration; love, etc., 897; appreciation, regard, account, popularity, credit, repute.

commendation, compliment, praise, laud, laudation; good word; encomium, eulogy, eulogium, panegyric, blurb [*slang*]; benediction, blessing, benison.

applause, plaudit, clap, clapping, acclaim, acclamation; cheer; paean, shout (*or* peal, chorus, thunders) of applause.

V. **approve**, esteem, value, prize, set great store by; honor, hold in esteem, look up to, admire, like, appreciate; stand up for, stick up for [*colloq.*], uphold, countenance, sanction, indorse, recommend.

commend, praise, laud, compliment, applaud, clap, cheer, acclaim, encore; eulogize, boost [*colloq.*], root for [*slang*], cry up, puff; extol, magnify, glorify, exalt, sing the praises of.

Adj. **commendatory**, complimentary, laudatory, panegyrical, eulogistic, lavish of praise, uncritical.

approved, praised, popular, in good odor; in high esteem, in favor, in high favor.

praiseworthy, commendable, worthy of praise, good, meritorious, estimable, creditable, unimpeachable.

Adv. with credit, to admiration.

932. DISAPPROBATION.—*N.* **disapprobation**, disapproval, disesteem, odium, dislike, black list, blackball, ostracism, boycott.

disparagement, depreciation, dispraise, detraction, etc., 934; denunciation, condemnation, stricture, objection, exception, criticism; blame, censure, obloquy, sarcasm, satire, insinuation, innuendo, sneer, taunt.

reproof, reprehension, remonstrance, expostulation, reprobation, admonition, reproach; rebuke, reprimand, lecture, curtain lecture; wigging, dressing down [*both colloq.*]; rating, scolding, correction, rebuff, home thrust, hit; frown, scowl, black look.

abuse, personalities, personal remarks, vituperation, invective, contumely, hard words; bad language.

diatribe, tirade, philippic.

clamor, outcry, hue and cry; hiss, hissing, catcall; execration.

V. **disapprove,** dislike, object to, take exception to, think ill of, view with disfavor, frown upon, look askance, look black upon, set one's face against.

blame, censure, reproach, reprobate, impugn, impeach, accuse, denounce, expose, brand, gibbet, stigmatize; show up [*colloq.*].

reprove, reprehend, chide, admonish, berate, take to task, overhaul, lecture, rebuke, blow up [*colloq.*], correct, reprimand, snub; chastise, castigate, lash, trounce.

remonstrate, expostulate, recriminate.

abuse, scold, rate, upbraid, fall foul of; jaw [*low*], rail, rail at, call names, execrate, revile, vilify.

decry, cry down, run down, backbite; insinuate, damn with faint praise; hiss, hoot, catcall, mob; ostracize, blacklist, boycott, blackball.

disparage, depreciate, knock [*colloq.*], dispraise, deprecate, speak ill of, condemn, scoff at, sneer at, satirize, lampoon, defame, criticize.

incur blame, scandalize, shock, revolt; get a bad name, forfeit one's good opinion, be under a cloud.

Adj. **disparaging,** condemnatory, denunciatory, reproachful, abusive, vituperative, defamatory.

critical, satirical, sarcastic, sardonic, cynical, dry, sharp, cutting, biting, severe, withering, trenchant, censorious, captious, hypercritical.

blameworthy, reprehensible, blamable, answerable, bad; vicious, etc., 945.

Adv. with a wry face.

933. FLATTERY.—*N.* **flattery,** adulation, cajolery, fawning, wheedling, obsequiousness, sycophancy, flunkeyism, toadyism.

honeyed words, flummery, buncombe [*cant or slang*]; blarney, soft soap [*both colloq.*].

V. **flatter,** overpraise, puff, wheedle, cajole, fawn upon, humor, pet, coquet, butter [*colloq.*], jolly [*slang or colloq.*]; truckle to, pander to, court, curry favor with.

Adj. **flattering,** adulatory; mealy-mouthed, honeyed, smooth, smooth-tongued; oily, unctuous, specious, plausible, servile, sycophantic, fulsome.

934. DETRACTION.—*N.* **detraction,** disparagement, depreciation, vilification, obloquy, scandal, defamation, slander, calumny, evil-speaking, backbiting; sarcasm, cynicism, criticism; invective.

personality, libel, lampoon, skit, squib.

V. **detract,** derogate, decry, depreciate, disparage, run down, cry down, belittle, criticize, pull to pieces, asperse, bespatter, blacken, vilify, brand, malign, backbite, libel, lampoon, traduce, slander, defame, calumniate.

Adj. **detracting**, defamatory, detractory, derogatory, disparaging, libelous; scurrilous, abusive, foul-mouthed; slanderous, calumnious.

935. FLATTERER.—*N.* **flatterer**, adulator, eulogist, euphemist; optimist; puffer, booster [*colloq.*], whitewasher.

toady, sycophant, parasite, hanger-on; courtier.

936. DETRACTOR.—*N.* **detractor**, censor, censurer; cynic, critic, caviler, carper.

defamer, knocker [*colloq.*], backbiter, slanderer, lampooner, satirist, traducer, libeler, calumniator, reviler, vituperator.

Adj. defamatory, etc., 934.

937. VINDICATION.—*N.* **vindication**, justification, warrant; exoneration, exculpation, acquittal; whitewashing, extenuation, palliation, softening, mitigation.

plea, apology, gloss, varnish; excuse, extenuating circumstances; allowance; reply, defense; recrimination.

apologist, vindicator, justifier; defendant, etc., 938.

V. **justify**, warrant, lend a color, vindicate, exculpate, acquit, clear, exonerate, whitewash.

extenuate, palliate, excuse, soften, apologize.

advocate, defend, plead one's cause; contend for, speak for; bear out, make good; support, plead, say in defense.

Adj. **vindicative**, vindicatory, vindicating, palliative, extenuating, exculpatory, apologetic.

excusable, defensible, pardonable; venial, plausible, justifiable.

938. ACCUSATION.—*N.* **accusation**, charge, imputation, slur, incrimination, recrimination, denunciation.

libel, challenge, citation, arraignment, impeachment, indictment, true bill, lawsuit, condemnation.

accuser, prosecutor, plaintiff, complainant, libelant, informant, informer.

accused, defendant, prisoner, respondent, litigant.

V. **accuse**, charge, tax, impute, twit, taunt with, reproach, stigmatize, slur; incriminate, inculpate, implicate.

inform against, indict, denounce, arraign; charge with, saddle with; impeach, show up [*colloq.*], challenge, cite, prosecute; blow upon [*colloq.*], squeal [*slang*].

Adj. **accusatory**, denunciatory, recriminatory.

inexcusable, indefensible, unpardonable, unjustifiable.

939. PROBITY.—*N.* **probity**, integrity, rectitude, uprightness, respectability, honesty, faith, honor, good faith; constancy, faith-fulness, fidelity, loyalty, trustworthiness, truth, veracity, candor, singleness of heart.

fairness, fair play, justice, equity, impartiality, principle.

punctiliousness, punctilio, delicacy, scrupulosity, scrupulousness, scruple; point of honor.

man of honor, man of his word, gentleman, trump [*slang*], brick [*slang or colloq.*].

V. be honorable, speak the truth, draw a straight furrow, make a point of; do one's duty, play the game [*colloq.*]; redeem one's pledge, keep one's promise (*or* word), keep faith with.

Adj. upright, honest, veracious, truthful, virtuous, noble, honorable, reputable, respectable; fair, right, just, equitable, impartial, square, white [*slang*].

manly, straightforward, frank, candid, openhearted.

loyal, constant, faithful, stanch; true; trusty, trustworthy; incorruptible.

conscientious, right-minded, high-principled, high-minded, scrupulous, religious, strict; nice, punctilious.

stainless, unstained, unsullied, inviolate, untainted, incorrupt, innocent, pure, undefiled, undepraved.

chivalrous, jealous of honor, high-spirited.

Adv. on the square [*colloq.*], in good faith, in all honor, by fair means, with clean hands.

940. IMPROBITY.—*N.* improbity, dishonesty, dishonor, disgrace; fraud, lying; bad faith, infidelity, faithlessness; Judas kiss, betrayal, perfidy, treachery, double-dealing; villainy, baseness, degradation, turpitude, moral turpitude.

breach of trust (*or* faith), disloyalty, divided allegiance, hyphenated allegiance [*cant*], treason, high treason; apostasy.

knavery, roguery, rascality, foul play; jobbing, jobbery, graft [*colloq.*], venality, corruption, sharp practice.

V. play false; break one's word (*or* promise), jilt, betray, forswear; grovel, sneak, lose caste; sell oneself, squeal [*slang*], go back on [*colloq.*].

Adj. dishonest, dishonorable; unconscientious, unscrupulous; fraudulent, knavish, falsehearted; unfair, one-sided; double, double-tongued, double-faced; timeserving, crooked, slippery; fishy [*colloq.*], questionable.

infamous, arrant, foul, base, vile, low, ignominious, perfidious, treacherous, perjured; contemptible, abject, mean, shabby, paltry, dirty, sneaking, groveling, rascally, corrupt, venal.

derogatory, degrading, undignified, unbefitting, ungentlemanly, unchivalric, unmanly, recreant, inglorious.

faithless, false, unfaithful, disloyal; untrustworthy; trustless, lost to shame, dead to honor.

Adv. like a thief in the night, by crooked paths, by foul means.

941. KNAVE.—*N.* **knave,** rogue, villain, rascal, etc., 949; shyster.

traitor, betrayer, archtraitor, conspirator, Judas; reptile, serpent, snake in the grass, wolf in sheep's clothing, sneak, squealer [*slang*], telltale, mischiefmaker; renegade, recreant, slacker.

942. DISINTERESTEDNESS.—*N.* **disinterestedness,** unselfishness, generosity; liberality, altruism, benevolence, loftiness of purpose, exaltation, magnanimity; honor, chivalry, heroism, sublimity.

self-denial, self-control, stoicism, self-abnegation, self-sacrifice, devotion, self-devotion; labor of love.

Adj. **disinterested,** unselfish, self-denying, self-sacrificing, altruistic.

magnanimous, high-minded; princely, great, high, elevated, lofty, exalted, greathearted, largehearted; generous, liberal; chivalrous, heroic, sublime.

943. SELFISHNESS.—*N.* **selfishness,** self-love, self-indulgence, self-worship, self-seeking, self-interest; egotism, egoism; illiberality, meanness.

self-seeker, timeserver, fortune hunter, monopolist, dog in the manger, trimmer; hog, roadhog [*colloq.*].

V. **be selfish,** feather one's nest; have an eye to the main chance, live for oneself alone.

Adj. **selfish,** self-seeking, self-indulgent, self-interested; self-centered; egotistic, egoistic.

illiberal, mean, ungenerous, narrow-minded; mercenary, venal; covetous.

worldly, unspiritual, earthly, earthly-minded, mundane, worldly-minded, worldly-wise; timeserving, interested.

Adv. from selfish motives.

944. VIRTUE.—*N.* **virtue,** morality, moral rectitude; integrity, probity, nobleness, well-doing, good actions, good behavior, well-spent life, innocence.

merit, worth, desert, excellence, credit; self-control, self-denial.

morals; ethics, duty, etc., 926; cardinal virtues.

V. **be virtuous,** practice virtue, do one's duty, fight the good fight; acquit oneself well, keep in the right path.

Adj. **virtuous,** good, innocent, meritorious, deserving, worthy, dutiful, duteous; moral, right, righteous, right-minded; creditable, laudable, commendable, praiseworthy; sterling, pure, noble; whole-souled.

exemplary; matchless, peerless; saintly, saintlike; angelic, god-like.

945. VICE.—*N.* **vice,** evildoing, wrongdoing, wickedness, viciousness, iniquity, sin, immorality, want of principle, knavery, obliquity, backsliding, infamy, brutality.

depravity, demoralization, corruption, profligacy, flagrancy.

weakness, infirmity, frailty, imperfection, error; foible; failing, failure; besetting sin; defect, defection.

fault, crime; guilt, etc., 947.

reprobate; sinner, etc., 949.

V. **be vicious,** sin, commit sin, err, transgress; misconduct one-self, misbehave; fall, lapse, slip, trip, offend, trespass, go astray; sow one's wild oats.

demoralize, brutalize; corrupt, degrade, etc., 659.

Adj.[1] **vicious,** sinful; wicked, iniquitous, immoral, unrighteous, wrong, criminal; unprincipled, lawless, disorderly, disgraceful, recreant, disreputable; demoralized, corrupt, depraved, degener-ate; evil-minded, heartless, graceless, shameless, abandoned.

base, sinister, foul, gross, vile, black, felonious, nefarious, shame-ful, scandalous, infamous, villainous, heinous; flagrant, atrocious.

diabolic *or* diabolical, devilish, fiendish, fiendlike, demoniacal, Mephistophelian, satanic, hellish, infernal, hellborn.

incorrigible, irreclaimable, obdurate, reprobate, reprehensible.

unjustifiable, indefensible, inexcusable, inexpiable, unpardon-able.

improper, unseemly, indecorous, indiscreet, unworthy, blame-worthy, discreditable; incorrect, undutiful, naughty.

weak, frail, lax, infirm, imperfect; spineless, invertebrate [*both fig.*].

946. INNOCENCE.—*N.* **innocence;** guiltlessness, incorrup-tion, impeccability; clean hands, clear conscience.

innocent, newborn babe; lamb, dove.

Adj. **innocent,** not guilty, unguilty; guiltless, faultless, sinless, stainless, spotless, clear, immaculate, unerring, undefiled, inculp-able, blameless, above suspicion, irreproachable, unimpeachable; virtuous, etc., 944.

harmless, inoffensive, innocuous, pure.

Adv. with clean hands; with a clear conscience.

947. GUILT.—*N.* **guilt,** guiltiness, culpability, criminality; vice, sinfulness, misconduct, misbehavior, misdeed; fault, sin, error, transgression; dereliction, delinquency.

indiscretion, lapse, slip, trip, flaw, blot, omission, failing, failure, blunder, break [*colloq.*].

[1] Most of these adjectives are applicable both to the act and to the agent.

offense, trespass: misdemeanor, malefaction, malversation, corruption, malpractice; crime, felony, capital crime.

enormity, atrocity, outrage; deadly sin, mortal sin.

Adj. guilty, blamable, culpable, reprehensible, blameworthy.

Adv. in the very act, red-handed.

948. GOOD MAN. GOOD WOMAN.—*N.* **good man,** worthy, model, paragon, pattern, good example; hero, demigod, angel, saint; benefactor, etc., 912; philanthropist, etc., 910.

salt of the earth; one in ten thousand; a man among men, white man [*slang*].

good woman, virgin, innocent; goddess, queen, Madonna, ministering angel, heaven's noblest gift.

949. BAD MAN. BAD WOMAN.—*N.* **bad man,** wrongdoer, worker of iniquity; evildoer, etc., 913; sinner, transgressor; bad example.

rascal, scoundrel, villain, knave, etc., 941; miscreant, wretch, reptile, viper, serpent, monster, devil, demon, devil incarnate, fallen angel, lost sheep, black sheep, castaway, prodigal.

bad woman, jade, Jezebel, hellcat.

ruffian, rowdy, bully, etc., 887; thief, murderer.

culprit, delinquent, criminal, malefactor, felon, convict, outlaw.

riffraff, scum of the earth; blackguard, loafer, sneak, vagabond.

scamp, scapegrace, ne'er-do-well, good for nothing, reprobate, scalawag [*colloq.*], limb [*colloq.*], rapscallion [*all the words in this paragraph are commonly applied jocularly or lightly*].

950. PENITENCE.—*N.* **penitence,** contrition, compunction, repentance, remorse, regret, self-reproach, self-reproof, self-accusation, self-condemnation, qualms of conscience.

acknowledgment, confession, apology, recantation; penance. **penitent,** Magdalen, prodigal son, returned prodigal.

V. **repent,** be sorry for, rue, regret, think better of, recant; plead guilty, acknowledge, confess, humble oneself, beg pardon, apologize; turn over a new leaf.

reclaim, reform, regenerate, redeem, convert, amend, make a new man of, restore self-respect.

Adj. **penitent,** repentant, contrite, softened, melted, touched, conscience-stricken; self-accusing, self-convicted.

951. IMPENITENCE.—*N.* **impenitence,** irrepentance, recusancy, hardness of heart, heart of stone, seared conscience, obduracy.

V. **be impenitent,** steel the heart, harden the heart; die and make no sign.

Adj. **impenitent,** obdurate, hard, hardened, seared, recusant, unrepentant; relentless, remorseless, graceless.

lost, incorrigible, irreclaimable; unreclaimed, unreformed.

952. ATONEMENT.—*N.* atonement, reparation, compromise, composition, compensation, quittance, expiation, redemption, reclamation, conciliation, propitiation; indemnification, redress, amends, apology, satisfaction; sacrifice.

penance, fasting, sackcloth and ashes, shrift, purgation, purgatory.

V. atone, atone for, expiate, propitiate, make amends; reclaim, redeem, repair, ransom, absolve, purge, shrive, do penance, pay the penalty.

apologize, express regret, beg pardon, give satisfaction.

Adj. propitiatory, expiatory, sacrifice, sacrificial.

953. [Moral Practice] TEMPERANCE.—*N.* temperance, moderation, frugality, sobriety, soberness, forbearance, abnegation; self-denial, self-restraint, self-control.

abstinence, abstemiousness, asceticism; vegetarianism, prohibition, teetotalism, total abstinence.

abstainer; teetotaler, etc., 958; vegetarian, fruitarian; ascetic.

V. be temperate, abstain, forbear, refrain, deny oneself, spare.

Adj. temperate, moderate, sober, frugal, sparing, abstemious.

954. INTEMPERANCE.—*N.* intemperance, sensuality, animalism, pleasure, luxury, luxuriousness, freeliving, indulgence, high living, dissipation, self-indulgence; voluptuousness, debauchery.

revel, revels, revelry, orgy; drunkenness, debauch, carousal, drinking bout, saturnalia.

V. be intemperate, indulge, exceed; live high (*or* on the fat of the land), dine not wisely but too well; plunge into dissipation, revel, carouse, run riot, sow one's wild oats.

Adj. intemperate, excessive; sensual, self-indulgent, voluptuous, wild, dissipated, dissolute, fast.

brutish, swinish, piggish, hoggish, beastlike, beastly.

luxurious, epicurean, sybaritical; nursed in the lap of luxury; indulged, pampered; full fed, high fed.

intoxicated, drunk, etc., 959.

954a. SENSUALIST.—*N.* sensualist, sybarite, voluptuary, man of pleasure, epicure, epicurean, gourmet; gourmand, glutton, pig, hog; free liver, hard liver.

955. ASCETICISM.—*N.* asceticism, puritanism, austerity; total abstinence; mortification, sackcloth and ashes, penance, fasting; martyrdom.

ascetic, anchorite, hermit, recluse; puritan, yogi [Hindu]; dervish, fakir [both Moham.]; martyr.

Adj. ascetic, austere, puritanical.

956. FASTING.—*N.* **fasting,** famishment, starvation.

fast, fast day, Lent, spare (*or* meager) diet, lenten diet, Barmecide feast; **short rations.**

V. **fast,** starve, famish, perish with hunger.

Adj. **fasting,** lenten, unfed; starved, half-starved, hungry.

957. GLUTTONY.—*N.* **gluttony;** greed, greediness, voracity; epicurism, gastronomy; high living; guzzling.

feast, banquet, good cheer, blow out [*slang*].

glutton, gormandizer, cormorant, hog, etc. (*sensualist*), 954a.
epicure, *bon vivant* [F.], gourmand [*obs. as* glutton], gourmet.

V. **gormandize,** gorge; overeat, glut, satiate, indulge, eat one's fill, cram, stuff, guzzle, bolt, devour, gobble up, gulp, raven, eat out of house and home.

Adj. **gluttonous,** greedy, gormandizing, omnivorous, voracious, devouring, overfed, gorged.

958. SOBRIETY.—*N.* **sobriety;** total abstinence, teetotalism.

water drinker; prohibitionist, dry [*slang*], teetotaler, total abstainer.

V. **take the pledge;** abstain, etc., 953.

Adj. **sober,** temperate, moderate, abstemious.

959. DRUNKENNESS.—*N.* **drunkenness,** intemperance, drinking, inebriety, inebriation, intoxication, winebibbing; bacchanalia; libations.

alcoholism, dipsomania; delirium tremens, d.t.'s [*colloq.*].

drink, alcoholic drinks, alcohol, blue ruin [*slang*], booze [*colloq.*]; grog, punch; punchbowl, cup, rosy wine, flowing bowl; liquor, dram, beverage, beer, etc.; cocktail, highball, peg [*slang*, orig. India]; stirrup cup, parting cup.

illicit distilling; bootlegging [*slang*], moonshining, moonshine *or* moonshine whisky [*colloq.*], hooch [*slang*], home-brew; moonshiner [*colloq.*]; bootlegger [*slang*].

drunkard, sot, toper, tippler, winebibber, hard drinker, soaker [*slang*], sponge [*slang*], boozer [*colloq.*], bum [*slang*]; reveler, carouser; dipsomaniac.

V. **get** (*or* be) **drunk,** see double; take a drop (*or* glass) too much; drink, tipple, booze [*colloq.*], soak [*slang*], have a jag on [*slang*], carouse; drink hard (*or* deep, like a fish).

liquor, liquor up [*both slang*], wet one's whistle [*colloq. or humorous*]; raise the elbow, hit the booze [*slang*], crack a bottle.

inebriate, fuddle [*colloq.*], befuddle.

sell illicitly, bootleg [*slang*].

Adj. **drunk,** tipsy, intoxicated, inebriate, inebriated; in a state of intoxication, overcome, fuddled [*colloq.*], boozy [*colloq.*], full [*vulgar*], lit up [*slang*], elevated [*colloq.*]; groggy [*colloq.*]; screwed, tight, primed [*all slang*], muddled, maudlin; blind drunk, dead drunk.

960. PURITY.—*N.* purity; decency, decorum, delicacy; continence, chastity, virtue, modesty; virginity.

virgin, vestal, prude; Diana.

Adj. **pure,** undefiled, modest, delicate, clean, decent, decorous; chaste, continent, virtuous, honest.

961. IMPURITY.—*N.* impurity, uncleanness; immodesty; grossness; indelicacy, indecency, obscenity; dissipation.

Adj. **impure,** unclean; immodest, shameless, indelicate, indecent, coarse, gross.

962. LIBERTINE.—*N.* **libertine,** voluptuary, rake, roué [F.], fast man.

5. Institutions

963. LEGALITY.—*N.* **legality,** legitimacy, legitimateness; legitimization.

law, code, constitution, charter, act, enactment, statute, rule, canon, ordinance, institution, regulation, bylaw, decree, standing order.

equity, common law; unwritten law; law of nations, international law; constitutionality; justice, etc., 922; jurisprudence; legislation.

V. **legalize,** legitimize; enact, ordain, decree, authorize, pass a law, legislate; codify, formulate, regulate.

Adj. **legal,** legitimate; according to law; vested, constitutional, chartered, legalized, lawful, statutory; legislative; judicial, juridical.

Adv. in the eye of the law.

964. [Absence or violation of law] ILLEGALITY.—*N.* **lawlessness,** illicitness; breach (*or* violation) of law; disobedience, violence, brute force, despotism, tyranny, outlawry; mob (*or* lynch) law.

illegality, informality, unlawfulness, illegitimacy; smuggling.

V. **violate the law,** set the law at defiance, make the law a dead letter, take the law into one's own hands.

smuggle, run, poach, bootleg [*slang*].

Adj. **illegal,** prohibited, unlawful, illegitimate, illicit, contraband, actionable.

unchartered, unconstitutional, lawless, unwarranted, unauthorized; unofficial.

arbitrary, despotic, summary, irresponsible.

Adv. with a high hand, in violation of law.

965. JURISDICTION. [Executive]—*N.* **jurisdiction,** judicature, administration of justice; judge, etc., 967; tribunal, etc., 966.

city government, municipal government, commission government, Oregon plan [U. S.]; municipality, corporation; police, police force, constabulary.

executive, officer, commissioner, lord lieutenant [Brit.], city manager, mayor, alderman, councilor, selectman; bailiff, beadle; sheriff, constable, policeman, police constable, police sergeant, patrolman, gendarme [F.].

bureau, department, portfolio, secretariat.

V. judge, adjudge, adjudicate, sit in judgment; have jurisdiction over.

Adj. executive, administrative; municipal; judiciary, judicial, juridical.

966. TRIBUNAL.—*N.* tribunal, court, board, bench, judicature, court of justice (*or* law); judgment seat, mercy seat; bar, bar of justice; town hall, statehouse, townhouse, courthouse; forum; sessions.

United States courts: U. S. Supreme Court, U. S. District Court, U. S. Circuit Court of Appeal; Federal Court of Claims, Court of Private Land Claims; Supreme Court, Superior Court, court of sessions, criminal court, police court, juvenile court.

court-martial, (*pl.* courts-martial), drumhead court-martial.
Adj. judicial, etc., 965; appellate; curial.

967. JUDGE.—*N.* judge, justice, justice (*or* judge) of assize; magistrate, police magistrate, beak [*slang*]; his worship [Eng.], his honor, his lordship [Brit.]; the court.

Lord Chancellor, Master of the Rolls, Vice-Chancellor, Lord Chief Justice [all Brit.], Chief Justice.

arbiter, arbitrator; moderator, receiver, master; umpire, referee; censor.

jury, grand jury, petty jury, inquest, panel.

juror, juryman, talesman; grand juror, grand juryman; petty juror, petty juryman.

V. adjudge, etc. (*determine*), 480; try a case, try a prisoner.
Adj. judicial, etc., 965.

968. LAWYER.—*N.* lawyer, jurist, legal adviser, advocate; barrister, barrister-at-law [Eng.]; counsel, counselor; king's counsel [Eng.]; pleader, special pleader.

attorney, solicitor; conveyancer, notary, notary public; pettifogger, shyster.

bar, legal profession; Inns of Court [Eng.].

V. practice law; practice at (*or* within) the bar, plead; be called to (*or* within) the bar; admitted to the bar.

disbar, degrade.
Adj. learned in the law; at the bar; forensic.

969. LAWSUIT.—*N.* lawsuit, suit, action, cause; litigation; suit in law.

writ, summons, subpoena, citation; habeas corpus [L.].

arraignment, prosecution, impeachment, accusation; present-ment, true bill, indictment.

arrest, apprehension, committal, commitment; imprisonment.

pleadings; declaration, bill, claim; affidavit, libel; answer, plea, demurrer, rebutter, rejoinder; surrebutter, surrejoinder.

litigant, suitor, libelant; plaintiff, defendant, etc., 938.

hearing, trial; judgment, sentence, finding, verdict; appeal, writ of error.

case, decision, decided case, precedent.

V. **litigate,** go to law, appeal to the law; bring to justice (*or* trial, the bar), put on trial, accuse, prefer (*or* file) a claim.

cite, summon, summons, serve with a writ, arraign; sue, prose-cute, indict, impeach; attach, distrain; commit, apprehend, arrest, give in charge.

try, hear a cause; sit in judgment; adjudicate, etc., 480.

970. ACQUITTAL.—*N.* acquittal, exculpation, acquittance, clearance, exoneration, discharge, release, absolution, reprieve, respite, pardon.

Exemption from punishment: impunity, immunity.

V. **acquit,** exculpate, exonerate, clear; absolve, whitewash, dis-charge, release, liberate, reprieve, respite, pardon.

Adj. **acquitted,** uncondemned, unpunished; recommend to mercy.

971. CONDEMNATION.—*N.* **condemnation,** conviction, judg-ment, penalty, sentence; death warrant.

V. **condemn,** convict, find guilty, damn, doom, sentence, pass sentence on, attaint, confiscate, sequestrate.

proscribe, interdict; disapprove, etc., 932; accuse, etc., 938.

Adj. **condemnatory,** damnatory, condemned, self-convicted.

972. PUNISHMENT.—*N.* **punishment,** punition, chastise-ment, chastening, correction, castigation; discipline, infliction, trial; judgment, penalty, retribution, nemesis, retributive justice.

Forms of punishment: lash, scaffold, etc. (*instrument of punishment*), 975; im-prisonment; transportation, banishment, expulsion, exile, involuntary exile, ostra-cism, penal servitude, hard labor, galleys; beating, flagellation, bastinado, blow, stripe, cuff, kick, buffet, pummel; torture, rack.

capital punishment, execution; hanging, shooting, electrocution, decapitation, strangling, strangulation, crucifixion, impalement, martyrdom, auto-da-fé (*pl.* autos-da-fé) [Pg.], hara-kiri [Jap.], happy dispatch [*jocular*], lethal chamber, hemlock.

V. **punish,** chastise, chasten, castigate, correct, inflict punish-ment; tar and feather; masthead, keelhaul.

visit upon, pay, settle, settle with, do for [*colloq.*], get even with, make an example of; give it one [*both colloq.*].

strike, etc., 276; smite; spank, thwack, thump, beat, buffet, thrash, pommel, drub, trounce, belabor; trim [*colloq.*], cowhide, lambaste [*slang*], lash, flog, scourge, whip, birch, cane, switch, horsewhip, lay about one, beat black and blue; sandbag, blackjack; pelt, stone.

execute; bring to the block (*or* gallows), behead, decapitate, guillotine; hang [*p. p.* hanged, *not* hung, *for the death penalty*], electrocute, shoot, burn, crucify, impale, lynch.

torture, agonize, rack, put on (*or* to) the rack, martyr, martyrize.

banish, exile, transport, deport, expel, ostracize; rusticate; drum out; dismiss, disbar; unfrock [*as a priest*].

Adj. punitive, penal, punitory, inflictive, castigatory.

973. REWARD.—*N.* reward, recompense, remuneration, prize, meed, guerdon, indemnity, indemnification; quittance, compensation, reparation, redress, acknowledgment, requital, amends, sop, consideration, return; atonement.

perquisite, perks [*slang*]; donation, etc., 784; tip, bribe, hush money, blackmail.

allowance, salary, stipend, wages; pay, payment, emolument; tribute; premium, fee, honorarium; hire; mileage.

V. reward, recompense, repay, requite, remunerate, compensate; fee, tip, bribe; pay, etc., 807; make amends, indemnify, redress, atone, satisfy, acknowledge.

Adj. remunerative, compensatory; retributive.

974. PENALTY.—*N.* penalty; retribution, etc. (*punishment*), 972; pain, penance.

fine, mulct, forfeit, forfeiture, damages, sequestration, confiscation.

V. penalize, fine, mulct, confiscate, sequestrate, sequester; forfeit.

975. [Instrument of punishment] SCOURGE.—*N.* scourge, whip, lash, strap, thong, cowhide, knout, cat, cat-o'-nine-tails; rope's end; black snake, bullwhack, quirt, rawhide.

rod, cane, stick, rattan, birch, birch rod; rod in pickle; switch, ferule, cudgel, truncheon.

Various instruments: pillory, stocks, whipping post, ducking stool, iron maiden; thumbscrew, boot, rack, wheel; treadmill, crank, galleys; bed of Procrustes.
scaffold; block, ax, guillotine; stake; cross, gallows, gibbet, tree; noose, rope, halter, bowstring; death chair, electric chair.

prison, jail, etc., 752; jailer.

executioner; electrocutioner, headsman, hangman; lyncher, torturer.

malefactor, criminal, culprit, felon, victim, gallows bird [*slang*].

V. RELIGIOUS AFFECTIONS

976. DEITY.—*N.* Deity, Divinity, Godhead, Omnipotence, Omniscience, Providence.

GOD, Lord, Jehovah, The King of Kings, The Lord of Lords, The Almighty, The Supreme Being, The Absolute, The First Cause, Author of all things, Creator of all things, The Infinite, The Eternal, The All-powerful, The Omnipotent, The All-wise, The All-merciful, The All-knowing, The Omniscient.

Deus [L.], *Theos* [Gr. Θεος], *Dieu* [F.], *Gott* [Ger.], *Dio* [It.], *Dios* [Sp.], *Deos* [Pg.], *Gud* [Nor., Sw., and Dan.], *God* [Du.], *Bog'* Russ.], Brahma [Skr.], *Deva* [Skr.], *Khuda* (Hind.), Allah (Ar.).

THE TRINITY, The Holy Trinity, The Trinity in Unity, Triunity, Threefold Unity.

I. GOD THE FATHER, The Maker, The Creator, The Preserver.
Functions: creation, preservation, divine government, thearchy.

II. GOD THE SON, Jesus Christ; The Messiah, The Anointed, The Saviour, The Redeemer, The Mediator, The Intercessor, The Advocate, The Judge; The Son of God, The Son of Man; The Only-Begotten, The Lamb of God, The Word, Logos; The Man of Sorrows; Jesus of Nazareth, King of the Jews, The Son of Mary, The Risen, Immanuel, The King of Kings and Lord of Lords, The King of Glory, The Prince of Peace, The Good Shepherd, The Way, The Door, The Truth, The Life, The Bread of Life, The Light of the World, The Vine, The True Vine.

The Incarnation, The Word made Flesh.
Functions: salvation, redemption, atonement, propitiation, mediation, intercession, judgment.

III. GOD THE HOLY GHOST, The Holy Spirit, Paraclete, The Comforter, The Consoler, The Intercessor, The Spirit of God, The Spirit of Truth, The Dove.
Functions: inspiration, regeneration, sanctification, consolation, grace.

The Deity in other religions: Brahmanism *or* **Hinduism:** Brahma (*neuter*), the Supreme Soul *or* Essence of the Universe; Trimurti *or* Hindu trinity *or* Hindu triad: (1) Brahma (*masc.*), the Creator; (2) Vishnu, the Preserver; (3) Siva, the Destroyer and Regenerator.
Buddhism: the Protestantism of the East; Buddha, the Blessed One, the Teacher.
Zoroastrianism: Zerâna-Akerana, the Infinite Being; Ahuramazda *or* Ormazd, the Creator, the Lord of Wisdom, the King of Light (*opposed by* Ahriman, the King of Darkness).
Mohammedanism *or* **Islam:** Allah.

V. **create,** fashion, make, form, mold, manifest.
preserve, uphold, keep, perpetuate, immortalize.
atone, redeem, save, propitiate, expiate; intercede, mediate.

predestinate, predestine, foreordain, preordain; elect, call, ordain.

bless, sanctify, hallow, justify, absolve, glorify.

Adj. almighty, all-powerful, omnipotent; omnipresent, all-wise, all-seeing, all-knowing, omniscient, supreme.

divine, heavenly, celestial; holy, hallowed, sacred, sacrosanct.

supernatural, superhuman, spiritual, ghostly, unearthly.

Adv. by God's will, by God's help, *Deo volente* [L.], God willing; in Jesus' name, in His name, to His glory.

977. [Beneficent spirits] ANGEL.—*N.* angel, archangel, messenger of God, guardian angel; ministering spirits, invisible helpers, choir invisible, heavenly host, sons of God; saint; seraphim (*sing.*, seraph, *E. pl.*, seraphs), Cherubim (*sing.*, cherub, *E. pl.*, cherubs; cherubim *or* cherubin *are often treated as sing.*).

Madonna, Our Lady, *Notre Dame* [F.], Holy Mary, The Virgin, The Blessed Virgin, The Virgin Mary.

Adj. angelic, seraphic, cherubic, archangelic.

978. [Maleficent spirits] SATAN.—*N.* Satan, the Devil, Lucifer, Belial, Beelzebub, Mephistopheles, Mephisto, Asmodeus, *le Diable* [F.], Deil [Scot.].

fallen angels, unclean spirits, devils; rulers of darkness, the powers of darkness; demon, etc.,980.

Moloch, Mammon; Belial, Beelzebub; Loki [*Norse Myth*].

diabolism, devil worship, demonism, demonology; Black Mass, black magic, demonolatry, witchcraft.

diabolist, demonologist.

V. demonize; bewitch, bedevil, etc. (*sorcery*), 992; possess, obsess.

Adj. satanic, diabolic *or* diabolical, devilish, demoniac *or* demoniacal, infernal, hellborn.

979. MYTHIC AND PAGAN DEITIES.—*N.* god, goddess; heathen gods and goddesses; pantheon.

Greek and Latin: Zeus, Jupiter *or* Jove (*King*); Apollo *or* Phoebus Apollo (*the sun*); Ares, Mars (*war*); Hermes, Mercury (*messenger*); Poseidon, Neptune (*ocean*); Hephaestus, Vulcan (*smith*); Dionysus, Bacchus (*wine*); Hades [Gr.], Pluto *or* Dis [L.] (*King of the lower world*); Kronos, Saturn (*time*); Eros, Cupid (*love*); Pan, Faunus (*flocks, herds, forests, and wild life*).

Hera, Juno (*Queen*); Demeter, Ceres (*fruitfulness*); Persephone, Proserpina *or* Proserpine (*Queen of the lower world*); Artemis, Diana (*the moon and hunting*); Athena, Minerva (*wisdom*); Aphrodite, Venus (*love and beauty*); Hestia, Vesta (*the hearth*); Rhea *or* Cybele ("Mother of the gods," *identified with* Ops, *wife of Saturn*); Gaea *or* Ge, Tellus (*earth goddess, mother of the Titans*).

Norse: Ymir (*primeval giant*), Odin *or* Woden (*the All-father* = *Zeus*); the Æsir: Thor (*the Thunderer*), Balder (= *Apollo*), Freyr (*fruitfulness*), Tyr (*war*), Bragi (*poetry and eloquence*), Höder (*blind god of the winter*), Heimdall (*warder of Asgard*), Loki (*evil*).

the Vanir: Njorth (*the winds and the sea*), Frey (*prosperity and love*), Freya (*goddess of love and beauty* = *Venus*).

Frigg *or* Frigga (*wife of Odin*), Hel (*goddess of death = Persephone*), Idun (*goddess of spring, wife of Bragi*), Sigyn (*wife of Loki*).

Egyptian: Ra *or* Amon-Ra (*the sun god*), Osiris (*judge of the dead*), Isis (*wife of Osiris*), Horus (*the morning sun; son of Osiris and Isis*), Anubis (*jackal-god, brother of Horus, a conductor of the dead*), Nephthys (*sister of Isis*), Set (*evil deity, brother of Osiris*), Thoth (*clerk of the underworld*), Bast *or* Bubastis (*a goddess with head of a cat*), the Sphinx (*wisdom*).

Various: Baal [Semitic]; Astarte *or* Ashtoreth (*goddess of fertility and love*) [Phoenician]; Bel [Babylonian]; The Great Spirit [N. Amer. Indian].

nymph, dryad, hamadryad, wood nymph; naiad, fresh-water nymph; oread, mountain nymph; nereid, sea nymph; Oceanid, ocean nymph; Pleiades, Hyades.

fairy, fay, sprite; nix (*fem.* nixie), water sprite; the good folk, brownie, pixy, elf (*pl.* elves), banshee; the Fates; kobold, troll, hobgoblin, gnome, kelpie; faun; peri, undine, sea maid, mermaid (*masc.* merman); Mab, Oberon, Titania, Ariel; Puck, Robin Goodfellow.

familiar spirit, familiar, genius, guide, good genius, daimon, demon.

mythology, mythical lore, folklore, fairyism, fairy mythology.

Adj. **mythical,** mythic, mythological, fabulous, legendary.

fairylike, sylphlike, elfin, elflike, elfish, nymphlike.

980. EVIL SPIRITS.—*N.* demon, fiend, devil, etc. (*Satan*), 978; evil genius, familiar, familiar spirit; bad (*or* unclean) spirit; incubus; ogre, ogress, ghoul, vampire, harpy; Fury, the Furies, the Erinyes, the Eumenides.

imp, bad fairy, sprite, jinni (*pl.* jinn), genius (*pl.* genii), dwarf. changeling, elf child, werewolf; satyr.

elemental, sylph, gnome, salamander, nymph [*Rosicrucian*]. siren, nixie, undine, Lorelei.

bugbear, bugaboo, bogy, goblin, hobgoblin.

Adj. demoniac, demoniacal, fiendish, fiendlike, evil, ghoulish; pokerish [*colloq.*], bewitched.

980a. SPECTER.—*N.* **specter,** ghost, apparition, vision, spirit, sprite, shade, shadow, wraith, banshee, spook [*now humorous*], phantom, phantasm, materialization [*spiritualism*], double.

will-o'-the-wisp, etc., 423.

Adj. **spectral,** ghostly, ghostlike, spiritual, wraithlike, weird, uncanny, eerie, spooky [*colloq.*] haunted; unearthly, supernatural.

981. HEAVEN.—*N.* **heaven;** kingdom of heaven (*or* God), heavenly kingdom; heaven of heavens, God's throne, throne of God; Paradise, Eden, Zion, Holy City, New Jerusalem, Heavenly City, City Celestial, abode of the blessed.

Mythological heaven or paradise: Olympus; Elysium, Elysian fields, Islands (*or* Isles) of the Blessed, Happy Isles, Fortunate Isles, garden of the Hesperides; third heaven, seventh heaven; Valhalla [Scandinavian]; Nirvana [Buddhist]; happy hunting grounds [N. Amer. Indian].

future state, life after death, eternal home, resurrection, translation; apotheosis, deification.

Adj. **heavenly,** celestial, supernal, unearthly, paradisaic, beatific; Elysian, Olympian.

982. HELL.—*N.* **hell,** bottomless pit, place of torment; pandemonium; hell-fire, everlasting fire (*or* torment); worm that never dies.

purgatory, limbo, Gehenna, abyss.

Mythological hell: Tartarus, Hades, Avernus; infernal regions, inferno, shades below, realms of Pluto.
Pluto, Rhadamanthus, Erebus, Charon, Cerberus; Persephone, Proserpina; Minos, Osiris.
Rivers of hell: Styx, Acheron, Cocytus, Phlegethon, Lethe.

Adj. **hellish,** infernal, stygian.

983. [Religious Knowledge] THEOLOGY.—*N.* **theology,** theosophy, divine wisdom, divinity, hagiography; monotheism, theism, religion; religious persuasion (*or* sect, denomination, affiliation); creed, articles (*or* declaration, profession, confession) of faith.

theologian, scholastic, divine, schoolman, the Fathers; monotheist, theist.

Adj. **theological,** religious, divine, canonical; denominational; sectarian.

983a. ORTHODOXY.—*N.* **orthodoxy;** strictness, soundness, religious truth, true faith; truth, etc., 494; soundness of doctrine; Christianity, Catholicism.

the church, Holy Church, Church Militant, Church Triumphant; Catholic (*or* Universal, Apostolic) Church; Established (*or* State) Church; The Bride of the Lamb; temple of the Holy Ghost; Church of Christ; Christians, Christendom.

canons; thirty-nine articles; Apostles' (*or* Nicene, Athanasian) Creed.

Adj. **orthodox,** sound, strict, faithful, catholic, Christian, evangelical, scriptural, literal, divine, monotheistic, true, etc., 494.

984. HETERODOXY. [Sectarianism]—*N.* **heterodoxy;** error, false doctrine, heresy, schism, recusancy, backsliding, apostasy; materialism, atheism; idolatry, superstition.

bigotry, fanaticism, iconoclasm; precisianism; sabbatarianism, puritanism, bibliolatry.

sectarianism, nonconformity, dissent, secularism; religious sects, the clash of creeds, the isms.

[*Generally speaking, each sect is* orthodox *to itself and* heterodox *to others.*]

paganism, heathenism, heathendom; animism, polytheism, pantheism; dualism.

pagan, heathen, paynim; kafir, non-Mohammedan; gentile; pantheist, polytheist, animist.

misbeliever, heretic, apostate; backslider; antichrist; idolater; skeptic, etc., 989.

bigot, dogmatist, fanatic, dervish, iconoclast.

sectarian, sectary; seceder, separatist, recusant, dissenter, non-conformist.

materialist, positivist, deist, agnostic, atheist, etc., 989.

Adj. **heterodox**, heretical, unorthodox, unscriptural, uncanonical, unchristian, apocryphal; antichristian; schismatic, recusant, iconoclastic; sectarian, dissenting, secular; agnostic, atheistic; skeptical, etc., 989.

bigoted, dogmatical, fanatical; superstitious, credulous; idolatrous.

pagan, heathen, heathenish, gentile, paynim; polytheistic, pantheistic, animistic.

985. REVELATION. [Biblical]—*N.* revelation, inspiration.

The Bible, the Book, the Book of Books, The Good Book, the Word, the Word of God, Scripture, the Scriptures, Holy Writ, Holy Scriptures, inspired writings, Gospel.

Old Testament, Septuagint, Vulgate, Pentateuch; the Law, the Prophets; Apocrypha.

New Testament; Gospels, Evangelists, Acts, Epistles, Apocalypse, Revelation; Good Tidings, Glad Tidings.

inspired writers, prophet, evangelist, apostle, disciple, saint; the Fathers, the Apostolic Fathers; Holy Men of old.

Adj. scriptural, biblical, sacred, prophetic; evangelical, evangelistic, apostolic, apostolical; inspired, apocalyptic, revealed; ecclesiastical, canonical.

986. SACRED WRITINGS. [Non-Biblical]—*N.* The Vedas, Upanishads, Puranas, Sutras, Bhagavad Gita [all Brahmanic]; Zendavesta, Avesta [Zoroastrian]; The Koran *or* Alcoran [Mohammedan]; Tripitaka, Dhammapada [Buddhist]; Granth, Adigranth [*Sikh*]; the Kings [Chinese]; the Eddas [Scandinavian].

Non-Biblical prophets and religious founders: Gautama (Buddha); Zoroaster, Confucius, Mohammed.

987. PIETY.—*N.* piety, religion, theism, faith; religiousness, religiosity, holiness, saintship; reverence, humility, veneration, devotion, worship, grace, sanctity, consecration.

beatification, regeneration, conversion, sanctification, salvation, inspiration, bread of life; Body and Blood of Christ.

believer, convert, theist, Christian, devotee, pietist, saint.

V. be pious, have faith, believe, receive Christ; venerate, adore, worship, revere, be converted, be on God's side, stand up for Jesus, fight the good fight, keep the faith, let one's light shine.

regenerate, convert, edify, sanctify, hallow, keep holy, beatify, inspire, consecrate, enshrine.

Adj. pious, religious, devout, devoted, reverent, godly, humble, pure, pure in heart, holy, spiritual, saintly, saintlike; believing, faithful, Christian.

regenerated; inspired, consecrated, converted, unearthly.

elected, adopted, justified, sanctified.

988. IMPIETY.—*N.* impiety, sin, irreverence; profaneness, profanity, blasphemy, profanation; desecration, sacrilege; scoffing.

Assumed piety: hypocrisy, pietism, cant, pious fraud; lip devotion, lip service; formalism, austerity; sanctimony, sanctimoniousness, pharisaism, sabbatarianism; sacerdotalism; bigotry; blue laws.

apostasy, recusancy, backsliding, perversion, reprobation.

bigot, pharisee, sabbatarian, formalist, pietist, precisian, devotee, ranter, fanatic.

sinner, scoffer, blasphemer, sabbath breaker; worldling; hypocrite.

the wicked, the evil, the unjust, the reprobate.

V. profane, desecrate, blaspheme, revile, scoff, swear; commit sacrilege.

dissemble, simulate, play the hypocrite, snuffle.

Adj. impious, irreligious, etc., 989; profane, irreverent, sacrilegious, blasphemous.

unhallowed, unsanctified, unregenerate; hardened, perverted, reprobate.

hypocritical, canting, pietistical, sanctimonious, unctuous, pharisaical, overrighteous.

bigoted, fanatical, hidebound, narrow, narrow-minded, illiberal, prejudiced, little; provincial, parochial, insular.

989. IRRELIGION.—*N.* irreligion, impiety, ungodliness, laxity, apathy, indifference.

skepticism, doubt; unbelief, disbelief, incredulity, agnosticism, freethinking; materialism, rationalism, positivism; atheism, infidelity.

unbeliever, infidel, atheist, heretic, heathen, alien, gentile, Nazarene; freethinker, skeptic, rationalist; materialist, positivist, nihilist, agnostic.

V. disbelieve, lack faith; doubt, question, deny the truth.

Adj. irreligious; undevout, godless, graceless, ungodly; unholy, unsanctified, unhallowed; atheistic.

skeptical, freethinking, unbelieving, unconverted; incredulous, faithless.

worldly, mundane, earthly, carnal, worldly, worldly-minded, unspiritual.

990. WORSHIP.—*N.* **worship,** cult, adoration, devotion, vow, aspiration, homage, service; kneeling, genuflection, prostration.

prayer, invocation, supplication, intercession, orison, petition; collect, litany, Lord's prayer, paternoster; *Ave Maria* [L.], Hail, Mary.

thanksgiving; grace, praise, glorification, paean, benediction, doxology, hosanna, hallelujah, alleluia, *Te Deum* [L.], *Gloria* [L.].

psalm, hymn, chant, response, anthem.

offering, oblation, sacrifice, incense, libation, offertory, collection.

divine service, office, duty; exercises; morning prayer; Mass, matins, evensong, vespers, vigils, lauds.

worshiper, congregation, communicant, celebrant.

V. **worship,** lift up the heart, aspire; revere, adore, do service, pay homage, offer one's vows, vow; bow down and worship.

pray, invoke, supplicate; beseech; offer up prayers, say one's prayers, tell one's beads, recite the rosary.

give thanks, say grace, bless, praise, laud, glorify, magnify, sing praises.

Adj. devout, devotional, reverent, solemn, fervid.

991. IDOLATRY.—*N.* **idolatry,** idolatrousness, demonism, demonology, devil worship, fetishism.

idolization, deification, apotheosis, canonization; hero worship.

sacrifice, hecatomb, holocaust; human sacrifices, immolation, self-immolation, suttee.

idol, golden calf, graven image, fetish, joss [Chinese], *lares et penates* [L.]; god (*or* goddess) of one's idolatry; Baal, Moloch, Juggernaut.

idolater, idolatress, idolizer, fetishist.

V. **idolize,** idolatrize, worship idols, put on a pedestal, prostrate oneself before; make sacrifice to, deify, canonize.

Adj. **idolatrous,** idolistic, prone before, prostrate before, in the dust before, at the feet of.

992. SORCERY.—*N.* **sorcery,** magic, black magic, the black art, necromancy, demonology, witchcraft, witchery, wizardry, fetishism, hoodoo, voodoo, voodooism; fire worship, incantation, enchantment, bewitchment, glamour; obsession, possession.

divination, etc. (*prediction*), 511; sortilege, ordeal, hocus-pocus.

V. **practice sorcery,** cast a nativity (*or* horoscope), conjure, charm, enchant, bewitch, bedevil, witch, voodoo, hoodoo [*colloq.*]; entrance, fascinate, hypnotize, cast a spell; call up spirits.

Adj. **magic,** magical, witching, weird, cabalistic, talismanic.

992a. PSYCHICAL RESEARCH.—*N.* **psychical research,** psychical (*or* psychic) investigation; abnormal (*or* mediumistic) phenomena; mysticism.

the subconscious, the subconscious self, the subliminal self, the higher self, ego, astral body; aura; subconsciousness, subliminal consciousness; intuition; dual personality, multiple personality, obsession, possession.

psychotherapy, psychotherapeutics, psychoanalysis; hysteria, neurasthenia, dreams, visions, apparitions, hallucinations.

mesmerism, animal magnetism; mesmeric trance; hypnotism; hypnosis.

Phenomena: **telepathy,** thought transference, thought transmission, telepathic transmission; second sight, clairvoyance, clairaudience, psychometry.

premonitions, previsions, premonitory apparition, fetch, wraith, double; death lights, ominous dreams.

automatism, automatic writing, planchette, ouija board, trance writing, spirit writing; trance speaking, inspirational speaking.

spiritualism, spiritism, spirit manifestations; trance, spirit control, spirit possession; mediumistic communications; séance; materialization.

medium, seer, clairvoyant, clairaudient, telepathist; guide, control; mesmerist, hypnotist.

V. **psychologize;** investigate the abnormal (*or* supernormal, subconscious, subliminal), traverse the borderland, know oneself.

mesmerize, magnetize, hypnotize, place under control, subject to suggestion, place in a trance, induce hypnosis.

Adj. **psychical,** psychic, psychological; spiritistic, spiritualistic, spiritual; subconscious, subliminal, supernormal, abnormal; mystic *or* mystical.

993. SPELL.—*N.* **spell,** charm, incantation, exorcism, abracadabra, open-sesame; evil eye.

talisman, amulet, phylactery, philter, fetish, wishbone; mascot, rabbit's foot, hoodoo [*colloq.*], jinx [*slang*], scarabaeus *or* scarab; veronica, swastika.

wand, caduceus, rod, divining rod, witch hazel, Aaron's rod.

Magic wish-givers: Aladdin's lamp, Aladdin's casket, magic casket, magic ring, magic belt, magic spectacles, wishing cap, Fortunatus' cap; seven-league boots; magic carpet; cap of darkness.

994. SORCERER.—*N.* **sorcerer,** magician, wizard, necromancer, conjuror, prestidigitator; charmer, exorcist, voodoo medicine man, witch doctor; astrologer, soothsayer, etc., 513.

sorceress, witch, hag; siren, harpy.

Cagliostro, Merlin; Circe, weird sisters, witch of Endor.

995. CHURCHDOM.—*N.* **churchdom;** church, ministry, priesthood, prelacy, hierarchy, church government; clericalism, sacerdotalism, episcopalianism.

monasticism, monkhood, monachism; celibacy.

Ecclesiastical offices and dignities: cardinalate, cardinalship; primacy, archbishopric, archiepiscopacy; prelacy, bishopric, episcopate, episcopacy, see, diocese; benefice, incumbency, living, cure, charge, cure of souls; rectorship, vicariate, vicarship; pastorate, pastorship, pastoral charge; deaconry, deaconship; curacy; chaplaincy, chaplainship, presbytery.

holy orders, ordination, institution, consecration, induction, installation, preferment, translation, presentation.

papacy, pontificate, See of Rome, the Vatican, the apostolic see.

V. **call,** ordain, induct, install, translate, consecrate, present, elect, bestow.

Adj. **ecclesiastical,** clerical, sacerdotal, priestly, pastoral, ministerial, hierarchical, episcopal, canonical; pontifical, papal, apostolic.

996. CLERGY.—*N.* **clergy,** clericals, ministry, priesthood, presbytery, the cloth, the pulpit, the desk.

clergyman, divine, ecclesiastic, priest, pastor, shepherd, minister, preacher, clerk in holy orders, parson, sky pilot [*slang*]; father, padre, *abbé* [F.], *curé* [F.]; reverend.

Dignitaries of the church: Pope, pontiff, Holy Father; cardinal, primate, metropolitan, archbishop, bishop, prelate, dean, archdeacon, canon, rector, vicar, beneficiary, incumbent, chaplain, curate; elder, deacon.

religious, abbot, prior, monk, friar, lay brother, pilgrim, palmer.

nun, sister, priestess, abbess, prioress, canoness; mother superior, the reverend mother; novice.

Adj. **ordained,** in orders, in holy orders, called to the ministry.

997. LAITY.—*N.* **laity,** flock, fold, congregation, assembly, brethren, people; society [U. S.]; class [Methodist].

layman, parishioner, catechumen.

V. **laicize,** secularize.

Adj. **secular,** lay congregational, civil, temporal, profane.

998. RITE.—*N.* **rite,** ceremony, observance, function, duty, form, solemnity, sacrament; service, ministry, ministration.

sermon, preaching, preachment, exhortation, religious harangue, homily, lecture, discourse.

worship, etc., 990; invocation of saints, confession, the confessional; absolution, remission of sins; reciting the rosary, telling one's beads.

Seven Sacraments: (1) baptism, immersion, christening; baptismal regeneration; font.

(2) **confirmation,** laying on of hands.

(3) **Eucharist,** Mass, Lord's supper, communion; the sacrament, the holy sacrament; consecrated elements, bread and wine, celebration; transubstantiation, real presence.

(4) **penance,** fasting, sackcloth and ashes, flagellation.

(5) **extreme unction,** last rites, viaticum.

(6) **holy orders,** ordination, etc. (*churchdom*), 995.

(7) **matrimony,** marriage, wedlock, etc., 903.

Sacred articles: relics, rosary, beads, reliquary, host, cross, rood, crucifix; pyx, censer, thurible; prayer wheel [Buddhist]; Sangraal, Holy Grail.

ritual, liturgy, rubric, canon, ordinal, missal, breviary, Mass book, beadroll, litany, prayer book, Book of Common Prayer; psalter, psalmbook, hymnbook, hymnal.

ritualism, ceremonialism; sabbatism, sabbatarianism; ritualist, sabbatarian.

V. **perform service,** do duty, minister, officiate, celebrate.

excommunicate; ban with bell, book, and candle.

preach, sermonize, address the congregation.

Adj. **ritual,** ritualistic, ceremonial, liturgic *or* liturgical; paschal.

999. CANONICALS.—*N.* **canonicals,** vestments, robe, gown, surplice, etc.

1000. TEMPLE.—*N.* **temple,** fane, place of worship; house of God, house of prayer; cathedral, minster, church, kirk [Scot.], chapel, meetinghouse.

synagogue, tabernacle; mosque [Moham.]; pagoda, Chinese temple, joss house [*colloq.*]; pantheon, shrine.

monastery, priory, abbey, friary, convent, nunnery, cloister.

parsonage, rectory, vicarage, manse, deanery, clergy house; bishop's palace; Vatican.

Adj. **churchly,** cloistered, monastic, monasterial, conventual.

INDEX

The numbers refer to the headings under which the words or phrases occur. When the same word or phrase can be used in various senses, the several headings under which it or its synonyms will be found are indicated by *italics*.

When the word given in the Index is itself the title or heading of a category, the word is printed in capitals and the reference number in bold-faced type, thus: **ACTIVITY 682.** When the word is the keyword to a group of synonyms, the reference number is also in bold-faced type.

Derivatives likewise have been sparingly admitted, since the allied or basic term will serve as a key to the various derived forms; thus *alarm* is given, but not *alarmed* or *alarming*. Adverbs ending in *-ly* should be looked for under the adjective, if not found in the Index.

IMPORTANT NOTE

The numbers following all references in this Index Guide refer to the *section* numbers in the text, and *not* to pages.

INDEX

A

abandon 624, 782
abandoned
   forsaken 893
   vicious 945
abandonment 757, 782
abase 879
abasement 874
abash 879
abashed 879
abatement 36
abbess 996
abbey 1000
abbot 996
abbreviation 201
abdicate 757
abdomen 250
abduct *repel* 289
   steal **791**
aberration 83
abet 707
abhor 867, 898
abhorrence 867, 898
abhorrent *painful* 830
   hateful 898
abide *endure* **1**, 106
   remain 110
   dwell 186
ability **157**, 698
abject *vile* 874
   servile 886
abjure *deny* 536
   renounce 607
ablaze 382
able *capable* 157
   skillful 698
able-bodied **159**
ablution 652
abnormal 83
aboard *present* 186
   afloat 273
abode 189
abolish 756
abolition 2, **162**, 756
abominable *bad* 649
   hateful 898
abominate *dislike* 867
   hate 898
abomination 867
aboriginal 66, 124
aborigine 188
abound 639
about *nearly* 32, **197**
   around 227

above 206
abracadabra 993
abrade 330,331
abrasion 330,331
abreast 216, 236
abridge 36, 201
   in writing **596**
abridgment 35, **201**
abroad 57, 196
abrupt *sudden* 113
   steep 217
abscond 623
ABSENCE 187
   –of mind 458
   –of time **107**
absent 187, 458
absentee 187
absent-minded 458
absolute *not relative* 1
   great **31**
   certain 474
absolution 918
absolve 918, 952
absorb *combine* 48
   take in 296
absorbed **451**
absorption 296
abstain *refrain* 623
   be temperate 953
abstainer **953**, **958**
abstemious **953**, **958**
abstention 623
abstinence 623, **953**
abstract, *v. take* 789
abstract, *n. epitome* 195, 596
abstracted *inattentive* 458
abstraction 38, 451, **458**
absurd 471, **497**, 583
ABSURDITY
   impossibility 471
   nonsense **497**
   ridiculousness 853
abundance 31, **639**
abundant *great* 31
   enough 639
abuse, *v. illtreat* 649
   misuse 679
abuse, *n. in-vective* **908, 932**
abusive 909, 932
abut 197
abysmal *deep* 208

abyss 198, **667**
academic 537
academy 542
accede *assent* 488
   submit 725
   consent 762
accelerate **132**, 274, 684
accent 402, **580**
accentuate 580, **642**
accept *assent* 488
   receive **785**
acceptable
   expedient 646
   agreeable 829
acceptance *security* **771**
access *approach* 286
accessible *possible* 470
   easy 705
accession *increase* 35
accessory *extrinsic* 6
   adjunct 37, 39
   accompanying 88
accident 151, 619, **735**
accidental *extrinsic* 6
   occasional 134
   fortuitous 156
acclaim 931
acclamation 488, **931**
acclivity 217
accommodate *suit* 23
   aid 707
accommodation
   adaptation 23
   space 180
ACCOMPANIMENT
   adjunct 37, 39
   coexistence **88**
   musical 415
accompany
   coexist **88**
   escort 664
accomplice 711
accomplish *execute* 161
   complete 729
accomplishment
   learning 490
   talent 698
accord
   agree 23
   assent 488
   grant 760, 784
accordance 16, 23
accordingly **8, 476**

311

aeronautics 267, **273**
aerostatics 267
aesthetic 845
afar 196
affable 894
affair *event* **151**
  battle 720
affect *relate to* 9
  qualify 469
  touch 824
  simper 855
  desire **865**
AFFECTATION **579**, 855
affected 579, **855**
affection 879
affectionate 897
AFFECTIONS **820**
affianced 903
affiliated 9, 11
affinitive 9
affinity *relation* 9
  similarity 17
affirm 535
AFFIRMATION 535
affirmative 535
affix *addition* **37**
  sequel 39
  precedence 62
afflict 830
affliction 828, 830
affluence 734, **803**
afford 803
affront 900, 929
afield 186
afire 382
afloat 267, **273**
afoot *ready* 673
aforesaid 104
afraid 860
afresh *repeated* **104**
  new 123
aft 235
after *in order* **63**
  in time 117
  rear 235
  in pursuit 281
aftermath 154
afternoon 126
afterpart 235
afterthought 451
afterward 117
again 104
  -and again 136
against 708
  -the grain 256, **704**
agape 455, 507
AGE *period* 108
  course 109
  long time 110
  oldness 124
  advanced life **128**
aged 128
AGENCY **170**
AGENT **690**
aggrandize 35
aggravate *increase* 35

heighten 835
AGGRAVATION 35, **835**
aggregate 50
aggression 716
aggrieve 830
aghast 860
agile 274
agitate *move* **315**
  excite 821, **824**
AGITATION
  [see *agitate*]
  energy 171
  motion 315
aglow 382, 420
agnostic **485**, 984, 989
agnosticism 989
ago 122
agonizing 830
agony *physical* 378
  mental 828
agree *accord* **23**, **714**
  concur 178
  assent 488
  -to 762
agreeable 82, **377**
AGREEMENT **23**, 82, 178
agriculture 371
agriculturist 342
aground *fixed* 150
  failure 732
ahead 234, 282, **303**
AID **707**, **906**
ail 655
aileron 267
ailment 655
aim *direction* 278
  purpose 620
aimless 615a
air *gas* 334
ATMOSPHERIC **338**, 349
  tune 415
  appearance 448
aircraft 273
air line 278
airman 269
AIR PIPE **351**
airplane 273, **726**
airs *affectation* 855
  vanity 880
airwoman 269a
airy [see *air*]
  visionary 4
  light 320
aisle 260
ajar 260
akimbo 244
akin *related* 11
alacrity 682, **836**
ALARM
  notice of danger **669**
  fear 860
alarmist 862
alarum 550, 669
album 593, 596
alcohol 959
alcove 191

alert *watchful* 457, 459
  active 682
alertness 457, 459
alias 18
alibi 187
alien *irrelevant* 10
  foreigner 57
alienate *disjoin* 44
  estrange 889
  set against 898
alight, v. *arrive* 292
  descend 306
alight, *adv. on fire* 382
align 278
alike 17
alive *living* 359
  intelligent 498
  active 682
all *whole* 50
  complete 52
allay 174, 834
allege 467, 535
allegiance *obedience* **743**
  duty 926
alleviate 174, 834
alleviation **174**
alley 260
alliance *relation* 9
  kindred 11
  co-operation **709**
allied 11, **48**
alliteration 104
allot 786
allow *admit* 529
  permit 760
allowable 760
allowance
  qualification 469
  gift 784
  salary **973**
alloy *mixture* 41
  combine **48**
allude 521, 526
allure 865
allusion 526
ally, v. 48
ally, n.
  auxiliary 711
  friend 890
almanac 86, 114
almighty 157, 976
Almighty, the 976
almost **32**
alms 784
aloft 206
alone 87
along 200
alongside *near* 197
  parallel 216
  laterally 236
aloof *distant* 196
  secluded 893
aloud 404
alphabet 561
already 118
also 37

altar 903
alter 15, 140
alteration *difference* 15
  variation 20a
  change 140
alternate *reciprocal* 12
  vary 20a
  periodic 138
  substitute 147
  oscillate 314
alternation 12, 138, **314**
alternative 147
although 179, 469
altitude 206
altogether 50, 52
altruism 910, 942
altruist 906, 910
alumnus 541
always *uniformly* **16**
  generally 78
  perpetually 112
amain *violent* 173
amalgamate 41, 48
amass 50, 72
amateur 602
amateurish 643
amaze 870
amazement 870
ambassador 534, 758
ambidexter 238
ambiguous *uncertain* 475
  unintelligible 519
  equivocal 520
ambition 620, 865
ambitious 865
amble 266
ambuscade 530
AMBUSH *hiding* **530**
  pitfall 667
amenable 602, 926
amend *improve* 658
amendment 658
amends 952
amenity 894
amiable 894, 906
amicable 888
amidst 41, 228
amiss 619
amity 714, 888
ammunition **727**
amnesty 918
among **41**, 228
amorous 897
amount *quantity* 25
  sum of money 800
amphitheater 728
ample *much* 31
  spacious 180
  large 192
  broad 202
amplify 194, 549
amputate 38
amulet *talisman* 747
  charm 993
amuse 840
AMUSEMENT 840

ANACHRONISM 115,
  135
anemia 160
anesthesia 376, 381
anesthetic 376
anesthetize 376
analogous **17**
analogy 9, 17
analysis
  decomposition 49
  inquiry 461
  reasoning 476
analyst 463
analytical [*see* analysis]
analyze [*see* analysis]
anarchist 891, 913
anarchy *disorder* 59
  social **738**
anathema 908
anathematize 908
anatomize *dissect* 44
  investigate 461
anatomy 44, 329
ancestor 166
ancestral 166
ancestry 69, **122,** 166
anchor *moor* 184
  stop 265
  safeguard 666
  hope 858
anchorage *location* 184
  roadstead **189**
  refuge **666**
anchorite 893, 955
ancient *old* 124
and 37
anecdote 594
anew 104, 123
ANGEL 977
angelic 977
anger 900
angle 244, 448
angry 900
anguish *physical* 378
  moral **828**
angular 244
ANGULARITY 244
ANIMAL 366, 370
  -life **364**
animalcule 193
animalism 954
animate 824, 836
animation *activity* 682
  vivacity 836
animosity 889, 900
annalist 553
annals 594
annex 37, 43
annihilate 2, 162
annihilation 2
anniversary **138,** 883
annotation 522
announce *predict* 511
  inform **527**
announcement
  [*see* announce]

annoy *molest* 907
  disquiet 830
annoyance 828, 830
annual 138
annul 756
ANNULMENT 756
anoint 332, 355
anointment 332, 355
anomaly 83
anonymous 565
another 15
ANSWER *reply* **462**
  go bail 806
answerable 177, 926
ant 366
antagonism *different* 24
  enmity 889
antagonist 710
antagonistic 14, 24, **179**
antecedence 62
antecedent 64
antedate 115
antediluvian 124
antelope 366
anthem 990
anthology *collection* 596
anthropology 368, 372
antic 840
anticipate
  foresee **121, 510**
  be early **132**
  expect 507
  hope 858
anticipation 115, 121
  [*see* anticipate]
anticlimax 853
antipathy *contrariety* 14
  repulsion 289
  dislike 898
  enemy 891
  hate 898
antipodes 14, 237
antiquary 122
antiquated
  aged 122, **124,** 128
  out of fashion 851
antique 124
antiquity 122, 124
antiseptic 662
antisocial 911
antithesis 14, 15
anxiety *solicitude* 459
  pain 828
  fear 860
anxious [*see* anxiety]
any 25
anybody 78
anyhow 627
apace 132
apache 361, 913
apart *irrelative* 10
  separate 15, 44
  singleness 87
  asunder 96
apartment 191
apathetic 275, 462, **823**

ARRANGEMENT 60
[*see* arrange]
arrant *great* 31
base 940
array *order* 58
multitude 102
dress 225
arrears *debt* 806
arrest *stop* 142
restrain 751
in law 969
ARRIVAL 292
arrive 265, **292**
arrogance 878, 880, 885
arrogant *proud* 878
vain 880
insolent 885
arrogate *assume* **739,** 885
claim 924
arrow 727
arsenal 691
arson 384
art *representation* 554
skill 698
cunning 702
artery 350, 627
artful 702
article *thing* 3
review 595
articulation *junction* 43
speech 580
artifice *plan* 626
cunning **702**
artificer 690
artificial *fictitious* 545
affected 855
-light **420**
artillery 727
artilleryman 726
artisan 690
ARTIST 559
artistic *skillful* 698
beautiful **845**
artistry 569
artless 703
ARTLESSNESS 703
as *motive* 615
ascend *increase* 35
rise 305
ascendancy *power* 157
influence 175
ascension [*see* ascend]
ASCENT *gradient* 217
rise 305
ascertain 480
ascertained 490
ascetic 953, **955**
ASCETICISM 953, 955
ascribe 155
aseptic 662
ashamed 879
ashen 429
ashes *corpse* 362
dirt 653
ashore 342
ashy 429

aside *laterally* 236
in a whisper 405
ask *inquire* 461
request 765
askance 217
askew 217, 243
aslant 217
asleep 683
aspect *feature* **5**
situation 183
appearance **448**
asperity *roughness* 256
discourtesy 895
asphyxiate 361
aspirant *candidate* 767
aspire *hope* 858
worship 990
asquint 217
ass *beast of burden* 271
fool 501
assail *attack* 716
assailant 716, 726
assassin 361
assault 716
ASSEMBLAGE 72
assembly *assemblage* 72
council 696
assembly room 189
ASSENT *agreement* **488**
be willing 602
assert *affirm* 535
assess *measure* 466
determine 480
tax 812
assessor *judge* 967
assets 780
asseverate 535
assiduous 682
assign *commission* 755
give 784
allot 786
assignable 270
assignee 785
assignment 155, 755
assimilate 16
assimilation 23, 161
assist 707, 906
assistant 711
assize *tribunal* 966
associate, *n.* 690, **890**
associate, *v. relate* **9**
mix 41
unite 43
combine 48
accompany 88
association
[*see* associate]
relation 9
co-operation 709
assonance 597
assort *arrange* 60
assortment 72
assuage *moderate* 174
relieve 834, 826
assume *suppose* 514
take 789

assumed 514
assuming *insolent* 885
assumption [*see* assume]
seizure **925**
assurance
certainty 474
belief 484
confidence **507**
promise 768
assure *render certain* 474
convince 484
promise 768
assuredly *assent* 488
astern 235
asteroid 318
astigmatism 443
astir *active* 682
astonish 870
astonishment 870
astound *excite* 824
frighten 860
astral 318
-body 317, 992a
astray 475
astute 498
asunder *separate* 44
distant 196
asylum *retreat* 666
atheism 989
atheist 984
athirst 865
athlete 159
athletic *strong* 159
gymnastic **720**
athletics 159, 720
athwart 219
at large **750**
atlas 86
atmosphere *air* 338
painting 556
atmospheric **338**
atom 32, **193**
atomize 336
atone 952, **976**
ATONEMENT
expiation 952
propitiation 976
atrocity 907, 947
atrophy 195
attach *join* 43
legal 969
attaché 746, 758
attachment 43, 969
ATTACK 716
attain *arrive* 292
succeed 731
attainable 470
attainment *knowledge* 490
attempt 675
attend *accompany* 88
be present 186
follow 281
apply the mind **457**
treat medically 662
serve 746
attendance [*see* attend]

B

battleship 726
baubel *trifle* 643
　　toy 840
bawl 411
bay, *n. gulf* 343
bay, *adj. brown* 433
bay, *v. cry* 412
bayonet 716, 727
bays *trophy* 733
bay window 260
be 1
beach 342
beacon 550
beadle *law officer* 965
beam *support* 215
　　light 420
bear, *n. brute* 895
　　stock exchange 797
bear, *v. endure* 151, 826
　　produce 161
　　sustain 215
　　carry 270
　　admit of 470
　　suffer 821
　　-fruit *prosper* 734
　　-upon *be relevant* 9
bearable 651
beard 253, 256
bearded 256
beardless 226
bearer 271
bearing *relation* 9
　　direction 278
　　meaning 516
　　demeanor 692
bearings *situation* 183
bearish 895
beast *animal* 366
　　brute 895
　　-of burden **271**
beastly *unclean* 653
beat, *n. periodicity* 138
　　verse 597
　　path 627
beat, *v. be superior* 33
　　surpass 303
　　oscillate 314
　　agitate 315
　　strike 972
　　-a retreat **623**
　　-down *cheapen* 819
beaten track *habit* 613
beatific 827, 981
beatification 987
beau *fop* 854
　　admirer 897
　　-ideal *perfect* 650
　　beauty 845
beautiful 845
beautify 845, 847
BEAUTY 845
becalm 265
because 476, **615**
beckon 550
becloud *befog* 353
become *change to* 144

behove 926
becoming *beautiful* 845
　　due 924
bed 215
bedaub 223
bedazzle 420
bedeck 847
bedevil *derange* 61
　　bewitch 992
bedizen 847
bedridden 655
bedrock 211
bee 366
beehive *for bees* 370
　　workshop 691
beeline 278
Beelzebub 978
beer 298
beetle *overhang* 206
　　project 250
befall 151
befit *agree* 23
　　behoove 924
befitting 924
before *in order* 62
　　in space **234**
　　ahead 280
beforehand **132**
befriend 707, 888
beg *ask* 765
　　-pardon 950
　　-the question 477
beggar *petitioner* **767**
　　poor man 804
　　low person 876
beggarly *vile* 874
begin 66
beginner 541
BEGINNING 66
begrudge 819
beguile *mislead* 495
behalf *advantage* 618
behave 692
　　-oneself 894
behavior 692
behead 361, 972
behind *in space* **235**
　　in sequence **281**
behindhand *late* 133
behold *see* 441
beholden *grateful* 916
behoove 926
being *abstract* 1
　　concrete 3
belated *late* 133
belie *deny* 536
　　falsify 544
BELIEF *credence* **484**
　　religious creed 983
believe 484, 987
believer 484, 987
belittle *decrease* 36
　　underestimate 483
　　detract 934
bell *alarm* 550
belle 854

belligerent
　　contentious 720
　　warlike 722
　　combatant 726
bellow *cry* 411
belly 250
belong to *related* 9
　　compose 56
　　property **777**
beloved 897
below 207
belt *outline* 230
　　ring 247
bemoan 839
bench *support* 215
　　tribunal 966
bend *fork* 244
　　curve 245
　　turn 311
　　give 324
beneath 207
benediction *gratitude* 916
　　approval 931
benefaction 784
BENEFACTOR **912**
beneficent 906
beneficial 648
beneficiary 785
benefit *profit* 618
　　do good 644, 648
　　assist 906
BENEVOLENCE
　　kindness 906, 910
benevolent 906
benighted *ignorant* 491
benignant 906
bent, *n. tendency* 176, 820
　　desire 865
bent, *adj. angular* 244
benumb *deaden* 381
　　blunt 823
bequeath 784
bequest 270, 784
berate 932
bereavement *death* 360
　　loss 776
bereft 776
berth *lodging* 189
　　office 625
beseech 765
beset *surround* 227
　　attack 716
beside 197, 236
besides 37
besiege *surround* 227
　　attack **716**
besmear 653
bespeak 755
best *good* 648
　　perfect 650
bestir oneself 682
bestow *give* 784
betimes 132
betoken 467
betray *disclose* 529
　　deceive 545

betroth 768, 903
betrothal 902
betrothed 897, 903
better *improve* **658**
between 228
betwixt 228
beverage 298
bevy 102
bewail 839
beware 668
bewilder *put out* **458**
 perplex 475
 astonish 870
bewitch *fascinate* **615**
 diabolize 978
 hoodoo 992
beyond *superior* **33**
 further 196
bias *influence* **175**
 tendency 176
 slope 217
 prepossession **481**
bib *pinafore* **225**
Bible **985**
bicentenary 98, 138
bicentennial 98, 138
bicker *quarrel* **713**
bicycle 272
bid *order* **741**
 offer 763
bide *wait* 133
 remain 141
biennial 138
bier 363
big *in degree* **31**
 in size 192, 206
bigot *dogmatist* **474**
 mule 606
 heterodox **984**
 impious **988**
bigoted 988
bigotry 474, 606, **984**
bill *money account* **811**
 -of fare 86, 298
billet, *n. office* **625**
billet, *v. locate* **184**
billingsgate 908
billows 341
bind *connect* 43
 compel 744
biography 594
biologist 357
biology 357, **359**
biplane 273
bird **366**
birth *beginning* 66
 production 161
birthday 138
birthright **924**
bisect 91
bisection **91**
bishop 996
bishopric 995
bit *small quantity* **32**
 part 51
 curb 752

bite *eat* 298
biting *cold* **383**
 pungent 392
bitter *cold* **383**
 acrid 395
 malevolent 907
bitterness [*see* bitter]
bivouac 265
bizzare 83, 853
black *color* **431**
 -sheep 949
blackball 893, 932
blacken 431
 defame 934
blacklist 932
blackmail 793
BLACKNESS 431
blade *edge tool* 253
blamable 932, 947
blame 155, **932**
blameless 946
blameworthy **932**, 947
blanch 429, 430
bland **894**
blandishment 902
blank *inexistent* 2
 unsubstantial 4
blanket 223
blare 404
blarney 933
blasé 869, 871
blasphemy **988**
blast, *n. destroy* 162
 explosion 173
blast, *v. wind* 349
blatant *loud* 404
blaze *heat* 382
 mark 550
blazer *coat* 225
blazon *publish* **531**
 inscribe 873
 -forth 882
bleach 429
bleachers 444
bleak **383**
blear-eyed 443
bleat 412
bleed *extort money* 814
 suffer 828
bleeding *hemorrhage* 299
BLEMISH *deface* 241
 imperfection 651
 defect **848**
blench *shrink* 821
blend *mix* 41
 combine 48
 harmonize 413
bless *sanctify* **976**
blessed 827
blessing 618, 931
blight 659
blighted 659
blind, *n. shade* 530
 pretext 617
blind, *adj. sightless* **442**
blind, *v. conceal* 528

blinders 443
blindfold 442, 491, **528**
BLINDNESS 442
blink *wink* 443
blinker **424**, 443, 530
bliss 827
blister 848
blithe 836
blithesome 836
blizzard 349
bloat *inflate* 194
bloated *expanded* **194**
 convex 250
block, *n. houses* 189
 mass 192
block, *v. hinder* 706
 execution 975
blockade *surround* **227**
 close 261
 seclude 893
blockhead 501
blonde 429
blood *consanguinity* 11
 -relation 11
bloodlessness 160
bloodshed 361
bloodthirsty 361
bloody *killing* 361
bloom *blossom* 367
 health 654
 flower 734
blossom
 flower 161, **365**, **367**
 flower 734
blot *blacken* **431**
 blemish 848
 disgrace 874
blotch *black* 431
 blemish 848
blotchy 431
blouse 225
blow *knock* **276**
 waft 349
 disappointment 509
 evil 619
 -up *explode* 173
 inflate 194, 349
 objurgate 932
blowhole 260, **351**
bludgeon 727
BLUE *color* **438**
bluestocking 492
bluff *high* 206
 brag 884
blunder *error* **495**
 absurdity **497**
 bungle 699
 failure 732
 indiscretion 947
blunt *obtuse* 254
 benumb 376
 plain-spoken **703**
BLUNTNESS 254
blur *dim* 443
 blemish 848
blurred *invisible* 447

blush *heat* 382
  redden **434**
  feel 821
bluster *violence* 173
  brag 884
  resent 900
  threaten 909
BLUSTERER 884, 887
blustering *insolent* **885**
boa 225
board *food* 298
  council 696
boarder 188
boast 855, **884**
boaster 482, **884**
boastful **884**
BOASTING 884
boat 273
boating 267
boatman 269
boatswain 269
bob *bow* 308
  oscillate 314
bodily 3, 50
body *substance* 3
  whole 50
  assemblage 72
  -clothes **225**
bodyguard 753
bog *swamp* 345
bogus 545
Bohemian 83
boil *be violent* 173
  effervesce 315
  bubble 353
  heat 382, 384
  flare up 824, 825
boisterous *violent* 173
  excitable 825
bold *prominent* 250
  unreserved 525
  defiant 715
  brave 861
boldness [see bold]
bolshevism 742
bolshevist 712, 742
bolster 707
bolt *sift* 42
  fasten 43
  close 261
  run away 623
  shackle 752
  -food 957
bomb 727
bombard 716
bombast 577
bombastic 577
bonanza *wealth* 803
bonbon 396
bond *tie* 9, 45
  security 771, 802
bondage 749
bonfire 382
bonnet 225
bonny *cheerful* 836
  pretty 845

bonus *gift* 784
  money 810
bony 323
BOOK, n. *volume* 593
book, *v. register* 86
bookish 490
bookkeeper 811
bookkeeping **811**
bookless *unlearned* **493**
bookshop 593
bookstore 593
bookworm **492**
boom *impulse* 276
  sound 404
  roll 407
boomerang *recoil* 277
  weapon 727
boon 784
boor *clown* 876
boorish *uncouth* 851
  rustic 876
boost *praise* 931
booster 935
boot 225
  to - *added* 37
booth 799
bootlegging 959
border, *n. edge* 231
  limit 233
border, *v. adjoin* 199
bordering 233
borderland 199
bore, *n. diameter* 202
  trouble 828
  plague 830
  wearier 841
bore, *v. perforate* 260
  satiate 869
boredom 841
borer 262
boring 275
born, be **359**
borough 189
borrow *imitate* 19
  receive 788
borrowed plumes
  deception 545
borrower 806
BORROWING 788
bosh 546
bosky 367
bosom *breast* 221
  affections 820
boss *knob* 250
  politician 694
  rule 737
  master 745
botanic 369
botanist 369
BOTANY 369
botch *disorder* 59
  bungle 699
both 89
bother *trouble* 828
  harass 830

bottle *receptacle* 191
  preserve 670
bottom *lowest part* **211**
  ship 273
bottomless **208**
boudoir 191
bough 51, 367
boulder 342
boulevards 627
bounce *jump* 309
  dismiss 756
bound
  circumscribe 195, 229
  leap 309
boundary 233, -line **233**
boundless 105
bounds 230, 233
bountiful 816
bounty 707, 906
bouquet *fragrance* **400**
  beauty 847
bourgeois *medium* 29
bout *turn* 138
  fight 720
boutonniere 400
bovine 366, 499
bow, *n. fore part* 234
  curve 245
  weapon 727
bow, *v. stoop* **308**
  greet 894
bower 189, **191**
bowie knife 727
bowl, *vessel* 191
  -along *walk* 266
bow-legged 243
bowman 726
bowsprit 234
box, *n. chest* 191
box, *v. fight* 720
boy 129
boycott *eject* 297
  resist 719
  disapprove 932
boyhood 127
boylike 129
brace, *n. two* 89
  support 215
  music 413
brace, *v. strengthen* 159
  refresh 689
bracing *salubrious* 656
bracken 367
bracket *tie* 43
  couple 89
brackish 392
brag *boast* 884
braggadocio 884
braggart 482, **884**
Brahmanism 976
braid 219
brain *intellect* 450
brainless 499
brainwork 451
brainy 450
brake, *n. copse* 367

C

coil *convolution* **248**
  circuit 311
coin, *n.* 800
coin, *v. fabricate* 161
coincide 13, 120, 488
coincidence *identity* 13
  in time 120
coincident **13**, 120, 178
coiner 792
COLD, *n. frigidity* **383**
cold, *adj.*
  frigid **383**
  insensible 823
  indifferent 866
cold-blooded 907
cold-bloodedness 871
coldhearted
  unfeeling 823
  malevolent 907
coldness *cold* 383
  unconcern 823
  indifference 866
collaboration 178
collaborator 711
collapse, *n.*
  prostration **158**
  failure 732
collapse, *v. fail* **304**
collar *dress* 225
  circlet 247
collateral *relative* 9
colleague
  associate 88, 690
  friend 890
collect *assemble* 72
  compile 596
collected *calm* 826
collection *assemblage* 72
  offertory 990
collective 78
collectively 50
college 542
collide 276
collision *clash* 179
  percussion 276
  opposition **708**
  encounter 720
colloquial 588
collusion *deceit* 545
  complicity 709
colonel 745
colonial 188
colonist 188, 294, 295
colonization 184
colonize 184
colony *region* 184
  settlement 188
COLOR, *n. hue* **428**
color, *v. redden* **434**
  be angry 900
colored 428
colorless *pale* **429**
colors *ensign* 550
colossal 106, 192
colossus **206**
colt *horse* 271

column *height* 206
  support 215
  monument 551
coma 683
comb, *n.* 253
comb, *v. clean* **652**
combat 720
COMBATANT **726**
combative 720, 722
COMBINATION **48**
combine *unite* **48**
  compose 56
  co-operate 709
combustible 384, 388
combustion 384
come *arrive* 292
  -after *succeed* 117
  -amiss 135
  -of age **131**
  -out *come of age* 131
  -together *assemble* 72
  converge 290
  -to nothing
    fail **732**
  -to pass 151
comedian 844
comedy 599, 853
comely 845
comfort *pleasure* 377
  delight 827
  relief 834
comfortable 377
Comforter 976
comforter *wrap* 223
comfortless 837
comic 842, 853
coming [*see* come]
  impending 152
  -out *debut* 883
COMMAND, *n.*
  requirement 630
  authority 737
  order **741**
command, *v. tower* 206
  order **737**, 741
  possess 777
commandant 745
commander 744, 789
commander
  mariner 269
  chief 745
commander-in-chief 745
commemorate 883
commemorative **883**
commence 66
commend 931
commendable 944
commendatory 931
comment 522, 595
commentary 522, **595**
commentator 595
commerce 794
commercial **794**
commingle 41
commiserate 914
commissariat 637

COMMISSION
  task 625
  delegate **755**
commissioner 745, 758
commit *do* 680
  delegate 755
  arrest 969
  -to memory 505
commitment 969
committee 696, 758
commodious 644
commodity 798
commodore 745
common, *n.* 367
common, *adj.*
  general 78
  ordinary 82
  habitual 613
  base 876
  -run 78
  -sense 498, 502
  in - *participated* **778**
commonalty 876
commoner 876
commonplace *mediocre* 29
  plain 576
  habit 613
  unimportant 643
commonweal
  mankind 372
  good 618
  utility **644**
commonwealth *region* 181
  mankind 372
  state 737
commotion 315
commune *township* 181
commune with 588
communicate *tell* 527
communication 43, 527
communicative 527
communion
  participation 778
  sacrament 998
communist 778
communistic 778
community *party* 712
communize 778
commutation
  substitution 147
  interchange 148
commute 774
commuter 268
COMPACT *joined* 43
  compressed 195
  compendious 201
  dense 321
  bargain **769**
compactness
  [*see* compact]
companion *match* 17
  accompaniment 88
  friend 890
companionable 892
companionship 892
company *assembly* **72**

convenient 646
convent 1000
conventicle *council* 696
convention *assembly* 72
  canon 80
  law 697
  compact 769
  social rule 852
conventional 82, 613, 852
conventionalism 613
conventionalist 82
conventionality 82, 852
conventionalize 82
conventual *monastic* 1000
converge 290
CONVERGENCE 290
convergent 286, 290
conversant 698
CONVERSATION 588
conversational 588
  sociable 892
converse *reverse* 14
  talk **588**
conversely 148
conversible 144
CONVERSION 144, 987
convert, *n.* 987
convert, *v.*
  change 140
  change to **144,** 484
  reclaim 950
convertible 13, 27
convex 250
CONVEXITY 250
convey *transfer* 270
  assign 783
conveyance
  transference 270
  vehicle 272
convict, *n. prisoner* 754
  condemned man 949
convict, *v. condemn* 971
conviction *belief* **484**
  guilt 971
convince *confute* 479
  assure 484
convivial 892
conviviality **892**
convocation
  assemblage 72
convoke 72
CONVOLUTION
  coil 248
convoy *accompany* 88
  transfer 270
  guard 664
convulse 315, 378
convulsion *revolution* 146
  fit 173, 315, 378
cook, *n. servant* 746
cook, *v. heat* 384
  prepare 673
cool, *adj. cold* 383
  refrigerate **385**
  inexcitable 826
  cautious 864

  indifferent 866
  imperturbable 871
  unfriendly 889
cool, *v. moderate* 174
coolheaded
  unexcitable 871
coolness [see cool]
caution **864**
  calmness 871
coop *restrain* 751
co-operate 709, 746
CO-OPERATION
  physical 178
  voluntary **709**
  participation 778
co-operative
  concurring 178
  helpful 746
co-ordinate *equal* 27
cope with *oppose* 708
  contend 720
copious *productive* 168
  abundant 639
copper *money* 800
copperish 433
coppice 367
copse 367
COPY, *n. facsimile* 21
  prototype **22**
  duplicate 90
copy, *v. imitate* 19
copyist *imitator* 19
coquet, *v. lie* 544
  change one's mind 607
  flirt 902
coquetry 855
coquette *belle* 854
  flirt 902
cord *tie* 45
  filament 205
cordial, *n. dram* 392
cordial, *adj.*
  pleasurable 377
  willing 602
  fervid 821
  grateful 829
cordiality *good will* 602
  fervor 821
cordon 232, 247
core *center* 68, **222**
  gist 5, 642
cork *plug* 263
corkscrew 248
corky *dry* 340
corner *plight* 7
  place 182
  angle **244**
  monopoly 777
corollary *adjunct* 39
coronation
  enthronement 755
  celebration 883
coronet 247, 747
corporal, *n.* 745
corporal, *adj. corporeal*
  316

corporate *joined* 43
corporation
  association **712,** 797
  jurisdiction 965
corporeal 3, 316
corps *assemblage* 72
  troops 726
CORPSE 362
corpulence **192**
corpulent 192
corral, *n. inclosure* 232
corral, *v. circumscribe* 229
  round up 370
correct, *adj. true* 494
correct, *v. inform* 527
  improve 658
  censure 932
  punish 972
correction [see correct]
  house of - 752
correctness [see correct]
CORRELATION
  relation 9
  reciprocity **12**
correlative 9, 12, 17
correspond *agree* 23
  write 592
CORRESPONDENCE
  correlation 12
  similarity 17
  agreement 23
  writing 592
correspondent
  letter writer **592**
  journalist 593
corridor 627
corrigible **658**
corroboration *evidence* 467
  assent 488
corrode *burn* 384
corrosion [see corrode]
corrosive [see corrode]
  caustic 171
  destructive 649
corrugate *roughen* 256
  rumple 258
  furrow 259
corrupt 659, 940
corrupting *noxious* **649**
corruption
  decomposition 49
  improbity 940
  vice 945
cortege *suite* 746
cosmic 318
cosmopolitan *urban* 189
cost 812
costly 809, 814
costume 225
cosy *snug* 377
  sociable 892
cot *abode* **189**
  bed 215
coterie *class* 75
  junto 712
cottage 189

compress 195
  shatter 328
  humble 879
crushed *unhappy* 828
crust 223
crusty *discourteous* 895
crutch *support* 215
crux *difficulty* 704
CRY *stridor* 410
  human **411**
  animal 412
  weep **839**
crying [*see* cry]
  urgent 630
crypt *cell* 191
  grave 207, 363
cryptic *uncertain* 475
  concealed 528
crystalline *dense* 321
  transparent 425
crystallization 321, 323
crystallize 321
cub *cad* 851
cubicle 191
cubist 556
cuddle 902
cudgel, *n.* 727
cudgel, *v. beat* 276
cue *hint* 527
  watchword 550
cuff *blow* 276
cuirass 717
cuisine 298
cul-de-sac 261
culinary 298
cull *choose* 609
  take 789
culminate *cap* 33
  tower 206
  crown 210
culprit 949, 975
cult 481, 990
cultivate *till* 371
  improve 658, 707
cultivated *courteous* 894
cultivation *tillage* 371
  knowledge 490
  improvement **658**
  courtesy 894
cultivator 371
cultural 537, 542
culture *knowledge* 490
  improvement 658
  courtesy 894
cumber 706
cumbersome *heavy* 319
  disagreeable 830
cumbrous 319, **830**
cumulative 467
CUNNING *artfulness* **702**
cup *vessel* 191

hollow 252
cupboard **191**
cupidity *avarice* 819
  desire 865
cupola *dome* 223, 250
cupping 662
cur *dog* 366
curable 658, 660
curate 996
curb, *n. bit* 752
curb, *v. moderate* 174
  slacken 275
  check 706
  restrain 751
curd 321
curdle *condense* 321
cure *reinstate* 660
  remedy 662
curio 847
CURIOSITY 455
  phenomenon 872
curious *exceptional* 83
  inquisitive **455**
curl *bend* 245
  convolution 248
  hair 256
curly 248
currency *publicity* 531
  money **800**
current, *n.*
  of air 349
current, *adj. existing* 1
  general 78
  present 118
  happening 151
  rife 531, 532
currycomb 253
curse, *n. bane* 663
  adversity 735
curse, *v. execrate* **908**
cursory *transient* 111
  hasty 684
curt *short* 201
  concise 572
curtail *retrench* 38
  shorten 201
curtailment
  decrease 36
  [*see* curtail]
curtain *shade* 424
  screen 530
curtsy 308
CURVATURE 245
curve 245, 252, 279
curved **245**
curvet *leap* 309
cushion *pillow* 215
cussedness 606
custodian 753
custody 664, 751
custom, *rule* 80

habit 124, **613**
  barter 794
  sale 796
  fashion 852
customary [*see* custom]
  regular 80
customer 795
cut, *n. bit* 51
  notch 257
  blow 276
  path 627
cut, *v. divide* 44
  absent 187
  curtail 201
  form 240
  depart 293
  reap 371
  carve 557
  ignore 893
  snub 895
  -*across* 302
  -*adrift* 44
  -*away* 38
  -*off subduct* 38
  disjoin 44
  bereft 776
  divorce 782
  -*out surpass* 33
  substitute 147
  -*short stop* 142
cuticle 223
cutlass 727
cutlery 253
cutter 273
cutthroat 361, 913
cutting *sharp* 253
  affecting 821
  painful 830
  -*edge* **253**
cuttings 596
cycle *period* 138
  circle 247
  vehicle **272**
cyclic 138
cyclist 268
cyclone *rotation* 312
  wind 349
cyclonic 349
cyclopedia 593
cylinder **249**, 272
cylindrical 249
cynic *recluse* 893
  misanthrope 911
  detractor 936
cynical *morose* 911
  contemptuous 930
  censorious 932
cynicism
  misanthropy 911
  discourtesy 895
czar 745

D

dab *morsel* 32
  slap 276
dabble *meddle* 682
  potter 683
dad 166
daft 503
dagger *weapon* 727
Dail Eireann 696
daily, *n. newspaper* 531
daily, *adj.*
  frequent 136
  periodic 138
dainty, *n. food* 298
dainty, *adj. savory* 394
  pleasing 829
  delicate 845
  fastidious 868
dais *support* 215
  throne 747
dale *valley* 252
dally *delay* 133
  idle 683
  fondle 902
dam, *n. parent* 166
dam, *v. close* 261, 348
  obstruct 706
damage, *n. loss* 776
damage, *v. injure* 659
dame 374
damn *curse* 908
  condemn 976
damoiselle 129
damp, *adj. moist* 339
damp, *v. dissuade* 616
  depress 837
damper *muffler* 405
  hindrance 706
damsel 129
dance, *n.* 840
dance, *v. jump* 309
  agitate 315
dancer 840
dandy *fop* 854
dandyism 855
DANGER 665
dangerous 665
dangle *hang* 214
  swing 314
  display 882
dangler 281
dank 339
dapper *elegant* 845
dapple-gray 432
dappled 432
dare *confront* 234
  defy 715
  face danger 861
dare-devil 863
daring 861
dark *obscure* 421
  dim 422
  invisible 447

unintelligible 519
darken
  obscure 421, 422
DARKNESS [*see* dark]
  421
darling *beloved* 897
darn 660
dart, *n. missile* 727
dart, *v.* 274
Darwinism 357
dash, *n. race* 274
  mark 550
  courage 861
dash *mix* 41
  speed 274
  -off *be active* 682
  haste 684
dashing *brave* 861
  ostentatious 882
dastard 862
data *evidence* 467
  reasoning 476
date 106, 114
datum [*see* data]
daub 223
daughter 167
daunt 860
dauntless 861
dawdle 133, 275
dawn, *n.* 125, 420, 422
dawn, *v. begin* 66
daybreak 125, 422
daydream *fancy* 515
  hope 858
daylight 125, 420
daze 420, 870
dazed *confused* 523
dazzle *daze* 420
  blind 443
  awe 928
deacon 996
dead *lifeless* 360
  mute 408a
  -of night
  midnight 126
  dark 421
deaden *weaken* 158
  numb 381
  muffle 405, 408a
deadened 381
deadlock *cessation* 142
  difficulty 704
deadly 361
deaf 419
deafen 419
DEAFNESS 419
deal, *n. much* 31
deal, *v. compact* 769
  allot 786
  -with *treat of* 595
dealings 769
dean *elder* 128

clergyman 996
dear *high priced* 809, **814**
  loved 897
DEARNESS **814**
dearth 640
DEATH 360
deathblow *end* 67
  killing 361
deathless *perpetual* 112
  famous 873
debar *hinder* 706
  restrain 751
  prohibit 761
debark 292, 342
debase *depress* 308
  deteriorate 659
  degrade 874
debased *lowered* 207
debatable 475
debate, *n.* 588
debate, *v. reason* 476
  hesitate 605
debility 160
debit *debt* 806
debonair 836
debouch 293
debris 645
DEBT 806
debtor 806
debut 883
decade *ten* 98
decadence 659
decamp 293, 623
decapitate 361, 972
decay, *n.*
  putrefaction 49, **653**
  deterioration 659
decay, *v. decrease* 36
  rot 49
  decline 124
decayed 160
  deteriorated **659**
decease 360
deceit *falsehood* 544
  deception 545
deceitful 544
deceive 545
deceived *in error* 495
  duped 486
DECEIVER 548
decennial 108
decennium 108
decent *mediocre* 651
  pure 960
DECEPTION 545, 702
deceptive *sophistical* 477
  deceiving 545
decide *turn the scale* 153
  judge 480
  resolve 604
  choose 609
decided *great* 31

resolved 604
deciduous *transitory* 111
  falling 306
decimal 99
decimate *kill* 361
decipher 522, 525
decision *judgment* 480
  resolution 604
  intention 620
decisive *certain* 474
  convincing 478
deck, *n. floor* 211
deck, *v. clothe* 225
declaim 582
declamatory 582
declaration *evidence* 467
  affirmation 535
  -of faith
    belief 484
    theology 983
  -of war 722
declare 535
declension [*see decline*]
  decrease 36
declination [*see decline*]
decline, *n. old age* 124
  descent 306
  deterioration 659
decline, *v. decrease* 36
  grow old 128
  reject 610
  refuse 764
declivity *slope* 217
  descent 306
decode 525
decoloration 429
decompose 49
DECOMPOSITION 49
decoration *ornament* 847
  title 877
decorous [*see decorum*]
  proper 924
  respectful 928
decorum *fashion* 852
  dignity 878
  purity 960
decoy, *n.* 548
decoy, *v. deceive* 545
  entice 615
DECREASE *in degree* 36
  in size 195
decree *judgment* 480
  order 741
  law 963
DECREMENT
  decrease 36
  thing deducted 40a
decrepit *old* 128
  impotent 158
  weak 160
decrepitude 128, 158
decrescendo 36
decry *underrate* 483
  censure 932
  detract 934
dedicate 677, 873

deduce *infer* 480
deducible 478
deduct *retrench* 38
deduction
  decrement 38, 40a
  reasoning 476
  inference 480
deed *record* 551
  act 680
  security 771
  exploit 861
deem 484
deep *great* 31
  profound 208
  sonorous 404
  cunning 702
deepen *increase* 35
  excavate 208
deeply [*see deep*]
deer 366
deface *destroy form* 241
  injure 659
  render ugly 846
defalcation 808
defamation 934
defamatory 932, 934
defame *shame* 874
  censure 932
  detract 934
defamer 936
default *shortcoming* 304
  debt 806
  nonpayment 808
defaulter *nonpayer* 808
defeat *confute* 479
  succeed 731
  failure 732
defect *decrement* 40a
  incompleteness 53
  shortcoming 304
  imperfection 651
  failing 945
defection
  disobedience 742
defective *incomplete* 53
  imperfect 651
defend 462
defendant 938
defender 717, 914
DEFENSE *answer* 462
  resistance 717
  vindication 937
defenseless *impotent* 158
  exposed 665
defensible *safe* 664
  excusable 937
defensive 717
defer *put off* 133
  neglect 460
  -to *assent* 488
  submit 725
  respect 928
deference *submission* 725
  obedience 743
  courtesy 894
  respect 928

deferment 460
DEFIANCE 715
defiant 715, 742
deficiency
  [*see deficient*]
deficient *unequal* 28
  inferior 34
  incomplete 53
  remiss 304
  imperfect 651
deficit *incompleteness* 53
  debt 806
defile, *n. gorge* 198
defile, *v. march* 266
  spoil 659
define *limit* 233
  explain 522
definite *special* 79
  limited 233
  certain 474
  exact 494
  manifest 525
definition
  interpretation 521
deflate 195
deflect *curve* 245
  deviate 279
deform 243, 846
deformed 243
deformity *distortion* 243
  ugliness 846
defraud *cheat* 545
  swindle 791
defray 807
deft *clever* 698
defunct 360
defy *confront* 234, 861
  set at defiance 715
degeneracy 659
degenerate
  deteriorate 659
  vice 945
degradation *shame* 874
  dishonor 940
degrade 874
DEGREE 26
deification 981
deify *honor* 873
  idolatry 991
deign *condescend* 879
deities 979
DEITY 976
DEJECTION
  melancholy 837
delay 133, 460
delectable *savory* 394
  agreeable 829
delegate, *n.* 524, 755, 758
delegate, *v. depute* 759
delegation 755
deliberate, *adj. slow* 275
deliberate, *v.* 451
deliberately 133, 275
deliberation 451
delicacy *weakness* 160
  dainty 298, 394

DIVERGENCE 291
difference 15
nonuniformity 16a
dissimilarity 18
variation 20a
disagreement 24
diverse 15, 81
diversified 16a
diversify [see diversity]
vary 18, 20a
change 140
diversion *change* 140
deviation 279
pleasure 377
amusement 840
diversity *difference* 15
irregularity 16a
dissimilarity 18
multiformity 81
divert *turn* 279
deceive 545
amuse 840
divest *denude* 226
-oneself of
DIVESTMENT 226
divide *separate* **44**
part 51
bisect 91
apportion 786
dividend *part* 51
portion 786
divination 511, 992
divine, *n. clergyman* 996
divine, *v. predict* 511
guess 514
divine, *adj. perfect* 650
of God **976, 983, 983a**
-service 990
Divinity *God* 976
theology 983
divisible 51
[see divide]
division [see divide]
separation 44
part 51
class 75
interval 198
discord 713
DIVORCE, n. 44, 905
divorce, *v. relinquish* 782
divulge 529
dizziness [see dizzy]
dizzy *confused* 458
vertigo 503
do *suit* 23
produce 161
act 680
complete **729**
-for *destroy* 162
kill 361
docile *willing* 602
dock, *n. wharf* 231
tribunal 966
dock, *v. shorten* 201
docket *list* 86

schedule 611
doctor *learned man* 492
physician 662
doctrinaire 855
doctrine *tenet* 484
document 551
documentary 467
dodder 160
dodge, *n. stratagem* 702
dodge, *v. change* 140
deviate 279
avoid 623
doer 680, 690
doff 226
dog, *n.* **366**
dog, *v. follow* 281
dogged *obstinate* 606
valorous 861
doggerel *verse* 597
ridiculous 851, 853
dogma 484
dogmatic *certain* 474
positive 481
dogmatism 474
dogmatist 474, 887
doings *events* 151
actions 680
doldrums *sulks* 901a
dole, *n. mite* 640
dole, *v. give* 784
doleful 837
doll 554
dollar 800
dolor *physical* 378
moral 828
dolorous 830
domain 75, 181
dome 206, 223, 250
domestic, *n. servant* 746
domestic, *adj.*
native 188, 367
tame 370
home 189, 221
secluded 893
-animals **366**
domesticate *locate* 184
acclimatize 613
-animals 370
domestication **184, 370**
domesticize 370
domicile 189
domiciled
inhabiting 186
domiciliary 188
-visit 461
dominant 175
dominate *influence* **175**
rule 737
domination 175, 737
domineer 739, **885**
dominion 181, 737
-rule 737
domino *dress* 225
mask 530
don, *n. scholar* 492
tutor 540

noble 875
don, *v. put on* 225
donate 784
donation 784
done
-for 732
failed 732
-up *tired* 688
donjon *defense* **717**
prison 752
donkey *ass* 271
fool 501
donor 784
doom, *n. fate* 152
destruction 162
death 360
necessity 601
doom, *v. sentence* 971
door *entrance* 66, 260
brink 231
barrier 232
doorkeeper 263
dormancy 172
dormant *inert* 172
dormitory 191
dory 273
dose *quantity* 25
medicine 662
dot *speck* 32, 193
dot *dowry* 784
dotage *age* 128
dotard 130, 501
dote *drivel* 499, 503
-upon 897
double *similar* 17
increase 35
duplex 90
substitute 147
fold 258
wraith 992a
double-dealing 544, 940
double-faced 940
DOUBT, n. uncertainty
475
disbelief 485
skepticism 989
doubtful 475, **485**
doubtless 474, 488
douceur *gift* 784
doughboy 726
doughty 159, 861
dour 739
douse 310
dovetail *agree* 23
join 43
insert 228
dowdy 851
dower *property* **780**
bequest 784
down, *n. upland* 180
down, *adj. below* 207
down, *v. cast down* 308
downcast *dejected* 837
downfall *destruction* 162
failure 732
misfortune **735**

E

erudite 490, 500, 539
erudition 490, 539
eruption *revolution* 146
  violence 173
  egress 295
  ejection 297
  explosion 406
eruptive [see eruption]
escalade 305
escalator 305, 307
escapade 608, 840
ESCAPE, *n. flight* **671**
escape, *v.* 671, 927
eschew *avoid* 623
  dislike 867
escort *companion* 88
  safeguard **664**
  keeper 753
esculent 298
escutcheon 550, 551
esophagus 350
esoteric 528
especial 79
especially 33
espionage 441, 461
esplanade 189
espouse *choose* 609
  marry 903
  -a cause *aid* 707
  co-operate 709
esprit de corps 709
espy 441
esquire 875
essay, *n.*
  experiment 463
  dissertation 595
ESSAY, *v.*
  endeavor **675**
essence *being* 1
  nature 5
  meaning 516
essential *real* 1
  intrinsic 5
  inherent 56
  important 642
establish *settle* **150**
  create 161
  place 184
  evidence **467**
  demonstrate 478
established 141
  church 983a
establishment
  fixture 150
  location 184
  shop 799
estate *condition* 7
  property **780**
esteem 928, 931
estimable 648
estimate *number* 85
  measure 466
  adjudge 480
estimation 480, **928**, 931
estrange *disjoin* 44
  alienate 889

  hate 898
estuary 343
etch 259, 558
etching 558
Eternal, The - 976
eternal 112
eternalize **112**
eternity 112
  an - 110
ether *space* 180
  vapor 334
  anaesthetic 376
ethereal 4, 820
etheric body 980a
ethical 926
ethics 926
ethnology 372
etiquette *custom* 613
  fashion 852
etymology 562
Eucharist 998
eulogist 935
eulogize **482**
eulogy 931
Eumenides 173, 900
euphemism *metaphor* 521
  phrase 566
  style 577
euphemist 935
euphony *melody* 413
  elegant style 578
euphuism 579, 855
eurythmic 542
eurythmics 242
evacuate *vacate* 185
  quit 293
  emit 297
evade *elude* 477
  not observe **773**
  exempt 927
evanescent 111
evangelical 983a, 985
Evangelists 985
evaporate *vanish* 4
  vaporize 336
  dry up **340**
evaporation
  vaporization 336
  dryness 340
evasion *sophistry* 477
  quirk 481
  concealment 528
  falsehood 544
  avoidance 623
evasive [see evasion]
eve 126
even, *adj.*
  uniform 16
  equal 27
  level 213
  parallel 216
  straight 246
  flat 251
  smooth 255
even, *v. level* 213
even, *adv.* 469

EVENING **126**
evenness
  [see even]
  symmetry 242
evensong 126, 990
event 151
  in the - of
  circumstance 8
  eventuality 151
  destiny 152
  supposition 514
  justified by the - 937
eventful **151**, 642
eventide 126
eventual 121
EVENTUALITY **151**
eventually 121, **151**, 154
eventuate 151
ever 16, 112
everlasting 112
evermore 16, 112
every 78, 138
  -other 138
everybody 78
every one 78
everywhere 180, 186
evict 297, 789
EVIDENCE **467**
evident *visible* 446
  certain **474**
  proved 478
  manifest 525
evidential 467
EVIL *harm* **619**
  badness 649
  -spirits 980
  -star 649
EVILDOER **913**, 949
evildoing 945
evil-minded 907, 945
evil speaking 908, 934
evince *show* **467**
  prove 478
evoke *cause* 153
  call upon 765
  excite 824
evolution 161, 311, **313**
evolutionary 313
evolve 161, **313**
ewer 191
exact, *adj. similar* **17**
  copy 21
  true **494**
  literal 516
exact, *v. require* 741
  claim 924, 926
exacting *discontented* 832
  fastidious 865
exaction 741
exactly *literally* 19
exactness [see exact]
  repetition 13
exaggerate *increase* 35
  overestimate 482
  magnify **549**
  misrepresent 555

F

fantastic *odd* 83
   absurd 497, 853
   imaginative 515
fantasy 515
far 196
   -and near 180
   -and wide 180, 196
farce *absurdity* **497, 853**
   drama 599
   wit 842
farcical 497, 853
fare, *n. food* 298
   price 812
fare, *v. do* 7
farewell 293
far-famed 31, 873
farfetched 10
far-flung 180
far-gone *much* 31
   insane 503
   spoiled 654
farinaceous 330
farm, *n. land* 780
farm, *v. till* 371
   rent 788
farmer 371
farmhouse 189
farsighted 441, 510
farther 196
   [see further]
farthing *coin* 800
fascinate *please* 829
   astonish 870
   love 897
   conjure 992
fascination [see fascinate]
   infatuation 825
   charm 829
   desire 870
FASHION, *n. state* 7
   custom 613
   mode 852
fashion, *v. form* 240
   create 976
fashionable 852
fast, *adj. joined* 43
   steadfast 150
   rapid 274
   intemperate 954
fast, *v.* **956**
fasten *join* 43
   restrain 751
fastening 45
fastidious 868
FASTIDIOUSNESS 868
FASTING *penance* 952
   abstinence **956**
fastness *defense* 717
fat, *n.* 356
fat, *adj. corpulent* 192
   bloated 194
   unctuous 355
fatal 361
fatalism 601
fatality 601
fate, *future* 152

   doom 360, 611
   necessity 601
fateful 601
Fates 601
father 166
   priest 996
Father, God the - 976
fatherland 189, **342**
fatherly 906
Fathers, the - 983
fathom, *n.* 466
fathom, *v. investigate* 461
   solve 462
   discover 480a
fathomless 208
FATIGUE 688
fatness [see fat]
fatten *expand* 194
   improve 658
   prosper 734
   -upon *feed* 298
fatuity 499
faucet 263, 295
fault *break* 70
   defect 304
   error 495
   imperfection 651
   failure 732
   at - *uncertain* 475
faultfinder 832
faultless *perfect* 650
   innocent 946
faulty *imperfect* 651
fauna 366
favor, *n. badge* 550
   indulgence 740
   gift 784
   partiality 923
favor, *v. resemble* 17
   aid 707
   permit 760
favorable *lucky* 134
   good 648
   aiding 707
   -to 709
FAVORITE **897, 899**
favoritism *friendship* 888
   wrong 923
fawn, *n. animal* 366
fawn, *adj. brown* 433
fawn, *v. cringe* 886
   flatter 933
fawning *servile* 746
fay 979
fealty *obedience* 743
   respect 928
FEAR 860
fearful *painful* 830
   timid 862
fearless 858, 861
feasible *possible* 470
feast *period* 138
   banquet 298, **957**
   revel 840
feat 680, 861
feather *class* 75

   tuft 256
   ornament 847
   -in one's cap
   honor 873
feathery 324
feature *character* 5
   form 240
   appearance 448
   lineament 234, 550
federal 712
federate 48
federation 709, 712
fee *pay* 809
   reward 973
feeble *weak* 160, **575**
   illogical 477
feeble-minded
   imbecile 499
   irresolute 605
FEEBLENESS *style* 575
feed *eat* 298
   fodder 370
   supply 637
feel *sense* 375
   touch 379
   respond 821
   -for 914
feeler *antenna* 379
   experiment 463
FEELING 821
feign 544, 546
feint 545
felicitate 896
felicitous *agreeing* 23
   happy 578
   pleasant 829
felicity 578, 827
feline, *n. cat* 366
feline, *adj. cunning* 702
fell, *v. destroy* 162
   lay flat 213
   lay low 308
fell, *adj.*
   dire 860
   malevolent 907
fellow *counterpart* 17
   equal 27
   companion 88
   man 373
   scholar 492
fellow countryman 890
fellow creature 372
fellow feeling
   friendship 888
   love 897
   benevolence 906
   pity 914
fellowship *friendship* 888
fellow student 541
felon 949, 975
felonious 945
felony 947
female **374**
feminine 374
femininity 374
fen 345

dismiss 756
excite 824
-at 716
-up *rage* 825
firearms 727
firebrand *fuel* 388
  instigator 615
fire bug 384, 949
fire-eater 863, 887
fire extinguisher 385
fireman *stoker* 268
  extinguisher 385
fireplace 386
fireproof 385
firm, *n. partnership* 712
  797
firm, *adj. fast* **43**
  steadfast 150
  hard 323
  resolute 604
firmness [*see* firm]
first 66
firstborn 124, 128
first-class *best* 648
first fruits 154
first-rate 648
firth 343
fiscal 800
fish, *n.* 366
fish, *v.* 622
  -for *pursue* 622
  desire 865
  -out *inquire* 461
  -up *raise* 307
fisherman 361
fissure 44, 198
fit, *n. paroxysm* **173**
  caprice 608
  disease 655
fit, *adj. expedient* 646
  right 922, 924
fit, *v. agree* 23
  -out *dress* 225
  prepare 673
fitful *irregular* 139
  changeable 149
fitness 23, 926
fitting 924
FIVE 98
fix, *n. dilemma* 7, 704
fix, *v. join* 43
  arrange 60
  establish 150
  place 184
fixed *intrinsic* 5
  durable 110
  permanent 141
  stable **150**
  -idea **825**
fixity 141, 265
fixture 150
fizz 353
fizzle 304, 353
flabby 324
flaccid 324, 326
flaccidity 326

flag, *n.* 550, 747
flag, *v. be weak* 160
  falter 275
  languish 683
  fatigue 688
flagon 191
flagrant *manifest* 525
  notorious 531
  atrocious 945
flagstaff 206
flake 204
flamboyant 577
flame *fire* 382
  light 420
  passion 824, 825
flank *side* 236
flap, *v. hang* 214
  move to and fro 315
flapper *girl* 129
flare *flash* 173
  glare 420
  -up *be excited* **824**
  get angry 900
flash *flare* 173
  fire 382
  light 420
flashy *gaudy* 428
  tawdry 851
flask 191
flat, *n. house* 191
  note 413
flat, *adj. low* 207
  horizontal 213
  even **251**
  vapid 391
  dull 843
flatiron 255
flatness 213, **251**
flatten 213, **251**
flatter *deceive* 545
  please 829
  adulate **933**
  -oneself 472, 858
FLATTERER 935
flattering 938
FLATTERY 933
flaunt *flourish* 873
  display 882
flaunting 882
flavor 390
flavoring 393
flaw *break* 70, 198
  error 495
  imperfection 651
  blemish 848
flaxen 436
flay 226
flea *insect* 366
fleck 440
fled *escaped* 671
flee 287
fleece, *n.* 223
fleece, *v. strip* 789
  rob 791
  surcharge 814
fleet, *n.* 273, 726

fleet, *adj. transient* 111
  swift 274
fleeting 111
flesh 364
flesh color 434
fleshy *of fruit* 354
flexible *pliant* 324
flicker *waver* 314
  flutter 315
  glimmer 420, 422
flier *aviator* 269a
  advertisement 531
flight *flying* 267
  swiftness 274
  departure 287, 293
  escape 671
flighty *inattentive* 458
  fanciful 515
flimsy *weak* 160
  slight 322
  soft 324
  sophistical 477
  trifling 643
finch *fear* 860, 862
fling *propel* 284
flippant *pert* 885
  discourteous 895
flirt 854, **902**
flirtation 902
flit *elapse* 109, 111
  move 264
  depart 293
  run away 623
flivver 272
float *navigate* **267**
  buoy up 305
  be light 320
flock *multitude* 72, 102
  laity 997
floe *ice* 383
flog 684, 972
flood 337, 348
floodgate 350
flood tide 206, 337
floor, *n.* 211
floor, *v. overthrow* 731
flop 315
flora 367, 369
floral 367
floriculture 371
florid 428, 434
  (*style*) 577
florist 371
flotation [*see* float]
flotilla 273, 726
flounce, *n. trimming* 231
flounce, *v. jump* 309
flounder *toss* 315
  be uncertain 475
  bungle 699
  fail **732**
flourish *brandish* 315
  vegetate 365, 367
  prosper 734
  flaunt 872
  boast 884

front 234
important **642**
forenoon 125
forensic 968
foreordain *destine* 152
forerun 62, 116, 280
forerunner 64, 673
foresee *expect* 121, 507
foreknow **510**
foreseen 871
foreshadow 511
foreshorten 201
FORESIGHT **510**
forest 367
forestall 132
forester 371
forestry 371
foretaste 510
foretell 511
forethought 510
forever 16, 112
forewarn *predict* 511
warn 668
foreword 64
forfeit, *n.* 974
forfeit, *v. lose* 776
forgather 72
forge *imitate* 19
swindle 791
-ahead 282
forger 792
forgery 21, 791
forget 506
forgetful 506
forgive 918
FORGIVENESS **918**
forgo [*see* forego]
forgotten 122, **506**
fork *divide* **91**
branch **244**
forlorn *dejected* 837
hopeless 859
deserted 893
-hope 859
FORM, *n. state* **7**
likeness 21
bench 215
shape 240
school class 541
manner 627
beauty 845
fashion 852
etiquette 882
form, *v. make up* 54
compose 56
order 58
arrange 60
convert 144
produce 161
shape **240**
organize 357

formalism 739, 988
formalist 82, 988
formality [*see* formal]
ceremony 882
formation
composition 54, 76
production 161
shape 240
formative *causal* 153
former *in order* 62
prior in time 116
past **122**
formerly 119, **122**
formidable 704
formless 241
formula 80, 697
formulate 590
forsake 624
forsaken 898
forswear *deny* 536
lie 544
refuse 764
fort 666, 717
forth 282
forthwith 132
fortification 717
fortify 159
fortitude *endurance* 826
courage 861
fortress 666, 717
fortuitous 6, 156, 621
fortuity 156
fortunate *opportune* 134
prosperous 734
fortune *destiny* 152, 601
chance 156
wealth 803
fortune teller 513
forum *place* 182
tribunal 966
forward, *adj. early* 132
front 234
onward **282**
active 682
insolent 885
uncourteous 895
forward, *v. transmit* 270
improve 658
help 707
fossil 40, **357**
fossilize 357
foster *aid* 707
excite 824
caress 902
foul, *adj. bad* 649
dirty 653
ugly 846
base 940
vicious 945
-play *wrong* 923
improbity 940
foul, *v. collide* 276
foul-mouthed 895
foulness [*see* foul]
foul-spoken 934
found *cause* 153

colonize 184
foundation *stability* 150
base 211
support 153, 215
founder, *n.* 164, 626
founder, *v. sink* **310**
fail 732
foundling 782, 893
fountain 153, 348
four 95
fourfold 96
Four Hundred 852, 875
fowl 366
fox *animal* 366
fox trot *dance* 840
fracas *noise* 404
discord 713
FRACTION *part* 51
less than one **100a**
fractional 51, 100a
fractious 901
fracture *disjunction* 44, 70
fissure 198
fragile *weak* 160
brittle 328
fragment *small part* 32
part 51, 100a
extract 596
fragmentary 100a
FRAGRANCE **400**
fragrant **400**
frail *weak* **160**
brittle 328
irresolute 605
failing 945
frailty [*see* frail]
frame, *n. condition* **7**
support 215
border 231
form 240
structure 329
frame, *v. make* 161
framework 215, 329
franchise *freedom* **748**
right 924
frangible 328
frank *open* 525
sincere 543
artless 703
frantic *violent* 173
delirious 503
excited 824
fraternal *brotherly* 11
leagued 712
friendly 888
-order 711
fraternity *brothers* 11
party 712
friends 888
fraternize *combine* 48, 709
sympathize 888
associate 892
fraud *deception* 545
impostor 548
fraudulent [*see* fraud]
fraught *full* 52

futile 645
futility 499, 645
FUTURE 117, **121,** 152

expected 507
-events **152**
-state *destiny* 152

heaven **981**
futurity **121**

G

gab 584
gabble **584**
gable *side* 236
gad 266
gag 403, 581
  muzzle 751
gage *measure* 466
gain *increase* 35
  prosper **618**
  acquisition **775**
  -time *protract* 110
  -upon *approach* 286
  pass 303
gainsay 536
gairish [*see garish*]
gait *walk* 264
galaxy *multitude* 102
  stars 318
gale 349
gall, *n. bitterness* 395
  insolence 885
gall, *v hurt* 378
  annoy 830
gallant *brave* 861
  courteous 894
gallantry 861, 902
gallery *room* 191
  passage 260
  spectators 444
galley *ship* 273
  cookroom 386
  printing 591
gallop 266, 274
gallows 361, 975
galore 102
galvanic *excitable* 825
galvanize 157
gamble 156, 621, 840
gambler 463, **621, 863**
gambling *chance* **621**
  rashness 863
gambol 309
game, *n. animal* 366
  amusement **840**
game, *adj. resolute* 604
game, *v. gamble* 621
gamester 840
gaming 156
gang 72, **712**
gangway 260
gaol [*see jail*]
gap 70, 198
gape, *yawn* **198,** 260
  stare 455
garage 191, 272
garb 225
garble *misinterpret* 523
  falsify **544**

garden 371
gardener 371
gargle 337
garish 851
garland *circle* 247
  fragrance 400
  ornament 847
garment 225
garner *store* 636
garnish 847
garret 210
garrison 717, 726
garrote 361
garrulity 584
garter *fastening* 45
gas *gaseity* 334
GASEITY 334
gaseous *unsubstantial* 4
  vaporous **334,** 336
gash *cut* 44
  internal 198
gasify 334
gasoline 356
gasp 688
gastronomy 957
gate 66, 232, 260
gather *collect* 72
  fold 258
  conclude 480
gathering *assemblage* 72
gaudy **428,** 851
gauge 466
gaunt 203
gauntlet *glove* 225
gawky *awkward* 699
  ugly 846
gay *bright* 428
  cheerful 836
  showy 882
gayety [*see gay*] 836
gaze 441
gazelle 366
gazette 531
gazetteer 86
gear *clothes* 225
  harness 633
gelatinous 352
gem *excellence* 648
  ornament 847
gendarme 726, 965
gender 75
genealogy 69
general, *adj. generic* 78
  habitual 613
general, *n.* 745
GENERALITY 78
generalize 78, 476
generally 16, 78

generalship 692, 722
generate 161, 168
generation
  consanguinity 11
  period 108
  production 161
generic 78
generosity *liberality* 816
  benevolence 906
  disinterestedness 942
generous [*see generosity*]
genesis *beginning* 66
  production 161
genial *cordial* 377
  warm 382
  willing 602
geniality 602
  [*see genial*]
genius *intellect* 450
  talent 498
  skill 698
  adept **700**
  familiar spirit 979
genteel 852
gentile *heterodox* 984
gentility 852
gentle *moderate* 174
  lenient 740
  meek 826
  courteous 894
  -breeding 894
gentlefolk 875
gentleman 373, 939
gentleness [*see gentle*]
gentry 875
genuflexion 308
genuine *true* 494
  good 648
genus 75
geography 183
geometry 466
germ *origin* 66
  cause 153
  stem 193
  -cell 357
germane *relevant* 23
germinate 194, 365
gesticulate 550
gesture 550
get *acquire* 775
  -back *regain* 775
  -down *descend* **306**
  -in 775
  -on *advance* 282
  prosper 734
gewgaw *trifle* 643
geyser 382, 384
ghastly *pale* 429

-nature 906
-offices *mediation* **724**
-taste 578, 850
-turn *kindness* **906**
-will *benevolence* **906**
-woman **948**
-word 931
make — *restore* **790**
  substantiate **924**
  vindicate **937**
good-for-**nothing** 158, **949**
good-**looking** 845
goodly *great* **31**
  handsome **845**
good-**natured** 906
GOODNESS 648
goods *effects* 780
  merchandise 798
goose *bird* 366
gore, *n. gusset* 43
  blood 361
gore, *v.* 260
gorge, *n. ravine* **198**
gorge, *v. glut* **869**
  gormandize 957
gorgeous *gay* **428**
  beautiful **845**
gorilla 366
gormandize **957**
gorse 367
gory *murderous* **361**
  red 434
gospel *doctrine* 484
  truth 494
Gospels **985**
gossamer 205
gossamery 320
gossip *news* 532
  babbler 584
  conversation 588
gouge 262
gourmand *glutton* 957
gourmet 868, 954a
govern 693, 737
governess 540
government **737, 745, 965**
governor *director* 694
  ruler 745
gown *dress* 225
grab *take* 789
grace *elegance* **845**
  polish 850
  pity 914
  forgiveness 918
  worship 990
graceful *elegant* 578
  beautiful **845**
  tasteful 850
graceless *inelegant* 579
  ugly 846
  impenitent 951
Graces **845**
gracious *courteous* **894**
  kind 906
gradation *degree* 26
  order 58

grade *degree* 26
  classify 60
  term 71
  obliquity 217
  ascent 305
  class 541
  crossing 219
gradual *degree* 26
  continuous 69
  slow 275
gradually 275
graduate, *n.* 492
graduate, *v. adjust* 23
  measure 26
  arrange 60
  initiate 537
graduation 537
graft, *v. insert* **300**
graft, *n. loot* 784
  improbity 940
grain *humor* 5
  tendency 176
  roughness 256
  texture 329
  powder 330
  against the-704
GRAMMAR 567
grammatical 567
gramophone 418
grand *august* 31
  important 642
  handsome **845**
  glorious 873
  ostentatious 882
  -*juror* 967
grandee 875
grandeur *greatness* 31
  repute 873
grandfather 130, 166
grandmother 166
grandness [see **grand**]
granny 30
grant *admit* 529
  permit 760
  consent 762
  confer 784
granular 330
graphic *intelligible* **518**
  vigorous 574
  descriptive 594
graphophone 418
grapnel 666
grapple 789
  -with
  -*a question* 461
  -*difficulties* 704
  oppose 708
  resist 719
grasp, *n. power* 737
grasp, *v. comprehend* 518
  retain 781
  -*at* 865
grasping *miserly* 819
  covetous 865
grass 367
  -*widow* 905

grassland **367**
grassplot **371**
grassy **367**
grate, *n. fireplace* **386**
grate, *v. rub* **330**
  -on the ear
    harsh sound **410**
grateful *enjoyable* **377**
  agreeable 829
  thankful **916**
gratification **377, 827**
gratify *permit* 760
  please 829
grating *lattice* 219
  stridor **410**
gratis 815
GRATITUDE 916
gratuitous
  inconsequent 477
  free 748, **815**
gratuity *gift* 784
grave, *n.* 363
grave, *adj. somber* **428**
  important 642
  distressing 830
  sad 837
graveclothes **363**
gravedigger **363**
gravestone 363
gravitate *descend* 306
  weigh 319
  -*towards* 176
GRAVITY *weight* **319**
  importance 642
  seriousness **837**
  [see **grave**]
GRAY *old* 128
  color 428, **432**
graybeard 130
graze *touch* 199, 379
  browse 298
  rub 331
grease *lubricate* 332
  oil 355, 356
greasy 355
great *much* **31**
  big 192
  glorious 873
greater 33
greatness 33
GREATNESS 31
greed *desire* 865
  gluttony 957
greedy 819, **865, 957**
Greek - deities **970**
GREEN, *n. lawn* 344, **371**
  color 435
green, *adj. new* **123**
  young 127
  sour 397
  credulous 486
  novice 701
  immature 674
greenhorn *novice* 493
  bungler 701
greenness **435**

hunchbacked 243
hundred 98
hunger 865
hungry 865, 956
hunt *pursuit* 286, 622
  inquiry 461
hunter *horse* 271
  pursuer 622
hurl 284
hurrah 838
hurricane *tempest* 349
hurry 274, 684
hurt, *n. physical pain* 378
  evil 619
hurt, *v.*
  cause (physical) pain 378
  maltreat 649
  injure 659, 907
  pain 830
  more frightened than-
    860
hurtful 649
hurtle 276
hurtless 648

husband *store* 636
  director 694
  spouse 903
husbandman 371
husbandry *agriculture* 371
  conduct 692
  economy 817
hush *moderate* 174
  stop 265
  silence 403
  taciturn 585
  -up *conceal* 528
  pacify 723
husk *covering* 223
husky *strong* 159
  hoarse 405, 581
hussar 726
hustings 728
hustle 682
hustler 682
hut 189
hybrid 41
hydroplane 273
hydroplaning 267

hygiene 656
hygienic 656
hygienics 670
Hymen 903
hymeneal 903
hymn *song* 415
  worship 990
hyperbole 549
hypercriticism 868
hyperphysical **450**
hyphen 45
hypnosis 376, 992*a*
hypnotic 683
hypnotism 683, 992*a*
hypnotize 615, 992
hypochondriac 837, 859
hypocrisy 544, 988
hypocrite 548
hypocritical **544, 988**
hypothesis 514
hypothetical 514
hysteria 992*a*
hysterical 821
hysterics 173

I

ice 383, 387
iceberg 383
ice chest 385
icon 554
iconoclasm 984
iconoclast 165
icy 383
IDEA *notion* **453**
ideal 515
idealism 450, 515
idealist 515
ideality 450, **515**
idealize 515
identical 13
identification 13
IDENTITY **13,** 27
idiocy 503
idiom 560, 566
idiosyncrasy 5, 79, 83
idiot 501
idiotic *foolish* 499
idle *trivial* 643
  slothful 683
idler 683
idol *favorite* 899
  fetich 991
idolater 991
IDOLATRY 991
idolize *love* 897
  idolatrize **991**
idyl 597
igneous 382
ignis fatuus 4, 443
ignite 384
ignition *calefaction* **384**
ignoble 876

ignominious 940
ignominy *shame* 874
  dishonor 940
IGNORAMUS **493**
IGNORANCE **491**
ignorant 491
ignore *neglect* 460
  not known 491
ill, *n. evil* 619
  badness 649
  sick 655
ill, *adj. bad* 649
  -usage 807
  -will 907, 921
ill-adapted 24
ill-advised *inexpedient* **647**
  unskillful **699**
ill-assorted 24
ill-behaved 895
ill-bred *vulgar* 851
  rude 895
ill-disposed 907
illegal 964
ILLEGALITY **964**
illegible 519
illegitimate **925,** 964
ill-fated 135, **735**
ill-favored 846
illiberal *stingy* 819
  selfish **943**
  bigoted 988
illicit 925, 964
illiteracy 491
illiterate **491,** 493
ill-made 243
ill-mannered **851**
ill-natured 907

illness 655
illogical **477**
ill-omened 135, 735
ill-proportioned 846
ill-spent 645
ill-starred 135
ill-timed 24, **135**
ill-treat 649, 907
ill-treatment 649
illuminant 420
illuminate *enlighten* 420
  comment 595
illumine *lighten* 420
  excite 824
ill-use 649
illusion
  fallacy of vision 443
  error 495
  deception **545**
illusive 4, **495**
illusory 4, 495
illustrate *exemplify* 82
  interpret 522
  represent 554
illustration 558
illustrious 873
image *likeness* 17
  appearance 448
  metaphor 521
imagery *fancy* 515
  metaphor 521
imaginable 470
imaginary 2, 4, 515
IMAGINATION 515
imaginative 515
imagine 515
imbecile, *adj. ignorant* 493

INEXPEDIENCE 647, 699
inexpedient 647
inexpensive 815
inexperience
  ignorance 491
  unskillfulness 699
inexpert 699
inexplicable 519
inexpressible *great* 31
  unintelligible 519
inexpressive 517
infallibility 474
infallible 474
infamous 940
infamy *shame* 874
  dishonor 940
infancy *beginning* 66
  youth 127
INFANT 129
infantile 129
infantine 129
infantry 726
infatuation *credulity* 486
  love 897
infect 659
infection 270, 655
infectious 270, **657**
infelicitous 24, 828
infelicity *misery* 828
infer *presume* 472
  deduce 480
inference 476, 480
inferior **34**, 207, **651**
INFERIORITY
  in degree 28, **34**
  in size 195
  imperfection 651
infernal *malevolent* 907
  wicked 945
infertility 169
infest 830
infidel 487, 989
infidelity *dishonor* 940
  irreligion 989
infiltrate *mix* 41
  interpenetrate 294
  ooze 295
infiltration 41, 302
infinite **105**, 180
infinite, the – 976
infinitely *great* 31
infinitesimal 32
INFINITY **105**
infirm *weak* 160
infirmary 662
infirmity 160, 655
inflame *give energy* 171
  render violent 173
  –*burn* 384
  excite 824
inflamed *red* 434
inflammatory *heated* 384
  [*see* inflame]
inflate *increase* 35

  expand 194
  blow 349
inflated *vain* **482**, 880
inflation [*see* inflate]
inflect 245
inflexible *straight* 246
  hard 323
  resolved 604
  obstinate 606
  stern 739
inflict 680, 739
infliction *adversity* 735
  mental pain 828, 830
  punishment 972
influence *cause* 153
  physical – **175**
  tendency 176
  inducement **615**
  instrumentality 631
  importance 642
  authority 737
  absence of – **175a**
influential **175**
influx 294
inform 527
  – *against accuse* 938
informal *irregular* 83
informality 83
informant 527, 938
INFORMATION
  knowledge 490
  communication **527**
infraction
  infringement 303
  disobedience 742
INFREQUENCY 103, **137**
infrequent 137
infringe *transgress* 303
  disobey 742
  not observe **773**
  violate **925**
infuriate *inflame* 173
  excite 824
  anger 900
infuse *mix* 41
  insert 300
  teach 537
infused 6
infusion [*see* infuse]
ingathering 72
ingenious *original* 515
  skillful 698
ingenuity 698
ingenuous *artless* 703
inglorious **374**
ingot 800
ingraft *join* 43
  insert 300
ingrafted 6
ingrain 329
ingrained *intrinsic* 5
  inborn 820
ingratiate 897
INGRATITUDE **917**
ingredient 56
INGRESS 294

inhabit 186, 188
INHABITANT 188
inhale *receive* 296
  breathe 349
inharmonious 15, 24
inhere in 56
inherence 5
inherent 56, 221, 820
inherit *acquire* 775
  possess 777
inheritance 777, 780
inherited 5
inheritor 779
inhibit *hinder* 706
  restrain 751
  prohibit 761
inhospitable 893
inhuman 907
inimical 14, 708
inimitable 20, 28, 650
iniquity 923, 945
initial 66
initiate *begin* 66
  receive 296
  teach 537
initiatory 296
inject 300, 337
injudicious 499, 863
injunction *command* 741
  prohibition 761
injure *harm* 619
  damage **659**
  spite 907
injurious 619, 923
injury *evil* 619
  badness 649
  damage **659**
injustice 923
inkling 514, 527
inland 221
inlay 300
inlet 66, **294**
  –*of the sea* 343
inmate 188, **221**
inmost 221
inn 189
innate 5, 221
inner 221
  – *reality* **1**
innkeeper 188, **637**
INNOCENCE **946**
innocent, *n. child* 167
  fool 501
innocent, *adj. good* 648
  artless 703
  guiltless **946**
innocuous *healthy* **656**
  innocent 946
innovation 20a, 123, 140
innuendo *hint* 527
innumerable 105
inobservance 773
inoculate *insert* 300
  influence **615**
inodorous 399
INODOROUSNESS 399

inoffensive *innocent* 946
inofficious 907
inoperative *powerless* 158
- *useless* 645
inopportune 135
inordinate 31, 641
inorganic 358
INORGANIZATION 358
inquest 461, 967
inquietude 828, 832
inquire 461
inquirer 461
inquiring 461
INQUIRY 461
inquisition *inquiry* 461
  severity 739
inquisitive 455
inroad *ingress* 294
  trespass 303
  invasion 716
insane 503
INSANITY 61, 503
insatiable 865
inscribe *write* 590
inscription 590
inscrutable 519
insect 193, 366
insecure 665
insensate *foolish* 499
  insane 503
INSENSIBILITY
  physical 376
  moral 823
insensible 376, 381
INSENSITIVENESS 823
inseparable *junction* 43
  coherence 46
insert *interpose* 228
  enter 294
  put in 300
  record 551
INSERTION 37, 228, 300
inside 221
-out 218
insidious *deceitful* 545
  cunning 702
insight 490
insignia 550
insignificance 32
insignificant 517, 643
insincere 544, 855
insinuate *intervene* 228
  insert 300
  hint 527
  blame 932
insipid *tasteless* 391
INSIPIDITY 391
insist *argue* 476
  command 741
-upon *affirm* 535
  be determined 604
insistence [see insist]
insaner 545
INSOLENCE 885
insolent *defiant* 715
  arrogant 885

disrespectful 929
insoluble *dense* 321
  unintelligible 519
insolvable 519
insolvency 808
insolvent 804, 806, 808
insomnia 682
inspect *look* 441
  attend to 457
inspector 694
inspiration *breathing* 349
  wisdom 498
  imagination 515
  motive 615
  revelation 985
inspire *breathe* 349
  prompt 615
  animate 824
  cheer 836
inspired 615
-writers 985
inspirit *incite* 615
  animate 824
  cheer 834
instability 149, 605
install 883, 883
installment *portion* 51
  payment 809
instance *example* 82
instant 113, 152
instantaneity 113
instantaneous 113
instanter 113
instate 883
instead 147
-of 755
instigate 615
instigator 615
instill *introduce* 296
  insert 300
  teach 537
instinct *intuition* 477
  impulse 601
instinctive 5, 477
institute, *n.* 542, 712
institute, *v. begin* 66
  cause 153
  produce 161
institution 542, 712
instruct *teach* 537
  advise 695
  order 741
instruction 537, 695
instructive 537
instructor 540
INSTRUMENT
  implement 633
  security 771
  musical - 417
  optical - 445
instrumental 631, 632
-music 415
INSTRUMENTALITY
  170, 631
insubordinate 742
insufferable 830, 867

INSUFFICIENCY 53, 640
insufficient 640
insufficiently 32
insular *apart* 44, 346
  narrow 481
  bigoted 988
insulate 44, 87, 346
  dull 843
insult *insolence* 885
  rudeness 895
  disrespect 929
insuperable 471
insupportable 830
insurance 768
insure *make sure* 474
  obtain security 771
insurgent 146, 742
insurmountable 471
insurrection 719, 742
insurrectionary 146
insusceptible 823
intact 52, 141
intaglio 22, 252
intangible 381
integer 50
integral 50
integrity *whole* 50, 52
  probity 939
integument 223
INTELLECT 450
  absence of - 405a
intellectual 450
INTELLIGENCE
  mind 450
  capacity 498
  news 532
intelligent 498
INTELLIGIBILITY 518
intelligible 518
INTEMPERANCE 954
  drunkenness 959
intemperate 954
intend 620
intense *great* 31
  energetic 171
intensify 35, 835
intensity *degree* 26
  greatness 31
  energy 171
intensive 35
intent, *adj.* 457
intent, *n. design* 620
INTENTION 620
intentional 620
inter 363
interact 12
interaction 170
intercalate 228
intercede *mediate* 724, 976
intercept *hinder* 706
  take 789
intercession 724, 976
  [see intercede]
intercessor 714
INTERCHANGE 12, 148
  barter 794

pray 990
involuntary **601**, 603
involution 248
  [see involve]
involve *include* 54
  evince 467
  mean 516
  imply **526**
involved 248
invulnerable 664
inward *intrinsic* 5
  inside 221
  incoming 294
inwrought 5
iota 32
IRASCIBILITY **901**
irate 900
ire 900
iridescent **440**
irksome *tiresome* 688
  difficult 704
iron *resolute* 604
ironclad, *adj.* 223
ironclad, *n.* 726
ironic [see irony]
irony *figure of speech* 521
  ridicule 856
irrational *illogical* 477
irreclaimable
  hopeless 859
  impenitent 951
irreconcilable 24
irrecoverable 122, 859
irregular, *adj. diverse* 16a

out of order 59
  fitful 70
  multiform 81
  against rule 83
  -in recurrence **139**
  distorted 243
irregular, *n. guerrilla* 722
  726
IRREGULARITY 16a, 59,
  139
IRRELATION 10
irrelevant *unrelated* **10**
  unaccordant 24
  unimportant 643
IRRELIGION **989**
irreligious **989**
irreparable 859
irrepressible *violent* 173
  excitable 825
irreproachable 946
irresistible *strong* 159
  impulsive 615
IRRESOLUTION 149,
  172, **605**
irrespective 10
irresponsible 605, 964
irretrievable 859
irreverence 929, 988
irrevocable *stable* 150
  necessary 601
  hopeless 859
irrigate 337
irriguous, 339
irritable *excitable* 825

irascible 901
irritate *excite* 173, **824**
  pain 830
  provoke 898, 900
irritation 900
  [see irritate]
  pain 828
Islam 976
ISLAND 44, **346**
isle 346
isolate *detach* 44, **87**
  seclude 893
isolated 10, 44
issue, *n. event* 151
  effect 154
  posterity 167
  inquiry 461
  denouement 729
issue, *v. distribute* 73
  depart 293
  emerge 295
  flow 348
  publish 531
  circulate 800
isthmus *connection* 45
  narrow 203
  land 342
itch *titillation* 380
itching 380
item 51
itemize 79
itinerant 266
itinerary *journey* **266**
  guidebook 527

J

jab 276
jabber 517
jacket **225**
jade, *n. horse* 271
jade, *v. fatigue* 688
jag 257
jagged 253, 256
jail 752
jailer *keeper* 753, 975
jam *squeeze* 43
jangle *harsh sound* 410
janitor 263
japan *coat* 223
jar *clash* 24
  vessel 191
  discord 713
jargon 497, 517, **563**
jaunt 266
jaunty *gay* 836
  pretty 845
javelin 727
jaws *eating* 298
jazz 415
jealous **920**
JEALOUSY **920**
jeer *flout* 929
Jehovah 976

jejune 391
  dull 843
jelly 352
jeopardy 665
jerk *start* 146
  throw 284
  pull 285
  agitate 315
jerky 315
jerry-built 160, 545
jersey *clothing* 225
jest *trifle* 643
  wit 842
jester 844
Jesus Christ 976
jet *stream* 348
jetty 666
jewel 847
jewelry **847**
jib, *n. front* 234
jib, *v. balk* 140
jibe *concur* 178
jig *dance* 840
jilt, *v.* 940
jimmy 633
jingle 408
jingo, *n. boaster* 884

jingo, *adj.* **885**
jingoism 884
jitney 272
job *business* 625
jobber *merchant* 797
jobbery 940
jobbing *barter* 794
  knavery 940
jockey *rider* 268
jocose 836, 842
jocular 636, 842
jocularity **842**
jocund *gay* 836
jog *push* 276
  shake 315
  -on
    trudge 266
    be slow 275
join *connect* **43**
  assemble 72
  adjoin 199
  arrive 272, 292
  unite 712
  -issue *quarrel* 713
joining 43
joint *junction* **43**
  accompanying 88

K

L

statute 697, 741
legality 963
law-abiding 743
lawful *permitted* 760
legal 924, 963
lawless *irregular* 83
mutinous 742
vicious 945
arbitrary 964
lawlessness 964
lawn 344
LAWSUIT 969
LAWYER 968
lax *incoherent* 47
soft 324
remiss 738
weak 945
laxative 652
LAXITY 47, 738
laxness 738, 773
lay, *n. ballad* 415
lay, *adj. secular* 997
lay, *v. place* 184
level 213
-aside *reject* 610
disuse 678
give up 782
-by *store* 636
disuse 678
-down the law 535
-to *attribute* 155
-up *store* 636
disuse 678
-waste 162
LAYER 204, 223
lay figure 4
layman 997
lazy *inactive* 683
lea 344
lead, *n. supremacy* 33
lead, *v. forerun* 62, 280
influence 175
tend 176
induce 615
direct 693
leaden *dim* 422
gray 432
leader *precursor* 64
dissertation 595
leadership 737
leading 280
leaf *part* 51
layer 204
plant 367
leafage 367
league, *n.* 712
league, *v. combine* 48
leak 295, 638
-out *disclose* 529
leakage [see leak]
leaky 295
lean *thin* 203
oblique 217
leaning *tendency* 176
willingness 602
desire 865

LEAP *jump* 309
leaping 309
learn 490, 539
learned 490, 539
LEARNER 492, 541
LEARNING 539
knowledge 490
lease, *n.* 780
lease, *v.* 787
leash *tie* 43
least 34
leave, *n. permission* 760
leave, *v. part company* 44
relinquish 624
bequeath 784
leaven, *n.* 153
leaven, *v. lighten* 320
leave-taking 293
leavings 40
lecture, *n.* 595
lecture, *v. teach* 537
speak 582
censure 932
lecturer *teacher* 540
speaker 582
ledge *shelf* 215
ledger 86
lee *side* 236
leer *stare* 441
lees 321
leeway 180
LEFT *residuary* 40
sinistral 239
left-handed 239
leg *support* 215
legacy 270, 784
legal *permitted* 760
legitimate 924
relating to law 963
LEGALITY 963
legalize 963
legation 755
legend 551, 594
legendary 515, 979
legerdemain 545
leggings 225
legible 518
legion *multitude* 102
legislation 963
legislator 694
legislature 72, 696
legitimate *permitted* 760
right 922
legal 924, 963
LEISURE *spare time* 685
opportunity 134
at one's - *late* 133
leisurely 133, 275
lend 787
lender 787
LENDING 787
LENGTH 200
lengthen *increase* 35
make long 200
lengthwise 200
lengthy *long* 200

diffuse 573
lenient *mild* 740
lenity 740
lens 445
Lent 956
lenten 956
leper *outcast* 892
less 34, 38
lessee 779
lessen - *in quantity or
degree* 36, 174
-*in size* 195
lesson *teaching* 537
warning 668
lessor 805
let *permit* 760
lend 787
-alone *avoid* 623
disuse 678
not do 681
-be *not do* 681
-fall *drop* 308
inform 527
speak 582
-go *neglect* 460
liberate 750
relinquish 782
-off *explode* 173
-out *lengthen* 200
disclose 529
liberate 750
lethal *deadly* 361
lethargy 683, 823
LETTER *character* 561
epistle 592
letter carrier 271, 534
letterpress 591
letters *knowledge* 490
language 560
levee *assemblage* 72
sociality 892
level, *adj. uniform* 16
equal 27
low 207
horizontal 213
flat 251
smooth 255
level, *v. destroy* 162
smooth 255
overturn 308
level-headed 826
lever 307, 633
leverage 175
LEVITY *lightness* 320
triviality 643
jocularity 836
levy *muster* 72
military 726
distrain 789
demand 812
lexicon 562
LIABILITY 177
debt 806
duty 926
liable 177
liar 548

libel *detraction* 934
   accusation 938
libelant 938
libeler 936
liberal *ample* 639
   expending 809
   generous 816
LIBERALITY 784, **816**
liberate *disjoin* 44
   deliver 672
   free 748, **750**
LIBERATION 750
LIBERTINE 962
liberty *freedom* 748
   permission 760
   right 924
library 593
lice 366
license *laxity* 738
   permission 760
   right 924
lid 223
lie, *n. untruth* 546
lie, *v. be situated* 183
   be present 186
   recline 213
   fib **544**
   -*in be* 1
lien *security* 771
   credit 805
lieutenant *officer* 745
   deputy 759
LIFE, *n. essence* 5
   events 151
   vitality **359**
   biography 594
   activity 682
   -*to come* 152
lifeboat 273
life-giving 168
lifeless *inert* 172
   dead 360
lifelike 17, 21
lifelong 110
lifetime 108
lift *raise* 307
ligament 45
ligature 45
LIGHT, *n. window* 260
   luminosity **420**
   luminary 423
   aspect 448
   knowledge 490
light, *adj. not heavy* **320**
   luminous 420
   trivial 643
   unburdened 705
   gay 836
light, *v. arrive* 292
   descend 306
   kindle 384
   illumine 420
light-colored **429**
lighten *illume* **420**
   facilitate 705
light-fingered 791

light-footed *fleet* 274
   active 682
lightheaded 503
lighthearted 836
lighthouse 550
lightning 420
like, *adj. similar* **17**
like, *v. relish* 394
   enjoy 827
   wish 865
   love 897
likely 472
likeness *similarity* 17, 21
   portrait 554
likewise 37
lilac *color* 437
Liliputian 193
limb *member* 51
limber *pliable* 324
LIMIT, *n. end* 67
   boundary **233**
limit, *v. circumscribe* 195, 229
   qualify 469
   restrain 751
limitation [*see* limit]
limited 32
limitless 105
limp, *adj. weak* 160
   supple 324
limp, *v.* 275
limpid 425, 570
line, *n. fastening* 45
   row 69
   lineage 69, 167
   length **200**
   direction **278**
   mark 550
   vocation 625
   armed force 726
line, *v.* **224**
lineage *kindred* 11
   series 69
   ancestry 122, 166
   posterity **167**
lineament *outline* 230
   appearance **448**
linear **200**
linen 225
liner 273
linger *delay* 133
   loiter 275, 281, 291
   -*on time* 106
lingo 563
lingua franca 563
lingual 560
linguistic 560
liniment *ointment* 356
LINING **224**
link, *n. tie* **9**
   vinculum 45
link, *v. connect* 43
lion *animal* 366
   celebrity 873
lion-hearted 861
lionize 873

lip 231
LIQUEFACTION 335
liquefy 335
liquid *fluid* **333**
liquidate 807
liquidity 333
liquor 298
lisp 583
LIST, *n. catalogue* 86
   leaning 217
   schedule 611
   arena 728
list, *v. classify* 69
   hear 418
   record 551
listen 418
listless *inactive* 683
   indifferent 866
literal *exact* **516**
literally **19**
literary 560
literature 490, **560**
lithe 324
litigant 938, 969
litigate 969
litigation 969
litigious 713
litter, *n. disorder* 59
litter, *v. derange* 61
   bed cattle 370
little -*in degree* 32
   -*in size* **193**
   bigoted 988
LITTLENESS 32, **193**
liturgy 998
live *exist* 1, **359**
   continue 141
   dwell 186
livelihood 803
liveliness **836** [*see* lively]
livelong 110
lively *frisky* 309
   keen 375
   active 682
   acute 821
   sensitive 822
   sprightly 836
livery 225
livid 431, 437
living *alive* **359**
   benefice 995
lizard 366
load, *n. quantity* **31**
   cargo **190**
   hindrance 706
   anxiety 828
load, *v. fill* 52
   lade 184, 190
loadstar [*see* lodestar]
loadstone *attraction* **288**
loaf *dawdle* 683
loafer 268, 927
loan 787
loath 603, 867
loathe *dislike* 867
   hate 898

relinquish 624
lure *charm* **288**
  deceive 545
  entice 615
lurid *dark* 421
  dim 422
lurk **526**, 528
luscious *savory* 394
luster **420**, 873

lustily *loud* 404
lustrous *shining* 420
lusty *strong* 159
  big 192
luxuriant *fertile* 168
  rank **365**
luxurious *pleasant* 377
  intemperate **954**
luxury

enjoyment 377, 827
  sensuality 954
lying 544
lymphatic *slow* 275
lynch 972
  -law 964
lyncher 975
lyric 597
lyrist 597

M

mace *weapon* 727
  scepter 747
machination 626, 702
machine *automobile* 272
  instrument 633
  party 712
machinery 633
machinist 690
mackintosh 225
mad *violent* 173
  insane 503
  excited 824
madam 374, 877
madden 824
MADMAN **504**
madness 503
Madonna 977
maelstrom *whirl* 312
magazine *book* 593
  store 636
magenta 434, 437
magic 992
magician 548, 994
magisterial 878, 885
magistrate 967
magnanimity 942
magnanimous **942**
magnate 875
magnet *attraction* 288
  desire 865
magnetic 157, 829
magnetism *power* 157
  influence 175
  attraction 288
magnetize 157, 288
magnificent *fine* 845
  grand 882
magnify *increase* 31, 35
  enlarge 194
  overrate 549
magnitude 25, 31, 192
maharajah 875
mahogany *color* 433
maid *girl* 129
  servant **746**
  spinster 904
maiden *first* 66
  girl 129
maidenly 374
mail *post* 270, **534**
  armor 717
maim *injure* 659

main, *n. ocean* 341
  land 342
  conduit 350
  in the - *principally* **642**
main, *adj. principal* 642
  -force *strength* 159
  violence 173
  compulsion 744
mainland 342
mainspring *cause* 153
mainstay *support* 215
  refuge 666
  hope 858
maintain *keep* 141
  continue 143
  sustain 170
  assert 535
  preserve 670
maintenance
  [*see* maintain]
majestic *grand* 31
  glorious 873
  stately 882
majesty 745, 873
major, *adj. greater* 33
major, *n. officer* 745
majority *superiority* 33
  plurality 100
  age 131
make *constitute* 54, 56
  render 144
  produce 161
  form 240
  complete 729
  compel 744
  create 976
  -believe **545**
  -good
  demonstrate 478
  -out *discover* 480*a*
  know 490
  interpret 522
  -up *complete* 52
maker *artificer* 690
Maker, the - 976
makeshift *substitute* 147
  excuse 617
make-up *composition* 54
makeweight 30
malady 655
malcontent **710**, **832**
male *man* **373**

MALEDICTION **908**
malefaction 947
malefactor 975
maleficent 907
MALEVOLENCE **907**
malevolent 907
malformation 243
malformed 241
malice *hate* 898
  spite 907
  bear - 907
malign, *adj. malevolent* 907
malign, *v. detract* 934
malignant 907
malignity 907
malinger 544
malison 908
malleable *soft* 324
maltreat *injure* **649**
  aggrieve **830**
  molest 907
mamma 166
mammal 366
Mammon 803
mammoth 192
MAN, *n. mankind* 372
  male **373**
  workman 690
  servant 746
  -of *action* **682**
man, *v. prepare* 673
  defend 717
manacle *fetter* 752
manage 175, 693
manageable *easy* **705**
management **692**, 693
manage *director* 694
mandate *requirement* 630
  command 741
mane 256
manege 370
maneuver *operation* 680
  stratagem 702
manful *strong* 159
  resolute 604
  brave 861
manger 191
mangle *smooth* 255
  injure 659
manhood 131, 861
mania *insanity* 503
  desire **865**

maniac 504
manifest, *n. list* 86
manifest, *adj. visible* 446
  obvious **525**
MANIFESTATION **525**
manifold 81
manipulate *handle* 379
  use 677
MANKIND **372**
manly *adolescent* 131
  strong **159**
  male 373
  brave 861
  upright 939
manna *food* 396
manner *kind* 75
  style 569
  way 627
  conduct 692
mannerism *special* 79
  affectation 855
manners *breeding* **852**
man-of-war 726
manse 1000
mansion 189
manslaughter 361
mantle, *n. dress* 225
mantle, *v. redden* 434
manual *schoolbook* 542
  book 593
  -labor 686
manufactory 691
manufacture 161
manufacturer 690
manuscript 590
many **102**
many-colored 428, 440
many-sided 81
map **554**
mar *deface* 241
  botch 699
maraud 791
marauder 792
marble *ball* 249
  sculpture 557
marbled 440
march *journey* 266
  music 415
  -with 199
marchioness 875
mare 271
margin *space* 180
  edge 231
marine, *n.* 269, 726
marine, *adj.* 273, 341
MARINER **269**
marital 903
maritime 267, 273, 241
mark, *n. degree* 26
  indication **550**
  object 620
  repute 873
mark, *v. take cognizance* 450
  attend to 457
  -out *choose* 609

  command 741
  -time *halt* 265
marked [*see* mark]
  special 79
market *consumer* 677
  mart 799
marksman 284, 700
maroon, *adj.* 433, 434
maroon, *v.* 782
marquis 875
marriage 43, **903**, 998
marriageable 131
married 903
  -man **903**
  -woman **903**
marrow 5, 221, 222
marry *combine* 43, 48
  wed **903**
MARSH **345**
marshal, *n. auxiliary* 711
  officer 745
marshal, *v.* 60
marshy 345
MART **799**
martial 722
martinet 739
martyr 828
  ascetic 955
martyrdom 828, 972
marvel *wonder* 870
  prodigy 872
marvelous 870
mascot 993
masculine *strong* **159**
  male 373
mash *soften* 324
  squash 352
mask *dress* 225
  shade 424
  concealment **528**
Masonic 712
masquerade 530, 840
masquerader **528**
Mass *worship* 990
  Eucharist 998
mass *quantity* 25
  much 31
  whole 50
  heap 72
  size 192
  density 321
massacre 361
massage 324, 331, 379
masses, the 876
masseur 662
massive *huge* 192
  heavy 319
  dense 321
mast 206
MASTER, *n. teacher* 540
  ruler **745**
  adept 700
  owner 779
master, *v. influence* 175
  understand 518
  learn 539

  succeed, conquer 731
  -of the situation 731
masterpiece 650, 698
mastery *success* **731**
masticate 298
mastiff 366
mat 215
match *fellow* 17
  copy 19
  equal **27**
  contest 720
  marriage 903
matchless *unequal* 28
  supreme 33
mate *similar* 17
  equal 27
  duality 89
  auxiliary 711
  friend 890
material, *n. substance* 316
  stuff 635
material, *adj.*
  important 642
materialism 984
materialist, 316, 984
MATERIALITY 3, **316**
materialize 316
MATERIALS **635**
materia medica 662
maternal 166
maternity, 166
mathematical *precise* 494
mathematician 85
mathematics 25
matin 125
matinée 892
matrimonial 903
matrimony 903, **998**
matrix *mold* 22
matron 374, 903
matronly 131
matter, *n. affair* 151
  material world **316**
  topic 454
  -of fact 1
matter, *v. signify* 642
matter-of-fact *prosaic* 576
  blunt **703**
  dull 843
mature, *adj. old* 124
  adolescent 131
  ripe 673
  -thought **451**
mature, *v. mellow* 144
  perfect 650
  prepare 673
maturity **124**
  [*see* mature]
maul *hurt* 649
maunder *prose* 573
  mumble 583
mausoleum 363
mauve 437
maw 191
MAXIM 80, **496**
maximum *supreme* 33

summit 210
mayor 745
maze *convolution* 248
  enigma 533
  difficulty 704
mazy 248
mead 344
meadow **344, 371**
meager *small* 32
  thin 203
  scanty 640
meal *repast* 298
MEAN, *n. average* **29**
  middle 68
mean, *adj. middle* 68
  contemptible 643
  stingy 819
  shabby 874
  ignoble 876
  selfish 943
mean, *v. signify* **516**
  intend 620
meander *wind* 248
  stroll 266
  deviate 279
MEANING **516**
meaningless 517
meanness *inferiority* 34
  [*see* mean]
MEANS *appliances* **632**
  wealth 803
meantime 106
meanwhile 106
measurable 466
measure, *n. extent* **25**
  degree 26
  proceeding 626
measure, *v.* 466
measureless 105
MEASUREMENT **25,**
  466
meat 298
mechanic 690
mechanical 601
  -powers **633**
mechanics 276
mechanism **633**
medal *record* 551
  palm 733
meddle **682**
meddlesome **682, 706**
medial 68
mediate *intervene* **631**
  intercede **724, 976**
MEDIATION
  instrumentality 631
  intercession **724**
  Christ 976
Mediator *Saviour* 976
mediator **724**
medical 662
medicine 662
  -man **548, 994**
medieval 124
mediocre *mean* 29
  ordinary 736

MEDIOCRITY
  average 29
  smallness 32
  -*of fortune* **736**
meditate *think* **450, 451**
meditation 451
medium, *n. mean* 29
  middle 68
  instrument 631
  seer 992a
medium, *adj.* **736**
medley *mixture* 41
  disorder 59
meed *reward* **973**
meek *gentle* **826**
  humble 879
meet, *v. agree* 23
  assemble 72
  converge 290
  fulfill 772
  -*with experience* 151
meeting [*see* meet]
  junction 43
  convergence 290
  arrival 292
  assembly 696
melancholy **830, 837**
mellow, *adj. old* 128
  soft 324, **428**
  ripe 673
mellow, *v.* 673
melodious 413
melodrama **599, 824**
melody 413
melt *vanish* 111
  convert 144
  liquefy 335
  heat 382
  fuse 384
  pity 914
  -*away cease to exist* 2
  vanish 4
melting pot **691**
member *part* 51
  component 56
  councilor 696
membrane 204
membranous 204
memento 505
memoir **594, 595**
memorable 151
memorandum 551
memorial *record* 551
memorialize 505
memorize 505
MEMORY 505
  fame 873
menace 909
ménage **692**
menagerie 370
mend *improve* **658**
  repair 660
mendacity 544
mendicancy 804
mendicant **800**
menial *servant* 746

mensuration 466
mental 450
  -*reservation* **528**
mentality 450
mention 527
menu 86, 298
mercantile **794**
mercenary, *n. soldier* **726**
  servant 746
mercenary, *adj.* **943**
MERCHANDISE 798
MERCHANT 797
merciful **914**
merciless 914a
mercurial *mobile* 264
  excitable 825
mercy *lenity* **740**
  pity 914
mere *simple* **32**
  trifling 643
meretricious 851
merge *combine* 48
  insert 300
  -*into become* 144
merit *goodness* **648**
  due 924
  virtue **944**
merited 924
meritorious 931
mermaid **979**
merriment **836, 840**
merry *cheerful* **836**
mesh 219
mesmerism **992**
mesmerist 992a
mess *mixture* 41
  disorder 59
  derangement 61
  difficulty 704
message *dispatch* **527**
  intelligence **532**
  command 741
MESSENGER
  traveler 268
  envoy **534**
Messiah **976**
messmate 890
metallic *harsh* **410**
metaphor *figure* **521**
metaphorical **521**
metaphysics 450
mete *measure* **466**
  distribute **786**
metempsychosis 140
meteoric *transient* 111
meteorology 338
meter *length* 200
  versification 597
METHOD *order* 58
  agency 170
  way **627**
methodical *orderly* 58
  regular **80, 138**
  businesslike 692
methodize 60
meticulous *exact* **494**

fastidious 868
metrical *measured* **466**
metropolis 189, 222
mettle *energy* 171
   spirit 820
   courage 861
mew *cry* 412
microbe 193
microscopic 32
mid 68
MID-COURSE **628**
midday 125
MIDDLE *-in degree* 29
   -in order **68**
   -in space 222
   -age **131**
middle-aged 131
middle-class 29
middleman 228
middling 736
midmost 68
midnight **126**
midriff 228
midshipman 269
midst 68
midsummer 125
midway 68
mien 448
might 31, 157
mighty *much* 31
   strong 157, 159
migrate 266
mild *moderate* 174
   warm 382
   lenient 740
   calm 826
MILDNESS **740**
mile 200
militant 722
military 722
   soldiers 726
   -authorities **745**
militia 726
milksop *coward* 862
milky 430
mill, *n.* 691
mill, *v. indent* 257
   pulverize 330
millennium *period* 108
   hope 858
millinery *ornament* 847
million 98, 876
millionaire 803
mimic *imitate* **19**
mince *step short* 275
   lisp 583
   affect 855
mind, *n. intellect* 450
   will 600
   purpose 620
   desire 865
   bear in - 505
mind, *v. attend to* 457
   dislike 867
mindful 457, 505
mine, *n.* 545, 636

mine, *v. sap* 162, 252, **717**
miner 252
   sapper and - 726
mineral 358
mineralize 358
mingle 41
miniature *small* 32
minimize 36
minimum 32, 34
minister *deputy* 759
   clergy 996
   -to help 707, 746
ministerial 995
ministration *aid* 707
ministry *direction* 693
   aid 707
   church 995
   clergy 996
minor *inferior* **34**
   infant 129
minority *few* 103
   youth 127
minster 1000
minstrel 416, 597
mint 22
minuend 38
minus *subtracted* 38
   absent 187
minute, *n. period* 108
   record 551
minute, *adj. -in degree* 32
   -in size 193
minutemen 726
minuteness **457**, 459
minutiae 32, **643**
miracle *exceptional* 83
   prodigy 872
miraculous *wonderful* 870
mirage 443
mire 653
mirror, *n. reflector* **445**
mirror, *v. imitate* 19
mirth 836
misadventure 735
misanthrope 911
MISANTHROPY **911**
misapply *misinterpret* 523
   misuse 679
   mismanage 699
misapprehend *mistake* 495
   misinterpret 523
misappropriate 679
misbehave 851, 945
misbehavior
   discourtesy 851, 895
   guilt 947
misbelief 485
misbeliever **984**
miscalculate 481, 495
miscall 565
miscarry 732
miscellany 41, **72, 78**
mischance *misfortune* 735
mischief 619
mischief-maker 913
mischievous 649

misconceive *mistake* 481,
   495
   misinterpret 523
misconception 481, 495
misconduct *guilt* 947
misconstrue 523
miscreant 949
misdate 115
misdeed 947
misdemeanor 947
misdoubt 485
misemploy 679
miser 819
miserable *unhappy* 828
miserably 32
miserly 819
misery **828**
misfire 732
misfortune *adversity* **735**
misgiving 485, 860
misguide 495, 538
misguided 699
mishap *failure* **732**
   misfortune 735
misinform 495, 538
misinstruct 538
MISINTERPRETATION
   523
MISJUDGMENT 481, 495
mislay *derange* 61
   lose 776
mislead **495**
mismanage 699
mismatch 15
misname 565
MISNOMER **565**
misplace *derange* 61
   displace 185
misprint 495
mispronounce 583
misproportioned *ugly* 846
misreckon 481
misrepresent
   misinterpret **523**
   misteach 538
   lie 544
   distort **555**
MISREPRESENTATION
   523, **555**
misrule 699, 738
miss, *n. girl* 129
   error 495
miss, *v. neglect* 460
   fail **732**
   lose 776
   want 865
misshapen *shapeless* **241**
   distorted 243
   ugly 846
missile **284, 727**
missing 2, 187
mission 625, 755
missionary 540
missive 592
misspell 523
misspend 818

O

oaf *fool* 501
oar *paddle* 267
   oarsman 269
oarsman 269
oasis 342
oath *assertion* 535
   bad language 908
obdurate *obstinate* 606
   impenitent 951
OBEDIENCE 743
obeisance *bow* 308
   submission 725
obelisk 206, 551
obesity 192
obey 743, 749
object, *n. thing* 3
   matter 316
   intention 620
object, *v.* disapprove 932
   -to *dislike* 867
objection 706, 932
objectionable
   inexpedient 647
   wrong 923
objective 6, **316**
OBJECTIVENESS 6
oblation 784, 990
obligation *necessity* 601
   promise 768
   debt 806
   duty 926
obligatory **926**
oblige *benefit* 707
   compel 744
obliging *helping* 707
   courteous 894
   kind 906
oblique 217
OBLIQUITY 217, 243
obliterate 2, 162, 552
OBLITERATION 552
OBLIVION 506
oblivious 506
obnoxious 898
obscure, *adj. dark* 421
   unseen 447
   unintelligible **519**
   ignoble 876
obscure, *v.* 874
OBSCURITY 421, 571
   [*see* obscure]
obsequies 363
obsequious 746, 886
OBSERVANCE *rule* 82
   habit 613
   fulfillment **772**
   duty **926**
observant 772
observation *attention* **457**
   assertion 535
observe 457, 772
observer *aviator* 269a

spectator 444
obsess *haunt* 860
obsession 481, 503, 992a
obsolete 122, 124, 851
obstacle 706
OBSTINACY 141, 606
obstinate 606
obstreperous 173
obstruct *close* 261
   hinder 706
obstructionist 710
obstructive **710**
obtain 775
obtainable 470
obtrude *interfere* 228
   insert 300
obtrusion 228, 706
obtrusive *interfering* 228
   rude 895
obtuse 254, 499
obverse 234
obviate 706
obvious *visible* 446
   manifest 525
occasion *juncture* 8
   opportunity 134
   cause 153
occasional **134**
occasionally 136
occult 526
occultism 526, 992a
occupancy 186, 777
occupant 188, 779
occupation *business* **625**
occupier *dweller* 188
   possessor 779
occupy 186, 777
   -oneself with 625
occur *exist* 1
   happen 151
   -to the mind 451
occurrence 151
OCEAN 341
oceanic 341
octave *eight* 98
   period 108
   poetry 597
octopus *mollusk* 366
   monster 913
ocular 441
odd *remaining* 40
   exceptional 83
   single 87
   insane 503
   ridiculous **853**
oddity 83, 503
odds *inequality* 28
   chance 156
   discord 713
ode 597
odious *disagreeable* 830
   hateful 898

odium *disgrace* 874
   hatred 898
ODOR 398
of course 478
offend *pain* 830
   anger 900
offense *attack* **716**
   anger 900
   guilt **947**
offensive *fetid* 401
   foul 653
   displeasing 830
   distasteful 867
   obnoxious 898
OFFER *volunteer* 602
   proposal 763
   give 784
offering *gift* **990**
offertory 990
offhand *careless* 460
   spontaneous 612
office 170, 625, 799
officer *director* **694**
   soldier 726
   commander 745
official, *n.* 694, 745
official, *adj. true* 494
   authoritative 737
officiate 625, 680
officious 682
offing *distance* 196
offset 30, 179
offshoot 39, 154
offspring *posterity* 167
often *repeated* 104
   frequent 136
ogle 441, 865
ogre 913, 980
OIL *grease* 355, **356**
oily *smooth* 255
   greasy 355
ointment 356, 662
old 124, 128
   -age 128
   -maid *spinster* 904
older 128
old-fashioned 851
oldness 124
oleaginous 355
oligarchy 737
olive *color* 435
olive branch
   pacification 723
olive green 435
OMEN 512
ominous *predicting* **511**
   hopeless 859
omission 53, 55, **773**
omit [*see* omission]
omitted *absent* 287
omnibus 272
omnipotence *power* 157

P

burden 706
pack, *v. locate* 184
package 72
packet 72
pact 769
pad *thicken* 194
  line 224
padding *lining* 224
  diffuseness 573
paddle, *n. oar* 267
paddle, *v. walk* 266
paean *rejoicing* 838
PAGAN 984
  -deities *979*
paganism **984**
page 746
pageant 448, 882
pagoda 206, 1000
pail 191
PAIN *physical* - **378**
  moral - **828**
  hurt 830
painful 378, 830
PAINFULNESS 830
painless 827
painstaking *active* 682
  laborious 686
paint *coat* 223
  color 428
  delineate **556**
  ornament 847
painter *rope* 45
  artist 559
PAINTING 556
pair, *n. similar* 17
  couple **89**
  horses 272
pair, *v. combine* 48
pajamas 225
pal *ally* 711
  chum 890
palace 189
palanquin 272
palatable *savory* 394
palate 390
palatial 882
palaver *colloquy* 588
  council 696
pale, *n. inclosure* 232
  limit 233
pale, *adj. dim* 422
  colorless 429
palfrey 271
paling *fence* 232
palisade 717
palisades *cliff* 212
pall, *v. weary* **841**
  satiate 869
palliate *moderate* 174
  relieve 834
  extenuate 937
palliative 174
pallid 429
pallor 429
palm *tree* 367
  trophy 733

laurel 877
  -off on 545
palmy *prosperous* 734
  joyous 836
palpable *material* 316
  obvious 446
  manifest 525
palpitate 315, 821
palter 605
paltry *small* 32
  unimportant **643**
  mean 940
pampas 344
pamper 954
pan 191
panacea 662
pandemonium 404, 414
pander to 933
panegyric 931
panel *list* 86
  partition 228
  jury 967
pang 378, 828
panic 860
panorama *view* 448
panoramic 78
pant *be hot* 382
  fatigue 688
  be excited 821
  pantomimist 599
pantheism 984
Pantheon *gods* 979
  temple 1000
pantomime 550
pantry 191
pap *pulp* 354
papa *father* 166
papacy **995**
papal 995
paper 590
  -money **800**
par 27
parable 521, 537
parabola *curve* 245
parade *procession* 69
  journey 266
  ostentation 882
Paradise 981
paradox *absurdity* 497
  difficulty 704
paradoxical *uncertain* 475
  absurd 497
paragon *perfect* 650
  glory 873
parallel, *n.* 17
parallel, *adj.* 17, 242
parallel, *v. imitate* 19
  agree 23
  equal **216**
PARALLELISM 17, 216,
  242
paralysis 158, 376, 823
paralyze 158, 376, 823
paramount *supreme* 33
parapet 717
paraphernalia 780

paraphrase *imitation* 19
  copy 21
  synonym 522
parasite *follower* **65**
  puppet 711
  flatterer 935
parasol 223
parboil 384
parcel *divide* 44
  group 72
parch 340, 382
parched 340
parchment 590
pardon 918
pardonable 937
pare *cut* 38
  reduce **195**
  peel 204
  divest 226
parent 166
parentage 11, 166
parental 166
parenthesis 198, 228
parenthetical 10, 228
pariah 876, 893
parish 181
parishioner 997
parity 27
park, *n.* 367, 840
park, *v.* 184
parlance 582
parley *talk* 588
  mediation 724
parliament 696
parliamentary 696
parlor 191
parochial *regional* 181
  narrow 481
parody *imitation* 19
  copy 21
  misrepresentation 555
  travesty 856
parole 768
  on - *restraint* 751
paroxysm *violence* 173
  agitation 315
  emotion 825
parquetry 440
parrot *imitation* 19
parrotism 19
parry *confute* 479
  avert 623
  defend 717
parsimonious **819**
PARSIMONY 819
parson 996
parsonage **1000**
PART, *n. portion* 51, **100a**
  role 599
  function 625
  duty 926
part, *v. divide* **44**
partake 778
partial *unequal* 28
  part 51
  fractional **100a**

misjudging 481
unjust 923
partiality desire 865
love 897
favor 923
partially 32, 51
participate co-operate 709
share 778
PARTICIPATION 778
participator 690
particle 32, 50, 193
particular, n. item 51
event 151
particular, adj. special 79
careful 494
exact 494
fastidious 868
particularize 79, 594
particularly 31, 33
particulars 79
parting 44
partisan follower 65
auxiliary 711
friend 890
partisanship 481, 709
partition divide 44
wall 228
partly 51
partner companion 88
auxiliary 711
partnership 88, 709
PARTY assemblage 72
person 372
association 712
sociality 892
-spirit warped judgment
481
co-operation 709
party-colored 428, 440
parvenu 123, 734, 876
paschal 998
pass, n. predicament 7
conjuncture 8
interval 198
defile 203
way 627
difficulty 704
thrust 716
pass, v. be superior 33
elapse 109, 122
happen 151
transfer 270
move through 302
vanish 449
an examination 648
away
cease 2, 142
-time 106
passable unimportant 643
imperfect 651
pretty 845
PASSAGE 302
conversion 144
corridor 191
opening 260
motion 264

navigation 267
transit 270
[see pass]
passenger 268
passing 31, 111
passion emotion 820
excitability 825
desire 865
love 897
anger 900
passionate impetuous 825
irascible 901
passionless 823
passive inert 172
obedient 743
passport 760
password 550
PAST 122
paste 352
pastime 840
pastor 996
pastoral 371
pastorate 995
pastry 396
pasture 232, 344
pat, adj. pertinent 23
pat, v. strike 276
patch change 140
blemish 848
-up restore 660
compromise 774
patchwork mixture 41
variegation 440
patent, n. 760
patent, adj. open 260
manifest 525
pater father 166
paternal father 166
benevolent 906
PATERNITY 166
paternoster 990
path direction 278
way 627
pathetic 830
pathless 180
pathos 821
patience
perseverance 604a
endurance 826
moderation 831
patient, n. 655
patriarch veteran 130
patriarchal 124, 166
patrician 875
patriot 910
patriotism 910
patrol safeguard 664
patrolman 664
patron auxiliary 711
customer 795
friend 890
patronage influence 175
aid 707
patronize aid 707
patter, n.
unmeaningness 517

talk 584
patter, v. strike 276
sound 407
pattern model 22
perfection 650
paucity 32, 103
Paul Pry 455
paunch 191, 250
pauper 640, 804
pause cessation 142
quiescence 265
pavement 211
pavilion 189
paving 211
paw handle 379
pawn 788
pawnbroker 787
pay, n. compensation 30
income 810
pay, v. defray 807
remunerate 973
PAYMENT 30, 807
remuneration 973
PEACE rest 265
silence 403
amity 721
peaceable 721
peaceful 174, 265, 721
peacemaker 714
peace offering 723
peace pipe 550
pea-coat 225
peak height 206
summit 33, 210
sharpness 253
peal 404, 407
pearly semitransparent 427
white 430
gray 432
peasant 876
peck, n. 31, 102
peculate 791
peculator 792
peculiar special 79
exceptional 83
peculiarity 5
peculiarly greatly 31
more 33
pecuniary 800
pedagogic 540
pedagogue scholar 492
teacher 450
pedal 633
pedant 492
pedantic 855
pedantry 491, 855
peddler 797
pedestal 215
pedestrain 268
pedigree 69, 166
pedlar [see peddler]
peek 441
peel pare 204
skin 223
uncover 226
peep chirp 412

improving 658
prohibit 761
PROHIBITION 761
   exclusion 55
prohibitionist 958
prohibitive 55, 761
project *bulge* **250**
   impel 284
   intend 620
   plan 626
projectile 284, 727
projecting 214, 250
projection 250, 283
projector *promoter* 626
proletariat 876
prolific 168
prolix 573
prolixity 573
prologue 64, 599
prolong *protract* 110
   delay 133
   continue 143
   lengthen 200
prolongation 117
   [*see* prolong]
prolonged 110
promenade *walk* 266
prominence
   [*see* prominent]
prominent *convex* **250**
   important 642
   eminent 873
promiscuous *mixed* 41
   indiscriminate 465a
PROMISE 768
promissory 768
   -note *security* **771**
promontory 206
promote *improve* 658
promoter *planner* 626
promotion 541, 658
prompt, *adj. early* 132
   active 682
prompt, *v. remind* 505
   tell 527
promulgate 531
prone *horizontal* **213**
   disposed **820**
proneness *tendency* 176
   disposition 820
prong 91
pronounce *judge* 480
   assert 535
   voice 580
   speak 582
pronounced 525
pronouncement 531
pronunciation 580
proof *test* 463
   demonstration 478
   printing 591
   -against 664
prop *support* 215
propaganda 673
propagate 161
propel 284

propensity *tendency* 176
   inclination 820
proper *individual* 79
   due 924
PROPERTY 342, **780**
prophecy 511
prophet *seer* 513
prophetic 511
prophylactic *healthful* 656
   preventive 706
propinquity 197
propitiate *pacify* 723
   mediate 724
   atone 952, 976
propitiator 724
propitiatory 952
propitious *timely* 134
   prosperous 734
   auspicious **858**
proportion *relation* 9
   symmetry 242
proportions *space* 180
   size 192
proposal 763, 765
propose *suggest* 514
   offer 763
   offer marriage 902
proposition *supposition* 454
   reasoning 476
   project 626
   offer 763
propound *suggest* **514**
proprietor 779
propriety *agreement* 23
   elegance 578
   fashion 852
   duty **926**
PROPULSION 284
propulsive 284
prorogue 133
prosaic *sober* 576
   dull 843
proscribe *interdict* 761
   curse 908
   condemn 971
PROSE, *n.* **598**
prose, *v.* 584
prosecute *pursue* 622
   arraign 969
prosecutor 938
proselyte 144, 607
prospect *destiny* 152
   futurity **121**
   view 448
   expectation **507**
prospector 463
prospective 120, **507**
prospectus *list* 86
   scheme 626
prosper 618, **734**
PROSPERITY 734
prostrate, *adj. powerless* 158
   low 207
   horizontal 213, 251

   submissive 725
   dejected 837
prostrate, *v. depress* 308
prostration
   [*see* prostrate]
   sickness 655
prosy *weary* 841
   dull 843
protect 664
protection *influence* 175
   defense 717
protectionist 751
protective 717
protector 664, 717, 912
protectorate 737
protest *dissent* **489**
   deprecate 766
   not pay **808**
protestant
   dissenting 489
protoplasm 357
PROTOTYPE 22
protract *prolong* 110
   delay 133
   lengthen 200
protrude 250
protrusive 250
protuberance 250
proud *dignified* 873
   lofty **878**
prove *arithmetic* 85
   demonstrate 478
   indicate 550
proverb 496
proverbial 490
provide *furnish* **637**
provided 8, **469**
providence 976
provident *careful* 459
   prepared 673
providential
   opportune 134
   fortunate 734
province *department* 75
   region 181
   office 625
provincial *rural* 189
   narrow 481
provincialism 563
PROVISION *food* 298
   supply **637**
   preparation 673
provisional
   conditional 8, **770**
   temporary 111
   contingent 134
proviso 469, 770
provocation 900
provoke *cause* 153
   excite 824
   vex 830
   anger 900
prow 234
prowess 861
prowl *walk* 266
   lurk 528

proximity 197
proxy 634, 755
prude 855
prudent *careful* 459
  wise 498
prudery *affectation* 855
  fastidiousness 868
prudish 855, 868
prune *take away* 38
  lop 201, 371
  repair 658
pry *look* 441
  search 455
  inquire 461
psalm 415, 990
pseudo *simulated* 17
  imitative 19
pseudonym 565
psychic 992a
PSYCHICAL 450, 992a
  -research 450, **992a**
psychoanalysis 450, 992a
psychological 450, 537
psychology 450
psychometry 450
psychotherapy **992a**
public 531
  -spirit 910
PUBLICATION 531
  production **161**
publicity 531
publish 531
publisher 593
pucker *fold* 258
puddle 343
pudgy 201
puerile *boyish* 129
  trifling 643
puff, *n. wind* 349
puff, *v. inflate* 194
  pant 688
  boast 883
  praise 931
  -up 880
puffy 194
pug *short* 201
  dog 366
pugnacity 720, 901
pull, *n. superiority* 33
  influence 175, 631
  attraction 288
pull, *v. row* 267
  draw 285
  -out 301
pulp 354
PULPINESS 354
pulpit 542

pulsate 138, 314
pulsation 138
pulse 314
pulverable **330**
pulverize 330
pump, *n. shoe* 225
  conduit 350
pump, *v. inflate* 349
  inquire 461
pun **497**, 842
punch, *n. mold* 22
  perforator 262
punch, *v. perforate* 262
  strike 276, 716
punctilio 882
punctilious *exact* 494
  observant 772
  formal 882
  scrupulous 939
punctual *early* 132
  periodical 138
  observant 772
punctuation **142**
puncture 260
pung 272
PUNGENCY 392
pungent 392
punish 972
PUNISHMENT 972
punitive 972
punt, *n. boat* 273
punt, *v. row* 267
puny 193
pup 366
pupil *student* 492, 541
puppet *cat's-paw* **711**
puppy *dog* 366
  fop 854
purblind 443
PURCHASE *support* 215
  buying **795**
purchaser 795
pure *simple* 42
  true 494
  clean 652
  virtuous 944
  innocent 946
  chaste 960
  devout 987
purely 31
purgatory 982
purge *cleanse* 652
  atone 952
purify 652
purist *style* **578**
puritan *prude* 855
  ascetic 955

puritanical *severe* 739
  prudish 855
  ascetic 955
PURITY 960
  [*see* pure]
purl 348, 405
purlieus 197
purloin 791
PURPLE *violet* 437
purport *meaning* 516
purpose 600, 620
  on - 620
purposeless 621
purr 405, 412
purse, *n.* 802
purse, *v. contract* 195
purse-proud 878
purser 801
pursuance 143
pursue
  follow 117, 281
  continue 143
  aim 622
pursuer 281, **622**
PURSUIT 281, 286, 622
purvey 637
push *impel* 276
  propel 284
pussy-foot *cautious* 864
put *place* 184
  invest 787
  -about *turn back* 283
  go round 311
  -down *destroy* 162
  record 551
  conquer 731
  -in motion **264**
  -off *delay* **133**
  -on *clothe* 225
  -out *extinguish* 385
  darken 421
  -together *join* 43
  -up *assemble* 72
  locate 184
  -up with *bear* 826
putrefy 49
putrid 653
puttee 225
putter *dally* 683
puzzle, *n.* 533
puzzle, *v. perplex* 475
puzzled **475**
puzzling 519
pygmy 193
pyramid 206
python *snake* 366

Q

quack *impostor* 548
quackery 855
quadrangle 95
quadrilateral 95

QUADRISECTION 97
quadroon 41
quadruped 366
QUADRUPLICATION 96

quaff 298
quagmire *marsh* 345
quail *fear* 860
  flinch 862

R

rostrum 542
rosy 434, 845
rosy-cheeked 845
rot *decay* 49, 659
  putrefy 653
rotate 312
ROTATION 138, **312**
rotten *foul* 653
  decayed 659
rotound 249
ROTUNDITY 249
rough, *n. bully* 876, 887
  913
rough, *adj. violent* 173
  shapeless 241
  uneven 256
  harsh 410
  churlish 895
roughen 256
roughhew 240
roughly *nearly* 197
ROUGHNESS 256
  [see rough]
roughrider 268
round, *n. series* 69
  revolution 138
round, *adj.*
  circular 247, 249
round, *v.* 245, 311
roundabout 279, 311
roundup 72
rouse *stimulate* 615
  excite 502
rout, *n. tumult* 315
rout, *v. overcome* 731
  discomfit 732
route 266, 627
routine *order* 58, 138
  custom 613
  business 625
rove *travel* 266
rover 268
roving 266
row, *n. series* 69
  violence 173
  street 189
row, *v.* 267
rowdy, *n. blusterer* 887
rowdyism 851
rower 269

royal 737
royalist 737
royalty 737
rub, *n. difficulty* 704
rub, *v.* **331**, 379, 662
rubber *overshoe* 225
  eraser 331
  masseur 662
rubbish 645
rube 876
Rubicon *limit* 233
rubicund 434
rubric *liturgy* 998
ruby *red* 434
ruck 876
rudder 273, 633, 693
ruddy *red* 434
rude *violent* 173
  shapeless 241
  vulgar 851
  unciviI 895
rudiment *beginning* 66
  cause 153
rudimentary 66
rudiments 66
rue *regret* 833
rueful *regretful* 833
  sad 837
ruff 225
ruffian *rough* 876, 913
  scoundrel 949
ruffianism 907
ruffle *disorder* 59
  derange 61
  roughen 256
  fold 258
  excite 824, 825
  irritate 898
rug *covering* 223
rugged
  shapeless 241
  rough 256
ruin *destruction* 162
  failure 732
  adversity 735
ruined 732, 859
ruinous *painful* 830
ruins *remains* 40
RULE *average* 29

regularity 80
influence 175
measure 466
decide 480
custom 613
precept 697
reign 737
ruler 737, 745
rumble 407
ruminate *chew* 298
  think 451
rummage 461
rumor 532
rump *remainder* 40
rumple *disorder* 59
  derange 61
  roughen 256
rumpus *confusion* 59
run, *n. rule* 29
  repetition 104
  motion 264
  speed 274
  habit 613
run, *v. flow* 109, 264, 348
  race 274
-down *depreciate* 932
runaway 623
rung 215
runner *branch* 51
  courier 268, 271, 534
rupture 44
  quarrel 713
rural 189, **371**
ruse *cunning* 702
rush *crowd* 72
  dash 274
  haste 684
russet 433
rust *decay* 659
rustic, *n.* 876
rustic, *adj.* 189, **371**
rustle 405, 407
rusty *decayed* 659
  unskillful 699
rut *regularity* 80
  furrow 259
ruthless
  savage 907
  revengeful 919

S

Sabbath 687
saber 727
sable 431
sabotage 162
saccharin 396
sacerdotal 995
sack, *n. bag* 191
  dismissal 756
sack, *v. plunder* 791
sacrament 998
SACRED *holy* 976

-writings **986**
sacrifice, *n. worship* 990
  holocaust **991**
sacrifice, *v.* 162
sacrilege 988
sad *dull* 428
  painful 830
  dejected 837
sadden 830, 837
saddle 155, 293
  -with *quarter on* 184

sadness 837
safe, *n.* 530
safe, *adj. secure* **664**
safeguard 717
SAFETY 664
sag *curve* 245
sagacious 498
SAGE, *n.* **500**
sage, *adj.* 498
said *repeated* 104
sail *navigate* 267

spurious *deceptive* 545
  illegitimate 925
spurn *reject* 610
  disdain 866, **930**
spurt *sprint* 274
  gush 348
spy, *n.* 444, 664
spy, *v.* 441
squabble 713
squad 72, 726
squadron 726
squalid *dirty* 653
  unsightly 846
squall, *n.* 349
squall, *v. cry* 411
squalor 653
squander 776, **818**
square, *n. four* **95**
  place 182
  rectangle 244
  measure 466
square, *adj. just* 922, 924
square, *v. compensate* 30
squash *quell* 162
  pulp 354
squat, *v.* 184, 308
squat, *adj. short* 201
  thick 202
  low 207
squatter 188
squaw 374
squeak *cry* 411
squeal 411
squeamish *sick* 655
  fastidious 868
squeeze *contract* 195
  condense 321
  -out *extract* **301**
squib *lampoon* 856
squint, *n.* 443
squint, *v. look* 441
squire *attendant* 746
  gentry 875
squirm 315
squirt *eject* 297
stab *pierce* 260
  kill 361
  pain 649
STABILITY 16, 141, **150**
stabilize 150
stable, *n.* 189, 370
stable, *adj.*
  permanent 141, 150
  quiescent 265
stack 72
staff *support* 215
  music 413
  council 696
  cast 712
  weapon 727
  retinue 746
stag *deer* 366
  male 373
  socialty 892
stage *degree* 26
  term 71

time 106
  position 183
  platform 215
  drama 599
stagecoach 272
stagger, *n. be slow* 275
  reel 314, 821
  shake belief 485
  startle 508
  astonish 870
stagnant *inert* 172
  quiescent 265
  unprogressive **659**
stagnate 265
stagnation *inertness* 172
  quiescence 265
staid *grave* 837
stain *color* 223, 428
  blemish 848
  disgrace 874
stainless *clean* 652
  honorable **939**
  innocent 946
staircase 305
stairs 305
stairway 305
stake *wager* 621
  security 771
  execution 975
stale *old* 124
  insipid 391
stalk, *n.* 215
stalk, *v. walk* 266
  chase 622
stall *cot* 189
  booth 799
stalwart *strong* 159
stamina *strength* 159
STAMMERING **583**
stamp *character* 7
  prototype 22
  kind 75
  form 240
  mark 550
  security 771
  -out *extinguish* 385
stampede 860
stanch, *adj.* 939
stanch, *v.* 348
stand, *n. time* 106
  support 215
  quiescence 265
stand, *v. resist* 719
  brook 821
  endure 826
  -by *near* 197
  aid 707
  -fast 141
  -for *indicate* 550
standard *model* 22
  degree 26
  average 29
  rule 80
  measure 466
  flag 550
  perfection 650

standardize 58
standing *footing* 8
  degree 26
  permanence 141
  situation 183
  rank 873
standpatter 150
standpoint 441
stanza 597
staple, *n. whole* 50
  material 635
staple, *adj.* 794
star *luminary* 318, **423**
  actor 599
  glory 873
  -s and stripes 550
starched *proud* 878
stare *look* 441
  gape 455
  wonder 870
stark *very* 31
  sheer 32
starry 318
start *begin* 66
  arise 151
  move **284**
  depart 293
  leap 309
  offer 763
  fear 860
  wonder 870
startle *doubt* 485
  stagger 508
  fear 860
  amaze 870
starvation [*see* starve]
  insufficiency 640
  fasting 956
starve *be poor* 804
  stint 819
  fast 956
STATE, *n. condition* **7**
  position 71
  realm 372, 780
  government **737**
state, *v.* 535
statehouse 966
stately *grand* 873
  pompous 882
statement 535
stateroom 191
statesman **694**
statesmanship **693**
static 319
statics 159, 319
station, *n. degree* 26
  term 71
  situation 183
  journey **266**
  prison 752
  rank 873
station, *v. locate* 184
stationary 265
statistical 85
statistics 85, 86
statue 554

discourteous 895
sulky 901a
SULLENNESS 901a
sully *dirty* 653
dishonor 874
sultan 745
sultry 382
sum *total* 50
number 84
money 800
-up *reckon* 37, 85
discriminate 465
review 596
summarize 201, 596
summary, *n.* 596
summary, *adj. transient* 111
short 201
concise 572
summer 125, 382
SUMMIT 33, 210
summon *command* 741
indict 969
summons 741, 969
sumptuous 882
sun **318, 423**
-god **423**
sunbeam 420
sunburnt 433
Sunday 687
sunder 44
sundial 114
sundry 102
sunny *warm* 382
cheerful 836
sunrise 125
sunset 126
sunshade 223
sunshine 420
sup *feed* 298
superabound **641**
superannuated 128, 158
superb 845
supercilious *proud* **878**
insolent 885
scornful 930
superficial *shallow* 209
extrinsic 220
ignorant 491
superficies 220
superfluity 40, 641
superfluous **641**
superhuman *godlike* 976
superintend **693**
superintendent 694
superior, *n. head* 694
superior, *adj. greater* **33**
high 206
SUPERIORITY 33
superlative 33
superman 33
supernatural 976, 980a
supersede *substitute* 147
relinquish **782**
superstition 486
superstitious 486, 984

supervene *succeed* 117
supervise 693
supervision **693**
supervisor 694
supervisory 693
supine *flat* 213, 251
sluggish 462
supplant 147
supple *soft* 324
supplement 37, 39
suppliant 767
supplicate *beg* 765
supplies 707
supply *store* **636**
provide 637
give 784
-deficiencies 52
SUPPORT, *n. footing* 175
foundation **215**
support, *v. perform* 170
evidence 467
escort 664
aid 707
feel 821
endure 826
supporter **215**
suppose 472, **514**
SUPPOSITION 514
suppress *destroy* 162
conceal 528
restrain 751
suppression [*see suppress*]
supremacy **33**
supreme *superior* **33**
highest 210
ruling 737
Supreme Being 976
sure *certain* 474
safe 664
sure-footed *careful* 459
skillful 698
cautious 864
sureness [*see sure*]
surety *certainty* 474
safety 664
sponsor 771
surf 348, 353
surface 220
surfeit *redundance* 641
satiety 869
surge *swarm* 72
swell 305
wave 348
surgeon 662
surgery 662
surly *gruff* 895
sullen 901a
surmise 514
surmount *tower* 206
overtop 210
ascend 305
surname 564
surpass *be superior* **33**
go beyond 303
outshine **873**
surplus *remainder* **40**

redundance 33, **641**
surprise, *n.* 508
surprise, *v.*
take unawares **674**
wonder 870
surrender *submit* **725**
relinquish 782
surreptitious
furtive 528
deceptive 545
surround 227
surrounding **227**
surroundings 227
surveillance *care* 459
direction 693
survey *view* 441
measure 466
surveyor 466
survive *remain* 40, 141
outlast 110
susceptibility
tendency 176
sensibility 375
impressibility 822
suspect *doubt* 485, 920
suppose 514
suspend *defer* 133
discontinue 142
hang **214**
suspense *cessation* 142
uncertainty 475
irresolution 605
suspension *lateness* 133
cessation 142
hanging 214
suspicion *doubt* 485
supposition 514
fear 860
jealousy 920
suspicious 485
sustain *continue* **143**
strengthen 159
support 215
aid 707
endure 821
sustenance 298, **707**
sustentation [*see sustain*]
swab *dry* 340
clean 652
swag *booty* 793
swagger, *n. pride* 878
swagger, *v. boast* 884
bluster 885
swain *man* 373
rustic 876
lover 897
swallow, *n.* 366
swallow, *v. gulp* **296**
be credulous 486
brook 826
swamp, *n. marsh* 345
swamp, *v.* 162
swampy 345
swan 366
swap *exchange* 148
barter 794

narrative 594
talebearer 532
talent 698
talented 698
talisman 747, 993
talk, n. rumor 532
  conversation 588
talk, v. speak 582
  -over confer 588
  persuade 615
  -together 588
talkative 584
talkativeness 584
talker 584, 588
tall lanky 200
  high 206
tally, n. numeration 85
  list 86
  sign 550
tally, v. agree 23
tame, adj. inert 172
  feeble 575
  mild 826
tame, v. moderate 174
  domesticate 370
  subjugate 749
tamper with alter 140
  injure 659
  meddle 682
tan color 433
tandem 200, 272
tang taste 390
  pungency 392
tangent 379
tangible material 316
  touching 379
  exact 494
tangle 61, 219
tangled disordered 59
tank reservoir 636
tankard 191
tantalize balk 509
  desire 865
tantamount equal 27
  synonymous 516
tap, n. faucet 263
tap, v. open 260
  hit 276
  let out 297
  sound 406
tape string 205
taper, n. candle 423
taper, adj. 203
taper, v. narrow 203
tapestry 847
tar sailor 269
  pitch 356a
tardy dilatory 133
  slow 275
target 620
tariff 812
tarnish soil 653
  deface 848
  disgrace 874
tarry remain 110
  delay 133

continue 141
  stay 265
tart, n. pastry 396
tart, adj. acid 397
  rude 895
tartan 440
task, n. lesson 537
  business 625
  fatigue 688
task, v. put to use 677
taskmaster 694
TASTE sapidity 390
  elegance 578
  good taste 850
tasteful 850
tasteless insipid 391
tasty 390, 394
tatters 225
tattle 588
tattler newsmonger 532
  gossip 588
tattoo, n. drumming 407
tattoo, v. 440
taunt, n. disrespect 929
taunt, v. reproach 938
taut 43
tautology repetition 104
  diffuse style 573
tavern 189
tawdry 851
tawny brown 433
  yellow 436
tax, n. impost 812
tax, v. inquire 461
  employ 677
  fatigue 688
  command 741
  accuse 938
taxable 812
taxation 812
taxi 272
taxicab 272
tea 892
teach 537
teachable 539
TEACHER 540, 673
TEACHING 537
team conveyance 272
  crew 712
  representative 759
tear, n. weeping 839
tear, v. separate 44
  move rapidly 274
  rave 825
tease annoy 830
technical 186
  -school 542
technicality 697
technique 698
Te Deum 990
tedious 841
tedium 841
teem produce 168
  abound 639
teeter 314
teetotalism 958

telegram 532
telegraph, n. 534, 550
telegraph, v. 527, 531
telepathic 450
telepathy 450, 992a
telephone, n. 418, 534
telephone, v. 527
telephony 402
telescope, n. 445
telescope, v. collide 276
telescopic 196
tell count 85
  influence 175
  inform 527
  speak 582
  describe 594
teller treasurer 801
telltale 532
temerity 863
temper, n. nature 5, 820
  state 7
  pliability 324
  irascibility 901
temper, v. moderate 174
  qualify 469
temperament
  nature 5, 820
  tendency 176
TEMPERANCE 174, 953
temperate moderate 174
  abstemious 953, 959
temperature 382
tempest 315, 349
TEMPLE 1000
temporal transient 111
temporary 111
temporize protract 110
  defer 133
  cunning 702
tempt entice 615
  desire 865
temptation 615, 865
tempter 615
  Satan 978
ten 98
tenable 664
tenacious 327, 861
TENACITY
  toughness 327
  coherence 46
  resolution 604
  obstinacy 606
  retention 781
tenancy 777
tenant, n. 188, 779
tenant, v. 186
tend conduce 176
  aid 707
  serve 746
  -stock 370
  -toward 278
TENDENCY 176
tender, n. boat 273
tender, adj. soft 324
  affectionate 897
  benevolent 906

traveling 266
traverse 302
travesty *imitate* 19
  copy 21
  misinterpret 523
  burlesque 555
trawl 285
trawler 273
tray 191
treacherous 907, 940
treachery *deception* 545
  dishonesty 940
tread 266
treason *revolt* 742
  treachery 940
treasure 636, 800
TREASURER 801
TREASURY 802
treat
  physical pleasure **377**
  bargain 769
  delight 827, 829
  -of 595
treatise 593, 595
treatment
  conduct 692
  medical - 662
treaty 769
treble *three* 93
  shrill 410
tree *pedigree* 166
  plant 367
trellis 219
tremble *totter* 160
  shake 315
  fear 860
tremendous *painful* 830
  fearful 860
tremor *agitation* 315
  emotion 821
  fear 860
tremulous *changeable* 149
  agitated 315
  fearful 860
trench *dike* 232
  furrow 259
  defense 717
trenchant *energetic* 171
  concise 572
  vigorous 574
  keen 821
trend *tendency* 176
  bend 278
trepidation *agitation* 315
  excitement 825
  fear 860
trespass *go beyond* 303
  sin 945
tress 256
triad 92
trial *inquiry* 461
  experiment 463
  essay 675
  adversity 735
  suffering 828
  lawsuit 969

TRIALITY 92
triangle 92
tribe *race* 11
  assemblage 72
  clan 166
tribulation 828
TRIBUNAL 966
tributary, *n. river* 348
tributary, *adj. giving* 784
tribute *donation* 784
  money paid 809
  reward 973
trick *deception* **545**
  habit 613
  contrivance 626
  skill 698
  artifice 702
trickery *deceit* 545
trickiness [see tricky]
trickle 295, 348
trickster *deceiver* **548**
  schemer 702
tricky *deceiving* 545
  cunning 702
tricycle 272
trident 92
trifle, *n.* 32, **643**
trifle, *v. neglect* 460
  fool 499
  -with *deceive* 545
trifler 460
trifling 643
trig 845
trill *sound* 407
  sing 416
trim, *n. state* 7
trim, *adj. neat* 652, **845**
trim, *v. adjust* 27
  form 240
  lie 544
  waver 605
  change sides **607**
  adorn 847
trimmer
  timeserver 607, 943
trimming *border* 231
  ornament 847
trinity 92
Trinity, Holy - **976**
trinket 643, 847
trio 92
trip, *n. jaunt* 266
  fall 306
trip, *v. run* 274
  leap 309
  mistake **495**
triple 93
triplet 92
TRIPLICATION 93
triplicity 92
TRISECTION 94
trite *known* 490
  conventional 613
triumph *succeed* **731**
  exult 838
trivial *unmeaning* 517

trifling 643
triviality 643
troglodyte 893
troll, *n.* 980
troll, *v.* 416
trolley 272
  -car 272
troop *assemblage* **72**
  soldiers 726
trooper 726
troopship 726
trope 521
TROPHY 733
tropical 382
trot *run* 266, 274
  translation 522
troth 768
troubadour 597
trouble, *n. turmoil* 59
  exertion 686
  adversity 735
  care 828
trouble, *v. derange* 61
troublesome
  inexpedient 647
  difficult 704
  painful 830
troublous 59
trough 259
trounce *censure* 932
  punish 972
trousers 225
trousseau 225
trow 484
truant 187, 623
truce 133, 142, **723**
truck *vehicle* 272
  barter 794
truckman 268
truculent 907
trudge *walk* 266
  move slowly 175
true *real* 1
  straight 246
  accurate 494
  veracious 543
  faithful 772
trueness [see true]
truism *axiom* 496
truly *really* **494**
trumpery 517, **643**
truncheon 727
trundle 284
trunk *stem* 166
  box 191
truss *bundle* 72
  support 215
trust, *n. belief* 484
  firm 712
  property 780
  credit 805
  hope 858
trust, *v.* 484, 858
trustee 758, 801
trustful 484, 486
trustworthy *certain* **474**

U

neutralize 179
not do 681
undoing ruin 735
undone ruined **732**
hopeless **859**
undoubted 474
undress, n. clothes 225
undress, v. strip 226
undue **925**
undulate wave 248
oscillate 314
undutiful 945
undying perpetual 143
unearth eject 297
disinter 363
discover 480a
unearthly immaterial 317
spectral 980a
heavenly 981
uneasy **828**
uneatable 867
uneducated ignorant 491
unprepared 674
unemotional 823
unemployed not used 678
inactive 681
unemployment 681
unenterprising 864
unequal **28**, 139
unequaled 28, 33
unequivocal great 31
sure 474
unerring certain 474
exact 494
unessential extrinsic 6
irrelative 10
unimportant 643
uneven diverse 16a
unequal 28
irregular 139
rough 256
unexampled
unimitated 20
unexpected sudden 132
unforeseen **508**
unfading 112
unfailing 141
unfair unjust 923
unfaithful 940
unfamiliar 83
unfashionable
unconventional 614
vulgar 851
unfasten 44
unfathomable infinite 105
deep 208
mysterious 519
unfavorable
out of season 135
obstructive **708**
adverse 735
unfeeling insensible 376
numb 381
heartless 823
unfeigned 543
unfetter release **750**

unfettered free 748
unfinished 53, 730
unfit inappropriate 24
impotence 158
inexpedient 647
unskillful 699
wrong 923
undue 925
unfitness inaptitude **24**
[see unfit]
unfitted not prepared **674**
unfledged young 127
callow 674
unflinching
persevering 604a
brave 861
unfold evolve 313
interpret 522
disclose 529
UNFOLDMENT **313**
unforeseen
unexpected 508
unforgiving 919
unfortunate ill-timed 135
unlucky **735**
unhappy **828**
unfriendly opposed 708
hostile **889**
malevolent 907
unfruitful 169
unfurl unfold 313
ungainly 846
ungenerous stingy 819
selfish 943
ungentlemanly rude 895
dishonorable 940
ungodly 989
ungovernable violent 173
passionate 825
ungraceful 846
ungracious uncivil 895
unfriendly 907
ungrammatical **568**
ungrateful **917**
ungrounded
unsubstantial 4
unguarded neglected 460
spontaneous 612
unguilty 946
unhallowed 988
unhappy unlucky 735
wretched 828
dejected 837
UNHEALTHINESS **657**
unhealthy ill 655
unwholesome **657**
unheard of
exceptional 83
improbable 473
ignorant 491
unhinge derange 61
make powerless 158
unholy 989
unhonored 874
unhurt 670
uniform. n. 225, 550

uniform, adj.
homogeneous **16**
regular 80
dress 225
symmetrical 242
UNIFORMITY 16, 80, 242
unimitated **20**
UNIMPORTANCE **643**
unimportant **643**
unimpressed 838
uninhabitable 187
uninhabited 187, **893**
uninitiated ignorant 491
unskillful 699
uninjured healthy **654**
preserved 670
unintellectual 452
unintelligent **499**
UNINTELLIGIBILITY
519
unintelligible **519**
unintentional 601
undesigned 621
uninteresting 841
uninterrupted
continuous 69
perpetual 112
uninvited **893**
uninviting 830
union agreement 23
junction 43
combination 48
party 712
concord 714
unique dissimilar 18
original 20
unequal 28
exceptional 83
alone 87
unison agreement 23
melody 413
unit 87
unite join 43, **712**
combine 48
compose 56
assemble 72
concur 178
converge 290
United States courts **966**
UNITY identity 13
uniformity 16
agreement 23
completeness 52
oneness 87
concord 714
universal **78**
-language 560
universe 318
university 542
unjust wrong 923
unjustifiable wrong **923**
inexcusable 938
wicked **945**
unkempt rough 256
vulgar 851
unkind 907

vacillating 605
precarious 665
unsteady *mutable* 149
unstable **665**
unstrung 160
unsubstantial
immaterial 2, 317
baseless 4
weak 160
erroneous 495
imaginary 515
UNSUBSTANTIALITY 4
unsuccess 732
unsuccessful **732**
unsuitable
incongruous 24
inexpedient 647
unsullied *clean* 652
honorable 939
unsurpassed 33
unsusceptible 826
unsuspecting *hopeful* 858
unsuspicious
believing 486
artless 703
hopeful 858
unswerving *straight* 246
direct 278
unsymmetrical
shapeless 241
distorted 243
unsympathetic 24
unsystematic 59, 139
untaught *ignorant* 491
untrained **674**
unteachable 499
untenable *illogical* 477
undefended **725**
unthankful 917
unthinkable 471
unthinking
unconsidered 452
involuntary 601
unthrifty 818
untidy 59, 653
untie *liberate* 750
until 106
UNTIMELINESS 135
untimely 135
untold *countless* 105
secret 528
untoward *ill-timed* 135
unprosperous 735
unpleasant 830
untrained
unaccustomed 614
unprepared 674
unskilled 699
untried 123
untrue *erroneous* 495
false **546**
untrustworthy
uncertain 475
erroneous 495
dishonorable 940
UNTRUTH 546

untruthfulness 544
untwine 313
untwist 313
unusual **83**
unutterable *great* 31
wonderful 870
unvalued *underrated* 483
unvaried *uniform* 16
monotonous 104
unvarying 16
unveil *disclose* 529
unventilated 261
unwarlike 862
unwarranted 925
unwary *neglectful* **460**
unwatchful 460
unwelcome
disagreeable 830
unsocial 893
unwholesome 657
unwieldy *large* **192**
heavy 319
cumbersome 647
unwilling 603
UNWILLINGNESS 603
unwind *evolve* 313
unwise 499
unwished 866
unwomanly 373
unwonted *unimitated* 20
unusual 83
unaccustomed 614
unworldly 939
unworthy *shameful* 874
vicious 945
unwritten *old* 124
spoken 582
unyielding
tough 323
obstinate 606
resisting 719
up 206, **305**
upbraid 932
upgrade 305
upgrowth 305
upheaval 146, 307
uphill *steep* **217**
laborious 686
uphold *continue* 143
support 215
evidence 467
aid 707
upholder **711**
upland, *n.* 180
upland, *adj.* **206**
uplands 206
uplift *raise* 206, 307
improve 658
upper 206
-hand *influence* 175
success 731
-ten thousand 875
uppermost 210
upraise 206, 307
uprear 206, 307
upright *vertical* 212

straight 246
honest **939**
uprising 146, 742
uproar *disorder* 59
violence 173
noise 404
uproarious 173
uproot *extract* 301
upset *destroy* 162
invert 218
throw down 308
disconcert 874
upshot *result* 154
upstart **123, 734, 876**
upturn 210, 218
upward 305
urban **189**
urbane 894
urchin *child* 129, 167
urge *impel* 276
incite 615
hasten 684
beg 765
urgency *need* 865
[see urgent]
urgent
pressing **630**
important 642
importunate 765
usage
custom 613
use 677
USE *habit* 613
utility 644
employ **677**
useful
instrumental 176, 633
serviceable **644, 677,** 746
useless
unproductive 169
futile **645**
user **677**
usher, *n.*
attendant 263, 746
usher, *v.*
receive 296
-in *begin* 66
herald 116
announce 511
usual *ordinary* 82
customary 613
usurer *lender* 787
miser 819
usurp *assume* 739
violate 925
usurpation [see usurp]
usurper 706, **925**
usury 806
utensil 633
utilitarian *useful* 677
UTILITY 644
utilize 677
utmost 33
utopia 858
utter, *v. distribute* 73
disclose 529

publish 531
speak 580, 582

money 800
utterance [*see* utter]

utterly *completely* 52
uttermost 31

V

vacancy [*see* vacant]
vacant *void* 4
  absent 187
  thoughtless **452**
  scanty 640
vacate *displace* **185**
  depart 293
  resign 757
vacation 687
vacillate *change* 149
  waver 605
vacuity 452
vacuous *unsubstantial* 14
  absent 187
vacuum 2, 187, 197
vagabond 268, **876**
vagary *fantasy* 515
  whim 608
vagrant, *n.* 268
vagrant, *adj.* 266
vague *unsubstantial* 4
  uncertain **475**
  obscure 519
vagueness **475**
vain *unprofitable* 645
  conceited **880**
vainglorious 878
vale 252
valediction *adieu* 293
valedictorian 293
valedictory 293, 582
valentine 902
valet 746
valiant 861
valid *powerful* 157
  true **494**
valise 191
valley 252
valor 861
valuable *useful* 644
  good 648
value, *n. color* 428
  importance **642**
  utility 644
  goodness 648
  price 812
value, *v.* 466, 480
valve 263, 350
vampire *evildoer* 913
  demon 980
van *front* **234**
  wagon 272
vandal 165, 913
vandalism 851
vane 349
vanguard 234
vanish *disappear* 2, **4**, 449
  be transient 111
VANITY *conceit* **880**

vanquish 731
vapid *insipid* 391
vapor *gas* 334, 353
VAPORIZATION 336
vaporize **336**
vaporizer 336
vaporous *unsubstantial* 4
  volatile 336
variable *irregular* 120
  changeable 140, 149
variance *difference* 15
  disagreement 24
  discord **713**
VARIATION
  difference 15
  dissimilarity 18
  diverseness **20a**
  chance 140
varied 15, 16a
variegated 428, 440
VARIEGATION 440
variety *difference* 15
  class 75
  multiformity 81
various *different* 15
  many 102
varnish, *n. resin* 356a
varnish, *v. overlay* 223
  decorate 847
vary *differ* 15, 18, **20a**
  change 140
  fluctuate 149
vase 191
vassal 746
vast *great* 31
  spacious 180
  large 192
vat 191
vaudeville 599
vault, *n. cellar* 191, 207
  dome 250
  tomb 363
vault, *v. leap* 309
vaunt 884
veer *change* 140
  deviate 279
  go back 283
VEGETABLE 367
  -*kingdom* 367
  -*life* 365
vegetarian 953
vegetarianism 298
vegetate *exist* 1
  grow **365**, 367
VEGETATION 365
  inaction 681
vegetative **365**, 367
vehemence *violence* 173
  emotion 825

vehement *violent* 173, **825**
  impassioned 574
VEHICLE *carriage* **272**
  instrument 631
veil, *n. covering* 225, 424
veil, *v. shade* **424**
  conceal 528
vein *conduit* 350
  humor 602, 820
  mine 636
VELOCITY
  rate of motion 264
  swiftness **274**
vender 796
vendetta 919
vendor 796
veneer 204, **223**
venerable *old* 124, 128
  sage **500**
  respected 928
veneration *respect* 928
  piety 987
vengeance 919
venom *bane* 663
  malignity 907
venomous *bad* 649
  poisonous 657
  rude 895
  maleficent 907
vent, *n. opening* 260, 295
vent, *v. disclose* 529
ventilate *air* 338
  discuss 595
venture, *n. chance* 621
  trial 675
  undertaking 676
venture, *v. experiment* 463
  presume 472
  risk 665
  try 675
  dare 861
venturesome
  enterprising 676
  brave 861
  rash 863
VERACITY *494*, **543**
veranda 191
verbal 562
verbatim 19, 516
verbiage 562, 573
verbosity *words* **562**
  diffuseness 573
verdant *green* 435
verdict *opinion* 480
  lawsuit 969
verdure *vegetation* 367
  green 435
verge, *n. edge* 231
  limit 233

verge, v. tend 176
  incline 278
  -upon 197
verification test 463
  warrant 771
verify test 463
  evidence 467
  find out 480a
verily truly 494
veritable 1, 494
verity 1, 494
vermin 366
vernacular, n. 560
vernacular, adj. native 188
  lingual 560
vernal 125
versatile changeable 149
verse poetry 597
versify 597
version 522
vertical 212, 246
VERTICALITY 212
vertigo 503
very 31
vesper 126
vespers 126
vessel receptacle 191
  ship 273
vest 225
vested fixed 150
  legal 963
vestibule entrance 66
vestige 551
vestment dress 225
  canonicals 999
vestry council 696
vesture 225
VETERAN old 130
  adept 700
  warrior 726
veterinarian 370
veto 761
vex 830, 898
vexation 830, 900
vexatious 830
vexed question 704
viaduct 627
vial 191
viands 298
vibrate 149, 314
vibration 138, 314, 408
vicar 996
vicarage 1000
vicarious substitute 147
VICE 945
vice-president 759
viceroy governor 745
vicinity 227
vicious 945
vicissitude 149
victim dupe 547
  sufferer 828
  culprit 975
victimize deceive 545
  injure 649
victor 731

victoria carriage 272
victory 731
victual provide 637
victuals 298
videlicet namely 79, 522
vie 648
view, n. sight 441
  appearance 448
  opinion 453, 484
  landscape 556
view, v. 441, 457
viewpoint 441, 453
vigil care 459
vigilance care 459
  activity 682
vigilant 459, 864
VIGOR energy 157, 171
  strength 159
  style 574
  resolution 604
  health 654
vigorous 574
vile hateful 649
  disgraceful 874
  plebeian 876
  dishonorable 940
  vicious 945
vilification 908
vilify censure 932
  detract 934
villa 189
village 189
villager 188
villain actor 599
  rascal 949
villainous evil 649
  wicked 945
villainy 940
vim 171, 682
VINCULUM 45
vindicate justify 937
VINDICATION 937
vindictive revengeful 919
vine 367
violate disobey 742
  infringe 925
  fail 927
VIOLENCE 173, 825
violent 173, 825
violet 437
violinist 416
viper snake 366, 913
virago 901
Virgin, The 977
virgin, n. girl 129
  spinster 904
  good woman 948, 960
virgin, adj. new 123
virile adolescent 131
  strong 159
  manly 373
virtu 847
virtual inexistent 2
  unsubstantial 5
virtually 5
VIRTUE power 157

  goodness 944
  purity 960
virtuous 944, 960
virulence noxiousness 649
  anger 900
  malevolence 907
virulent energetic 171
  corrupting 649, 657
  angry 900
  malevolent 907
virus disease 655
visage front 234
  appearance 448
viscount 875
VISIBILITY 446
visible 446
vision phantom 4, 980a
  sight 441
  dream 515
visionary inexistent 2
  unsubstantial 4
  imaginary 515
visit arrival 292
  sociality 892
visitation disease 655
  adversity 735
  suffering 828
visitor friend 890
vista glade 260
  sight 441
  appearance 448
visual 441
  -organ 441
visualize 220
vital living 359
  important 642
  -principle 1
vitality stability 150
  strength 159
  life 359
vitalize 359
vitiate deteriorate 659
vituperate 908, 932
vituperation 908, 932
vivacious active 682
  sensitive 822
  cheerful 836
vivid bright 420, 428
  graphic 518
vivification 359
vivify 359
vixen fox 366
  shrew 901
viz. [see videlicet]
vizor 530
vocabulary 86, 562
vocal musical 415
  oral 580
  -music 415
vocalist 416
vocalize 562, 580
vocation business 625
vociferate 411
vociferation loudness 404
  cry 411
  voice 580

W

FOREIGN WORDS AND PHRASES

à bas. [F.] Down, down with.

ab initio. [L.] From the beginning.

à bon marché. [F.] Cheap; a good bargain.

ab origine. [L.] From the origin.

ab ovo. [L.] From the egg; from the beginning.

à cheval. [F.] On horseback.

addenda. [L.] Things to be added; list of additions.

ad finem. [L.] To the end.

ad hoc. [L.] To or with respect to this (object); said of a body elected or appointed for a definite work (as a school board for education).

ad infinitum. [L.] To infinity.

ad libitum. [L.] At pleasure; as much as one pleases.

ad nauseam. [L.] To the point of disgust or satiety.

ad rem. [L.] To the purpose; to the point.

adsum. [L.] I am present; here!

ad valorem. [L.] According to the value.

advocatus diaboli. [L.] Devil's advocate; a person chosen to dispute before the papal court the claims of a candidate for canonization.

æquo animo. [L.] With an equable mind; with equanimity.

ære perennius. [L.] More lasting than brass (or bronze).

affaire d'amour. [F.] A love affair.

affaire de cœur. [F.] An affair of the heart.

affaire d'honneur. [F.] An affair of honor; a duel.

a fortiori. [L.] With stronger reason.

Agnus Dei. [L.] Lamb of God.

à haute voix. [F.] Aloud.

à la belle étoile. [F.] Under the stars; in the open air.

à la bonne heure. [F.] In good time; very well.

à la carte. [F.] According to the bill of fare.

à la mode. [F.] According to the custom (or fashion).

al fresco. [It.] In the open air.

alter ego. [L.] Another self.

amende honorable. [F.] Satisfactory apology; reparation.

à merveille. [F.] Admirably; marvelously.

amour propre. [F.] Self-love; vanity.

ancien régime. [F.] The former order of things.

anglice. [NL.] In the English language or fashion.

anguis in herba. [L.] A snake in the grass; an unsuspected danger.

anno urbis conditæ. [L.] In the year (or from the time) of the founded city (Rome).

à outrance. [F.] To the utmost.

aperçu. [F.] A general sketch or survey.

à perte de vue. [F.] Till beyond one's view.

à peu près. [F.] Nearly.

à pied. [F.] On foot.

a posteriori. [L.] From effect to cause; empirical.

a priori. [L.] From cause to effect; presumptive.

arbiter elegantiarum. [L.] A judge or supreme authority in matters of taste.

arcana imperii. [L.] State secrets.

argumentum ad hominem. [L.] An argument to the individual man; *i.e.*, to his interests and prejudices.

arrière-pensée. [F.] Mental reservation.

ars est celare artem. [L.] It is true art to conceal art.

ars longa, vita brevis. [L.] Art is long, life is short.

au contraire. [F.] On the contrary.

au courant. [F.] Fully acquainted with matters.

au désespoir. [F.] In despair.

au fait. [F.] Well acquainted with; expert.

au fond. [F.] At bottom.

au reste. [F.] As for the rest; besides.

au revoir. [F.] Until we meet again.

autant d'hommes, autant d'avis. [F.] So many men, so many minds.

avant-propos. [F.] Preliminary matter; preface.

à votre santé! [F.] To your health!

ballon d'essai. [F.] A trial balloon; a device to test opinion.

bas bleu. [F.] A bluestocking; a literary woman.

beau idéal. [F.] The ideal of perfection.

beau monde. [F.] The world of fashion.

beaux esprits. [F.] Men of wit.

beaux yeux. [F.] Fine eyes; good looks.

bel esprit. [F.] A person of wit or genius; a brilliant mind.

ben trovato. [It.] Well found.

bête noire. [F.] A bugbear; a special aversion; *lit.*, black beast.

bis dat qui cito dat. [L.] He gives twice who gives quickly.

bona fides (bona fide). [L.] Good faith (in good faith).

bon ami. [F.] Good friend.

bon gré, mal gré. [F.] With good or ill grace; willing or unwilling.

bon jour. [F.] Good day; good morning.

bon mot. [F.] A witty saying.

bonne foi. [F.] Good faith.

bon naturel. [F.] Good nature.

bon soir. [F.] Good evening.

bon ton. [F.] Fashionable society; good style.

bon vivant. [F.] A lover of good living; a gourmet.

bon voyage! [F.] A good voyage or journey to you!

campo santo. [It.] A burying-ground; *lit.*, a holy field.

canaille. [F.] Rabble.

carpe diem. [L.] Enjoy the present day; improve the time.

casus belli. [L.] That which causes or justifies war.

catalogue raisonné. [F.] A catalogue arranged according to subjects.

cause célèbre. [F.] A celebrated or notorious case (in law).

caveat emptor. [L.] Let the purchaser beware (*i.e.*, he buys at his own risk).

cave canem. [L.] Beware of the dog.

cela va sans dire. [F.] That goes without saying; that is a matter of course.

c'est-à-dire. [F.] That is to say.

c'est égal. [F.] It's all one.

c'est magnifique, mais ce n'est pas la guerre. [F.] It is magnificent, but it is not war.

c'est autre chose. [F.] That's quite another thing.

ceteris paribus. [L.] Other things being equal.

chacun à son goût. [F.] Every one to his taste.

chef-d'œuvre. [F.] Masterpiece.

cherchez la femme. [F.] Look for the woman (who is at the bottom of the affair).

chère amie. [F.] A dear (female) friend.

chevalier d'industrie. [F.] One who lives by his wits; a swindler.

ci-gît. [F.] Here lies.

circa. [L.] About.

cogito, ergo sum. [L.] I think, therefore I exist.

comme il faut. [F.] As it should be; in good form.

compte rendu. [F.] An account rendered; a report.

con amore. [It.] With love; very earnestly.

confrère. [F.] Colleague.

contretemps. [F.] An unex- pected or untoward event; a hitch.

coram populo. [L.] Publicly; in public.

corpus delicti. [L.] The body of the crime.

corrigenda. [L.] Things to be corrected; a list of errors.

coup. [F.] A stroke.—**coup d'essai**, a first attempt.— **coup d'état**, a sudden decisive blow in politics; a stroke of policy.—**coup de grâce**, a finishing stroke.—**coup de main**, a sudden attack or en- terprise.—**coup de maître**, a master stroke.—**coup d'œil**, a rapid glance of the eye.— **coup de pied**, a kick.—**coup de soleil**, sunstroke.—**coup de théâtre**, a theatrical effect.

coûte que coûte. [F.] Cost what it may.

credat Judæus Apella. [L.] Let Apella, the superstitious Jew, believe it; I won't.

credo quia absurdum. [L.] I believe because it is absurd, or contrary to reason.

cui bono? [L.] For whose ad- vantage?

cul-de-sac. [F.] A blind alley (often used figuratively).

cum grano salis. [L.] With a grain of salt; with some al- lowance.

d'accord. [F.] In agreement.

débâcle. [F.] The break-up of ice in a river; *hence*, a general, confused rout.

de bonne grâce. [F.] With good grace; willingly.

de facto. [L.] In point of fact; actual or actually.

dégagé. [F.] Free; easy; unconstrained.

de gustibus non est disputandum. [L.] There is no disputing about tastes.

Dei gratia. [L.] By the grace of God.

de jure. [L.] From the law; by right.

delenda est Carthago. [L.] Carthage must be destroyed.

de mortuis nil nisi bonum. [L.] (Say) nothing but good of the dead.

dénoûement. [F.] The issue; the end of a plot.

de novo. [L.] Anew.

Deo gratias. [L.] Thanks to God.

de profundis. [L.] Out of the depths.

de rigueur. [F.] Indispensable; obligatory.

dernier ressort. [F.] A last resort.

de trop. [F.] Too much; more than is wanted; out of place.

deus ex machina. [L.] A god from a machine; used in reference to forced or unlikely events introduced in a drama, novel, etc., to resolve a difficult or awkward situation; derived from the use of deities in the ancient drama.

dies iræ. [L.] Day of wrath.

Dieu et mon droit. [F.] God and my right (British royal motto).

distingué. [F.] Distinguished; of elegant appearance.

dolce far niente. [It.] Sweet doing-nothing; sweet idleness.

Dominus vobiscum. [L.] The Lord be with you.

double entente (or, esp. in English, **entendre**). [F.] A double meaning; a play upon words.

dramatis personæ. [L.] Characters of the drama or play.

dulce et decorum est pro patria mori. [L.] It is sweet and glorious to die for one's country.

dum spiro, spero. [L.] While I breathe, I hope.

dum vivimus, vivamus. [L.] While we live, let us live.

ecce homo. [L.] Behold the man!

édition de luxe. [F.] A splendid and expensive edition of a book.

editio princeps. [L.] The first printed edition of a book.

ego et rex meus. [L.] I and my king.

élite. [F.] The best part; the pick.

emeritus. [L.] Retired or superannuated after long service.

en avant. [F.] Forward.

en déshabillé. [F.] In undress.

en effet. [F.] In effect; substantially; really.

en famille. [F.] With one's family; in a domestic state.

enfant gâté. [F.] A spoiled child.

enfants perdus. [F.] Lost children; a forlorn hope.

enfant terrible. [F.] A terrible child, *that is*, one who makes disconcerting remarks.

enfant trouvé. [F.] A foundling.

enfin. [F.] In short; at last; finally.

en masse. [F.] In a mass (*or* body).

en rapport. [F.] In harmony; in agreement.

en route. [F.] On the way.

en suite. [F.] In company; in a set.

entente cordiale. [F.] Cordial understanding, especially between two states.

entourage. [F.] Surroundings; friends, confidants, etc., closely associated with a person.

entre nous. [F.] Between ourselves.

en vérité. [F.] In truth; verily.

e pluribus unum. [L.] One out of many; one composed of many (motto of the United States).

errata. [L.] Errors; list of errors.

esprit de corps. [F.] The animating spirit of a collective body, *as* a regiment.

est modus in rebus. [L.] There is a medium in all things.

et cætera (or **et cetera.**) [L.] And the rest.

et id genus omne. [L.] And everything of the sort.

et tu, Brute! [L.] And thou also, Brutus!

eureka! [Gr.] I have found (it)!

Ewigkeit. [G.] Eternity.

ex cathedra. [L.] From the chair; with high authority.

excelsior. [L.] Higher, *that is*, taller, loftier.

exeunt omnes. [L.] All go out (*or* retire).

exit. [L.] He goes out.

ex nihilo nihil fit. [L.] Out of nothing, nothing comes.

ex officio. [L.] In virtue of (his) office.

ex parte. [L.] From one party or side.

ex pede Herculem. [L.] From the foot we recognize a Hercules; we judge of the whole from the specimen.

experto crede. [L.] Trust one who has had experience.

exposé. [F.] A statement; a recital.

ex post facto. [L.] After the deed is done; retrospective.

extra muros. [L.] Beyond the walls.

ex uno disce omnes. [L.] From one judge of the rest.

facile princeps. [L.] Easily preeminent; indisputably the first.

facilis est descensus Averni. [L.] The descent to Avernus (*or* hell) is easy.

façon de parler. [F.] Way of speaking.

fait accompli. [F.] A thing already done.

faux pas. [F.] A false step; a slip in behavior.

femme de chambre. [F.] A chambermaid; lady's maid.

festina lente. [L.] Hasten slowly.

feu de joie. [F.] A discharge of firearms as a sign of rejoicing.

fiat justitia, ruat cœlum. [L.] Let justice be done though the heavens should fall.

fiat lux. [L.] Let there be light.

fides Punica. [L.] Punic (*or*

Carthaginian) faith; treachery.

fidus Achates. [L.] Faithful Achates; a true friend.

fin de siècle. [F.] End of the (nineteenth) century.

finis coronat opus. [L.] The end crowns the work.

flagrante delicto. [L.] In the commission of the crime; red-handed.

fons et origo. [L.] The source and origin.

force majeure. [F.] Greater force or strength; overwhelming force; compulsion.

fortiter in re. [L.] With firmness in acting.

fortuna favet fortibus. [L.] Fortune favors the bold.

furor loquendi. [L.] A rage for speaking.

furor scribendi. [L.] A rage for writing.

gaucherie. [F.] Awkwardness.

gaudeamus igitur. [L.] So let us be joyful.

genius loci. [L.] The genius (or guardian spirit) of a place.

gens d'armes. [F.] Men at arms.

gloria in excelsis (Deo). [L.] Glory (to God) in the highest.

gloria Patri. [L.] Glory be to the Father.

goût. [F.] Taste; relish.

grâce à Dieu. [F.] Thanks to God.

habitué. [F.] One in the habit of frequenting a place.

hic et ubique. [L.] Here and everywhere.

hic jacet. [L.] Here lies.

hinc illæ lacrimæ. [L.] Hence these tears.

hodie mihi, cras tibi. [L.] Mine today; yours tomorrow.

hoi polloi. [Gr.] The many; the vulgar; the rabble.

homme d'esprit. [F.] A man of wit or genius.

homo sum; humani nihil a me alienum puto. [L.] I am a man; I count nothing human indifferent to me.

honi soit qui mal y pense. [O. F.] Shamed be he who thinks evil of it (motto of the Order of the Garter).

horribile dictu. [L.] Horrible to relate.

hors de combat. [F.] Out of the combat; disabled.

hors d'œuvre. [F.] A relish.

hôtel de ville. [F.] A town hall.

hôtel-Dieu. [F.] A hospital.

humanum est errare. [L.] To err is human.

ibidem. [L.] At the same place (in a book).

ich dien. [G.] I serve (motto of the Prince of Wales).

ici on parle français. [F.] French is spoken here.

ignotum per ignotius. [L.] The unknown (explained) by the still more unknown.

il n'y a pas de quoi. [F.] Don't mention it; it's not worth speaking of.

il n'y a que le premier pas qui coûte. [F.] It is only the first step that costs.

il penseroso. [It.] The pensive man.

impasse. [F.] A deadlock; an insurmountable difficulty.

impedimenta. [L.] Encumbrances; luggage; baggage.

in æternum. [L.] Forever.

in articulo mortis. [L.] At the point of death; in the last struggle.

index expurgatorius. [L.] A list of prohibited works.

in esse. [L.] In being; in actuality.

in extenso. [L.] At full length.

in extremis. [L.] At the point of death.

infra dignitatem. [L.] Below one's dignity.

in loco. [L.] In the place; in the natural (*or* proper) place.

in loco parentis. [L.] In the place of a parent.

in medias res. [L.] Into the midst of things.

in memoriam. [L.] To the memory of; in memory.

in nomine. [L.] In the name of.

in omnia paratus. [L.] Prepared for all things.

in perpetuum. [L.] Forever.

in posse. [L.] In possible existence; in possibility.

in præsenti. [L.] At the present moment.

in propria persona. [L.] In one's own person.

in puris naturalibus. [L.] Quite naked.

in re. [L.] In the matter of.

in rerum natura. [L.] In the nature of things.

in sæcula sæculorum. [L.] For ages on ages.

in situ. [L.] In its original position.

in statu quo. [L.] In the former state.

inter alia. [L.] Among other things.

inter nos. [L.] Between ourselves.

in terrorem. [L.] As a warning.

in toto. [L.] In the whole; entirely.

intra muros. [L.] Within the walls.

in transitu. [L.] In course of transit.

in vacuo. [L.] In empty space; in a vacuum.

in vino veritas. [L.] There is truth in wine; truth is told under the influence of liquor.

invita Minerva. [L.] Against the will of Minerva; without genius or natural abilities.

ipse dixit. [L.] He himself said it; a dogmatic saying or assertion.

ipsissima verba. [L.] The very words.

ipso facto. [L.] By that very fact.

ipso jure. [L.] By the law itself.

jacquerie. [F.] French peasantry; a revolt of peasants.

je ne sais quoi. [F.] I know not what; a something or other.

jeu de mots. [F.] A play on words; a pun.

jeu d'esprit. [F.] A display of wit; a witticism.

jeunesse dorée. [F.] Gilded youth; rich and fashionable young men.

jubilate Deo. [L.] Rejoice in God; be joyful in the Lord.

jure divino. [L.] By divine law.

jure humano. [L.] By human law.

juste milieu. [F.] The golden mean.

laborare est orare. [L.] To labor is to pray; work is worship.

labor omnia vincit. [L.] Labor conquers everything.

laissez-faire. [F.] Let alone; noninterference.

l'allegro. [It.] The merry man.

lapsus calami. [L.] A slip of the pen.

lapsus linguæ. [L.] A slip of the tongue.

lapsus memoriæ. [L.] A slip of the memory.

lares et penates. [L.] Household gods.

lasciate ogni speranza voi ch'entrate. [It.] All hope abandon ye who enter here (inscription on the entrance to the hell of Dante's Inferno).

laudator temporis acti. [L.] A praiser of past times.

laus Deo. [L.] Praise to God.

l'avenir. [F.] The future.

le beau monde. [F.] The fashionable world.

lebe wohl. [G.] Farewell.

la grand monarque. [F.] The great monarch; Louis XIV of France.

le pas. [F.] Precedence in place or rank.

le roi est mort, vive le roi! [F.] The king is dead, long live the king (his successor)!

le roy le veult. [Norm. F.] The king wills it; the formula used by the sovereign in assenting to a bill.

le roy s'avisera. [Norm. F.] The king will consider; the formula formerly used by the sovereign in rejecting a bill.

lèse-majesté. [F.] High treason.

l'état c'est moi. [F.] It is I who am the state.

le tout ensemble. [F.] The whole (taken) together.

lettre de cachet. [F.] A sealed letter containing private orders; a royal warrant.

lex non scripta. [L.] Unwritten law; common law.

lex scripta. [L.] Statute law.

l'homme propose, et Dieu dispose. [F.] Man proposes, and God disposes.

l'inconnu. [F.] The unknown.

littera scripta manet. [L.] The written word remains.

locum tenens. [L.] One occupying the place of another; a substitute.

longo intervallo. [L.] By *or* at a long interval.

lucus a non lucendo. [L.] Used as typical of an absurd derivation—*lucus*, a grove, having been derived by an old grammarian from *luceo*, to shine—"from not shining."

lusus naturæ. [L.] A sport or freak of nature.

ma chère. [F.] My dear (fem.).

ma foi. [F.] Upon my faith.

magna est veritas, et prevalebit. [L.] Truth is mighty, and will prevail.

magnum opus. [L.] A great work.

maison de santé. [F.] A private asylum *or* hospital.

maître d'hôtel. [F.] A house steward.

mala fide. [L.] With bad faith; treacherously.

mal-à-propos. [F.] Ill-timed; out of place.

mal de mer. [F.] Seasickness.

malgré nous. [F.] In spite of us.

mañana. [Sp.] Tomorrow.

mardi gras. [F.] Shrove Tuesday.

mare clausum. [L.] A closed sea; a sea belonging to a single nation.

mariage de convenance. [F.] Marriage from motives of interest rather than of love.

materfamilias. [L.] Mother of a family.

matériel. [F.] Baggage and munitions of an army; material equipment as opposed to men.

mauvaise honte. [F.] Bashfulness; shamefacedness.

mauvais goût. [F.] Bad taste.

mauvais sujet. [F.] A bad subject; a worthless scamp.

mea culpa. [L.] My fault; by my fault.

me judice. [L.] I being judge; in my opinion.

mêlée. [F.] A confused conflict.

memento mori. [L.] Remember that you must die; a reminder of death.

mens sana in corpore sano. [L.] A sound mind in a sound body.

mens sibi conscia recti. [L.] A mind conscious of rectitude.

meo periculo. [L.] At my own risk.

mésalliance. [F.] A bad match; marriage with one of a lower rank.

meum et tuum. [L.] Mine and thine.

mirabile dictu. [L.] Wonderful to relate.

mirabile visu. [L.] Wonderful to see.

mise en scène. [F.] Stage setting.

modus operandi. [L.] Manner of working.

modus vivendi. [L.] Manner of living; used of a temporary working agreement or compromise.

mon ami. [F.] My friend (masc.).

mon cher. [F.] My dear (masc.).

mont-de-piété. [F.] A public or municipal pawnshop.

monumentum ære perennius. [L.] A monument more lasting than brass.

more majorum. [L.] After the manner of our ancestors.

morituri te salutamus. [L.] We, about to die, salute thee:—said by the Roman gladiators to the emperor.

mot d'ordre. [F.] Watchword.

motu proprio. [L.] Of his own accord.

moyen âge. [F.] Middle Ages.

multum in parvo. [L.] Much in little.

mutatis mutandis [L.] With the necessary changes.

natura non facit saltum [L.] Nature does not make a leap.

née. [F.] Born used in giving

the maiden name of a married woman.

négligé. [F.] Morning dress; an easy loose dress.

nemine contradicente. [L.] No one speaking in opposition; without opposition.

nemine dissentiente. [L.] No one dissenting; with a dissenting voice.

nemo me impune lacessit. [L.] No one assails me with impunity (motto of Scotland).

ne plus ultra. [L.] Nothing further; the uttermost point; perfection.

ne quid nimis. [L.] Avoid excess.

n'est-ce pas? [F.] Isn't that so?

nicht wahr? [G.] Isn't that so?

nil admirari. [L.] To be astonished at nothing.

nil desperandum. [L.] There is no reason for despair.

n'importe. [F.] It matters not.

nisi Dominus, frustra. [L.] Except the Lord (build the house, they labor) in vain (that build it). Ps. cxxvii. (motto of Edinburgh).

noblesse oblige. [F.] Rank imposes obligations.

Noël. [F.] Christmas.

nolens volens. [L.] Unwilling or willing.

noli me tangere. [L.] Touch me not.

nom de guerre. [F.] A war name; a pseudonym; a pen name.

nom de plume. [F.] A pen name. (Incorrect for Nom de guerre.)

non Angli sed angeli. [L.] Not Angles but angels.

non compos mentis. [L.] Not of sound mind.

non est. [L.] He (or it) is not.

non est inventus. [L.] He has not been found.

non libet. [L.] It does not please (me).

non liquet. [L.] The case is not clear.

non multa, sed multum. [L.] Not many things, but much.

non nobis solum. [L.] Not for ourselves alone.

non omnis moriar. [L.] I shall not wholly die.

non sequitur. [L.] It does not follow.

nosce te ipsum. [L.] Know thyself.

nota bene. [L.] Note well; take notice.

Notre Dame. [F.] Our Lady.

nous avons changé tout cela. [F.] We have changed all that.

nous verrons. [F.] We shall see.

novus homo. [L.] A new man; one who has raised himself from obscurity.

nuance. [F.] Shade; tint.

nulla dies sine linea. [L.] Not a day without a line; no day without something done.

nunc aut nunquam. [L.] Now or never.

obiit. [L.] He (or she) died.

obiter dictum. [L.] A thing said by the way.

odi profanum vulgus. [L.] I loathe the profane rabble.

odium theologicum. [L.] The hatred of theologians.

œuvres. [F.] Works.

ohne Hast, ohne Rast. [G.] Without haste, without rest: —motto of Goethe.

omnia vincit amor. [L.] Love conquers all things.

on dit. [F.] They say.

onus probandi. [L.] The burden of proof.

operæ pretium est. [L.] It is worth while.

ora et labora. [L.] Pray and work.

ora pro nobis. [L.] Pray for us.

ore rotundo. [L.] With round full voice; well-turned speech.

O! si sic omnia. [L.] Oh, if all things (were) so; Oh, if he had always so spoken or acted.

O tempora! O mores! [L.] Alas for the times! Alas for the manners (*or* morals)!

otium cum dignitate. [L.] Ease with dignity.

ouï-dire. [F.] Hearsay.

ouvrage de longue haleine. [F.] A work of long breath; a long work *or* one which lasts.

pace. [L.] By leave of; not to give offence to.

palmam qui meruit ferat. [L.] Let him who has won the palm wear it.

pardonnez-moi. [F.] Pardon me; I beg your pardon.

par excellence. [F.] Pre-eminently.

par exemple. [F.] For example.

par hasard. [F.] By chance.

pari passu. [L.] With equal pace; side by side.

par nobile fratrum. [L.] A noble pair of brothers; two just alike.

parole d'honneur. [F.] Word of honor.

particeps criminis. [L.] An accomplice in a crime.

parti pris. [F.] Preconceived opinion.

parvenu. [L.] A person of low origin who has risen suddenly to wealth or position; an upstart.

pas. [F.] A step; precedence.

passim. [L.] Everywhere; throughout; in all parts of the book, chapter, etc.

pâté de foie gras. [F.] Goose-liver pie.

paterfamilias. [L.] Father of a family; head of a household.

pater patriæ. [L.] Father of his country.

pax vobiscum. [L.] Peace be with you.

peccavi. [L.] I have sinned (*or* been to blame).

peine forte et dure. [F.] Strong and severe punishment; a kind of judicial torture.

penchant. [F.] A strong liking.

pensée. [F.] A thought.

per. [L.] For; through; by.— **per contra.** On the contrary. —**per annum.** By the year; annually.—**per capita.** By heads; for each individual.— **per centum.** By the hundred. —**per diem.** By the day; daily.—**per fas et nefas.** Through right and wrong.— **per se.** By itself.

persona non grata. [L.] An unacceptable person.

peu à peu. [F.] Little by little.

peu de chose. [F.] A trifle.

pièce de résistance. [F.] A resistance piece; the main dish of a meal.

pied-à-terre. [F.] A resting-place; a temporary lodging.

pis aller. [F.] The worst or last shift.

place aux dames. [F.] Make room for the ladies.

plebs. [L.] The common people.

poco a poco. [It.] Little by little.

point d'appui. [F.] Point of support; basis.

pons asinorum. [L.] The asses' bridge; a name for the fifth proposition of the first book in Euclid.

poste restante. [F.] To remain in the post office till called for.

post hoc ergo propter hoc. [L.] After this, therefore, on account of this; subsequent to, therefore due to this—an illogical way of reasoning.

pour faire rire. [F.] To excite laughter.

pour le mèrite. [F.] For merit.

pour passer le temps. [F.] To pass the time.

preux chevalier. [F.] A brave knight.

prima donna. [It.] First lady; the chief female singer in an opera, etc.

prima facie. [L.] At first view (or consideration).

primo. [L.] In the first place.

primum mobile. [L.] The source of motion; the mainspring.

principia, non homines. [L.] Principles, not men.

pro bono publico. [L.] For the good of the public.

procès-verbal. [F.] An authenticated minute or statement.

pro et contra. [L.] For and against.

profanum vulgus. [L.] The profane herd.

pro forma. [L.] For the sake of form.

pro patria. [L.] For our country.

pro rata. [L.] According to rate or proportion.

pro tanto. [L.] For so much; as far as it goes.

protégé. [F.] One under the protection of another.

Punica fides. [L.] Punic (or Carthaginian) faith; treachery.

qualis rex, talis grex. [L.] Like king, like people.

quand même. [F.] Even if; whatever may happen.

quantum libet. [L.] As much as you please.

quantum sufficit. [L.] As much as suffices.

quelque chose. [F.] Something; a trifle.

quid pro quo. [L.] Something in return; an equivalent.

quién sabe? [Sp.] Who knows?

quis custodiet ipsos custodes? [L.] Who shall guard the guards themselves?

qui s'excuse s'accuse. [F.] He who excuses himself accuses himself.

qui va là? [F.] Who goes there?

qui vive? [F.] Who lives? Who goes there? To be on the qui vive means to be alert or watchful.

quoad hoc. [L.] To this extent.

quoad sacra. [L.] As far as sacred things are concerned; for ecclesiastical purposes only.

quem Deus vult perdere, prius dementat. [L.] Those whom God wishes to destroy, he first makes mad.

quod erat demonstrandum. [L.] Which was to be proved or demonstrated.

quod vide. [L.] Which see.

quorum pars magna fui. [L.] Of which things, I was an important part.

quot homines, tot sententiæ. [L.] Many men, many minds.

raconteur. [F.] A teller of stories.

raison d'être. [F.] The reason for a thing's existence.

rapprochement. [F.] The act of bringing (*or* coming) together.

rara avis. [L.] A rare bird; a paragon.

réchauffé. [F.] *Lit.*, something warmed up; *hence*, old literary material worked up into a new form.

reductio ad absurdum. [L.] A reducing to the absurd; a method of proof in which a proposition is shown to be true by demonstrating the absurdity of its contradictions.

rencontre. [F.] An encounter; a hostile meeting.

répondez, s'il vous plaît. [F.] Please reply. *R. S. V. P.*

requiescat in pace. [L.] May he rest in peace.

res angusta domi. [L.] Narrow circumstances at home; poverty.

res gestæ. [L.] Things done; exploits; history.

respice finem. [L.] Look to the end.

résumé. [F.] A summary or abstract.

resurgam. [L.] I shall rise again.

revenons à nos moutons. [F.] Let us return to our sheep; let us return to our subject.

rôle. [F.] A character represented on the stage; also other similar meanings.

rouge et noir. [F.] Red and black; a game of chance.

rus in urbe. [L.] The country in town.

salle à manger. [F.] Dining room

sanctum sanctorum. [L.] Holy of holies.

sang froid. [F.] Coolness; indifference.

sans façon. [F.] Without ceremony.

sans peur et sans reproche. [F.] Without fear and without reproach.

sans souci. [F.] Without care.

sartor resartus. [L.] The patcher repatched; the tailor patched (*or* mended).

satis superque. [L.] Enough, and more than enough.

satis verborum. [L.] Enough of words; no more need be said.

sauve qui peut. [F.] Let him save himself who can.

savoir-faire. [F.] The knowing how to act; tact.

savoir-vivre. [F.] Good breeding; refined manners.

scripsit. [L.] Wrote (it).

sculpsit. [L.] Engraved (it).

secundum artem. [L.] According to art (*or* rule).

semper idem. [L.] Always the same.

semplice. [It.] Simple; plain.

seriatim. [L.] In a series; one by one.

sic itur ad astra. [L.] Such is the way to the stars, or to immortality.

sic passim. [L.] So here and there throughout; so everywhere.

sic transit gloria mundi. [L.] Thus passes away the glory of this world.

sicut ante. [L.] As before.

similia similibus curantur. [L.] Like things are cured by like.

simplex munditiis. [L.] Elegant in simplicity.

sine cura. [L.] Without charge or care.

sine die. [L.] Without a day being appointed.

sine qua non. [L.] Without which, not; something indispensable.

siste, viator. [L.] Stop, traveler.

sit tibi terra levis. [L.] Light lie the earth upon thee.

soi-disant. [F.] Self-styled.

sotto voce. [It.] In an undertone.

spero meliora. [L.] I hope for better things.

splendide mendax. [L.] Nobly untruthful; untrue for a good object.

sponte sua. [L.] Of one's (*or* its) own accord.

status quo. [L.] The state in which; the existing condition.

stet. [L.] Let it stand; do not delete.

suaviter in modo, fortiter in re. [L.] Gentle in manner, resolute in execution.

sub judice. [L.] Under consideration.

sub rosa. [L.] Under the rose; confidentially.

succès d'estime. [F.] A partial success, or one based on certain merits.

sui generis. [L.] Of its own peculiar kind; in a class by itself.

summum bonum. [L.] The chief good.

sunt lacrimæ rerum. [L.] There are tears for things; misfortunes call for tears.

suppressio veri. [L.] A suppression of the truth.

sursum corda. [L.] Lift up your hearts.

suum cuique. [L.] Let every one have his own.

tableau vivant. [F.] A living picture; the representation of some scene by a group of persons.

table d'hôte. [F.] A public dinner at an inn or hotel.

tabula rasa. [L.] A smooth or blank tablet.

tant mieux. [F.] So much the better.

tant pis. [F.] So much the worse.

te Deum laudamus. [L.] We praise Thee, O God (*or rather*, as God).

te judice. [L.] You being the judge.

tempus fugit. [L.] Time flies.

terminus ad quem. [L.] The term (*or* limit) to which.

terminus a quo. [L.] The term (*or* limit) from which.

terra firma. [L.] Solid earth; a secure foothold.

terra incognita. [L.] An unknown country.

tertium quid. [L.] A third something; a nondescript.

tiers état. [F.] The third estate; the commons.

timeo Danaos et dona ferentes. [L.] I fear the Greeks, even when they bring gifts.

tot homines, quot sententiæ. [L.] So many men, so many minds.

toto cælo. [L.] By the whole heavens; diametrically opposite.

tour de force. [F.] A notable feat of strength or skill.

tout à fait. [F.] Wholly; entirely.

tout à l'heure. [F.] Instantly.

tout au contraire. [F.] On the contrary.

tout de suite. [F.] Immediately.

tout ensemble. [F.] The whole taken together.

tu quoque. [L.] You also.

ubi supra. [L.] Where above mentioned.

ultima Thule. [L.] Most distant Thule; utmost limit.

una voce. [L.] With one voice; unanimously.

und so weiter. [G.] And so forth.

urbi et orbi. [L.] To the city and to the world.

utile dulci. [L.] The useful with the agreeable.

ut infra. [L.] As below.

ut supra. As above.

væ victis. [L.] Woe to the vanquished.

vale. [L.] Farewell.

valet de chambre. [F.] A personal attendant; a body servant.

varium et mutabile semper femina. [L.] Woman is ever a changeful and capricious thing.

veni, vidi, vici. [L.] I came, I saw, I conquered. (Cæsar's message to the senate when he conquered Pharnaces, king of Pontus.)

verbatim et literatim. [L.] Word for word and letter for letter.

verbum sat sapienti. [L.] A word is enough for a wise man.

via, veritas, vita. [L.] The way, the truth, the life.

vice versa. [L.] The terms of the case being interchanged or reversed; conversely.

videlicet. [L.] Namely (*lit.*, one may see).

vide ut supra. [L.] See what is stated above.

vi et armis. [L.] By force and arms; by main force.

vincit qui se vincit. [L.] He conquers who conquers himself.

virginibus puerisque. [L.] For maidens and boys.

vis a tergo. [L.] A force from behind.

vis-à-vis. [F.] Opposite; face to face.

vis inertiæ. [L.] The power of

inertia; resistance to force applied.

vis medicatrix naturæ. [L.] The healing power of nature.

vis vitæ. [L.] Living force; energy.

vivat regina (rex)! [L.] Long live the queen (king)!

viva voce. [L.] By the living voice; orally.

vive la bagatelle! [F.] Long live trifles (*or* frivolity)!

vive le roi! [F.] Long live the king!

vogue la galère! [F.] Row the galley; come what may!

voilà. [F.] Behold; there is; there are.

voilà tout. [F.] That's all.

vox et præterea nihil. [L.] A voice and nothing more; sound but no sense.

vox populi, vox Dei. [L.] The voice of the people is the voice of God.

vraisemblance. [F.] Probability; apparent truth.

vulgo. [L.] Commonly.

Wanderjahr. [G.] Year of wandering.

Wanderlust. [G.] Passion for traveling (*or* wandering).

Weltanschauung. [G.] World view; theory or conception of life or of the world in all its aspects.

Weltschmerz. [G.] World sorrow; sentimental pessimism.

Zeitgeist. [G.] Time-spirit; spirit of the age.

zum Beispiel. [G.] For example.

ABBREVIATIONS USED
IN WRITING AND PRINTING

A

a. About; acre; adjective; afternoon; answer; are (metric system); at.

A. Academician; Academy; America; American; artillery.

A. A. A. Amateur Athletic Association.

A. A. A. S. American Association for the Advancement of Science.

A. A. of A. Automobile Association of America.

A. A. U. Amateur Athletic Union.

ab. About.

A. B. Artium Baccalaureus (L., Bachelor of Arts); (also l. c.) able-bodied (seaman).

abbr., *or* **abbrev.** Abbreviated; abbreviation.

abd. Abdicated.

A. B. F. M. American Board of Foreign Missions.

abl. Ablative.

Abp. Archbishop.

abr. Abridged; abridgment.

abs. Absolutely; abstract.

A. B. S. American Bible Society.

A. C. Alpine Club; ambulance corps; ante Christum (L., before Christ); Army Corps.

Acad. Academy.

acc. Acceptance; account; accusative.

acct. Account.

ad. (*pl.* ads.) Advertisement.

a. d. After date; ante diem (L., before the day).

A. D. Anno Domini (L., in the year of our Lord).

A. D. C. Aid-de-camp; aide-de-camp.

ad fin. Ad finem (L., at the end).

ad inf. Ad infinitum (L., to infinity).

ad int. Ad interim (L., in the meantime).

adj. Adjective.

Adj., *or* **Adjt.** Adjutant.

Adj. Gen. Adjutant General.

ad. lib. Ad libitum (L., at pleasure).

Adm. Admiral; Admiralty.

admix. Administratrix.

admr. Administrator.

admx. Administratrix.

adv. Ad valorem; adverb; advocate.

Adv. Advent.

Adv. Gd. Advance guard.

advt. Advertisement.

æ., æt., ætat. Ætatis (L., of age, aged).

A. E. F. American Expeditionary Forces.

AF. *or* **A.-F.** Anglo-French.

aff. Affectionate; affirmative; affirming.

afft. Affidavit.

Afr. Africa; African.

A. G. Adjutant General; Advance guard; Attorney-general.

agr., *or* **agric.** Agriculture; agricultural.

agt. Agent.

A. H. Anno Hegiræ (L., in the year of the Hegira).

A. H. C. Army Hospital Corps.

A. I. American Institute.

Ala. Alabama.

A. L. A. American Library Association; Automobile Legal Association.

ald., *or* **aldm.** Alderman.

Alex. Alexander.

alg. Algebra.

alt. Alternate; altitude; alto.

Alta. Alberta (Canada).

Am. America; American; ammunition.

a. m. Ante meridiem (L., before noon).

A. M. Anno mundi (L., in the year of the world); Annus Mirabilis (L., the Wonderful Year, i.e., 1666); Artium Magister (L., Master of Arts).

A. M. D. Army Medical Department.

Amer. America; American.

A. M. S. Army Medical Staff.

amt. Amount.

anal Analogous, analogy; analysis; analytic.

anat Anatomy.

anc. Ancient; anciently.

anon Anonymous.

ans Answer.

ant. Antonym; antiquarian.

Ant. Anthony; Antigua.

anthrop. Anthropology; anthropological.

antiq. Antiquities; antiquarian.

A. N. Z. A. C., *or* **Anzac.** Australian and New Zealand Army Corps.

A. O. Army order.

A. O. C. Army Ordnance Corps.

A. O. D. Army Ordnance Department.

A. O. F. Ancient Order of Foresters.

A. O. H. Ancient Order of Hibernians.

aor. Aorist.

A. P. C. Army Pay Corps.

A. P. D. Army Pay Department.

Apoc. Apocalypse; Apocrypha; Apocryphal.

app. Appendix; appointed.

App. Apostles.

approx. Approximately.

Apr. April.

aq., Aq. Aqua (L., water).

Ar. Arabian; Arabic.

A. R. Anno regni (L., in the year of the reign); Army Regulations.

A. R. A. Associate of the Royal Academy (of Arts, London).

Arab. Arabian; Arabic.

arch. Archaic; archaism; archery; archipelago; architect; architecture.

Arch. Archibald.

archaeol. Archæology.

Archd. Archdeacon; Archduke.

arith. Arithmetic.

Ariz. Arizona.

Ark. Arkansas.

Arm. Armenian.

arr. Arranged; arrived; arrivals.

art. Article; artificial; artillery; artist.

Art. *or* **A.** Artillery.

AS., *or* **A.-S.** Anglo-Saxon.

A. S. C. Army Service Corps; Army Staff Corps (British Army).

A. S. C. E. American Society of Civil Engineers.

A. S. M. E. American Society of Mechanical Engineers.

assd. Assigned.

assn. Association.

assoc. Associate; association.

asst. Assistant.

A. S. S. U. American Sunday School Union.

astr., astron. Astronomer; astronomy.

astrol. Astrologer; astrology.

Atl. Atlantic.

att., atty. Attorney.

at. wt. Atomic weight.

A. U. C. Ab urbe condita (L., from the founding of the city; i.e., Rome, about 753 B. C.).

Aug. August.

Aus., Aust. Austria; Austrian.

Austral. Australasia; Australia.

Auth. Ver. Authorized Version.

auxil. Auxiliary.

av. Avenue; average.

A. V. Artillery Volunteers; Authorized Version.

A. V. C. Army Veterinary Corps.

A. V. D. Army Veterinary Department.

ave. Avenue.

A. W. L. Absent with Leave.

A. W. O. L. Absent without Leave.

ax. Axiom.

az. Azure.

B

b. Base; bass; battery; bay; book; born; brother.

B. A. Bachelor of Arts; British Academy; British America.

B. Agr. Bachelor of Agriculture.

bal. Balance.

bap. Baptized.

Bapt. Baptist.

bar. Barometer; barometric; barrel.

Barb. Barbados.

barr. Barrister.

Bart. Baronet.

bat., batt., *or* **bn.** Battalion.

batt. *or* **b.** Battery.

bbl. (*pl.* bbls.) Barrel.

B. C. Before Christ; British Columbia.

B. C. L. Bachelor of Civil Law.

bd. Board; bond; bound.

B. D. Bachelor of Divinity.

bdl. (*pl* bdls.) Bundle.

b. e. Bill of exchange.

B. E. F. British Expeditionary Forces.

Belg. Belgian; Belgium.

Benj. Benjamin.

B. ès L. Bachelier ès Lettres (F. Bachelor of Letters).

bg. (*pl.* bgs.) Bag.

b. h. p. Brake horse power.

B. I. British India.

Bib. Bible; Biblical.

biog. Biographer; biography.

biol. Biologist; biology.

bk. Bank; book.

bkg. Banking.

bkt. (*pl.* bkts.) Basket.

b. l. Bill of lading; breech-loading.

B. L. Bachelor of Laws.

bldg. (*pl.* bldgs.) Building.

B. Litt. Bachelor of Literature, *or* of Letters.

B. L. R. Breech-loading rifle.

b. m. Board measure.

B. M. Bachelor of Medicine; Brigade Major.

B. Mus. Bachelor of Music.

b. o. Branch office; buyer's option.

Boh. Bohemia; Bohemian.

Bol. Bolivia.

bor. Borough.

bot. Botanical; botanist; botany.

Bp. Bishop.

b. p. Below proof; bill of parcels; bills payable.

B. P. O. E. Benevolent and Protective Order of Elks.

br. Brig; brother; brown.

Br. British.

Br. Am. British America.

b. rec. Bills receivable.

brig. Brigade; brigadier.

Brit. Britain; British.

bro. (*pl.* bros.) Brother.

b. s. Balance sheet; bill of sale.

B. S. Bachelor of Surgery.

B. Sc. Bachelor of Science.

bu., bus. Bushel; bushels.

bul. Bulletin.

Bulg. Bulgaria; Bulgarian.

B. V. M. Beata Virgo Maria (L., Blessed Virgin Mary).

Bvt. Brevet; breveted.

Brig. Gen. Brigadier General.

C

c. Carton; cathode; cent; centime; centimeter; century; chapter, child; circa (L., about); cost; cubic; current.

C. Cape; Catholic; centigrade (thermometer); Chancellor; Congress; Conservative; Consul; Corps; Court.

C. A. Chartered Accountant; Chief Accountant; Confederate Army; Controller of Accounts; Court of Appeal.

cal. Calendar; calends; calorie.

Calif. California.

Cam., Camb. Cambridge.

Can. Canada; Canadian.

Cant. Canterbury, Canticles.

Cantab. Cantabrigiensis (L., of Cambridge).

Cantuar. Cantuaria (LL., Canterbury); Cantuariensis (LL., of Canterbury).

cap. Capital; capitalize; capitulum (L., chapter); captain.

Capt. Captain.

car. Carat; carpentry.

Card. Cardinal.

cash. Cashier.

cat. Catalogue; catechism.

cath. Cathedral.

Cath. Catherine; Catholic.

cav. Cavalry.

C. B. Cape Breton; Cavalry Brigade; Chief Baron; Common Bench; Companion of the Bath; Confined to Barracks.

cc. Cubic centimeter, *or* centimeters.

c. c. Compte courant (F., account current); cubic centimeter, *or* centimeters.

C. C. Caius College (Cambridge, Eng.); Circuit Court; Civil Court; County Clerk.

C. C. D. Commander of Coast Defenses.

C. C. P. Court of Common Pleas.

c. d. v. Carte de visite.

C. E. Church of England; Civil Engineer; Corps of Engineers.

cel. Celebrated.

Celt. Celtic.

cen. Central; century.

cent. Centigrade; central; century; centum.

cert. Certificate; certify.

certif. Certificate; certificated.

cf. Confer (i.e., compare).

C. F. A. Chief of Field Artillery.

c. f. & i. or c. f. i. Cost, freight, and insurance.

cg. Centigram.

C. G. Captain General; Captain of the Guard; Coast Guard; Commanding General; Consul General.

C. G. H. Cape of Good Hope.

C. G. S. or c. g. s. Centimeter-gram-second (system of units); Chief of General Staff in the field.

ch. Chapter; chief; child, church.

Ch. Chancery; Charles; China; Church.

C. H. Captain of the Horse; Courthouse; Customhouse.

chanc. Chancellor; chancery.

chap. Chaplain; chapter.

Chas. Charles.

chem. Chemical; chemist; chemistry.

Chin. China; Chinese.

Ch. J. Chief Justice.

Chr. Christ; Christian; Christopher.

chron. Chronological; chronology.

Chron. Chronicles.

chs. Chapters.

c. i. f. Cost, insurance, and freight.

circ. Circa. circiter, circum (L., about).

cit. Citation, cited; citizen.

civ. Civil; civilian.

C. J. Chief Justice.

cl. Centiliter; class; clause; clergyman; cloth.

class. Classic; classical; classification.

cld. Cleared; colored.

clk. Clerk.

cm. Centimeter.

cml. Commercial.

C. M. Certificated Master; common meter; Corresponding Member; court-martial.

C. M. G. Companion of St. Michael and St. George.

cml. Commercial.

Co. Company; county.

c. o. Care of; carried over.

C. O. Colonial Office; Commanding Officer; Crown Office.

coad. Coadjutor.

C. O. D. Cash, or collect, on delivery.

C. of S. Chief of Staff.

cog. Cognate.

col. College; collegiate; colonial; colony; colored; column.

Col. Colonel; Colossians.

coll. Colleague; collection; collector; college.

collat. Collateral; collaterally.

colloq. Colloquial; colloquially.

Colo. Colorado.

Col. Sergt. Color Sergeant.

com. Comedy; commentary; commerce; common; commonly; communication.

Com. Commander; Commission; Commissioner; Committee; Commodore.

comdg. Commanding.

Comdr. Commander.

Comdt. Commandant.

comp. Compare; comparative; composer; compositor; compound; comprising.

Com. Ver. Common Version.

con. Contra (L., against).

Cong. Congregational; Congress; Congressional.

conj. Conjunction.

Conn. Connecticut.

const. Constable; constitution.

cont. Containing; contents; continent; continue; continued.

contemp. Contemporary.

contr. Contracted; contraction; contrary.

cor. Corner; cornet; corrected; correction; correlative; correspondent; corresponding.

Cor. Corinthians.

Corp. Corporal.

cos. Cosine.

cosec. Cosecant.

cot. Cotangent.

cp. Compare.

c. p. Candle power; chemically pure.

C. P. Common Pleas; Common Prayer; Court of Probate.

C. P. A. Certified public accountant.

cps. Coupons.

C. P. S. Clerk of Petty Sessions.

cr. Created; credit; creditor; crown.

cresc. Crescendo.

C. S. Christian Science; Civil Service.

C. S. A. Confederate States Army; Confederate States of America.

C. S. C. Conspicuous Service Cross.

C. S. I. Companion of the Star of India (Brit. order).

C. S. N. Confederate States Navy.

C. S. O. Chief Signal Officer.

ct. Cent; county

cts. Cents; centimes.

cu., cub. Cubic.

cur. Currency; current.

C. V. Common Version.

c. w. o. Cash with order.

cwt. Hundredweight or hundredweights.

cyc., or cyclo. Cyclopedia; cyclopedic.

C. in C. Commander in Chief.

D

d. Date; daughter; day; dead; degree; denarius, or denarii (L., penny or pence); deputy; died; dime; dollar; dose.

D. Democrat; department; Deus (L., God); Duke; Dutch.

Dan. Danish, Daniel.

D. A. R. Daughters of the American Revolution.

dat. Dative.

dau. Daughter.

D. C. Da capo (It., from the beginning); Dental Corps; District Court; District of Columbia.

D. C. L. Doctor of Civil Law.

d. d. Days after date.

D. D. Divinitatis Doctor (L., Doctor of Divinity).

D. D. S. Doctor of Dental Surgery.

Dea. Deacon.

deb. Debenture.

dec. Declension; declination; decorative.

Dec. December.

def. Defendant; definition.

deft. Defendant.

deg. Degree.

del. Delegate; delineavit (L., he, *or* she, drew it).

Del. Delaware.

Dem. Democrat; Democratic.

Den. Denmark.

dep. Department; departs; deponent; deputy.

dept. Department; deponent.

der., *or* **deriv.** Derivation; derivative; derived.

Deut. Deuteronomy.

D. F. Dean of the Faculty; Defensor Fidei (L., Defender of the Faith).

dft. Defendant; draft.

dg. Decigram.

D. G. Dei gratia (L., by the grace of God); Deo gratias (L., thanks to God); Director General; Dragoon Guards.

diam. Diameter.

dict. Dictator; dictionary.

dim., *or* **dimin.** Diminuendo; diminutive.

dis. Discipline; discount.

disc. Discount; discovered.

disct. Discount.

disp. Dispensatory.

dist. Distant; distinguished; district.

div. Divide; divided; dividend; divine; division; divisor.

dl. Deciliter.

D. Lit. Doctor of Literature.

D. L. O. Dead Letter Office.

dm. Decimeter.

do. Ditto.

dol. (*pl.* dols.) Dollar; dollars.

dom. Domestic; dominion.

D. O. M. Deo Optimo Maximo (L., to God, the Best, the Greatest).

D. O. R. C. Dental Officers' Reserve Corps.

dow. Dowager.

doz. Dozen; dozens.

dpt. Department; deponent.

dr. Dram; drawer.

Dr. Debtor; doctor.

dram. pers. Dramatis personæ.

d. s. Dal segno (It., from the sign; — *musical direction*); day's sight; days after sight.

D. S. Director of Supplies.

D. Sc. Doctor of Science.

D. S. C. Distinguished Service Cross.

D. S. O. Distinguished Service Order (British, Army and Navy).

D T Double Time; "rush." (Signal).

D. T.'s. Delirium tremens. *Colloq.*

Du. Dutch.

D. V. Deo volente (L., God willing).

D. V. M. Doctor of Veterinary Medicine.

D. V. S. Director of Veterinary Services.

dwt. Pennyweight *or* pennyweights.

E

E. Earl; Earth; East; Eastern; Engineer; English.

ea. Each.

Ebor. Eboracum (L., York); Eboracensis (L., of York).

E. C. Eastern Central (Postal District, London); Established Church.

eccl., or eccles. Ecclesiastical.

Eccl., or Eccles. Ecclesiastes.

Ecclus. Ecclesiasticus.

Ecua. Ecuador.

ed. Edition; editor.

E. D. Eastern Department; Extra Duty.

Edin. Edinburgh.

edit. Edition.

Edw. Edward.

E. E. Early English; Electrical Engineer; errors expected.

E. E. & M. P. Envoy Extraordinary and Minister Plenipotentiary.

Eg. Egypt; Egyptian.

e. g. Exempli gratia (L., for example).

E. I. East India; East Indies.

elec. Electrical; electrician; electricity.

Eliz. Elizabeth; Elizabethan.

Em. Emmanuel; Emily; Emma.

E. M. F. Electromotive force.

Emp. Emperor; Empress.

ency., or encyc. Encyclopedia.

ENE. East-northeast.

eng. Engineer; engraving.

Eng. England; English.

engin. Engineer; engineering.

entom. Entomology.

E. O. Engineer Officer.

E. O. R. C. Engineer Officers' Reserve Corps.

Eph. Ephesians, Ephraim.

Epiph. Epiphany.

Epis., or Episc. Episcopal.

eq. Equal; equivalent.

ESE. East-southeast.

esp., or espec. Especially.

Esq. Esquire.

est., or estab. Established.

Esth. Esther.

et al. Et alibi (L., and elsewhere); et alii (L., and others).

etc. Et cetera (L., and others, and so forth).

et seq. Et sequens (L., and the following).

et sqq. Et sequentes (L., and the following), *masc.* & *fem. pl.*, or sequentia, *neut. pl.*

etym., or etymol. Etymology.

ex. Examined; example; excursion; executed; executive; export; extract.

ex div. Without dividend.

Exod. Exodus.

exp. Export; express.

Expl. Explosives.

exr. Executor.

exrx. Executrix.

ext. External; extinct; extra; extract.

Ezek. Ezekiel.

F

f. Farthing; fathom; feminine; fine; flower; folio; foot; forte; franc.

F. Fahrenheit; French.

F. A. Field Artillery.

fac. Facsimile.

Fahr. Fahrenheit.

F. A. I. A. Fellow of the American Institute of Architects.

fam. Familiar; family.

F. A. M. Free and Accepted Masons.

far. Farriery; farthing.

F. A. R. C. Field Artillery Reserve Corps.

F. B. A. Fellow of the British Academy (scientific society).

F. C. Free Church (of Scotland).
fcap. Foolscap.
fcp. Foolscap.
F. D. Fidei Defensor (L., Defender of the Faith).
Feb. February.
fem. Feminine.
ff. Folios; following (pages); fortissimo.
F. F. V. First Families of Virginia.
f. i. For instance.
fict. Fiction.
fig. Figurative; figuratively; figure.
Fin. Finland; Finnish.
fir. Firkin; firkins.
fl. Florin; flourished; fluid.
Fl. Flanders; Flemish.
Fla. Florida.
Flem. Flemish.
fm. Fathom.
F. M. Field Marshal; Foreign Mission.
fo. Folio.
F. O. Field Officer; Field Order.
f. o. b. Free on board.
fol. Folio; following.
for. Foreign.
fort. Fortification.
fr. Fragment; franc; from.
Fr. Father; France; Frau; French; Friar.
Fred. Frederick.
freq. Frequent; frequentative.
F. R. G. S. Fellow of the Royal Geographical Society (London).
Fri. Friday.
F. R. S. Fellow of the Royal Society (London).
frs. Francs.
F. S. Field Service.
ft. Feet; foot; fort; fortified.

fur. Furlong; further.
fut. Future.

G

g. Gauge; genitive; gram; guide; guinea or guineas; gulf.
G. German.
Ga. Georgia.
G. A. General Assembly.
gal. (*pl.* gals.) Gallon.
Gal. Galatians.
G. A. R. Grand Army of the Republic.
gaz. Gazette; gazetteer.
G. B. Great Britain.
G. B. & I. Great Britain and Ireland.
G. C. Grand Chancellor (*or* Chaplain, Chapter, Council, Conclave, etc.).
g. c. d. Greatest common divisor.
g. c. m. Greatest common measure.
G. C. M. General Court Martial.
Gd. Guard.
gen. Gender; general; generic; genitive; genus.
Gen. General; Genesis.
gent. Gentleman.
Geo. George.
geog. Geographer; geographic; geographical; geography.
geol. Geologic; geological; geologist; geology.
geom. Geometry.
ger. Gerund.
Ger. German; Germany.
G. H. Q. General Headquarters.
gi. Gill; gills.
G. L. Grand Lodge.

gm. Gram.

G. M. Grand Master.

G. O. General order.

G. O. C. General Officer Commanding.

gov. Government; governor.

Gov. Gen. Governor General.

govt. Government.

G. P. Gloria Patri (L., Glory to the Father); Graduate in Pharmacy.

G. P. O. General Post Office.

gr. Grain; grand; great; gross.

Gr. Greece; Greek; Grecian.

gram. Grammar.

Gr. Br., Gr. Brit. Great Britain.

G. S. General Secretary; General Service; General Staff; Grand Scribe; Grand Secretary.

gt. Gilt; great; gutta (L., drop).

gtt. Guttæ (L., drops).

gun. Gunnery.

H

h. Harbor; hard; hardness; height; high; hour; husband.

H., HQ., or Hqrs. Headquarters.

ha. Hectare.

H. A. Horse Artillery.

Hab. Habakkuk.

Hag. Haggai.

H. B. C. Hudson's Bay Company.

H. B. M. His (or Her) Britannic Majesty.

H. C. Heralds' College, House of Commons.

h. c. f. Highest common factor.

H. E. High explosive; His Eminence; His Excellency.

Heb. Hebrew; Hebrews.

hectol. Hectoliter.

hectom. Hectometer.

H. E. I. C. Honorable East India Company.

her. Heraldry.

hg. Hectogram; heliogram.

H. G. His (or Her) Grace; Horse Guards, High German.

H. H. His (or Her) Highness; His Holiness (the Pope).

hhd. Hogshead; hogsheads.

H. I. H. His (or Her) Imperial Highness.

H. I. M. His (or Her) Imperial Majesty.

Hind. Hindustan; Hindustani.

hist. Historian; historical; history.

H. J. Hic jacet (L., here lies).

hl. Hectoliter.

H. L. House of Lords.

hm. Hectometer.

H. M. His (or Her) Majesty.

H. M. S. His (or Her) Majesty's Service; or Ship.

ho. House.

Hon. Honorable; honorary.

hort. Horticulture.

Hos. Hosea.

Hosp. Hospital.

H. P., or h. p. Half pay; high pressure; horse power.

hr. (pl. hrs.) Hour.

H. R. House of Representatives.

H. R. E. Holy Roman Emperor, or Empire.

H. R. H. His (or Her) Royal Highness.

H. S. H. His (or Her) Serene Highness.

ht. Height.

Hun., Hung. Hungarian; Hungary.

H. W. M. High-water mark.
Hy. Henry.
hyd. Hydrostatics.
hyp. Hypothesis; hypothetical.

I

I. Imperator (L., Emperor); island.
I. A. Indian Army.
ib., *or* **ibid.** Ibidem (L., in the same place).
Ice., Icel. Iceland; Icelandic.
id. Idem (L., the same).
I. D. R. Infantry Drill Regulations.
i. e. Id est. (L., that is).
i. h. p. Indicated horse power.
IHS. A symbol representing Greek IH (ΣΟΥ) Σ Jesus.
ill., illus., illust. Illustrated; illustration.
Ill. Illinois.
imp. Imparted; imperative; imperfect; imperial; impersonal; imported; importer.
in. (*pl.* ins.) Inch.
inc. Including; inclusive; incorporated; increase.
incl. Including; inclusive.
incog. Incognito.
incor. Incorporated.
ind. Independent; indicative; indigo.
Ind. India; Indian; Indiana.
inf. Infantry; infinitive.
I. N. R. I. Iesus Nazarenus, Rex Iudæorum (L., Jesus of Nazareth, King of the Jews).
ins. Inches; inscribed; inspector; insurance.
insp. Inspector.
inst. Instant; institute; institution.

int. Interest; interior; interjection; internal; international; interpreter; intransitive.
interj. Interjection.
intrans. Intransitive.
in trans. In transitu (L., on the way).
introd. Introduction; introductory.
I. O. O. F. Independent Order of Odd Fellows.
I. O. U. I owe you.
I. R. Inland Revenue; Internal Revenue.
I. R. C. Infantry Reserve Corps.
Ire. Ireland.
is. Island; isle.
Isa. Isaiah.
isl. Island; isle.
It. Italian; Italy.
ital. Italic, italics.
Ital. Italian; Italy.
I. W. Isle of Wight.

J

J. Judge; Justice.
J. A. Judge Advocate.
Jam. Jamaica.
Jan. January.
Jap. Japan; Japanese.
Jas. James.
Jav. Javanese.
J. C. Jesus Christ; Julius Cæsar; jurisconsult.
J. C. D. Juris Civilis Doctor (L., Doctor of Civil Law).
Jer. Jeremiah.
JJ. Justices.
Jno. John.
Jon., Jona. Jonathan.
Jos. Joseph.
Josh. Joshua.
Jour. Journal; journeyman

J. P. Justice of the Peace.
Jr. Junior.
Judg. Judges.
Jun., *or* jun. Junior.
Junc. Junction.
jus., just. Justice.

K

K. King; Kings; Knight.
Kans. Kansas.
K. B. King's Bench.
K. C. Knights of Columbus.
K. C. B. Knight Commander of the Bath (Brit. order).
kg. Kilogram.
K. G. Knight of the Garter.
Ki. Kings.
kilom. Kilometer.
K. K. K. Ku-Klux Klan.
kl. Kiloliter.
km. Kilometer; kingdom.
K. M. Knight of Malta (European religious order).
knt. Knight.
K. O. Commanding Officer.
K. P. Kitchen Police; Knight *or* Knights of Pythias.
K. T. Knight Templar.
Ky. Kentucky.

L

l. Lake; land; latitude; leaf; league; left; length; libra (L., a pound); line; link; liter.
L. Lady; Latin; Law; Liber (L., book); Liberal; Low.
La. Louisana.
Lab. Labrador.
Lam. Lamentations.
lat. Latitude.
Lat. Latin.
lb. (*pl.* lbs.) Libra *or* libræ (L., pound *or* pounds).

l.c. Loco citato (L., in the place cited); lower case.
L. C. Lord Chamberlain; Lord Chancellor.
L/C Letter of Credit.
L. C. J. Lord Chief Justice.
l. c. m. Least common multiple.
Ld., ld. Lord.
L. D. Lady Day; (*or* LD.) Low Dutch.
Ldp. Lordship.
lea. League.
leg. Legal; legate; legato; legislative; legislature.
Lev. Leviticus.
LG., *or* L. G. Low German.
LGr., *or* L. Gr. Low Greek.
l. h. Left hand.
L. H. A. Lord High Admiral.
L. I. Light Infantry; Long Island.
lib. Liber (L., book); librarian; library.
Lieut. *or* Lt. Lieutenant.
lin. Lineal; linear.
liq. Liquid; liquor.
lit. Liter; literal; literally; literary; literature.
Lit. D. Literarum Doctor (L., Doctor of Letters).
Lith. Lithuanian.
Litt. D. Litterarum Doctor (L., Doctor of Letters).
LL., *or* L. L. Late Latin; Low Latin.
L. L. Lord Lieutenant.
LL. B. Legum Baccalaureus (L., Bachelor of Laws).
LL. D. Legum Doctor (L., Doctor of Laws).
log. Logarithm.
lon., *or* long. Longitude.
L. S. Licentiate in Surgery.
L. S. D., *or* £. s. d., *or* l. s. d.

Libræ, solidi, denarii (L., pounds, shillings, pence).
Lt. *or* Lieut. Lieutenant.
l. t. Long ton.

M

m. Male; manual; married; masculine; measure; medicine; medium; meridian; meter; middle; mile; mill; minute; month; moon; morning; mountain.
M. Majesty; Manitoba; Marshal; Marquis; Monsieur.
M. A. Magister Artium (L., Master of Arts); Military Academy.
Mac., Macc. Maccabees.
mach. Machinery.
Mad. Madam.
mag. Magazine; magnitude.
Maj. Major.
Mal. Malachi.
man. Manège; manual.
Manit. Manitoba.
manuf. Manufactory; manufacture.
mar. Maritime.
Mar. March.
March. Marchioness.
Marq. Marquis.
mas., *or* masc. Masculine.
Mass. Massachusetts.
math. Mathematician; mathematics.
Matt. Matthew.
max. Maximum.
M. C. Medical Corps; Member of Congress.
Md. Maryland.
M. D. Medicinæ Doctor (L., Doctor of Medicine).
mdse. Merchandise.

Me. Maine.
ME., *or* M. E. Middle English.
M. E. Mechanical, Military, *or* Mining Engineer; Methodist Episcopal; Most Excellent.
meas. Measure.
mech. Mechanics; mechanical.
med. Medical; medicine; medieval; medium.
Medit. Mediterranean.
mem. Memento; memoir; memorandum; memorial.
mer. Meridian; meridional.
Messrs. Messieurs.
metal. Metallurgy.
meteor. Meteorology.
Meth. Methodist.
Mex. Mexican; Mexico.
Mf., *or* mf. Mezzo forte (It., moderately loud).
mfg. Manufacturing.
mfr. (*pl.* mfrs.) Manufacturer.
mg. Milligram.
Mgr. Monseigneur; Monsignore.
M. H. G., *or* MHG. Middle High German.
M. H. R. Member of the House of Representatives.
M. I. Mounted Infantry.
Mic. Micah.
Mich. Michaelmas; Michigan.
mid. Middle; midshipman.
mil. Military; militia.
min. Minim; minimum; mining; minister; minor; minute.
Minn. Minnesota.
Min. Plen. Minister Plenipotentiary.
misc. Miscellaneous.
Miss. Mississippi.
ml. Mail; milliliter.
M. L. A. Modern Language Association.

M. L. G., *or* **MLG.** Middle Low German.

Mlle. Mademoiselle.

mm. Millimeter.

MM. Their Majesties; Messieurs.

Mme. (*pl.* **Mmes.**) Madame (*pl.* Mesdames).

mo. (*pl.* mos.) Month.

Mo. Missouri.

M. O. Medical officer; money order.

mod. Moderate; moderato (It., moderately); modern.

Moham. Mohammedan.

mol. wt. Molecular weight.

Mon. Monastery; Monday.

Monsig. Monseigneur; Monsignor.

Mont. Montana.

Mor. Morocco.

M. O. R. C. Medical Officers' Reserve Corps.

M. P. Member of Parliament.

M. P. C. Member of Parliament, Canada.

m. p. h. Miles per hour.

Mr. Mister.

M. R. C. Medical Reserve Corps.

Mrs. Mistress.

MS., *or* **ms.** Manuscript.

M. S. Master of Science; Master of Surgery.

m. s. l. Mean sea level.

MSS. *or* **mss.** Manuscripts.

mt. (*pl.* mts.) Mount; mountain.

mun. Municipal.

mus. Museum; music; musician.

Mus. B. Musicæ Baccalaureus (L., Bachelor of Music).

Mus. D. *or* **Musc. Doc.** Musicæ Doctor (L., Doctor of Music).

M. W. Most Worshipful; Most Worthy.

myg. Myriagram.

myl. Myrialiter.

mym. Myriameter.

myth. Mythology.

N

n. Natus (L., born); nephew; neuter; new; nominative; note; noun; number.

N. Navy; Noon; Norse; North; Northern.

N. A. National Academy; National Army; North America; North American.

N. A. A. National Automobile Association.

Nah. Nahum.

nat. National; native; natural.

Nath. Nathanael; Nathaniel.

naut. Nautical.

nav. Naval; navigable; navigation.

N. B. New Brunswick; North Britain; North British; nota bene (L., note well, *or* take notice).

N. C. New Church; Nurses' Corps; North Carolina.

N. C. O. Noncommissioned Officer.

n. d. No date.

N. Dak. North Dakota.

N. E. New England.

N. E. A. National Education Association.

Nebr. Nebraska.

N. E. D. New English Dictionary;—better, O. E. D. (which see).

neg. Negative.

Neh. Nehemiah.

Neth. Netherlands.

neut. Neuter.

Nev. Nevada.

N. F. Newfoundland; (or NF.) Norman French.

Ng. Norwegian.

N. G. National Guard; New Granada; (Slang) no good.

N. Gr., or NGr. New Greek.

N. H. New Hampshire.

Nicar. Nicaragua.

N. J. New Jersey.

N. L., or NL. New Latin.

N. Lat. North latitude.

N. Mex. New Mexico.

NNE. North-northeast.

NNW. North-northwest.

N. O. Natural order (Bot.); New Orleans.

No., or no. (pl. Nos., nos.) Numero (L., [by] number).

nol. pros. Nolle prosequi (L., to be unwilling to prosecute).

nom. Nominative.

non seq. Non sequitur (L., it does not follow).

Nor. Norman; North.

Norw., or Nor. Norway; Norwegian.

Nov. November.

N. P. New Providence; Notary Public.

nr. Near.

N. R. North Riding; North River.

N. S. National Society; New Series; New Style (since 1752); Novia Scotia.

N. S. W. New South Wales.

N. T. New Testament; Northern Territory.

Num. Numbers.

NW. Northwest; Northwestern.

N. W. T. Northwest Territories.

N. Y. New York.

N. Z. New Zealand.

O

O. Old; Ontario; Order.

o/a. On account (of).

ob. Obiit (L., he, or she, died).

Obad. Obadiah.

obdt. Obedient.

obj. Object; objection; objective.

obl. Oblique; oblong.

obs. Observation; observatory; obsolete.

obt. Obedient.

oc. Ocean.

Oct. October.

O. D., or OD. Old Dutch.

O. E., or OE. Old English.

O. E. Omissions excepted.

O. E. D. Oxford English Dictionary.

O. F., or OF. Old French.

off. Offered; officer; official; officinal.

O. H. G., or OHG. Old High German.

O. H. M. S. On His (or Her) Majesty's Service.

O. K., or OK. Correct; all right. Cant.

Okla. Oklahoma.

ol. Oleum (L., oil).

O. M. Old measurement; Order of Merit.

Ont. Ontario.

O. O. R. C. Ordnance Officer ' Reserve Corps.

op. Opera; opposite, opus.

opp. Opposed; opposite.

opt Optative; optics.

Or. Oriental.

O. R. C. Order of the Red Cross; Officers' Reserve Corps.

ord. Ordained; order; ordinance; ordinary; ordnance.

Oreg. Oregon.

orig. Original; originally.

O. S. Old School; Old Series; Old Style; ordinary seaman.

O. T. Old Testament.

O. T. C. Officers' Training Camp.

Oxon. Oxonia (L., Oxford); Oxoniensis (L., Oxonian).

oz. Ounce; ounces.

P

p. Page; part; participle; past; penny; piano (It., softly); pint; pipe; pole; population; professional.

P. Pastor; pater (L., father); père (F., father); post; president; priest; prince.

Pa. Pennsylvania.

p. a. Participial adjective; per annum (L., by the year).

P/A. Power of attorney; private account.

Pac. Pacific.

pam. Pamphlet.

Pan. Panama.

par. Paragraph; parallel; parenthesis; parish.

Para. Paraguay.

parl. Parliament; parliamentary.

part. Participle.

pass. Passive.

P. B. Prayer Book.

p. c. Per cent; postal card; post card.

pd. Paid.

P. E. Presiding Elder; Protestant Episcopal,

P. E. I. Prince Edward Island.

pen. Peninsula.

Pent. Pentecost.

per an. Per annum (L., by the year).

per ct. Per cent.

perf. Perfect.

perh. Perhaps.

pers. Person; personal.

Pers. Persia; Persian.

pert. Pertaining.

Pet. Peter.

pf. Preferred.

Pg. Portugal; Portuguese.

P. G. M. Past Grand Master.

Phar. Pharmacy; Pharmacopœia.

Ph. B. Philosophiæ Baccalaureus (L., Bachelor of Philosophy).

Ph. D. Philosophiæ Doctor (L., Doctor of Philosophy).

Ph. G. Graduate in Pharmacy.

Phil. Philemon; Philip; Philippians; Philippine.

Phila. Philadelphia.

philol. Philology; philologist.

philos. Philosopher; philosophical; philosophy.

physiol. Physiologist; physiology.

P. I. Philippine Islands.

pinx. Pinxit (L., he, *or* she, painted it).

pk. (*pl.* pks.) Peck.

pkg. (*pl.* pkgs.) Package.

pl. Place; plural.

plf., *or* **plff.** Plaintiff.

plup., *or* **plupf.** Pluperfect.

plur. Plural.

pm. Premium.

P. M., *or* **p. m.** Post meridiem.

(L., afternoon); post mortem.

P. M. G. Postmaster-General.

P. O. Post office; Province of Ontario.

P. O. B. Post-office box.

P. O. D. Pay on delivery; Post Office Department.

Pol. Poland; Polish.

pol., polit. Political.

pol. econ. Political economy.

pop. Popular; population.

Port. Portugal; Portuguese.

pos. Positive; possessive.

poss. Possession; possessive.

pp. Pages; past participle; pianissimo.

p. p. Past participle; postpaid.

P. P. C. or p. p. c. Pour prendre congé (F., to take leave).

pph. Pamphlet.

p. pr. Present participle.

P. Q. Previous question; Province of Quebec.

pr. Pair; present; price; priest; prince.

Pr. Preferred stock.

P. R. Puerto Rico.

prep. Preparatory; preposition.

pres. President; presidency.

Presb. Presbyterian.

pret. Preterit.

prin. Principal.

priv. Privative.

prob. Probably; problem.

Prof. Professor.

pron. Pronominal; pronoun; pronounced; pronunciation.

propr. Proprietor.

pros. Prosody.

Prot. Protestant.

pro tem. Pro tempore (L., temporarily).

prov. Provident; province; provisional.

Prov. Provençal; Proverbs; Provost.

prox. Proximo (L., next, of the next month).

prs. Pairs.

Prus. Prussia; Prussian.

Ps. Psalm; Psalms.

P. S. Postscriptum (L., postscript); Privy Seal.

pseud. Pseudonym.

psychol. Psychologist; psychology.

pt. (pl. pts.) Part; payment; pint; point; port.

P. T., or p. t. Post town.

p. v. Post village.

pwt. Pennyweight; pennyweights.

pxt. See pinx.

Q

q. Quart; queen; query; question; quintal; quire.

Q. Quebec (province)

Q. E. D. Quod erat demonstrandum (L., which was to be demonstrated).

Q. F. Quick-Fire, or quick-firing.

ql. Quintal.

Q. M. Quartermaster.

Q. M. G. Quartermaster-General.

Q. M. O. R. C. Quartermaster Officers' Reserve Corps.

Q. M. S. Quartermaster-Sergeant.

qr. (pl. qrs.) Quadrans (L., a farthing); quarter; quire.

qt. Quantity; (pl. qts.) quart.

qu. Quart; quarterly; queen; query; question.

ques. Question.

qy. Query.

R

r. Railroad; railway; rare; received; rector; resides; retired; right; river; rises; road; rod; rood; royal.

R. Rabbi; Radical; Réaumur; Republican; response.

R. A. Rear Admiral; Regular Army; Royal Academy; Royal Artillery.

rad. Radical; radix.

R. C. Red Cross; Roman Catholic.

R. C. A. Reformed Church in America.

Re. Rupee.

R. E. Reformed Episcopal; Right Excellent; Royal Engineers.

Réaum. Réaumur.

rec. Receipt; recipe; record; recorded; recorder.

recd. Received.

rec. sec. Recording secretary.

rect. Receipt; rector; rectory.

ref. Referee; reference; referred; reformation; reformed.

Ref. Ch. Reformed Church.

reg. Regent; region; register; registered; registry; regular.

Reg. Regina (L., queen).

regt. Regiment.

rel. Relating; relative (-ly); religion; religious.

rep. Repeat; report; reporter; representative; republic.

Rep. Republican.

Repub. Republic; Republican.

retd. Returned.

rev. Revenue; reverse; review; revise; revised; revision; revolution.

Rev. Revelation; Reverend.

Rev. Ver. Revised Version.

R. F., or **r. f.** Rapid-fire.

R. F. D. Rural Free Delivery.

R. G. S. Royal Geographical Society (London).

r. h. Right hand.

R. H. Royal Highness.

rhet. Rhetoric; rhetorical.

R. I. Rhode Island.

R. I. P. Requiescat in pace (L., may he, or she, rest in peace).

riv. River.

rm. Ream.

R. M. Resident Magistrate; Royal Marines.

R. M. S. Royal Mail Steamer.

R. N. Royal Navy.

R. N. R. Royal Naval Reserve.

ro. Rood.

Robt. Robert.

Rom. Roman; Romance; Romans.

Rom. Cath. Roman Catholic.

R. O. T. C. Reserve Officers' Training Corps (or Camp).

R. P. O. Railroad Post Office.

rpt. Report.

R. R. Railroad.

Rs. Rupees.

R. S. Recording Secretary; Revised Statutes.

R. S. V. P. Répondez, s'il vous plaît (F., reply, if you please).

Rt. Hon. Right Honorable.

Rt. Rev. Right Reverend.

Rum. Rumania; Rumanian.

Rus., or **Russ.** Russia; Russian.

R. V. Revised Version; Rifle Volunteers.

R. W. Right Worshipful; Right Worthy.

Ry. Railway.

R. Y. S. Royal Yacht Squadron.

S

s., *or* S. Section; see; series; shilling; signed; singular; son; stem; sun; surplus.

S. Sabbath; Saint; Saxon; school; senate; Socialist; Society; Socius (L., Fellow); soprano; South; Southern.

S. A. Salvation Army; Small-arms; South Africa; South America; South Australia.

sa. Sable.

Sab. Sabbath.

S. Afr. South Africa; South African.

Salv. Salvador.

Sam. Samaritan; Samuel.

S. Amer., *or* S. Am. South America; South American.

S. & T. Supply and Transport.

Sans. Sanskrit.

S. A. R. South African Republic.

Sar. Sardinia; Sardinian.

Sask. Saskatchewan.

Sat. Saturday.

Sax. Saxon; Saxony.

sb. Substantive.

S. B. Bachelor of Science; South Britain.

sc. Scene; and see sci., scil., scr., sculp.

Sc. Scotch; Scottish.

s. c. Small capitals.

S. C. Signal Corps; South Carolina; Staff Corps; Supreme Court.

Scand. Scandinavia; Scandinavian.

S. caps. Small capitals.

sch. Scholium; schooner.

sci. Science; scientific.

scil. Scilicet (L., namely).

Scot. Scotch; Scotland; Scottish.

scr. Scruple.

Script. Scripture.

sculp. Sculpsit (L., he, *or* she, carved it).

s. d. Sine die (L., without [appointing] a day).

S. Dak. South Dakota.

SE. Southeast.

sec. Secant; second; secretary; section; secundum (L., according to).

Sec. Leg. Secretary of Legation.

sect. Section.

Sem. Seminary; Semitic.

Sen. Senate; Senator; Senior.

Sep., *or* Sept. September; Septuagint.

ser. Series; sermon.

serg., sergt., *or* Sgt. Sergeant.

Serv. Servian.

s. g. Specific gravity.

S. G. Solicitor-general; Surgeon-General.

Sgt. Maj. Sergeant-Major.

Sh., *or* sh. Share; shilling; shillings.

Shak. Shakespeare.

S. I. Sandwich Islands; Staten Island.

Sib. Siberia; Siberian.

Sic. Sicilian; Sicily.

sing. Singular.

S. J. Society of Jesus.

S. J. C. Supreme Judicial Court.

Skr., *or* Skt. Sanskrit.

S. L. Solicitor at Law.

S. Lat. South latitude.

Slav. Slavic; Slavonic.

sld. Sailed.

S. M. Sa Majesté (F., His, *or* Her, Majesty); Sergeant-Major; Society of Mary

sm. c., *or* **sm. caps.** Small capitals.

S. O., *or* **s. o.** Seller's option.

S. O. Staff Officer; Signal Officer; Special Order.

soc. Society.

S. of Sol. Song of Solomon.

sol. Solution.

sop. Soprano.

S. O. R. C. Signal Officers' Reserve Corps.

sov. Sovereign.

sp. Species; specimen; spelling; spirit.

Sp. Spain; Spaniard; Spanish.

s. p. Sine prole (L., without issue).

S. P. C. A. Society for Prevention of Cruelty to Animals.

S. P. C. C. Society for Prevention of Cruelty to Children.

specif. Specifically.

sp. gr. Specific gravity.

S. P. Q. R. Senatus Populusque Romanus (L., the Senate and People of Rome); small profits, quick returns.

spt. Seaport.

sq. Squadron.

sq. Sequens (L., the following [one]); square.

sqq. Sequentes (L., the following [ones]).

Sr. Sir; Senior.

S. R. S. Fellow (L., Socius) of the Royal Society.

ss. Scilicet (L., namely); semis (L., half).

S. S. Steamship; Supply Sergeant.

SSE. South-southeast.

SSW. South-southwest.

st. Stanza; stone; stet (L., let it stand).

St. Saint; Strait; Street.

stat. Statuary; statue; statutes.

S. T. D. Sacræ Theologiæ Doctor (L., Doctor of Sacred Theology).

str. Steamer.

Sub. Subaltern.

subj. Subject; subjunctive.

subst. Substantive; substitute.

suff. Suffix.

Sun. Sunday.

sup. Superior; superlative; supine; supplement; supra (L., above).

Sup. C. Superior Court; Supreme Court.

superl. Superlative.

Sup. O. Supply Officer.

supp. Supplement.

Supt. Superintendant.

surg. Surgeon; surgery.

surv. Surveying; surveyor.

s. v. Sub verbo (L., under the word); sub voce (L., under the title).

S. V. Sancta Virgo (L., Holy Virgin); Sanctitas Vestra (L., Your Holiness).

SW. Southwest.

Sw., *or* **Swed.** Sweden; Swedish.

Switz. Switzerland.

syn. Synonym; synonymous.

Syr. Syria; Syriac.

T

t. Temperature; tenor; time; tome; ton; town; township; transitive.

T. Territory; Testament; trains; Turkish.

tan. Tangent.

tel. Telegram; telegraph; telephone.

Tenn. Tennessee.
ter. Terrace; territory.
Test. Testament.
Teut. Teuton; Teutonic.
Tex. Texas.
Th. Thomas.
Theo. Theodore; Theodosia.
Theoph. Theophilus.
Thess. Thessalonians.
Tho., or **Thos.** Thomas.
Thurs. Thursday.
Tim. Timothy.
T. M. True mean.
T. N. T. Trinitrotoluene or Trinitrotoluol.
t. o. Telegraph office; turn over.
topog. Topographical; topography.
tp. Township.
tr. Translated; translation; translator; transpose; treasurer; trustee.
trav. Travel; traveler.
treas. Treasurer; treasury.
trig. Trigonometric; trigonometrical; trigonometry.
Trin. Trinity.
trop. Tropic; tropical.
T. S. Transport and Supply.
T. T. Telegraphic transfer; Trinity term.
T. U. Trade Union.
Tues. Tuesday.
Turk. Turkey; Turkish.
typ. Typographer; typographic (-ical); typography.

U

U. Uncle; Unionist; upper.
U. K. United Kingdom.
ult. Ultimately; ultimo.
Unit. Unitarian.
univ. Universally; university.

Univ. Universalist.
U. of S. Afr. Union of South Africa.
U. P. C. United Presbyterian Church.
Uru. Uruguay.
U. S. Uncle Sam; United States.
U. S. A. United States Army; United States of America.
U. S. C. United States of Colombia.
U. S. M. United States Mail; United States Marine.
U. S. M. A. United States Military Academy.
U. S. N. United States Navy.
U. S. N. A. United States Naval Academy.
U. S. N. G. United States National Guard.
U. S. S. United States Senate; United States Ship or Steamer.
usu. Usual; usually.
u. s. w. Und so weiter (G., and so forth).

V

v. Verb; verse; version; versus; very; vicar; vice-; vide (L., see); village; vocative; volume; von (G., of).
V. Venerable; Victoria; Viscount; Volunteers.
Va. Virginia.
v. a. Verb active.
V. A. Vicar Apostolic; Vice Admiral.
var. Variant; variation; variety; various.
Vat. Vatican.
vb. n. Verbal noun.
V. C. Veterinary Corps; Vice Chancellor; Victoria Cross.

Ven. Venerable; Venice.

Venez. Venezuela.

ver. Verse; verses.

Vet. Veterinary.

V. G. Vicar-general.

v. i. Verb intransitive.

Vic. Victoria.

vid. Vide (L., see).

vil. Village.

Vis., *or* **Visc.** Viscount.

viz. Videlicet (L., namely).

V. M. D. Veterinariæ Medicinæ Doctor (L., Doctor of Veterinary Medicine).

v. n. Verb neuter.

voc. Vocative.

vocab. Vocabulary.

vol. (*pl.* **vols.**) Volume; volunteer.

vol. Volcano; volcanic.

V. P. Vice-President.

v. r. Verb reflexive.

V. R. Victoria Regina (L., Queen Victoria).

V. Rev. Very Reverend.

vs. Versus.

v. s. Vide supra (L., see above).

V. S. Veterinary Surgeon.

Vt. Vermont.

v. t. Verb transitive.

Vul. Vulgate.

vv. Verses; violins.

W

w. Wanting; week; wide; wife; with.

W. Wales; Washington; Welsh; West; Western.

W. A. West Africa; Western Australia.

Wash. Washington.

W. C. Wesleyan Chapel; Western Central (Postal District, London).

W. C. T. U. Woman's Christian Temperance Union.

W. D., *or* **War D.** War Department.

Wed. Wednesday.

w. f. Wrong font.

w. g. Wire gauge.

W. G. C. Worthy Grand Chaplain.

W. G. M. Worthy Grand Master.

whf. Wharf.

W. I., *or* **W. Ind.** West Indies; West Indian.

Wis. Wisconsin.

Wisd. of Sol. Wisdom of Solomon.

wk. Week.

W. long. West longitude.

Wm. William.

W. M. Worshipful Master.

WNW. West-northwest.

W. O. War Office.

wp. Worship.

W. R. Water reserve; West Riding.

WSW. West-southwest.

wt. Weight.

W. Va. West Virginia.

Wyo. Wyoming.

X

X. Χριστος (Gr., Christ).

X-c., *or* **X-cp.** Ex coupon.

Xmas [no period] Christmas.

Xn. Christian.

Xnty., *or* **Xty.** Christianity.

Xper., *or* **Xr.** Christopher.

Xt. Christ.

Y

y. Yard; year.

yd. (*pl.* yds.) Yard.

Y. M. C. A. Young Men's Christian Association.

Y. M. Cath. A. Young Men's Catholic Association.

Y. M. C. U. Young Men's Christian Union.

Y. P. S. C. E. Young People's Society of Christian Endeavor.

yr. (*pl.* yrs.) Year; younger; your.

Y. W. C. A. Young Women's Christian Association.

Z

Zach. Zacharias; Zachary.

Zeb. Zebadiah; Zebedee.

zoogeog. Zoogeography.

zool. Zoological; zoologist; zoology.

Z. S. Zoological Society.

Zech. Zechariah.

Zeph. Zephaniah.

About

ROGET'S INTERNATIONAL THESAURUS

from which

ROGET'S POCKET THESAURUS

is derived

In 1852, Peter Mark Roget, an English doctor, published the first thesaurus. It filled an important need and became an immediate success. That little book with the long title—*Thesaurus of English Words and Phrases Classified and Arranged so as to Facilitate the Expression of Ideas and Assist in Literary Composition*—was the father of all thesauruses. Fortunately, perhaps, his title has been shortened; but that is the only thing about it which has shrunk. Today *Roget's Pocket Thesaurus* and the bigger volume from which it is derived, *Roget's INTERNATIONAL Thesaurus,* are lineal descendants of Roget's *Thesaurus of English Words.* In these two volumes reside not only the genius of Roget himself, but the work of many subsequent compilers and editors who have expanded the original book into one of the largest and certainly one of the most useful word books in the English language.

Peter Roget was surely inspired when he devised his *Thesaurus.* Known as a brilliant physician, a Fellow of the Royal Society, and a founder of the Society for the Diffusion of Knowledge, this amazing and versatile man invented a slide rule, did pioneer work on a calculating machine, and wrote volumes on phrenology, electricity, physiology, and other scientific problems of his time. But today he is best known for his *Thesaurus*, a book which, ironically enough, he always considered a mere side line.

The basic principle of Roget's *Thesaurus*, which has been scrupulously observed in *Roget's Pocket Thesaurus* and in *Roget's INTERNATIONAL Thesaurus*, is the *grouping of words according to their ideas* rather than the listing of words, as the dictionaries do, according to the alphabet. This is the secret of a genuine thesaurus and is the basis for its remarkable usefulness.

Good writing depends on using the exact word; but how often do you have to grope—usually without success— for the exact word to fit the idea you have in mind? A thesaurus solves just that problem. With a thesaurus you start with an idea and find the word or phrase that suits it. A dictionary, on the other hand, is just the reverse: you start with a word and find its definition. It is impossible, because of the very nature of these two basic reference books, to compile a thesaurus in dictionary form, and it was the genius of Roget which saw this first and the wisdom of subsequent editors which has warned them not to tamper with a proved success.

Roget's Pocket Thesaurus and the more complete *Roget's INTERNATIONAL Thesaurus* are arranged in two basic sections. The first, or main text, consists of hundreds of lists of related words and phrases. These lists cover all areas of knowledge. Originally devised by Peter Roget, they represent a famous breakdown of knowledge which, in its own right, was a feat of human intelligence. Within these lists are placed words and phrases of related meanings; the words themselves are clustered into tiny groups of almost synonymous meanings. But these groups grow and spread like animal cells into a network of related meanings so that if, for example, you want to find a word similar in meaning, though not completely synonymous, to "gay," a thesaurus can help you where a dictionary of synonyms cannot. No dictionary of synonyms has been so useful or enjoyed such success as Roget's *Thesaurus*.

The second section is the all-important index. Here are listed in alphabetical order all the words of the first section and the exact places where they appear. "Gay," for example, appears several places in the text: it is listed in its senses of bright, cheerful, and showy. The index tells you this, and shows you where to turn to find the lists of related words and phrases for every one of these basic meanings of "gay." Without this index a thesaurus is useless. It is the quick and efficient key that unlocks the hundreds of lists of related words and phrases—it is the essential key that is lacking in so-called "dictionary thesauruses."

The extraordinary usefulness of *Roget's Pocket Thesaurus* and *Roget's INTERNATIONAL Thesaurus* is attested to by many famous writers. Kenneth Roberts has written: "I can't possibly remember how many copies of this book I've owned and worn to tatters; but ever since the days when I was writing verse for the old *Life,* I have regarded it as the most valuable reference book that an author could have." Mary Roberts Rinehart said that she has "used at least four of these books since I first commenced to write, and even the fourth one is now in poor shape." And Philip Van Doren Stern wrote that "with the exception of the dictionary, it is the reference book I most often use and find indispensable for that elusive word that slips the mind when you want it most. To the professional writer whose everyday job has to do with words the book is an absolute necessity."

Roget's Pocket Thesaurus, then, and *Roget's INTERNATIONAL Thesaurus* derive their extraordinary usefulness from the fidelity with which they adhere to Peter Mark Roget's original concept. Naturally both volumes have been expanded. For example, many new listings have had to be added to Roget's original divisions of knowledge to provide room for the advances in science and technology which even this amazing doctor did not dream of. Altogether, in the larger edition, there are more than 200,000 words and phrases, and in both editions appear contemporary American colloquialisms and slang.

Pocket Books and the Thomas Y. Crowell Company have taken exceptional pride in bringing this famous reference book to a peak of usefulness for the modern American; it is pre-eminently suitable for the student, teacher, housewife, business and professional man, writer —in short, for everyone who ever has need of writing anything from a letter to a play, from a business report to a scientific treatise.